SECOND EDITION

THIRTEEN QUESTIONS IN ETHICS AND SOCIAL PHILOSOPHY

SECOND EDITION

THIRTEEN QUESTIONS IN ETHICS AND SOCIAL PHILOSOPHY

G. LEE BOWIE   *Mount Holyoke College*

MEREDITH W. MICHAELS   *Hampshire College*

KATHLEEN HIGGINS   *University of Texas at Austin*

Under the general editorship of ROBERT J. FOGLEIN
Dartmouth College

HARCOURT BRACE COLLEGE PUBLISHERS
Fort Worth   Philadelphia   San Diego   New York   Orlando   Austin   San Antonio
Toronto   Montreal   London   Sydney   Tokyo

Publisher **Earl McPeek**
Acquisitions Editor **David Tatom**
Product Manager **Steven K. Drummond**
Project Editor **Tamara Neff Vardy**
Production Manager **Serena B. Manning**
Art Director **Brian Salisbury**

ISBN: 0-15-503684-X
Library of Congress Catalog Number: 97-74862

Address Orders to:
Harcourt Brace & Company
6277 Sea Harbor Drive
Orlando, FL 32887-6777
1-800-782-4479

Address editorial correspondence to:
Harcourt Brace College Publishers
301 Commerce Street, Suite 3700
Fort Worth, TX 76102

Web site address:
http://www.hbcollege.com

Printed in the United States of America

8 9 0 1 2 3 4 5 6   039   9 8 7 6 5 4 3 2

PREFACE

This book originated as a companion to *Twenty Questions: An Introduction to Philosophy* (Bowie, Michaels, and Solomon). An underlying assumption of that book, and of this one, is that philosophy, though a discipline in its own right, can nevertheless be located in and generated by a variety of different intellectual endeavors. Our experience as teachers has persuaded us that, far from disturbing the disciplinary sanctity of philosophy, the incorporation of a wide array of readings from a wide array of sources actually promotes the virtues of philosophical critique and reflection. *Thirteen Questions in Ethics* attempts to create a generous and imaginative context within which students can struggle with and come to understand some of the central problems in ethics. We have deliberately made the boundaries flexible between ethics and other regions of philosophy—political and social philosophy, metaphysics, and epistemology—so that students can appreciate the conceptual complexity of ethical deliberation.

We have also been careful, both in the questions that we chose to address and in the particular selections we adopted, to include issues and points of view that are too often missing from textbooks in ethics. Thus, we have included a chapter on racism and incorporated questions about race into other chapters. Similarly, we have endeavored to represent feminist perspectives throughout the text. Our assumption is that the inclusion of particular, socially located perspectives reinforces the view that ethics itself is morally responsive.

Many different courses can be constructed from the readings in this book. Some instructors will want to include a theory section in their course. We have organized the readings to accommodate this. Although these boundaries are sure to be somewhat artificial, we have supposed that Part I could be approached pretheoretically, as a way of getting a "hook" into moral issues to which students will have an immediate connection. Instructors can easily insert a section on ethical theory after this part and then take up topics in Parts II and III. It is also easy to imagine courses that focus on feminist approaches to ethics or on classical approaches.

We hope there are many ways this book can be used that we have not been able to anticipate. We encourage the instructor and the student to play with the readings and create even more ways of involving students in their development of some perspective on the problems of ethics. One great hope of a book that achieves the sort of diversity that we have sought here is that students will be inspired to browse beyond the range of the approach adopted by their particular instructor. The wise instructor will encourage students to range freely through these selections in the expectation that they will discover material that will lead them further, possibly in unforeseen directions. We have tried, throughout, to foster a view of the nature of ethical inquiry that encourages such exploration.

In preparing this second edition of *Thirteen Questions in Ethics,* we have revisited nearly every chapter, updating and reconceptualizing in light of new directions in contemporary discussions of these central questions. In some cases, this has resulted in a substantial reconfiguration—for example in the chapters "What Kind of Person Do I Want to Be?" (Chapter 1), "How Should I Make Money?" (Chapter 6), "How Does

Racism Affect My Life?" (Chapter 8), and "Can We Control Violence?" (Chapter 10). In other chapters, a key modern classic has been added—for example an exerpt from Annette Baier's now classic *Trust and Anti-Trust* in Chapter 5 ("Is It Ever Right to Lie?"). In some chapters, the revisions are intended to focus more effectively on aspects that are becoming more prominent—for example the addition of material on welfare in the chapter "How Should I Respond to Poverty?" (Chapter 12).

The efforts involved in the development of this text have been nearly as diverse as the materials included. David Tatom at Harcourt Brace has carefully fostered our ideas and has supplied a valued critical voice. Bill McLane was an enormous help early on in developing the original concept. We would also like to thank the rest of the book team at Harcourt Brace: Serena Manning, production manager; Brian Salisbury, art director; and Tamara Vardy, project editor. Kathy Dennis has been particularly helpful, both in dealing with permissions, and in nudging the project along when it needed to be prodded. Anna May Dion and Laurie Dion have worked unstintingly on the details of bringing such a collection together. Quyen Tran's creativity, eye for detail, and relentless energy have made this collection far better than it could otherwise have been. In addition, Jenene Allison, Roger Ames, Baruch Brody, Douglas Buhrer, Susan Douglas, T. R. Durham, Elizabeth During, Betty Sue Flowers, Dale Flowers, Janice Frey, Marlene Fried, Paula Fulks, Jay Garfield, Robert Gooding-Williams, Cynthia Gordon, Julie Inness, Robert Kane, Sam Keen, Allesandra Lippucci, Sandra Lynch, Steve Moninger, Linda E. Patrik, Henry Rosemont, Ed Stein, Laura Syron, David Tebaldi, Jorge Valadez, Martha C. Nussbaum, and Garret Sokoloss have made valuable contributions. We are grateful to all of them.

Contents

CHAPTER 9
Can There Be Equality between Men and Women?   382

CHAPTER 10
Can We Control Violence?   440

CHAPTER 11
What Should We Sacrifice for Animals and the Environment?   489

CHAPTER 12

How Should I Respond to Poverty?   555

CHAPTER 13

Who Should Decide When I Die?   606

PART ONE
Preliminary Questions

CHAPTER 1

What Kind of Person Do I Want to Be?

Throughout your childhood, you were probably asked on a regular basis, "What do you want to be when you grow up?" If you were like most children, you had different answers at different times. One year, perhaps you wanted to be a fire-fighter; the next year, perhaps your goal was to become a professional dancer. Maybe every now and then a new experience motivated you to contemplate a life that you never before considered. After your first science class, for instance, you may have imagined what it would be like to work in a laboratory, perhaps discovering a new element or a cure for cancer. Television probably had an impact on your thinking as well. Maybe televised accounts of various space missions made you fantasize about being an astronaut. Some of you are probably continuing to reconsider your plans as a consequence of your experiences during college.

You may have had less concrete aspirations as well. Maybe you wanted to be "just like" an admired aunt or uncle. You probably had heroes, both among the people you knew personally and among the characters (fictitious or actual) that you encountered through movies, television, books, and magazines. Although your childhood choice of heroes and your style of expressing enthusiasm for them may seem an embarrassment to you now, you may still find that your lifetime's experience has left you with some strong ideas about what you do and do not admire in a person.

One of the most basic concerns of ethics has to do with the way you believe you should conduct your life. Ethical questions about how to resolve particular moral quandaries arise from this concern. Reflection on such questions constitute the greater part of this book. But another type of question that is fundamental to one's personal ethics deals with the general habits, policies, and organization of one's everyday way of living. Are some ways of arranging one's life better than others, and on what basis can one determine this?

Philosophers have often discussed these concerns by appealing to the notion of *virtue*. A virtue is a trait that is desirable for a person to possess. Some philosophers (called *teleologists*) argue that particular traits are desirable because they lead to particular results. Others (called *deontologists*) contend that certain types of behavior are desirable whether or not they are rewarded with desirable consequences—they are simply the "right" way to live.

Aristotle, an ancient Greek philosopher, emphasized virtue as central to good living, and a number of contemporary American philosophers have endorsed this view. Among these is Laurence Thomas. In "Justice, Happiness, and Self-Knowledge," Thomas defends an argument advanced by Plato, Aristotle's teacher, regarding the virtue of justice. Plato, in his dialogue *The Republic*, argued (through his character Socrates) that unjust people are necessarily unhappy. Thomas focuses on a particular kind of unjust person, specifically, the unjust person who pretends not to be unjust, but instead to be caring. By developing the habit of disguising his or her real attitude, such a person, argues Thomas, renders him or herself vulnerable to self-deception.

Lynne McFall considers another long-heralded virtue, integrity, as important for the modern individual. Observing that integrity involves being "undivided; an integral whole," she considers what such a state of being involves. Among the requisite characteristics of a person who exhibits integrity, she concludes, are coherence among one's principles, motivations, and actions; a commitment to values that genuinely are important; and an unconditional commitment to certain personal values. This last requirement has a surprising consequence. Although moral principles are frequently thought to demand impartiality toward everyone, personal integrity may require unconditional commitment to family and friends, which amounts to a very partial attitude. Thus, certain conceptions of morality may be in tension with the kind of personal integrity that McFall defends. But she concludes that personal integrity is nonetheless invaluable. Not only is it fundamental to a fulfilled sense of individual identity; it is essential to our having values in a fundamental sense.

Cheshire Calhoun agrees with McFall that integrity is important. But she thinks that many conceptions of integrity, including McFall's, offer incomplete pictures of what is involved. Commonly, integrity is described as being a matter of either (1) unifying oneself into a coherent whole, (2) being true to one's character, or (3) taking a firm stand on some principles. What all of these descriptions miss, Calhoun argues, is the fact that integrity is a social virtue. It involves formulating one's own best judgment about what is worth doing in a context in which others, too, are deliberating. To act with integrity means to behave in a way that is consistent with one's own best judgment. It is to behave as though one's endorsements matter, and ought to matter, to others as well as to oneself. A person who acts without integrity is not only letting him or herself down; such a person is letting others down as well, even when social pressure motivates the person to be hypocritical in the first place.

Robert C. Solomon reminds us of some of the difficulties involved in being a deliberator in a community of deliberators. Especially when we are convinced that something important is at stake, we are often dismayed to find that others deliberate differently and reach conclusions that differ from our own. Solomon suggests that it is important to remember that people have different ethical styles. Different individuals, equally well motivated, can nevertheless focus on different aspects of the same issue; and they may disagree on which of several considerations is most important in resolving an ethical problem. Solomon thinks that recognizing personal differences in ethical style can help us to avoid the temptation to vilify well-meaning individuals whose styles differ from our own. It can also help us assess what is really going on in a disagreement. Before assuming that a conflict is a battle between good and evil, it is worth considering whether the clash is based on an honest philosophical disagreement about the best way of resolving a problem.

Joe Dominguez and Vicki Robin also consider our deliberations, particularly those concerning money. Although many people in American society aspire to become wealthy, Dominguez and Robin suggest that this may not be the best goal. We get money, they observe, by trading for it our "life energy"—the amount of time and energy available to us. They suggest that in our personal economic decisions, we would do well to focus on getting the most value from our experience and all the things we use. Dominguez and Robin suggest that we reconsider "frugality," a word for a virtue that is no longer popular. Properly, frugality should be understood as using material things wisely and getting as much joy as possible from them. Dominguez and Robin see frugality as particularly important in our time, for they think that many people trade too much life energy for money.

Jungian psychotherapist Thomas Moore also urges us to try to get more joy from our experiences. Moore believes that many of us fail to appreciate the extent to which everyday beauty can nurture us. He encourages us to attend to those things that invite our contemplation and to care for what we encounter in our everyday environments. If we as a culture are to develop an ecological sensibility, we must begin by putting beauty high on our agendas. By doing so, Moore believes, our world will appear, not as a hostile environment, but as a supportive home, filled with soul.

Bertrand Russell, too, offers advice about gaining more satisfaction from our experiences. He advises us to take up what he calls "impersonal interests." He argues that hobbies and any other interest that does not pertain to one's practical affairs are valuable aids to happiness, for they help us overcome pettiness and replenish us after being worn from our efforts and the cares of which adult life is full. Being open to ideas and pursuits that we value for their own sake is, in Russell's view, an indication of greatness of soul. Even when things go wrong, Russell argues, having an interest in things that lie outside the scope of one's practical concerns is a source of consolation. Such interests help us to see things in proportion.

In our century, some disasters have seemed catastrophic beyond proportion. In the face of them, the question of what traits one wants to have may seem dwarfed. Etty Hillesum, a young Jewish woman who died in Auschwitz, confronted her era with the conviction that only personal virtue—courage, faith, and particularly love—could challenge the evil she saw around her. This chapter closes with some selections from her diaries, in which she discusses her endeavors to respond to her experiences by becoming more, not less, humane.

LAURENCE THOMAS

Justice, Happiness, and Self-Knowledge

LAURENCE THOMAS teaches philosophy at Syracuse University and writes in the areas of social philosophy and moral psychology. He is the author of *Living Morally* (1989).

No man can, for any considerable time, wear one face to himself and another to the multitude without finally getting bewildered as to which is the true one.

NATHANIEL HAWTHORNE

The Platonic view that every just person is, in virtue of being such, happier than any unjust person, since all among the latter are unhappy, strikes a most responsive chord in the hearts of a great many persons. But it would seem that this idea has less of a foothold in reality than it does in our hearts. It is far too difficult to deny that there are unjust persons who are happy. Indeed, some even seem to be happier than many a just person.

So I shall lower my sights. Rather than attempting to defend as sound the Platonic view, I shall argue that the just person is favored to be happier than a certain kind of unjust person whom I shall simply call a masquerader—this is, an individual who is frequently concerned to masquerade as a deeply caring person. To this end, I shall defend two theses. One is the Justice/Self-Knowledge (JSK) thesis: when it comes to interpersonal relationships the just person has more self-knowledge than a masquerader. The other is the Happiness/Self-Knowledge (HSK) thesis: other things equal, a person's happiness is more secure if it stems from the self-knowledge which he possesses with respect to the realization of his endeavors. Though obviously weaker than what Plato was after, I take it that the view which I am concerned to defend is very much in keeping with the spirit of his thought. . . .

Unjust treatment being what it is, willing targets of injustice are hard to come by. Thus, an unjust person can carry out his unjust exploits only if he is sufficiently powerful that he can simply beat into submission all who stand in his way or he is fairly good at catching people off guard. Given the latter, it in no way follows that every or any unjust person must be what I have called a masquerader. For we can imagine an exceedingly clever and crafty unjust person who always manages to catch his targets of injustice unaware and then to escape without detection. Presumably, anyone who possessed Gyges' ring could do these things. We can even imagine that this person is widely known to be unjust, but nonetheless successfully thwarts all attempts to apprehend him. Again, a person with Gyges' ring could presumably pull this off. So, we can imagine a viciously unjust person who never has to give the impression that he will act unjustly.

But so much for what we can imagine. In the actual world, no unjust person possesses anything remotely resembling a Gyges' ring. Accordingly, an unjust person could not be within striking range of some of his targets of injustice but for the fact that he gives them every reason to believe that he will not treat them unjustly. That is, in general an unjust person cannot carry out his unjust exploits without, upon occasion,

6

having to deceive some others into thinking that he will not treat them unjustly. Again, from none of this does it follow that every or any unjust person must be a masquerader. However, once it is seen that deceiving people can very much facilitate leading an unjust life, it becomes obvious that it will suit the purposes of some unjust persons to be masqueraders, since a person can have no better reason to think that she will not be treated unjustly by another than that she has reason to believe that the person cares deeply about her. But one pays an enormous price for being a masquerade.

For, if we believe that we genuinely care deeply about a person, then we do not want it to turn out, at least not too often, that the primary explanation for our displaying caring behavior toward him is other than that we genuinely care about him. And as we shall see, if an unjust person is a masquerader, then on that account alone, he cannot help but be less certain than the just person as to why he is moved to display caring behavior toward his friends and loved ones. . . .

There are two reasons cum explanations why the masquerader will be moved to display caring behavior toward someone: (a) an intrinsic one, that is, he cares deeply about the person or (b) an extrinsic one, that is, he stands to gain some benefit which is not simply that of taking delight in displaying caring behavior toward the person in question. More precisely, in the latter case the behavior is not motivated by love or concern for the person in question. Respectively, we have genuine and simulated caring behavior. It goes without saying that these two explanations are not mutually exclusive. Quite the contrary, because having close ties with some person or the other is essential to our psychological well-being and displays of caring behavior serve to maintain such ties, then it is clearly to a person's advantage to display such behavior from time to time towards those with whom he has close ties. In other words, a person always has an extrinsic reason for displaying caring behavior towards those with whom he has close ties. . . . [I]f we take ourselves to care deeply about a person, then we want the fact that we care deeply about him to be the primary explanation, if not the only explanation, for our displaying caring behavior toward him. We do not want the explanation to be that we will benefit in return, even if we know this to be so, as in the maintenance of close ties. We want the reason for our displaying caring behavior to be an intrinsic one rather than an extrinsic one.

Now, in view of the fact that it is a characteristic feature of the unjust person who is a masquerader that, except when it comes to those about whom he cares deeply, he is moved to display caring behavior toward others precisely because it is to his extrinsic advantage to do so, the obvious question is this: How can he be sure that this is not also the explanation for why he is moved to display caring behavior toward his friends and loved ones? How can he be sure that his caring behavior toward them is genuine rather than simulated? Or, to put the question in terms of intrinsic and extrinsic reasons: How can he be sure that it is for intrinsic rather than extrinsic reasons that he displays caring behavior towards his friends and loved ones? At first blush, it might seem natural to suppose that the masquerader can simply rely upon the difference in the way he would feel when, on the one hand, displaying caring behavior toward those whom he cares deeply about and, on the other, displaying caring behavior toward his targets of injustice. But can he? I think not.

Obviously enough, the best substitute for something is one that is all but indistinguishable from the genuine article. Now, the fact of the matter is that in general human beings are fairly good monitors of human behavior. Over time, especially, we become quite good at sizing up the depth of a person's sincerity. And the key element in our assessment is a person's non-verbal behavior, which refers to all bodily behavior including how a person says what he says. So, by verbal behavior alone what is meant is simply the words which a person utters. Given that utterances of the appropriate sort can be produced at will, it should come as no surprise that non-verbal behavior plays a fundamentally important role in our assessment. Moreover, among friends and loved ones, especially, much of the nonverbal behavior is spontaneous and affective. If Jones and Smith are close friends and Jones tells Smith that she, Jones, has just won a Nobel Prize or has just lost her son, then Smith should respond with joy in the first case, sadness in the second, and spontaneously in either case. That he should so respond is not really a matter open for discussion. Smith's attitude toward Jones should be such that the appropriate feelings (emotions) are automatically engaged, as it were, depending on the news conveyed to him. He does not need to deliberate about whether to have them. Hence, the feelings he displays are, and come across as being, a natural outcome of what he actually feels. Putting the point this way allows for the fact that we do not always deem it appropriate to display our feelings, though presumably the story I have just told is not one where this holds.

As the preceding remarks should make clear, a person is best able to simulate deeply caring behavior, and will be most successful at passing himself off as a close friend or loved one if, simply upon cue, he is actually able to bring himself to experience the feelings that are appropriate for the occasion. For only then will his simulated caring behavior have the spontaneity and naturalness to it that is characteristic of behavior among those who are close to one another when one party informs the other of either his good fortune or his misfortune.

Now, to be sure, on the view which I have presented if a person is simulating deeply caring behavior, then his experiencing the appropriate feelings constitutes an act on his part, since he brings it about that he experiences them, whereas this is not the case for the person who experiences feelings on account of actually caring deeply about a person. Here, only an event occurs; for the person's attitude toward the individual in question is such that the appropriate feelings automatically come about upon learning what has happened to that individual. So it might be thought that a person who is adept at simulating deeply caring behavior should have no difficulty in distinguishing such behavior from that which is genuine. But . . . this surmise is mistaken. . . .

After all, our automatically experiencing the appropriate sorts of feelings towards a person is what serves as the bedrock of our belief that we care deeply about him. We cannot become adept at simulating deeply caring behavior without causing a severe fault to run through this bedrock. For precisely what this adeptness comes to is our being able to bring it about that we will automatically experience the appropriate feelings though we do not, in fact, care deeply about the person. We cannot have it both ways. We cannot be adept at experiencing the feelings we want to experience toward others and not have an erosion in our confidence to judge correctly whether our deeply caring behavior is simulated or genuine. And the feelings which we automatically experience cannot serve as the bedrock of our belief that we care deeply about a person if we are not confident that we would not experience them but for the fact that we have the appropriate attitude toward that person.

The masquerader has no immunity in this regard. An inevitable consequence of his adeptness at simulating deeply caring behavior is that he will find eroded his confidence in his judgment that his displays of caring behavior toward those whom he takes himself to care about are indeed genuine rather than simulated.

We can make the argument tighter. What is characteristic of the masquerader is that extrinsic reasons for displaying caring behavior can cause him to experience spontaneously, in the appropriate circumstances, the very feelings that intrinsic reasons of this sort can cause him to experience spontaneously. He has come to be this way on account of his concern to be able to pass himself off as a deeply caring person from time to time. But it will be remembered that there is always an extrinsic reason why a person should display caring behavior toward those with whom he has close ties. The problem for the masquerader, then, is this: Since (1) there is always an extrinsic reason for him to display caring behavior toward those with whom he has close ties, (2) he can easily enough be moved to display such behavior for extrinsic reasons, since he is a basically unjust person, and (3) extrinsic reasons for displaying caring behavior can result in his experiencing spontaneously, the appropriate circumstances, the very same feelings that intrinsic reasons of this sort can cause him to experience spontaneously, then it follows that (4) the masquerader cannot simply rely upon his feelings as evidence that his displays of caring behavior toward those with whom he has close ties is genuine. Now, if (5) the just person can rely upon such feelings whereas the masquerader cannot or, at any rate, the former can do so to a significantly greater extent than the latter, then it follows that the masquerader cannot be as confident as the just person as to why he (the masquerader) is moved to display caring behavior toward his friends and loved ones. It is not a characteristic feature of the just person that, because he desires to treat others justly, he will be moved to pass himself off as one who cares deeply about others when actually he does not. The just life does not require that one be adept at simulating deeply caring behavior; nor, a fortiori, does it require that one be adept at simulating just behavior.

Hence, leading a just life does not require a skill the very having of which casts an enormous shadow of doubt upon why one is moved to display caring behavior toward a person. It can even be allowed that the just person masks his feelings upon occasion. Parents who have just been dismissed from their jobs might manage to hide, at least for the moment, their situation from their daughter, who has received word that she has won a Rhodes Scholarship, since they do not wish to detract from her moment of glory. Notice, however, that this masking on their part cannot in any way be considered a constitutive part of leading a just life; whereas for the masquerader, simulating caring feelings is a constitutive part of his leading an unjust life. If these remarks are sound, then the JSK thesis holds. . . .

Let us turn now to the Happiness/Self-Knowledge thesis: other things equal, a person's happiness is more secure if it stems from the self-knowledge which he possesses with respect to the realization of his endeavors. The truth of this thesis can be easily made out.

Occasional luck can truly be a wonderful thing; too much of it, though, will destroy our self-confidence. For the more it turns out that the explanation for our successes is luck the less our successes reflect positively upon us, since the more it turns out that luck is the explanation for our successes the less they can be credited to our own abilities, skills, and ingenuity. So, for the overwhelming majority of cases, we want the explanation of our successes to be none other than that we have properly and skillfully employed our natural assets. We want to be the author of our successes, let us say. These remarks are not meant to be an aside. On the contrary, they make it abundantly clear that we do not wish to be plagued with self-doubt as to whether or not we are the author of our successes. This is significant for the simple reason that, other things equal, the less a person is plagued with self-doubt in this regard, the happier he is. Needless to say, it matters not whether the endeavors are constitutive of our interpersonal relationships. These remarks should suffice to show that the Happiness/Self-Knowledge thesis is sound.

It should be obvious how the HSK thesis bears on the unjust person who is a masquerader. As I have said, whether we are basically just or unjust, we want our displays of caring behavior toward those whom we deeply care about to be genuine. The problem for the masquerader is just that in this regard he is plagued with significantly more self-doubt than the (basically) just person. In this very important respect, then, the masquerader is favored to be less happy than the (basically) just person.

LYNNE MCFALL

Integrity

LYNNE McFALL teaches philosophy at Syracuse University. She publishes fiction as well as philosophy. Her books include *The One True Story of the World* and *Happiness*.

> *Olaf (upon what were once knees)*
> *does almost ceaselessly repeat*
> *'there is some shit I will not eat'*
>
> e. e. cummings

COHERENCE

Integrity is the state of being "undivided; an integral whole." What sort of coherence is at issue here? I think there are several.

One kind of coherence is simple consistency: consistency within one's set of principles or commitments. One cannot maintain one's integrity if one has unconditional commitments that conflict, for example, justice and personal happiness, or conditional commitments that cannot be ranked, for example, truth telling and kindness.

Another kind of coherence is coherence between principle and action. Integrity requires "sticking to one's principles," moral or otherwise, in the face of temptation, including the temptation to redescription.

Take the case of a woman with a commitment to marital fidelity. She is attracted to a man who is not her husband, and she is tempted. Suppose, for the purity of the example, that he wants her too but will do nothing to further the affair; the choice is hers. Now imagine your own favorite scene of seduction.

After the fact, she has two options. (There are always these two options, which makes the distinction between changing one's mind and weakness of the will problematic, but assume that this is a clear case.) She can (1) admit to having lost the courage of her convictions (retaining the courage of her mistakes) or (2) rewrite her principles in various ways (e.g., by making fidelity a general principle, with exceptions, or by retroactively canceling her "subscription"). Suppose she chooses the latter. Whatever she may have gained, she has lost some integrity. Weakness of the will is one contrary of integrity. Self-deception is another. A person who admits to having succumbed to temptation has more integrity than the person who sells out, then fixes the books, but both suffer its loss.

A different sort of incoherence is exhibited in the case where someone does the right thing for (what he takes to be) the wrong reason. For example, in Dostoevsky's *The Devils*, Stepan Verkhovensky says, "All my life I've been lying. Even when I spoke the truth. I never spoke for the sake of the truth, but for my own sake." Coherence between principle and action is necessary but not sufficient. One's action might *correspond* with one's principle, at some general level of description, but be inconsistent

11

with that principle more fully specified. If one values not just honesty but honesty for its own sake, then honesty motivated by self-interest is not enough for integrity.

So the requirement of coherence is fairly complicated. In addition to simple consistency, it puts constraints on the way in which one's principles may be held (the "first-person" requirement), on how one may act given one's principles (coherence between principle and action), and on how one may be motivated in acting on them (coherence between principle and motivation). Call this *internal coherence*. . . .

To summarize the argument so far: personal integrity requires that an agent (1) subscribe to some consistent set of principles or commitments and (2), in the face of temptation or challenge, (3) uphold these principles or commitments, (4) for what the agent takes to be the right reasons.

These conditions are rather formal. Are there no constraints on the *content* of the principles or commitments a person of integrity may hold?

INTEGRITY AND IMPORTANCE

Consider the following statements.

Sally is a person of principle: pleasure.

Harold demonstrates great integrity in his single-minded pursuit of approval.

John was a man of uncommon integrity. He let nothing—not friendship, not justice, not truth—stand in the way of his amassment of wealth.

That none of these claims can be made with a straight face suggests that integrity is inconsistent with such principles.

A person of integrity is willing to bear the consequences of her convictions, even when this is difficult, that is, when the consequences are unpleasant. A person whose only principle is "Seek my own pleasure" is not a candidate for integrity because there is no possibility of conflict—between pleasure and principle—in which integrity could be lost. Where there is no possibility of its loss, integrity cannot exist.

Similarly in the case of the approval seeker. The single-minded pursuit of approval is inconsistent with integrity. Someone who is describable as an egg sucker, brownnose, fawning flatterer cannot have integrity, whatever he may think of the merits of such behavior. A commitment to spinelessness does not vitiate its spinelessness—another of integrity's contraries.

The same may be said for the ruthless seeker of wealth. A person whose only aim is to increase his bank balance is a person for whom nothing is ruled out: duplicity, theft, murder. Expedience is *contrasted* to a life of principle, so an ascription of integrity is out of place. Like the pleasure seeker and the approval seeker, he lacks a "core," the kind of commitments that give a person character and that makes a loss of integrity possible. In order to sell one's soul, one must have something to sell. . . .

Most of us, when tempted to "sell out," are tempted by pleasure, approval, money, status, or personal gain of some other sort. The political prisoner under the thumbscrew wants relief, however committed he may be to the revolution. Less dramatically, most of us want the good opinion of others and a decent standard of living. Self-interest in these forms is a legitimate aim against which we weigh our other concerns. But most of us have other "higher," commitments, and so those who honor most what we would re- sist are especially liable to scorn.

This tendency to objectify our own values in the name of personal integrity can best be seen, I think, in a more neutral case. Consider the following claim:

> The connoisseur showed real integrity in preferring the Montrachet to the Moun- tain Dew.

Even if he was sorely tempted to guzzle the Mountain Dew and forbore only with the greatest difficulty, the connoisseur, we would say, did not show integrity in preferring the better wine. Why? Resisting temptation is not the only test of integrity; the chal- lenge must be to something *important*. . . .

One may die for beauty, truth, justice, the objection might continue, but not for Montrachet. Wine is not that important. . . .

When we grant integrity to a person, we need not *approve* of his or her principles or commitments, but we must at least recognize them as ones a reasonable person might take to be of great importance and ones that a reasonable person might be tempted to sacrifice to some lesser yet still recognizable goods. It may not be possible to spell out these conditions without circularity, but that this is what underlies our judgments of integrity seems clear enough. Integrity is a personal virtue granted with social strings attached. By definition, it precludes "expediency, artificiality, or shallowness of any kind." The pleasure seeker is guilty of shallowness, the approval seeker of artificiality, and the profit seeker of expedience of the worst sort. . . .

INTEGRITY, FRIENDSHIP, AND THE OLAF PRINCIPLE

An attitude essential to the notion of integrity is that there are some things that one is not prepared to do, or some things one *must* do. I shall call this the "Olaf Principle," in honor of e. e. cummings's poem about Olaf, the "conscientious objector." This principle requires that some of one's commitments be unconditional.

In what sense?

There are, in ordinary moral thought, expressions of the necessity or impossibility of certain actions or types of actions that do not neatly correspond to the notions of ne- cessity and impossibility most often catalogued by moral theorists. "I *must* stand by my friend (or "I *cannot* let him down") may have no claim to logical, psychological, ra- tional, or moral necessity in any familiar sense. There is nothing logically inconsistent in the betrayal of friendship, or one could never be guilty of it. It is not psychologically impossible, since many have in fact done it and survived to do it again. Rationality does not require unconditional allegiance, without some additional assumptions, for one may have better reason to do a conflicting action, for example, where the choice is between betraying a friend and betraying one's country (although I am sympathetic to

E. M. Forster's famous statement to the contrary). Nor is the necessity expressed one that has a claim to universality, for different persons may have different unconditional commitments. Impartiality and absoluteness are not what is at stake, for the choice may be between a friend and ten innocent strangers, and one person may have different unconditional commitments at different times. It is not clear, then, what sense of *unconditional commitment* is at issue.

Unless corrupted by philosophy, we all have things we think we would never do, under any imaginable circumstances, whatever we may give to survival or pleasure, power and the approval of strangers; some part of ourselves beyond which we will not retreat, some weakness however prevalent in others that we will not tolerate in ourselves. And if we do that thing, betray that weakness, we are not the persons we thought; there is nothing left that we may even in spite refer to as *I*.

I think it is in this sense that some commitments must be unconditional: they are conditions of continuing as ourselves.

Suppose, for example, that I take both friendship and professional advancement to be great goods, and my best friend and I are candidates for a promotion. Suppose, too, that I know the person who has the final decision has an unreasoned hatred of people who drink more than is socially required, as my friend does. I let this be known, not directly of course, with the predictable result that I am given the promotion.

Now in one sense I have not done anything dishonest. My friend may be the first to admit the pleasure he takes in alcohol. It may even be one of the reasons I value his friendship. (Loyal drinking companions are not easy to come by.) But this is clearly a betrayal of friendship. Is it so obviously a failure of integrity?

In *any* conflict between two great goods, I may argue, one must be "betrayed." And between you and me, I choose me.

What is wrong with this defense?

To beat someone out of a job by spreading vicious truths is proof that I am no friend. It is in the nature of friendship that one cannot intentionally hurt a friend in order to further one's own interests. So if I claim to be this person's friend, then I am guilty of incoherence, and therefore lack integrity.

Why does incoherence seem the wrong charge to make? The answer, I think, is that it is much too weak.

Some of our principles or commitments are more important to us than others. Those that can be sacrificed without remorse may be called *defeasible* commitments. For many of us, professional success is an important but defeasible commitment. I would like to be a successful philosopher, esteemed by my colleagues and widely published, but neither success nor failure will change my sense of personal worth.

Contrasted to defeasible commitments are *identity-conferring* commitments: they reflect what we take to be most important and so determine, to large extent, our (moral) identities. . . .

For many of us, friendship is an identity-conferring commitment. If we betrayed a friend in order to advance our careers, we could not "live with" ourselves; we would not be the persons we thought we were. This is what it means to have a "core": a set of principles or commitments that makes us who we are. Such principles cannot be justified by reference to other values, because they are the most fundamental commitments we have; they determine what, for us, is to *count* as a reason. . . .

MORAL INTEGRITY

If integrity is a moral virtue, then it is a special sort of virtue. One cannot be solely concerned with one's own integrity, or there would be no object for one's concern. Thus integrity seems to be a higher-order virtue. To have moral integrity, then, it is natural to suppose that one must have some lower-order moral commitments; that moral integrity adds a moral requirement to personal integrity. . . .

What makes something a moral principle?

One commonly accepted view is that moral principles are characterized by impartiality and universality. Assuming this is true, it follows that moral integrity will require that these conditions be met.

Is this plausible?

Let us return to the principled adulterer and look at it from the husband's point of view. At first he feels betrayed and is hurt. Then he stops to consider what impartiality requires. Perhaps my wife's new lover makes her happier than I can, he reasons, and the affair will certainly make her lover happier, so there is all that happiness to be weighed against my pain. The children are grown, so it is not hurting them. Impartiality seems to require that I grant her this freedom, even encourage it.

Second example. Suppose you are having a bad day. The car breaks down on the way to teach a class in which three students fall asleep and the rest are bored or belligerent. Your latest philosophical masterpiece has come back in the mail with a note from the editor saying that the referees' comments were too abusive to decently pass on to you. During office hours your best student wonders aloud what moral theory has to do with anything that genuinely worries anyone. You have been worrying about that yourself. You wait an hour for a friend who was supposed to meet you at noon but who seems to have forgotten. On the way back from drinking your lunch, just as despair is about to take over for self-pity, you run into K. He sees by your wild eyes that you are in a bad way. He is just going to lunch, he says, and invites you along. You agree, having had nothing to eat since the English muffin your toaster burned for breakfast. While waiting to order, he listens sympathetically to your litany of unrelieved bad luck and real failure. He tries to cheer you up. Feeling better, you express your appreciation, tell him that he is a good friend. He says he is only doing his moral duty. You smile, thinking this philosophical irony. His blank expression suggests you are wrong. Over Caesar salad he tells you about his dear wife, whom he married because no one was more in need of love, nor so unlikely to find it. Somewhere between the main course and the coffee you realize he was not kidding. He is only doing for you what he would do for anyone in your sorry state—his duty.

The fairly simple point of these examples is that impartiality is incompatible with friendship and love, and so incompatible with personal integrity where friendship and love are identity-conferring commitments.

What does moral integrity require?

Any identity-conferring commitment *except* to impartiality will be inconsistent with impartiality. If moral integrity presupposes personal integrity, and personal integrity requires identity-conferring commitments, then moral integrity is, generally, inconsistent with impartiality. . . .

CONCLUSION

Moral integrity is as much a threat to social morality as personal integrity. The difference is that the attack comes from *within* the moral point of view, and its target is impartiality. Perhaps, then, integrity should be given up, as having a moral cost that is too great.

I think this would be a mistake. The reason is made graphically clear in a story by the science fiction writer Theodore Sturgeon, called "The Dark Room." In this story the narrator, Conway, has a friend named Beck who regularly gives cocktail parties at which everyone who attends is eventually humiliated. A sweet old woman, the author of children's books, tells an obscene story. A man who prides himself on his dignity and decorum urinates on the living room floor. An undercover agent walks up to a CIA man and spills his guts. And at the most recent party, Conway's loyal wife ends up in bed with one of the other guests. This gets his attention; on reflection he sees the pattern of humiliation and resolves to find out what's going on. Breaking into Beck's house while he's out of town Conway comes upon an alien being who has the ability to take on any form, to be whatever people want to see. The alien confesses that he feeds on the humiliation of humans. Without it he will die. He finances the parties for Beck in order to get new victims, whose humiliation he causes. This explanation satisfies Conway except for one thing: why, having attended every party, has *he* never been humiliated? The alien explains that Conway is an "immune": a creature who cannot be humiliated because there is nothing he would not do.

Without integrity, and the identity-conferring commitments it assumes, there would be nothing to fear the loss of, not because we are safe but because we have nothing to lose.

CHESHIRE CALHOUN

Standing for Something

CHESHIRE CALHOUN teaches philosophy at Colby College. She specializes in ethics, social philosophy, and feminism. She has written extensively in these areas, and she coedited a book titled *What Is an Emotion?*

We admire and trust those who have integrity, take pride in our own, rue its absence in politics, and regret our own failures to act with integrity. Clearly, integrity is a virtue, but it is less clear what it is a virtue *of* or why we might prize it.

Three pictures of integrity have gained philosophical currency, particularly through the work of Bernard Williams, Gabriele Taylor, Lynne McFall, and Jeffrey Blustein. I shall call these the integrated-self, identity, and clean-hands pictures of integrity. On the integrated-self view, integrity involves the integration of "parts" of oneself—desires, evaluations, commitments—into a whole. On the identity view, integrity means fidelity to those projects and principles which are constitutive of one's core identity. On the clean-hands view, integrity means maintaining the purity of one's own agency.

I. THE INTEGRATED-SELF PICTURE OF INTEGRITY

Etymologically, 'integrity' is related to integer, a whole number, and to integration, the unification of parts into a whole. The integrated-self picture of integrity begins from this etymological observation, and the resulting description of the person of integrity as a whole integrated self owes a good deal to Harry Frankfurt's work on freedom and responsibility.

On this view, the integration of the self, and hence integrity, requires first of all that one not be a "wanton." Frankfurt imagines wantons to be individuals who either lack the capacity or simply fail to deliberate and make up their minds about which of their desires they want to be volitionally effective. As a result, wantons act on whichever desire happens to be psychologically strongest at the moment. Because the wanton is passive in relation to what moves him, Frankfurt concludes that the wanton's desires are, in an important sense, not *his* and, as a result, neither are his actions. Such a being lacks integrity altogether. He does not, in Frankfurt's view, have a self, since it is only by endorsing a particular desire that an agent claims it as his own and thereby constitutes his self. . . .

II. THE IDENTITY PICTURE OF INTEGRITY

A second picture of integrity owes a good deal to Bernard Williams's work. On this view, integrity is a matter of having a character and being true to it. To have a character, as Williams sees it, is to have some ground projects with which one is so strongly identified that in their absence one would not be able to find meaning in one's life or have a reason for going on. Because both Kantianism and utilitarianism require that agents be prepared to give up their ground projects in the name of impartial good ordering or the maximization of good states of affairs, both moral systems are, in his view, hostile to agents' integrity. . . .

III. THE CLEAN-HANDS PICTURE OF INTEGRITY

Running throughout both pictures of integrity presented so far is the thought that integrity is importantly connected to an agent's endorsements. The clean-hands picture offers a different take on this same theme. On this picture, integrity is a matter of endorsing and, should the occasion arise, standing on some bottom-line principles that define what the agent is willing to have done through her agency and thus the limits beyond which she will not cooperate with evil. A person has integrity when there are some things she will not do regardless of the consequences of this refusal. In bottom-line situations, she places the importance of principle and the purity of her own agency above consequentialist concerns. . . .

IV. PERSONAL AND SOCIAL VIRTUES

. . . Some virtues are personal, others are social, yet others are both. A personal virtue, like temperance, consists in having the proper relation to oneself—in this case, to one's desires. Social virtues consist in having the proper relation to others. Civility, for instance, is a social virtue, a desirable mode of conducting oneself among others. Some virtues are both personal and social. Self-respect, for instance, might be thought to involve having both a proper regard for one's own moral status (and thus the right relation to oneself) and a proper regard for one's place among other moral beings (and thus the right relation to others); it is a virtue exercised both by holding oneself to standards and by demanding rightful treatment from others. . . .

Characterizing integrity as a purely personal virtue does not imply that there is anything self-indulgent about striving to have integrity. But it does imply that integrity is not essentially connected to how we conduct ourselves among others and that its fitting us for proper social relations is not what makes it a virtue. Is there any reason to think that integrity is less like temperance, a purely personal virtue, and more like self-respect, a personal and social virtue? Taking the notion of "standing for something" and the self-indulgence criticism of integrity in turn, I want to suggest two reasons for not confining the analysis of integrity to understanding its nature as a personal virtue. First, doing so fails to provide us with an adequate explication of what it means to stand for something. Second, although such analyses can counter the self-indulgence charge, they cannot make the person of integrity's relation to other persons central to that defense.

Standing For

I take it that the notion of standing for something is central to the meaning of integrity. Indeed, part of the intuitive appeal of the integrated-self, identity, and clean-hands pictures lay in their articulating part of what is meant by standing for something. When, however, the analysis of integrity is confined to understanding it as a personal virtue, "standing *for*" something ultimately reduces to "standing *by*" the line that demarcates self from not-self. On the integrated-self, identity, and clean-hands pictures, the adoption of principles and values as one's own establishes the line between self and not-self. Acting with integrity, that is, on one's own judgment, is thus intimately tied to protecting the boundaries of the self—to protecting it against disintegration, against loss of self–identity, and against pollution by evil. Acting without integrity undermines the boundaries of the self, whether that be accomplished through the abandonment of one's autonomy, the betrayal of one's deepest commitments, or the contamination of one's agency through association with evil. On all three views, loss of integrity signals loss of some important dimension of selfhood.

To the extent that integrity is, indeed, a personal virtue, this account of the significance of standing by one's principles and values rings true. What drops out of these accounts, however, is the centrality of standing *for* principles and values that, in one's own best judgment, are worthy of defense because they concern how *we*, as beings interested in living justly and well, can do so.

. . . I am strongly inclined to think that integrity is a *social* trait and that its fitting us for community membership is precisely what makes it a social *virtue*. Looking at integrity as a social virtue enables us to see persons of integrity as insisting that it is in some important sense for us, for the sake of what ought to be our project or character as a people, to preserve what ought to be the purity of our agency that they stick by their best judgment. It is to a picture of integrity as a social virtue that I now turn.

V. STANDING FOR SOMETHING

What then is the social virtue of integrity? I begin with this picture: I am one person among many persons, and we are all in the same boat. None of us can answer the question—'What is worth doing?'—except from within our own deliberative points of view. This 'What is worth doing?' question can take many specific forms. What evils, if any, ought one morally to refuse doing no matter the consequences? What, for philosophers, is worth writing about? What is worth keeping, what worth reforming in the social identity "Black" or "woman" or "gay"? What principles take precedence over what others? What is one, if not the only, worthwhile way of conducting a good life? That they are answerable only from within each person's deliberative viewpoint means that all of our answers will have a peculiar character. As one among many deliberators, each can offer only her own judgment. Although each aims to do more than this—to render a judgment endorsable by all—nothing guarantees success. The thought, "It is just my judgment and it may be wrong," cannot be banished no matter how carefully deliberation proceeds. But given that the only way of answering the 'What is worth doing?'

question is to plunge ahead using one's own deliberate viewpoint, one's best judgment becomes important. As one among many deliberators who may themselves go astray, the individual's judgment acquires gravity. It is, after all, not *just* her judgment about what it would be wrong or not worthwhile to do. It is also her *best* judgment. Something now hangs for all of us, as co-deliberators trying to answer correctly the 'What is worth doing?' question, on her sticking by her best judgment. Her standing for something is not just something she does for herself. She takes a stand for, and before, all deliberators who share the goal of determining what is worth doing.

To have integrity is to understand that one's own judgment matters because it is only within individual persons' deliberative viewpoints, including one's own, that what is worth our doing can be decided. Thus, one's own judgment serves a common interest of co-deliberators. Persons of integrity treat their own endorsements as ones that matter, or ought to matter, to fellow deliberators. Absent a special sort of story, lying about one's views, concealing them, recanting them under pressure, selling them out for rewards or to avoid penalties, and pandering to what one regards as the bad views of others, all indicate a failure to regard one's own judgment as one that should matter to others. The artist who alters his work of genius, making it saleable to a tasteless public, lacks integrity because he does not regard his best aesthetic judgment as important to anyone but himself. He abandons the co-deliberative perspective. And those who act for the sake of preserving their identity without asking whether it is worth preserving lack of integrity, because they do not even raise the 'What is worth doing?' question. 'Whatever sells' and 'whatever is me' cannot ground action with integrity because these reasons do not address the co-deliberative question of what is worth doing.

That hypocrites lack integrity is a common observation. Analyses of integrity as a personal virtue, however, do not plausibly explain why. On the integrated-self and identity pictures of integrity, one would have to say that hypocrites lack integrity because their actions are not integrated with their endorsements; or because in the course of pretending commitment, they are untrue to their real, identity-conferring commitments; or because sustained pretense undermines the agent's ability to be clear and un-self-deceived about what she really does endorse. Although hypocrisy may be bad in these ways for the hypocrite, this is not typically why we charge hypocrites with lacking integrity. Hypocrites mislead. And it is because they deliberately mislead us or others about what is worth doing that they lack integrity. Jim Bakker, for instance, persuaded a lot of people to invest money in his doing God's work. His embezzling revealed that he had misled them either about the value of doing God's work or the value of his doing it. Neither the integrated-self nor the identity picture of integrity can explain why misleading others, by itself and not because of its deleterious effects on the hypocrite, has anything to do with lacking integrity. If, however, integrity is not a merely personal virtue, but the social virtue of acting on one's own judgment because doing so matters to deliberators' common interest in determining what is worth doing, then hypocritical misrepresentation of one's own best judgment clearly conflicts with integrity.

This view of integrity also helps to explain the shame at failure to abide by one's own judgment as something more than mere shame at the unsturdiness of one's will or the guilty awareness of violating a standard. If an agent passes herself off as someone who insists on the importance of private spaces and then secretly indulges in reading another's private letters, the thoughts, "I have no self-control" and "This is wrong," are different from the thought, "I have no integrity." Neither the weakness nor the wrong-ness of the act immediately reveals lack of integrity. Rather, the thought, "I have no in-tegrity," accompanies the revelation of one's inability to stand for something before others.

Finally, looking at integrity not as the personal virtue of keeping oneself intact but as the social virtue of standing for something before fellow deliberators helps explain why we care that persons have the courage of their convictions. The courageous pro-vide spectacular displays of integrity by withstanding social incredulity, ostracism, contempt, and physical assault when most of us would be inclined to give in, compro-mise, or retreat into silence. Social circumstances that erect powerful deterrents to speaking and acting on one's own best judgment and undermine the possibilities for deliberating about what is worth doing. We thus have reason to be thankful when per-sons of integrity refuse to be cowed.

Understanding integrity as a social virtue also shifts our sense of what the obstacles to integrity might be. On the integrated-self picture, the primary obstacles to integrity are internal—self-deception, weakness of will, shoddy practical reasoning, incoher-ence in and ambivalence about one's endorsements. These are no doubt obstacles. But what of contempt, ostracism, loss of a job, penal sanctions, the breakdown of friendships and familial relations, being labeled 'confrontational', 'difficult', 'overly sensitive', or 'militant', not to mention the inexhaustible confidence of others that one is wrong? These are public obstacles to acting with integrity. Even the thickest skinned and tough-est willed may find them hard to stand up against, especially on a continuing basis.

But if integrity is the virtue of having a proper regard for one's own judgment as a deliberator among deliberators, it would seem that integrity is not just a matter of sticking to one's guns. Arrogance, pomposity, bullying, haranguing, defensiveness, in-civility, close-mindedness, deafness to criticism (traits particularly connected with fa-naticism) all seem incompatible with integrity. All reflect a basic unwillingness or inability to acknowledge the singularity of one's own best judgment and to accept the burden of standing for it in the face of conflict. Moreover, acknowledging others as de-liberators who must themselves abide by their best judgment seems part of, not exte-rior to, acting with integrity. Untempered by the thought, "This is just my own best judgment," standing for something puts one's own and others' integrity at risk—one's own because of the temptation to supplement "standing for" with coercive pressure, and others' because coercion may work. This is to say that when what is worth doing is under dispute, concern to act with integrity must pull us both ways. Integrity calls us simultaneously to stand behind our convictions and to take seriously others' doubts about them. Thus, neither ambivalence nor compromise seem inevitably to betoken lack of integrity. If we are not pulled as far as uncertainty or compromise, integrity would at least demand exercising due care in how we go about dissenting. Because we so of-ten look for exemplars of integrity retrospectively, looking for those who championed causes that to us now are clearly worthy, it is easy to overlook what from their vantage point acting with integrity must have looked like. Socrates, Galileo, Luther, and King acted against the best judgment of their peers, including some whom they admired. To think that caving in to their peers posed the only threat to their integrity oversimplifies the nature of integrity. Hubristic denial that others' best judgment matters posed an equal threat. However admirable those with the confrontational courage of their con-victions may be, even protesters risk losing their integrity to arrogance.

VI. CONCLUDING REMARK

What I have had to say about integrity suggests that integrity may be a master virtue, that is, less a virtue in its own right than a pressing into service of a host of other virtues—self-knowledge, strength of will, courage, honesty, loyalty, humility, civility, respect, and self-respect. My aim was to understand that service. What is a person who tries to have integrity trying to do? I have not rejected (though I have revised) the ideas that she is trying to be autonomous, or loyal to deep commitments, or uncontaminated by evils. But I have tried to argue that this is not the whole story. She is also trying to stand for what, in her best judgment, is worth persons' doing.

ROBERT C. SOLOMON

Ethical Styles

ROBERT C. SOLOMON is the Quincy Lee Centennial Professor of philosophy and business at the University of Texas at Austin. He has written on many topics in philosophy, and his books include *The Passions* (1976), *In the Spirit of Hegel* (1983), *The Bully Culture* (1992), and *About Love* (1988).

One of the most important but least often addressed aspects of ethics is the difference among ethical styles. It is a problem that surfaces in almost every discussion of actual cases, whether in business school or in the boardroom, whether the topic is South Africa or advertising for children on television. Different people have different premises, different ways of arguing, different ways of doing the right thing. There are ethical styles just as there are social styles and styles of management and marketing. A clash of ethical styles can be far more disruptive and destructive to business tranquility than differences of opinion or clashes of personality. In a conflict of ethical styles, each party typically thinks the other "immoral"—or worse. Negotiation breaks down, not because there is no common point of interest but because there is not even agreement on the kinds of interests that are relevant to the case.

The most familiar clash of ethical styles—one that emerges in almost every management context—is the sort of seemingly irresolvable conflict that we find between Manny K., who feels absolutely constrained by the letter of the law, and John Stuart, who is more concerned with the practical specifics of the case at hand. For Manny K., it does not matter that the rule in question is outdated or impractical. It does not matter that it became a matter of law or policy under another administration, which is now out of office. It does not matter that the rule will no doubt be changed someday. Manny K. believes that one should obey rules, whatever their origins and whatever the consequences. Any other way of thinking, from his standpoint, is amoral.

John Stuart, on the other hand, is a self-consciously practical person. Rules serve a purpose, a function, and they are to be obeyed just because—but only because—they serve that purpose or function. A rule that proves to be impractical no longer deserves our respect or obedience. A rule that was formulated under very different circumstances or was legislated by a different administration should be carefully scrutinized and not given too much weight. John Stuart makes his decisions on the sole ground that a certain course of action has the best consequences for everyone involved. If that fits the rules (as it usually does), then so much the better. If it does not, then so much the worse for the rules—and so much too for that stubborn Manny K., who for some unfathomable reason refuses to see the point.

Manny K. considers John Stuart to be nothing but an amoral opportunist, a man who does not respect authority and the rules. John Stuart considers Manny K. to be utterly unreasonable and impractical, if not "impossible." When general utility conflicts with an established rule, John and Manny are certain to misunderstand each other. There can be no compromise, because each of them considers his own position to be beyond question and cannot understand the other, except, perhaps, as pathology.

Why has so familiar a scenario found so minimal a role in studies of organizational behavior and business ethics? Ethical styles have been ignored by business writers because we tend to assume that ethical principles, unlike personalities and public policies, are universal and nonnegotiable. One executive interrupted at the beginning of one of our seminars and, crossing his arms in defiance, challenged the very purpose of our discussion, saying, "There is right, and there is wrong. There is nothing more to discuss, in business or anywhere else." We responded, of course, with a case designed to bring out the conflict of established rules with practical necessities, and the John Stuarts in the group soon rose to the occasion, making our point for us. One of the more destructive legacies of our Judeo-Christian tradition in ethics is that it tends to encourage dogmatic and intolerant thinking precisely where understanding and tolerance are most necessary.

There are a number of ethical styles, of which Manny K. and John Stuart exemplify but two. There are styles that emphasize painful wrestling with problems and styles that rely on sheer intuition. There are styles that emphasize pity and compassion, and there are styles that stress the importance of being detached and objective. Not every attitude in ethics is an ethical style, of course. Being immoral is not an ethical style. Selfishness, despite its occasional vogue as an "enlightened" ethics, is not an ethical style. There are, however, many styles of ethics. . . . Here are eight of them:

1. RULE-BOUND. Thinking and acting on the basis of rules and principles, paying only secondary regard to circumstances or exceptions. (Manny K.)
2. UTILITARIAN. Weighing probable consequences, both to the company and to the public well-being. Principles are important only as rules of thumb. "The greatest good for the greatest number of people" is the ultimate test for any action or decision. (John Stuart.)
3. LOYALIST. Evaluating all decisions first in terms of benefit to the company and its reputation. The concern with reputation (motivated by one's own pride in the company) also ensures general conformity to laws and principles and concern with the company's role in the larger social picture. (Also called the "company man.")
4. PRUDENT. Weighing probable consequences to oneself and one's own concerns but always including long-range considerations of company reputation, public trust, customer and supplier relations, ability to obtain loans, etc. Prudence is not the same as selfishness or crude self-interest (though it is sometimes called "enlightened self-interest") since it has built into it the mutual dependence of one's own interests and company interests. The primary difference between the prudent strategist, the loyalist, and the utilitarian is that the first is concerned primarily with himself and only secondarily with the rest of the world; the second is concerned primarily with the well-being of the company without special regard for him- or herself. The utilitarian takes the broader social view and, though naturally concerned with one's own and one's company's success, thinks in terms of the overall good. The prudent strategist lives on the border between ethics and self-interest and unlike the loyalist and the utilitarian is not unlikely to give up his tentative ethical stance under pressure or conflict. A special case is the person Maccoby calls the "gamesman," whose ethical commitment might be said to be limited to the "rules of the business game,"

within which the primary motivations are to be challenged and to win, without respect for the rules he has to obey (in order to play) and without regard for the actual
consequences of his actions.

5. VIRTUOUS. Every action is measured in terms of its reflection of one's character or
the company reputation, without immediate regard to consequences and often
without paying much attention to general principles. The virtuous style can vary in
both scope and method; it can be identical in its concerns to the company concerns
of the loyalist, or it can encompass the social world—as in the actions of some of the
great business philanthropists. It can pride itself on obedience to the rules, or it can
pride itself for its unerring intuitions, but it is one's own virtue that is the source of
pride rather than the autonomous motive to obey the rules, for example.

6. INTUITIVE. Making decisions on the basis of "conscience" and without deliberation,
argument, or reasons, the intelligence of which may not be immediately apparent.
Intuitive thinkers tend to be extremely impatient with more deliberative, rule-
bound, and utilitarian types. It is a style that usually flourishes only at the top of the
decision-making hierarchy, and continued success (by moral, utilitarian, and prudential standards) is essential, since errors in intuition, unlike errors in deliberation
and strategy, cannot be readily explained or rationalized.

7. EMPATHETIC. Following one's feelings, in particular feelings of sympathy and compassion. "Putting oneself in the other's place" is the modus operandi of the sentimental style, whether the "other" be a competitor ("How would we like it if he . . .")
or a customer ("Suppose you found yourself stuck with . . .").

8. DARWINIAN. Whoever survives must be right. In some versions, this is clearly not an
ethical position (e.g., "If we win, we're right, but if they win, we were wronged").
But a consistent Darwinian fully accepts the possibility and even the desirability of
his or her own failure to a superior competitor, without complaint.

Ethics is thinking in terms of the "larger picture," not ignoring or neglecting one's
own interests and well-being (a faulty view of ethics) but not overemphasizing one's
own interests either. When, as is usual, one's own interests coincide with company interests, the distinction does not even arise (which is why the prudential strategist can
be tentatively included in the list of ethical styles). And when, which is also usual, the
(long-term) well-being of the company coincides with its positive contributions to society, there need be no distinction made between company loyalty and the more general good (which is why the loyalist has an ethical style rather than just a sociological
attachment). In fact, in such amiable circumstances, ethical styles overlap or remain
hidden from view; "business as usual" usually takes ethical considerations for granted
(which is not to be confused, as it so often is, with the supposed irrelevance of ethical
considerations in business). It is in times of conflict or crisis that differences in ethical
styles become prominent, and it is in those times that such differences must be understood and negotiated instead of—as happens so often—being allowed to make a bad
situation that much more explosive.

We said that each of these styles has its characteristic advantages and disadvantages; for example, the lack of practical flexibility in rulebound moral thinking, the
sometimes impossible complexity of utilitarian calculations, and the untrustworthy
(because only tentative) ethical dependability of the prudential strategist. But this is
not the place to explore these in detail; rather we wish to stress the variety of ethical

styles, each of which defines its own criteria for right thinking (e.g., in the rule-bound style, thinking about applying the right rules; in the intuitive style, minimal thinking) and right action (good for the company, good for society, good for others). Understanding the differences and resolving conflicts among ethical styles can sometimes be as important and as difficult as resolving the ethical problems themselves.

ETHICAL STYLES

1. Rule-bound   obedience to law, rule, principle
2. Utilitarian   consequences for everybody
3. Loyalist   the company first
4. Prudent   our long-term advantage
5. Virtuous   character, reputation are all-important
6. Intuitive   spontaneous judgments
7. Empathetic   "how must he feel?"
8. Darwinian   whoever survives is right

JOE DOMINGUEZ AND VICKI ROBIN

Your Money or Your Life

JOE DOMINGUEZ was a financial analyst on Wall Street who retired at age 31. He and **VICKI ROBIN** founded *New Road Map Foundation,* an all-volunteer, non-profit organization that promotes living toward a sustainable future. Both live in Seattle.

All our false notions about money thus far have one common flaw—they identify money as something external to ourselves. It is something we all too often don't have, which we struggle to get, and on which we pin our hopes of power, happiness, security, acceptance, success, fulfillment, achievement and personal worth. Money is the master and we the slaves. Money is the victor and we the vanquished.

What, then, is the way out? What is the one consistently true statement we can make about money that will allow us to be clear, masterful and powerful in our relationship with it?

Money is something we choose to trade our life energy for.

We will repeat this because you may have missed its full significance: **Money is something we choose to trade our life energy for.**

Our life energy is our allotment of time here on earth, the hours of precious life available to us. When we go to our jobs we are trading our life energy for money. This truth, while simple, is profound. Less obvious but equally true, when we go to the welfare office, we are trading our life energy for money. When we go to Reno, we are trading our life energy for money (we hope). Even windfalls like inheritances must in some way be "earned" to actually belong to the heir—life energy must be exchanged. Time is spent with lawyers, accountants, trustees, brokers and investment counselors to handle the money. Or time is spent in therapy working out the relationship with the deceased or the guilt at receiving all that money. Or time is spent investigating worthy causes to fund. All this is life energy traded for money.

This definition of money gives us significant information. Our life energy is more *real* in our actual experience than money. You could even say money *equals* our life energy. So, while money has no intrinsic reality, our life energy does—at least to us. It's tangible, and it's finite.

Life energy is all we have. It is precious because it is limited and irretrievable and because our choices about how we use it express the meaning and purpose of our time here on earth. . . .

Having Enough

Global citizens living sustainably in a global community of communities—what kind of world would that be? Let's try to imagine for a moment such a world, a world in which everyone had enough—enough for his or her survival, enough for comforts and even enough extra for those special times that represent real pleasure. . . .

The dream of "everyone having enough" has been with us as a species for thousands of years, yet has never been fulfilled. . . . The dream of a sustainable world might begin to seem quite possible if what wasn't needed, the clutter of life, faded away. Does this sound like an impossible dream? Perhaps . . . but if you agree with Viktor Frankl that we each possess a will to have meaning, then possibilities abound.

The Japanese have a wonderful saying: "The gods only laugh when people ask them for money."

And the Tao Te Ching, the ancient Chinese book of wisdom, puts it this way: "He who knows he has enough is rich. . . ."

THE PLEASURES OF FRUGALITY

We looked up "frugal" in a 1986 Merriam-Webster dictionary and found "characterized by or reflecting economy in the expenditure of resources." That sounds about right—a serviceable, practical and fairly colorless word. None of the elegance or grace of the "enoughness" that . . . [some] experience. But when we dig deeper, the dictionary tells us that "frugal" shares a Latin root with *frug* (meaning virtue), *frux* (meaning fruit or value) and *frui* (meaning to enjoy or have the use of). Now we're talking. Frugality is **enjoying** the **virtue** of getting good **value** for every minute of your life energy and from everything you **have the use of.**

That's very interesting. In fact, it's more than interesting. It's transforming. Frugality means we are to *enjoy* what we have. If you have ten dresses but still feel you have nothing to wear, you are probably a spendthrift. But if you have ten dresses and have enjoyed wearing all of them for years, you are frugal. Waste lies not in the number of possessions but in the failure to enjoy them. Your success at being frugal is measured not by your penny-pinching but by your degree of enjoyment of the material world.

Enjoyment of the material world? Isn't that hedonism? While both have to do with enjoying what you have, frugality and hedonism are opposite responses to the material world. Hedonism revels in the pleasures of the senses and implies excessive consumption of the material world and a continual search for more. Frugal people, however, get value from everything—a dandelion or a bouquet of roses, a single strawberry or a gourmet meal. A hedonist might consume the juice of five oranges as a prelude to a pancake breakfast. A frugal person, on the other hand, might relish eating a single orange, enjoying the color and texture of the whole fruit, the smell and the light spray that comes as you begin to peel it, the translucence of each section, the flood of flavor that pours out as a section bursts over the tongue . . . and the thrift of saving the peels for baking.

To be frugal means to have a high joy-to-stuff ratio. If you get one unit of joy for each material possession, that's frugal. But if you need ten possessions to even begin registering on the joy meter, you're missing the point of being alive.

There's a word in Spanish that encompasses all this: *aprovechar.* It means to use something wisely—be it old zippers from worn-out clothing or a sunny day at the beach. It's getting full value from life, enjoying all the good that each moment and each thing has to offer. You can "*aprovechar*" a simple meal, a flat of overripe strawberries or a cruise in the Bahamas. There's nothing miserly about *aprovechar*; it's a succulent word, full of sunlight and flavor. If only "frugal" were so sweet.

The "more is better and it's never enough" mentality in North America fails the frugality test not solely because of the excess, but because of the lack of enjoyment of what we already have. Indeed, North Americans have been called materialists, but that's a misnomer. All too often it's not material things we enjoy as much as what these things symbolize: conquest, status, success, achievement, a sense of worth and even favor in the eyes of the Creator. Once we've acquired the dream house, the status car or the perfect mate, we rarely stop to enjoy them thoroughly. Instead, we're off and running after the next coveted acquisition.

Another lesson we can derive from the dictionary definition of "frugal" is the recognition that we don't need to possess a thing to enjoy it—we merely need to *use* it. If we are enjoying an item, *whether or not we own it,* we're being frugal. For many of life's pleasures it maybe far better to "use" something than to "possess" it (and pay in time and energy for the upkeep). So often we have been like feudal lords, gathering as many possessions as possible from far and wide and bringing them inside the walls of our castle. If we want something (or wanted it in the past, or imagine we might want it in the future), we think we must bring it inside the boundaries of the world called "mine." What we fail to recognize is that what is outside the walls of "mine" doesn't belong to the enemy; it belongs to "the rest of us." And if what lies outside our walls is not "them" but "us," we can afford to loosen our grip a bit on our possessions. We can gingerly open the doors of our fortress and allow goods (material and spiritual) to flow into and out of our boundaries.

Frugality, then, is also learning to share, to see the world as "ours" rather than as "theirs" and "mine." And, while not explicit in the word, being frugal and being happy with having enough mean that more will be available for others. Learning to equitably share the resources of the earth is at the top of the global agenda, and some creative frugality in North America could go a long way toward promoting that balance.

Frugality *is* balance. Frugality is the Greek notion of the golden mean. Frugality is being efficient in harvesting happiness from the world you live in. Frugality is right-use (which sounds, appropriately, like "righteous")—the wise stewarding of money, time, energy, space and possessions. Goldilocks expressed it well when she declared the porridge "not too hot, not too cold, but just right." Frugality is something like that— not too much, not too little, but just right. Nothing is wasted. Or left unused. It's a clean machine. Sleek. Perfect. Simple yet elegant. It's that magic word—enough. The peak of the Fulfillment Curve. The jumping-off point for a life of being fulfilled, learning and contributing to the welfare of the planet.

"Frugal, man." That's the cool, groovy way to say "far out" in the nineties. Surfers will talk about frugal waves. Teenage girls will talk about frugal dudes. Designers will talk about frugal fashions. Mark our words!

Keep this in mind as we explore ways to save money. We aren't talking about being cheap, making do or being a skinflint or a tightwad. We're talking about *creative* frugality, a way of life in which you get the maximum fulfillment for each unit of life energy spent.

In fact, now that you know that money is your life energy, it seems foolish to consider wasting it on stuff you don't enjoy and never use. . . . if you are 40 years old, . . . you have just 329,601 hours of life energy in your bank. That may seem like a lot now, but those hours will feel very precious at the *end* of your life. Spend them well now and you won't have regrets later.

In the end, this creative frugality is an expression of self-esteem. It honors the life energy you invest in your material possessions. Saving those minutes and hours of life energy through careful consuming is the ultimate in self-respect.

THOMAS MOORE

Beauty and the Reanimation of Things

THOMAS MOORE is a psychotherapist and author who writes on Jungian psychology and mythology, as well as the arts. He is author of *The Planets Within, Rituals of the Imagination, Care of the Soul: A Guide for Cultivating Depth and Sacredness in Everyday Life,* and *Soul Mates: Honoring the Mysteries of Love and Relationship.* In this excerpt, Moore argues that beauty can help us to care for our souls.

Attending a Roman Catholic Mass recently, I was struck by the translation of an ancient prayer I knew well from the old days, when the Mass was sung in Latin. The exact translation of the prayer from the Latin is "Lord, only say the word, and my soul shall be healed." The new English version is: "Lord, only say the word and I shall be healed." It's a small difference, but a very telling one: we no longer make a distinction between soul and self. It could be tempting to place the idea of care of the soul in the category of self-improvement, which is much more of an ego project than is care of the soul. But the soul is not the ego. It is the infinite depth of a person and of a society, comprising all the many mysterious aspects that go together to make up our identity.

The soul exists beyond our personal circumstances and conceptions. The Renaissance magus understood that our soul, the mystery we glimpse when we look deeply into ourselves, is part of a larger soul, the soul of the world, *anima mundi*. This world soul affects each individual thing, whether natural or human-made. You have a soul, the tree in front of your house has a soul, but so too does the car parked under that tree.

To the modern person who may think of the psyche as a chemical apparatus, the body as a machine, and the manufactured world as a marvel of human brainpower and technology, the idea of *anima mundi* might seem strange indeed. The best some forms of psychology can do with our occasional intuitive sensation that all things are alive is to explain the phenomenon as projection, the unconscious endowment of human fantasy onto an "inanimate" object. *Inanimate* means "without *anima*"—no *anima mundi*.

The trouble with the modern explanation that we *project* life and personality onto things is that it lands us deeply in ego: "All life and character comes from me, from how I understand and imagine experience." It is quite a different approach to allow things themselves to have vitality and personality.

In this sense, care of the soul is a step outside the paradigm of modernism, into something entirely different. My own position changes when I grant the world its soul. Then, as the things of the world present themselves vividly, I watch and listen. I respect them because I am not their creator and controller. They have as much personality and independence as I do.

James Hillman and Robert Sardello, both of whom have written extensively about the world soul in our own time, explain that objects express themselves not in language but in their remarkable individuality. An animal reveals its soul in its striking

31

appearance, in its life habits, and in its style. The things of nature similarly show themselves with extraordinary particularity. A river's power and beauty give it an imposing presence. A striking building stands before us as an individual every bit as soulful as we are.

Everyone knows that we can be deeply affected by the things of nature. A certain hill or mountain can offer a deep emotional focus to a person's life or to a family or community. When my great-grandparents settled in upstate New York after emigrating from Ireland, they created a thriving small farm in the countryside. They raised many kinds of animals, sowed fields with a variety of crops, and planted and tended an orchard with great care. The house that they built was graceful to look at from the outside, and inside it was filled with old paintings and photographs. A player piano stood against the wall of a small parlor, and the kitchen served as the main social center. In front of the house were two grand chestnut trees that offered shade and beauty for the family and the many people who visited the farm for over fifty years.

Not long ago I joined up with some cousins and paid a visit to the old homestead, which had been sold to a man who wanted the land only for hunting. We found that the barn had fallen to the ground and was now completely hidden by brush; even the house was no longer visible among the tall grasses that had grown up around its foundation. But a piece of the orchard was still visible, and the chestnut trees had not lost their nobility and kindliness. My cousins and I talked about those trees and some of the people who had sat under them on hot summer days telling tall tales and innumerable stories about the past. I remembered an uncle making a slanted cut on a small twig from the tree, showing me the marks of horseshoe nails in the cross-section—his explanation of why the tree was called a horse chestnut.

If someone thinking of widening the road or building a new house should ever come to cut down those chestnut trees, it would be a painful loss for me and many members of my family, not just because the trees are symbols of time past, but because they are living beings filled with beauty and surrounded by a huge aura of memory. In a real sense they are part of the family, bound to us as individuals of another species but not another community.

Made things also have soul. We can become attached to them and find meaningfulness in them, along with deeply felt values and warm memories. A neighbor told me he wanted to move to a different town, but his children loved their house so much they wouldn't let him make the move. We know these feelings of attachment to things, but we tend not to take them seriously and allow them to be part of our world view. What if we took more seriously this capacity of things to be close to us, to reveal their beauty and expressive subjectivity? The result would be a soul-ecology, a responsibility to the things of the world based on appreciation and relatedness rather than on abstract principle. Our felt relationship to things wouldn't allow us to pollute or to perpetuate ugliness. We couldn't let a beautiful ocean bay become a sewer system for shipping and manufacturing because our hearts would protest this violation of soul. We can only treat badly those things whose souls we disregard.

The attachment I am describing is not a sentimentalizing or idealizing of things, but rather a sense of a common life that extends to objects. Because the attachment is superficial, sentimentalizing nature can actually foster abuse of nature. It also seems possible to love the earth intellectually without feeling the emotional relationship; a real relationship with nature has to be fostered by spending time with it, observing it, and being open to its teachings. Any true relationship requires times, a certain vulnerability, and openness to being affected and changed.

A deep ecological sensibility can come only from the deep soul, which thrives in community, in thinking that is not detached from the heart, and in relatedness to particulars. It's a simple idea: if you don't love things in particular, you cannot love the world, because the world doesn't exist except in individual things. *Anima mundi* refers to the soul in each thing, and therefore psychology, as a discipline of the soul, is properly concerned with things. Ultimately, then, the fields of psychology and ecology overlap, because care of the world is a tending to the soul that resides in nature as well as in human beings.

Let's return to the world *ecology*. As we have already seen, *oikos* means "home." Speaking from the point of view of soul, ecology is not earth science, it is *home* science; it has to do with cultivating a sense of home wherever we are, in whatever context. The things of the world are part of our home environment, and so a soulful ecology is rooted in the feeling that this world is our home and that our responsibility to it comes not from obligation or logic but from true affection.

Without a felt connection to things we become numb to the world and lose that important home and family. The homelessness we see on our city streets is a reflection of a deeper homelessness we feel in our hearts. Homeless people embody a deprivation of soul which we all experience to the extent that we live in an inanimate world without the sense of a world soul to connect us to things. We assume that our loneliness has to do with other people, but it also comes from our estrangement from a world that we have depersonalized by our philosophies. We assume that homelessness has to do with economics, when it is more the mirror of the society and culture we have made.

• • •

Care of our actual houses, then, however humble, is also care of the soul. No matter how little money we have, we can be mindful of the importance of beauty in our homes. No matter where we live, we live in a neighborhood, and we can cultivate this wider piece of earth, too, as our home, as a place that is integrally bound to the condition of our hearts.

Every home is a microcosm, the archetypal "world" embodied in a house or a plot of land or an apartment. Many traditions acknowledge the archetypal nature of a house with some kind of cosmic ornament—a sun and moon, a band of stars, a dome that obviously reflects the canopy of the sky. In its architecture and ornamentation, Shakespeare's Globe Theatre was the planet in miniature. Each of us lives in the Globe Theatre of our own homes; what happens to us there happens in our entire world.

Marsilio Ficino recommended that we should all have images in our houses that remind us of our relationship to the cosmos. He suggested, for example, that we place either a model of the universe or an astrological painting on the ceiling of our bedroom. Not so long ago we still carved moons into our outhouses. But now one rarely sees a cosmic architectural motif, except perhaps for a pointed roof, which could function for use as a spire pointing to the heavens, if we did not explain the geometry of our roofs as a solution to drainage problems.

The Zuni Indians of New Mexico express the idea of the cosmic home in their mythology. In their creation story, the location of their village is found by a water strider, a bug; it stretches its body across the continent, and its heart rests at Zuni. We could all tell a similar myth of our own homes, about how they correspond to our beating animal hearts. When the Zuni sing about this Middle Place, they acknowledge the mystery that a real home is always at once a particular place and the entire world. "When it rained at Zuni," they chant, "it would rain all over the earth." This profound conception of our own homes and locales is the basis of a real, soulful ecology. As long as the heart is involved, care of the place will follow. . . .

•   •   •

BEAUTY, THE FACE OF THE SOUL

Throughout history we find certain schools of thought, such as the Renaissance Platonists and the Romantic poets, that have focused on the soul. It's interesting to note that these soul-minded writers have emphasized certain common themes. Relatedness, particularity, imagination, mortality, and pleasure are among them; another is beauty.

In a world where soul is neglected, beauty is placed last on its list of priorities. In the intellect-oriented curricula of our schools, for instance, science and math are considered important studies, because they allow further advances in technology. If there is a slash in funding, the arts are the first to go, even before athletics. The clear implication is that the arts are dispensable: we can't live without technology, but we can live without beauty.

This assumption that beauty is an accessory, and dispensable, shows that we don't understand the importance of giving the soul what it needs. The soul is nurtured by beauty. What food is to the body, arresting, complex, and pleasing images are to the soul. If we have a psychology rooted in a medical view of human behavior and emotional life, then the primary value will be health. But if our idea of psychology is based on the soul, then the goal of our therapeutic efforts will be beauty. I will go so far as to say that if we lack beauty in our lives, we will probably suffer familiar disturbances in the soul—depression, paranoia, meaninglessness, and addiction. The soul craves beauty and in its absence suffers what James Hillman has called "beauty neurosis."

Beauty assists the soul in its own peculiar ways of being. For example, beauty is arresting. For the soul, it is important to be taken out of the rush of practical life for the contemplation of timeless and eternal realities. Tradition named this need of the soul *vacatio*—a vacation from ordinary activity in favor of a moment of reflection and wonder. You may find yourself driving along a highway when you suddenly pass a vista that catches your breath. You stop the car, get out for just a few minutes, and behold the grandeur of nature. This is the arresting power of beauty, and giving in to that sudden longing of the soul is a way of giving it what it needs. Discussions of beauty can sometimes sound ethereal and philosophical, but from the soul viewpoint, beauty is a necessary part of ordinary life. Every day we will find moments when the soul glimpses an occasion for beauty, if only passing a store window and stopping for a second to notice a beautiful ring or an arresting pattern in a dress.

Some scholars say that the Three Graces dancing in a circle in Boticelli's famous painting *Primavera* represent Beauty, Restraint, and Pleasure. According to Renaissance writings, these three are the graces of life. What would a modern equivalent be—technology, information, and communication? The Renaissance graces have to do directly with the soul. Botticelli's painting shows Eros or Desire shooting his flaming arrow at Restraint. The arrow of desire and attachment stops us in our tracks—we are taken by the beauty, and feel its pleasure. Outwardly, of course, nothing is accomplished. We may not buy the ring that has caught our eye, or photograph the vista. The point of the momentary seizure is simply to feed the soul with its preferred diet—a sight that invites contemplation.

For the soul, then, beauty is not defined as pleasantness of form but rather as the quality in things that invites absorption and contemplation. Sōetsu Yanagi, founder of Japan's modern craft movement, defines beauty as that which gives unlimited scope to the imagination; beauty is a source of imagination, he says, that never dries up. A thing so attractive and absorbing may not be pretty or pleasant. It could be ugly, in fact, and yet seize the soul as beautiful in this special sense. James Hillman defines beauty for the soul as things displaying themselves in their individuality. Yanagi's and Hillman's point is that beauty doesn't require prettiness. Some pieces of art are not pleasing to look at, and yet their content and form are arresting and lure the heart into profound imagination.

• • •

If we are going to care for the soul, and if we know that the soul is nurtured by beauty, then we will have to understand beauty more deeply and give it a more prominent place in life. Religion has always understood the value of beauty, as we can see in churches and temples, which are never built for purely practical considerations, but always for the imagination. A tall steeple or a rose window are not designed to allow additional seating or better light for reading. They speak to the soul's need for beauty, for love of the building itself as well as its use, for a special opportunity for sacred imagination. Couldn't we learn from our churches and temples, our kivas and mosques, to give attention and funding to this same need in our homes, our commercial buildings, our highways, and our schools?

In a symptomatic way vandalism—which favors schools, cemeteries, and churches—paradoxically draws attention to the sacredness of things. Frequently when we have lost a sense of the sacred, it reappears in a negative form. The work of dark angels is not altogether different from those who wear white. Here, then, is another way to interpret the abuse of things—as an underworld attempt to reestablish their sacredness.

An appreciation for beauty is simply an openness to the power of things to stir the soul. If we can be affected by beauty, then soul is alive and well in us, because the soul's great talent is for being affected. The word *passion* means basically "to be affected," and passion is the essential energy of the soul. The poet Rilke describes this passive power in the imagery of the flower's structure, when he calls it a "muscle of infinite reception." We don't often think of the capacity to be affected as strength and as the work of a powerful muscle, and yet for the soul, as for the flower, this is its toughest work and its main role in our lives.

BERTRAND RUSSELL

Impersonal Interests

BERTRAND RUSSELL (1872–1970) was one of the greatest philosophers of this century. He wrote an enormous number of books and articles, from *Principia Mathematica* (1910–1913, with Alfred North Whitehead) to some notorious poems in favor of "free love" and atheism. He was too controversial for most universities, and a famous court case prevented him from teaching at City College of New York. He did, however, win the Nobel Prize for Literature in 1950. At the age of 89, he was jailed for protesting against nuclear arms.

I wish to consider not those major interests about which a man's life is built, but those minor interests which fill his leisure and afford relaxation from the tenseness of his more serious preoccupations. In the life of the average man his wife and children, his work and his financial position occupy the main part of his anxious and serious thought. Even if he has extra-matrimonial love affairs, they probably do not concern him as profoundly in themselves as in their possible effects upon his home life. The interests which are bound up with his work I am not for the present regarding as impersonal interests. A man of science, for example, must keep abreast of research in his own line. Towards such research his feelings have the warmth and vividness belonging to something intimately concerned with his career, but if he reads about research in some quite other science with which he is not professionally concerned he reads in quite a different spirit, not professionally, less critically, more disinterestedly. Even if he has to use his mind in order to follow what is said, his reading is nevertheless a relaxation, because it is not connected with his responsibilities. If the book interests him, his interest is impersonal in a sense which cannot be applied to the books upon his own subject. It is such interests lying outside the main activities of a man's life that I wish to speak about in the present chapter.

One of the sources of unhappiness, fatigue and nervous strain is inability to be interested in anything that is not of practical importance in one's own life. The result of this is that the conscious mind gets no rest from a certain small number of matters, each of which probably involves some anxiety and some element of worry. Except in sleep the conscious mind is never allowed to lie fallow while subconscious thought matures its gradual wisdom. The result is excitability, lack of sagacity, irritability, and a loss of sense of proportion. All these are both causes and effects of fatigue. As a man gets more tired, his external interests fade, and as they fade he loses the relief which they afford him and becomes still more tired. This vicious circle is only too apt to end in a breakdown. What is restful about external interests is the fact that they do not call for any action. Making decisions and exercising volition are very fatiguing, especially if they have to be done hurriedly and without the help of the subconscious. Men who feel that they must "sleep on it" before coming to an important decision are profoundly right. But it is not only in sleep that the subconscious mental processes can work. They can work also while a man's conscious mind is occupied elsewhere. The man who can forget his work when it is over and not remember it until it begins again next day is likely to do his work far better than the man who worries about it through-out the intervening hours. And it is very much easier to forget work at the times when it ought to be forgotten if a man has many interests other than his work than it is if he has not. It is, however, essential that these interests should not exercise those very fac-ulties which have been exhausted by his day's work. They should not involve will and quick decision, they should not, like gambling, involve any financial element, and they should as a rule not be so exciting as to produce emotional fatigue and preoccupy the subconscious as well as the conscious mind.

A great many amusements fulfill all these conditions. Watching games, going to the theater, playing golf, are all irreproachable from this point of view. For a man of a book-ish turn of mind reading unconnected with his professional activities is very satisfac-tory. However important a worry may be, it should not be thought about throughout the whole of the waking hours.

In this respect there is a great difference between men and women. Men on the whole find it very much easier to forget their work than women do. In the case of women whose work is in the home this is natural, since they do not have the change of place that a man has when he leaves the office to help them to acquire a new mood. But if I am not mistaken, women whose work is outside the home differ from men in this re-spect almost as much as those who work at home. They find it, that is to say, very difficult to be interested in anything that has for them no practical importance. Their purposes govern their thoughts and their activities, and they seldom become absorbed in some wholly irresponsible interest. I do not of course deny that exceptions exist, but I am speaking of what seems to me to be the usual rule. In a women's college, for example, the women teachers, if no man is present, talk shop in the evening, while in a man's col-lege the men do not. This characteristic appears to women as a higher degree of con-scientiousness than that of men, but I do not think that in the long run it improves the quality of their work. And it tends to produce a certain narrowness of outlook leading not infrequently to a kind of fanaticism.

All impersonal interests, apart from their importance as relaxation, have various other uses. To begin with, they help a man to retain his sense of proportion. It is very easy to become so absorbed in our own pursuits, our own circle, our own type of work, that we forget how small a part this is of the total of human activity and how many things in the world are entirely unaffected by what we do. Why should one remember this? you may ask. There are several answers. In the first place, it is good to have as true a picture of the world as is compatible with necessary activities. Each of us in the world for no very long time, and within the few years of his life has to acquire what-ever he is to know of this strange planet and its place in the universe. To ignore our op-portunities for knowledge, imperfect as they are, is like going to the theater and not listening to the play. The world is full of things that are tragic or comic, heroic or bizarre or surprising, and those who fail to be interested in the spectacle that it offers are forgoing one of the privileges that life has to offer.

Then again a sense of proportion is very valuable and at times very consoling. We are all inclined to get unduly excited, unduly strained, unduly impressed with the im-portance of the little corner of the world in which we live, and of the little moment of time comprised between our birth and death. In this excitement and overestimation of our own importance there is nothing desirable. True, it may make us work harder, but it will not make us work better. A little work directed to a good end is better than a great deal of work directed to a bad end, though the apostles of the strenuous life seem to think otherwise. Those who care much for their work are always in danger of falling into fanaticism, which consists essentially in remembering one or two desirable things while forgetting all the rest, and in supposing that in the pursuit of these one or two any incidental harm of other sorts is of little account. Against this fanatical temper there is no better prophylactic than a large conception of the life of man and his place in the universe. This may seem a very big thing to invoke in such a connection, but apart from this particular use, it is in itself a thing of great value.

It is one of the defects of modern higher education that it has become too much a training in the acquisition of certain kinds of skill, and too little an enlargement of the mind and heart by an impartial survey of the world. You become absorbed, let us say, in a political contest, and work hard for the victory of your own party. So far, so good. But it may happen in the course of the contest that some opportunity of victory presents itself which involves the use of methods calculated to increase hatred, violence and suspicion in the world. For example, you may find that the best road to victory is to insult some foreign nation. If your mental purview is limited to the present, or if you have imbibed the doctrine that what is called efficiency is the only thing that matters, you will adopt such dubious means. Through them you will be victorious in your immediate purpose, while the more distant consequences may be disastrous. If, on the other hand, you have as part of the habitual furniture of your mind the past ages of man, his slow and partial emergence out of barbarism, and the brevity of his total existence in comparison with astronomical epochs—if, I say, such thoughts have molded your habitual feelings, you will realize that the momentary battle upon which you are engaged cannot be of such importance as to risk a backward step towards the darkness out of which we have been slowly emerging. Nay, more, if you suffer defeat in your immediate objective, you will be sustained by the same sense of its momentariness that made you unwilling to adopt degrading weapons. You will have, beyond your immediate activities, purposes that are distant and slowly unfolding, in which you are not an isolated individual but one of the great army of those who have led mankind towards a civilized existence. If you have attained to this outlook, a certain deep happiness will never leave you, whatever your personal fate may be. Life will become a communion with the great of all ages, and personal death no more than a negligible incident.

If I had the power to organize higher education as I should wish it to be, I should seek to substitute for the old orthodox religions—which appeal to few among the young, and those as a rule the least intelligent and the most obscurantist—something which is perhaps hardly to be called religion, since it is merely a focusing of attention upon well-ascertained facts. I should seek to make young people vividly aware of the past, vividly realizing that the future of man will in all likelihood be immeasurably longer than his past, profoundly conscious of the minuteness of the planet upon which we live and of the fact that life on this planet is only a temporary incident; and at the same time with these facts which tend to emphasize the insignificance of the individual, I should present quite another set of facts designed to impress upon the mind of the young the greatness of which the individual is capable, and the knowledge that throughout all the depths of stellar space nothing of equal value is known to us. Spinoza long ago wrote of human bondage and human freedom; his form and his language make his thought difficult of access to all students of philosophy, but the essence of what I wish to convey differs little from what he has said.

A man who has once perceived, however temporarily and however briefly, what makes greatness of soul, can no longer be happy if he allows himself to be petty, self-seeking, troubled by trivial misfortunes, dreading what fate may have in store for him. The man capable of greatness of soul will open wide the windows of his mind, letting the winds blow freely upon it from every portion of the universe. He will see himself and life and the world as truly as our human limitations will permit; realizing the brevity and minuteness of human life, he will realize also that in individual minds is concentrated whatever of value the known universe contains. And he will see that the man whose mind mirrors the world becomes in a sense as great as the world. In emancipation from the fears that beset the slave of circumstance he will experience a profound joy, and through all the vicissitudes of his outward life he will remain in the depths of his being a happy man.

Leaving these large speculations and returning to our more immediate subject, namely the value of impersonal interests, there is another consideration which makes them a great help towards happiness. Even in the most fortunate lives there are times when things go wrong. Few men except bachelors have never quarreled with their wives; few parents have not endured grave anxiety owing to the illnesses of their children; few business men have avoided times of financial stress; few professional men have not known periods when failure stared them in the face. At such times a capacity to become interested in something outside the cause of anxiety is an immense boon. At such times when in spite of anxiety there is nothing to be done at the moment, one man will play chess, another will read detective stories, a third will become absorbed in popular astronomy, a fourth will console himself by reading about the excavations at Ur of the Chaldees. Any one of these four is acting wisely, whereas the man who does nothing to distract his mind and allows his trouble to acquire a complete empire over him is acting unwisely and making himself less fit to cope with his troubles when the moment for action arrives. Very similar considerations apply to irreparable sorrows such as the death of some person deeply loved. No good is done to any one by allowing oneself to become sunk in grief on such an occasion. Grief is unavoidable and must be expected, but everything that can be done should be done to minimize it. It is mere sentimentality to aim, as some do, at extracting the very uttermost drop of misery from misfortune. I do not of course deny that a man may be broken by sorrow, but I do say that every man should do his utmost to escape this fate, and should seek any distraction, however trivial, provided it is not in itself harmful or degrading. Among those I regard as harmful and degrading I include such things as drunkenness and drugs, of which the purpose is to destroy thought, at least for the time being. The proper course is not to destroy thought but to turn it into new channels, or at any rate into channels remote from the present misfortune. It is difficult to do this if life has hitherto been concentrated upon a very few interests and those few have now become suffused with sorrow. To bear misfortune well when it comes, it is wise to have cultivated in happier times a certain width of interests, so that the mind may find prepared for it some undisturbed place suggesting other associations and other emotions than those which are making the present difficult to bear.

A man of adequate vitality and zest will surmount all misfortunes by the emergence after each blow of an interest in life and the world which cannot be narrowed down so much as to make one loss fatal. To be defeated by one loss or even by several is not something to be admired as a proof of sensibility, but something to be deplored as a failure in vitality. All our affections are at the mercy of death, which may strike down those whom we love at any moment. It is therefore necessary that our lives should not have that narrow intensity which puts the whole meaning and purpose of our life at the mercy of accident.

For all these reasons the man who pursues happiness wisely will aim at the possession of a number of subsidiary interests in addition to those central ones upon which his life is built.

ETTY HILLESUM

A Precious Slice of Life

ETTY HILLESUM was a Dutch Jew living in Amsterdam during the Holocaust. In September 1943 she was deported to Auschwitz and died soon after turning 29.

27 FEBRUARY, FRIDAY MORNING, 10 O'CLOCK

. . . How rash to assert that man shapes his own destiny. All he can do is determine his inner responses. You cannot know another's inner life from his circumstances. To know that you must know his dreams, his relationships, his moods, his disappointments, his sickness and his death. . . .

Very early on Wednesday morning a large group of us were crowded into the Gestapo hall, and at that moment the circumstances of all our lives were the same. All of us occupied the same space, the men behind the desk no less than those about to be questioned. What distinguished each one of us was only our inner attitudes. I noticed a young man with a sullen expression, who paced up and down looking driven and harassed and making no attempt to hide his irritation. He kept looking for pretexts to shout at the helpless Jews: 'Take your hands out of your pockets . . .' and so on. I thought him more pitiable than those he shouted at, and those he shouted at I thought pitiable for being afraid of him. When it was my turn to stand in front of his desk, he bawled at me, 'what the hell's so funny?' I wanted to say, 'Nothing's funny here except you,' but refrained. 'You're still smirking,' he bawled again. And I, in all innocence, 'I didn't mean to, it's my usual expression.' And he, 'Don't give me that, get the hell out of here,' his face saying, 'I'll deal with you later.' And that was presumably meant to scare me to death, but the device was too transparent.

I am not easily frightened. Not because I am brave but because I know that I am dealing with human beings and that I must try as hard as I can to understand everything that anyone ever does. And that was the real import of this morning: not that a disgruntled young Gestapo officer yelled at me, but that I felt no indignation, rather a real compassion, and would have liked to ask, 'Did you have a very unhappy childhood, has your girlfriend let you down?' Yes, he looked harassed and driven, sullen and weak. I should have liked to start treating him there and then, for I know that pitiful young men like that are dangerous as soon as they are let loose on mankind. But all the blame must be put on the system that uses such people. What needs eradicating is the evil in man, not man himself.

Something else about this morning: the perception, very strongly borne in, that despite all the suffering and injustice I cannot hate others. All the appalling things that happen are no mysterious threats from afar, but arise from fellow beings very close to us. That makes these happenings more familiar, then, and not so frightening. The terrifying thing is that systems grow too big for men and hold them in a satanic grip, the builders no less than the victims of the system, much as large edifices and spires, created

41

by men's hands, tower high above us, dominate us, yet may collapse over our heads and bury us.

12 MARCH 1942, THURSDAY EVENING, 11.30

How indescribably beautiful it all was, Max, our cup of coffee, the cheap cigarette and that walk through the darkened city, arm in arm, and the fact that we two were together. Anyone who knew about our past would have found it strange and quite incredible, this meeting out of the blue—just because Max intends to get married and wants me of all people to give him advice. But that's what was so beautiful—to be able to come back to a friend of one's youth and see oneself reflected in the light of his own greater maturity. At the start of the evening he said, 'I don't know what it is, but something in you has changed. I think you have turned into a real woman.' And at the end, 'The change is not for the worse, believe me, your features, your gestures, they're as lively and expressive as ever, but now there's so much more wisdom behind them, it's so nice to be with you,' and he shone his flashlight briefly in my face, nodded in recognition and said decidedly, 'It's you all right.' And then, half clumsily and half familiarly, our cheeks brushed and we moved on and drew apart. It really was beautiful. And paradoxical though it must sound: perhaps it was our first real meeting. As we walked on he said suddenly, 'I think that perhaps over the years we can grow into real friends.' And so nothing is ever lost. People do return to you, you live with them inside you until a few years later they are back with you again.

On 8 March I had written to S., 'My passion used to be nothing but a desperate clinging to—to what, exactly? To something one cannot cling to with the body.'

And it was the body of this man, who now walked beside me like a brother, to which I had once clung in terrible despair. That, somehow, was the most gladdening thing: something had survived, the pleasing and familiar exchange of ideas, the sharing of each other's presence, the revival of memories that no longer haunted us, who once had lived so destructively off each other. Although by the end, of course, we were both emotionally exhausted.

Still, it was the old Max who suddenly asked, 'Have you had an affair with anyone else since then?' I held up two fingers. Later when I said I might marry a refugee so that I could be with him when they sent him to a camp, he pulled a face. As we took our leave, he said, 'You won't do anything foolish, will you? I'm so afraid you'll come to grief.' And I, 'I Won't come to grief, don't worry.' And I wanted to add something, but by then we had moved too far away from each other. If you have a rich inner life, I would have said, there probably isn't all that much difference between the inside and outside of a camp. Would I myself be able to life up to such sentiments? There are few illusions left to us. Life is going to be very hard. We shall be torn apart, all who are dear to one another. I don't think the time is very far off now. We shall have to steel ourselves inwardly more and more.

I would love to read the letters I wrote to him when I was eighteen. He said, 'I always had such ambitions for you, I expected great works from you.' I said, 'Max, they'll come. There's no hurry. Can't we be patient?' 'Yes, I know you can write. Now and then I read over the letters you wrote to me; you can write.'

Still, it's a comforting thought that things like that can still happen in this riven world of ours. Many more things perhaps than we are prepared to admit to ourselves. A youthful love suddenly rediscovering itself, smiling back at its own past. And reconciled to it. That's what had happened to me. I set the tone that evening and Max went along with it, and that said a good deal.

So, everything is no longer pure chance, a bit of a game now and then, an exciting adventure. Instead I have the feeling that I have a destiny, in which the events are strung significantly together. When I think how we talked together through the dark city, older now, softened by the past, feeling that we still had so much to tell each other but vague about when we should meet again, I am filled with a profound and solemn gratitude that this could happen in my life. It is now close on midnight and I'm going to bed. It's been a good day. At the end of each day I feel the need to say: life is very good after all. I have my own philosophy now, one I'm prepared to speak up for, which is saying a lot for the self-conscious girl I've always been. . . .

SATURDAY MORNING, 10 O'CLOCK

. . . That was my day, then, a long day. And the most important thing about it all? That the branches of the tree outside my window have been lopped off.

The night before the stars had still hung like glistening fruit in the heavy branches, and now they climbed, unsure of themselves, up the bare, ravaged trunk. Oh, yes, the stars: for a few nights, some of them, lost, deserted, grazed over the wide, forsaken, heavenly plain.

For a moment, when the branches were being cut, I became sentimental. And for that moment I was deeply sad. Then I suddenly knew: I should love the new landscape, too, love it in my own way. Now the two trees rise up outside my window like imposing, emaciated ascetes, thrusting into the bright sky like two daggers.

And on Thursday evening the war raged once again outside my window and I lay there watching it all from my bed. Bernard was playing a Bach record next door. It had sounded so powerful and glowing, but then, suddenly, there were planes, ack-ack fire, shooting, bombs—much noisier than they have been for a long time. It seemed to go on right beside the house. And it suddenly came to me again: there must be so many houses all over the world which are collapsing each day under just such bombs as these.

And Bach went gallantly on, now faint and small. And I lay there in my bed in a very strange mood. Filaments of light along the menacing bare trunk outside my window. A constant pounding. And I thought to myself: any minute now a piece of shrapnel could come through that window. It's quite possible. And it's equally possible that there would be a lot of pain. And yet I felt so deeply peaceful and grateful, there in my bed, and meekly resigned to all the disasters and pains that might be in store for me.

All disasters stem from us. Why is there a war? Perhaps because now and then I might be inclined to snap at my neighbour. Because I and my neighbour and everyone else do not have enough love. Yet we could fight war and all its excrescences by releasing, each day, the love which is shackled inside us, and giving it a chance to live. And I believe that I will never be able to hate any human being for his so-called 'wickedness,' that I shall only hate the evil that is within me, though hate is perhaps putting it too strongly even then. In any case, we cannot be lax enough in what we demand of others and strict enough in what we demand of ourselves.

Yes, the trees, sometimes at night their branches would bow down under the weight of the fruit of the stars, and now they are menacing daggers piercing the bright spring air. Yet even in their new shape and setting they are unspeakably beautiful. I remember a walk along an Amsterdam canal, one dreamlike summer night, long, long ago. I had visions then of ruined cities. I saw old cities vanish and new cities arise and I thought to myself, even if the whole of this world is bombed to bits, we shall build a new world, and that one too will pass, and still life will be beautiful, always beautiful.

Even ill-fated Rotterdam. What a bizarre new landscape, so full of eerie fascination, yet one we might also come to love again. We human beings cause monstrous conditions, but precisely because we cause them we soon learn to adapt ourselves to them. Only if we become such that we can no longer adapt ourselves, only if, deep inside, we rebel against every kind of evil, will we be able to put a stop to it. Aeroplanes, streaking down in flames, still have a weird fascination for us—even aesthetically—though we know, deep down, that human beings are being burnt alive. As long as that happens, while everything within us does not yet scream out in protest, so long will we find ways of adapting ourselves, and the horrors will continue.

Does that mean I am never sad, that I never rebel, always acquiesce, and love life no matter what the circumstances? No, far from it. I believe that I know and share the many sorrows and sad circumstances that a human being can experience, but I do not cling to them. I do not prolong such moments of agony. They pass through me, like life itself, as a broad, eternal stream, they become part of that stream, and life continues. And as a result all my strength is preserved, does not become tagged on to futile sorrow or rebelliousness.

And finally: ought we not, from time to time, open ourselves up to cosmic sadness? One day I shall surely be able to say to Ilse Blumenthal, 'Yes, life is beautiful, and I value it anew at the end of every day, even though I know that the sons of mothers, and you are one such mother, are being murdered in concentration camps. And you must be able to bear your sorrow; even if it seems to crush you, you will be able to stand up again, for human beings are so strong, and your sorrow must become an integral part of yourself, part of your body and your soul, you mustn't run away from it, but bear it like an adult. Do not relieve your feelings through hatred, do not seek to be avenged on all German mothers, for they, too, sorrow at this very moment for their slain and murdered sons. Give your sorrow all the space and shelter in yourself that is its due, for if everyone bears his grief honestly and courageously, the sorrow that now fills the world will abate. But if you do not clear a decent shelter for your sorrow, and instead reserve most of the space inside you for hatred and thoughts of revenge—from which new sorrows will be born for others—then sorrow will never cease in this world and will multiply. And if you have given sorrow the space its gentle origins demand, then you may truly say: life is beautiful and so rich. So beautiful and so rich that it makes you want to believe in God.'. . .

And the people, the friends, my many friends! Nowadays there are hardly any accidental relationships left; you have a deep if subtly different relationship with each person, and must not be disloyal to one for the sake of the other. There are no wasted and boring minutes any longer, one has to keep learning how to take one's rest between two deep breaths or in a five-minute chat. . . .

21 JULY, TUESDAY EVENING, 7 O'CLOCK

. . . I feel as if I were the guardian of a precious slice of life, with all the responsibility that entails. . . .

29 SEPTEMBER

Let me just note down one more thing for myself: Matthew 6:34: Take therefore no thought for the morrow: for the morrow shall take thought for the things of itself. Sufficient unto the day is the evil thereof.

We have to fight them daily, like fleas, those many small worries about the morrow, for they sap our energies. We make mental provision for the days to come and everything turns out differently, quite differently. Sufficient unto the day. The things that have to be done must be done, and for the rest we must not allow ourselves to become infested with thousands of petty fears and worries, so many motions of no confidence in God. Everything will turn out all right with my residence permit and with my ration book; right now there's no point in brooding about it, and I would do much better to write a Russian essay. Ultimately, we have just one moral duty: to reclaim large areas of peace in ourselves, more and more peace and to reflect it towards others. And the more peace there is in us, the more peace there will also be in our troubled world.

Just had a short telephone conversation with Toos. Jopie writes, 'Don't send anymore parcels. Everything is in turmoil.' Haanen sent a letter to his wife: too short to make sense but long enough to make everyone nervous. Nasty. And it set off a bad reaction in me as well. We have to fight that. Must turn our backs on all these pointless rumours, which spread like an infectious disease. Now and then I get an inkling of what goes on in all these unhappy people. Their lives are so impoverished and so empty. And then they say what I have heard from so many of them, 'I can't read any books these days, I just can't concentrate any longer. In the past my house was always full of flowers, but now, well, I no longer care for that sort of thing.' Impoverished, empty lives. Can they be taught to 'work' on themselves, to find peace in themselves? To live a productive and confident life despite all these fears and rumours? To know that one can fling oneself down on one's knees in the farthest and quietest corner of one's inner life and stay there kneeling until the sky above looks sunny and clear again? I felt it once more in the flesh, last night, what human beings have to suffer these days. It is good to be reminded of that from time to time, if only to learn how to fight it. And then to continue undisturbed through the wide and open landscape that is one's own heart. But I haven't reached that point yet. First to the dentist, and this afternoon to my appointment at the Jewish Council in Keizersgracht.

30 SEPTEMBER

To be true to one's own spontaneity, to what one set out to do in an all too spontaneous moment.

To be true to every feeling and thought that has started to germinate.

To be true in the fullest sense of the word, to be true to God, to one's own best moments.

If I have one duty in these times, it is to bear witness. I think I have learned to take it all in, to read life in one long stretch. And in my youthful arrogance I am often sure that I can remember every least thing I see and that I shall be able to relate it all one day. Still, I must try to put it down now.

I seem able to see ever more clearly the gaping chasms which swallow up man's creative powers and *joie de vivre*. They are holes in our own mind. Sufficient unto the day is the evil thereof. And: man suffers most through his fears of suffering. The body keeps leading the spirit, when it should be the other way round. 'You live too cerebral a life.' And why now? Because I would not surrender my body to your greedy hands? How strange men are! How much I want to write. Somewhere deep inside me is a workshop in which Titans are forging a new world. I once wrote in despair: 'it is inside my little skull that this world must be rethought, that it must be given fresh clarity.' I still occasionally think so, with the same, almost diabolical, presumption. I know how to free my creative powers more and more from the snares of material concerns, from the idea of hunger and cold and danger. They are, after all, imaginary phantoms, not the reality. Reality is something one shoulders together with all the suffering that goes with it, and with all the difficulties. And as one shoulders them so one's resilience grows stronger. But the *idea* of suffering (which is not the reality, for real suffering is always fruitful and can turn life into a precious thing) must be destroyed. And if you destroy the ideas behind which life lies imprisoned as behind bars, then you liberate your true life, its real mainsprings, and then you will also have the strength to bear real suffering, your own and the world's. . . .

LATER

I have the feeling that my life is not yet finished, that it is not yet a rounded whole. A book, and what a book, in which I have got stuck half-way. I would so much like to read on. There have been moments when I have felt as if my whole life had been one great preparation for community living, when in fact I have always led a very private life. . . .

9 OCTOBER

. . . Paradoxical though it may sound: whenever one tries too desperately to be physically close to some beloved person, whenever one throws all one has into one's longing for that person, one is really giving him short change. For one has no reserves left then for a true encounter. . . .

CHAPTER 2

How Should
I Treat
My Family
and Friends?

Your best friend has started dating someone, and you are pleased when he or she wants you to meet this new important person. You plan to meet your friend and the date for dinner. You arrive at the chosen restaurant at the appointed time and are horrified to discover that the date is someone that you know and had hoped to start dating. The slogan "All's fair in love and war" crosses your mind. But you feel that it would be wrong to interfere. You might be able to attract your friend's date, but that would be the wrong way to treat your friend.

Certain interpersonal relationships—friendship, marriage, dating relationships, and close ties of kinship—carry with them particular ethical obligations. The ethical issues that pertain to interpersonal relationships do not generally stem from disagreement regarding whether or not special relationships obligate us in special ways. Moral debate often has to do with how we ought to resolve the tensions that sometimes arise between obligations to those who are close to us and other moral obligations. (Peter Singer's "Famine, Affluence, and Morality," included in abridged form in Chapter 12, considers, for instance, the competing aims of helping poor people and providing for one's family.)

These concerns are made more complicated by the fact that the obligations one has to family members and friends are usually taken to be the kind of obligations that German philosopher Immanuel Kant terms **meritorious duties.** Unlike duties that can be fulfilled by performing (or refraining from) a particular act (**necessary duties,** in Kant's terminology), meritorious duties are ongoing moral demands that will never be satisfied once and for all. The obligation that one has to care for elderly parents, for instance, is not generally thought to be of the sort of obligation for which one can write a large check and be done with the matter. Part of the reason that a check sounds like a deficient response to the obligation involved is that family and friends are typically thought to be objects of particular *care* and *concern.* Our concerns determine not just particular steps we ought to take but also the central priorities in our lives. Our relationships to our families and friends are not just one more source of obligations among many—for most of us, they are among the most important concerns of our lives.

The Chinese philosopher Confucius, who lived in the sixth century B.C.E., thought that the importance of our families to our lives should be recognized in ethics. Confucius defends a notion of graduated love, in which our love for family members is most fundamental. Confucius does not claim that we should love *only* our relatives; but he does think that family members, particularly parents, should come first. Confucius also places great emphasis on choosing virtuous friends and treating them with respect. Confucius urges empathy with others in a version of the Golden Rule: we should not do anything to others that we would not want done to ourselves. More positively, we should respond to others as appropriately as possible in the particular situation in which we interact with them. (This emphasis on particular circumstances in ethics is sometimes called **ethical particularism,** as distinguished from the view that ethical principles should be universal, applicable to every situation.)

Not all thinkers would agree with Confucius that our obligations to family members should always take precedence over other obligations. (This was true even in ancient China, where Confucius was criticized by the thinker Mo Zi, who argued that one should love everyone equally.) The problem of conflicting loyalties has been a disturbing moral problem for generations, as is evident in Sophocles' *Antigone*, written in the fifth century B.C.E. In this play, a young woman named Antigone is the sister of Polyneices, who has been killed in a dispute for the kingship of Thebes. The new king, Creon, has ordered that Polyneices' body be left unburied. But this creates a dilemma for Antigone. Should she obey the law, as pronounced by the king? Or should she fulfill her familial obligation to her brother by burying him? She decides to bury Polyneices. Creon responds by ordering that she be walled up in a tomb, ignoring the protestations of his son Haemon, who is engaged to Antigone. The excerpt included in this chapter includes Antigone's confrontation with Creon as well as Haemon's attempt to change his father's mind. (Things do not go well in the rest of the play. While in the tomb, Antigone hangs herself. Haemon breaks into the tomb, discovers that Antigone is dead, and kills himself. And Creon's wife, Eurydice, hearing the news, also commits suicide.)

Daniel Callahan considers what specific moral and legal obligations grown children have to their elderly parents in contemporary America. He observes that typical moral language seems ill suited for the parent-child bond. Children's obligations to parents are not merely special cases of children's obligations to friends, as some have argued—children might have obligations to their parents whether or not their parents have been their "friends" over the course of their lives. Nor are parents contractual parties to whom children "owe" specific kinds of support. In today's America, many elderly parents need the support of their children, lacking support from any other source; although this fact does not obviously establish that children have a moral obligation, it does suggest the importance of this bond in the lives of many Americans. The fact that some children have not chosen to act on this moral obligation, if in fact they perceive one, has led a few states to pass laws mandating that children contribute to their elderly parents' support, although few are enforcing such laws. But Callahan concludes that such laws may be extremely destructive. They may, he argues, undercut the nurturing ties of affection and loyalty, substituting mere monetary support for a richer kind of support that elderly people really need.

The moral dilemma presented in the excerpt from Mark Twain's *Huckleberry Finn* is dated and somewhat startling. It portrays Huck Finn's moral quandary about whether his loyalty to his friend Jim, an escaped slave, outweighs his responsibility to Jim's owner to restore her property. Loyalty wins out, in what we might see as a clear victory of right thinking over racism. But from Huck's perspective, given his conditioning, he follows his emotions rather than his reason, which reminds him that "reason is wrong." This portrait of Huck raises the question of which is a firmer guide in matters of interpersonal relationships: reason or emotion, principle or a sense of caring?

Janice Raymond emphasizes the importance of same-sex friendships for personal fulfillment, focusing in particular on relationships between women. She stresses, however, the difficulties involved in developing such friendships. She believes that women's friendships suffer from the conditions of modern life and that women have been too brainwashed by a male-dominated ideology to hold their female friendships in high esteem. Nevertheless, we should consider friendships a major priority in our lives, especially in contemporary America where many adults do not find their lives fully satisfying.

Dorothy Dinnerstein explores the origins of the ideology that values men more highly than women and its impact on adult relationships. She contends that the usual child-rearing scenario, in which infants are nurtured predominantly by their mothers, results in infantilism and sexism in adults of both sexes. The mother is the first other person that the infant learns to recognize. Traditionally, she is the absolute authority over the infant, checking some of the infant's efforts, as well as the first supportive audience for the baby's assertions of will. Because the mother does not always provide everything the infant wants when the child wants it, the mother is also the original object of anger. As a consequence, the infant feels ambivalence toward its mother, an ambivalence that becomes projected onto women generally. In traditional families in our society, the father comes into clear focus only when a child is somewhat older. Accordingly, the child's relationship with the father does not have the same complex ambivalence that the relationship with the first "other" had, and the father comes to symbolize a clearer kind of authority than that associated with the mother. Children generalize from fathers to men generally, and the consequence is that children of both sexes accept male authority figures because they are an alternative to the distress of their early relationship to the mother. Insofar as infantile rage continues to operate in adults, adults direct this rage at women and seek male authority figures as a refuge. Dinnerstein thinks that sexism will continue until adults outgrow this psychological infancy, and the essential change required if this is to happen throughout society, she believes, is for parents of both sexes to play a significant nurturing role from the beginning of a child's life.

The Confucian Analects

CONFUCIUS (Kong Fuzi, 551–479 B.C.E.) was a Chinese philosopher and the founder of an important philosophical tradition. Confucian ethics emphasizes the respect of children for their parents and the observance of traditional rituals and roles in one's behavior. Confucius is a particularist in ethics. In other words, he believes that appropriate behavior depends on the circumstances.

BOOK I

1. The Master said, To learn and at due times to repeat what one has learnt, is that not after all[1] a pleasure? That friends should come to one from afar,[2] is this not after all delightful? To remain unsoured even though one's merits are unrecognized by others, is that not after all what is expected of a gentleman?
2. Master Yu said, Those who in private life behave well towards their parents and elder brothers, in public life seldom show a disposition to resist the authority of their superiors. And as for such men starting a revolution, no instance of it has ever occurred. It is upon the trunk[3] that a gentleman works. When that is firmly set up, the Way grows. And surely proper behaviour towards parents and elder brothers is the trunk of Goodness?

• • •

6. The Master said, A young man's duty is to behave well to his parents at home and to his elders abroad, to be cautious in giving promises and punctual in keeping them, to have kindly feelings towards everyone, but seek the intimacy of the Good. If, when all that is done, he has any energy to spare, then let him study the polite arts.[4]
7. Tzu-hsia said, A man who

> Treats his betters as betters,
> Wears an air of respect,
> Who into serving father and mother
> Knows how to put his whole strength,
> Who in the service of his prince will lay down his life,
> Who in intercourse with friends is true to his word—

---

[1] The 'after all' implies 'even though one does not hold office.'

[2] Several of the disciples belonged to other States (e.g. Wei and Ch'i); but there is no evidence that they came to Lu on account of Confucius. Unless, however, there is here some allusion that escapes us, the phrase must refer to the visits of admirers from abroad, perhaps friends made during the Master's journeys in Honan.

[3] i.e. upon what is fundamental, as opposed to 'the twigs,' i.e. small arts and accomplishments, which the gentleman leaves to his inferiors.

[4] i.e. learn to recite the *Songs*, practice archery, deportment, and the like.

others may say of him that he still lacks education, but I for my part should certainly call him an educated man.

• • •

11. The Master said, While a man's father is alive, you can only see his intentions; it is when his father dies that you discover whether or not he is capable of carrying them out. If for the whole three years of mourning he manages to carry on the household exactly as in his father's day, then he is a good son indeed.

• • •

BOOK II

4. The Master said, At fifteen I set my heart upon learning. At thirty, I had planted my feet firm upon the ground. At forty, I no longer suffered from perplexities. At fifty, I knew what were the biddings of Heaven. At sixty, I heard them with docile ear. At seventy, I could follow the dictates of my own heart; for what I desired no longer overstepped the boundaries of right.

5. Mêng I Tzu[5] asked about the treatment of parents. The Master said, Never disobey! When Fan Ch'ih[6] was driving his carriage for him, the Master said, Mêng asked me about the treatment of parents and I said, Never disobey! Fan Ch'ih said, In what sense did you mean it? The Master said, While they are alive, serve them according to ritual. When they die, bury them according to ritual and sacrifice to them according to ritual.[7]

6. Mêng Wu Po[8] asked about the treatment of parents. The Master said, Behave in such a way that your father and mother have no anxiety about you, except concerning your health.

7. Tzu-yu[9] asked about the treatment of parents. The Master said, 'Filial sons' nowadays are people who see to it that their parents get enough to eat. But even dogs and horses are cared for to that extent. If there is no feeling of respect, wherein lies the difference?

8. Tzu-hsia[10] asked about the treatment of parents. The Master said, It is the demeanour that is difficult. Filial piety does not consist merely in young people undertaking the hard work, when anything has to be done, or serving their elders first with wine and food. It is something much more than that.

---

[5] A young grandee of Lu, whose father sent him to study with Confucius. He died in 481 B.C.

[6] A disciple.

[7] Evidently by 'disobey' Confucius meant 'disobey the rituals.' The reply was intended to puzzle the enquirer and make him think. In *Mencius*, III, 1, II, 2, 'While they are alive . . . ', etc., is given as a saying of Master Tsêng. Here and elsewhere 'sacrifice' means offerings in general and not only animal-sacrifice.

[8] Son of Mêng I Tzu.

[9] A disciple.

[10] This is Chêng Hsüan's interpretation. Pao Hsien (6 B.C.–65 A.D.) takes *sê* to mean the expression of one's parents, which must be watched for hints of approval or disapproval.

21. Someone, when talking to Master K'ung, said, How is it that you are not in the public service? The Master said, The Book[11] says: 'Be filial, only be filial and friendly towards your brothers, and you will be contributing to government.' There are other sorts of service quite different from what you mean by 'service.'

BOOK III

7. The Master said, Gentlemen never compete. You will say that in archery they do so. But even then they bow and make way for one another when they are going up to the archery-ground, when they are coming down and at the subsequent drinking-bout. Thus even when competing, they still remain gentlemen.

BOOK IV

18. The Master said, In serving his father and mother a man may gently remonstrate with them. But if he sees that he has failed to change their opinion, he should resume an attitude of deference and not thwart them; may feel discouraged, but not resentful.
26. Tzu-yu said, In the service of one's prince repeated scolding can only lead to loss of favour; in friendship, it can only lead to estrangement.

BOOK V

16. The Master said, Yen P'ing Chung is a good example of what one's intercourse with one's fellowmen should be. However long he has known anyone he always maintains the same scrupulous courtesy.

BOOK XV

23. Tzu-kung asked saying, Is there any single saying that one can act upon all day and every day? The Master said, Perhaps the saying about consideration: 'Never do to others what you would not like them to do to you.'

---

[11] i.e. what Europeans call the *Book of History*. The passage does not occur in the genuine books. . . . What it meant in its original context no doubt was 'Be pious to your ancestors . . . be generous in rewarding your officers of State.' Confucius 'reanimates' the ancient text, in order to prove that a virtuous private life makes a real contribution towards the public welfare.

SOPHOCLES

Antigone

SOPHOCLES was an Athenian tragedian and statesman of the fifth century B.C. His best-known works are the Theban Plays: Oedipus the King, Oedipus at Colonus, and Antigone.

CHORUS
What strange vision meets my eyes,
Fills me with a wild surprise?
Sure I know her, sure 'tis she,
The maid Antigone.
Hapless child of hapless sire,
Didst thou recklessly conspire,
Madly brave the King's decree?
Therefore are they haling thee?

[ENTER GUARD BRINGING ANTIGONE]

GUARD
Here is the culprit taken in the act
Of giving burial. But where's the King?

CHORUS
There from the palace he returns in time.

[ENTER CREON]

CREON
Why is my presence timely? What has chanced?

GUARD
No man, my lord, should make a vow, for if
He ever swears he will not do a thing.
His afterthoughts belie his first resolve.
When from the hail-storm of thy threats I fled
I sware thou wouldst not see me here again;
But the wild rapture of a glad surprise
Intoxicates, and so I'm here forsworn.
And here's my prisoner, caught in the very act,
Decking the grave. No lottery this time;
This prize is mine by right of treasure-trove.
So take her, judge her, rack her, if thou wilt.
She's thine, my liege; but I may rightly claim
Hence to depart well quit of all these ills.

CREON
Say, how didst thou arrest the maid, and where?

GUARD

Burying the man. There's nothing more to tell.

CREON

Hast thou thy wits? Or know'st thou what thou say'st?

GUARD

I saw this woman burying the corpse
Against thy orders. Is that clear and plain?

CREON

But how was she surprised and caught in the act?

GUARD

It happened thus. No sooner had we come,
Driven from thy presence by those awful threats,
Than straight we swept away all trace of dust,
And bared the clammy body. Then we sat
High on the ridge to windward of the stench,
While each man kept his fellow alert and rated
Roundly the sluggard if he chanced to nap.
So all night long we watched, until the sun
Stood high in heaven, and his blazing beams
Smote us. A sudden whirlwind then upraised
A cloud of dust that blotted out the sky.
And swept the plain, and stripped the woodlands bare,
And shook the firmament. We closed our eyes
And waited till the heaven-sent plague should pass.
At last it ceased, and lo! there stood this maid.
A piercing cry she uttered, sad and shrill,
As when the mother bird beholds her nest
Robbed of its nestlings; even so the maid
Wailed as she saw the body stripped and bare,
And cursed the ruffians who had done this deed.
Anon she gathered handfuls of dry dust.
Then, holding high a well-wrought brazen urn,
Thrice on the dead she poured a lustral stream.
We at the sight swooped down on her and seized
Our quarry. Undismayed she stood, and when
We taxed her with the former crime and this,
She disowned nothing. I was glad—and grieved;
For 'tis most sweet to 'scape oneself scot-free,
And yet to bring disaster to a friend
Is grievous. Take it all in all, I deem
A man's first duty is to serve himself.

CREON

Speak, girl, with head bent low and downcast eyes,
Dost thou plead guilty or deny the deed?

ANTIGONE

Guilty. I did it, I deny it not.

CREON

[TO GUARD]

Sirrah, begone whither thou wilt, and thank
Thy luck that thou hast 'scaped a heavy charge.

[TO ANTIGONE]

Now answer this plain question, yes or no,
Wast thou acquainted with the interdict?

ANTIGONE

I knew, all knew; how should I fail to know?

CREON

And yet wert bold enough to break the law?

ANTIGONE

Yea, for these laws were not ordained of Zeus,
And she who sits enthroned with gods below,
Justice, enacted not these human laws.
Nor did I deem that thou, a mortal man,
Could'st by a breath annul and override
The immutable unwritten laws of Heaven.
They were not born to-day nor yesterday;
They die not; and none knoweth whence they sprang.
I was not like, who feared no mortal's frown,
To disobey these laws and so provoke
The wrath of Heaven. I know that I must die,
E'en hadst thou not proclaimed it; and if death
Is thereby hastened, I shall count it gain.
For death is gain to him whose life, like mine,
Is full of misery. Thus my lot appears
Not sad, but blissful; for had I endured
To leave my mother's son unburied there,
I should have grieved with reason, but not now.
And if in this thou judgest me a fool,
Methinks the judge of folly's not acquit.

CHORUS

A stubborn daughter of a stubborn sire,
This ill-starred maiden kicks against the pricks.

CREON

Well, let her know the stubbornest of wills
Are soonest bended, as the hardest iron,
O'er-heated in the fire to brittleness.
Flies soonest into fragments, shivered through.

A snaffle curbs the fieriest steed, and he
Who in subjection lives must needs be meek.
But this proud girl, in insolence well-schooled,
First overstepped the established law, and then—
A second and worse act of insolence—
She boasts and glories in her wickedness.
Now if she thus can flout authority
Unpunished, I am woman, she the man.
But though she be my sister's child or nearer
Of kin than all who worship at my hearth,
Nor she nor yet her sister shall escape
The utmost penalty, for both I hold,
As arch-conspirators, of equal guilt.
Bring forth the other; even now I saw her
Within the palace, frenzied and distraught.
The workings of the mind discover oft
Dark deeds in darkness schemed, before the act.
More hateful still the miscreant who seeks
When caught, to make a virtue of a crime.

ANTIGONE
Would'st thou do more than slay thy prisoner?

CREON
Not I, thy life is mine, and that's enough.

ANTIGONE
Why dally then? To me no word of thine
Is pleasant: God forbid it e'er should please;
Nor am I more acceptable to thee.
And yet how otherwise had I achieved
A name so glorious as by burying
A brother? so my townsmen all would say,
Were they not gagged by terror. Manifold
A king's prerogatives, and not the least
That all his acts and all his words are law.

CREON
Of all these Thebans none so deems but thou.

ANTIGONE
These think as I, but bate their breath to thee.

CREON
Hast thou no shame to differ from all these?

ANTIGONE
To reverence kith and kin can bring no shame.

CREON
Was his dead foeman not thy kinsman too?

ANTIGONE
One mother bare them and the self-same sire.

CREON
Why cast a slur on one by honouring one?

ANTIGONE
The dead man will not bear thee out in this.

CREON
Surely, if good and evil fare alike.

ANTIGONE
The slain man was no villain but a brother.

CREON
The patriot perished by the outlaw's brand.

ANTIGONE
Nathless the realms below these rites require.

CREON
Not that the base should fare as do the brave.

ANTIGONE
Who knows if this world's crimes are virtues there?

CREON
Not even death can make a foe a friend.

ANTIGONE
My nature is for mutual love, not hate.

CREON
Die then, and love the dead if love thou must,
No woman shall be master while I live. . . .

CHORUS
Thy might, O Zeus, what mortal power can quell?
Not sleep that lays all else beneath its spell,
Nor moons that never tire: untouched by Time,
  Throned in the dazzling light
  That crowns Olympus' height,
Thou reignest King, omnipotent, sublime.
  Past, present, and to be,
  All bow to thy decree,
  All that exceeds the mean by Fate
  Is punished, Love or Hate.
Hope flits about on never-wearying wings;
Profit to some, to some light loves she brings,
But no man knoweth how her gifts may turn,
Till 'neath his feet the treacherous ashes burn.
Sure 'twas a sage inspired that spake this word;

If evil good appear
To any, Fate is near;
And brief the respite from her flaming sword.
   Hither comes in angry mood
   Haemon, latest of thy brood;
   Is it for his bride he's grieved,
   Of her marriage-bed deceived,
   Doth he make his mourn for thee,
   Maid forlorn, Antigone?

[ENTER HAEMON]

CREON

Soon shall we know, better than seer can tell.
Learning my fixed decree anent thy bride,
Thou mean'st not, son, to rave against thy sire?
Know'st not whate'er we do is done in love?

HAEMON

O father, I am thine, and I will take
Thy wisdom as the helm to steer withal.
Therefore no wedlock shall by me be held
More precious than thy loving governance.

CREON

Well spoken: so right-minded sons should feel,
In all deferring to a father's will.
For 'tis the hope of parents they may rear
A brood of sons submissive, keen to avenge
Their father's wrongs, and count his friends their own.
But who begets unprofitable sons,
He verily breeds trouble for himself,
And for his foes much laughter. Son, be warned
And let no woman fool away thy wits.
Ill fares the husband mated with a shrew,
And her embraces very soon wax cold.
For what can wound so surely to the quick
As a false friend? So spue and cast her off,
Bid her go find a husband with the dead.
For since I caught her openly rebelling,
Of all my subjects the one malcontent,
I will not prove a traitor to the State.
She surely dies. Go, let her, if she will,
Appeal to Zeus the God of Kindred, for
If thus I nurse rebellion in my house,
Shall not I foster mutiny without?
For whoso rules his household worthily,
Will prove in civic matters no less wise.
But he who overbears the laws, or thinks

To overrule his rulers, such an one
I never will allow. Whome'er the State
Appoints, must be obeyed in everything,
Both small and great, just and unjust alike.
I warrant such an one in either case
Would shine, as King or subject; such a man
Would in the storm of battle stand his ground,
A comrade leal and true; but Anarchy —
What evils are not wrought by Anarchy!
She ruins States, and overthrows the home,
She dissipates and routs the embattled host;
While discipline preserves the ordered ranks.
Therefore we must maintain authority
And yield no tittle to a woman's will.
Better, if needs be, men should cast us out
Than hear it said, a woman proved his match.

CHORUS
To me, unless old age have dulled my wits,
Thy words appear both reasonable and wise.

HAEMON
Father, the gods implant in mortal men
Reason, the choicest gift bestowed by heaven.
'Tis not for me to say thou errest, nor
Would I arraign thy wisdom, if I could;
And yet wise thoughts may come to other men
And, as thy son, it falls to me to mark
The acts, the words, the comments of the crowd.
The commons stand in terror of thy frown,
And dare not utter aught that might offend,
But I can overhear their muttered plaints,
Know how the people mourn this maiden doomed
For noblest deeds to die the worst of deaths.
When her own brother slain in battle lay
Unsepulchred, she suffered not his corse
To lie for carrion birds and dogs to maul:
Should not her name (they cry) be writ in gold?
Such the low murmurings that reach my ear.
O father, nothing is by me more prized
Than thy well-being, for what higher good
Can children covet than their sire's fair fame,
As fathers too take pride in glorious sons?
Therefore, my father, cling not to one mood,
And deem not thou art right, all others wrong.
For whoso thinks that wisdom dwells with him,
That he alone can speak or think aright,
Such oracles are empty breath when tried.

The wisest man will let himself be swayed
By others' wisdom and relax in time.
See how the trees beside a stream in flood
Save, if they yield to force, each spray unharmed,
But by resisting perish root and branch.
The mariner who keeps his mainsheet taut,
And will not slacken in the gale, is like
To sail with thwarts reversed, keel uppermost.
Relent then and repent thee of thy wrath;
For, if one young in years may claim some sense,
I'll say 'tis best of all to be endowed
With absolute wisdom; but, if that's denied,
(And nature takes not readily that ply)
Next wise is he who lists to sage advice.

CHORUS
If he says aught in season, heed him, King.

[TO HAEMON]

Heed thou thy sire too; both have spoken well.

CREON
What, would you have us at our age be schooled,
Lessoned in prudence by a beardless boy?

HAEMON
I plead for justice, father, nothing more.
Weigh me upon my merit, not my years.

CREON
Strange merit this to sanction lawlessness!

HAEMON
For evil-doers I would urge no plea.

CREON
Is not this maid an arrant law-breaker?

HAEMON
The Theban commons with one voice say, No.

CREON
What, shall the mob dictate my policy?

HAEMON
'Tis thou, methinks, who speakest like a boy.

CREON
Am I to rule for others, or myself?

HAEMON
A State for one man is no State at all.

CREON
The State is his who rules it, so 'tis held.

HAEMON
As monarch of a desert thou wouldst shine.

CREON
This boy, methinks, maintains the woman's cause.

HAEMON
If thou be'st woman, yes. My thought's for thee.

CREON
O reprobate, would'st wrangle with thy sire?

HAEMON
Because I see thee wrongfully perverse.

CREON
And am I wrong, if I maintain my rights?

HAEMON
Talk not of rights; thou spurn'st the due of Heaven.

CREON
O heart corrupt, a woman's minion thou!

HAEMON
Slave to dishonour thou wilt never find me.

CREON
Thy speech at least was all a plea for her.

HAEMON
And thee and me, and for the gods below.

CREON
Living the maid shall never be thy bride.

HAEMON
So she shall die, but one will die with her.

CREON
Hast come to such a pass as threaten me?

HAEMON
What threat is this, vain counsels to reprove?

CREON
Vain fool to instruct thy betters; thou shalt rue it.

HAEMON
Wert not my father, I had said thou err'st.

CREON
Play not the spaniel, thou a woman's slave.

HAEMON

When thou dost speak, must no man make reply?

CREON

This passes bounds. By heaven, thou shalt not rate
And jeer and flout me with impunity.
Off with the hateful thing that she may die
At once, beside her bridegroom, in his sight.

HAEMON

Think not that in my sight the maid shall die,
Or by my side; never shalt thou again
Behold my face hereafter. Go, consort
With friends who like a madman for their mate.

[EXIT HAEMON]

CHORUS

Love resistless in fight, all yield at a glance of thine eye,
Love who pillowed all night on a maiden's cheek dost lie,
Over the upland folds thou roam'st, and the trackless sea.
Love the gods captive holds. Shall mortals not yield to thee?
Mad are thy subjects all, and even the wisest heart
Straight to folly will fall, at a touch of thy poisoned dart.
Thou didst kindle the strife, this feud of kinsman with kin,
By the eyes of a winsome wife, and the yearning her heart to win.
For as her consort still, enthroned with Justice above,
Thou bendest man to thy will, O all invincible Love.
    Lo I myself am borne aside,
    From Justice, as I view this bride.
    (O sight an eye in tears to drown)
    Antigone, so young, so fair,
      Thus hurried down
    Death's bower with the dead to share.

ANTIGONE

Friends, countrymen my last farewell I make;
    My journey's done.
One last fond, lingering, longing look I take
    At the bright sun.
For Death who puts to sleep both young and old
    Hales my young life,
And beckons me to Acheron's dark fold,
    An unwed wife.
No youths have sung the marriage song for me,
    My bridal bed
No maids have strewn with flowers from the lea,
    'Tis Death I wed.

CHORUS

But bethink thee, thou art sped,
Great and glorious, to the dead.
Thou the sword's edge hast not tasted,
No disease thy frame hath wasted.
Freely thou alone shalt go
Living to the dead below.

ANTIGONE

Nay, but the piteous tale I've heard men tell
   Of Tantalus' doomed child,
Chained upon Siphylus' high rocky fell,
   That clung like ivy wild,
Drenched by the pelting rain and whirling snow,
   Left there to pine,
While on her frozen breast the tears aye flow—
   Her fate is mine.

CHORUS

She was sprung of gods, divine,
Mortals we of mortal line.
Like renown with gods to gain
Recompenses all thy pain.
Take this solace to thy tomb
Hers in life and death thy doom.

ANTIGONE

Alack, alack! Ye mock me. Is it meet
   Thus to insult me living, to my face?
Cease, by our country's altars I entreat,
   Ye lordly rulers of a lordly race.
O fount of Dirce, wood-embowered plain
   Where Theban chariots to victory speed,
Mark ye the cruel laws that now have wrought my bane
   The friends who show no pity in my need!
Was ever fate like mine? O monstrous doom,
   Within a rock-built prison sepulchred.
To fade and wither in a living tomb.
   An alien midst the living and the dead.

CHORUS

In thy boldness over-rash
Madly thou thy foot didst dash
'Gainst high Justice' altar stair.
Thou a father's guilt dost bear.

ANTIGONE

At this thou touchest my most poignant pain,
   My ill-starred father's piteous disgrace,
The taint of blood, the hereditary stain,

That clings to all of Labdacus' famed race.
Woe worth the monstrous marriage-bed where lay
    A mother with the son her womb had borne;
Therein I was conceived, woe worth the day,
    Fruit of incestuous sheets, a maid forlorn,
And now I pass, accursèd and unwed,
    To meet them as an alien there below;
And thee, O brother, in marriage ill-bestead,
    'Twas thy dead hand that dealt me this deathblow.

CHORUS

Religion has her claims, 'tis true,
Let rites be paid when rites are due.
Yet is it ill to disobey
The powers who hold by might the sway.
Thou hast withstood authority,
A self-willed rebel, thou must die.

ANTIGONE

Unwept, unwed, unfriended, hence I go,
    No longer may I see the day's bright eye;
Not one friend left to share my bitter woe,
    And o'er my ashes heave one passing sigh.

CREON

If wail and lamentation aught availed
To stave off death, I trow they'd never end.
Away with her, and having walled her up
In a rock-vaulted tomb, as I ordained,
Leave her alone at liberty to die,
Or, if she choose, to live in solitude,
The tomb her dwelling. We in either case
Are guiltless as concerns this maiden's blood.
Only on earth no lodging shall she find.

ANTIGONE

O grave, O bridal bower, O prison house
Hewn from the rock, my everlasting home,
Whither I go to join the mighty host
Of kinsfolk, Persephassa's guests long dead,
The last of all, of all most miserable,
I pass, my destined span of years cut short.
And yet good hope is mine that I shall find
A welcome from my sire, a welcome too,
From thee, my mother, and my brother dear;
For with these hands, I laved and decked your limbs
In death, and poured libations on your grave.
And last, my Polyneices, unto thee
I paid due rites, and this my recompense!
Yet am I justified in wisdom's eyes.

For even had it been some child of mine,
Or husband mouldering in death's decay,
I had not wrought this deed despite the State.
What is the law I call in aid? 'Tis thus
I argue. Had it been a husband dead
I might have wed another, and have borne
Another child, to take the dead child's place.
But, now my sire and mother both are dead,
No second brother can be born for me.
Thus by the law of conscience I was led
To honour thee, dear brother, and was judged
By Creon guilty of a heinous crime.
And now he drags me like a criminal,
A bride unwed, amerced of marriage-song
And marriage-bed and joys of motherhood,
By friends deserted to a living grave.
What ordinance of heaven have I transgressed?
Hereafter can I look to any god
For succour, call on any man for help?
Alas, my piety is impious deemed.
Well, if such justice is approved of heaven,
I shall be taught by suffering my sin;
But if the sin is theirs, O may they suffer
No worse ills than the wrongs they do to me!

CHORUS
The same ungovernable will
Drives like a gale the maiden still.

CREON
Therefore, my guards who let her stay
Shall smart full sore for their delay.

ANTIGONE
Ah, woe is me! This word I hear
Brings death most near.

CHORUS
I have no comfort. What he saith,
Portends no other thing than death.

ANTIGONE
My fatherland, city of Thebes divine,
Ye gods of Thebes whence sprang my line,
Look, puissant lords of Thebes, on me;
The last of all your royal house ye see.
Martyred by men of sin, undone.
Such meed my piety hath won.

[EXIT ANTIGONE]

DANIEL CALLAHAN

What Do Children Owe Elderly Parents?

DANIEL CALLAHAN is director of The Hastings Center for Biomedical Ethics. A philosopher by training, he received his Ph.D. from Harvard. He has written extensively on medical ethics and abortion.

In the spring of 1983 the Reagan administration announced that states may under Medicaid legally require children to contribute to the support of their elderly parents. At the time a number of states were considering or enacting just such laws. The administration, one spokesman said, was not proposing anything inherently new. It was simply responding to a state request for clarification of the existing Medicaid law, and wanted only to say that state statutes enforcing family responsibility laws were not in conflict with federal policy.

As it turned out, the administration's initiative was a policy shift whose time had not come. While a number of states flirted for a time with new family responsibility policies, only a few (Virginia, Idaho, and Mississippi, for example) actually adopted them, and even fewer seem to be enforcing them. As pressing as the state Medicaid nursing home burden is, it rapidly became clear that there is little general sentiment to force children to provide financially for their elderly parents.

Nonetheless, Reagan's initiative was an important social and policy event and raises significant moral issues. In one form or another, the idea is likely to arise again. Anything that can be done to raise revenue to reduce the Medicaid burden probably will be done. Three questions are thus worth considering. What kind of a moral obligation do children have toward the welfare of their elderly parents? Can it be said that the changed health, longevity, and social circumstances of the elderly justify a shift in traditional moral obligations? Even if children do have some significant duties to parents, is it still legitimate to ask the state to take over much of the direct burden of care?

The first question is of course an old one. Each generation has had to make its own sense of the biblical injunction that we should honor our fathers and mothers. It neither tells us in what "honor" consists nor how far filial obligation should be carried. As a piece of practical advice, however, it once made considerable sense. In most traditional and agricultural societies, parents had considerable power over the lives of their offspring. Children who did not honor their parents risked not only immediate privation, but also the loss of the one inheritance that would enable them to raise and support their own families—land they could call their own.

The advent of industrialization brought about a radical change. It reduced the direct coercive power of parents over their children, setting into motion a trend toward the independence of both parents and children that has been a mark of contemporary society. Though the affective bond between parents and children has so far endured in the face of industrialization and modernity, the combination of actual attachment and potential independence frames the question of the obligation of children toward their elderly parents.

The moral ideal of the parent-child relationship is that of love, nurture, and the mutual seeking for the good of the other. While the weight of the relationship will or-dinarily shift according to the age of children and their parents, mutual respect and reci-procity have been a central part of the moral standard. Yet the reality of human lives can stand in the way of the realization of moral ideals. Just as not all children are lovable, neither do all parents give the welfare of their children their serious attention and high-est priority. Many children do not find their parents lovable and feel no special sense of duty toward them. Many parents are not happy with the way their children turn out, or with the kind of lives they live, and do not seek to remain intertwined with them.

To what extent, and under what circumstances, flaws and faults of that kind can be said to alter the mutual obligations is obviously an important question. Yet even when the affectional bonds between parent and child are strong, it is still by no means clear what each morally owes to the other. If parents ought to help their children to grow up and flourish, should they go so far as to seriously jeopardize their own future welfare in doing so? If children should honor their elderly parents, how great a sacrifice ought that to entail?

THE CHANGING STATUS OF THE ELDERLY

The present relationship between children and their elderly parents is shaped in part by the changing status of the elderly in society. A rising number and increasing pro-portion of our population are elderly. The "young old" (65–75) appear to be in better health than ever, but as people live longer, there is also an increasing number of the "old old" (75 +) who are frail and dependent. Despite a variety of public programs and considerable improvement in recent decades, a significant proportion of the elderly (about 25 percent in 1980) still live in poverty or near-poverty. A large proportion do not have immediate family or relatives to whom they can turn for either financial or emotional assistance, and many—particularly women—live alone or in institutions. Even so, as Victor Fuchs notes in summarizing available data, rising income has "made it possible for an ever higher percentage [of the elderly] to maintain their own house-holds, health permitting."

Independence, however, need not mean an absence of family ties. Gerontologists take great pleasure in demolishing what they tell us are two prevalent myths, that the caring family has disappeared, and that the elderly are isolated from their children. There has indeed been a decline in the number of elderly who live with their children or other relatives, from three-fifths in 1960 to one-third in 1980, and an equally sharp drop—down to 1 percent—in the number of elderly who depend upon their children for financial support. Yet it still seems to be true, as Ethel Shanas has noted, that "most old people live close to at least one of their children and see at least one child often. Most old people see their siblings and relatives often, and old people, whether bedfast or housebound because of ill health, are twice as likely to be living at home as to be res-idents in an institution. . . ." In addition, it is estimated that 60–80 percent of all dis-abled or impaired persons receive significant family help.

One important change involves the proportion of young and old who believe that children should be financially responsible for their elderly parents. This has shifted downward (from about 50 percent in the mid-fifties to 10 percent in the mid-seventies), and a simultaneous reduction in financial assistance has occurred. However, this need not be taken as an indication of a diminished sense of filial responsibility. The advent of Social Security, and the increasing financial strength of the elderly for other reasons, all indicate important social variables that have reduced financial pressure on children to support parents.

Other social changes could eventually alter that situation. The increasing number of divorced families, of small families, and of families where both spouses work, have created the possibility of a reduced sense of obligation in the future, though that has yet clearly to materialize. In his 1981 book *New Rules*, the pollster Daniel Yankelovich wrote that "one of the most far-reaching changes in [moral] norms relates to what parents believe they owe their children and what their children owe them. Nowhere are the changes in the unwritten social contract more significant or agonizing. The overall pattern is clear: today's parents expect to make fewer sacrifices for their children than in the past, but they also demand less from their offspring in the form of future obligations than their parents demanded of them. . . . Sixty-seven percent [of Americans surveyed] believe that 'children do not have an obligation to their parents regardless of what their parents have done for them.'". . . .

WHAT THE LAW SAYS

Some twenty-six states at present have statutes that can require children to provide financial support for needy parents. Though erratically administered, difficult to implement, and of doubtful financial value, they remain as testimony to an effort dating back to the early seventeenth century to shift from the public to the private sphere the care of poverty-stricken elderly. While such laws had no precedent in either common law or medieval law, they came into being in England with the Elizabethan Poor Law of 1601, representing a culmination of at least three centuries of efforts to cope with the problem of the poor in general. The Poor Law did not concentrate on the children of the elderly, but extended the network of potential support to include the fathers and mothers, and the grandfathers and grandmothers, of the poor. The family, as a unit, was to be responsible for poverty-stricken kinfolk.

When these laws passed over into the American scene, during the seventeenth and eighteenth centuries, the focus was on the responsibility of children toward their elderly parents, though a few states have retained the wider scope. Blackstone's famous *Commentaries* succinctly state the moral basis of such a responsibility: "The duties of children to their parents arise from a principle of natural justice and retribution. For to those who gave us existence we naturally owe subjection and obedience during our minority, and honor and reverence ever after; they who protected the weakness of our infancy are entitled to our protection in the infirmity of their age; they who by sustenance and education have enabled their offspring to prosper ought in return to be supported by that offspring in case they stand in need of assistance."

The American state laws were little invoked during the eighteenth and nineteenth centuries, but they were increasingly turned to during the twentieth century, particularly in the aftermath of the depression and World War II. While there is broad historical agreement that the primary purpose of the laws was to protect the public from the burden of caring for the poor, including the elderly, the laws were buttressed by a variety of moral assumptions.

Martin R. Levy and Sara W. Gross have identified three moral premises that underlie the American laws and developed some cogent criticisms of them. First, "the duty of a child to support his parents is a mirror-image of the parents' responsibility to support a child." They point out the doubtful logic of that position. In procreation parents not only bring a child into the world, but by the same action undertake the moral obligation of sustaining that child, whose existence is entirely dependent upon the parents. As Levy and Gross put it, "In the converse situation of the duty of a child to support a parent, there is no proximate cause, no volitional act, and no rational basis for the demand of support. The child has not acted to bring about the life of the parent. While the father assumes the voluntary status of fatherhood, the child assumes no duty by having been born. His birth is the result of the act of the father and mother, and such a result cannot logically or physically be turned into a proximate cause." While they do not deny that there can be a moral bond of love and affection, "moral duty and gratitude, or lofty ideals, cannot be used as a justification for the taking of property." By focusing on "the taking of property," the authors focus on a relatively narrow point.

The second general moral premise turns on what they call "the relational interest of family status." They mean that the simple fact of a family relationship—creating a special tie between parent and child, both biological and social—may itself engender the basis for a demand made upon children to support their elderly parents. Yet they point out that the relational interests are both too broad and too narrow to serve as a reasonable criterion for determining the duty to provide support. "It is too broad in . . . that not all children love and revere their parents. The status of a child confers no special emotional tie in and of itself." It is too narrow in that, if emotional commitment is the standard, then a child would logically be bound to support everyone to whom he or she is tied by emotional commitment, whether family member or not.

The analogy of a contract provides the third moral premise. Since the child was at one time supported by the parent, does not that create an implicit contract requiring that the child in turn support the parent when that becomes necessary? Levy and Gross point out that no direct contract is negotiated between parent and child when the child is procreated, and that any analogy must thus be based on an implied or quasi-contract. But the analogy of an implied contract does not work: the two parties necessary to the making of a contract did not exist simultaneously. A common standard in the law, moreover, is that neither the carrying out of a duty, nor the promise of rendering a performance already required by duty, is a sufficient condition of a return promise—an obligation to do likewise.

PARENTS AS "FRIENDS"

Although Levy and Gross effectively dispatch the argument that the benefits bestowed by parents upon children automatically entail a duty of the children in return to aid parents, there is considerably more that needs to be said. Are we to hold that the obligation flows in one direction only, that because children were given no choice about being born, they owe nothing whatever to their parents? That seems too extreme. At the least, it fails to explain why in fact many children feel an obligation toward their parents, nor does it sufficiently plumb the moral depths of the family relationship.

The late Jane English also argued that the language of "owing" is mistakenly applied in the circumstances. Children "owe" parents nothing at all—which is not to say that there are not many things that children ought to do for their parents. Instead, she held that "the duties of grown children are those of friends and result from love between them and their parents, rather than being things owed in repayment for the parents' earlier sacrifices." In situations where one person does a favor for another, there may be an obligation to reciprocate, but parents do not do favors for their children in the same sense that strangers or acquaintances may do them for each other. The bond that should unite parents and children is that of friendship, and "friendship ought to be characterized by *mutuality* rather than reciprocity: friends offer what they can give and accept what they need without regard for the total amount of benefits exchanged. And friends are motivated by love rather than by the prospect of repayment. Hence, talk of 'owing' is singularly out of place in friendship." Thus children ought to do things for their parents, but the "ought" is that which follows from friendship; it resists both quantitative measurement and the stricter language of owing something in return for earlier benefits.

While English's argument has some plausibility, it is ultimately unsatisfying. Friendship can certainly exist between parent and child, but it often does not. Quite apart from those circumstances where parents have neglected their children or otherwise alienated their affection, they may have little in common other than their biological origins. Moreover, the nature of the friendship that exists between parent and child can and usually will be different from the kind that exists between and among those who are unrelated. A child might plausibly say that, while he is not a friend of his parents, he nonetheless feels toward them respect and love. To push the same point further, many children actively dislike their parents, find no pleasure in their company, and yet feel they ought to do things for them despite those feelings. In distinguishing between favors and friendship, English says that "another difference between favors and friendships is that after a friendship ends, the duties of friendship end." That may be true enough in the case of nonfamily relationships, but it then raises all the more forcefully the question of whether friendship, however much it may mark a relationship between parent and child, can catch the fullness of the moral bond.

The origin and nature of the parent-child bond—or whatever other relationship may exist—is unique. By the procreation of children parents create a social unit that otherwise would not and could not exist. If children do not select their parents, neither do parents select their individual children (they choose to have *a* child, not *this* child). Even so, the family relationship is not something one can simply take or leave. It is a fundamental and unavoidable part of our social nature as human beings. That psychotherapists can spend a good deal of time untangling problems between parents and children provides at least a clue to the emotional depth of the biological relationship, whether marked by unhappiness or happiness. We can and do drift away from ordinary friendships, but parents stay in our memory and exert their influence even in the face of distance or active hostility. Whether we like it or not, we are in some sense always one with our parents, both because of the unique circumstances by which we came to know them and because of the long period of nurture when we were utterly dependent upon them. The mutual interaction of parents and children, even when friendships exist, cannot then entirely be reduced to the category of friendship. The emotional and biological bond between parent and child gives the relationship a permanent and central place in our lives, quite apart from whether that relationship turns out well or poorly. That cannot be said of friendship in the usual sense of the term.

CAPTURING INTIMACY IN MORAL LANGUAGE

Ferdinand Schoeman catches some of this flavor when he argues that the traditional language of morality, that of rights and obligations, does not seem to fit well in describing the bond among family members: "We *share ourselves* with those with whom we are intimate and are aware that they do the same with us. Traditional moral boundaries, which give rigid shape to the self, are transparent to this kind of sharing. This makes for nonabstract moral relationships in which talk about rights of others, respect for others, and even welfare of others is to a certain extent irrelevant." Perhaps Schoeman takes things a bit far, but he tries to make clear that the intimacy of family relationships forces us into revealing and sharing a self that may not be revealed to others on the public stage. While it is often the case that parents do not really know their own child, just as often they do, even when their perceptions differ from those of the child. Whether they understand their child or not, the fact that they shared considerable intimacy when the child was young gives them access to a self that others may never see. For their part, children have unique access to parents, seeing a side of them that may never be revealed to others.

Another powerful candidate for the source of obligation is that of gratitude on the part of children toward their parents. Gratitude would be due, not simply because parents discharged their obligations toward the children, but because in their manner of doing so they went beyond the demands of mere duty, giving voluntarily of themselves in a way neither required nor ordinarily expected of them. As Jeffrey Blustein notes, "Duties of gratitude are owed only to those who have helped or benefited us freely, without thought of personal gain, simply out of a desire to protect or promote our well-being. The givers may hope for some return, but they do not give in expectation of it." A consequence of this line of reasoning, however, is that only those parents who did more than was morally required could be said to have a right to the gratitude of their children. And it is by no means obvious that a "debt of gratitude" carries with it a strict obligation to provide like goods or services, that is, to go beyond what is otherwise required.

I am searching here with some difficulty for a way to characterize the ethical nature of the parent-child relationship, a relationship that appears almost but not quite self-evident in its reciprocal moral claims and yet oddly elusive also. We seem to say too much if we try to reduce the relationship to mutual moral duties, rights and obligations. That implies a rigor and formalism which distorts the moral bond. We say too little if we try to make it a matter of voluntary affection only. Yet we cannot, I suspect, totally dismiss the language of obligation nor would we want to give up the ideal of mutual affection either. If the procreation and physical rearing of a child does not automatically entail reciprocal duties toward the parents when they are needy and dependent, it is certainly possible to imagine a sense of obligation arising when parents have done far more for children than would morally be required of them. My own parents, for example, did not throw me out on my own when I reached eighteen. They sacrificed a good deal to provide me with a higher education, and in fact provided financial support for my graduate education until I was thirty, topping that off by giving my wife and me a down-payment on our first house. They did it out of affection, rather than duty, but I certainly felt I owed them something in return in their old age. There need not be, then, any necessary incompatibility between feeling both affection and a sense of duty. But we lack a moral phrase that catches both notions in one concept; and neither taken separately is quite right.

THE POWER OF DEPENDENCE

Another aspect of the relationship between children and their elderly parents bears reflection. Much as young children will have a special dependence upon parents, as those human beings above all others who have a fateful power over their destinies, so many elderly parents can come in dire circumstances similarly to depend upon their children. In a world of strangers or fleeting casual acquaintances, of distant government agencies and a society beyond their control, elderly parents can see in their children their only hope for someone who ought to care for them. Neither parent nor child may want this kind of emotional dependence, and each might wish that there were an alternative. Nonetheless, parents may be forced to throw themselves upon their children simply because there is no other alternative. Who else is likely to care?

Can that sense of utter need, if not for money then only for affection and caring, in and of itself create a moral obligation? It is surely a difficult question whether, as a general matter, a moral obligation is incurred when one human being is rendered by circumstance wholly dependent upon another—whether, that is, the dependency itself creates the obligation, quite apart from any other features of the relationship. A moral claim of that kind will inevitably be controversial, if only because it is (regretfully) common to rest claims of obligation upon implicit or explicit contracts of one kind or another; or upon features of the relationship that can be subjected to a utilitarian calculation. It is difficult in this case plausibly to invoke such norms. Still, the power of sheer dependence—whether of newborn child upon parent or elderly, dependent parent upon child—can be potent in its experienced moral demands. The fate of one or more persons rests in the hands of another. The issue, as it presents itself, may be less one of trying to discover the grounds of obligation that would require a response than one of trying to find grounds for ignoring a demand that so patently assaults the sensibilities. It is not so much "must I?" as it is "how can I not?"

Joel Feinberg, commenting on the moral place of gratitude, moves in a similar direction when he writes, "My benefactor once freely offered me his services when I needed them. . . . But now circumstances have arisen in which he needs help, and I am in a position to help him. Surely, I owe him my services now, and he would be entitled to resent my failure to come through." A qualification is in order here: gratitude is ordinarily thought due only when, as noted above, a benefactor has gone beyond ordinary duties. In some cases, parents may have only done their duty, and in such a minimal way that no gratitude seems due them. We are then brought back to the starkest moral situation—in which the dependency only seeks to establish a claim on us.

In trying to unravel the nature of the possible moral obligations, it may be helpful to speak of some specific claims or demands that might be made. Money is by no means the only, or necessarily the most important, benefit that parents can ask of their children. Children can also contribute their time and physical energy, and provide affection and psychological support. On a scale of moral priorities, it would be difficult to persuasively argue that parents have an obligation to deprive their own dependent children of necessary financial support in order to support their elderly parents. By virtue of procreating those children, the latter have a claim upon them that their parents cannot equal. Of course, where a surplus exists after their own children have been taken care of, the financial support of needy parents might become obligatory, particularly if there were no other available sources of support. Ordinarily, however, their principal economic duties will be toward their own children.

The same cannot necessarily be said of providing either physical help or affection to their parents. While the giving of physical help or affection could readily be merged, I think it is useful to distinguish between them. Physical help—such as assistance in moving, cleaning, shopping, and trips to visit friends or doctors—is a somewhat different contribution to the welfare of the elderly than simply talking with them. Parents of young children may not readily be able to adapt their schedules to such demands upon their time or energy. Yet they may be able to provide affection, either by visits at times they find convenient, or through letters and telephone calls. An inability to provide some kinds of care does not exempt children from providing other forms. In fact, the available evidence suggests that affection is most wanted, and it is not difficult to understand why. The uncertainties of old age, the recognition of growing weakness and helplessness, can above all generate the desire to believe that at least some people in the world care about one's fate, and are willing to empathetically share that burden which few of us would care to bear alone—a recognition that life is gradually coming to an end and that nature is depriving us of our body, our individuality, and our future.

In terms of financial obligations, there is considerable evidence from human experience in general, and from state efforts to impose financial burdens upon children in particular, that enforced legal obligations of children toward parents are mutually destructive. If only from the viewpoint of promoting family unity and affection, the provision of economic and medical care for the elderly by the government makes considerable sense. Ben Wattenberg quotes someone who nicely catches an important point: "We [older folks] don't like to take money from our kids. We don't want to be a burden. They don't like giving us money, either. We all get angry at each other if we do it that way. So we all sign a political contract to deal with what anthropologists would call the 'intergenerational transfer of wealth.' The young people *give* money to the government. I *get* money from the government. That way we can both get mad at the government and keep on loving each other."

If the burden of economic care of the elderly can be difficult even for the affluent, it can be impossible for the poor. Moreover, adults with elderly parents ought not to be put in the position of trying to balance the moral claims of their own children against those of their parents, or jeopardizing their own old age in order to sustain their parents in their old age. Though such conflicts may at times be inescapable, society ought to be structured in a way that minimizes them. The great increase in life expectancy provides a solid reason, if one was ever needed, for arguing that all of us collectively through the state—rather than the children of the elderly—should supply their basic economic support. Both parents and children legitimately want an appropriate independence, not the kind that sunders their relationship altogether or makes it merely contingent upon active affection. A balance is sought between that independence which enables people to have a sense of controlling their own destinies, and those ties of obligation and affection that render each an indispensable source of solace in the face of a world that has no special reason to care for them.

A minimal duty of any government should be to do nothing to hinder, and if possible do something to protect, the natural moral and filial ties that give families their power to nurture and sustain. To exploit that bond by coercively taxing families is, I believe, to threaten them with great harm. It is an action that presupposes a narrower form of moral obligation of children to parents than can rationally be defended. At the same time it promises to rupture those more delicate moral bonds, as powerful as they are conceptually elusive, that sustain parents and children in their lives together. Such bonds do not necessarily rule out financial incentives for children to care for their aged parents, as some recent legislative proposals suggest. But if such incentives are to receive support, in that case considerable care would be needed to guard against an exploitation of parents by avaricious children. There are, I ruefully note, as many ways to corrupt the parent-child relationship as ways to sustain it.

MARK TWAIN

You Can't Pray a Lie

MARK TWAIN (born SAMUEL LANGHORNE CLEMENS; 1835–1910) was a noted humorist and novelist. He is especially known for his highly autobiographical stories of boyhood on the Mississippi: *The Adventures of Tom Sawyer* (1876) and *The Adventures of Huckleberry Finn* (1884). Twain's writing is regarded as one of the most representative of nineteenth-century American life.

We went drifting down into a big bend, and the night clouded up and got hot. The river was very wide, and was walled with solid timber on both sides; you couldn't see a break in it hardly ever, or a light. We talked about Cairo, and wondered whether we would know it when we got to it. I said likely we wouldn't because I had heard say there warn't but about a dozen houses there, and if they didn't happen to have them lit up, how was we going to know we was passing a town? Jim said if the two big rivers joined together there, that would show. But I said maybe we might think we was passing the foot of an island and coming into the same old river again. That disturbed Jim—and me too. So the question was, what to do? I said, paddle ashore the first time a light showed, and tell them pap was behind, coming along with a trading scow, and was a green hand at the business, and wanted to know how far it was to Cairo. Jim thought it was a good idea, so we took a smoke on it and waited.

There warn't nothing to do now but to look out sharp for the town, and not pass it without seeing it. He said he'd be mighty sure to see it, because he'd be a free man the minute he seen it, but if he missed it he'd be in a slave country again and no more show for freedom. Every little while he jumps up and says:

"Dah she is!"

But it warn't. It was Jack-o'-lanterns, or lightning-bugs; so he set down again, and went to watching, same as before. Jim said it made him all over trembly and feverish to be so close to freedom. Well, I can tell you it made me all over trembly and feverish, too, to hear him, because I began to get it through my head that he *was* most free—and who was to blame for it? Why, *me.* I couldn't get that out of my conscience, no how nor no way. It got to troubling me so I couldn't rest; I couldn't stay still in one place. It hadn't ever come home to me before, what this thing was that I was doing. But now it did; and it stayed with me, and scorched me more and more. I tried to make out to myself that *I* warn't to blame, because *I* didn't run Jim off from his rightful owner; but it warn't no use, conscience up and says, every time, "But you knowed he was running for his freedom, and you could 'a' paddled ashore and told somebody." That was so—I couldn't get around that no way. That was where it pinched. Conscience says to me, "What had poor Miss Watson done to you that you could see her nigger go off right under your eyes and never say one single word? What did that poor old woman do to you that you could treat her so mean? Why, she tried to learn you your book, she tried to learn you your manners, she tried to be good to you every way she knowed how. *That's* what she done."

I got to feeling so mean and miserable I most wished I was dead. I fidgeted up and down the raft, abusing myself to myself, and Jim was fidgeting up and down past me. We neither of us could keep still. Every time he danced around and says, "Dah's Cairo!" it went through me like a shot, and I thought if it *was* Cairo I reckoned I would die of miserableness.

Jim talked out loud all the time while I was talking to myself. He was saying how the first thing he would do when he got to a free state he would go to saving up money and never spend a single cent, and when he got enough he would buy his wife, which was owned on a farm close to where Miss Watson lived; and then they would both work to buy the two children, and if their master wouldn't sell them, they'd get an Ab'litionist to go and steal them.

It most froze me to hear such talk. He wouldn't ever dared to talk such talk in his life before. Just see what a difference it made in him the minute he judged he was about free. It was according to the old saying "Give a nigger an inch and he'll take an ell." Thinks I, this is what comes of my not thinking. Here was this nigger, which I had as good as helped to run away, coming right out flat-footed and saying he would steal his children—children that belonged to a man I didn't even know; a man that hadn't ever done me no harm.

I was sorry to hear Jim say that, it was such a lowering of him. My conscience got to stirring me up hotter than ever, until at last I says to it, "Let up on me—it ain't too late yet—I'll paddle ashore at the first light and tell." I felt easy and happy and light as a feather right off. All my troubles was gone. I went to looking out sharp for a light, and sort of singing to myself. By and by one showed. Jim sings out:

"We's safe, Huck, we's safe! Jump up and crack yo' heels! Dat's de good ole Cairo at las', I jis knows it!"

I says:

"I'll take the canoe and go and see, Jim. It mightn't be, you know."

He jumped and got the canoe ready, and put his old coat in the bottom for me to set on, and give me the paddle; and as I shoved off, he says:

"Pooty soon I'll be a-shout'n for joy, en I'll say, it's all on accounts o' Huck; I's a free man, en I couldn't ever ben free ef it hadn' ben for Huck; Huck done it. Jim won't ever forgit you, Huck; you's de bes' fren' Jim's ever had; en you's de *only* fren' ole Jim's got now."

I was paddling off, all in a sweat to tell on him; but when he says this, it seems to kind of take the tuck all out of me. I went along slow then, and I warn't right down certain whether I was glad I started or whether I warn't. When I was fifty yards off, Jim says:

"Dah you goes, de old true Huck; de on'y white genlman dat ever kep' his promise to old Jim."

Well, I just felt sick. But I says, I *got* to do it—I can't get *out* of it. Right then along comes a skiff with two men in it with guns, and they stopped and I stopped. One of them says:

"What's that yonder?"

"A piece of a raft," I says.

"Do you belong on it?"

"Yes, sir."

"Any men on it?"

"Only one, sir."

"Well, there's five niggers run off tonight up yonder, above the head of the bend. Is your man white or black?"

I didn't answer up prompt. I tried to, but the words wouldn't come. I tried for a second or two to brace up and out with it but I warn't man enough—hadn't the spunk of a rabbit. I see I was weakening; so I just give up trying up and says:

"He's white."

"I reckon we'll go and see for ourselves."

"I wish you would," says I, "because it's pap that's there, and maybe you'd help me tow the raft ashore where the light is. He's sick—and so is mam and Mary Ann."

"Oh, the devil! we're in a hurry, boy. But I s'pose we've got to. Come, buckle to your paddle, and let's get along."

I buckled to my paddle and they laid to their oars. When we had made a stroke or two I says:

"Pap'll be mighty much obleeged to you, I can tell you. Everybody goes away when I want them to help me tow the raft ashore, and I can't do it by myself."

"Well, that's infernal mean. Odd, too. Say, boy, what's the matter with your father?"

"It's the—a—the—well, it ain't anything much."

They stopped pulling. It warn't but a mighty little ways to the raft now. One says:

"Boy, that's a lie. What *is* the matter with your pap? Answer up square now, and it'll be the better for you."

"I will, sir, I will, honest—but don't leave us, please. It's the—the—Gentlemen, if you'll only pull ahead, and let me heave you the headline, you won't have to come a-near the raft—please do."

"Set her back. John, set her back!" says one. They backed water. "Keep away, boy—keep to looard. Confound it, I just expect the wind has blowed it to us. Your's pap's got the smallpox, and you know it precious well. Why didn't you come out and say so? Do you want to spread it all over!"

"Well," says I, a-blubbering, "I've told everybody before, and they just went away and left us."

"Poor devil, there's something in that. We are right down sorry for you, but we—well, hang it, we don't want the smallpox, you see. Look here, I'll tell you what to do. Don't you try to land by yourself, or you'll smash everything to pieces. You float along down about twenty miles, and you'll come to a town on the left-hand side of the river. It will be long after sunup then, and when you ask for help you tell them your folks are all down with chills and fever. Don't be a fool again, and let people guess what is the matter. Now we're trying to do you a kindness; so you just put twenty miles between us, that's a good boy. It wouldn't do any good to land yonder where the light is—it's only a woodyard. Say, I reckon your father's poor, and I'm bound to say he's in pretty hard luck. Here, I'll put a twenty-dollar gold piece on this board, and you get it when it floats by. I feel mighty mean to leave you; but my kingdom! it won't do to fool with smallpox, don't you see?"

"Hold on, Parker," says the man, "here's twenty to put on the board for me. Good-by, boy; you do as Mr. Parker told you, and you'll be all right."

"That's so, my boy—good-by, good-by. If you see any runaway niggers you get help and nab them, and you can make some money by it."

"Good-by, sir," says I; "I won't let no runaway niggers get by me if I can help it."

They went off and I got aboard the raft, feeling bad and low, because I knowed very well I had done wrong, and I see it warn't no use for me to try to learn to do right; a body that don't get *started* right when he's little ain't got no show—when the pinch comes there ain't nothing to back him up and keep him to his work, and so he gets beat. Then I thought a minute, and says to myself, hold on; s'pose you'd 'a' done right and give Jim up would you felt better than what you do now? No, says I, I'd feel bad— I'd feel just the same way I do now. Well, then, says I, what's the use you learning to do right when it's troublesome to do right and ain't no trouble to do wrong, and the wages is just the same? I was stuck. I couldn't answer that. So I reckoned I wouldn't bother no more about it, but after this always do whichever come handiest at the time. . . .

I went to the raft, and set down in the wigwam to think. But I couldn't come to nothing. I thought till I wore my head sore, but I couldn't see no way out of the trouble. After all this long journey, and after all we'd done for them scoundrels, here it was all come to nothing, everything all busted up and ruined, because they could have the heart to serve Jim such a trick as that, and make him a slave again all his life, and amongst strangers, too, for forty dirty dollars.

Once I said to myself it would be a thousand times better for Jim to be a slave at home where his family was, as long as he'd *got* to be a slave, and so I'd better write a letter to Tom Sawyer and tell him to tell Miss Watson where he was. But I soon give up that notion for two things: she'd be mad and disgusted at his rascality and ungratefulness for leaving her, and so she'd sell him straight down the river again; and if she didn't, everybody naturally despises an ungrateful nigger, and they'd make Jim feel it all the time, and so he'd feel ornery and disgraced. And then think of *me*! It would get all around that Huck Finn helped a nigger to get his freedom; and if I was ever to see anybody from that town again I'd be ready to get down and lick his boots for shame. That's just the way: a person does a low-down thing, and then he don't want to take no consequences of it. Thinks as long as he can hide, it ain't no disgrace. That was my fix exactly. The more I studied about this the more my conscience went to grinding me, and the more wicked and low-down and ornery I got to feeling. And at last, when it hit me all of a sudden that here was the plain hand of Providence slapping me in the face and letting me know my wickedness was being watched all the time from up there in heaven, whilst I was stealing a poor old woman's nigger that hadn't ever done me no harm, and now was showing me there's One that's always on the lookout, and ain't a-going to allow no such miserable doings to go only just so fur and no further. I most dropped in my tracks I was so scared. Well, I tried the best I could to kinder soften it up somehow for myself by saying I was brung up wicked, and so I warn't so much to blame; but something inside of me kept saying, "There was the Sunday school, you could 'a' gone to it; and if you'd 'a' done it they'd 'a' learnt you there that people that acts as I'd been acting about that nigger goes to everlasting fire."

It made me shiver. And I about made up my mind to pray, and see if I couldn't try to quit being the kind of a boy I was and be better. So I kneeled down. But the words wouldn't come. Why wouldn't they? It warn't no use to try and hide it from Him. Nor from *me*, neither. I knowed very well why they wouldn't come. It was because my heart warn't right; it was because I warn't square; it was because I was playing double. I was letting *on* to give up sin, but away inside of me I was holding on to the biggest one of all. I was trying to make my mouth *say* I would do the right thing and the clean thing, and go and write to that nigger's owner and tell where he was; but deep down in me I knowed it was a lie, and He knowed it. You can't pray a lie—I found that out.

So I was full of trouble, full as I could be; and didn't know what to do. At last I had an idea; and I says, I'll go and write the letter—and *then* see if I can pray. Why, it was astonishing, the way I felt as light as a feather right straight off, and my troubles all gone. So I got a piece of paper and a pencil, all glad and excited, and set down and wrote:

> Miss Watson, your runaway nigger Jim is down here two mile below Pikesville, and Mr. Phelps has got him and he will give him up for the reward if you send.
>
> HUCK FINN

I felt good and all washed clean of sin for the first time I had ever felt so in my life, and I knowed I could pray now. But I didn't do it straight off, but laid the paper down and set there thinking—thinking how good it was all this happened so, and how near I come to being lost and going to hell. And went on thinking. And got to thinking over our trip down the river; and I see Jim before me all the time: in the day and in the nighttime, sometimes moonlight, sometimes storms, and we a-floating along, talking and singing and laughing. But somehow I couldn't seem to strike no places to harden me against him, but only the other kind. I'd see him standing my watch on top of his'n, 'stead of calling me, so I could go on sleeping; and see him how glad he was when I come back out of the fog; and when I come to him again in the swamp, up there where the feud was; and such-like times; and would always call me honey, and pet me, and do everything he could think of for me, and how good he always was; and at last I struck the time I saved him by telling the men we had smallpox aboard, and he was so grateful, and said I was the best friend old Jim ever had in the world, and the *only* one he's got now; and then I happened to look around and see that paper.

It was a close place. I took it up, and held it in my hand. I was a-trembling, because I'd got to decide, forever, betwixt two things, and I knowed it. I studied a minute, sort of holding my breath, and then says to myself:

"All right, then, I'll *go* to hell"—and tore it up.

JANICE RAYMOND

The Conditions of Female Friendship

JANICE RAYMOND teaches women's studies at the University of Massachusetts at Amherst. She writes extensively about issues in feminist ethics. Her books include *A Passion for Friends* (1986) and (edited with Dorchen Leidholdt) *The Sexual Liberals and the Attack on Feminism* (1990).

THOUGHTFULNESS

Thinking is a necessary condition of female friendship. The thinking I advocate is better described by the word *thoughtfulness.* In my use of it, *thoughtfulness* is characterized on the one hand by ability to reason and on the other by considerateness and caring. It is this kind of thoughtfulness that is necessary for Gyn/affection.

The commonly accepted definition of *thoughtfulness* is concern for others, attentiveness to others' needs, and considerateness for others. However, the word in its primary sense means literally "full of thought." Other meanings are "absorbed in thought," "meditative," or "characterized by careful reasoned thinking." Thus the word thoughtfulness contains a dual meaning and poses another tension. I contend that these two meanings must come together and be expressed in Gyn/affection.

Thoughtfulness has contributed much to the divisions and dissensions among women. . . .

Many women have expressed disappointment and frustration at the lack of thoughtfulness that pervades many women's groups and that women seem to accept as a matter of course in feminist relationships and gatherings.

On the other hand, many women have been socialized to react almost instinctually to other people's needs, mostly those of men and children. Women have been drained by a kind of thoughtfulness that is really lacking in thought to the extent that it is indiscriminately given, without thinking about the conditions under which it is extended and the fact that it is left to women in any context to be thoughtful. Here the thinking is missing from thoughtfulness so that women give and give, extend themselves constantly, and deal and deal with the needs of others in what has at times almost amounted to a feminine compulsion. The thoughtfulness that most women are trained to extend in a hetero-relational context is not born out of Self-directed thinking. Many women "go into robot" performing "emotional labor" to fulfill all sorts of others' needs. For women, the cost of this kind of thoughtfulness has been the obliteration of thinking.

A vision of female friendship restores the thinking to thoughtfulness. At the same time, it restores a thoughtfulness to thinking, that is a respect and considerateness for another's needs. Only thoughtfulness, in its more expanded meaning, can sustain female friendship and give it daily life. A thinking friendship must become a thoughtful friendship in the full sense of the word *thoughtfulness.* Many women may be brilliant

81

thinkers, but that thinking has to be accompanied by a genuine attentiveness and respect for other women if female friendship is to flourish. On the other hand, many women may be caring and considerate of others, but if this thoughtfulness lacks a Self-directed thinking that "prepares us ever anew to meet whatever we must meet in our daily lives," it reinforces socialized femininity rather than female friendship. The word *thoughtfulness* conveys the meaning of a thinking considerateness and a considerate thinking. It is not accidental that it has such a dual meaning. A woman who truly thinks is, more expansively, full of thought in many realms. . . .

"*Intercourse with oneself*" is crucial to both the idea of thinking and that of friendship, for it is where both come together. Thinking is where I keep myself company, where I find my original friend, if you will. It is the solitude, as opposed to loneliness, where I am alone with, but not lonely in, the companionship of myself. Thinking is where I am at home with myself when, for all sorts of reasons, I withdraw from the world. "The partner who comes to life when you are alert and alone is the only one from whom you can never get away—except by ceasing to think." This is one of the major reasons why women have lost their Selves—because they have stopped thinking. By not thinking, an individual loses her original friendship with her Self. Through thinking, a person discovers that she can be her real Self. In discovering this, she also realizes that the conversation that took place in the duality of thinking activity—that is, the duality of "myself with myself," the "two-in-one," or "the one who asks and the one who answers"—enables conversation with others. When I discover, through thinking, that I can converse with my real Self, I have to realize that such a conversation is possible with others. This is the awakening of female friendship in which the search for others like my Self begins. . . .

A woman must be at the same time a friend to her original Self and to others. Which comes first is hard to determine. What is clear is that thinking and friendship go hand in hand. . . .

PASSION

As female friendship is characterized by thoughtfulness, it is also marked by passion. Friendship is a passion but, in my vision, it is a thoughtful passion. It manifests a thinking heart.

The tension between thinking and feeling, as signified in the phrase "thoughtful passion," is evident in the etymology of the word *passion*. Passion derives from Old French and Latin roots meaning "suffering, pain or some disorder of body or spirit." It also means being "affected by external agency." However, etymologies are often multidimensional, and so we find another meaning of *passion* defined as "any kind of feeling by which the mind is powerfully affected or moved . . . an eager outreaching of the mind toward something" (*Oxford English Dictionary*).

A passionate friendship upholds the integrity between thought and passion. In passionate friendship, there is no separation between the two. It is not so much that they merge, but that they have not been fractured to begin with. . . .

A thoughtfully passionate friendship is passion at its most active. It keeps passion active and does not allow it to degenerate into its more passive modes. More concretely, it helps two women to become their own person. There is a dynamic integrity of existence in a thoughtful passion that is missing in more sentimental friendship. Friendship that is characterized by thoughtful passion ensures that a friend does not lose her Self in the heightened awareness of and attachment to another woman.

The loss of Self has happened most frequently in lover relationships. And, in fact, passion is generally associated with lovers, not with friends, or not with friends who aren't lovers. There has been much discussion of passion within the lover relationship, but not much talk of friendship within love. It is my opinion that when a lover finds that she is losing her Self in the heightened awareness of and attachment to another woman in a sexually passionate relationship, the friendship is problematic. Either the friendship wasn't strong initially or it got swallowed up in the sexual passion of the lover relationship. Thus passion deteriorates into its more passive mode, engulfing a necessary friendship and eclipsing its ability to generate a needed thoughtfulness about the friendship that is required for passion to survive and thrive.

In any kind of lover relationship that is committed, one's lover should be one's best friend. And if one's best friend is one's lover, she should also be the primary passion of her lover's life. A truly passionate love life, above all, must be pervaded by a thoughtful passion. . . .

When a woman lives as a woman, among women, among men, she at the same time questions the man-made world but does not dissociate from it, assimilate to it, or allow it to define her as a victim in it. She demands her place in it as a woman whose affinities are with women. She takes on the existence of what Mary Daly might refer to as "defiant deviant." Hannah Arendt might have named her a "conscious pariah," and Virginia Woolf would have probably welcomed her into the "Society of Outsiders." I prefer the term *inside outsider* because it helps to make clear the dual tension of women who see the man-made world for what it is and exist in it with worldly integrity, while at the same time seeing beyond it to something different. The term also highlights the reality of women who know that they can never really be insiders yet who recognize the liabilities of the dissociated outsider.

The inside outsider lives in the world with worldly integrity, weaving the strands of feminist wisdom into the texture of the world and paving the way for the entrance of women as women, that is, women on our own terms, into the world. As an inside outsider, a woman's work is characterized by the dual tension between her feminism and her worldliness. Her worldliness is dependent on her feminist vision, yet her feminist vision is actualized in her worldly location. . . .

The practical question, however, is How and where do women participate in the world? The worldliness I am advocating is not necessarily that of joining the anti-nuclear movement, the state legislature, or any other such worldly activities on their own terms. The terms of such endeavors are rarely woman-defined or woman-oriented. If participation in such worldly activities, or in others, is to be engaged in with worldly integrity, this participation must be on our terms, not in an absolute sense but in a way that enables woman-identified women to work within these worlds with integrity and with the ability to effect change—in other words, to work as inside outsiders.

If integrity means "that from which nothing can be taken," women must learn a few lessons from the feminist political past. Historically, women have been the mainstays of the abolitionist movements, peace movements, and other movements for human rights and social justice worldwide. In all of these movements, the feminist question was rarely highlighted. As a result, women did not participate in such movements on our own terms, and a worldly integrity was lacking. There are, of course, exceptions to this, but I am speaking in general.

On a more particular level, it might be helpful to give some concrete examples of how a woman functions as an inside outsider. Or, in other words, how does a woman live and act with worldly integrity? There are individual women and women's groups explicitly dedicated to women's causes. They may work in organizations specifically devoted to battered women, to the feminist campaign against pornography, or in various service organizations that meet women's needs. Or, as individuals, they may defend women in court, institute legislation against rape or for equal pay, or dismantle discriminatory and oppressive structures in which many women live their domestic and work lives. They may edit feminist journals, provide women-centered health care, and/or teach Women's Studies. All these types of feminist work have made a profound impact on the man-made world, changing, for example, the face of patriarchal legislation, health care, and learning, as well as creating more woman-centered and institutional structures. . . .

In the final analysis, worldliness is a materializing of dual vision, of two sightsseeing. Liberation, if it requires "seeing with more than ordinary sight," also requires "seeing with ordinary sight." As vision radically upheaves the existent man-made world, it must at some point give rise to coherent groups, lasting structures, and patterns of worldly activity. As vision disturbs, it must also stabilize. The structures of women living in the world must also be built.

> It is a fact of social/political movements that radicalism does not sustain a movement. For a movement to endure, its broad base and widespread influence must be assured. But radicalism is *essential* for the life of a movement, as it will bring to it the most uncompromising critique of the abusive, exploitative power that the movement seeks to undermine and overcome. It is the presence of radical critique which assures us that the movement will not devolve to simple reform—that is, patchwork on an exploitative, corrupt, and ruthless power structure.

Women must use this radicalism to re-fashion women's existence in the real world. However, without structure and stability, radicalism will be frantic, bursting with energy, but short-lived. In this process, we must keep the tension between movement and stasis. Feminist farsighted vision is meaningless unless it is accompanied by nearsighted realism which gives it shape and staying power. It is also meaningless unless such dual vision can translate into happiness—a happiness in this world.

HAPPINESS

There has not been much talk or writing about happiness in the women's movement. It is almost as if feminists expected that happiness could come about only in some future life, after the struggle is won and the revolution over. Malraux once noted that in the twentieth century, the so-called intellectuals found in revolution what many others formerly sought in eternal life; that is, the revolution "saves those that make it."

Many women have defined feminism only in political terms, accentuating struggle against male tyranny. They have failed to see that just as feminism is a politics of risk and resistance, it must hold out to women some promise of happiness now. Organized sisterhood against the conditions of female oppression and the feminist fight against all states of atrocities against women serve as a powerful bulwark against the forces and structures of patriarchy. However, a purely political feminism, emphasizing only conflict and resistance, bears too strong a resemblance to religious eschatologies (theologies of the future) that would have women believe that the true happiness is achievable only in some life to come.

What is happiness? We use the term today more in a psychological sense, that is, as a disposition, feeling, or state of being that a person experiences. Originally, however, the term had an ethical meaning. In its earliest philosophical usage, happiness was connected with moral purpose, with teleology. Happiness was found in the fulfillment of some activity, end, or goal of life. Aristotle reminds us that happiness is an activity of the mind, of contemplation. Combining these meanings, happiness has also been defined as the feeling that accompanies the activity of the whole self, or the feeling of self-realization. Along with this, happiness means the harmonious life itself.

My own definition of happiness is an amalgam and rephrasing of these meanings. On the one hand happiness, as I am describing it, is striving for the full use of one's powers. It is attained in fulfilling certain ends or purposes. On the other hand, one must experience happiness. Therefore, it is a state of existence which I think can best be summarized in Nadezhda Mandelstam's translation of the Russian word *zhizneradostny* as "life-glad." Literally, she means to be glad in/about/with life. To be "life-glad" adds a certain depth and substance to the word *happiness.* In short, then, happiness is striving for the full use of one's powers that make one "life-glad."

I do not mean to speak about happiness as if it is an all-or-nothing existence. For example, a woman can be happy in her work but unhappy at home. Happiness implies, however, that one is constantly seeking for the integrity of the Self and that it is a process. It is, as I said, a striving. But the more that endeavor is transformed into existence, the more one is "life-glad." It should not be, as Charlotte Brontë noted, a task. "No mockery in this world ever sounds to me so hollow as that of being told to cultivate happiness. What does such advice mean? Happiness is not a potato, to be planted in mould, and tilled with manure."

Female friendship gives women the context in which to be "life-glad." It creates a private and public sphere where happiness can become a reality. It provides encouragement and environment for the full use of one's powers. And since the profession of friendship means that the one who befriends has a greater interest in her friend's happiness than in that of others in general, female friendship strives for the full use of the friend's powers.

DOROTHY DINNERSTEIN

The Roots of Patriarchal Despotism

DOROTHY DINNERSTEIN is the author of *The Mermaid and the Minotaur: Sexual Arrangements and Human Malaise*, from which the following excerpt is taken.

THE NATURE OF MATERNAL AUTHORITY

Maternal will emanates, first of all, from a subjectivity that we encounter before our own sense of subjectivity is at all clearly established. It is the first separate subjectivity of which we become aware, and its separateness . . . is a fact to which most of us are never fully reconciled. To recognize the actuality of any subjectivity outside our own—which means recognizing the actuality of our own as well—is a momentous intellectual step. It would be a huge, difficult step in any case: the discovery that any fellow creature exists revolutionizes the nature of existence. And the difficulty is immensely complicated by the difference between the mother's adult sentience and our own infant one, and by our grief at the separation, at the cutting off of our initial sense of fusion with her, that this step involves. We necessarily take this step so far as we must. But few of us carry it to its logical conclusion, which is a matter of coming to see in retrospect that the first parent was after all no more and no less than a fellow creature. To come to see this is not a task wholly beyond human strength, even under present conditions. But it is a task that is rarely taken on, since it is arduous and our male-female arrangements make it easy to shirk.

Female sentience, for this reason, carries permanently for most of us the atmosphere of that unbounded, shadowy presence toward which all our needs were originally directed. And the intentionality that resides in female sentience comes in this way to carry an atmosphere of the rampant and limitless, the alien and unknowable. It is an intentionality that needs to be conquered and tamed, corralled and subjugated, if we (men most urgently, but women too) are to feel at all safe in its neighborhood.

It needs to be corralled, controlled, not only because its boundaries are unclear but also because its wrath is all-potent and the riches it can offer or refuse us bottomless. *What makes female intentionality so formidable—so terrifying and at the same time so alluring—is the mother's life-and-death control over helpless infancy:* an intimately carnal control exerted at a time when mind and body—upon whose at least partial separability it later becomes a matter of human dignity to insist—are still subjectively inseparable. This *power* that the mother exerts is felt before the existence of her *will* can be perceived. When the child, in the process of coming to know itself as a center of will, starts to be aware of hers, it faces the will of a being at whose touch its flesh has shuddered with joy, a being the sound of whose footsteps has flooded its senses with a relief more total than it can ever know again. For a long time to come, her kiss will still make bumps and bruises better; her voice will still dispel terror. Yet she is a being who on other occasions has mysteriously withheld food, who has mysteriously allowed loneliness, terror, and pain to continue. She is still—and will be for years to come—a being whose moods of inattention or indifference cast an ominous shadow over existence, a being whose displeasure is exile from warmth and light.

But *what makes female intentionality formidable* is something more than the mother's power to give and withhold while we are passive. It *is also the mother's power to foster or forbid, to humble or respect, our first steps toward autonomous activity.* It is just as we begin to discover the drastic limits of our own will's scope that we start to be aware of her separate intentionality, and this awareness is inevitably pervaded with the feeling evoked by that discovery. We meet her will just as we start to struggle with the human chagrin of confinement in a circumscribed body, a body whose efforts to impose the wishes of its imaginative adventurous inhabitant on the indifferent physical world prove enragingly puny. And this outside will of hers easily prevails, when it so chooses, over our own emerging will: it prevails not only through passive resistance to our wishes, as the physical world does, but also through personal and purposeful force exerted upon this weak, circumscribed body. This coincidence multiplies the newly discovered bodily chagrin, makes it intimate and social, transmutes it into humiliation. . . .

• • •

. . . The child feels confidence within the predictable, customary shape of the life over which she presides; it feels power in joining forces with her power; it feels pride in acquiring the self-command (control over its muscles and its sphincters, ability to contain its own angry or grabby or otherwise importunate impulses) that will win her approval. But all of these feelings of strength are inseparable from the sense of obeying, or collaborating with, her female will. It may be a gentle or a harsh will, a sympathetic or an overbearing or a woundingly indifferent will, but it is in any case a uniquely potent will. And the vital strengths that are developed under its auspices must be tested out against it; otherwise they remain the mother's strengths, not the child's.

The child's will, then, is poised, for dear life's sake, to confront and resist the will of woman. But to live up to this challenge is to contend with appalling complications. For woman is not merely the first, permanently nebulous, outside "I" and the first, all-giving, provider, not merely the first, all-mighty, adversary and protector, lover and ruler. *She is also the first "you,"* and this "you"ness of hers contributes in a number of ways to the lifelong emotional impact of female intentionality.

It means, first of all, that her weight as an adversary rests not just on her strength in contrast with the child's puniness but also on the child's realization that she is consciously aware—and aware of the child's awareness—of this contrast. *In confronting her the child faces an old, devastatingly knowledgeable witness.* . . .

But woman is also the audience who has acclaimed our first triumphs ("Look!" my mother and my aunts would cry out to each baby in turn as it shook a rattle, stood up, peed in a pot, took the cover off a box and fitted it on again: "Look"—in joyous amazement, as if such a thing had never been seen before—"what the baby can *do!*") and the invincible ally whose help made possible our first landmark achievements. What we feel, along with vulnerability in the face of woman's old awareness of our weakness, is a deep sense of need, rooted in her old support of our nascent strength. *It is woman's will that nurtures*—celebrates, stimulates, shelters—*the growth of the child's own will.*

The child, then, in purposefully opposing the mother, takes a double risk. On the one hand she can retaliate by crushing her opponent's pride as only she is in a position to do: she can point up, dwell upon, the child's early failures instead of minimizing and smoothing them over; she can make the child knuckle under again as it has done before instead of acknowledging its growing strength, and its right to win sometimes, by compromising with its wishes. But on the other hand she can give way too far: she can leave the child in possession of an empty field; she can abandon it to a hollow victory, bereft of its mighty sponsor. Faced with this double risk, a naturally keen childhood fantasy-wish (lived out widely by adult men with the women whom they rule) is to keep female will in live captivity, obediently energetic, fiercely protective of its captor's pride, ready always to vitalize his projects with its magic maternal blessing and to support them with its concrete, self-abnegating maternal help. . . .

● ● ●

THE NATURE OF PATERNAL AUTHORITY

To mother-raised humans, male authority is bound to look like a reasonable refuge from female authority. We come eventually, of course, to resent male authority too: regardless of its gender, or of our gender, authority generates resentment. But the primitive swing between need and rage described just above is oriented originally, and stays oriented mainly, toward the will behind the hand that rocks the cradle. On the whole, our attitudes toward the second parent—the parent who ordinarily orbits, at the beginning, outside the enchanted mother-infant pair, and who then enters it so gradually that it remains for a long time a very lopsided triangle indeed—are far less infantile, far less inchoate, than our attitudes toward the first.

We do, needless to say, both love and fear a father's strength, both need and resent his feeling of responsibility for us. But his strength and his feeling of responsibility do not ordinarily become tangible to us until after the world has started to lose its initial magic. His presence is apt to be relatively peripheral until after we have started to organize the realm of inner feeling into reasonably discrete regions or units, and to recognize that a creature can have multiple aspects, shifting moods, and still be a permanent, unitary individual. For this reason he is perceived from the beginning (unless, of course, he is an abnormally rejecting or frightening person) as a more *human* being than the mother, more like an adult version of oneself, less engulfing, less nebulously overwhelming.

Even if a father inflicts corporal punishment, it is punishment endured by a body that we perceive as clearly separate from his. We experience opposition between his will and ours, even if he is autocratic and even though he easily wins, through an awareness that we have come to recognize as uniquely our own; and he experiences this opposition through an awareness on which we do not centrally depend to keep us oriented to the environment. What he mainly inspires is not so much ambivalence as a mixture of sentiments. The mixture can be disturbing, but the disturbance cannot come as close to the heart of our sense of existence itself as the ambivalence of the earlier, more vital, maternal tie.

A father can be quite tyrannical, then, and still be felt as in some sense a refreshing presence. His power is more distinct and clearly defined than the mother's, his wisdom less eerily clairvoyant. Because he is a creature more separate from ourselves, our resentment of him is less deeply tinged with anxiety and guilt. And our love for him, like our anger at him, lies outside the shadowy maternal realm from which all children, to grow up, must escape.

The father, as de Beauvoir has pointed out, is respected for an achievement to which every child, with some part of itself, aspires: He moves in a world that lies safely outside the maternal aura. His spirit eludes, and even partly controls, that wilderness of forces which is both nature and feminine. Even if his work in the world is menial, he has the status of a participant in history, because he is above female authority: he has identity outside the immediate family circle.

So the essential fact about paternal authority, the fact that makes both sexes accept it as a model for the ruling of the world, is that it is under prevailing conditions a sanctuary from maternal authority. It is a sanctuary passionately cherished by the essential part of a person's self that wants to come up (like Andersen's mermaid) out of the drowning sweetness of early childhood into the bright dry light of open day, the light of the adult realm in which human reason and human will—not the boundless and mysterious intentionality, the terrible uncanny omniscience, of the nursery goddess—can be expected, at least ideally, to prevail.

THE HEART OF THE PROBLEM

The main use man makes of woman in the face of unfreedom is to hide from himself the depth of his capitulation to societal coercion, the depth of his failure to leave childhood behind and take his fate in his own hands. Woman uses woman in this way too; her mechanism for doing so is not so different from his as it looks on the surface.

For both, the essential fact is this: Few of us ever outgrow the yearning to be guided as we were when we were children, to be told what to do, for our own good, by someone powerful who knows better and will protect us. Few of us even wholeheartedly try to outgrow it. What we do try hard to outgrow, however, is our subjugation to female power: the power on which we were dependent before we could judge, or even wonder, whether or not the one who wielded it knew better and was bossing us for our own good; the power whose protectiveness—although we once clung to it with all our might, and although it was steadier and more encompassing than any we are apt to meet again—seemed at that time both oppressive and imperfectly reliable.

Having escaped that power, or at least learned how to keep it within bounds, all but a few of us have exhausted our impulse toward autonomy: the relatively limited despotism of the father is a relief to us. In some part of ourselves we do not really want to be our own bosses; all we want is to be bossed a little more finitely and comprehensibly. And this part of ourselves tells the other part, the part that wants to shake off submission, that really we have already shaken off submission: the boss we have now is a much better boss, a boss we have chosen of our own free will.

The central opportunity for self-deception, then, that lies in the shift from dependence on female authority to dependence on male, patriarchal, authority is seized by both sexes. In the original self-reversing revolution it is daughters as well as sons who revolt, and the revolt is not against a father but against a mother. What makes it possible to replace that deposed sovereign with another and still feel triumphant is that the new sovereign is of a new gender: *If a different, apparently blameless, category of person were not temptingly available as a focus for our most stubborn childhood wish—the wish to be free and at the same time to be taken care of—we would be forced at the beginning, before our spirit was broken, to outgrow that wish and face the ultimate necessity to take care of ourselves.*

As things are, having achieved the shift and found ourselves still unfree, we make the best of our new situation. At the thought of tampering with it too far, we are faced with the specter of reversion to the greater helplessness we have escaped. Patriarchy remains a refuge that we are afraid to dismantle. We feel that the reign of the early mother is waiting for us just outside its walls; and besides, we must balance our dislike of constraint against our fears of freedom. Our stance, in submission to patriarchy, is the stance of tired old revolutionaries: our self-assertion is on the record, so to speak. We have, after all, overthrown the first and worst tyrant, and we are still defending ourselves against the everpresent threat of her return to power. What more can we expect of ourselves?

The sense that our refuge from maternal power is besieged is constantly reinforced, unfortunately, by the surprising vicissitudes of life outside the nursery. Our hopes for this splendid life out from under female dominion are bound to be in part disappointed, and this fact acts, paradoxically, not to undermine our trust in the patriarchal refuge but rather to reinforce our dread of that from which it shields us. The paradox works as follows: Male authority carries the breath of the rationally controllable world, the world that the child—even, in a qualified way, the girl child—looks forward to being part of when it becomes an adult. But this world, as we enter it, turns out of course to be far less controllable, far less rational, than it looked from a distance. We find in it many of the constraints we met in the nursery. What we learn, when we finally manage to escape the enforced obedience of childhood, is that we are still not our own bosses. And we feel in this shocking lesson an echo of the related lesson that we learned at the beginning under female auspices: that our powers to manipulate the environment are limited, and that there exist other human wills strong enough to prevail over our own. The echo adds depth to the mother-raised human's fear and resentment of female authority. That we are never, after all, wholly our own bosses means that the early mother has after all won. We have not escaped helplessness as well as we thought we would when we left her; the proof is that we must still submit to unconquerable forces: to the indignity of bodily illness, and the inexorability of bodily aging; to the thwarting of ambition; to unwelcome orders from more powerful adults; to the pressure of social custom and economic need and the ravages of natural disasters. Every such proof of our weakness and fragility silently activates a rage that goes far back to our first encounters with the angry pain of defeat. *If these first encounters had not taken place under all-female auspices, if women were not available to bear the whole brunt of the unexamined infantile rage at defeat that permeates adult life, the rage could not so easily remain unexamined; the infantilism could more easily be outgrown.* Under present conditions, what happens is that each setback imprisons us more firmly than ever in the patriarchal trap: inside it, safe under the control of a new boss, we can go on raging at the old one.

On an inarticulate level, then, *both men and women use the unresolved early threat of female dominion to justify keeping the infantilism in themselves alive under male dominion.* Patriarchy provides woman, like man, with a boss for the baby in her at the same time that it affirms her freedom from the boss she had when she was in fact a baby. It provides her—vicariously, through him—with the satisfaction of making the old tyrant knuckle under, bow down, and at the same time lets her enjoy directly a slave's freedom under a new tyrant.

For her, some of the sting is taken out of her capitulation to this new tyrant by the sense that he fears the old one in her, that she is a magic captive, that he handles her gingerly. For him, what takes the sting out, what makes life under the dominion of other males livable, is in part his ownership of her, his access to her resources. This neutralizes his sense of being himself owned and exploited by the social order: He may be a slave, but he is a rich, a slave-owning, slave. He is a free slave, too, free to vent, in his bullying of her, the rage he feels at other men's bullying of him. Feminists have been pointing out for a long time that the subordination of woman helps maintain societal oppression by way of this mechanism.

But there is something more that also helps take the sting out for man, helps blunt the edge of his impulse to resist tyranny: Woman's old power over him is not wholly dead. It is contained, fenced in, but it is still potent enough to help counterbalance the male power to which he has chosen (freely, he can believe) to attach and subordinate himself. A part of him is held back from vassalage to men; he still pays some homage to the old tyrant, who, tamed and corralled, rules him now at his pleasure, with his permission.

Even in the efforts man makes to *overthrow* male tyranny—male tyranny over males, that is—he rests on the vassalage of woman. Reassured that he has the original despot under control, he can play with the notion of emerging from under the wing of the new one. He needed that refuge while he was escaping her power. But now his unilateral dependence on her seems to be behind him; she and he are mutually dependent: he still needs her, but most of the overt power is securely in his hands. He can draw on her vitality, take heart from her obedience, and fight for brotherhood. He can even deny to himself that she is helping him: in Freud's account of brothers banding together against the primal patriarch there is no mention of support from sisters or wives.

But such efforts are inevitably abortive, given our present sexual arrangements. What makes them abortive is not only the inner ambivalence toward the mighty old man that Freud so well describes. What keeps the rebel helpless to surmount that ambivalence is the gender-related instability of his stance in this kind of fight. He is drawing strength from the subservience of woman for a struggle against the tyranny of man; but he can keep woman subservient only with the strength he draws from the sponsorship of the male tyrant. If he wins the struggle, what he at once begins to miss is not only the old man himself, and the intrinsic sweetness of subjugation to him, but also the super-male backing that the old man provided, which made his control of woman emotionally possible. The ground he stands on as he fights melts under him as his adversary retreats. He is balancing terrors, dependencies, against each other; the balance keeps tipping, and he keeps slipping back into the patriarchal trap.

This must happen, again and again, until we start outgrowing the original dependency, the original terror of eternal helplessness, instead of trying all our lives to keep it at bay. And we will take on this emotional task only when we no longer have the option, at the beginning, of shirking it by running for refuge from the first tyrant to another of a new gender. When we can not run away from the task we will face it: we will then put tyranny in its place instead of trying to keep woman in hers. The project of brotherhood cannot be achieved until it includes sisters. It is inseparable from the project of sexual liberty.

CHAPTER 3

How Can I Make Sense of Sex?

During the past several years, a conservative political movement has been advocating the boycott of Barbie dolls. According to their spokespeople, Barbie dolls, with their voluptuous figures and suggestive clothing, encourage children to think about sex and so contribute to a social climate that condones early sexual activity, teenage pregnancy, and the deterioration of family values. Simultaneously, and with less concentrated efforts, feminist organizations have also urged parents to avoid purchasing Barbie and her pals. On this line of reasoning, Barbie is to be shunned because she, and Ken, represent the sort of gender stereotyping that has contributed to gender inequality. In addition, Barbie represents female sexuality in its most oppressive form. Barbie exists principally as an object of male desire. Her exaggerated proportions remind us that women are valued only in so far as they meet the demands of male sexual fantasy.

These Barbie Doll Wars provide us with a sense of the complexities of sexual morality. It probably strikes you as odd that conservatives and feminists should line up together against the Barbie doll, given that they have entirely different conceptions of what is wrong with prevailing sexual ethics and behavior. After all, conservatives tend to worry about preserving the traditional family, whereas feminists generally regard the traditional family as a principal site of the oppression of women. What seems clear enough from this odd coincidence of views regarding Barbie dolls is that any particular sexual morality has to be understood not simply in relation to those things that it encourages and prohibits, but also with reference to the motivations for its proscriptions. If the Barbie doll case does not persuade you, think about the fact that in the nineteenth century, a fair number of middle-class women encouraged their husbands to visit prostitutes because middle-class women believed themselves to be devoid of sexual desire, whereas their husbands were prone to intense sexual "urges."

This chapter provides a wide-ranging introduction to various issues that fall within the boundaries of sexual ethics. As Robert C. Solomon notes in his essay, though sex may have a clearly defined biological purpose, its biological purpose is only rarely why one worries or fantasizes about it, wants to engage in it, or actually does engage in it. Human sexuality intersects with other human characteristics and capacities in complex ways. That is precisely why sex cannot be reduced to a purely biological phenomenon. Sex and sexuality actually do pervade our lives. This is exactly why we find people worrying about the dangers of Barbie. So you should not be surprised that the issues addressed in this chapter begin with contraception and end with sexual harassment after considering adultery and homosexuality.

One of the principal themes that inform all of these issues is that of sexual freedom. It is not surprising that many people believe, for example, that advances in contraceptive technology result in increases in sexual freedom. Solomon argues, however, that though user-friendly contraceptives may make sexual activity more congenial for heterosexual couples, contraceptives alone cannot account for changes in attitudes about sex. In addition, it is important to realize that sexual behavior is constrained, not only by fear of pregnancy, but by social pressures as well. The attitudes about sex are what determine the acceptability of contraception.

Solomon's arguments regarding the nature and purpose of sex remind us that sexuality is not a simple function of individual choice and desire. What we desire and what we choose are constructed within particular social settings. According to prevailing moral canon, to desire someone else's spouse, and then to act on that desire, is to betray the sanctity of marriage. Richard Wasserstrom explores the presuppositions behind this view of adultery and wonders whether it promotes an excessively restrictive concept of intimate, interpersonal relationships. His essay encourages us to examine critically the reasons for and consequences of the general societal proscription against sexual behavior that falls outside the bounds of what we might imagine that Ozzie and Harriet do in their bedroom. Morris Kaplan explores the public face of homosexuality in relation to the emergence of a vocal demand for equality on the part of gays and lesbians. He provides a comprehensive account of the various legal and political arenas within which rights claims are negotiated. Audre Lorde's essay, by focusing on the struggles of black women, and black lesbians in particular, emphasizes the importance of looking at the relationship between sexuality and political power in our effort to understand sexual morality.

The final essay, by Crosthwaite and Priest, turns our attention to the issue of sexual harassment, a phenomenon that has received widespread attention in the media as businesses and other institutions struggle to develop and enforce antiharrassment codes. Crosthwaite and Priest argue that sexual harassment can only be understood in the context of gender inequality. An adequate definition of sexual harassment would help to illuminate how disparate cases—from a boss extracting sexual favors from his secretary on threat of dismissal, to men hanging pornographic posters on the walls of police barracks—fall into the category of sexually harmful behavior.

ROBERT C. SOLOMON

Sex, Contraception, and Conceptions of Sex

ROBERT C. SOLOMON teaches philosophy and business at the University of Texas at Austin. His books include *In the Spirit of Hegel, From Hegel to Existentialism, About Love, Its Good Business,* and *A Passion for Justice.*

> *... males and females united without any premeditated design, as chance, occasion, or desire brought them together, nor had they any great occasion for language to make known what they had to say to each other. They parted with the same ease.*
>
> JEAN-JACQUES ROUSSEAU

There is the myth: 'free sex', as told by a philosophical libertine who practiced it freely. It is a distinctively male fantasy, of course; one might say, a paradigm of irresponsibility. But suppose the problem of unwanted pregnancy—and to see it as a problem at all is already an enormous philosophical and political leap—could be solved. Could sex not then become as Jean-Jacques fantasized it, 'free' and divorced from morals and even manners? 'Liberated from our biology' as Shulamith Firestone once put it: how different would our sexual world be?

Does effective contraceptive technology alter our conception of sex? Does it 'free' sex from extraneous fears and moral concerns? When I started my research into the topic, I thought I knew; what had had a more direct and dramatic effect on sexual conduct than the availability of the pill in the 1960s, and what could be more obvious than the 'sexual revolution' then set in motion? But on further investigation and reflection, I began to realize that our modern medical miracles had ancient, however less effective counterparts, and that sexual revolutions, looking at the whole of history, have been a dime-a-dozen. With that in mind, and without lacking gratitude for the advances of modern medicine, I want to answer the question with a qualified 'No.' Our new contraceptive technology has not altered our conceptions of sex in anything like the radical 'revolutionary' ways we sometimes imagine.

> Sexual intercourse began
> In nineteen sixty-three
> (Which was rather late for me)—
> Between the end of the
> CHATTERLEY ban
> And the Beatles' first LP.
> PHILLIP LARKIN
High Windows

I would like to throw open to question the concept taken most for granted in contemporary discussions of contraception—sex. For a philosopher to even ask 'what, really,

95

is sex?' is to open him or herself up to ridicule. (Who else would ask such a question?) 'What is the problem?' it is replied curtly, with a smirk, occasionally coupled with an offer of an ostensive definition. 'Sex is,—well, sex is—just what it is'. It is straightforward biology, which happens (usually) to involve two people, and more importantly, which happens to be fun. Unfortunately, fun has its price, for nature's purpose is not the same as our purposes. But, fortunately, in sex as in so much of modern life, human technology has taken control of nature. Sex is one thing; reproduction is something else. A thousand generations have enjoyed one only along with the other. We, finally, have separated them.

Reproduction, because it involves the lives of other human beings in the most dramatic way imaginable, their very creation, is at the center of our moral concerns; indeed, until recently, the very concept of a person's 'morals' was far more concerned with his or her sexual behavior than with any other virtues or vices. But now, severing sex and reproduction, also threatens to divorce sex and morals, according to the fears of many contemporary moralists. In fact, this has not happened. What current technology, coupled with the current sexual counter revolution, shows us is that sexuality is still at the heart of morality, and though there are the most serious questions of life and death involved in questions of reproduction there remain equally ethical—if not so mortal—questions of morals in our non-reproductive conception of sex. Sex, in other words, is not as 'free' as the sexual revolutionaries once thought.

What is sex? It is, in some sense, the coupling of bodies in certain, not so strictly circumscribed ways. There is a central paradigm, which provides the continuity with most of the animal kingdom and even a small minority of plants—heterosexual intercourse. Indeed, given the flat and untitillating use of the word 'sex' in biology textbooks to describe the behavior of scorpions and fish, not to mention pine trees, one gets the idea that sex for us is much the same physical process, except that we alone in the kingdoms of life have chosen to make a moral issue of it. But this is wholly misleading, if it is not actually fraudulent. In fact, most human sex has about as much continuity with arachnids and dicotyledons as eating the Sunday wafer and sipping the Passover wine have to do with nutrition.

Sex is ideas. Sex is not about conception—at least, not usually; our conceptions about sex are far more tied to our morals than our gonads, though, to be sure, one can easily and amusingly imagine how different our sexual fantasies might be if our organs were differently constituted, say, on the bottom of one foot or—reminiscent of a once popular but physiologically dubious movie—inside of the mouth or the throat. This essay, accordingly, is about our sexual conceptions, not about conception or contraception as such. Indeed, what continues to strike me as remarkable is that, despite the dramatic developments two decades ago, changes in contraceptive technology are not the major determinants of our conceptions of sex. My historical thesis in a nutshell: attitudes about sex determine the acceptability of contraception, at least as much as the availability of effective contraception determines attitudes about sex.

THE TELEOLOGY OF SEX: THE PURPOSE OF SEX

Sex is not just 'matter in motion' (we may refrain from mentioning the many more imaginative metaphors), plus the pleasurable sensations thereby promoted and produced.

Sex, like virtually all human activities and like most biological phenomena, has a purpose, or purposes. In the perspective of biology, of course, that purpose is clear enough: the perpetuation of the species. Pleasure, the expression or the stimulation of romantic love, getting even with the husband or getting a good grade the hard way are at most epiphenomena, perhaps effective motivation, but probably of no real relevance at all. Yet only rarely, if ever, does one 'have sex' within the biological perspective. The purpose of sex is therefore only rarely, if ever, the same as 'nature's purpose'—the perpetuation of the species. There is also OUR purpose or purposes, what we desire over and above—or instead of—fulfilling our biological roles as self-perpetuating links in a chain that extends from Adam and Eve or perhaps rather Lucy to Nietzsche's *Übermensch* or 'the last man.'

Philosophers—following the ancient Greeks—like to refer to the purpose of a phenomenon as its 'telos'; thus we can speak of the 'teleology of sex'—its ultimate purpose. But our teleology immediately splits at least in two, for there is what we have called, with evolutionary naivete, 'nature's purpose,' and then there are our various purposes, which are not the same thing. Indeed, once we introduce that distinction, we immediately begin to wonder how the two have ever been connected, except for the contingencies of biology—in the same way that one might wonder how it is that the miracle that we call 'language' has such an intimate connection with the organ of ingestion (Jacques Derrida aside, I should add).

'Nature's Purpose'

To talk of 'nature's purpose' is, of course, naive. We no longer talk so easily of the teleology of the world—as Aristotle did so long ago and as Hegel and his henchmen did with less ease a century and a half ago. We prefer causal models, efficient rather than final causes, physiochemical processes rather than instincts and collectively unconscious cunning. Nevertheless, we can say, controversially but a bit oddly, that sex does serve a purpose—whether or not we want to say that sex has a purpose. Sex provides— for the moment—the only means of reproduction of human beings, though whether this is a good thing in the eyes of some larger telos is an awesome question I would not want to broach here. And sometimes, about 2.3 periods per lifetime for most Americans, considerably less for many couples in other cultures whose birth rate is inversely higher, nature's purpose does indeed coincide with at least one of the purposes of the heterosexual couple having intercourse. (It is logically possible, of course, that a homosexual couple might also adopt this telos, but this possibility is not a fruitful topic of discussion.) This happy harmony is not our concern here, however; it is the divorce rather than the marriage of sex and conception that interests us. Let us turn, therefore, to persons' purposes, leaving nature to fend for herself.

Persons' Purposes

It is with persons' purposes that the teleology of sex becomes complicated. I have not mentioned some parallel complications in nature, for example, male dogs or chimps mounting other males, not in procreative confusion but as an unchallengeable gesture of dominance. I do want to consider such behavior, however, in the context of human sexuality. To take a more common example, it is often said, in many languages, that to have intercourse with a woman is to 'possess' her. I do not take such talk lightly, and the fact that the woman in question may or may not conceive as the result of the possessive act does not seem to be relevant to the matter. I choose this somewhat feudal example to underscore the sometimes less-than-romantic theme of the theory that I will be presenting here; sex is not, in addition to its biological functions, just a matter of pleasure or the expression of love. The human purposes of sex are spread across an enormous range of symbolic and practical concerns, from love and intentional debasement to a mere sleep aid. To talk about 'the purpose' of sex, even confining ourselves to 'our purposes' is a serious mistake. It does not follow, however, that this diversity makes impossible a unified theory of sexuality. Indeed, it is the diversity itself that has to be explained.

By 'persons' purposes,' I do not mean conscious purposes, nor, of course, do I refer only to explicit and mutually agreed upon purposes. The cooperative telos of the transparently self-reflective and psychologically explicit sado-masochist couple is one thing; the fumbling, confused clash of desires, fantasies, habits, expectations and aims that most of us take to bed with us is quite different as well as more common. Indeed, it is part of the ethics of sex (as opposed to the ethics of reproduction) that most of our purposes remain unspoken; it is a matter of curiosity as well as 'liberation' that we have recently been encouraged to make explicit our fantasies and desires. Not surprisingly, most of these tend to be rather mechanical ('touch me here') rather than the more significant messages and meanings that such behavior expresses, knowingly or not.

I do not want to attack the profound question of 'the unconscious,' much less the even more problematic Jungian notion of a 'collective' unconscious. There is no doubt that such a thing, consisting at least of those most basic biological impulses and residual instincts, which Kraft-Ebbing misleadingly calls 'the 6th, genital sense.' But whether there is an extinct-laden unconscious is quite another matter, and at least one proto-Jungian philosopher, Nietzsche, vehemently denied the collectivity of our impulses, turning the tables to insist that our 'herd-consciousness' is to be found in consciousness, our individuality in our instincts. Our own view of sexuality, as opposed to some of our theories about it, seems to side with Nietzsche. Each of us appears to belabor the illusion—against all evidence—that each of us sexually unique. But—back to the point—many of our purposes, individual or collective, instinctual or learned, are not conscious. When told about them—if we have not already been too jaded by 80 years of Freud—we would probably deny them, or, at least, dismiss them as minor aberrations, and 'out of character.'

WHAT DO I WANT WHEN I WANT YOU?

Any discussion of human sexuality involves more than a catalog of organs, feelings, physiological and behavioral responses; sex is first of all desire, both temporally and, less obviously, phenomenologically. Indeed, one might make a case that sex without desire is not sexuality at all, though one hesitates to suggest or imagine what it might be. But what is it that one desires?

The glib answers are soon forthcoming, along with that familiar smirk and a number of rude responses. Such responses, however, are largely limited to adolescents and academic seminars. A novice may think that the 'end' (telos as well as terminus) of sex is successful intercourse (though even the notion of 'success' should be carefully scrutinized here). But clearly despite certain philosophical protests, sex is not one of those activities that is 'desired for its own sake' (if anything is so desired). It is not just that sex sometimes serves a telos, but that it always does. If there is anything like a purely sexual impulse (and they are very rare if they exist in us at all), we still have to say something such as 'it is the satisfaction of the impulse' that is in question, not sex for sex's sake. Indeed, we should want to know more about this alleged 'impulse' (which was 'discovered' or 'postulated', in fact fabricated—at the end of the 19th century). Some animals perhaps may experience something like 'pure sexual desire,' but this is noteworthy only insofar as it is also isolated and empty, virtually unrelated to any other activities and something of a mystery to the animal itself. Dennett, in an unusual bit of anthropomorphizing, imagines a bird in the midst of its instinctual behavior, musing to itself, 'Why am I doing this?' Clearly few mammals enjoy such an impulse; sex becomes a matter of status as well as species-preservation, and, watching my male dog's behavior around a female in heat, it is clear that sexual desire supplies only a small if not minimal motive, and is interwoven inseparably with a half dozen other concerns. When we return to human sexuality, we might be far closer to the mark by beginning, not with the obvious but with the obscure, not with the simpleminded aim of wanting intercourse but with the 'infinite yearning' of *eros* suggested by Aristophanes in Plato's *Symposium*. In philosophy, it is always better to err towards the infinite than to get trapped in the picayune.

So, what is sexual desire? Indeed, is it possible (as Michel Foucault hints) that we ought to give up such talk as quite misleading and mythological, as if sex were indeed a distinct and isolated impulse with only the most peculiar and often antagonistic connections with our other motives and desires? Without going quite so far, we can begin to appreciate the complexity of what we call 'sexual desire' and its intricate connections with other desires and motives. Sex is not a distinct activity, except according to certain customs and rituals which make it so. Accordingly, sexual desire is not an easily distinguished mode of desire—which is how it is possible to produce those yearly disclosures that football, Pac-Man, quoits, metaphysics, process philosophy and eating artichokes are sexual. Who can say where one desire starts and another ends? How is it that Eric Rohmer's obsessive desire to touch Claire's Knee is highly sexual while the practiced intercourse of a jaded Don Juan may be just about as sexual as his desire to get it over with and go home to watch the Tonight Show? When we begin to analyse sexual desire, therefore, we should not be surprised that there is much more to it than sex. Indeed, sometimes sex might not even be part of it at all.

How could this be? And what does it have to do with the topic of contraception and conceptions of sex. First of all, the example of Claire's Knee—and if that sounds too fantastic consider your day-to-day furtive glance around the office—shows, if not yet convincingly, that the end of sex and sexual desire need not be sexual intercourse. Indeed, one might be obsessed with sex but find the very idea of intercourse unthinkable. One should therefore not leap to the now nearly automatic conclusion that such a desire must be 'repressed' or 'suppressed' or any other 'pressed' including 'un-expressed.' If sexual desire is not necessarily aimed at intercourse—heterosexual intercourse in particular—then the supposed essential tie between sex and sexual desire and those rather constricted activities in which pregnancy is possible is dramatically weakened. This is not to deny that most heterosexual couplings do end (terminus if not telos) in intercourse of the most often-prescribed variety. It is only to say that sexual desire is not so firmly connected to intercourse as is often supposed. Our sexual conceptions are far more independent of considerations concerning the consequences of intercourse than the linkage between contraceptive technology and sexual freedom suggests.

FUNCTIONALISM

In a society schooled in efficiency, in which ethics and utility are often thought to be the same, in which even physical exercise is supposed to serve a purpose, we should not be surprised that our conceptions of sex tend to turn to questions of function—to the uses of sex. My discussion of the teleology of sex might be viewed as part and parcel of this pragmatist orientation, and desirable as it might seem 'for its own sake,' sex in America is almost always defended in terms of some further goal—good health, happiness and interpersonal satisfaction. The idea of chastity horrifies us, and medical science has not been slow to catalog through the ages the various malfunctions that cruelly follow this unnatural abstinence.

Yet, the pragmatic notion of 'having a function,' like the more classical notion of teleology, is not a singular notion. It admits a variety of interpretations, from the traditional biological accounts of 'instinct' and 'species preservation' (that is, 'nature's purpose'—serving that natural function), to the Freudian account of pleasure as the purpose, however construed, in terms of the hydraulics of the 'psychic apparatus,' not the phenomenal sensations of 'fun.' But of particular interest to us here is the first of these interpretations, sex's natural function, reproduction. (Note that 'procreation,' even in the word itself, takes us at least one infinite step beyond nature.) What are we to make of the inescapably close connection—some philosophers even suggest entailment—between sexual desire and heterosexual intercourse?

The standard view, I take it, is this: sexuality changes with changes in its circumstances, the technology of contraception in particular. Taken as a hypothesis, the view suggests the following reading of history: in epochs where contraception is effective and available, sex is plentiful, relatively unrepressed and 'free.' Where contraception is not effective or available, sex tends to be prohibited, timid and fearful. But even a casual reading of the literature shows that not only is this hypothesis wrong, but its very foundation is upsidedown. (I refer here to the study of John Reed[s] who demonstrates this hypothesis with intriguing detail.) The correlation between contraceptive efficiency and sexual attitudes is most unclear; indeed there are cultures with no 'protection' against pregnancy that are highly promiscuous, and just as many cultures with relatively effective contraception that are, in our terms, 'Victorian.' (Oddly enough, many of the actual Victorians fall into the first class, rather than the second.) Thus the whole notion that contraceptive apparatus determines the nature of sexuality is inverted; it is rather attitudes toward sexuality—and, of course, attitudes towards population growth and the practicalities of having children—that determine the interest in, the effectiveness of, and the availability of contraception. Of course, there are societies in which readily available contraception is withheld from the public precisely in order to counteract a casual or promiscuous attitude towards sexuality. Witness the Reagan Administration's abortive and stupidly misconceived 'Squeal Rule,' according to which the parents of a young girl must be notified if she is to receive birth control information. Conservatives quickly respond, though for the wrong reasons, that information about birth control has not proven to lower the bastard birth rate, and some come to the correct conclusion—though with the wrong motives—that attitudes toward sex are not determined and are not therefore alterable through technological know-how alone. But these are standard twists and turns in the history of sexuality, not its primary path. It is the utter failure of the 'Squeal Rule,' not its paternalistic intentions, that has made us aware that sexual attitudes do not depend on technological availability; technological availability pivots on sexual attitudes, in this case, an atavistic nostalgia for the days of virginity, when sex was more feared than desired.

Functionalism, crudely conceived, is the view that sex serves the conveniences of life; it is desired when it is convenient, not desired when inconvenient, with contraception high on the list of conveniences. This is, however, a crude view of sex, and a crude view of life as well. Again let's remember Aristophanes' reference to eros and an 'infinite yearning.' We will not understand that yearning unless we give up the functional, as well as the biological, view of sex.

WHAT IS "SEX"?

The genealogy of 'sex' begins, no doubt, with the birds and the bees. But it is a thin 'natural' history of love that does not soon see that the very word "natural"—in a cultural context—is a *moral* term. 'Nature' might aim at propagation of the genotype, but cultures are concerned with group solidarity, rank and status, rules, respect and, for the sake of authority as well as order, prohibitions. To think that all of this is functional in the crude sense, aimed at population control or convenience, is nonsense. Indeed, much of the history of the availability of contraception is the history of power politics: the priests against the witches, the Republicans against the remnants of the counterculture. What is 'natural' depends not on biology but on ideology.

Our concept of 'nature' is inherited from Aristotle, the Greeks, the church, the Enlightenment. In all of its forms, it displays one of the more glamorous sophistries in Western thinking: the appeal to a silent and therefore incontrovertible Nature in the defense of particularly provincial practices. Indeed, it is rarely biological nature that is in question: it is more usually 'natural reason,' which is, as often suggested, most unnatural, even 'a bit of the divine.' When philosophers sought a 'natural religion,' for example, they were not after nature worship or what Santayana called 'animal faith': they were after rational arguments. And when there are demands for 'natural sex,' it is not bestiality or rear-entry intercourse that is preferred; the call is rather to 'rational sex,' which means, that for which there are accepted standards and arguments (most notably what I have elsewhere called 'the two-minute emissionary-missionary male-superior ejaculation service,' with some credit to John Barth). Whether or not sex is the danger to civilization that Freud thought it was, the traditional emphasis has been on quick and efficient sex, just enough to satisfy what D. H. Lawrence called 'evacuation lust' and, in the larger scheme of things, to ensure an adequate supply of progeny to maintain the status quo. Indeed, in our genealogy of sex and 'sex,' we should look to the social politics of classes and inheritance rights before the technological availability of contraception.

What then is sex? Like most loaded terms in our vocabulary, 'sex' defies definition. It is rather a political term, to be used in ways more defined by power than by established semantics. Like most loaded philosophical terms, it shifts, suspiciously, between an indisputable paradigm and abstract arguments of the sort we have gotten used to since Kraft-Ebbing and Freud. The paradigm is heterosexual intercourse, embellished with perhaps minimal preparatory passion ('foreplay') and typically succeeded by sleep or television rather than pregnancy. One might say, following some Oxford philosophers, that 'if that isn't sex, nothing is.' Perhaps, but the difficult task, hidden in this paradigm case argument, is to specify the feature of that paradigm. Is it the presence of male and female, or just the presence of two people? Is orgasm necessary to the paradigm? For both or only for the male? Is ejaculation of the male sufficient? (Ejaculation being the physical event of which orgasm is the more holistic phenomenon.) Must two people go 'all the way' or is it sufficient just that they want to? Indeed, is it even necessary for the paradigm that the genitals are the focus of attention, though, as a matter of contingency, we might quickly note that there are certain non-logical advantages to their inclusion.

'Sex' is a plastic, political term: the presence of an indisputable paradigm does not lessen its flexibility or its controversiality. The test case, perhaps, will always be homosexuality. Is it included in the paradigm? Does it count in a culture as 'natural sex'? In our own society, there are clearly no agreed upon answers to these questions. But before we try to tighten the link between ideological questions about sexual conceptions and technological questions about contraception, we should focus our attention on homosexuality. Here is, to say the obvious, a mode of sexuality in which pregnancy and contraception are not issues. But what we find is that homosexuality displays a history that is parallel to and usually a part of the history of heterosexuality. Its values are typically the same. Even its gestures and gender (not sex) identities are the same. To say that this is because it models itself after heterosexuality is to betray both a bias and a woeful historical blindness. Indeed, the most celebrated example of a homosexual culture— the ancient Greeks—despised women and heterosexuality, so much so that, in Plato's symposium virtually all of the speakers take pains to point out the inferiority of that merely functional domestic *eros* in contrast to the divine status of that 'higher' *eros* between men (more properly, between youths and men). What do we find when we look at Greek homosexuality—a licentious free-for-all with no restrictions, given the irrelevance of conception? Not at all. Indeed, the best books on the subject as well as the ancient texts themselves show us quite clearly that the sexual ethic among the Greeks was, if anything, more precise and much less hypocritical than the sexual mores of modern heterosexual cultures. Again, sex is determined by ethics, not biology (though once again I hasten to add that the contingencies of our bodies surely provide the material for that ethics; as the Marquis de Sade once commented, against the popular 'argument from design' that was circulating in natural theology: if God had not intended the anus to be used for sex he would not have shaped and positioned it so conveniently).

SEXUAL PARADIGMS

I have by now, I hope, conveyed some sense of my thesis that our sexual conceptions are not wholly determined by the more mechanical contingencies of medical research.

There is a logical and, more importantly, a cultural gap between functions and ideas, and it is more often the ideas that influence the functions rather than the other way around. (Even Marx and Engels would agree with this version of idealism, given that I have included most of the political and economic influences on the side of the 'ideas.') Our conception of sex is to a certain extent centered on a paradigm, the two minute emissionary-missionary male-superior ejaculation service.

The Paradigm need not be an ideal; indeed most paradigms tend to be boring examples, even in discussions of sex. But this paradigm has many facets, and so too draws upon many perspectives. In fact, heterosexual intercourse is not itself a paradigm so much as it is the convergence of many paradigms, and the job of a philosopher in addition to enjoying the practice, is to develop a theory in which these various paradigms are distinguished and played off against one another. There are four basic paradigms:

(1) the reproductive or procreative paradigm; (2) the pleasure or 'recreational' paradigm; (3) the metaphysical or 'Platonic' paradigm; and (4) the intersubjective communication paradigm.

The Reproductive Paradigm

The reproductive model has perhaps always been overemphasized, but, in the religious dress of 'procreation,' it has been especially well-nourished under the auspices of the Christian church. It is a paradigm which distills off the pleasures and Romantic overtones of sex and reduces it to a matter of dutiful service to the species—or to God. The paradigm is typically embellished and not left in its cold biological state, but even so it is distinctively unconcerned with questions of mutual expression and tenderness. (The union of souls as well as bodies is a secondary development.) The paradigm of reproductive sexuality is the effective and efficient ejaculation of the male into the female. His orgasm is a bonus; hers is of no importance whatever. Indeed, excess enjoyment, wasting time and—most essentially—'wasting seed,' is perversion. Indeed, although the concept of 'perversion' did not really enter into sexual ethics and medicine until the 19th century, the prohibitions against masturbation, sodomy, and all other manners of 'wasting seed' are found clearly even in the Old Testament. Needless to say, the sole paradigm here is heterosexual intercourse. Homosexuality has no place whatever, and even love and pleasure are at most of secondary importance as enticements, not telos.

Though nourished by religion, the reproductive model does not depend on religion for its persistence. Kant once argued that our sexual appetites are justified only insofar as they serve Nature's End, not our own. So too partisan politics or simple excessive biological conscientiousness can promote the reproductive paradigm. A Darwinian might see sex this way; a couple desperate to have children may temporarily conceive of their sexuality in this way, a sexual moralist might literally refer to 'natural sex'—in an argument against homosexuality for example—without invoking religion at any point. Indeed, this is often the more powerful and harder to refute version of moral arguments concerning sexuality, that our 'natural' desires are aimed at reproduction, whether consciously or not. 'Natural sex' is therefore sex aimed at reproduction, whether or not *we* aim at reproduction—or even thwart it—in our sexual activities. One might suggest, for instance, that such sex in general is 'practice' for the real thing, an odd suggestion which has, nevertheless, a considerable history behind it.

A paradigm is not necessarily an exclusive perspective, a set of blinders which permit only a single telos or conception. It is rather a matter of focus, a way of picking out certain features as essential and pushing others into the background. The reproductive paradigm highlights the biological consequences and minimizes the recreational and expressive features of sex. The procreational version of the paradigm adds to this the theology of divine design. Neither version need eliminate or ignore the other aspects of sexuality, but their emphasis already establishes an ethical framework. It is this framework within which the morals of contraception become heated issues, and it is within this framework that the technology of contraception has the greatest effect on our sexual conceptions. But there are other paradigms, and with them, other ethics and other concerns.

The Pleasure Paradigm

The pleasure paradigm might be called 'liberal' as a reaction against the more conservative reproductive/procreative paradigm. It is, for the most part, the paradigm that provided the ideology of the sexual revolution of the 1960's and it is no coincidence that the most effective means of birth control ever invented coincided with this new ideology. But 'most effective' does not mean new or novel, and effectiveness is only one factor in the determination of sexual attitudes. Morals are often more effective than technological effectiveness or, in the case of the sexual revolution, some say the 'lack of morals,' Which is cause, which is effect? But here again we run up against that too simpleminded deterministic thesis. It is absurd to say that 'the pill' had nothing to do with the new attitude of freedom that defined the so-called 'revolution,' but it is equally nonsense to insist that it is by itself the cause of that cultural explosion. Contrary to traditional Freudian imagery, the 1960's were not the time of '*eros* unchained' (one popular phrase of the period). There was not a massive libido suddenly released. Rather, there was a shift in paradigms, a swing of the *Zeitgeist* which included, not coincidentally, a new technology.

The real father of the sexual revolution is not Doctor Rock or Doctor Hertig but that ideologist of the libido, Sigmund Freud. It is Freud, for all of his personal sexual conservatism, who most soundly attacks the traditional reproductive procreational paradigm and puts in its place a model of sex with pleasure as its telos and its defining characteristic. Sex, for Freud, is not Nature's purpose, but rather the primary drive of the 'psychic apparatus' to discharge itself. The pleasure paradigm, like the reproductive paradigm, rests on a biological foundation. It is the nervous system that is the locus of Freud's theory, and its physiological basis that determines the telos of sex. The goal of the nervous system, and of the organism, is Catharsis, Freud tells us. Its principle is homeostasis, or 'the constancy principle.' Its ultimate aim is emptiness and relaxation (a formulation that later led Freud into his flirtation with 'the Nirvana principle' and 'the death instinct'). The release of built-up tension is pleasure; the retention of tension is pain. The release or 'catharsis' of tension in sexuality produces the orgasm, and it is the pleasure of the orgasm—that is, the pleasure of release—that is the end of sexuality, not the procreative consequences of ejaculation. Thus it is important to note how central Freud's distinction between physical and psychic satisfaction becomes; it is the latter that is essential to successful sex, not the former. This simple picture is complicated by the fact that in addition to this 'primary process' there is a complex system of ego-needs, which involves identification with certain sexual 'objects.' Accordingly, sex becomes concerned with the satisfaction of these secondary drives as well, and the simple pleasure of sex is complicated if not thwarted by the need for acceptance, security, and love. One might note the echo of Jean-Jacques Rousseau here, for Freud was also a 'romantic' of sorts, but a pessimist *à la* Schopenhauer rather than a hopeful visionary like Rousseau. It is worth taking full note of the fact that, as release of tension, masturbation plays a central role in Freud's notion of sex, while in the reproductive paradigm this is at best a perversion, if not irrelevant to sex altogether.

The notion of 'discharge' or 'catharsis' in Freud's paradigm is obviously based on a male-oriented perspective. In this as well as in its biological foundation, it is not entirely distinct from the reproductive model. Understanding Freud, however, is not primarily a matter of the history of medicine so much as it is a socio-cultural concern; and his rebellion against the reproductive model is part and parcel of a far more general rebellion against a certain kind of society. So too, the pleasure model in its more modern version, whether the American Civil Liberties Union version which allows any sexual activity between 'mutually consenting adults,' or the more vulgar version that simply insists, 'if it feels good, do it,' consists in part of a rebellion against restrictions no longer acceptable, paradigms no longer unchallengeable. As a 'liberating' paradigm, the pleasure model needs no defense. A more difficult question is whether it is the best paradigm, a question that has become increasingly urgent in the counter-revolutionary years of the last decade.

What ails the pleasure paradigm? Fifteen years ago Rollo May wrote in a best-selling book, *Love and Will*, that the sexual revolution has wrought its own forms of repression and unhappiness. His argument turns too much—in accord with that psychiatric genre—on the pathological, on the failures and victims of the revolution rather than its beneficiaries. Nevertheless, as both Freud and May warn us, with some justification, the plight of the neurotic may be a mirror—if a distorting mirror—of the pathology of everyday life. If the reproductive model makes sex too restrictive, the pleasure model makes it too conceptually permissive. Furthermore, any model of sexuality which makes masturbation as central or more central than intercourse, any model that refers to the other person in sexual desire as an 'object,' is an unlikely candidate for an adequate model of most of our sexual lives. Again, the paradigm may be liberating, but that does not mean that it is wholly adequate in itself.

Three main points of contention against the pleasure paradigm are the following:

(a) Aristotle argued 2500 years ago that pleasure is never the end of any of our activities, including sex. It is rather the accompaniment of good activity, the enjoyment that comes from being virtuous and fulfilling one's telos. Thus the question becomes: What is the telos of sex that it gives us so much pleasure? What is it that we satisfy? What do we want? To say that pleasure is the *telos* of sex is to confuse the play with its musical accompaniment. (In that context, a consideration of the very different moods of making love, and the music that one might play along with them, is revealing.)

(b) Sex is mutual activity; masturbation, no matter how satisfying, is not our paradigm. At least part of the answer to the questions in (a) above is that there is satisfaction in being with or 'having' another person, not as a 'secondary' concern, as Freud has it, but as a primary concern. The promiscuity and lack of discrimination of aroused males aside, it is not an 'object' of sex we seek, but a partner.

(c) Moreover, because sex depends on concepts and paradigms as well as basic biology, our sexual behavior is never 'without meaning.' Some meanings, however, are demeaning, and every sexual act has its significance. To think that one can indulge in the traditionally most powerful symbolic activity in almost every culture without its meaning anything is an extravagant self-deception, which, nonetheless, does not prevent its wide-spread appearance in libertines and rakes of all ages.

The Metaphysical Paradigm

The metaphysical paradigm is by far the most poetic of the four. We demand "meaningful" relationships; this paradigm provides meaning. The metaphysical paradigm is Romantic love or eros; its classic text is Plato's *Symposium* (thus I would also call it 'the Platonic paradigm,' which is not to be conflated with the asexual notion of 'Platonic love' that emerged 15 centuries later). In simpleminded parlance, it is the vision that two people are 'made for each other.' Protestant Christianity often supplements or even replaces the procreative paradigm with this metaphysical paradigm, thus shifting the religious as well as the sexual emphasis to love (*agape* not *eros*). The best picture of the metaphysical paradigm, however, is Aristophanes' wonderful tale in the *Symposium*, of a double creature cleft in two ('like an apple') by Zeus and ever since trying to find its 'other half.' And indeed sex does sometimes seem like that, an experience so overwhelming and filled with significance that questions about the technology of contraception are not even plausible candidates for the defining features of our sexual conceptions.

The Intersubjective Paradigm

The intersubjective or communication paradigm is the paradigm I would most like to defend, but I will not try to do so here. What I will do here is offer it through an example, and then use it to conclude why it is that, in the course of my research, I have decided to minimize the seemingly obvious influence of sexual technology on sexual attitudes and concepts. The example comes from Jean-Paul Sartre. For Sartre, unlike Freud, sex is essentially interpersonal. He does not deny that masturbation is sexual; there just is not anything very interesting to say about it. It is not just the consequences of sex that count; it is its meaning. But where the metaphysical paradigm tends to take a rather rosy view of meaning, Sartre sees quite clearly that meanings can be different. His dark vision is summarized in his famous play, *Huis Clos (No Exit):* 'Hell is other people.' Sex, accordingly, is essentially conflict, or, rather, it is the central battleground of our interpersonal wars. Sex is intersubjective: it is primarily concerned not with pregnancy or pleasure nor even togetherness, but rather with effecting as definitively as possible the other person's constitution of both him or herself, and oneself as well. It is a battle of domination and freedom, Sartre tells us. Sex focuses the most inert parts of the body — breasts and buttocks — not for pleasure and not for the sake of reproduction but, symbolically, Sartre says, 'to turn the other into an object,' to reduce him or her to a mere body in one's control. Every caress is manipulation; pleasure is an instrument, and one's own pleasure — far from being the goal of sex — may easily be a distraction and a defeat.

   I do not endorse this gloomy view which, if taken whole, would put most of us in the land of the voluntary chaste. But its structure I consider nothing less than revolutionary — more revolutionary than even Freud's pleasure paradigm and the much touted sexual revolutions of the past. What Sartre does for us is to shift the paradigm once again, to sex as expression. It is not one's own pleasure that counts primarily (though one need not be indifferent to it) nor is it even the pleasure one produces in one's partner. Mutual pleasure production is not the telos of sex, even when, as so often, it is the most explicit focus of sex. (Kant, who died a virgin, once described sex as 'mutual masturbation.') One can correct Sartre's pessimistic picture by noting that love, too, is expressed through sex, but it is essential not to leap too quickly to the naive romanticism that says that only love is, or ought to be, expressed by sex. Sex is like a language, and there is no clear limit to the interpersonal feelings that it can express, given an adequate vocabulary and what we might call sexual literacy.

CONCLUSION: CONCEPTIONS AND CONCEPTION

My purpose here has been to demonstrate the conceptual complexity of a phenomenon too often viewed as primitive and uncomplicated, as if only the consequences are complications, not sex itself. I have shown that there is much more to sexuality than an enjoyable and occasionally productive biological process, and that the technology of sexual consequences—if I may call it that—is only part of, not the essential determinant of, the nature of our sexual lives.

RICHARD WASSERSTROM

Is Adultery Immoral?

RICHARD WASSERSTROM taught philosophy at the University of California, Santa Cruz. He has published widely in ethics and legal philosophy.

Many discussions of the enforcement of morality by the law take as illustrative of the problem under consideration the regulation of various types of sexual behavior by the criminal law. It was, for example, the Wolfenden Report's recommendation concerning homosexuality and prostitution that led Lord Devlin to compose the now famous lecture, "The Enforcement of Morals." And that lecture in turn provoked important philosophical responses from H. L. A. Hart, Ronald Dworkin, and others.

Much, if not all, of the recent philosophical literature on the enforcement of morals appears to take for granted the immorality of the sexual behavior in question. The focus of discussion, at least, is whether such things as homosexuality, prostitution, and adultery ought to be made illegal even if they are immoral, and not whether they are immoral.

I propose in this paper to think about the latter, more neglected topic, that of sexual morality, and to do so in the following fashion. I shall consider just one kind of behavior that is often taken to be a case of sexual immorality—adultery. I am interested in pursuing at least two questions. First, I want to explore the question of in what respects adulterous behavior falls within the domain of morality at all. For this surely is one of the puzzles one encounters when considering the topic of sexual morality. It is often hard to see on what grounds much of the behavior is deemed to be either moral or immoral, for example, private homosexual behavior between consenting adults. I have purposely selected adultery because it seems a more plausible candidate for moral assessment than many other kinds of sexual behavior.

The second question I want to examine is that of what is to be said about adultery, without being especially concerned to stay within the area of morality. I shall endeavor, in other words, to identify and to assess a number of the major arguments that might be advanced against adultery. I believe that they are the chief arguments that would be given in support of the view that adultery is immoral, but I think they are worth considering even if some of them turn out to be nonmoral arguments and considerations.

A number of the issues involved seem to me to be complicated and difficult. In a number of places I have at best indicated where further philosophical exploration is required without having successfully conducted the exploration myself. The paper may very well be more useful as an illustration of how one might begin to think about the subject of sexual morality than as an elucidation of important truths about the topic.

Before I turn to the arguments themselves there are two preliminary points that require some clarification. Throughout the paper I shall refer to the immorality of such things as breaking a promise, deceiving someone, etc. In a very rough way, I mean by this that there is something morally wrong that is done in doing the action in question. I mean that the action is, in a strong sense of *"prima facie,"* prima facie wrong or unjustified. I do not mean that it may never be right or justifiable to do the action; just that the fact that it is an action of this description always does count against the rightness of the action. I leave entirely open the question of what it is that makes actions of this kind immoral in this sense of "immoral."

The second preliminary point concerns what is meant or implied by the concept of adultery. I mean by "adultery" any case of extramarital sex, and I want to explore the arguments for and against extramarital sex, undertaken in a variety of morally relevant situations. Someone might claim that the concept of adultery is conceptually connected with the concept of immorality, and that to characterize behavior as adulterous is already to characterize it as immoral or unjustified in the sense described above. There may be something to this. Hence the importance of making it clear that I want to talk about extramarital sexual relations. If they are always immoral, this is something that must be shown by argument. If the concept of adultery does in some sense entail or imply immorality, I want to ask whether that connection is a rationally based one. If not all cases of extramarital sex are immoral (again, in the sense described above), then the concept of adultery should either be weakened accordingly or restricted to those classes of extramarital sex for which the predication of immorality is warranted.

One argument for the immorality of adultery might go something like this: what makes adultery immoral is that it involves the breaking of a promise, and what makes adultery seriously wrong is that it involves the breaking of an important promise. For, so the argument might continue, one of the things the two parties promise each other when they get married is that they will abstain from sexual relationships with third persons. Because of this promise both spouses quite reasonably entertain the expectation that the other will behave in conformity with it. Hence, when one of the parties has sexual intercourse with a third person he or she breaks that promise about sexual relationships which was made when the marriage was entered into, and defeats the reasonable expectations of exclusivity entertained by the spouse.

In many cases the immorality involved in breaching the promise relating to extramarital sex may be a good deal more serious than that involved in the breach of other promises. This is so because adherence to this promise may be of much greater importance to the parties than is adherence to many of the other promises given or received by them in their lifetime. The breaking of this promise may be much more hurtful and painful than is typically the case.

Why is this so? To begin with, it may have been difficult for the nonadulterous spouse to have kept the promise. Hence that spouse may feel the unfairness of having restrained himself or herself in the absence of reciprocal restraint having been exercised by the adulterous spouse. In addition, the spouse may perceive the breaking of the promise as an indication of a kind of indifference on the part of the adulterous spouse. If you really cared about me and my feelings—the spouse might say—you would not have done this to me. And third, and related to the above, the spouse may see the act of sexual intercourse with another as a sign of affection for the other person and as an additional rejection of the nonadulterous spouse as the one who is loved by the adulterous spouse. It is not just that the adulterous spouse does not take the feelings of the spouse sufficiently into account, the adulterous spouse also indicates through the act of adultery affection for someone other than the spouse. I will return to these points later. For the present, it is sufficient to note that a set of arguments can be developed in support of the proposition that certain kinds of adultery are wrong just because they involve the breach of a serious promise which, among other things, leads to the intentional infliction of substantial pain by one spouse upon the other.

Another argument for the immorality of adultery focuses not on the existence of a promise of sexual exclusivity but on the connection between adultery and deception. According to this argument, adultery involves deception. And because deception is wrong, so is adultery.

Although it is certainly not obviously so, I shall simply assume in this paper that deception is always immoral. Thus the crucial issue for my purposes is the asserted connection between extramarital sex and deception. Is it plausible to maintain, as this argument does, that adultery always does involve deception and is on that basis to be condemned?

The most obvious person on whom deceptions might be practiced is the nonparticipating spouse; and the most obvious thing about which the nonparticipating spouse can be deceived is the existence of the adulterous act. One clear case of deception is that of lying. Instead of saying that the afternoon was spent in bed with A, the adulterous spouse asserts that it was spent in the library with B, or on the golf course with C.

There can also be deception even when no lies are told. Suppose, for instance, that a person has sexual intercourse with someone other than his or her spouse and just does not tell the spouse about it. Is that deception? It may not be a case of lying if, for example, the spouse is never asked by the other about the situation. Still, we might way, it is surely deceptive because of the promises that were exchanged at marriage. As we saw earlier, these promises provide a foundation for the reasonable belief that neither spouse will engage in sexual relationships with any other persons. Hence the failure to bring the fact of extramarital sex to the attention of the other spouse deceives that spouse about the present state of the marital relationship.

Adultery, in other words, can involve both active and passive deception. An adulterous spouse may just keep silent or, as is often the fact, the spouse may engage in an increasingly complex way of life devoted to the concealment of the facts from the nonparticipating spouse. Lies, half-truths, clandestine meetings, and the like may become a central feature of the adulterous spouse's existence. These are things that can and do happen, and when they do they make the case against adultery an easy one. Still, neither active nor passive deception is inevitably a feature of an extramarital relationship.

It is possible, though, that a more subtle but pervasive kind of deceptiveness is a feature of adultery. It comes about because of the connection in our culture between sexual intimacy and certain feelings of love and affection. The point can be made indirectly at first by seeing that one way in which we can, in our culture, mark off our close friends from our mere acquaintances is through the kinds of intimacies that we are prepared to share with them. I may, for instance, be willing to reveal my very private thoughts and emotions to my closest friends or to my wife, but to no one else. My sharing of these intimate facts about myself is from one perspective a way of making a gift to those who mean the most to me. Revealing these things and sharing them with those who mean the most to me is one means by which I create, maintain, and confirm those interpersonal relationships that are of most importance to me.

Now in our culture, it might be claimed, sexual intimacy is one of the chief currencies through which gifts of this sort are exchanged. One way to tell someone—particularly someone of the opposite sex—that you have feelings of affection and love for them is by allowing to them or sharing with them sexual behaviors that one doesn't share with the rest of the world. This way of measuring affection was certainly very much a part of the culture in which I matured. It worked something like this. If you were a girl, you showed how much you liked someone by the degree of sexual intimacy you would allow. If you liked a boy only a little, you never did more than kiss—and even the kiss was not very passionate. If you liked the boy a lot and if your feeling was reciprocated, necking, and possibly petting, was permissible. If the attachment was still stronger and you thought it might even become a permanent relationship, the sexual activity was correspondingly more intense and more intimate, although whether it would ever lead to sexual intercourse depended on whether the parties (and particularly the girl) accepted fully the prohibition on nonmarital sex. The situation for the boy was related, but not exactly the same. The assumption was that males did not naturally link sex with affection in the way in which females did. However, since women did, males had to take this into account. That is to say, because a woman would permit sexual intimacies only if she had feelings of affection for the male and only if those feelings were reciprocated, the male had to have and express those feelings, too, before sexual intimacies of any sort would occur.

The result was that the importance of a correlation between sexual intimacy and feelings of love and affection was taught by the culture and assimilated by those growing up in the culture. The scale of possible positive feelings toward persons of the other sex ran from casual liking at the one end to the love that was deemed essential to and characteristic of marriage at the other. The scale of possible sexual behavior ran from brief, passionless kissing or hand-holding at the one end to sexual intercourse at the other. And the correlation between the two scales was quite precise. As a result, any act of sexual intimacy carried substantial meaning with it, and no act of sexual intimacy was simply a pleasurable set of bodily sensations. Many such acts were, of course, more pleasurable to the participants because they were a way of saying what the participants feelings were. And sometimes they were less pleasurable for the same reason. The point is, however, that in any event sexual activity was much more than mere bodily enjoyment. It was not like eating a good meal, listening to good music, lying in the sun, or getting a pleasant back rub. It was behavior that meant a great deal concerning one's feelings for persons of the opposite sex in whom one was most interested and with whom one was most involved. It was among the most authoritative ways in which one could communicate to another the nature and degree of one's affection.

If this sketch is even roughly right, then several things become somewhat clearer. To begin with, a possible rationale for many of the rules of conventional sexual morality can be developed. If, for example, sexual intercourse is associated with the kind of affection and commitment to another that is regarded as characteristic of the marriage relationship, then it is natural that sexual intercourse should be thought properly to take place between persons who are married to each other. And if it is thought that this kind of affection and commitment is only to be found within the marriage relationship, then it is not surprising that sexual intercourse should only be thought to be proper within marriage.

Related to what has just been said is the idea that sexual intercourse ought to be restricted to those who are married to each other as a means by which to confirm the very special feelings that spouses have for each other. Because the culture teaches that sexual intercourse means that the strongest of all feelings for each other are shared by the lovers, it is natural that persons who are married to each other should be able to say this to each other in this way. Revealing and confirming verbally that these feelings are present is one thing that helps to sustain the relationship; engaging in sexual intercourse is another.

In addition, this account would help to provide a framework within which to make sense of the notion that some sex is better than other sex. As I indicated earlier, the fact that sexual intimacy can be meaningful in the sense described tends to make it also the case that sexual intercourse can sometimes be more enjoyable than at other times. On this view, sexual intercourse will typically be more enjoyable where the strong feelings of affection are present than it will be where it is merely "mechanical." This is so in part because people enjoy being loved, especially by those whom they love. Just as we like to hear words of affection, so we like to receive affectionate behavior. And the meaning enhances the independently pleasurable behavior.

More to the point, moreover, an additional rationale for the prohibition on extramarital sex can now be developed. For given this way of viewing the sexual world, extramarital sex will almost always involve deception of a deeper sort. If the adulterous spouse does not in fact have the appropriate feelings of affection for the extramarital partner, then the adulterous spouse is deceiving that person about the presence of such feelings. If, on the other hand, the adulterous spouse does have the corresponding feelings for the extramarital partner but not toward the nonparticipating spouse, the adulterous spouse is very probably deceiving the nonparticipating spouse about the presence of such feelings toward that spouse. Indeed, it might be argued, whenever there is no longer love between the two persons who are married to each other, there is deception just because being married implies both to the participants and to the world that such a bond exists. Deception is inevitable, the argument might conclude, because the feelings of affection that ought to accompany any act of sexual intercourse can only be held toward one other person at any given time in one's life. And if this is so, then the adulterous spouse always deceives either the partner in adultery or the nonparticipating spouse about the existence of such feelings. Thus extramarital sex involves deception of this sort and is for this reason immoral even if no deception vis-à-vis the occurrence of the act of adultery takes place.

What might be said in response to the foregoing arguments? The first thing that might be said is that the account of the connection between sexual intimacy and feelings of affection is inaccurate. Not inaccurate in the sense that no one thinks of things that way, but in the sense that there is substantially more divergence of opinion than that account suggests. For example, the view I have delineated may describe reasonably accurately the concepts of the sexual world in which I grew up, but it does not capture the sexual *Weltanschauung* of today's youth at all. Thus, whether or not adultery implies deception in respect to feelings depends very much on the persons who are involved and the way they look at the "meaning" of sexual intimacy.

Second, the argument leaves to be answered the question of whether it is desirable for sexual intimacy to carry the sorts of messages described above. For those persons for whom sex does have these implications, there are special feelings and sensibilities that must be taken into account. But it is another question entirely whether any valuable end—moral or otherwise—is served by investing sexual behavior with such significance. That is something that must be shown and not just assumed. It might, for instance, be the case that substantially more good than harm would come from a kind of demystification of sexual behavior: one that would encourage the enjoyment of sex more for its own sake and one that would reject the centrality both of the association of sex with love and of love with only one other person.

I regard these as two of the more difficult, unresolved issues that our culture faces today in respect to thinking sensibly about the attitudes toward sex and love that we should try to develop in ourselves and in our children. Much of the contemporary literature that advocates sexual liberation of one sort or another embraces one or the other of two different views about the relationship between sex and love.

One view holds that sex should be separated from love and affection. To be sure sex is probably better when the partners genuinely like and enjoy each other. But sex is basically an intensive, exciting sensuous activity that can be enjoyed in a variety of suitable settings with a variety of suitable partners. The situation in respect to sexual pleasure is no different from that of the person who knows and appreciates fine food and who can have a very satisfying meal in any number of good restaurants with any number of congenial companions. One question that must be settled here is whether sex can be so demystified; another, more important question is whether it would be desirable to do so. What would we gain and what might we lose if we all lived in a world in which an act of sexual intercourse was no more or less significant or enjoyable than having a delicious meal in a nice setting with a good friend? The answer to this question lies beyond the scope of this paper.

The second view seeks to drive the wedge in a different place. It is not the link between sex and love that needs to be broken; rather, on this view, it is the connection between love and exclusivity that ought to be severed. For a number of the reasons already given, it is desirable, so this argument goes, that sexual intimacy continue to be reserved to and shared with only those for whom one has very great affection. The mistake lies in thinking that any "normal" adult will only have those feelings toward one other adult during his or her lifetime—or even at any time in his or her life. It is the concept of adult love, not ideas about sex, that, on this view, needs demystification. What are thought to be both unrealistic and unfortunate are the notions of exclusivity and possessiveness that attach to the dominant conception of love between adults in our and other cultures. Parents of four, five, six, or even ten children can certainly claim and sometimes claim correctly that they love all of their children, that they love them all equally, and that it is simply untrue to their feelings to insist that the numbers involved diminish either the quantity or the quality of their love. If this is an idea that is readily understandable in the case of parents and children, there is no necessary reason why it is an impossible or undesirable ideal in the case of adults. To be sure, there is probably a limit to the number of intimate, "primary" relationships that any person can maintain at any given time without the quality of the relationship being affected. But one adult ought surely be able to love two, three, or even six other adults at any one time without that love being different in kind or degree from that of the traditional, monogamous, lifetime marriage. And as between the individuals in these relationships, whether within a marriage or without, sexual intimacy is fitting and good.

The issues raised by a position such as this one are also surely worth exploring in detail and with care. Is there something to be called "sexual love" which is different from parental love or the nonsexual love of close friends? Is there something about love in general that links it naturally and appropriately with feelings of exclusivity and possession? Or is there something about sexual love, whatever that may be, that makes these feelings especially fitting here? Once again the issues are conceptual, empirical, and normative all at once: What is love? How could it be different? Would it be a good thing or a bad thing if it were different?

Suppose, though, that having delineated these problems we were now to pass them by. Suppose, moreover, we were to be persuaded of the possibility and the desirability of weakening substantially either the links between sex and love or the links between sexual love and exclusivity. Would it not then be the case that adultery could be free from all of the morally objectionable features described so far? To be more specific, let us imagine that a husband and wife have what is today sometimes characterized as an "open marriage." Suppose, that is, that they have agreed in advance that extramarital sex is—under certain circumstances—acceptable behavior for each to engage in. Suppose, that as a result there is no impulse to deceive each other about the occurrence or nature of any such relationships, and that no deception in fact occurs. Suppose, too, that there is no deception in respect to the feelings involved between the adulterous spouse and the extramarital partner. And suppose, finally, that one or the other or both of the spouses then has sexual intercourse in circumstances consistent with these understandings. Under this description, so the agreement might conclude, adultery is simply not immoral. At a minimum, adultery cannot very plausibly be condemned either on the ground that it involves deception or on the ground that it requires the breaking of a promise.

At least two responses are worth considering. One calls attention to the connection between marriage and adultery; the other looks to more instrumental arguments for the immorality of adultery. Both issues deserve further exploration.

One way to deal with the case of the "open marriage" is to question whether the two persons involved are still properly to be described as being married to each other. Part of the meaning of what it is for two persons to be married to each other, so this argument would go, is to have committed oneself to have sexual relationships only with one's spouse. Of course, it would be added, we know that that commitment is not always honored. We know that persons who are married to each other often do commit adultery. But there is a difference between being willing to make a commitment to marital fidelity, even though one may fail to honor that commitment, and not making the commitment at all. Whatever the relationship may be between the two individuals in the case described above, the absence of any commitment to sexual exclusivity requires the conclusion that their relationship is not a marital one. For a commitment to sexual exclusivity is a necessary although not a sufficient condition for the existence of a marriage.

Although there may be something to this suggestion, as it is stated it is too strong to be acceptable. To begin with, I think it is very doubtful that there are many, if any, *necessary* conditions for marriage; but even if there are, a commitment to sexual exclusivity is not such a condition.

To see that this is so, consider what might be taken to be some of the essential characteristics of a marriage. We might be tempted to propose that the concept of marriage requires the following: a formal ceremony of some sort in which mutual obligations are undertaken between two persons of the opposite sex; the capacity on the part of the persons involved to have sexual intercourse with each other; the willingness to have sexual intercourse only with each other; and feelings of love and affection between the two persons. The problem is that we can imagine relationships that are clearly marital and yet lack one or more of these features. For example, in our own society, it is possible for two persons to be married without going through a formal ceremony, as in the common-law marriages recognized in some jurisdictions. It is also possible for two persons to get married even though one or both lacks the capacity to engage in sexual intercourse. Thus, two very elderly persons who have neither the desire nor the ability to have intercourse can, nonetheless, get married, as can persons whose sexual organs have been injured so that intercourse is not possible. And we certainly know of marriages in which love was not present at the time of the marriage, as, for instance, in marriages of state and marriages of convenience.

Counterexamples not satisfying the condition relating to the abstention from extramarital sex are even more easily produced. We certainly know of societies and cultures in which polygamy and polyandry are practiced, and we have no difficulty in recognizing these relationships as cases of marriages. It might be objected, though, that these are not counterexamples because they are plural marriages rather than marriages in which sex is permitted with someone other than with one of the persons to whom one is married. But we also know of societies in which it permissible for married persons to have sexual relationships with persons to whom they were not married, for example, temple prostitutes, concubines, and homosexual lovers. And even if we knew of no such societies, the conceptual claim would still, I submit, not be well taken. For suppose all of the other indicia of marriage were present: suppose the two persons were of the opposite sex. Suppose they had the capacity and desire to have intercourse with each other, suppose they participated in a formal ceremony in which they understood themselves voluntarily to be entering into a relationship with each other in which substantial mutual commitments were assumed. If all these conditions were satisfied, we would not be in any doubt about whether or not the two persons were married even though they had not taken on a commitment of sexual exclusivity and even though they had expressly agreed that extramarital sexual intercourse was a permissible behavior for each to engage in.

A commitment to sexual exclusivity is neither a necessary nor a sufficient condition for the existence of a marriage. It does, nonetheless, have this much to do with the nature of marriage: like the other indicia enumerated above, its presence tends to establish the existence of a marriage. Thus, in the absence of a formal ceremony of any sort, an explicit commitment to sexual exclusivity would count in favor of regarding the two persons as married. The conceptual role of the commitment to sexual exclusivity can, perhaps, be brought out through the following example. Suppose we found a tribe which had a practice in which all the other indicia of marriage were present but in which the two parties were *prohibited* ever from having sexual intercourse with each other. Moreover, suppose that sexual intercourse with others was clearly permitted. In such a case we would, I think, reject the idea that the two were married to each other and we would describe their relationship in other terms, for example, as some kind of formalized, special friendship relation—a kind of heterosexual "blood-brother" bond.

Compare that case with the following. Suppose again that the tribe had a practice in which all of the other indicia of marriage were present, but instead of a prohibition on sexual intercourse between the persons in the relationship there was no rule at all. Sexual intercourse was permissible with the person with whom one had this ceremonial relationship, but it was no more or less permissible than with a number of other persons to whom one was not so related (for instance, all consenting adults of the opposite sex). Although we might be in doubt as to whether we ought to describe the persons as married to each other, we would probably conclude that they were married and that they simply were members of a tribe whose views about sex were quite different from our own.

What all of this shows is that *a prohibition* on sexual intercourse between the two persons involved in a relationship is conceptually incompatible with the claim that the two of them are married. The *permissibility* of intramarital sex is a necessary part of the idea of marriage. But no such incompatibility follows simply from the added permissibility of extramarital sex.

These arguments do not, of course, exhaust the arguments for the prohibition on extramarital sexual relations. The remaining argument that I wish to consider—as I indicated earlier—is a more instrumental one. It seeks to justify the prohibition by virtue of the role that it plays in the development and maintenance of nuclear families. The argument, or set of arguments, might, I believe, go something like this.

Consider first a farfetched nonsexual example. Suppose a society were organized so that after some suitable age—say, 18, 19, or 20—persons were forbidden to eat anything but bread and water with anyone but their spouse. Persons might still choose in such a society not to get married. Good food just might not be very important to them because they have underdeveloped taste buds. Or good food might be bad for them because there is something wrong with their digestive system. Or good food might be important to them, but they might decide that the enjoyment of good food would get in the way of the attainment of other things that were more important. But most persons would, I think, be led to favor marriage in part because they preferred a richer, more varied, diet to one of bread and water. And they might remain married because the family was the only legitimate setting within which good food was obtainable. If it is important to have society organized so that persons will both get married and stay married, such an arrangement would be well suited to the preservation of the family, and the prohibitions relating to food consumption could be understood as fulfilling that function.

It is obvious that one of the more powerful human desires is the desire for sexual gratification. The desire is a natural one, like hunger and thirst, in the sense that it need not be learned in order to be present within us and operative upon us. But there is in addition much that we do learn about what the act of sexual intercourse is like. Once we experience sexual intercourse ourselves—and in particular once we experience orgasm—we discover that it is among the most intensive, short-term pleasures of the body.

Because this is so, it is easy to see how the prohibition upon extramarital sex helps to hold marriage together. At least during that period of life when the enjoyment of sexual intercourse is one of the desirable bodily pleasures, persons will wish to enjoy those pleasures. If one consequence of being married is that one is prohibited from having sexual intercourse with anyone but one's spouse, then the spouses in a marriage are in a position to provide an important source of pleasure for each other that is unavailable to them elsewhere in the society.

The point emerges still more clearly if this rule of sexual morality is seen as of a piece with the other rules of sexual morality. When this prohibition is coupled, for example, with the prohibition on non-marital sexual intercourse, we are presented with the inducement both to get married and to stay married. For if sexual intercourse is only legitimate within marriage, then persons seeking that gratification which is a feature of sexual intercourse are furnished explicit social directions for its attainment; namely marriage.

Nor, to continue the argument, is it necessary to focus exclusively on the bodily enjoyment that is involved. Orgasm may be a significant part of what there is to sexual intercourse, but it is not the whole of it. We need only recall the earlier discussion of the meaning that sexual intimacy has in our own culture to begin to see some of the more intricate ways in which sexual exclusivity may be connected with the establishment and maintenance of marriage as the primary heterosexual, love relationship. Adultery is wrong, in other words, because a prohibition on extramarital sex is a way to help maintain the institutions of marriage and the nuclear family.

Now I am frankly not sure what we are to say about an argument such as this one. What I am convinced of is that, like the arguments discussed earlier, this one also reveals something of the difficulty and complexity of the issues that are involved. So, what I want now to do—in the brief and final portion of this paper—is to try to delineate with reasonable precision what I take several of the fundamental, unresolved issues to be.

The first is whether this last argument is an argument for the *immorality* of extramarital sexual intercourse. What does seem clear is that there are differences between this argument and the ones considered earlier. The earlier arguments condemned adulterous behavior because it was behavior that involved breaking of a promise, taking unfair advantage, or deceiving another. To the degree to which the prohibition on extramarital sex can be supported by arguments which invoke considerations such as these, there is little question but that violations of the prohibition are properly regarded as immoral. And such a claim could be defended on one or both of two distinct grounds. The first is that things like promise-breaking and deception are just wrong. The second is that adultery involving promise-breaking or deception is wrong because it involves the straightforward infliction of harm on another human being—typically the nonadulterous spouse—who has a strong claim not to have that harm so inflicted.

The argument that connects the prohibition on extramarital sex with the maintenance and preservation of the institution of marriage is an argument for the instrumental value of the prohibition. To some degree this counts, I think, against regarding all violations of the prohibition as obvious cases of immorality. This is so partly because hypothetical imperatives are less clearly within the domain of morality than are categorical ones, and even more because instrumental prohibitions are within the domain of morality only if the end they serve or the way they serve it is itself within the domain of morality.

What this should help us see, I think, is the fact that the argument that connects the prohibition on adultery with the preservation of marriage is at best seriously incomplete. Before we ought to be convinced by it, we ought to have reasons for believing that marriage is a morally desirable and just social institution. And this is not quite as easy or obvious a task as it may seem to be. For the concept of marriage is, as we have seen, both a loosely structured and complicated one. There may be all sorts of intimate, interpersonal relationships which will resemble but not be identical with the typical marriage relationship presupposed by the traditional sexual morality. There may be a number of distinguishable sexual and loving arrangements which can all legitimately claim to be called *marriages*. The prohibitions of the traditional sexual morality may be effective ways to maintain some marriages and ineffective ways to promote and preserve others. The prohibitions of the traditional sexual morality may make good psychological sense if certain psychological theories are true, and they may be purveyors of immense psychological mischief if other psychological theories are true. The prohibitions of the traditional sexual morality may seem obviously correct if sexual intimacy carries the meaning that the dominant culture has often ascribed to it, and they may seem equally bizarre when sex is viewed through the perspective of the counterculture. Irrespective of whether instrumental arguments of this sort are properly deemed moral arguments, they ought not to fully convince anyone until questions like these are answered.

MORRIS KAPLAN

Sexual Justice

MORRIS KAPLAN teaches philosophy at Purchase College, State University of New York. He served as a trial attorney with the Legal Aid Society of New York and has published widely on issues related to the ethics and politics of sexuality.

Claims of lesbian and gay rights encompass a range of arguments regarding the right relationships between gay people and the state. As the movement for these rights has developed in the United States since the 1960s, claims have come to include disparate demands on the political order, supported by diverse and potentially conflicting conceptions of the scope and limits of legitimate state action. This political situation has been exacerbated and made more urgent by the impact of the AIDS epidemic. However, it remains important to identify and clarify the divergent strands of a movement for lesbian and gay rights. It may be useful to indicate three primary categories for such claims: 1) decriminalization of homosexual activities between consenting adults; 2) the prohibition of discrimination against lesbians and gays in employment, housing, education, and public accommodations; and 3) the legal and social recognition of the ethical status of lesbian and gay relationships and community institutions.

Approximately one-half of the states continue to prohibit specified sexual activities (usually anal and oral intercourse) even when pursued in private between consenting adults: some jurisdictions proscribe such activities among "persons," others specifically target "persons of the same sex." Moral and political opposition to such criminalizing of intimate sexual behavior is generally articulated in terms derived from John Stuart Mill's classic essay *On Liberty*. Legal strategies seeking to invalidate such legislation as an unconstitutional infringement of individual "rights of privacy" culminated in the Supreme Court's five-to-four decision of *Bowers v. Hardwick*, when the Court refused to overturn Georgia's laws banning consensual sodomy. Litigation in state courts premised on the provisions of state constitutions has met with some success. The claim underlying demands for decriminalization is an individual's right "to be let alone." At issue is the limitation of the state's authority to regulate individual behavior between consenting adults in which no one is harmed. A number of important academic debates . . . have in recent decades used the example of consensual homosexual relations among adults in private as a lens through which to consider the limits on the coercive authority of the state. In political terms, libertarians of the right sometimes join with traditionally liberal civil libertarians in condemning state intrusion into the domain of private sexual behavior between consenting adults.

A somewhat different range of concerns informs opposition to invidious discrimination against lesbians and gays. Here the movement for lesbian and gay rights joins African Americans, women, religious and ethnic minorities, and the disabled in seeking the protections provided to some of these groups by the United States Congress in the Civil Rights Acts of 1964 and 1965 and by subsequent similar enactments by states and localities. When couched in constitutional terms, these claims invoke the "Equal

Protection Clause" of the Fourteenth Amendment, whereas privacy claims depend on
the "Due Process Clause." Currently fashionable libertarian advocacy of "minimal government" and some versions of liberalism that reject the criminalization of private homosexual behavior nonetheless oppose the extension of civil rights protections as an
unjustifiable intrusion into private decisionmaking by employers, landlords, and others. Only nine states include sexual orientation among the categories protected against
discrimination in their civil rights laws. The federal civil rights laws do not include sexual orientation as a protected category (although the Clinton administration supported
proposals to do so in a 1995 bill with virtually no chance for passage in the 104th United
States Congress). Civil rights legislation in general prohibits discrimination against
specified groups in employment, housing, education, and public accommodations and
provides a range of remedies from injunctive relief through compensatory damages to
punitive damages. Claims by lesbians and gays for such protection envision a more
positive role of the state in assuring these rights. Indeed, libertarians and other defenders of a minimal state are correct in seeing that the demand for protection against discrimination asks the state to prohibit individuals from exercising their prejudices
against queers when they occupy positions empowered to dispense jobs, housing, or
other economic opportunities. However, their objection conflates individual freedom
of association, the right to choose your friends, with the collective economic and social
power of large-scale employers, financial institutions, real estate enterprises, and the
like; it engages not only questions about private property, but also the legal fiction that
corporations are persons. The philosopher Richard Mohr, no friend to state power, has
effectively marshaled the arguments favoring the inclusion of lesbians and gays in
civil rights legislation, emphasizing the crucial importance of such legislation as a
guarantor of fundamental political rights. He describes the role of the state in this context as that of a "civil shield." . . .

The highly contested political character of this issue, in a period of widespread
reaction against all civil rights legislation—and growing moral panic about homosexuality—is evidenced by efforts in Oregon, Colorado, and elsewhere to forbid by refer-
endum the enactment of laws to protect homosexuals against discrimination. These
campaigns have invidiously labeled as demands for "special rights" the efforts of lesbian and gay citizens to gain equal citizenship. These referenda themselves raise fundamental questions as to the authors of popular majorities to deny to some groups
equal access to normal political processes. In May 1996, the Supreme Court invalidated
Proposition Two amending the Colorado Constitution as a violation of the U.S. Constitution's guarantee of "equal protection of the laws" to lesbian and gay citizens. . . . .

A related but distinct class of claims emerge when we turn to the growing demand
on states and the law for recognition of the status of lesbian and gay relationships, institutions, and communal needs. Among the practical issues addressed here are: the
right of lesbians and gays to marry or otherwise establish domestic partnerships; the
entitlement of lesbian and gay partners to the benefits of health insurance, lease or rent
stabilization privileges provided spouses or family members, or the dignity of recognition within the institutions that provide care for the sick and dying; the recognition
of lesbian mothers and gay fathers as fit custodians of their own children and of lesbians and gay men generally as potential foster or adoptive parents; the demands of
lesbian and gay organizations for official status in public schools, universities, or professional associations; the rights of queers to gather at bars, bathhouses, and social clubs

without police harassment; the status of lesbian and gay institutions in the politics and provision of healthcare during the AIDS crisis. These are among the most controversial claims, and some advocates of liberal tolerance see them as going too far. During the 1996 Presidential campaign, President Bill Clinton, who supported federal civil rights protections for lesbians and gay men, emphasized his opposition to same-sex marriage. Nonetheless, litigation challenging the denial of marital status to same-sex couples is proceeding in several jurisdictions; the Supreme Court of the State of Hawaii in *Baehr v. Lewin* held that this exclusion violates a state constitutional ban on discrimination based on sex and must survive "strict scrutiny" if it is to be upheld. Efforts to secure recognition of same-sex domestic partnerships have met with some success from local governments and in negotiating agreements with private employers. Moreover, throughout the country, lesbians and gay men in increasing numbers are sharing "commitment ceremonies" with their families and friends, bearing and adopting children, and establishing families of their own. The ethical and social attitudes underlying these claims present a provocative and unstable juncture of conservative and radical impulses.

At issue is the demand for the recognition and respect of lesbian and gay relations and institutions within the broader legal, social, and ethical context. The state functions in this context not only as a civil shield protecting lesbians and gay men against invidious discrimination by private citizens, but also as a positive agency for actualizing the aspirations of queer citizens. Moreover, the rights in question are not simply those of individuals, but of couples, families, and voluntary associations. Ultimately what is at stake is the moral legitimacy and ethical validity of lesbian and gay ways of life. These claims reveal the political and philosophical heart of the movement for lesbian and gay rights. Far from being "icing on the cake," such demands are the real "bread and butter" underlying more abstract and formal conceptualizations of lesbian and gay rights. These issues provide a focal point for comprehending the resistance to lesbian and gay rights as well as a perhaps surprising locus for potential reconciliation between lesbian and gay rights and traditionally formulated "family values" and community norms. Indeed, attention to the ethical and social status of lesbian/gay relationships and institutions requires us to probe and to clarify the problematic role of "community" in contemporary democratic theory and practice. . . . The emergence of a social and political movement for equality among lesbian, gay, and other queer citizens raises important questions about the ways in which sexual identities intersect with the status of citizenship in modern democracies. We cannot avoid the question of how one's sexuality contributes to shaping a sense of individuality and of the goods to be pursued in the course of life. In applying the principle of democratic equality to lesbian and gay rights, . . . urge that the desire for erotic expression and the ability freely to form intimate associations with others are frequently integral components of a full and meaningful life. This argument is vulnerable to the objection that some choices may be not only violations of conventional morality, but also destructive of the well-being of the person making them. Some argue that people should not be permitted to make choices deleterious to their own best interests. In its starkest terms, the view is that homosexuality is a form of mental illness and that same-sex desire itself, far from being an expression of autonomous choice, is a pathological symptom from which its sufferers must be protected. Less dramatically, some see homosexuality as a developmental deficit that cuts off lesbians and gay men from the full maturity of genital heterosexuality in the context of monogamy and the nuclear family. Others claim that it is somehow impossible for homosexuals in our society to be happy, whether as a result of their own condition or of social prejudice. In any event, the culture is infused with attitudes that support the active discouragement if not the complete prohibition of lesbian and gay intimacies and identities. In personal terms, these feelings are captured in the complex and ambiguous responses that many otherwise liberal folks have to the prospects of their own children growing up gay. . . . Claims for the recognition of lesbian and gay relationships and community institutions directly challenge these objections to the legitimacy of lives that affirm same-sex desires and associations. J. S. Mill's argument in *On Liberty* rejects this kind of paternalism as strongly as it does moral conformism:

> . . . the only purpose for which power can be rightfully exercised over any member of a civilized community, against his will, is to prevent harm to others. His own good, either physical or moral, is not a sufficient warrant. He cannot rightfully be compelled to do or forbear because it will make him happier, because, in the opinions of others, to do so would be wise or even right.

This position derives from the same recognition of the centrality of individual moral autonomy as does Rawls's use of the original position to clarify the egalitarian implications of moral agency: "Over himself, over his own body and mind, the individual is sovereign." . . . Although some readers may question the strict application of Mill's anti-paternalism in cases of suicide prevention or the involuntary treatment of self-destructive mental illnesses, it is hard to see how such reservations could be extended to the exercise of erotic choice. In those extreme cases, what is in question is the continued capacity of the individual to make any decisions at all, not the wisdom or prudence of a particular pattern of choices. Even if one acknowledges some need to restrain individuals from ending or irreversibly damaging their own agency, the freedom of individuals finally to determine what matters most to them and what sort of persons they will become is an irreducible component of moral autonomy.

Psychoanalytic theory and psychiatric practice may provide the most important contemporary locus for working through these issues; they have played an important ethical and political role in American culture, especially during the social transformations since World War II. At a time of increasing secularization, and within a constitutional context of religious pluralism, models of mental health have figured importantly as vehicles, sometimes as disguises, for ethical judgment and authority. Metaphysical embarrassment over the difficulty of sustaining claims to know the good, combined with political reservations about imposing sectarian religious moralities, has encouraged the extension of scientific and medical conceptions of health and illness to encompass a wide variety of behavioral and social matters. Not only sexual issues but also matters of substance abuse, addiction, efficiency at work, and the conduct of interpersonal relations are couched in terms of the language of mental health and illness. The use of therapeutic models of intervention to justify involuntary forms of treatment in civil settings and to reshape programs in criminal justice has been widespread and increasingly controversial. However, arguments against homosexuality grounded in notions of mental illness and health no longer command support from authorized experts in the fields of psychiatry and psychology; in 1973, the American Psychiatric Association, after protracted debate within the field and in response to challenges from lesbian and gay activists, struck homosexuality from the classification of mental disorders in the *Diagnostic and Statistical Manual.* The American Psychological Association soon followed suit. In the final analysis, the use of medical and psychological opinion about human behavior to support the coercive intervention of the state to overrule individual choice must be governed by same principles that apply to the enforcement of other ethical judgments. Whatever may be said about therapeutic approaches to sexuality when voluntarily undertaken, they cannot be used to justify overriding the wishes of a mature individual otherwise entitled to democratic liberty. This sort of medical paternalism collapses into moralism, albeit of a secular variety.

In terms of the cultural influence of the discourse of mental health, it is worth noting that Sigmund Freud was at odds with his followers among psychiatrists in the United States over just this issue, seeing their insistence on the pathological status of homosexuality as a symptom of their moralizing and conformist tendencies. Freud's own understanding of this question regarding the legal, medical, and ethical status of homosexuality set him against the normative judgments and normalizing practices of American psychiatry. His writing on the subject undercuts their claim to scientific and moral authority and offers reasons for a more positive evaluation of homosexuals' capacities and contributions to ethical life. Equally important, his ongoing theoretical accounts of human sexuality provide grounds for a continuing critique of conventional social attitudes and a basis for constructing a positive defense of diverse sexualities. Psychoanalytic theory argues that all persons have deep needs for sexual expression and relation; that sexuality is a basic source of human motivation; and, that it is inherently multivalent and diverse, gaining its importance from complex connections with individual life histories, unconscious fantasies, and social convention. . . . The major opinions in *Bowers v. Hardwick* display conflicting analyses of the construction of sexual identity and the place of sexual conduct in personal life. . . . For Blackmun, at issue in *Bowers v. Hardwick* is the right of individuals to pursue happiness and to shape personal identities through freely chosen intimate associations with others. He finds this moral and legal principle central to the scheme of constitutional protections of individual autonomy. By emphasizing the place of "intimate association" within a broader context of equal citizenship and moral pluralism, Blackmun incorporates substantive ethical concern for human flourishing into a liberal conception of personal rights. Although some have seen Blackmun as deploying an assimilationist strategy that eradicates homosexual difference and domesticates sexual desires, I read him as urging the expansion and enrichment of a generalized conception of human rights to include sexual desire and erotic expression within the context of an individual's life choices. The result is to construct a thicker conception of constitutional liberty and of the range of rights it entails. As a result, Blackmun translates "the alleged right to homosexual sodomy" from a decontextualized domain of possible sexual practices into the realm of emotional and interpersonal relationships. Although such scholars as Daniel Ortiz and Cheshire Calhoun see a "desexualization" of homosexual identity at work here, I discern recognition of an erotic component in all "intimate associations" and a sexual dimension to the identities to which they contribute. Blackmun adumbrates a conception of legal personality in which individuals situated in diverse and overlapping social contexts become the locus for the construction of mutually interacting personal identities. "Freedom of intimate association" transcends the definition of privacy as a right of solitary individuals to be left alone and emphasizes the creation of intimate spaces within which persons can establish, maintain, revise, and transform both relationships and identities. Blackmun does not shy away from the conclusion that there may be many "right" ways to conduct one's sexual and emotional life.

On the other hand, Justice White in the opinion of the Court and Chief Justice Warren Burger in his concurring opinion construct homosexuals in terms of an invidious *difference*. Despite the plain language of the Georgia statute that outlawed all sexual acts involving the sexual organs of one person and the mouth or anus of another, the Court considered the legitimacy of criminalizing "homosexual sodomy" only. Indeed, as Jonathan Goldberg emphasizes, the Court sees homosexuals as so different that the same physical acts that are permissible when performed by heterosexuals may be criminalized when the actors are homosexual. A number of commentators have observed a certain slippage in the Court's reliance on history and tradition to buttress their deference to the Georgia law. . . . Not only did the Georgia law apply in its terms to all persons, not just homosexuals, but the historical condemnation of sodomy itself applied to a range of "unnatural acts" that shared a tendency to frustrate the procreative aspects of sexual intercourse. The definition of "homosexual sodomy" as a distinct and proper concern of legislative action reflects more recent medical and juridical discourses defining "homosexuals" as a distinct class of *persons* rather than the historical interest of state and church in restricting the sexual *acts* of all persons to marital settings in which procreation is a likely outcome.

The historical prohibition of sodomy constructs human sexuality as directed toward procreation; it intersects with the alleged state interest in protecting and promoting marriage and the family unit that figures importantly in the privacy jurisprudence. The instability of such an appeal under contemporary circumstances is evidenced by the facts that the right of privacy was first articulated in overturning a state ban on contraception, and that its most far-reaching and controversial application has been in the abortion cases. Constitutional rights of privacy have protected decisions by married and unmarried couples alike to use contraception and by all women to decide whether or not to terminate pregnancies through abortion. These cases have displayed an unstable tension between protecting individual autonomy in decision making and promoting the institutional integrity of marriage and the family unit.

There is a related tension between disparate constructions of the *person* as bearer of fundamental rights; on the one hand, the autonomous decision maker with a fundamental right to determine the conditions of her life; on the other, a potential procreator charged with deploying her sexuality on behalf of the reproduction of the species. *Roe v. Wade* decisively resolves this tension in favor of individual decisional autonomy. Perhaps surprisingly, these tensions within the privacy jurisprudence mirror strains that Freud identifies as fundamental to modern civilization with its disparate demands for altruism from men and women in the regulation of their sexual desires and the maintenance of a reproductive imperative. . . . Seen in this light, the Supreme Court's decision in *Bowers v. Hardwick* is very much a rear-guard action, locking the barn after the horse has been stolen. The historical sexual moralities invoked by White and Burger construct sexuality in terms of an imperative of biological reproduction and a culture of familial integrity. When the Court subordinates the interests of families to the choices of individual women, the reproductive imperative itself is called into question.

What's left for traditional moralists is the struggle against an enemy whose very identity has been constructed in opposition to both families and reproduction, the "homosexual sodomite." This imputed identity is a hybrid produced from psychiatric discourses that define homosexuality as a perverted identity and religious moralities that condemn sodomy as a sinful act. . . . The diverse opinions in *Hardwick* show how deeply homosexual difference is implicated when judgments of disease and immorality, constructions of family relations and personal choice. Effectively, the Court consigns those of us marked by this difference to second-class citizenship by denying that the constitutional right of privacy applies to "homosexual sodomy."

AUDRE LORDE

Scratching the Surface

Some Notes on Barriers to Women and Loving

AUDRE LORDE, a black lesbian feminist poet, has written extensively in prose and poetry on feminism, heterosexism, racism, and the interrelation of oppressions.

Racism: *The belief in the inherent superiority of one race over all others and thereby the right to dominance.*

Sexism: *The belief in the inherent superiority of one sex and thereby the right to dominance.*

Heterosexism: *The belief in the inherent superiority of one pattern of loving and thereby its right to dominance.*

Homophobia: *The fear of feelings of love for members of one's own sex and therefore hatred of those feelings in others.*

The above forms of human blindness stem from the same root—the inability to recognize or tolerate the notion of difference as a beneficial and dynamic human force, and one which is enriching rather than threatening to the defined self.

To a large degree, at least verbally, the black community has moved beyond the "two steps behind her man" mode of sexual relations sometimes mouthed as desirable during the sixties. This was a time when the myth of the black matriarchy as a social disease was being presented by racist forces for an excuse or diversion, to redirect our attentions away from the real sources of black oppression.

For black women as well as black men, it is axiomatic that if we do not define ourselves for ourselves, we will be defined by others—for their use and to our detriment. The development of self-defined black women, ready to explore and pursue our power and interests within our communities, is a vital component in the war for black liberation. The image of the Angolan woman with a baby on one arm and a gun in the other is neither romantic nor fanciful. Black women in this country coming together to examine our sources of strength and support, and to recognize our common social, cultural, emotional, and political interests, is a development which can only contribute to the power of the black community as a whole. For it is only through the coming together of self-actualized individuals, female and male, that any real advances can be made. The old sexual power-relationships based on a dominant/subordinate model between unequals have not served us as a people, nor as individuals.

Black women who define ourselves and our goals beyond the sphere of a sexual relationship can bring to any endeavor the realized focus of a completed and therefore empowered individual. Black women and black men who recognize that the development of their particular strengths and interests does not diminish the other, do not diffuse their energies fighting for control over each other. We focus our attentions against the real economic, political and social forces at the heart of this society which are ripping ourselves and our children and our worlds apart.

Increasingly, despite opposition, black women are coming together to explore and to alter those manifestations of our society which oppress us in ways different from the oppression of black men. This is no threat to black men, and is only seen as one by those black men who choose to embody within themselves those same manifestations of female oppression. For instance, enforced sterilization and unavailable abortions are tools of oppression against black women, as is rape. Only to those black men who are unclear as to the paths of their own self-definition can the self-actualization and self-protective bonding of black women be seen as a threatening development.

● ● ●

Today, the red herring of homophobia and lesbian-baiting is being used in the black community to obscure the true double face of racism/sexism. Black women sharing close ties with each other, politically or emotionally, are not the enemies of black men. Too frequently, however, an attempt to rule by fear tactics is practiced by some black men against those black women who are more ally than enemy. These tactics are sometimes expressed as threats of emotional rejection: "Their poetry wasn't too bad but I couldn't take all those lezzies (lesbians)." The man who says this is warning every black woman present who is interested in a relationship with men—and most black women are—that (1) if she wishes to have her work considered she must eschew any other allegiance except to him and (2) any woman who wishes his friendship and/or support had better not be "tainted" by woman-identified interests.

If such threats of labelling, vilification and/or emotional isolation are not enough to bring black women docilely into camp as followers, or persuade them to avoid each other as political or emotional support for each other, then the rule by terror can be expressed physically, as on the campus of a New York college recently, where black women sought to come together around feminist concerns. Violently threatening phone calls were made to those black women who dared to explore the possibilities of a feminist connection with non-black women. Some of these women, intimidated by these threats and the withdrawal of male approval, did turn against their sisters. When threats did not prevent the attempted coalition of black feminists, the resulting hysteria left some black women beaten and raped. Whether the threats by black men actually led to these assaults, or merely encouraged the climate of hostility within which they could occur, the results upon the women attacked were the same.

Wars and jails have decimated the ranks of black males of marriageable age. The fury of many black heterosexual women against white women who date black men is rooted in this unequal sexual equation, since whatever threatens to widen that equation is deeply and articulately resented. But this is essentially unconstructive resentment because it extends sideways, and can never result in true progress on the issue, because it does not question the vertical lines of power or authority, nor the sexist assumptions which dictate the terms of the competition. And the racism of white women can be better addressed where it is less complicated by their own sexual oppression. In this situation it is not the non-black woman who calls the tune, but rather the black man who turns away from himself in his sisters, or who, through a fear borrowed from white men, reads her strength not as a resource but as challenge.

All too often the message comes loud and clear to black women from black men: "I am the prize and there are not too many of me and remember I can always go elsewhere. So if you want me you'd better stay in your place which is away from each other, or I will call you lesbian and wipe you away." Black women are programmed to define themselves within this male attention and to compete with each other for it, rather than to recognize their common interests.

The tactic of encouraging horizontal or lateral hostility to becloud the real and more pressing issues of oppression is by no means new, nor limited to relations between women. The same tactic is used to continue or exacerbate the separation between black women and black men. In discussions around the hiring and firing of black faculty at universities, the charge is frequently heard that black women are more easily hired than are black men. For this reason, black women's problems of promotion and tenure are not to be considered as important, since they are only "taking jobs away from black men." Here again, energy is being wasted on battles which extend horizontally, over the pitifully few crumbs allowed us, rather than being used in a joining of forces to fight for a more realistic representation of black faculty. This would be a vertical battle against the racist policies of the academic structure itself, one which could result in real power and change. And of course, it is the structure at the top which desires changelessness, and so profits from these apparently endless kitchen wars.

Instead of keeping our attentions focused upon the real enemies, enormous energy is being wasted in the black community today by both black men and heterosexual black women, in anti-lesbian hysteria. Yet women-identified women—those who sought their own destinies and attempted to execute them in the absence of male support—have been around in all of our communities for a long time. As Yvonne Flowers of York College pointed out in a recent discussion, the unmarried aunt, childless or otherwise, whose home and resources were often a welcome haven for different members of the family, was a familiar figure in many of our childhoods. And within the homes of our black communities today, it is not the black lesbian who is battering and raping our under-age girl-children, out of displaced and sickening frustration.

The black lesbian has come under increasing attack from both black men and heterosexual black women. In the same way that the existence of the self-defined black woman is no threat to the self-defined black man, the black lesbian is an emotional threat only to those black women who are unsure of, or unable to, express their feelings of kinship and love for other black women, in any meaningful way. For so long, we have been encouraged to view each other with suspicion, as eternal competitors, or as the visible face of our own self-rejection.

But traditionally, black women have always bonded together in support of each other, however uneasily and in the face of whatever other allegiances which militated against that bonding. We have banded together with each other for wisdom and strength and support, even when it was only a relationship to one man. We need only look at the close—although highly complex and involved—relationship between African co-wives; or at the Amazon warriors of ancient Dahomey, who fought together as the Kings' main and most ferocious bodyguard. We need only look at the more promising power wielded by the West African Market Women Associations of today, and those governments which have risen and fallen at their pleasure.

In a verbatim retelling of her life, a 92-year-old Efik-Ibibio woman of Nigeria recalls her love for another woman:

I had a woman friend to whom I revealed my secrets. She was very fond of keeping secrets to herself. We acted as husband and wife. We always moved hand in glove and my husband and hers knew about our relationship. The villagers nicknamed us twin sisters. When I was out of gear with my husband, she would be the one to restore peace. I often sent my children to go and work for her in return for her kindnesses to me. My husband being more fortunate to get more pieces of land than her husband, allowed some to her, even though she was not my co-wife.

The Fon of Dahomey still have 12 different kinds of marriage, one of which is known as "giving the goat to the buck," where a woman of independent means marries another woman who then may or may not bear children, all of whom will belong to the blood line of the other woman. Some marriages of this kind are arranged to provide heirs for women of means who wish to remain "free," and some are homosexual relationships. Marriages of this kind occur throughout Africa, in several different places among different peoples.

In all of these cases, the women involved are recognized parts of their communities, evaluated not by their sexuality but by their respective places within the community.

While a piece of each black woman remembers the old ways of another place and time, when we enjoyed each other in a sisterhood of work and play and power, other pieces of us, less functional, eye each other with suspicion as we have been programmed to do. In the interests of separation, and to keep us out of touch with our own power, black women have been taught to view each other as always suspect, heartless competitors for the scarce male, the all-important prize that will legitimize our existence. This becomes an ultimate and dehumanizing denial of self, no less lethal than that dehumanization of racism which is so closely allied to it.

If the recent hysterical rejection of lesbians in the black community is based solely upon an aversion to the idea of sexual contact between members of the same sex (a contact existing for ages in most of the female compounds across the African continent, from reports) why then is the idea of sexual contact between black men so much more easily accepted, or unremarked? Is the reality of the imagined threat the existence of a self-motivated, self-defined black woman who will not fear nor suffer some terrible retribution from the gods because she does not necessarily seek her face in a man's eyes, even if he has fathered her children? Female-headed households in the black community are not always situations by default.

The distortion of relationship which says "I disagree with you, or I do not share your lifestyle, so I must destroy you" leaves black people with basically uncreative victories, defeated in any common struggle. That is jugular vein psychology, based on a fallacy which holds that your assertion or affirmation of your self must mean an attack upon my self—or that my defining myself will somehow prevent or retard your self-definition. The supposition that one sex needs the other's acquiescence in order to exist prevents both from moving together as self-defined persons toward a common goal.

● ● ●

This is a prevalent mistake among oppressed peoples, and is based upon the false notion that there is only a limited and particular amount of freedom that must be divided up between us, with the largest and juiciest pieces going as spoils to the victor or the stronger. So instead of joining together to fight for more, we quarrel between ourselves for a larger slice of the one pie. Black women fight between ourselves over men instead of pursuing and using who we are and our strengths; black women and men fight between ourselves over who has more of a right to freedom, instead of seeing each other's struggles as part of our own; black and white women fight between ourselves over who is the more oppressed, instead of seeing those areas in which our causes are the same. (Of course, this last separation is worsened by the intransigent racism that white women too often fail to, or cannot, address in themselves.)

As black women we have the right and responsibility to define ourselves, and to seek our allies in common cause with black men against racism, and with white women against sexism. But most of all as black women we have a right to recognize each other without fear and to love where we choose, for both homosexual and heterosexual black women today share a history of bonding and strength that our particular sexual preferences should not blind us to.

JAN CROSTHWAITE AND GRAHAM PRIEST

The Definition of Sexual Harassment

JAN CROSTHWAITE teaches philosophy at the University of Auckland.
GRAHAM PRIEST teaches philosophy at the University of Queensland.

Sexual harassment is a pervasive feature of the society in which we live. It occurs in both public and private life. It is distinctive both in the role that it plays in social interactions and in its phenomenology for those who experience it. A common response to the subject, particularly amongst men, is to consider it a trivial and unimportant one. This, we think, could not be further from the truth: it is a phenomenon of no little importance, not only to those who experience it, but to our understanding of the nature of the society in which we live. . . .

We will try to . . . [provide] a definition of sexual harassment. We are not after what is often called a nominal definition, that is, an analysis of the meaning of the phrase 'sexual harassment'. We are after a real definition of the phenomenon itself. Sexual harassment is a social phenomenon with a particular nature. The nature manifests itself in the causal role that sexual harassment plays in our society. An adequate grasp of this nature provides an explanation of various things whose connection is not immediately apparent, and a fuller understanding of the society in which we function. . . .

In approaching a definition, it helps to have before us some paradigm examples of the thing to be defined. So we shall start with a list of examples of sexual harassment. A diverse range of actions and situations have been identified as sexual harassment, from rape and coercive sexual intercourse through to actions which create a 'hostile environment' for women in the workplace. Some of these examples are contentious. In some cases a given action may have significance as sexual harassment only in the context of a pattern of behaviour. However, we think that the most unproblematic examples of sexual harassment fall into the following categories. This list is not intended to be exhaustive, but we do think that it captures the most significant cases in an illuminating way.

1) A position of power or authority may be used to secure sexual access of some sort to a subordinate. This includes such classic examples as an employer, teacher, etc., using either incentives (such as promotion or higher grades) or, more commonly, threats of sanction (such as dismissal or failure) to secure his sexual aims with respect to an employee or student. The threat of sanction is often explicit, but need not be. Victims may feel threatened simply because they know there is an institutional power inequality. (We are using 'institution' here in a conventional and rather narrow sense, to refer to economic, political (in the traditional sense), professional, etc., institutions—such things as businesses, universities, churches, etc., rather than in the wider sense it is sometimes given where any conventional social practice—like marriage or heterosexuality—is regarded as an 'institution'.)

   The sexual access involved may be of many kinds, from a sort of voyeurism, through sexual talk and touching, to sexual intercourse. A complaint by a woman in her mid-thirties, H, about her employer, E, gives an indication of the range of behaviour which can be involved.

> The behaviour complained of included: a 'peeping tom' incident where E visited H's home late one night; remarks about H's sexual habits and the colour of her underwear; pinning H to the work bench; E asking H if he could have a 'peep' at her; attempts to lift her skirt and to kiss her; E exposing his erect penis and trying to force H to touch him; and discussions of a sexual nature.

Such behaviour can occur outside contexts of institutional power, but we would then categorise it differently. The distinguishing characteristic of this first category of examples is the use (indeed, abuse) of institutional power, in some form, for sexual ends.

2) Sexual access can also be sought and taken in contexts where there is no institutional power difference to serve as a source of threat or incentive. Groping, persistent sexual invitations, etc., by fellow workers and fellow students are common examples of this category. At the extreme of this category are acts of rape, including rape through violence or threat of violence. These interactions, like those in category 1, are directed towards some form of sexual access or gratification of the perpetrator. This distinguishes them from examples in the following groups.

3) Sexually harassing behaviour need not be directed towards sexual access or gratification. Its aim may be rather to make the victim aware of the presence of the perpetrator and her vulnerability to his sexual appraisal. Sometimes this awareness is the perpetrator's explicit aim; sometimes it is a corollary of another intention, such as showing oneself to be 'one of the boys'. Leering, wolf-whistles, etc., fall into this category. Rarely does a wolf-whistler expect to obtain sexual favours. There may, but need not be, some sexual gratification from eliciting a response in the victim, but the point is really to force the presence and attention of the harasser on the harassee in a certain way. Ostentatious leering at a woman's breasts is unlikely to be a matter of obtaining sexual pleasure from looking at her breasts; it is better explained as forcing her to be aware of her sexuality as perceived by (some) men and of herself as vulnerable to the sexual predation of men. Sexual harassment of this kind may occur within or outside institutional power relationships.

4) Sexual behaviour may also result unintentionally in a similar response to that intended in examples of group 3. Telling 'dirty' jokes, and displaying sexually explicit pictures, etc., will be examples of this kind in certain contexts. The major difference between this group and the previous group of examples is that the intention of the harasser to have an effect on the harassee may be quite absent. Consider, for example, the case of a woman who reported feeling humiliated every time she came to work and 'saw this picture of a woman with her legs wide open, looking passive and provocative'. She explained that 'I felt it reflected on me, my work status, even my ability to do my job'. This response, though understandable and even predictable, need not have been foreseen, let alone intended, in displaying the picture concerned.

Unwelcome or inappropriate compliments on someone's physical appearance might be included in this category, in that while they are usually intended to have an effect on the victim, it need not be one which highlights the presence of the harasser in the way of examples in 3. (Of course, some compliments are offered and function in the same way as wolf-whistles characteristically do, and hence would fall into group 3.) Hadjifotiou cites a complaint by a woman manager which seems to provide an example of sexual harassment of this sort, though without further details the intention behind the comments (and hence categorisation as group 3 or group 4) is unclear.

> My boss is incapable of having a meeting or discussion with me without some comment about my sex. There are constant references to the fact that you are a woman, your dress, etc., and remarks such as 'you're looking attractive today' or 'I know you will be able to influence so-and-so by fluttering your eyelashes'. I try to ignore it.

So much for the examples. It is clear from these that a range of morally problematic features is exhibited by actions classified as sexual harassment: abuse of power, injustice, failure of respect for the wishes and interests of victims, treating women as sex objects, causing distress or otherwise harming the victim, and creating sexually discriminatory work and study environments. While each of these has provided the focus for some account of sexual harassment, we don't think that any of them captures its real nature.

We are also concerned that, while a definition of sexual harassment should include all the examples above, it should not be so wide as to rule out the possibility of morally acceptable sexual interaction in the variety of situations in which people find themselves, even those where there is an institutional power imbalance. Nor do we think that every form of immoral or unacceptable sexual interaction counts as sexual harassment. Some sorts of sexual interaction might count as unprofessional conduct but not sexual harassment; for example, where a female academic has an affair with an older male graduate student she is supervising. With these points, and the above examples in mind, let us now turn to the question of a definition. We will start by considering an appealing but misleading approach, and then suggest a better one. . . .

An obvious starting place for defining sexual harassment is the surface structure of the term itself, which suggests that sexual harassment is harassment of a sexual nature, as religious harassment and racial harassment are harassment of a religious or racial nature respectively. We will argue, though, that such an approach yields a definition which is both too narrow and too broad. To avoid this suggestion that we think is misleading, we will refer to sexual harassment as SH from now on.

The Shorter Oxford English Dictionary says that to harass is: to trouble or vex by repeated attacks; to worry, distress. But applying this gives too narrow a definition of SH. There are classic examples of SH which do not involve harassment in this sense, such as the following example (of category 1) of SH of a college student by her teacher.

> Well, [in] my freshman year I took a class. I didn't understand all of the readings and by the time the final came around I found myself with an F. So I asked him if I could talk to him about grades in his office. So I went to his office and he gave me a choice—either be with him or take the F. So I met him at his house, and spent three hours with him in his bed. . . . I felt dirty but I didn't get the F. He gave me a D. Was it worth it? Yes and no. I felt it was something I had to do to save myself.

There is no repeated attack here; nor does the student's further description of her response to this choice fit our usual conception of being troubled or worried. (Though her feeling dirty does indicate a sense of humiliation or degradation.) Hence this is not harassment according to the above definition, but it is still SH.

Any account of SH as a species of the genus harassment is also too broad. To make this clear, it will be useful first to note an ambiguity in the idea of harassing behaviour being *of a sexual nature*. This could mean harassment *by means of sexual behaviour*, or harassment *on the basis of the sex* of the victim. Definitions of SH sometimes run these two aspects together. We think both meanings of 'sexual' are significant, though neither separately nor in combination do they define a category of harassment which is sexual harassment.

Religious and racial harassment are not harassment by religious or racial behaviour (though the latter will include some *racist* behaviour). Rather, the victim is subject to harassment *because of* his/her race or religion. Such parallels suggest that sexual harassment is harassment on the basis of sex. There is some truth to the idea that the sex of the victim is a determining feature of SH, as our analysis will make clear. But not all harassment on the basis of sex is SH, as [this] example makes clear: A 'female academic whose male colleagues continually ridicule her ideas and opinions may be the object of sexist harassment' though not thereby of SH.

Is SH then harassment by means of sexual behaviour? The sexual nature of the behaviour involved is an important component of SH, but not all harassment by means of sexual behaviour is SH. For example, one male might harass another who is modest or prudish by explicitly sexual behaviour towards women in his presence. Or consider a more contentious case. A woman employee wants to court her employer. Over a period of time she persistently asks him to go out with her, gives him gifts, etc., all in a very open and non-threatening way. The employer, we may suppose, does not want to have a sexual relationship with his employee, and comes to find the constant advances embarrassing and annoying. He is harassed, and the harassment is of a sexual nature. But we are inclined not to call this SH, for reasons we will make clear shortly.

We think then that SH is not best understood as harassment of a sexual nature; it is not a species of the genus harassment at all. To that extent, the terminology is unfortunate and misleading. We must look for another definition. Rather than explore other dead ends, we will turn now to the definition we think correct. We will then consider some reasons for preferring this to alternative analyses. . . .

We approach the issue of providing a definition of SH in good traditional form; first we locate its genus, and then its species. SH is a form of behaviour, but of what genus? Our answer is that SH is a form of oppressive behaviour. This, of course, raises the question of what oppression is. Various analyses of oppression have been given, particularly by feminist theorists. What they share, and what for our purposes is sufficient, is that oppression is a relation between social groups which involves one group wielding power which is illegitimate, in some sense, over another group in the society. Oppression is systematic and systemic, though not necessarily intentional. And it involves a limitation of the prospects for self-development, realisation of goals and material success, of members of the oppressed group, often through the psychological impact on these people of the behaviour and structures which sustain the oppression.

The illegitimacy of the exercise of group power or dominance involved in oppression is to be understood in terms of wider notions of political or moral rightness, rather than the narrower conventions of the particular society. Thus, slave-owners oppress slaves, but police do not oppress the general public in a democratic society. (At least, according to liberal political theory they do not. In practice police clearly do play an oppressive role sometimes, e.g., in race relations.) The room for debate about when power is illegitimate captures in part the room for contention about whether a particular group is oppressed.

Next, what species of oppressive behaviour is SH? Our answer is, essentially, that SH is a pattern of sexual behaviour that constitutes or contributes to the oppression of one gender group by another. ('Constitutes' because SH can itself be an exercise of illegitimate power; and 'contributes to' because SH has a role in creating and maintaining the general situation of men's oppression of women.) This, however, still lacks adequate specificity. For, as SH is normally practised, it constitutes or contributes to oppression in a quite distinctive way. Feminist analyses of oppression have pointed out the role of effects on the psychological states of victims in maintaining oppression. We believe that SH contributes to the maintenance of gender power particularly through its psychological impact on victims. We therefore propose that SH is any form of sexual behaviour by members of a dominant gender group towards members of a subordinate gender group whose typical effect is to cause members of the subordinate group to experience their powerlessness as a member of that group. To say that the effect is typical does not imply, of course, that it is invariable. Nor do we wish to suggest that the experience is one of complete powerlessness; all that is required is that the behaviour be of a kind which promotes in its recipients an awareness of having less power than the harasser, in virtue of their respective genders. This is the definition we will defend in the rest of the paper.

As given, the definition is gender-neutral. In our society, it is men who are the dominant gender group, and so only men who can harass. (This is an important point, and we will return to it later.) But if there were, or could be, a society where the power roles between men and women were reversed, behaviour of the kind we are talking about directed by women against men would constitute SH.

So much for the definition. We think that it has some initial plausibility, but not that it wears the mark of its correctness on its face. In what follows we will discuss the definition and try to show how it makes sense of a number of issues, including the paradigm examples. That it does so provides further evidence of the correctness of the definition. . . .

The definition we have given locates SH as an abuse of power of a certain kind. Many have seen the issue of power, and the abuse or misuse of power, as central to SH. We think that SH cannot adequately be characterised just as abuse of power for sexual ends, for reasons we will give shortly. But by placing it as we have in the context of the gender power of a group, and, specifically, the procedures that men use (collectively) for disempowering women, the power connection is made clear.

Abuse of power is a feature of the examples we mentioned in category 1. However, it is not this which constitutes their nature as SH. Institutional power may be abused in many ways, and misusing it for sexual ends shares the moral wrongness of any other form of corruption. Some misuses of institutional power for sexual ends will, in addition to being corrupt, be SH and wrong in this further way. But it is possible to misuse power for sexual ends without this being SH. Consider, for example, a club treasurer who uses club funds to take a prospective lover to dinner.

Moreover, focussing on SH as an abuse of power for sexual ends does not satisfactorily account for examples of SH in the other categories we have outlined. Examples such as wolf-whistling make clear that SH can occur in situations where there is no institutional power structure involved, and it is possible, even common, for male employees and students to sexually harass their female peers. Particularly, a definition directly in terms of the abuse of power would exclude category 2 examples, even though they may share all other features of examples in category 1.

One response to this problem might be to generalise the notion of power to include non-institutional power inequalities. Men are characteristically more powerful physically than women, and this difference is often present and carries an implicit threat in situations of SH. A harasser might also have some other non-institutional source of power through which he threatens the harassee—for example, information about her which she does not wish disclosed. However, appeal to a range of possible power inequalities is unsatisfactory. First, no power inequality need be present for SH (other than the background social inequality of the sexes to which our account appeals). Second, even if a satisfactory general account of the exercise of power can be given, it is difficult to give a clear content to the idea of an *abuse* of power outside institutional contexts. We think that the appeal to the socially structured power difference between gender groups, as it functions in our account, best captures the intuitions which have sometimes seen all SH as a function of power inequalities. . . .

The definition also makes sense of what is, emotionally, the dominant feeling that women experience when subjected to SH: one of powerlessness. This has two aspects; one general and one specific. First, the general: being subjected to SH makes women aware of their less powerful position in society in general, in sexual interactions with men particularly, and also in various other contexts such as the workplace. Women are aware that they are subject to sexual harassment in a way in which men are not subject to harassment as men. This brings home to women not just the existence of a gender-based power differential, but that it is peculiarly encoded in sexual behaviour.

The second, and specific, aspect of the sense of powerlessness is the common feeling of women subjected to SH of being unable to do anything about the behaviour in question. Typically, what strikes home hardest is not being the object of such behaviour, but being unable to respond effectively. Other than flirtatious playfulness, the appropriate feminine response to sexual solicitation is meant to be a 'polite but firm' rejection. This is unlikely to be effective in stopping the SH behaviour, because feminine 'no-saying' is not to be taken seriously, particularly in the domain of sexual behaviour. Standard sexual stereotypes take sexual predation of women to be a natural expression and prerogative of masculinity. Any aggression or stridency in response is held to be unfeminine, and to diminish a woman's right to respectful treatment. No acceptable response allows the victim of SH to make clear her view that the behaviour is quite unacceptable and often humiliatingly inappropriate. Indeed, to make this clear one would have to address many cultural assumptions embedded in masculine and feminine sex and social roles, including assumptions of male dominance.

To be unable to counter effectively behaviour one finds humiliating is to be further humiliated. Many studies indicate that a frequent response of women to SH is to try and ignore it (and add that this is not effective: the problem does not go away). Another common response is to remove oneself from the situation, often at great personal cost where this is a workplace or educational context. Both attempting to ignore a problem-situation and leaving or withdrawing from it are indications of feeling powerless to respond effectively to the source of one's problems. Examples of category 3 make particularly clear the situation of lacking any effective response. Protest is the only response available to wolf-whistles, and protest is ineffectual because it is precisely the response desired. But it is true of other cases also that what rankles is, typically, not being able to do anything effective about the unacceptable behaviour.

The definition also explains why there is typically a difference between the responses of women and of men subjected to apparently the same kind of sexually harassing behaviour. Again, this is most obvious with respect to cases of category 3. If a man is subjected to wolf-whistles, comments about his sexual attractiveness, etc., his reaction, though possibly mixed with embarrassment, will normally be one of some pleasure. He does not feel any lack of power, and the experience is not an unpleasant one. This is precisely because of the asymmetry in power relations. Similar comments apply to situations like category 2. Sexual advances towards a man typically flatter him. And if he really does not want them, he just says so, and that is that. This is not true when the roles are reversed. Such gender differences in experience are explained in our account of SH by the role of power inequalities between the sexes. . . .

It is a consequence of the account we offer that, in societies where males are the dominant gender, women cannot commit SH, nor men be victims. This may seem counter-intuitive when both sexes can exhibit the sort of behaviour described in our paradigm examples of SH.

Analyses of SH differ about such gender asymmetry. Some feminist analyses explicitly define SH as something only males can do. For example, Lin Farley says:

> Sexual harassment is best described as unsolicited nonreciprocal male behaviour that asserts a woman's sex role over her function as worker.

Philosophical analyses, though, are usually deliberately gender-neutral. . . . So some further discussion and defence of our position on this issue seem in order.

We think our definition captures genuine and significant gender asymmetries with respect to SH which are often obscured by gender-neutral analyses. As well as the phenomenological differences mentioned above, our account explains, for example, the salient fact that women rarely engage in SH-type behaviour. SH is behaviour of a kind involved in the maintenance of an asymmetric power-structure, and one should therefore expect the dominant to employ it more than the subordinate. But because these gender asymmetries are contingent on particular, society-specific, gender power relations, we avoid the arbitrariness of stipulatively excluding the possibility of women committing SH. It is not an essential feature of SH that women cannot commit it; it is a contingent consequence of gender power relations in our society.

It is easy to think of situations apparently similar to cases of SH, but in which the roles of the sexes are reversed. For example, a woman employer might solicit sexual attention from a male employee under threat of firing him if he does not comply. Or a group of women, out for a night on the town, might harass a man in a restaurant with ribald jokes, sexual gestures and innuendo. While such behaviour is similar in various ways to SH, it is not SH. Crucially, it has a different typical phenomenology and nett social effect.

Take the first (employer/employee) case. This is similar to SH of category 1. But even if the man feels powerless in the face of the threat of firing, he is unlikely to feel powerless *in virtue of his gender*: he feels powerless *qua* employee. Moreover, such cases clearly do not have the effect of sustaining gender/power structures—quite the contrary. The fact that the behaviour is not SH does not, of course, mean that it is morally acceptable. It is clearly an abuse of institutional power, as it is when a man does it.

The second sort of example (women out on the town) is more analogous to a case of SH of category 3. But again, the phenomenology is typically different. The man may be annoyed, even to the point of leaving the restaurant; he may even feel embarrassed; but he is unlikely to be reminded of his lack of power *qua* male. And again, such acts are hardly an affirmation of social power, more a subversion of it. This is simply harassment by sexual behaviour, which, as we have already argued, is different.

It might still be asked why the same behaviour should count as SH when done by one sex but not the other. What lurks behind this question is a simple empiricist assumption to the effect that phenomena must be defined in terms of their empirical manifestations. Such empiricism is, in general, quite unsustainable in the social sciences. Empirical manifestations do not float in mid-air: they draw their nature from both the social structure in which they are embedded and the effects they have on this structure. For example, the same utterance could be a request or an order depending simply on the social relationship between the persons involved. There are also familiar cross-cultural examples of very different behaviour having the same empirical manifestation. The point of distinguishing between behaviour of men and women which appears the same is that (as things are) it differs in the much more fundamental ways we have indicated; specifically, in its relation to one of the fundamental structural features of our society: patriarchy. To focus simply on the observable behaviour of SH is to be superficial and miss its essence.

It is, of course, possible for someone to say that they intend to use the term 'sexual harassment' just to mean harassment of a sexual nature. And if someone wishes to do this, we are prepared to yield the term. As we said before, we are not interested in lexicography; we are interested in understanding a certain social phenomenon, the maintenance of a power structure by certain kinds of sexual behaviour. In the last instance, it does not really matter what you call it. . . .

We have argued that the background social context of power relations between the sexes means that only sexual behaviour by men directed towards women can be SH in our society. But does it also mean that all such behaviour is SH? Obviously, all sexual activity in our society takes place in the social context of gender inequality we have identified as crucial to SH. So won't any heterosexual interaction (or at least any which is male initiated) count as SH? We think not, because we believe that heterosexual interactions (even where male initiated) need not all be of a kind that serves to sustain women's oppression and make them feel powerless. However, we do acknowledge that there are analyses of heterosexual activity according to which all such activity expresses and contributes to the maintenance of male dominance. If one were to accept such an analysis (which we most certainly do not), then all heterosexual activity could turn out to be SH on our account.

One final point in this context. We'd like to return to the question why SH should be called harassment if, as we claim, it is not in fact a species of the genus harassment. We can now give a simple answer. Harassment is a gradual process of wearing down. While some cases of SH, including paradigmatic cases like a boss soliciting sex under threat of firing, may be single and isolated incidents for the individuals concerned, any isolated event of SH fits a much more general pattern of sexual behaviour as used in the disempowerment of women. The process of wearing down applies to women as a group, not necessarily to particular individuals. In that sense, the name 'harassment' is, after all, appropriate. . . .

Let us, finally, reiterate some of our central points by way of reviewing our paradigm examples.

Examples of category 3: wolf-whistling, etc., fit the pattern of our definition most obviously. Behaviour of this kind typically impresses on the woman harassed a feeling of impotence, as we have pointed out. Notice that even though the harasser typically intends to have some effect on the harassee, this need not be, and usually is not, that of making her feel powerless. The feeling of powerlessness comes from the recognition that men have, and feel they have, the power to publicly express uninvited sexual appraisals of women. The significant point in classifying behaviour as SH is not the subjective intentions of the harasser, but its objective effect on the harassee, which is partly a reminder of, partly constitutive of, the power asymmetry.

Examples of category 4, jokes, posters, etc., reinforce this point. Since SH is not a matter of the intentions of the harasser, what he thinks is going on, whether or not he intends to offend, etc., are quite irrelevant. This is not to say that everyone who displays explicit sexual material is guilty of SH. Rather, the point is that if this is done in a context where it has the effect in question on women, it is SH. It is then explicable why sexual displays of this sort in the work-place in particular should be taken as SH by women. Highlighting women's sexuality in such a context may both denigrate women's status as workers and assert the dominance of masculine values and interests in the work-place. Hence it affirms and contributes to women's inequality to men in this area of common life.

Examples of category 2 also fit our definition well. Standard discussions of this kind of example tend to stress the taking of sexual liberties. This, though certainly morally objectionable, is not what constitutes SH. The point is, rather, the effect that this has on the harassee, and how this fits into the bigger picture of power relations in society. A woman can take sexual liberties, of course; but as we have already observed, the effect of this on men is typically quite different from the effect of men taking sexual liberties with women.

Finally, similar comments apply to examples of category 1. What makes this kind of example SH is not the attempt to obtain sexual favours. More serious is the effect that this has on people who are already in a vulnerable position (students, employees, etc.). This kind of example is also misleading in a certain way. SH has something to do with an abuse of power, and examples of this kind suggest that it is power of an institutional nature (that of an employer, teacher, etc.). It is not; it is power of a gender nature. What makes it so easy to confuse the two is just the fact that these are, or at least, have been, pretty much coextensive in our society. . . .

Life is full of behaviour that is sexual in one way or another. Some of this is unacceptable. With the recognition, brought about by feminism, that much traditionally accepted male sexual behaviour is of this kind, it has become common to lump together much unacceptable sexual behaviour as SH. Though this has a political point, it can be quite misleading, and, in the end, it is harmful. We have located SH by the role it plays in the constitution and preservation of asymmetric gender power relations, i.e., patriarchy. As such, it is a quite specific form of unacceptable sexual behaviour. Lumping it together with other things merely cloaks this, and so cloaks the important political role that it plays in our society. We hope that our account, by cleanly isolating its specificity, produces a clearer understanding of the kind of society in which we live and how it works, and so contributes, if only a little, to changing it.

PART TWO
Individual Ethics

CHAPTER 4

What Is Reproductive Freedom?

Frank and Gertrude fall in love. They talk about getting married, moving to California, getting good jobs, and several years later having two beautiful children. Their children will be three years apart in age. The little girl will look just like Gertrude, the little boy just like Frank.

This story is probably familiar. Even if this isn't exactly how you imagine your own life, you have to agree that the story represents a fairly typical fantasy of the circumstances surrounding reproduction, at least in our culture. We tend to think of reproduction as a matter of choice. Most people want to have children and when they are ready to do so, then they do. Some people don't want any children, and so they don't have them. Of course, a little reflection reminds us that this picture of reproduction is far from complete. It ignores the ways in which both the complexities of human biology and the constraints of human society affect our reproductive desires, choices, and possibilities. Pregnancy is not the result of an act of will alone. It requires the cooperation of two fully functioning reproductive systems. And, just as a woman cannot get pregnant simply by *wanting* to, so can she get pregnant when she *does not* want to.

In this chapter, we first explore a controversial issue that focuses our attention on the nature and limits of reproductive freedom, namely, the issue of abortion. What we think is at stake morally in the abortion controversy is a function of what we think about sex, reproduction, responsibility, sexual equality, and religion. Looking at abortion from a philosophical point of view can help to sort out the principal moral questions that make it the subject of so much disagreement.

When thinking about abortion as a philosophical topic, it is helpful to begin by considering what women actually think about when they are trying to decide whether or not to have an abortion. Obviously, the factors that a woman considers will be a function of her particular circumstances. Sometimes, the pregnancy itself might present difficulties. A teenager may feel that being pregnant while at school would cause enormous personal and social problems for her. An astronaut about to take off for several months on a space station may feel that being pregnant would interfere with her work. Sometimes, the pregnancy itself is not so much of a problem; rather, the problem is the child that will be its end result. A student might feel that having a child at this point would seriously jeopardize her chances of finishing school; a mother of two children might feel that having another child would impair her emotional and financial capacity to care for her existing ones. Whatever we ultimately decide about the morality of abortion, it is important to keep in mind that it is always a concrete act that is undertaken for particular reasons in particular circumstances.

Most opposition to abortion is based on the claim that human life begins at conception and thus a human embryo or fetus is a person like any of us and so has a right to life. Although philosophers disagree as to all that a right to life involves, we can assume that at the very least that it guarantees that one not be killed unjustifiably. Unwarranted or unjustified killing is murder. Murder is not permissible. Those opposed to abortion typically believe that the killing of an "innocent" embryo is unwarranted. If so, they conclude, abortion is murder and hence is impermissible. When the problem of abortion is framed in this way, it appears that those who wish to defend the practice of abortion against this conclusion are forced to argue that personhood does not begin at conception, but at some later stage of pregnancy or at birth. Ann Druyan and Carl Sagan present the principal arguments for and against fetal personhood.

Judith Jarvis Thomson, on the other hand, urges those who are concerned to establish the permissibility of abortion to avoid the entanglements of the debate over the beginnings of personhood. For the sake of argument, she grants those opposed to abortion their major premise, namely, that the fetus is a person from the moment of conception. She then proceeds to argue that, even if the fetus is a person, it does not follow that a woman is required to carry it to term. The woman's right to control her own body outweighs the rights of the fetus. She hopes to set abortion in a context that displays clearly what she takes to be the central moral issue that it raises: does a woman have an *obligation* to maintain, for the sake of the fetus, an unwanted pregnancy to term? Thomson's example of the unconscious violinist who requires the use of your kidneys to stay alive has become legendary. It is up to you to decide whether or not you take this, or any of her other suggestive analogies, to be persuasive. It is also useful to consider Mary Anne Warren's argument for the significance of birth in determining moral obligations to fetuses/infants and Alan Donagan's argument for its irrelevance in the context of Thomson's general claims about the sorts of obligations that people have to help others in need.

We then turn our attention to other moral dimensions of reproduction, dimensions that may well be complicated by prevailing concerns about the legitimacy of abortion. Laura Purdy asks us to consider the conditions under which it might be morally impermissible to have children. In order to illuminate the general range of considerations morally relevant to a judgment that a person ought not procreate, Purdy focuses on the specific case of genetically transmittable diseases and argues that it is morally wrong to reproduce when a high risk of transmitting a serious disease or defect exists.

Several controversial cases involving adoption have captured considerable media attention. Prominent among them is the case of Baby Girl Clausen, in which a judge awarded an adopted child to her biological father on the grounds that his parental rights had never been properly terminated. Mary Shanley turns our attention to the tension between "father's rights" and "maternal autonomy" in relation to the custodial claims of unwed biological parents. She argues that it makes no sense to consider parental rights as individual rights, given that they necessarily involve a relationship with another (dependent) person. Her essay helps to illuminate the complexity of societal views about the moral and political dimensions of reproduction.

ANN DRUYAN AND CARL SAGAN

The Question of Abortion

ANN DRUYAN is secretary of the Federation of American Scientists, founded in 1945 by the original atomic scientists to combat the misuse of science and technology. She is also a writer and television producer.

CARL SAGAN (1934–1997) taught and did research at Cornell University. The idea that fetal brain activity might help provide a rational compromise in the abortion debate was raised in his 1977 book, *The Dragons of Eden,* for which he received the Pulitzer Prize.

The issue had been decided years ago. The court had chosen the middle ground. You'd think the fight was over. Instead, there are mass rallies, bombings and intimidation, arrests, intense lobbying, legislative drama, Congressional hearings, Supreme Court decisions and clerics threatening politicians with perdition. Partisans fling accusations of hypocrisy and murder. The intent of the Constitution and will of God are equally invoked. Doubtful arguments are trotted out as certainties. The contending factions call on science to bolster their positions. Families are divided, husbands and wives agree not to discuss it, old friends are no longer speaking. Politicians check the latest polls to discover the dictates of their consciences. Amid all the shouting, it is hard for the adversaries to hear one another. Opinions are polarized. Minds are closed.

Is it wrong to abort a pregnancy? Always? Sometimes? Never? How do we decide? We wrote this article to understand better what the contending views are and to see if we ourselves could find a position that would satisfy us both. We had to weigh the arguments of both sides for consistency and to pose test cases, some of which are purely hypothetical. If in some of these tests we seem to go too far, we ask the reader to be patient with us—we're trying to stress the various positions to the breaking point to see their weaknesses and where they fail.

In contemplative moments, nearly everyone recognizes that the issue is not wholly one-sided. Many partisans of differing views, we find, feel some disquiet, some unease when confronting what's behind the opposing arguments. (This is partly why such confrontations are avoided.) And the issue surely touches on deep questions: What are our responsibilities to one another? Should we permit the state to intrude into the most intimate and personal aspects of our lives? Where are the boundaries of freedom? What does it mean to be human?

TESTING "FREEDOM OF CHOICE"

Of the many actual points of view, it is widely held—especially in the media, which rarely have the time or the inclination to make fine distinctions—that there are only two: "pro-choice" and "pro-life." This is what the two principal warring camps like to call themselves, and that's what we'll call them here. In the simplest characterization, a

145

pro-choicer would hold that the decision to abort a pregnancy is to be made only by the woman; the state has no right to interfere. And a pro-lifer would hold that, from the moment of conception, the embryo or fetus is alive; that this life imposes on us a moral obligation to preserve it; and that abortion is tantamount to murder. Both names—pro-choice and pro-life—were picked with an eye toward influencing those whose minds are not yet made up; few people wish to be counted as being against freedom of choice or as opposed to life. Indeed, freedom and life are two of our most cherished values, and here they seem to be in fundamental conflict.

Let's consider these two absolutist positions in turn. A newborn baby is surely the same being it was just before birth. There is good evidence that a late-term fetus responds to sound—including music, but especially its mother's voice. It can suck its thumb or do a somersault. Occasionally, it generates adult brain wave patterns. Some people say they remember being born, or even the uterine environment. Perhaps there is thought in the womb. It's hard to maintain that a transformation to full personhood happens abruptly at the moment of birth. Why, then, should it be murder to kill an infant the day after it was born but not the day before?

As a practical matter, this isn't very important: less than one percent of all tabulated abortions in the United States are listed in the last three months of pregnancy (and, on closer investigation, most such reports turn out to be due to miscarriage or miscalculation). But third-trimester abortions provide a test of the limits of the pro-choice point of view. Does a woman's "innate right to control her own body" include the right to kill a near-term fetus who is, for all intents and purposes, identical to a newborn child?

We believe that many supporters of reproductive freedom are troubled at least occasionally by this question. But they are reluctant to raise it because it is the beginning of a slippery slope. If it is impermissible to abort a pregnancy in the ninth month, what about the eighth, seventh, sixth . . . ? Once we acknowledge that the state can interfere at *any* time in the pregnancy, doesn't it follow that the state can interfere at all times?

This conjures up the specter of predominantly male, predominantly affluent legislators telling poor women they must bear and raise alone children they cannot afford to bring up; forcing teenagers to bear children they are not emotionally prepared to deal with; saying to women who wish for a career that they must give up their dreams, stay home and bring up babies; and, worst of all, condemning victims of rape and incest to carry and nurture the offspring of their assailants. Legislative prohibitions on abortion arouse the suspicion that their real intent is to control the independence and sexuality of women. Why should legislators have any right at all to tell women what to do with their bodies? To be deprived of reproductive freedom is demeaning. Women are fed up with being pushed around.

And yet, by consensus, all of us think it proper that there be prohibitions against, and penalties exacted for, murder. It would be a flimsy defense if the murderer pleads that this is just between him and his victim and none of the government's business. If killing a fetus is truly killing a human being, is it not the *duty* of the state to prevent it? Indeed, one of the chief functions of government is to protect the weak from the strong.

If we do not oppose abortion at *some* stage of pregnancy, is there not a danger of dismissing an entire category of human beings as unworthy of our protection and respect? And isn't that dismissal the hallmark of sexism, racism, nationalism and religious fanaticism? Shouldn't those dedicated to fighting such injustices be scrupulously careful not to embrace another?

TESTING THE "RIGHT TO LIFE"

There is no right to life in any society on Earth today, nor has there been at any former time (with a few rare exceptions, such as among the Jains of India): We raise farm animals for slaughter; destroy forests; pollute rivers and lakes until no fish can live there; kill deer and elk for sport, leopards for their pelts and whales for fertilizer; entrap dolphins, gasping and writhing, in great tuna nets; club seal pups to death; and render a species extinct every day. All these beasts and vegetables are as alive as we. What is (allegedly) protected is not life, but *human* life.

And even with that protection, casual murder is an urban commonplace, and we wage "conventional" wars with tolls so terrible that we are, most of us, afraid to consider them very deeply. (Tellingly, state-organized mass murders are often justified by redefining our opponents—by race, nationality, religion or ideology—as less than human.) That protection, that right to life, eluded the 40,000 children under 5 who died on our planet today—as every day—from preventable starvation, dehydration, disease and neglect.

Those who assert a "right to life" are for (at most) not just any kind of life, but for—particularly and uniquely—human life. So they too, like pro-choicers, must decide what distinguishes a human being from other animals, and when, during gestation, the uniquely human qualities—whatever they are—emerge.

Despite many claims to the contrary, life does not begin at conception: It is an unbroken chain that stretches back nearly to the origin of the Earth, 4.6 billion years ago. Nor does *human* life begin at conception: It is an unbroken chain dating back to the origin of our species, tens or hundreds of thousands of years ago. Every human sperm and egg is, beyond the shadow of a doubt, alive. They are not human beings, of course. However, it could be argued that neither is a fertilized egg.

In some animals, an egg develops into a healthy adult without benefit of a sperm cell. But not, so far as we know, among humans. A sperm and an unfertilized egg jointly comprise the full genetic blueprint for a human being. Under certain circumstances, after fertilization, they can develop into a baby. But most fertilized eggs are spontaneously miscarried. Development into a baby is by no means guaranteed. Neither a sperm and egg separately, nor a fertilized egg, is more than a *potential* baby or a *potential* adult. So if a sperm and an egg are as human as the fertilized egg produced by their union, and if it is murder to destroy a fertilized egg—despite the fact that it's only *potentially* a baby—why isn't it murder to destroy a sperm or an egg?

Hundreds of millions of sperm cells (top speed with tails lashing: 5 inches per hour) are produced in an average human ejaculation. A healthy young man can produce in a week or two enough spermatozoa to double the human population of the Earth. So is masturbation mass murder? How about nocturnal emissions or just plain sex? When the unfertilized egg is expelled each month, has someone died? Some lower animals can be grown in the laboratory from a single body cell. If such cloning technology were ever developed for humans, would we be committing genocide by shedding a drop of blood?

All human sperm and eggs are genetic halves of "potential" human beings. Should heroic efforts be made to save and preserve all of them, everywhere, because of this "potential"? Is failure to do so immoral or criminal? Of course, there's a difference between taking a life and failing to save it. And there's a big difference between the probability of survival of a sperm cell and that of a fertilized egg. But the absurdity of a corps of high-minded semen-preservers moves us to wonder whether a fertilized egg's mere "potential" to become a baby really does make destroying it murder.

Opponents of abortion worry that, once abortion is permissible immediately after conception, no argument will restrict it at any later time in the pregnancy. Then, they fear, one day it will be permissible to murder a fetus that is unambiguously a human being. Both pro-choicers and pro-lifers (at least some of them) are pushed toward absolutist positions by parallel fears of the slippery slope.

Another slippery slope is reached by those pro-lifers who are willing to make an exception in the agonizing case of a pregnancy resulting from rape or incest. But why should the right to live depend on the *circumstances* of conception? If the same child were to result, can the state ordain life for the offspring of a lawful union but death for one conceived by force or coercion? How can this be just? And if exceptions are extended to such a fetus, why should they be withheld from any other fetus? This is part of the reason some pro-lifers adopt what many others consider the outrageous posture of opposing abortions under any and all circumstances—only excepting, perhaps, when the life of the mother is in danger.

By far the most common reason for abortion is birth-control. So shouldn't opponents of abortion be handing out contraceptives? That would be an effective way to reduce the number of abortions. Instead, the United States is far behind other nations in the development of safe and effective methods of birth control—and, in many cases, opposition to such research (and to sex education) has come from the same people who oppose abortions.

WHEN DO WE BECOME HUMAN?

The attempt to find an ethically sound and unambiguous judgment on when, if ever, abortion is permissible has deep historical roots. Often, especially in Christian tradition, such attempts were connected with the question of when the soul enters the body—a matter not readily amenable to scientific investigation and an issue of controversy even among learned theologians. Ensoulment has been asserted to occur in the sperm before conception, at conception, at the time of "quickening" (when the mother is first able to feel the fetus stirring within her) and at birth. Or even later.

Different religions have different teachings. Among hunter-gatherers, there are usually no prohibitions against abortion, and it was common in ancient Greece and Rome. The Assyrians impaled women on stakes for attempting abortions. The Jewish Talmud teaches that the fetus is not a person and has no rights. The Old and New Testaments— rich in detailed prohibitions on dress, diet and permissible words—contain not a word specifically prohibiting abortion. The only passage that's remotely relevant (*Exodus* 21: 22) decrees that if there's a fight and a woman bystander is accidentally injured and made to miscarry, the assailant must pay a fine. The Catholic Church's first and long-standing collection of canon law (according to the leading historian of the Church's teachings on abortion, John Connery, S.J.) held that abortion was homicide only after the fetus was already "formed"—roughly, the end of the first trimester. It was not until 1869 that abortion at any time for any reason became grounds for excommunication.

If you deliberately kill a human being, it's called murder. If you deliberately kill a chimpanzee—biologically, our closest relative—whatever else it is, it's not murder. To date, murder uniquely applies to killing human beings. Therefore, the question of when personhood (or, if we like, ensoulment) arises is key to the abortion debate. When does the fetus become human? When do distinct and characteristic human qualities emerge?

We recognize that specifying a precise moment will overlook individual differences. Therefore, if we must draw a line, it ought to be drawn conservatively—that is, on the early side. There are people who object to having to set some numerical limit, and we share their disquiet; but if there is to be a law on this matter, and it is to effect some useful compromise between the two absolutist positions, it must specify, at least roughly, a time of transition to personhood.

Every one of us began from a dot. A fertilized egg is roughly the size of the period at the end of this sentence. The momentous meeting of sperm and egg generally occurs in one of the two fallopian tubes. One cell becomes two, two become four, and by the sixth day the fertilized egg has become a kind of hollow sphere wandering off to another realm: the womb. It destroys tissue in its path. It sucks blood from capillaries. It establishes itself as a kind of parasite on the walls of the uterus.

- By the third week, around the time of the first missed menstrual period, the forming embryo is about 2 millimeters long and is developing various body parts. But it looks a little like a segmented worm.

- By the end of the fourth week, it's approximately 5 millimeters (about 1/5 inch) long. It's recognizable as a vertebrate, its tube-shaped heart is beginning to beat, something like the gill arches of a fish or an amphibian have become conspicuous, and there is a pronounced tail. It looks something like a newt or a tadpole. This is the end of the first month after conception.

- By the fifth week, the gross divisions of the brain can be distinguished. What will later develop into eyes is apparent, and little buds appear—on their way to becoming arms and legs.

- By the sixth week, the embryo is 13 millimeters (about 1/2 inch) long. The eyes are still on the side of the head, as in most animals, and the reptilian face has connected slits where the mouth and nose eventually will be.

- By the end of the seventh week, the tail is almost gone, and sexual characteristics can be discerned (although both sexes look female). The face is mammalian but somewhat piglike.

- By the end of the eighth week, the face resembles a primate's but is still not quite human. Most of the human body parts are present in their essentials. Some lower brain anatomy is well-developed. The fetus shows some reflex response to delicate stimulation.

- By the tenth week, the face has an unmistakably human cast. It is beginning to be possible to distinguish males from females. Nails and major bone structures are not apparent until the third month.

- By the fourth month, you can tell the face of one fetus from that of another. Quickening is most often first felt in the fifth month. The bronchioles of the lungs do not begin developing until approximately the sixth month, the alveoli still later. Recognizably human brain activity begins intermittently around the middle of the seventh month.

So, if only a person can be murdered, when does the fetus attain personhood? When its face becomes distinctly human, near the end of the first trimester? When the fetus becomes responsive to stimuli—again, at the end of the first trimester? When the fetus becomes active enough to be felt as quickening, typically in the middle of the second trimester? When the lungs have reached a stage of development sufficient that the fetus might, just conceivably, be able to breathe on its own in the outside air?

The trouble with such developmental milestones is not just that they're arbitrary. More troubling is the fact that none of them involves *uniquely human* characteristics— apart from the superficial matter of facial appearance. All animals respond to stimuli and move of their own volition. Large numbers are able to breathe. But that doesn't stop us from slaughtering them. Reflexes and motion and respiration are not what makes us human.

Other animals have advantages over us—in speed, strength, endurance, climbing or burrowing skills, camouflage, sight or smell or hearing, mastery of the air or water. Our one great advantage, the secret of our success, is thought—characteristically human thought. We are able to think things through, imagine events yet to occur, figure things out. That's how we invented agriculture and civilization. Thought is our blessing and our curse, and it makes us who we are.

Thinking occurs, of course, in the brain—principally in the top layers of the convoluted "gray matter" called the cerebral cortex. The roughly 100 billion neurons in the brain constitute the material basis of thought. The neurons are connected to each other, and their linkups play a major role in what we experience as thinking. But large-scale linking up of neurons doesn't begin until the 24th to 27th week of pregnancy—the sixth month.

By placing harmless electrodes on a subject's head, scientists can measure the electrical activity produced by the network of neurons inside the skull. Different kinds of mental activity show different kinds of brain waves. But brain waves with regular patterns typical of adult human brains do not appear in the fetus until about the 30th week of pregnancy—near the beginning of the third trimester. Fetuses younger than this— however alive and active they may be—lack the necessary brain architecture. They cannot yet think.

Acquiescing in the killing of any living creature, especially one that might later become a baby, is troublesome and painful. But we've rejected the extremes of "always" and "never," and this puts us—like it or not—on the slippery slope. If we are forced to choose a developmental criterion, then this is where we draw the line: when the beginning of characteristically human thinking becomes barely possible. It is, in fact, a very conservative definition: Regular brain waves are rarely found in fetuses. More research would help. If we wanted to make the criterion still more stringent, to allow for precious fetal brain development, we might draw the line at six months. This, it so happens, is where the Supreme Court drew it in 1973—although for completely different reasons.

VIABILITY AND THE COURT

Its decision in the case of *Roe v. Wade* changed American law on abortion. It permits abortion at the request of the woman without restriction in the first trimester and, with some restrictions intended to protect her health, in the second trimester. It allows states to forbid abortion in the third trimester, except when there's a serious threat to the life or health of the woman. In a recent reassessment, the Supreme Court declined explicitly to overturn *Roe v. Wade* but in effect invited the 50 state legislatures to decide for themselves.

What was the reasoning in *Roe v. Wade?* There was no legal weight given to what happens to the children once they are born, or to the family. Instead, a woman's right to reproductive freedom is protected, the court ruled, by constitutional guarantees of privacy. But that right is not unqualified. The woman's guarantee of privacy and the fetus's right to life must be weighed—and when the court did the weighing, priority was given to privacy in the first trimester and to life in the third. The transition was decided not from any of the considerations we have been dealing with so far in this article—not when "ensoulment" occurs, not when the fetus takes on sufficient human characteristics to be protected by laws against murder. Instead, the criterion adopted was whether the fetus could live outside the mother. This is called "viability" and depends in part on the ability to breathe. The lungs are simply not developed, and the fetus cannot breathe—no matter how advanced an artificial lung it might be placed in—until about the 24th week, near the start of the sixth month. This is why *Roe v. Wade* permits states to prohibit abortions in the last trimester. It's a very pragmatic criterion.

If the fetus at a certain stage of gestation would be viable outside the womb, the argument goes, then the right of the fetus to life overrides the right of the woman to privacy. But just what does "viable" mean? Even a full-term newborn is not viable without a great deal of care and love. There was a time before incubators, only a few decades ago, when babies in their seventh month were unlikely to be viable. Would aborting in the seventh month have been permissible then? After the invention of incubators, did aborting pregnancies in the seventh month suddenly become immoral? What happens if, in the future, a new technology develops so that an artificial womb can sustain a fetus even before the sixth month by delivering oxygen and nutrients through the blood—as the mother does through the placenta and into the fetal blood system? We grant that this technology is unlikely to be developed soon or become available to many. But *if* it were available, does it then become immoral to abort earlier than the sixth month, when previously it was moral? A morality that depends on, and changes with, technology is a fragile morality; for some, it is also an unacceptable morality.

And why, exactly, should breathing (or kidney function, or the ability to resist disease) justify legal protection? If a fetus can be shown to think and feel but not be able to breathe, would it be all right to kill it? Do we value breathing more than thinking and feeling? Viability arguments cannot, it seems to us, coherently determine when abortions are permissible. Some other criterion is needed. Again, we offer for consideration the earliest onset of human thinking as that criterion.

Since, on average, fetal thinking occurs even later than fetal lung development, we find *Roe v. Wade* to be a good and prudent decision addressing a complex and difficult issue. With prohibitions on abortion in the last trimester—except in cases of grave medical necessity—it strikes a fair balance between the conflicting claims of freedom and of life.

JUDITH JARVIS THOMSON

A Defense of Abortion

JUDITH JARVIS THOMSON teaches philosophy at the Massachusetts Institute of Technology. Some of her extensive writings on ethics are collected in *Rights, Restitution and Risk* (1986). She is also author of *The Realm of Rights* (1990).

Most opposition to abortion relies on the premise that the fetus is a human being, a person, from the moment of conception. The premise is argued for, but, as I think, not well. Take, for example, the most common argument. We are asked to notice that the development of a human being from conception through birth into childhood is continuous; then it is said that to draw a line, to choose a point in this development and say "before this point the thing is not a person, after this point it is a person" is to make an arbitrary choice, a choice for which in the nature of things no good reason can be given. It is concluded that the fetus is, or anyway that we had better say it is, a person from the moment of conception. But this conclusion does not follow. Similar things might be said about the development of an acorn into an oak tree, and it does not follow that acorns are oak trees, or that we had better say they are. Arguments of this form are sometimes called "slippery slope arguments"—the phrase is perhaps self-explanatory—and it is dismaying that opponents of abortion rely on them so heavily and uncritically.

I am inclined to agree, however, that the prospects for "drawing a line" in the development of the fetus look dim. I am inclined to think also that we shall probably have to agree that the fetus has already become a human person well before birth. Indeed, it comes as a surprise when one first learns how early in its life it begins to acquire human characteristics. By the tenth week, for example, it already has a face, arms and legs, fingers and toes; it has internal organs, and brain activity is detectable. On the other hand, I think that the premise is false, that the fetus is not a person from the moment of conception. A newly fertilized ovum, a newly implanted clump of cells, is no more a person than an acorn is an oak tree. But I shall not discuss any of this. For it seems to me to be of great interest to ask what happens if, for the sake of argument, we allow the premise. How, precisely, are we supposed to get from there to the conclusion that abortion is morally impermissible? Opponents of abortion commonly spend most of their time establishing that the fetus is a person, and hardly any time explaining the step from there to the impermissibility of abortion. Perhaps they think the step too simple and obvious to require much comment. Or perhaps instead they are simply being economical in argument. Many of those who defend abortion rely on the premise that the fetus is not a person, but only a bit of tissue that will become a person at birth; and why pay out more arguments than you have to? Whatever the explanation. I suggest that the step they take is neither easy nor obvious, that it calls for closer examination than it is commonly given, and that when we do give it this closer examination we shall feel inclined to reject it.

I propose, then, that we grant that the fetus is a person from the moment of conception. How does the argument go from here? Something like this, I take it. Every person has a right to life. So the fetus has a right to life. No doubt the mother has a right to decide what shall happen in and to her body; everyone would grant that. But surely a person's right to life is stronger and more stringent than the mother's right to decide what happens in and to her body, and so outweighs it. So the fetus may not be killed; an abortion may not be performed.

It sounds plausible. But now let me ask you to imagine this. You wake up in the morning and find yourself back to back in bed with an unconscious violinist. A famous unconscious violinist. He has been found to have a fatal kidney ailment, and the Society of Music Lovers has canvassed all the available medical records and found that you alone have the right blood type to help. They have therefore kidnapped you, and last night the violinist's circulatory system was plugged into yours, so that your kidneys can be used to extract poisons from his blood as well as your own. The director of the hospital now tells you, "Look, we're sorry the Society of Music Lovers did this to you— we would never have permitted it if we had known. But still, they did it, and the violinist now is plugged into you. To unplug you would be to kill him. But never mind, it's only for nine months. By then he will have recovered from his ailment, and can safely be unplugged from you." Is it morally incumbent on you to accede to this situation? No doubt it would be very nice of you if you did, a great kindness. But do you *have* to accede to it? What if it were not nine months, but nine years? Or longer still? What if the director of the hospital says, "Tough luck, I agree, but you've now got to stay in bed, with the violinist plugged into you, for the rest of your life. Because remember this. All persons have a right to life, and violinists are persons. Granted you have a right to decide what happens in and to your body, but a person's right to life outweighs your right to decide what happens in and to your body. So you cannot ever be unplugged from him." I imagine you would regard this as outrageous, which suggests that something really is wrong with that plausible-sounding argument I mentioned a moment ago.

In this case, of course, you were kidnapped; you didn't volunteer for the operation that plugged the violinist into your kidneys. Can those who oppose abortion on the ground I mentioned make an exception for a pregnancy due to rape? Certainly. They can say that persons have a right to life only if they didn't come into existence because of rape; or they can say that all persons have a right to life, but that some have less of a right to life than others, in particular, that those who came into existence because of rape have less. But these statements have a rather unpleasant sound. Surely the question of whether you have a right to life at all, or how much of it you have, shouldn't turn on the question of whether or not you are the product of a rape. And in fact the people who oppose abortion on the ground I mentioned do not make this distinction, and hence do not make an exception in case of rape.

Nor do they make an exception for a case in which the mother has to spend the nine months of her pregnancy in bed. They would agree that would be a great pity, and hard on the mother; but all the same, all persons have a right to life, the fetus is a person, and so on. I suspect, in fact, that they would not make an exception for a case in which, miraculously enough, the pregnancy went on for nine years, or even the rest of the mother's life.

Some won't even make an exception for a case in which continuation of the pregnancy is likely to shorten the mother's life; they regard abortion as impermissible even to save the mother's life. Such cases are nowadays very rare, and many opponents of abortion do not accept this extreme view. All the same, it is a good place to begin: a number of points of interest come out in respect to it.

1. Let us call the view that abortion is impermissible even to save the mother's life "the extreme view." I want to suggest first that it does not issue from the argument I mentioned earlier without the addition of some fairly powerful premises. Suppose a woman has become pregnant, and now learns that she has a cardiac condition such that she will die if she carries the baby to term. What may be done for her? The fetus, being a person, has a right to life, but as the mother is a person too, so has she a right to life. Presumably they have an equal right to life. How is it supposed to come out that an abortion may not be performed? If mother and child have an equal right to life, shouldn't we perhaps flip a coin? Or should we add to the mother's right to life her right to decide what happens in and to her body, which everybody seems to be ready to grant—the sum of her rights now outweighing the fetus' right to life?

The most familiar argument here is the following. We are told that performing the abortion would be directly killing the child, whereas doing nothing would not be killing the mother, but only letting her die. Moreover, in killing the child, one would be killing an innocent person, for the child has committed no crime, and is not aiming at his mother's death. And then there are a variety of ways in which this might be continued. (1) But as directly killing an innocent person is always and absolutely impermissible, an abortion may not be performed. Or, (2) as directly killing an innocent person is murder, and murder is always and absolutely impermissible, an abortion may not be performed. Or, (3) as one's duty to refrain from directly killing an innocent person is more stringent than one's duty to keep a person from dying, an abortion may not be performed. Or, (4) if one's only options are directly killing an innocent person or letting a person die, one must prefer letting the person die, and thus an abortion may not be performed.

Some people seem to have thought that these are not further premises which must be added if the conclusion is to be reached, but that they follow from the very fact that an innocent person has a right to life. But this seems to me to be a mistake, and perhaps the simplest way to show this is to bring out that while we must certainly grant that innocent persons have a right to life, the theses in (1) through (4) are all false. Take (2), for example. If directly killing an innocent person is murder, and thus is impermissible, then the mother's directly killing the innocent person inside her is murder, and thus is impermissible. But it cannot seriously be thought to be murder if the mother performs an abortion on herself to save her life. It cannot seriously be said that she *must* refrain, that she *must* sit passively by and wait for her death. Let us look again at the case of you and the violinist. There you are, in bed with the violinist, and the director of the hospital says to you, "It's all most distressing, and I deeply sympathize, but you see this is putting an additional strain on your kidneys, and you'll be dead within the month. But you *have* to stay where you are all the same. Because unplugging you would be directly killing an innocent violinist, and that's murder, and that's impermissible." If anything in the world is true, it is that you do not commit murder, you do not do what is impermissible, if you reach around to your back and unplug yourself from that violinist to save your life.

The main focus of attention in writings on abortion has been on what a third party may or may not do in answer to a request from a woman for an abortion. This is in a way understandable. Things being as they are, there isn't much a woman can safely do to abort herself. So the question asked is what a third party may do, and what the mother may do, if it is mentioned at all, is deduced, almost as an afterthought, from what it is concluded that third parties may do. But it seems to me that to treat the matter in this way is to refuse to grant to the mother that very status of person which is so firmly insisted on for the fetus. For we cannot simply read off what a person may do from what a third party may do. Suppose you find yourself trapped in a tiny house with a growing child. I mean a very tiny house, and a rapidly growing child—you are already up against the wall of the house and in few minutes you'll be crushed to death. The child on the other hand won't be crushed to death; if nothing is done to stop him from growing he'll be hurt, but in the end he'll simply burst open the house and walk out a free man. Now I could well understand it if a bystander were to say, "There's nothing we can do for you. We cannot choose between your life and his, we cannot be the ones to decide who is to live, we cannot intervene." But it cannot be concluded that you too can do nothing, that you cannot attack it to save your life. However innocent the child may be, you do not have to wait passively while it crushes you to death. Perhaps a pregnant woman is vaguely felt to have the status of house, to which we don't allow the right of self-defense. But if the woman houses the child, it should be remembered that she is a person who houses it.

I should perhaps stop to stay explicitly that I am not claiming that people have a right to do anything whatever to save their lives. I think, rather, that there are drastic limits to the right of self-defense. If someone threatens you with death unless you torture someone else to death, I think you have not the right, even to save your life, to do so. But the case under consideration here is very different. In our case there are only two people involved, one whose life is threatened, and one who threatens it. Both are innocent: the one who is threatened is not threatened because of any fault, the one who threatens does not threaten because of any fault. For this reason we may feel that we bystanders cannot intervene. But the person threatened can.

In sum, a woman surely can defend her life against the threat to it posed by the unborn child, even if doing so involves its death. And this shows not merely that the theses in (1) through (4) are false; it shows also that the extreme view of abortion is false, and so we need not canvass any other possible ways of arriving at it from the argument I mentioned at the outset.

2. The extreme view could of course be weakened to say that while abortion is permissible to save the mother's life, it may not be performed by a third party, but only by the mother herself. But this cannot be right either. For what we have to keep in mind is that the mother and the unborn child are not like two tenants in a small house which has, by an unfortunate mistake, been rented to both: the mother *owns* the house. The fact that she does adds to the offensiveness of deducing that the mother can do nothing from the supposition that third parties can do nothing. But it does more than this: it casts a bright light on the supposition that third parties can do nothing. Certainly it lets us see that a third party who says "I cannot choose between you" is fooling himself if he thinks this is impartiality. If Jones has found and fastened on a certain coat, which he needs to keep him from freezing, but which Smith also needs to keep him from freezing, then it is not impartiality that says "I cannot choose between you" when Smith owns the coat. Women have said again and again "This body is *my* body!" and they have reason to feel angry, reason to feel that it has been like shouting into the wind. Smith, after all, is hardly likely to bless us if we say to him. "Of course it's your coat anybody would grant that it is. But no one may choose between you and Jones who is to have it."

We should really ask what it is that says no one may choose in the face of the fact that the body that houses the child is the mother's body. It may be simply a failure to appreciate this fact. But it may be something more interesting, namely the sense that one has a right to refuse to lay hands on people, even where it would be just and fair to do so, even where justice seems to require that somebody do so. This justice might call for somebody to get Smith's coat back from Jones and yet you have a right to refuse to be the one to lay hands on Jones, a right to refuse to do physical violence to him. This, I think, must be granted. But then what should be said is not "no one may choose," but only "*I* cannot choose," and indeed not even this, but "*I* will not *act*," leaving it open that somebody else can or should, and in particular that anyone in a position of authority, with the job of securing people's rights, both can and should. So this is no difficulty. I have not been arguing that any given third party must accede to the mother's request that he perform an abortion to save her life, but only that he may.

I suppose that in some views of human life the mother's body is only on loan to her, the loan not being one which gives her any prior claim to it. One who held this view might well think it impartiality to say "I cannot choose." But I shall simply ignore this possibility. My own view is that if a human being has any just, prior claim to anything at all, he has a just, prior claim to his own body. And perhaps this needn't be argued for here anyway, since, as I mentioned, the arguments against abortion we are looking at do grant that the woman has a right to decide what happens in and to her body.

But although they do grant it, I have tried to show that they do not take seriously what is done in granting it. I suggest the same thing will reappear even more clearly when we turn away from cases in which the mother's life is at stake, and attend, as I propose we now do, to the vastly more common cases in which a woman wants an abortion for some less weighty reason than preserving her own life.

3. Where the mother's life is not at stake, the argument I mentioned at the outset seems to have a much stronger pull. "Everyone has a right to life, so the unborn person has a right to life." And isn't the child's right to life weightier than anything other than the mother's own right to life, which she might put forward as ground for an abortion?

This argument treats the right to life as if it were unproblematic. It is not, and this seems to me to be precisely the source of the mistake.

For we should now, at long last, ask what it comes to, to have a right to life. In some views having a right to life includes having a right to be given at least the bare minimum one needs for continued life. But suppose that what in fact *is* the bare minimum a man needs for continued life is something he has no right at all to be given? If I am sick unto death, and the only thing that will save my life is the touch of Henry Fonda's cool hand on my fevered brow, then all the same, I have no right to be given the touch of Henry Fonda's cool hand on my fevered brow. It would be frightfully nice of him to fly in from the West Coast to provide it. It would be less nice, though no doubt well meant, if my friends flew out to the West Coast and carried Henry Fonda back with them. But I have no right at all against anybody that he should do this for me. Or again, to return to the story I told earlier, the fact that for continued life that violinist needs the continued use of your kidneys does not establish that he has a right to be given the continued use of your kidneys. He certainly has no right against you that *you* should give him continued use of your kidneys. For nobody has any right to use your kidneys unless you give him such a right; and nobody has the right against you that you shall give him this right—if you do allow him to go on using your kidneys, this is a kindness on your part, and not something he can claim from you as his due. Nor has he any right against anybody else that *they* should give him continued use of your kidneys. Certainly he had no right against the Society of Music Lovers that they should plug him into you in the first place. And if you now start to unplug yourself, having learned that you will otherwise have to spend nine years in bed with him, there is nobody in the world who must try to prevent you, in order to see to it that he is given something he has a right to be given.

Some people are rather stricter about the right to life. In their view, it does not include the right to be given anything, but amounts to, and only to, the right not to be killed by anybody. But here a related difficulty arises. If everybody is to refrain from killing that violinist, then everybody must refrain from doing a great many different sorts of things. Everybody must refrain from slitting his throat, everybody must refrain from shooting him—and everybody must refrain from unplugging you from him. But does he have a right against everybody that they shall refrain from unplugging you from him? To refrain from doing this is to allow him to continue to use your kidneys. It could be argued that he has a right against us that *we* should allow him to continue to use your kidneys. That is, while he had no right against us that we should give him the use of your kidneys, it might be argued that he anyway has a right against us that we shall not now intervene and deprive him of the use of your kidneys. I shall come back to third-party interventions later. But certainly the violinist has no right against you that *you* shall allow him to continue to use your kidneys. As I said, if you do allow him to use them, it is a kindness on your part, and not something you owe him.

The difficulty I point to here is not peculiar to the right to life. It reappears in connection with all the other natural rights; and it is something which an adequate account of rights must deal with. For present purposes it is enough just to draw attention to it. But I would stress that I am not arguing that people do not have a right to life—quite to the contrary, it seems to me that the primary control we must place on the acceptability of an account of rights is that it should turn out in that account to be a truth that all persons have a right to life. I am arguing only that having a right to life does not guarantee having either a right to be given the use of or a right to be allowed continued use of another person's body—even if one needs it for life itself. So the right to life will not serve the opponents of abortion in the very simple and clear way in which they seem to have thought it would.

4. There is another way to bring out the difficulty. In the most ordinary sort of case, to deprive someone of what he has a right to is to treat him unjustly. Suppose a boy and his small brother are jointly given a box of chocolates for Christmas. If the older boy takes the box and refuses to give his brother any of the chocolates, he is unjust to him, for the brother has been given a right to half of them. But suppose that, having learned that otherwise it means nine years in bed with that violinist, you unplug yourself from him. You surely are not being unjust to him, for you gave him no right to use your kidneys, and no one else can have given him any such right. But we have to notice that in unplugging yourself, you are killing him; and violinists, like everybody else, have a right to life, and thus in the view we were considering just now, the right not to be killed. So here you do what he supposedly has a right you shall not do, but you do not act unjustly to him in doing it.

The emendation which may be made at this point is this: the right to life consists not in the right not to be killed, but rather in the right not to be killed unjustly. This runs a risk of circularity, but never mind: it would enable us to square the fact that the violinist has a right to life with the fact that you do not act unjustly toward him in unplugging yourself, thereby killing him. For if you do not kill him unjustly, you do not violate his right to life, and so it is no wonder you do him no injustice.

But if this emendation is accepted, the gap in the argument against abortion stares us plainly in the face: it is by no means enough to show that the fetus is a person, and to remind us that all persons have a right to life—we need to be shown also that killing the fetus violates its right to life, i.e., that abortion is unjust killing. And is it?

I suppose we may take it as a datum that in a case of pregnancy due to rape the mother has not given the unborn person a right to the use of her body for food and shelter. Indeed, in what pregnancy could it be supposed that the mother has given the unborn person such a right? It is not as if there were unborn persons drifting about the world, to whom a woman who wants a child says "I invite you in."

But it might be argued that there are other ways one can have acquired a right to the use of another person's body than by having been invited to use it by that person. Suppose a woman voluntarily indulges in intercourse, knowing of the chance it will issue in pregnancy, and then she does become pregnant; is she not in part responsible for the presence, in fact the very existence, of the unborn person inside her? No doubt she did not invite it in. But doesn't her partial responsibility for its being there itself give it a right to the use of her body? If so, then her aborting it would be more like the boy's taking away the chocolates, and less like your unplugging yourself from the violinist— doing so would be depriving it of what it does have a right to, and thus would be doing it an injustice.

And then, too, it might be asked whether or not she can kill it even to save her own life: If she voluntarily called it into existence, how can she now kill it, even in self-defense?

The first thing to be said about this is that it is something new. Opponents of abortion have been so concerned to make out the independence of the fetus, in order to establish that it has a right to life, just as its mother does, that they have tended to overlook the possible support they might gain from making out that the fetus is *dependent* on the mother, in order to establish that she has a special kind of responsibility for it, a responsibility that gives it rights against her which are not possessed by any independent person—such as an ailing violinist who is a stranger to her.

On the other hand, this argument would give the unborn person a right to its mother's body only if her pregnancy resulted from a voluntary act, undertaken in full knowledge of the chance a pregnancy might result from it. It would leave out entirely the unborn person whose existence is due to rape. Pending the availability of some further argument, then, we would be left with the conclusion that unborn persons whose existence is due to rape have no right to the use of their mothers' bodies, and thus that aborting them is not depriving them of anything they have a right to and hence is not unjust killing.

And we should also notice that it is not at all plain that this argument really does go even as far as it purports to. For there are cases and cases, and the details make a difference. If the room is stuffy, and I therefore open a window to air it, and a burglar climbs in, it would be absurd to say, "Ah, now he can stay, she's given him a right to the use of her house—for she is partially responsible for his presence there, having voluntarily done what enabled him to get in, in full knowledge that there are such things as burglars, and that burglars burgle." It would be still more absurd to say this if I had had bars installed outside my windows, precisely to prevent burglars from getting in, and a burglar got in only because of a defect in the bars. It remains equally absurd if we imagine it is not a burglar who climbs in, but an innocent person who blunders or falls in. Again, suppose it were like this: people-seeds drift about in the air like pollen, and if you open your windows, one may drift in and take root in your carpets or uphol-stery. You don't want children, so you fix up your windows with fine mesh screens, the very best you can buy. As can happen, however, and on very, very rare occasions does happen, one of the screens is defective; and a seed drifts in and takes root. Does the person-plant who now develops have a right to the use of your house? Surely not—despite the fact that you voluntarily opened your windows, you knowingly kept car-pets and upholstered furniture, and you knew that screens were sometimes defective. Someone may argue that you are responsible for its rooting, that it does have a right to your house, because after all you *could* have lived out your life with bare floors and furniture, or with sealed windows and doors. But this won't do—for by the same token anyone can avoid a pregnancy due to rape by having a hysterectomy, or anyway by never leaving home without a (reliable!) army.

It seems to me that the argument we are looking at can establish at most that there are *some* cases in which the unborn person has a right to the use of its mother's body, and therefore *some* cases in which abortion is unjust killing. There is room for much dis-cussion and argument as to precisely which, if any. But I think we should sidestep this issue and leave it open, for at any rate the argument certainly does not establish that all abortion is unjust killing.

5. There is room for yet another argument here, however. We surely must all grant that there may be cases in which it would be morally indecent to detach a person from your body at the cost of his life. Suppose you learn that what the violinist needs is not nine years of your life, but only one hour: all you need do to save his life is to spend one hour in that bed with him. Suppose also that letting him use your kidneys for that one hour would not affect your health in the slightest. Admittedly you were kidnapped. Admittedly you did not give anyone permission to plug him into you. Nevertheless it seems to me plain you *ought* to allow him to use your kidneys for that hour—it would be indecent to refuse.

Again, suppose pregnancy lasted only an hour, and constituted no threat to life or health. And suppose that a woman becomes pregnant as a result of rape. Admittedly she did not voluntarily do anything to bring about the existence of a child. Admittedly she did nothing at all which would give the unborn person a right to the use of her body. All the same it might well be said, as in the newly emended violinist story, that she *ought* to allow it to remain for that hour—that it would be indecent in her to refuse.

Now some people are inclined to use the term "right" in such a way that it follows from the fact that you ought to allow a person to use your body for the hour he needs, that he has a right to use your body for the hour he needs, even though he has not been given that right by any person or act. They may say that it follows also that if you re-fuse, you act unjustly toward him. This use of the term is perhaps so common that it cannot be called wrong; nevertheless it seems to me to be an unfortunate loosening of what we would do better to keep a tight rein on. Suppose that box of chocolates I men-tioned earlier had not been given to both boys jointly, but was given only to the older boy. There he sits, stolidly eating his way through the box, his small brother watching enviously. Here we are likely to say "You ought not to be so mean. You ought to give your brother some of those chocolates." My own view is that it just does not follow from the truth of this that the brother has any right to any of the chocolates. If the boy refuses to give his brother any, he is greedy, stingy, callous—but not unjust. I suppose that the people I have in mind will say it does follow that the brother has a right to some of the chocolates, and thus that the boy does act unjustly if he refuses to give his brother any. But the effect of saying this is to obscure what we should keep distinct, namely the difference between the boy's refusal in this case and the boy's refusal in the earlier case, in which the box was given to both boys jointly, and in which the small brother thus had what was from any point of view clear title to half.

A further obligation to so using the term "right" that from the fact that A ought to do a thing for B, it follows that B has a right against A that A do it for him, is that it is going to make the question of whether or not a man has a right to a thing turn on how easy it is to provide him with it; and this seems not merely unfortunate, but morally unacceptable. Take the case of Henry Fonda again. I said earlier that I had no right to the touch of his cool hand on my fevered brow, even though I needed it to save my life. I said it would be frightfully nice of him to fly in from the West Coast to provide me with it, but that I had no right against him that he should do so. But suppose he isn't on the West Coast. Suppose he has only to walk across the room, place a hand briefly on my brow—and lo, my life is saved. Then surely he ought to do it, it would be indecent to refuse. Is it to be said "Ah, well, it follows that in this case she has a right to the touch of his hand on her brow, and so it would be an injustice in him to refuse"? So that I have a right to it when it is easy for him to provide it, though no right when it's hard? It's rather a shocking idea that anyone's rights should fade away and disappear as it gets harder and harder to accord them to him.

So my own view is that even though you ought to let the violinist use your kidneys for the one hour he needs, we should not conclude that he has a right to do so—we should say that if you refuse, you are, like the boy who owns all the chocolates and will give none away, self-centered and callous, indecent in fact, but not unjust. And similarly, that even supposing a case in which a woman pregnant due to rape ought to allow the unborn person to use her body for the hour he needs, we should not conclude that he has a right to do so; we should conclude that she is self-centered, callous, indecent, but not unjust, if she refuses. The complaints are no less grave; they are just different. However, there is no need to insist on this point. If anyone does wish to deduce "he has a right" from "you ought," then all the same he must surely grant that there are cases in which it is not morally required of you that you allow that violinist to use your kidneys, and in which he does not have a right to use them, and in which you do not do him an injustice if you refuse. And so also for mother and unborn child. Except in such cases as the unborn person has a right to demand it—and we were leaving open the possibility that there may be such cases—nobody is morally *required* to make large sacrifices, of health, of all other interests and concerns, of all other duties and commitments, for nine years, or even for nine months, in order to keep another person alive.

6. We have in fact to distinguish between two kinds of Samaritan: the Good Samaritan and what we might call the Minimally Decent Samaritan. The story of the Good Samaritan, you will remember, goes like this:

> A certain man went down from Jerusalem to Jericho, and fell among thieves, which stripped him of his raiment, and wounded him, and departed, leaving him half dead.
>
> And by chance there came down a certain priest that way; and when he saw him, he passed by on the other side.
>
> And likewise a Levite, when he was at the place, came and looked on him, and passed by on the other side.

But a certain Samaritan, as he journeyed, came where he was; and when he saw him he had compassion on him.

And went to him, and bound up his wounds, pouring in oil and wine, and set him on his own beast, and brought him to an inn, and took care of him.

And on the morrow, when he departed, he took out two pence, and gave them to the host, and said unto him, "Take care of him; and whatsoever thou spendest more, when I come again, I will repay thee." (Luke 10:30–35)

The Good Samaritan went out of his way, at some cost to himself, to help one in need of it. We are not told what the options were, that is, whether or not the priest and the Levite could have helped by doing less than the Good Samaritan did, but assuming they could have, then the fact they did nothing at all shows they were not even Minimally Decent Samaritans, not because they were not Samaritans, but because they were not even minimally decent.

These things are a matter of degree, of course, but there is a difference, and it comes out perhaps most clearly in the story of Kitty Genovese, who, as you will remember, was murdered while thirty-eight people watched or listened, and did nothing at all to help her. A Good Samaritan would have rushed out to give direct assistance against the murderer. Or perhaps we had better allow that it would have been a Splendid Samaritan who did this, on the ground that it would have involved a risk of death for himself. But the thirty-eight not only did not do this, they did not even trouble to pick up a phone to call the police. Minimally Decent Samaritanism would call for doing at least that, and their not having done it was monstrous.

After telling the story of the Good Samaritan, Jesus said "Go, and do thou likewise." Perhaps he meant that we are morally required to act as the Good Samaritan did. Perhaps he was urging people to do more than is morally required of them. At all events it seems plain that it was not morally required of any of the thirty-eight that he rush out to give direct assistance at the risk of his own life, and that it is not morally required of anyone that he give long stretches of his life—nine years or nine months—to sustaining the life of a person who has no special right (we were leaving open the possibility of this) to demand it.

Indeed, with one rather striking class of exceptions, no one in any country in the world is *legally* required to do anywhere near as much as this for anyone else. The class of exceptions is obvious. My main concern here is not the state of the law in respect to abortion, but it is worth drawing attention to the fact that in no state in this country is any man compelled by law to be even a Minimally Decent Samaritan to any person; there is no law under which charges could be brought against the thirty-eight who stood by while Kitty Genovese died. By contrast, in most states in this country women are compelled by law to be not merely Minimally Decent Samaritans, but Good Samaritans to unborn persons inside them. This doesn't by itself settle anything one way or the other, because it may well be argued that there should be laws in this country—as there are in many European countries—compelling at least Minimally Decent Samaritanism. But it does show that there is a gross injustice in the existing state of the law. And it shows also that the groups currently working against liberalization of abortion laws, in fact working toward having it declared unconstitutional for a state to permit abortion, had better start working for the adoption of Good Samaritan laws generally, or earn the charge that they are acting in bad faith.

I should think, myself, that Minimally Decent Samaritan laws would be one thing, Good Samaritan laws quite another, and in fact highly improper. But we are not here concerned with the law. What we should ask is not whether anybody should be compelled by law to be a Good Samaritan, but whether we must accede to a situation in which somebody is being compelled—by nature, perhaps—to be a Good Samaritan. We have, in other words, to look now at third-party interventions. I have been arguing that no person is morally required to make large sacrifices to sustain the life of another who has no right to demand them, and this even where the sacrifices do not include life itself; we are not morally required to be Good Samaritans or anyway Very Good Samaritans to one another. But what if a man cannot extricate himself from such a situation? What if he appeals to us to extricate him? It seems to me plain that there are cases in which we can, cases in which a Good Samaritan would extricate him. There you are, you were kidnapped, and nine years in bed with that violinist lie ahead of you. You have your own life to lead. You are sorry, but you simply cannot see giving up so much of your life to the sustaining of his. You cannot extricate yourself, and ask us to do so. I should have thought that—in light of his having no right to the use of your body—it was obvious that we do not have to accede to your being forced to give up so much. We can do what you ask. There is no injustice to the violinist in our doing so.

7. Following the lead of the opponents of abortion, I have throughout been speaking of the fetus merely as a person, and what I have been asking is whether or not the argument we began with, which proceeds only from the fetus' being a person, really does establish its conclusion. I have argued that it does not.

But of course there are arguments and arguments, and it may be said that I have simply fastened on the wrong one. It may be said that what is important is not merely the fact that the fetus is a person, but that it is a person for whom the woman has a special kind of responsibility issuing from the fact that she is its mother. And it might be argued that all my analogies are therefore irrelevant—for you do not have that special kind of responsibility for that violinist, Henry Fonda does not have that special kind of responsibility for me. And our attention might be drawn to the fact that men and women both *are* compelled by law to provide support for their children.

I have in effect dealt (briefly) with this argument in section 4 above; but a (still briefer) recapitulation now may be in order. Surely we do not have any such "special responsibility" for a person unless we have assumed it, explicitly or implicitly. If a set of parents do not try to prevent pregnancy, do not obtain an abortion, and then at the time of birth of the child do not put it out for adoption, then they have assumed responsibility for it, they have given it rights, and they cannot *now* withdraw support from it at the cost of its life because they now find it difficult to go on providing for it. But if they have taken all reasonable precautions against having a child, they do not simply by virtue of their biological relationship to the child who comes into existence have a special responsibility for it. They may wish to assume responsibility for it, or they may not wish to. And I am suggesting that if assuming responsibility for it would require large sacrifices, then they may refuse. A Good Samaritan would not refuse— or anyway, a Splendid Samaritan, if the sacrifices that had to be made were enormous. But then so would a Good Samaritan assume responsibility for that violinist; so would Henry Fonda, if he is a Good Samaritan, fly in from the West Coast and assume responsibility for me.

8. My argument will be found unsatisfactory on two counts by many of those who want to regard abortion as morally permissible. First, while I do argue that abortion is not impermissible, I do not argue that it is always permissible. There may well be cases in which carrying the child to term requires only Minimally Decent Samaritanism of the mother, and this is a standard we must not fall below. I am inclined to think it a merit of my account precisely that it does *not* give a general yes or a general no. It allows for and supports our sense that, for example, a sick and desperately frightened fourteen-year-old schoolgirl, pregnant due to rape, may *of course* choose abortion, and that any law which rules this out is an insane law. And it also allows for and supports our sense that in other cases resort to abortion is even positively indecent. It would be indecent in the woman to request an abortion, and indecent in a doctor to perform it, if she is in her seventh month, and wants the abortion just to avoid the nuisance of postponing a trip abroad. The very fact that the arguments I have been drawing attention to treat all cases of abortion, or even all cases of abortion in which the mother's life is not at stake, as morally on a par ought to have made them suspect at the outset.

Secondly, while I am arguing for the permissibility of abortion in some cases, I am not arguing for the right to secure the death of the unborn child. It is easy to confuse these two things in that up to a certain point in the life of the fetus it is not able to survive outside the mother's body; hence removing it from her body guarantees its death. But they are importantly different. I have argued that you are not morally required to spend nine months in bed, sustaining the life of that violinist; but to say this is by no means to say that if, when you unplug yourself, there is a miracle and he survives, you then have a right to turn round and slit his throat. You may detach yourself even if this costs him his life; you have no right to be guaranteed his death, by some other means, if unplugging yourself does not kill him. There are some people who will feel dissatisfied by this feature of my argument. A woman may be utterly devastated by the thought of a child, a bit of herself, put out for adoption and never seen or heard of again. She may therefore want not merely that the child be detached from her, but more, that it die. Some opponents of abortion are inclined to regard this as beneath contempt—thereby showing insensitivity to what is surely a powerful source of despair. All the same, I agree that the desire for the child's death is not one which anybody may gratify, should it turn out to be possible to detach the child alive.

At this place, however, it should be remembered that we have only been pretending throughout that the fetus is a human being from the moment of conception. A very early abortion is surely not the killing of a person, and so is not dealt with by anything I have said here.

MARY ANNE WARREN

The Moral Significance of Birth

MARY ANNE WARREN currently teaches at San Francisco State University. She has published widely in applied ethics and feminist philosophy.

English common law treats the moment of live birth as the point at which a legal person comes into existence. Although abortion has often been prohibited, it has almost never been classified as homicide. In contrast, infanticide generally is classified as a form of homicide, even where (as in England) there are statutes designed to mitigate the severity of the crime in certain cases. But many people—including some feminists—now favor the extension of equal legal rights to some or all fetuses. The extension of legal personhood to fetuses would not only threaten women's right to choose abortion, but also undermine other fundamental rights. I will argue that because of these dangers, birth remains the most appropriate place to mark the existence of a new legal person. . . .

SPEAKING OF RIGHTS

. . . Some feminist philosophers have suggested that the very concept of a moral right may be inconsistent with the social nature of persons. Elizabeth Wolgast argues convincingly that this concept has developed within an atomistic model of the social world, in which persons are depicted as self-sufficient and exclusively self-interested individuals whose relationships with one another are essentially competitive. As Wolgast notes, such an atomistic model is particularly inappropriate in the context of pregnancy, birth, and parental responsibility. . . . But is the concept of a moral right necessarily incompatible with the social nature of human beings? Rights are indeed individualistic, in that they can be ascribed to individuals, as well as to groups. But respect for moral rights need not be based upon an excessively individualistic view of human nature. A more socially perceptive account of moral rights is possible, provided that we reject two common assumptions about the theoretical foundations of moral rights. These assumptions are widely accepted by mainstream philosophers, but rarely stated and still more rarely defended.

The first is what I shall call the intrinsic-properties assumption. This is the view that the only facts that can justify the ascription of basic moral rights or moral standing to individuals are facts about *the intrinsic properties of those individuals.* Philosophers who accept this view disagree about which of the intrinsic properties of individuals are relevant to the ascription of rights. They agree, however, that relational properties—such as being loved, or being part of a social community or biological ecosystem—cannot be relevant.

The second is what I shall call the single-criterion assumption. This is the view that there is some single property, the presence or absence of which divides the world into

164

those things which have moral rights or moral standing, and those things which do not. Christopher Stone locates this assumption within a more general theoretical approach, which he calls "moral monism." Moral monists believe that the goal of moral philosophy is the production of a coherent set of principles, sufficient to provide definitive answers to all possible moral dilemmas. Among these principles, the monist typically assumes, will be one that identifies some key property which is such that, "Those beings that possess the key property count morally . . . [while those] things that lack it are all utterly irrelevant, except as resources for the benefit of those things that do count."

Together, the intrinsic-properties and single-criterion assumptions preclude any adequate account of the social foundations of moral rights. The intrinsic-properties assumption requires us to regard all personal or other relationships among individuals or groups as wholly irrelevant to basic moral rights. The single-criterion assumption requires us to deny that there can be a variety of sound reasons for ascribing moral rights, and a variety of things and beings to which some rights may appropriately be ascribed. Both assumptions are inimical to a feminist approach to moral theory, as well as to approaches that are less anthropocentric and more environmentally adequate. The prevalence of these assumptions helps to explain why few mainstream philosophers believe that birth can in any way alter the infant's moral rights.

PROTECTING NONPERSONS

If we are to justify a general moral distinction between abortion and infanticide, we must answer two questions. First, why should infanticide be discouraged, rather than treated as a matter for individual decision? And second, why should sentient fetuses not be given the same protections that law and common sense morality accord to infants? But before turning to these two questions, it is necessary to make a more general point.

Persons have sound reasons for treating one another as moral equals. These reasons derive from both self-interest and altruistic concern for others—which, because of our social nature, are often very difficult to distinguish. Human persons—and perhaps all persons—normally come into existence only in and through social relationships. Sentience may begin to emerge without much direct social interaction, but it is doubtful that a child reared in total isolation from human or other sentient (or apparently sentient) beings could develop the capacities for self-awareness and social interaction that are essential to personhood. The recognition of the fundamentally social nature of persons can only strengthen the case for moral equality, since social relationships are undermined and distorted by inequalities that are perceived as unjust. There may be many nonhuman animals who have enough capacity for self-awareness and social interaction to be regarded as persons, with equal basic moral rights. But, whether or not this is true, it is certainly true that if any things have full and equal basic moral rights then persons do.

However we cannot conclude that, because all persons have equal basic moral rights, it is always wrong to extend strong moral protections to beings that are not persons. Those who accept the single-criterion assumption may find that a plausible inference. By now, however, most thoughtful people recognize the need to protect vulnerable elements of the natural world—such as endangered plant and animal species, rainforests, and rivers—from further destruction at human hands. . . . Although destroying them is not murder, it is an act of vandalism which later generations will mourn.

It is probably not crucial whether or not we say that endangered species and natural habitats have a moral right to our protection. What is crucial is that we recognize and act upon the need to protect them. Yet certain contemporary realities argue for an increased willingness to ascribe rights to impersonal elements of the natural world. Americans, at least, are likely to be more sensitive to appeals and demands couched in terms of rights than those that appeal to less familiar concepts, such as inherent value. So central are rights to our common moral idiom, that to deny that trees have rights is to risk being thought to condone the reckless destruction of rainforests and redwood groves. If we want to communicate effectively about the need to protect the natural world—and to protect it for its own sake as well as our own—then we may be wise to develop theories that permit us to ascribe at least some moral rights to some things that are clearly not persons.

Parallel issues arise with respect to the moral status of the newborn infant. As Wolgast argues, it is much more important to understand our responsibilities to protect and care for infants than to insist that they have exactly the same moral rights as older human beings. Yet to deny that infants have equal basic moral rights is to risk being thought to condone infanticide and the neglect and abuse of infants. Here too, effective communication about human moral responsibilities seems to demand the ascription of rights to beings that lack certain properties that are typical of persons. But, of course, that does not explain why we have these responsibilities towards infants in the first place.

WHY PROTECT INFANTS?

. . . Although the human newborn may have no intrinsic properties that can ground a moral right to life stronger than that of a fetus just before birth, its emergence into the social world makes it appropriate to treat it as if it had such a stronger right. This, in effect, is what the law has done, through the doctrine that a person begins to exist at birth. Those who accept the intrinsic-properties assumption can only regard this doctrine as a legal fiction. However, it is a fiction that we would have difficulty doing without. If the line were not drawn at birth, then I think we would have to draw it at some point rather soon thereafter, as many other societies have done.

Another reason for condemning infanticide is that, at least in relatively privileged nations like our own, infants whose parents cannot raise them can usually be placed with people who will love them and take good care of them. This means that infanticide is rarely in the infant's own best interests, and would often deprive some potential adoptive individual or family of a great benefit. It also means that the prohibition of infanticide need not impose intolerable burdens upon parents (especially women). A rare parent might think it best to kill a healthy infant rather than permitting it to be reared by others, but a persuasive defense of that claim would require special circumstances. For instance, when abortion is unavailable and women face savage abuses for supposed sexual transgressions, those who resort to infanticide to conceal an "illegitimate" birth may be doing only what they must. But where enforcement of the sexual double standard is less brutal, abortion and adoption can provide alternatives that most women would prefer to infanticide.

Some might wonder whether adoption is really preferable to infanticide, at least from the parent's point of view. Judith Thomson notes that, "A woman may be utterly devastated by the thought of a child, a bit of herself, put out for adoption and never seen or heard of again." From the standpoint of narrow self-interest, it might not be irrational to prefer the death of the child to such a future. Yet few would wish to resolve this problem by legalizing infanticide. The evolution of more open adoption procedures which permit more contact between the adopted child and the biological parent(s) might lessen the psychological pain often associated with adoption. But that would be at best a partial solution. More basic is the provision of better social support for child-rearers, so that parents are not forced by economic necessity to surrender their children for adoption.

These are just some of the arguments for treating infants as legal persons, with an equal right to life. A more complete account might deal with the effects of the toleration of infanticide upon other moral norms. But the existence of such effects is unclear. Despite a tradition of occasional infanticide, the Arapesh appear in Mead's descriptions as gentle people who treat their children with great kindness and affection. The case against infanticide need not rest upon the questionable claim that the toleration of infanticide inevitably leads to the erosion of other moral norms. It is enough that most people today strongly desire that the lives of infants be protected, and that this can now be done without imposing intolerable burdens upon individuals or communities. . . .

WHY BIRTH MATTERS

I have defended what most regard as needing no defense, i.e., the ascription of an equal right to life to human infants. Under reasonably favorable conditions that policy can protect the rights and interests of all concerned, including infants, biological parents, and potential adoptive parents.

But if protecting infants is such a good idea, then why is it not a good idea to extend the same strong protections to sentient fetuses? The question is not whether sentient fetuses ought to be protected: of course they should. Most women readily accept the responsibility for doing whatever they can to ensure that their (voluntarily continued) pregnancies are successful, and that no avoidable harm comes to the fetus. Negligent or malevolent actions by third parties which result in death or injury to pregnant women or their potential children should be subject to moral censure and legal prosecution. A just and caring society would do much more than ours does to protect the health of all its members, including pregnant women. The question is whether the law should accord to late-term fetuses *exactly the same* protections as are accorded to infants and older human beings.

The case for doing so might seem quite strong. We normally regard not only infants, but all other postnatal human beings as entitled to strong legal protections *so long as they are either sentient or capable of an eventual return to sentience.* We do not also require that they demonstrate a capacity for thought, self-awareness, or social relationships before we conclude that they have an equal right to life. Such restrictive criteria would leave too much room for invidious discrimination. The eternal propensity of powerful groups to rationalize sexual, racial, and class oppression by claiming that members of the oppressed group are mentally or otherwise "inferior" leaves little hope that such restrictive criteria could be applied without bias. Thus, for human beings past the pre-natal stage, the capacity for sentience—or for a return to sentience—may be the only pragmatically defensible criterion for the ascription of full and equal basic rights. If so, then both theoretical simplicity and moral consistency may seem to require that we ex-tend the same protections to sentient human beings that have not yet been born as to those that have.

But there is one crucial consideration which this argument leaves out. It is impossible to treat fetuses *in utero* as if they were persons without treating women as if they were something less than persons. The extension of equal rights to sentient fetuses would inevitably license severe violations of women's basic rights to personal autonomy and physical security. In the first place, it would rule out most second-trimester abortions performed to protect the woman's life or health. Such abortions might sometimes be construed as a form of self-defense. But the right to self-defense is not usually taken to mean that one may kill innocent persons just because their continued existence poses some threat to one's own life or health. If abortion must be justified as self-defense, then it will rarely be performed until the woman is already in extreme danger, and perhaps not even then. Such a policy would cost some women their lives, while others would be subjected to needless suffering and permanent physical harm.

Other alarming consequences of the drive to extend more equal rights to fetuses are already apparent in the United States. In the past decade it has become increasingly common for hospitals or physicians to obtain court orders requiring women in labor to undergo Caesarean sections, against their will, for what is thought to be the good of the fetus. Such an extreme infringement of the woman's right to security against physi-cal assault would be almost unthinkable once the infant has been born. No parent or relative can legally be forced to undergo any surgical procedure, even possibly to save the life of a child, once it is born. But pregnant women can sometimes be forced to un-dergo major surgery, for the supposed benefit of the fetus. As George Annas points out, forced Caesareans threaten to reduce women to the status of inanimate objects—containers which may be opened at the will of others in order to get at their contents.

Perhaps the most troubling illustration of this trend is the case of Angie Carder, who died at George Washington University Medical Center in June 1987, two days after a court-ordered Caesarean section. Ms. Carder had suffered a recurrence of an earlier cancer, and was not expected to live much longer. Her physicians agreed that the fetus was too undeveloped to be viable, and that Carder herself was probably too weak to survive the surgery. Although she, her family, and the physicians were all opposed to a Caesarean delivery, the hospital administration—evidently believing it had a legal obligation to try to save the fetus—sought and obtained a court order to have it done. As predicted, both Carder and her infant died soon after the operation. This woman's rights to autonomy, physical integrity, and life itself were forfeit—not just because of her illness, but because of her pregnancy.

Such precedents are doubly alarming in the light of the development of new tech-niques of fetal therapy. As fetuses come to be regarded as patients, with rights that may be in direct conflict with those of their mothers, and as the *in utero* treatment of fetuses becomes more feasible, more and more pregnant women may be subjected against their will to dangerous and invasive medical interventions. If so, then we may be sure that there will be other Angie Carders.

Another danger in extending equal legal protections to sentient fetuses is that women will increasingly be blamed, and sometimes legally prosecuted, when they miscarry or give birth to premature, sick, or abnormal infants. It is reasonable to hold to the caretakers of infants legally responsible if their charges are harmed because of their avoidable negligence. But when a woman miscarries or gives birth to an abnormal infant, the cause of the harm might be traced to any of an enormous number of actions or circumstances which would not normally constitute any legal offense. She might have gotten too much exercise or too little, eaten the wrong foods or the wrong quantity of the right ones, or taken or failed to take certain drugs. She might have smoked, consumed alcohol, or gotten too little sleep. She might have "permitted" her health to be damaged by hard work, by unsafe employment conditions, by the lack of affordable medical care, by living near a source of industrial pollution, by a physically or mentally abuse partner, or in any number of other ways.

Are such supposed failures on the part of pregnant women potentially to be construed as child abuse or negligent homicide? If sentient fetuses are entitled to the same legal protections as infants, then it would seem so. The danger is not a merely theoretical one. Two years ago in San Diego, a woman whose son was born with brain damage and died several weeks later was charged with felony child neglect. It was said that she had been advised by her physician to avoid sex and illicit drugs, and to [go to] the hospital immediately if she noticed any bleeding. Instead, she had allegedly had sex with her husband, taken some inappropriate drug, and delayed getting to the hospital for what might have been several hours after the onset of bleeding.

In this case, the charges were eventually dismissed on the grounds that the child protection law invoked had not been intended to apply to cases of this kind. But the multiplication of such cases is inevitable if the strong legal protections accorded to infants are extended to sentient fetuses. A bill recently introduced in the Australian state of New South Wales would make women liable to criminal prosecution if they are found to have smoked during pregnancy, eaten unhealthful foods, or taken any other action which can be shown to have adversely affected the development of the fetus. Such an approach to the protection of the fetuses authorizes the legal regulation of virtually every aspect of women's public and private lives, and thus is incompatible with even the most minimal right to autonomy. Moreover, such laws are apt to prove counterproductive, since the fear of prosecution may deter poor or otherwise vulnerable women from seeking needed medical care during pregnancy. I am not suggesting that women whose apparent negligence causes prenatal harm to their infants should always be immune from criticism. However, if we want to improve the health of infants we would do better to provide the services women need to protect their health, rather than seeking to use the law to punish those whose prenatal care has been less than ideal.

There is yet another problem, which may prove temporary but which remains significant at this time. The extension of legal personhood to sentient fetuses would rule out most abortions performed because of severe fetal abnormalities, such as Down's Syndrome or spina bifida. Abortions performed following amniocentesis are usually done in the latter part of the second trimester, since it is usually not possible to obtain test results earlier. Methods of detecting fetal abnormalities at earlier stages, such as chorion biopsy, may eventually make late abortion for reasons of fetal abnormality unnecessary; but at present the safety of these methods is unproven.

The elimination of most such abortions might be a consequence that could be accepted, were the society willing to provide adequate support for the handicapped children and adults who would come into being as a result of this policy. However, our society is not prepared to do this. In the absence of adequate communally funded care for the handicapped, the prohibition of such abortions is exploitative of women. Of course, the male relatives of severely handicapped persons may also bear heavy burdens. Yet the heaviest portion of the daily responsibility generally falls upon mothers and other female relatives. If fetuses are not yet persons (and women are), then a respect for the equality of persons should lead to support for the availability of abortion in cases of severe fetal abnormality.

Such arguments will not persuade those who deeply believe that fetuses are already persons, with equal moral rights. How, they will ask, is denying legal equality to sentient fetuses different from denying it to any other powerless group of human beings? If some human beings are more equal than others, then how can any of us feel safe? The answer is twofold.

First, pregnancy is a relationship different from any other, including that between parents and already-born children. It is not just one of innumerable situations in which the rights of one individual may come into conflict with those of another; it is probably the *only* case in which the legal personhood of one human being is necessarily incompatible with that of another. Only in pregnancy is the organic functioning of one human individual biologically inseparable from that of another. This organic unity makes it impossible for others to provide the fetus with medical care or any other presumed benefit, except by doing something to or for the woman. To try to "protect" the fetus other than through her cooperation and consent is effectively to nullify her right to autonomy, and potentially to expose her to violent physical assaults such as would not be legally condoned in any other type of case. The uniqueness of pregnancy helps to explain why the toleration of abortion does not lead to the disenfranchisement of other groups of human beings, as opponents of abortion often claim. For biological as well as psychological reasons, "It is all but impossible to extrapolate from attitudes towards fetal life attitudes toward [other] existing human life."

But, granting the uniqueness of pregnancy, why is it *women's* rights that should be privileged? If women and fetuses cannot both be legal persons then why not favor fetuses, e.g., on the grounds that they are more helpless, or more innocent, or have a longer life expectancy? It is difficult to justify this apparent bias towards women without appealing to the empirical fact that women are already persons in the usual, non-legal sense—already thinking, self-aware, fully social beings—and fetuses are not. Regardless of whether we stress the intrinsic properties of persons, or the social and relational dimensions of personhood, this distinction remains. Even sentient fetuses do not yet have either the cognitive capacities or the richly interactive social involvements typical of persons.

This "not yet" is morally decisive. It is wrong to treat persons as if they do not have equal basic rights. Other things being equal, it is worse to deprive persons of their most basic moral and legal rights than to refrain from extending such rights to beings that are not persons. This is one important element of truth in the self-awareness criterion. If fetuses were already thinking, self-aware, socially responsive members of communities, then nothing could justify refusing them the equal protection of the law. In that case, we would sometimes be forced to balance the rights of the fetus against those of the woman, and sometimes the scales might be almost equally weighted. However, if women are persons and fetuses are not, then the balance must swing towards women's rights.

CONCLUSION

Birth is morally significant because it marks the end of one relationship and the beginning of others. It marks the end of pregnancy, a relationship so intimate that it is impossible to extend the equal protection of the law to fetuses without severely infringing women's most basic rights. Birth also marks the beginning of the infant's existence as a socially responsive member of a human community. Although the infant is not instantly transformed into a person at the moment of birth, it does become a biologically separate human being. As such, it can be known and cared for as a particular individual. It can also be vigorously protected without negating the basic rights of women. There are circumstances in which infanticide may be the best of a bad set of options. But our own society has both the ability and the desire to protect infants, and there is no reason why we should not do so.

We should not, however, seek to extend the same degree of protection to fetuses. Both late-term fetuses and newborn infants are probably capable of sentience. Both are precious to those who want children; and both need to be protected from a variety of possible harms. All of these factors contribute to the moral standing of the late-term fetus, which is substantial. However, to extend equal legal rights to fetuses is necessarily to deprive pregnant women of the rights to personal autonomy, physical integrity, and sometimes life itself. *There is room for only one person with full and equal rights inside a single human skin.* That is why it is birth, rather than sentience, viability, or some other prenatal milestone that must mark the beginning of legal parenthood.

ALAN DONAGAN

The Moral Status
of the Foetus

ALAN DONAGAN (1925–1991), originally from Australia, taught philosophy at the California Institute of Technology in Pasadena. His works include *Choice: The Essential Element in Human Action* (1987) and *Spinoza* (1989).

In investigating duties to others, it is convenient to begin with those that can arise between one man and another independently of any institution with which either may be associated. . . . The most familiar institutions, like those of civil society, such as parliament and the legal system, invest certain official positions with certain rights, duties, and immunities; specify certain kinds of action as impermissible and others as permissible; and provide for the adjudication of whether the rules have been violated, and for the imposition of penalties if they have. However, I shall consider any system of constitutive rules whatever to be an institution, even that for a game of patience played by a solitary man, which he has invented and has divulged to nobody else.

The first set of noninstitutional duties to others to be considered are those having to do with force and violence. Since respect for human beings as rational creatures entails, in general, treating every normal adult as responsible for the conduct of his own affairs, to interfere by force with anybody else's conduct of his life, unless there is a special and adequate reason, is not to respect him as a rational creature. The principle may therefore be laid down that *it is impermissible for anybody at will to use force upon another.*

Not all human beings are normal, however, and not all are adult. . . .

Children also are rational creatures, whose reason is in process of development. Although it must be recognized that the power or normal children to look after themselves is constantly growing, while they remain children they are not fully capable of doing so: and, in a measure as they are not, those in charge of them may forcibly prevent them from harming themselves or others, and may compel them to submit to education reasonably thought to be of benefit to them.

The question of when a given human being's life as an individual begins is of great importance in the Hebrew-Christian system. The duties of human beings to others are duties to them as human beings, that is, as rational creatures of a certain kind. The forms which may be taken by the fundamental moral duty of respect for a rational creature as such will vary with the degree to which that creature is actually in possession of the reason a mature creature of that kind would normally possess; but such variations in no way annul the duty. In simpler ages, it was practically sufficient to treat duties to others as beginning with their birth. However, as medical knowledge has grown, and as techniques have been developed by which the unborn can be both benefited and injured, the theoretical issue cannot set aside on the ground of practical unimportance.

The question of when the life of a human being begins is a biological one, since human beings are rational *animals*; and biology answers it simply and unequivocally:

172

a human life begins at conception, when the new being receives the genetic code. Although a zygote does not, even when made visible through a microscope, look like a human being, and although adult human beings cannot have the kind of relations with it that they can have to other adults, or even to children, its status as a rational creature is in no way compromised. Attempts to deny the humanity of zygotes, by declaring that humanity begins at birth, or at viability (that is, at the point when an unborn child, extruded from the womb, could be kept alive) are scientifically obscurantist. An eight-month-old premature baby is biologically less mature than an eight-and-three-quarter-month-old unborn one; and viability has no biological significance. Whether an unborn child is viable or not depends on the state of medical technology. It is reasonable to forecast that, in a century or so, a zygote will be viable.

It follows that the principle *it is impermissible for anybody at will to use force upon another* applies to adult and child alike, to born and unborn. However, just as it is legitimate to use force on children for purposes for which it would not be legitimate to use it on adults, so very difficult questions are raised about the extent to which it is legitimate to use force upon an unborn child. . . . These questions bring into doubt the consistency of Hebrew-Christian morality. . . .

By far the most familiar charge of inconsistency against traditional Hebrew-Christian morality, and the only one that is plausible, has to do with its doctrine of the family. For, while its principle of parental responsibility presupposes . . . that it is impermissible voluntarily to become a parent or a child you cannot rear, traditional moralists have been agreed in condemning many of the methods by which a couple can limit the number of children they have. Now it is at least possible to argue that, in some societies at least, unless the forbidden methods of limiting families are resorted to, in some cases individual parents, in others society at large, will not be able to discharge the duty owed to the children who will be born. Such problems are fittingly described as "Malthusian," after T. R. Malthus, whose *Essay on the Principle of Population as It Affects the Future Emprevement of Society* (1st ed., 1798) first persuasively presented the hypothesis that population always tends to outrun the growth of production.

Since the precepts of a moral system are inconsistent on a question only if they give rise to perplexity *simpliciter* with regard to it, in considering whether traditional Hebrew-Christian morality is inconsistent on Malthusian problems, attention must be confined to situations that can occur even though all its precepts have been observed. Hence only problems of overpopulation that could arise in a society in which the great majority of births occur in monogamous families are to be considered.

The precepts of traditional morality that bear upon Malthusian problems fall into two groups.

On one side, parents are held to have the duty of feeding, clothing, sheltering, and educating their children, and the right to noninterference in their doing so. Should either parent die or be incapacitated, the relatives of the bereaved children, and if they cannot or will not, society at large, must share or undertake the responsibility. In simpler times, any healthy laborer and his wife were supposed to be able to feed and clothe the children that would naturally be born to them, and to bring them up to be laborers or laborers' wives. That the supposition did not necessarily correspond to reality appears in many accounts of nineteenth-century England, such as this from Richard Jefferies' *Toilers of the Field*:

He minded when that sharp old Miss—was always coming round with tracts and blankets, like taking some straw to a lot of pigs, and lecturing his missis about economy. What a fuss she made, and scolded his wife as if she were a thief for having her fifteenth boy! His missis turned on her at last and said: "Lor miss, that's all the pleasure me an' my old man got."

This anecdote places in an unlovely light the presupposition of the Hebrew-Christian precept of parental responsibility, that it is impermissible voluntarily to become a parent of a child you cannot rear. For the indomitable laborer's wife also expresses a position sanctioned by Hebrew-Christian morality, which from the beginning has looked askance at any requirement of prolonged continence in marriage. Hence, without recent contraceptive techniques, in any society in which most people are healthy and marry young, a normal Jewish or Christian married life ensures that most families will be large. And so inevitably, by Malthusian calculations, a time will come of the kind deplored by Jefferies' intrusive bringer of tracts and blankets, when many parents will not be able adequately to bring up those children, and the population of the society will outrun its natural resources.

Yet Hebrew-Christian morality condemns the most common practice by which preindustrial societies have limited their populations, namely, infanticide. Sterilization is also rejected, as violating the precept forbidding nontherapeutic mutilation. And, although not expressly prohibited, the method described in the following grim passage from A. J. P. Taylor's *English History: 1914–1945* is undoubtedly contrary to the sexual ideal of both Jewish and Christian marriage:

> in the eighteen-eighties, when the decline in the birthrate first appears statistically, the middle class, who were the first to limit their families, simply abstained from sexual intercourse.

Two methods of limiting families have nevertheless been proposed as satisfying the requirements of common morality. One is to abstain from intercourse during those days in the menstrual cycle in which the wife is fertile; the other is to make the act of intercourse infertile by physical devices such as the sheath or diaphragm, or by pharmacological treatments rendering either husband or wife temporarily infertile.

The development of effective methods of both kinds in the past fifty years has posed a new set of problems for moralists. At first contraceptive intercourse was condemned as perverse. . . . Jewish moralists seem to have found least difficulty in drawing the necessary distinction, but Protestant opinion was not far behind. In Protestantism, lay opinion makes itself felt more promptly and directly than in Roman Catholicism; and Protestant parents of modest means not only accepted it as a duty to bring their children up in a way that was not possible if they had many, but also failed to see anything wrong with the new contraceptive methods. In the Roman Catholic church, however, all forms of contraception remain condemned. . . .

Yet even among Roman Catholics the force of the argument [against contraception] has widely been found obscure. There is undoubtedly a genuine distinction between the approved "rhythm" method of bringing it about that intercourse only takes place when the wife is infertile, and the condemned contraceptive method of having intercourse only when it has been brought about by one of a variety of devices, that she, her husband, or the act is infertile. The two methods are not on a par. But what is wrong with the second is not clear. . . . [I]ntercourse within marriage which is normal in every way, except for having been artificially made what most intercourse is naturally, may reasonably be held to have an erotic significance quite different from that of deviant sexual acts. If it does, and if the wrongness of deviant sexual acts derives from their significance and not from their merely physical character, a demonstration of their wrongness would be unlikely to apply also to contraceptive intercourse. And if that is so, it will be difficult to find any premise from which the impermissibility of contraception can be derived that anybody would take for a principle of common morality apart from his position on the issue in dispute.

Granting the legitimacy of contraception, any society which can produce contraceptive devices or medicines cheaply, and which can teach its members to use them, can solve Malthusian problems. But what of societies lacking those productive or educational capabilities?

The most common answer [is that] the duties of bringing up one's children well, and of promoting a reasonable balance between population and terrestrial resources, are duties of beneficence, and contain the qualification "by all lawful means in one's power." The duties not to commit abortion or infanticide, and not to mutilate oneself by sterilization, are all absolute prohibitions. Hence it is not inconsistent with the duty to bring up one's children adequately, or to contribute to the limitation of the population, to refuse to adopt unlawful means of doing so. Evil is not to be done that good may come of it.

Although this argument is logically adequate, its premises are disputable. To begin with, is it merely a duty of beneficence to bring one's children up adequately? Is it not rather an absolute obligation, a perfect duty in Kant's sense, arising from the impermissibility of procreating any child who cannot be so brought up? If it is, and if every self-supporting couple is entitled to marry, and to have a normal sexual relationship in marriage, are there not possible situations in which perplexity *simpliciter* would arise?

It appears so; but, on closer scrutiny, the appearance begins to dissolve. Despite Malthus, human population generally did not outrun natural resources until technology had become advanced, and it did so partly because of it. . . . It is doubtful whether, in any environment in which a race of rational animals could naturally evolve, the societies formed by members of that race could not prevent overpopulation except by killing the innocent or invading morally legitimate forms of the family. In sum: it has not been shown that, if contraception is permissible, the traditional prohibitions of abortion, infanticide, and sterilization on the one side, and of invading legitimate forms of the family on the other, would give rise to perplexity *simpliciter* in any conceivable society of rational animals. Nor, if it were to be demonstrated that such a society is possible, would it follow that traditional common morality is inconsistent in principle. It is far more likely that the demonstration would disclose some flaw in the specificatory premises by which the traditional doctrine of the family is derived, and indicate how it may be corrected.

Finally, it should be mentioned that a further possible solution of Malthusian problems would be effected if the recent revival of the pagan doctrine that abortion is permissible could be reconciled with common morality. Two distinct lines of argument have been offered.

The first is that procuring an abortion does not, as was traditionally believed, violate the rights of a human child. This is sometimes asserted on the ground that a foetus is not a human being at all. But that is forced. It would be superfluous to rehearse the argument, neatly summed up in a brilliant if occasionally perverse paper by Roger Wertheimer, for the conclusion that "fertilization . . . [is] a nonarbitrary point marking the inception of a particular object, a human being." It is difficult, in view of modern scientific biology, to maintain that, although a newborn child, or a twenty-weeks-old unborn one, is a human being, a zygote is not.

Yet it is tautological to assert that the relations between a nonviable foetus and the world are different from those of a viable one or of a newborn child: namely, that the nonviable foetus can only survive in its mother's womb. And it has been argued that it has no absolute right to be there; and that the mother, under certain circumstances, has the right to have her womb evacuated. Judith Jarvis Thomson has put the matter thus:

> If a set of parents . . . have taken all reasonable precautions against having a child, they do not simply by virtue of their biological relationship to the child who comes into existence have a special responsibility for it. They may wish to assume responsibility for it, or they may not wish to. And . . . if assuming responsibility for it would require large sacrifices, then they may refuse.

As she recognizes, it may be objected that the parents of an unborn child brought into existence, although unintentionally, by their joint voluntary action, stand to it in a relation utterly different from that in which they would stand to a child left on their doorstep, or from that in which either would stand to another human being whose bloodstream had, without permission, been surgically connected with either of theirs, and who would die if the connection were broken.

That what matters here is not "simply . . . their biological relationship" is shown by the related case of a woman who has conceived as a result of rape. Here the unborn child has not been brought into existence by any voluntary action of hers. And so, in my opinion, for her to refuse to have it in her womb would not fail to respect it as a rational creature. Although the child is formally innocent, it is an involuntary intruder whom the mother may have removed from her body, even should that cause its death, without violating the prohibition of causing the death of the materially innocent. Of course, she would have no right to object to its being reared in an artificial womb, if that were possible, as presumably one day it will be. And it would be a supererogatory act of great nobility for her to choose to give birth to it, out of reverence for its innocent humanity.

Accordingly, as Mary Anne Warren has acknowledged in a strong and original defence of abortion, if a foetus is human, and if moral duties are owed to human beings as such, then Thomson's argument "can provide a clear and persuasive defence of a woman's right to obtain an abortion only with respect to those cases in which the woman is in no way responsible for her pregnancy." If the absolute right of a pregnant woman to procure an abortion is to be sustained, it must be on the ground that a human being is not, as such, owed moral duties. That is the foundation of the second line of argument for the permissibility of abortion.

In Warren's version, that line is as follows. Only "full-fledged members of the moral community" have moral rights. A being becomes such a full-fledged member by virtue of being a person, not by virtue of being a member of the species *homo sapiens,* or of any other species of rational animal. The characteristics that make for personhood are: consciousness, developed reason, self-motivated activity, the power to communicate messages of an indefinite variety of types, and self-awareness. Hence "highly-advanced, self-aware robots or computers, should such be developed," would be persons, as would "intelligent inhabitants of other worlds." Unborn human children, human infants, and senile human dotards, would not—nor would their counterparts among nonterrestrial rational animals.

This argument implies that moral rights are acquired and lost according as one comes to be capable of certain sorts of mental activity, or ceases to be. To be a person, in Warren's sense, is not the nature of any being, but a stage through which some beings pass. And the concept of that stage varies with those who conceive it, despite Warren's belief that it "is very nearly universal (to people)"—that is, to persons. Michael Tooley, her ally in maintaining that moral rights go with personhood and not with membership of a rational species, let the cat out of the bag when he defined a person as a being having "a (serious) moral right to life." Tooley himself would grant this right to any organism that possesses the concept of a self as a continuing subject of experiences and other mental states, and that believes itself to be such a continuing entity. Hence his persons are not identical with Warren's. But that is the nature of our contemporary concept of personhood: it is a do-it-yourself kit for constructing a "moral community" to your own taste.

Yet within the concepts of traditional morality, could not the core of positions like Warren's and Tooley's be preserved without recourse to the factitious concept of personhood? A being whose actions are subject to moral judgement must be a full rational agent; and is not full rational agency a stage through which rational animals pass? Why then, should not traditional morality be revised by recognizing only beings in a state of full rational agency as proper objects of moral duties, and possessors of moral rights?

Although it has been asserted that the dispute between those who take moral rights to go with a state ("personhood," or full moral agency, or what you will), and those who take them to go with membership of a rational species, probably cannot be settled objectively, there nevertheless seems to be an objective ground for settling it.

Duties owed to any being arise out of the respect that is owed to it. Let it, then, be provisionally conceded that, in the first instance, respect is recognized as owed to beings by virtue of a state they are in: say, that of rational agency. If there are beings who reach that state by a process of development natural to normal members of their species, given normal nurture, must not respect logically be accorded to them, whether they have yet reached that state or not? The principle underlying this reasoning is: if respect is owed to beings because they are in a certain state, it is owed to whatever, by its very nature, develops into that state. To reject this principle would be arbitrary, if indeed it would be intelligible. What could be made of somebody who professed to rate the state of rational agency as of supreme value, but who regarded as expendable any rational creature whose powers were as yet undeveloped?

Since it would be arbitrary to accord the respect that generates moral duties to beings in a state of developed rationality, while refusing it to beings who naturally develop into that state, there is a fundamental moral difference between a member of the species *homo sapiens,* or of any other species of rational animal there may be in the universe, and a cat or a sparrow. "Ye are of more value than many sparrows" even when your natural development is at the foetal stage.

Abortion is therefore not a possible solution of Malthusian problems within common morality.

LAURA PURDY

Can Having Children Be Immoral?

LAURA PURDY teaches philosophy in the Division of Social Sciences at Wells College. Her most recent book is *Reproducing Persons: Issues in Feminist Bioethics* (1996), from which the following selection is taken.

Is it morally permissible for me to have children? A decision to procreate is surely one of the most significant decisions a person can make. So it would seem that it ought not be made without some moral soul searching.

There are many reasons why one might hesitate to bring children into this world if one is concerned about their welfare. Some are rather general, such as the deteriorating environment or the prospect of poverty. Others have a narrower focus, such as continuing civil war in one's country or the lack of essential social support for childrearing in the United States. Still others may be relevant only to individuals at risk of passing harmful diseases to their offspring.

There are many causes of misery in this world, and most of them are unrelated to genetic disease. In the general scheme of things, human misery is most efficiently reduced by concentrating on noxious social and political arrangements. Nonetheless, we should not ignore preventable harm just because it is confined to a relatively small corner of life. So the question arises, Can it be wrong to have a child because of genetic risk factors?

Unsurprisingly, most of the debate about this issue has focused on prenatal screening and abortion: much useful information about a given fetus can be made available by recourse to prenatal testing. This fact has meant that moral questions about reproduction have become entwined with abortion politics, to the detriment of both. The abortion connection has made it especially difficult to think about whether it is wrong to prevent a child from coming into being, because doing so might involve what many people see as wrongful killing; yet there is no necessary link between the two. Clearly, the existence of genetically compromised children can be prevented not only by aborting already existing fetuses but also by preventing conception in the first place.

Worse yet, many discussions simply assume a particular view of abortion without recognizing other possible positions and the difference they make in how people understand the issues. For example, those who object to aborting fetuses with genetic problems often argue that doing so would undermine our conviction that all humans are in some important sense equal. However, this position rests on the assumption that conception marks the point at which humans are endowed with a right to life. So aborting fetuses with genetic problems looks morally the same as killing "imperfect" people without their consent.

This position raises two separate issues. One pertains to the legitimacy of different views on abortion. Despite the conviction of many abortion activists to the contrary, I believe that ethically respectable views can be found on different sides of the debate, including one that sees fetuses as developing humans without any serious moral claim on continued life. There is no space here to address the details, and doing so would be once again to fall into the trap of letting the abortion question swallow up all others. However, opponents of abortion need to face the fact that many thoughtful individuals do *not* see fetuses as moral persons. It follows that their reasoning process, and hence the implications of their decisions, are radically different from those envisioned by opponents of prenatal screening and abortion. So where the latter see genetic abortion as murdering people who just don't measure up, the former see it as a way to prevent the development of persons who are more likely to live miserable lives, a position consistent with a worldview that values persons equally and holds that each deserves a high-quality life. Some of those who object to genetic abortion appear to be oblivious to these psychological and logical facts. It follows that the nightmare scenarios they paint for us are beside the point: many people simply do not share the assumptions that make them plausible.

How are these points relevant to my discussion? My primary concern here is to argue that conception can sometimes be morally wrong on grounds of genetic risk, although this judgment will not apply to those who accept the moral legitimacy of abortion and are willing to employ prenatal screening and selective abortion. If my case is solid, then those who oppose abortion must be especially careful not to conceive in certain cases, as they are, of course, free to follow their conscience about abortion. Those like myself who do not see abortion as murder have more ways to prevent birth. . . .

There is always some possibility that reproduction will result in a child with a serious disease or handicap. Genetic counselors can help individuals determine whether they are at unusual risk and, as the Human Genome Project rolls on, their knowledge will increase by quantum leaps. As this knowledge becomes available, I believe we ought to use it to determine whether possible children are at risk *before* they are conceived.

. . . I want to defend the thesis that it is morally wrong to reproduce when we know there is a high risk of transmitting a serious disease or defect. This thesis holds that some reproductive acts are wrong, and my argument puts the burden of proof on those who disagree with it to show why its conclusions can be overridden. Hence it denies that people should be free to reproduce mindless of the consequences. However, as moral argument, it should be taken as a proposal for further debate and discussion. It is not, by itself, an argument in favor of legal prohibitions of reproduction.

There is a huge range of genetic diseases. Some are quickly lethal; others kill more slowly, if at all. Some are mainly physical, some mainly mental; others impair both kinds of function. Some interfere tremendously with normal functioning, others less. Some are painful, some are not. There seems to be considerable agreement that rapidly lethal diseases, especially those, such as Tay-Sachs, accompanied by painful deterioration, should be prevented even at the cost of abortion. Conversely, there seems to be substantial agreement that relatively trivial problems, especially cosmetic ones, would not be legitimate grounds for abortion. In short, there are cases ranging from low risk of mild disease or disability to high risk of serious disease or disability. Although it is difficult to decide where the duty to refrain from procreation becomes compelling, I believe that there are some clear cases. I have chosen to focus on Huntington's disease to illustrate the kinds of concrete issues such decisions entail. However, the arguments are also relevant to many other genetic diseases.

The symptoms of Huntington's disease usually begin between the ages of thirty and fifty:

> Onset is insidious. Personality changes (obstinacy, moodiness, lack of initiative) frequently antedate or accompany the involuntary choreic movements. These usually appear first in the face, neck, and arms, and are jerky, irregular, and stretching in character. Contradictions of the facial muscles result in grimaces; those of the respiratory muscles, lips, and tongue lead to hesitating, explosive speech. Irregular movements of the trunk are present; the gait is shuffling and dancing. Tendon reflexes are increased. . . . Some patients display a fatuous euphoria; others are spiteful, irascible, destructive, and violent. Paranoid reactions are common. Poverty of thought and impairment of attention, memory, and judgment occur. As the disease progresses, walking becomes impossible, swallowing difficult, and dementia profound. Suicide is not uncommon.

The illness lasts about fifteen years, terminating in death.

Huntington's disease is an autosomal dominant disease, meaning it is caused by a single defective gene located on a non-sex chromosome. It is passed from one generation to the next via affected individuals. Each child of such an affected person has a 50 percent risk of inheriting the gene and thus of eventually developing the disease, even if he or she was born before the parent's disease was evident.

Until recently, Huntington's disease was especially problematic because most affected individuals did not know whether they had the gene for the disease until well into their childbearing years. So they had to decide about childbearing before knowing whether they could transmit the disease or not. If, in time, they did not develop symptoms of the disease, then their children could know they were not at risk for the disease. If unfortunately they did develop symptoms, then each of their children could know there was a 50 percent chance that they, too, had inherited the gene. In both cases, the children faced a period of prolonged anxiety as to whether they would develop the disease. Then, in the 1980s, thanks in part to an energetic campaign by Nancy Wexler, a genetic marker was found that, in certain circumstances, could tell people with a relatively high degree of probability whether or not they had the gene for the disease. Finally, in March 1993, the defective gene itself was discovered. Now individuals can find out whether they carry the gene for the disease, and prenatal screening can tell us whether a given fetus has inherited it. These technological developments change the moral scene substantially.

How serious are the risks involved in Huntington's disease? Geneticists often think a 10 percent risk is high. But risk assessment also depends on what is at stake: the worse the possible outcome, the more undesirable an otherwise small-risk seems. In medicine, as elsewhere, people may regard the same result quite differently. But for devastating diseases such as Huntington's this part of the judgment should be unproblematic: no one wants a loved one to suffer in this way.

There may still be considerable disagreement about the acceptability of a given risk. So it would be difficult in many circumstances to say how we should respond to a particular risk. Nevertheless, there are good grounds for a conservative approach, for it is reasonable to take special precautions to avoid very bad consequences, even if the risk is small. But the possible consequences here *are* very bad: a child who may inherit

Huntington's disease has a much greater than average chance of being subjected to severe and prolonged suffering. And it is one thing to risk one's own welfare, but quite another to do so for others and without their consent.

Is this judgment about Huntington's disease really defensible? People appear to have quite different opinions. Optimists argue that a child born into a family afflicted with Huntington's disease has a reasonable chance of living a satisfactory life. After all, even children born of an afflicted parent still have a 50 percent chance of escaping the disease. And even if afflicted themselves, such people will probably enjoy some thirty years of healthy life before symptoms appear. It is also possible, although not at all likely, that some might not mind the symptoms caused by the disease. Optimists can point to diseased persons who have lived fruitful lives, as well as those who seem genuinely glad to be alive. One is Rick Donohue, a sufferer from the Joseph family disease: "You know, if my mom hadn't had me, I wouldn't be here for the life I have had. So there is a good possibility I will have children." Optimists therefore conclude that it would be a shame if these persons had not lived.

Pessimists concede some of these facts but take a less sanguine view of them. They think a 50 percent risk of serious disease such as Huntington's is appallingly high. They suspect that many children born into afflicted families are liable to spend their youth in dreadful anticipation and fear of the disease. They expect that the disease, if it appears, will be perceived as a tragic and painful end to a blighted life. They point out that Rick Donohue is still young and has not experienced the full horror of his sickness. It is also well-known that some young persons have such a dilated sense of time that they can hardly envision themselves at thirty or forty, so the prospect of pain at that age is unreal to them.

More empirical research on the psychology and life history of suffers and potential sufferers is clearly needed to decide whether optimists or pessimists have a more accurate picture of the experiences of individuals at risk. But given that some will surely realize pessimists' worst fears, it seems unfair to conclude that the pleasures of those who deal best with the situation simply cancel out the suffering of those others when that suffering could be avoided altogether.

I think that these points indicate that the morality of procreation in such situations demands further investigation. I propose to do this by looking first at the position of the possible child, then at that of the potential parent. . . .

The first task in treating the problem from the child's point of view is to find a way of referring to possible future offspring without seeming to confer some sort of morally significant existence on them. I follow the convention of calling children who might be born in the future but who are not now conceived "possible" children, offspring, individuals, or persons.

Now, what claims about children or possible children are relevant to the morality of childbearing in the circumstances being considered? Of primary importance is the judgment that we ought to try to provide every child with something like a minimally satisfying life. I am not altogether sure how best to formulate this standard, but I want clearly to reject the view that it is morally permissible to conceive individuals so long as we do not expect them to be so miserable that they wish they were dead. I believe that this kind of moral minimalism is thoroughly unsatisfactory and that not many people would really want to live in a world where it was the prevailing standard. Its lure is that it puts few demands on us, but its price is the scant attention it pays to human well-being.

How might the judgment that we have a duty to try to provide a minimally satisfying life for our children be justified? It could, I think, be derived fairly straightforwardly from either utilitarian or contractarian theories of justice, although there is no space here for discussion of the details. The net result of such analysis would be to conclude that neglecting this duty would create unnecessary unhappiness or unfair disadvantage for some persons.

Of course, this line of reasoning confronts us with the need to spell out what is meant by "minimally satisfying" and what a standard based on this concept would require of us. Conceptions of a minimally satisfying life vary tremendously among societies and also within them. *De rigeur* in some circles are private music lessons and trips to Europe, whereas in others providing eight years of schooling is a major accomplishment. But there is no need to consider this complication at length here because we are concerned only with health as a prerequisite for a minimally satisfying life. Thus, as we draw out what such a standard might require of us, it seems reasonable to retreat to the more limited claim that parents should try to ensure something like normal health for their children. It might be thought that even this moderate claim is unsatisfactory as in some places debilitating conditions are the norm, but one could circumvent this objection by saying that parents ought to try to provide for their children health normal for that culture, even though it may be inadequate if measured by some outside standard. This conservative position would still justify efforts to avoid the birth of children at risk for Huntington's disease and other serious genetic diseases in virtually all societies.

This view is reinforced by the following considerations. Given that possible children do not presently exist as actual individuals, they do not have a right to be brought into existence, and hence no one is maltreated by measures to avoid the conception of a possible person. Therefore, the conservative course that avoids the conception of those who would not be expected to enjoy a minimally satisfying life is at present the only fair course of action. The alternative is a laissez-faire approach that brings into existence the lucky, but only at the expense of the unlucky. Notice that attempting to avoid the creation of the unlucky does not necessarily lead to *fewer* people being brought into being; the question boils down to taking steps to bring those with better prospects into existence, instead of those with worse ones.

I have so far argued that if people with Huntington's disease are unlikely to live minimally satisfying lives, then those who might pass it on should not have genetically related children. This is constant with the principle that the greater the danger of serious problems, the stronger the duty to avoid them. But this principle is in conflict with what people think of as the right to reproduce. How might one decide which should take precedence?

Expecting people to forego having genetically related children might seem to demand too great a sacrifice of them. But before reaching that conclusion we need to ask what is really at stake. One reason for wanting children is to experience family life, including love, companionship, watching kids grow, sharing their pains and triumphs, and helping to form members of the next generation. Other reasons emphasize the validation of parents as individuals within a continuous family line, children as a source of immortality, or perhaps even the gratification of producing partial replicas of oneself.

Children may also be desired in an effort to prove that one is an adult, to try to cement a marriage, or to benefit parents economically.

Are there alternative ways of satisfying these desires? Adoption or new reproductive technologies can fulfill many of them without passing on known genetic defects. Sperm replacement has been available for many years via artificial insemination by donor. More recently, egg donation, sometimes in combination with contract pregnancy, has been used to provide eggs for women who prefer not to use their own. Eventually it may be possible to clone individual humans, although that now seems a long way off. All of these approaches to avoiding the use of particular genetic material are controversial and have generated much debate. I believe that tenable moral versions of each do exist.

None of these methods permits people to extend both genetic lines or realize the desire for immortality or for children who resemble both parents; nor is it clear that such alternatives will necessarily succeed in proving that one is an adult, cementing a marriage, or providing economic benefits. Yet, many people feel these desires strongly. Now, I am sympathetic to William James's dictum regarding desires: "Take any demand, however slight, which any creature, however weak, may make. Ought it not, for its own sole sake be satisfied? If not, prove why not." Thus a world where more desires are satisfied is generally better than one where fewer are. However, not all desires can be legitimately satisfied, because as James suggests, there may be good reasons, such as the conflict of duty and desire, why some should be overruled.

Fortunately, further scrutiny of the situation reveals that there are good reasons why people should attempt with appropriate social support to talk themselves out of the desires in question or to consider novel ways of fulfilling them. Wanting to see the genetic line continued is not particularly rational when it brings a sinister legacy of illness and death. The desire for immortality cannot really be satisfied anyway, and people need to face the fact that what really matters is how they behave in their own lifetimes. And finally, the desire for children who physically resemble one is understandable, but basically narcissistic, and its fulfillment cannot be guaranteed even by normal reproduction. There are other ways of proving one is an adult, and other ways of cementing marriages—and children don't necessarily do either. Children, especially prematurely ill children, may not provide the expected economic benefits anyway. Nongenetically related children may also provide benefits similar to those that would have been provided by genetically related ones, and expected economic benefit is, in many cases, a morally questionable reason for having children.

Before the advent of reliable genetic testing, the options of people in Huntington's families were cruelly limited. On the one hand, they could have children, but at the risk of eventual crippling illness and death for them. On the other, they could refrain from childbearing, sparing their possible children from significant risk of inheriting this disease, perhaps frustrating intense desires to procreate—only to discover, in some cases, that their sacrifice was unnecessary because they did not develop the disease. Or they could attempt to adopt or try new reproductive approaches.

Reliable genetic testing has opened up new possibilities. Those at risk who wish to have children can get tested. If they test positive, they know their possible children are at risk. Those who are opposed to abortion must be especially careful to avoid conception if they are to behave responsibly. Those not opposed to abortion can responsibly conceive children, but only if they are willing to test each fetus and abort those who carry the gene. If individuals at risk test negative, they are home free.

What about those who cannot face the test for themselves? They can do prenatal testing and abort fetuses who carry the defective gene. A clearly positive test also implies that the parent is affected, although negative tests do not rule out that possibility. Prenatal testing can thus bring knowledge that enables one to avoid passing the disease to others, but only, in some cases, at the cost of coming to know with certainty that one will indeed develop the disease. This situation raises with peculiar force the question of whether parental responsibility requires people to get tested.

Some people think that we should recognize a right "not to know." It seems to me that such a right could be defended only where ignorance does not put others at serious risk. So if people are prepared to forego genetically related children, they need not get tested. But if they want genetically related children, then they must do whatever is necessary to ensure that affected babies are not the result. There is, after all, something inconsistent about the claim that one has a right to be shielded from the truth, even if the price is to risk inflicting on one's children the same dread disease one cannot even face in oneself.

In sum, until we can be assured that Huntington's disease does not prevent people from living a minimally satisfying life, individuals at risk for the disease have a moral duty to try not to bring affected babies into this world. There are now enough options available so that this duty needn't frustrate their reasonable desires. Society has a corresponding duty to facilitate moral behavior on the part of individuals. Such support ranges from the narrow and concrete (such as making sure that medical testing and counseling is available to all) to the more general social environment that guarantees that all pregnancies are voluntary, that pronatalism is eradicated, and that women are treated with respect regardless of the reproductive options they choose.

MARY L. SHANLEY

Fathers' Rights, Patriarchy, and Sex Equality

MARY SHANLEY, who teaches political science at Vassar College, has published widely on feminist law and politics.

The . . . case of *Baby Girl Clausen,* involving a custody dispute between the biological parents, Cara Clausen and Daniel Schmidt of Iowa, and the adoptive parents, Roberta and Jan DeBoer of Michigan, over who should be recognized as the legal parents of baby Jessica, focused national attention on the issue of the rights biological unwed fathers may have to custody of their infant offspring. When Cara Clausen, at the time unmarried, gave birth to a baby girl, she gave her irrevocable consent to the child's adoption two days after its birth, as did the man she named as the child's father on the birth certificate. Within weeks, however, Clausen regretted her decision and informed Daniel Schmidt that he was the baby's father. Schmidt responded by filing a petition to establish paternity and by initiating legal action to block the adoption. Schmidt contended that a biological father has a right to custody of his child unless it is shown that he is "unfit" to be a parent. After some two years of litigation, Michigan declared it did not have jurisdiction in the matter. Iowa proceeded to enforce its decree that Schmidt's parental rights had never properly been terminated and that the child had to be returned to his physical custody.

Many of those who commented on the case asked whether Daniel Schmidt's alleged rights should be enforced in the face of the trauma Jessica, now a toddler, would suffer in being removed from the only family she had known. While this matter merits serious attention, I want to focus on a different issue raised by the case, namely the basis and nature of an unwed biological father's right to veto an adoption decision of an unwed mother. This question was obscured in the case of *Baby Girl Clausen* because Daniel Schmidt initiated his action with the full cooperation of Cara Clausen, who had come to regret her decision. But it was *his* rights that the Iowa courts upheld, holding that an unwed biological father had a right to preclude an adoption initiated by the biological mother or the state.

There have been a significant number of cases in which an unwed biological father has sought to reverse the biological mother's decision to allow a child to be adopted, and legal thinking on the matter is quite unsettled. Many courts continue to apply the traditional rule that they must consider the "best interest" of the child in making any decision about custody. Supporters of biological fathers' rights, by contrast, argue that when the biological mother does not wish to retain custody, the biological father's claim automatically takes precedence over that of some "stranger" or potential adoptive parent. Interestingly, some advocates of women's rights have also criticized the best-interest standard as too subject to the biases of individual judges, but have argued that women's unique role in human gestation and childbirth, as well as various aspects of their social and economic vulnerability, dictate that an unwed biological mother must be able to make the decision to have her child adopted without interference by the father or the state. According to this view, neither the biological mother nor the state has an obligation to seek the biological father's consent to the adoption decision, or even to inform him of his paternity. From such a perspective, statutes requiring that biological mothers, but not biological fathers, consent to the adoption of their newborn infant do not deny men equal protection. The debate between advocates of these two perspectives takes us to the difficult issue of what, indeed, should be the grounding of anyone's claim to parental rights.

From my perspective, neither the "fathers' rights" nor the "maternal autonomy" position provides a fully satisfactory basis of thinking about the custodial claims of unwed biological parents. I am persuaded by considerations advanced by advocates in both camps that the best interest standard is unsuitable for cases involving newborns surrendered by their mothers for adoption. But almost all arguments for unwed fathers' rights are based on a notion of gender neutrality that is misleading, not only because of women's biological experience of pregnancy but also because of the inequality inherent in the social structures in which sexual and reproductive activity currently take place. Many arguments in favor of a mother's right to decide on the custody of her child, by contrast, expose the ways in which purportedly gender-neutral rules applied to situations of inequality simply reintroduce patriarchal inequality and run the risk of reinforcing the gender stereotype that women, not men, are the natural and proper nurturers of children.

The theoretical question of who should have parental rights, and on what grounds, is complicated by the practical consideration of what will prove to be the best means of moving toward both greater sexual equality and acceptance of diverse family forms. (I am, for example, concerned that any principles I develop here be compatible with enabling lesbian life-partners to parent a child free from threats by a known sperm donor to seek parental rights after agreeing prior to conception not to do so.) It is possible that the best way to counter the patriarchal tendencies of so much public policy and law dealing with families would be to give women complete or at least preponderant decision-making authority about all reproductive matters, at least until present social and economic inequalities based on sex diminish. I am tempted by such a position, but fear that along with empowering women in the short run it would reinforce traditional gender roles in the long run. I am also influenced by my belief in the desirability of sexual equality in both the public and private spheres, which requires not only free access to jobs and public activity for women, but also the assumption of concrete, day-to-day, "hands on" responsibility for child rearing by men. Law and social policy in the area of parental rights must walk a very fine line between adopting false gender neutrality by treating men and women identically, on the one hand, and reinforcing gender stereotypes on the other.

I argue here that a liberal polity interested in protecting the possibility for intimate association and family life for all its members should articulate norms that ground parental claims in a mixture of genetic relationship, assumption of responsibility, and provision of care to the child (including gestation). In the case of a newborn, this means that the biological father must take concrete steps to demonstrate his commitment to the child prior to the biological mother's relinquishment of the child for adoption, and courts must have the authority to judge both his efforts and the mother's objections to his claim. Only some such standard, I believe, recognizes the complexity of the sexual, genetic, biological, economic, and social relationships between adults and among adults and children that are involved in human reproductive activity.

Beyond the legal issues raised by unwed biological fathers' claims to custody, considering the rights of unwed biological parents also raises issues about individual rights in situations dealing with family relationships. By looking behind abstract assertions of individual rights to examine the dependency, reciprocity, and responsibility involved in family relationships, I suggest that the traditional liberal understanding of autonomous individuals must be revised to take account of the fact that persons are not fundamentally isolated and discrete but constructed in and by their relationships to others. . . .

If unwed biological fathers should have some custodial claim to their children but not the extreme claim qualified only by "fitness," what standards should define the extent of their rights? The law needs to adopt stringent criteria for assessing the biological father's intention to take responsibility for and act as a parent to his child even prior to birth. Such criteria will require us to shift our thinking and mode of augmentation away from an emphasis on parents as owners to parents as stewards, from parental rights to parental responsibilities, and from parents viewed as individuals to parents as persons-in-relationship with a child.

Many discussions of the "rights" of biological mothers and fathers reveal the inherent tension in liberal theory and legal practice between protecting individuals and their freedoms and protecting and fostering those relationships which in fundamental ways constitute every individual. The language of parental rights emphasizes the parent's status as an autonomous rights-bearer, and invoking individual rights has proved useful in minimizing the role of the state in people's procreative and child-rearing decisions. For example, begetting, bearing, and raising children are for many people part of the good or fulfilling life that the liberal state is obligated to protect. No one seriously proposes that children should simply be assigned at birth to the best possible or next available parents without regard to who begot and bore them. Courts have recognized the importance of intergenerational ties for many people and protected the liberty to procreate and parent a child not only in custody cases like *Stanley* and *Caban* but in decisions prohibiting forced sterilization, such as *Skinner v. Oklahoma* (316 U.S. 535 [1942]). And since biological parents have a variety of incentives to care for their children to the best of their abilities, assigning custody to them simultaneously protects children's rights as well as those of adults, and sets important bounds to the exercise of state power.

Yet in other contexts, use of the language of parental rights inappropriately focuses on the individual parent rather than on the relationships that are inherent in being a "parent." Katharine Bartlett has advocated recasting many legal disputes that involve parents and children in such a way that the language used does not pit one "right" against another, but emphasizes the view that parenthood implies deep and sustained human connection and must be grounded in adult responsibility for children: "the law should force parents to state their claims . . . not from the competing, individual perspectives of either parent or even of the child, but from the perspective of each parent-child relationship. And in evaluating (and thereby giving meaning to) that relationship, the law should focus on parental responsibility rather than reciprocal 'rights.' . . ." Bartlett suggests that language based more explicitly on open-ended responsibility toward children would capture the nature of the parent-child relationship better than discussions framed in terms of parental rights.

When someone is considered in the role of parent, he or she cannot be viewed apart from the child that makes him or her a parent; an "autonomous" (in the sense of unfettered or atomistic) individual is precisely what a parent is *not*. A "parental right" should not be viewed as pertaining to an individual per se, but only to an individual-in-relationship with a dependent child. It is therefore entirely appropriate for the law to require that efforts be made to establish a relationship before a parental right can be recognized.

Asking a court to determine whether a man has made efforts to establish a parental relationship with a newborn is, however, fraught with difficulties that involve pregnancy and the different physical relationship of biological father and mother to the fetus, the social relationships between biological father and mother, and the need to minimize both intrusiveness by the courts and subjectivity in their judgments. Indeed, part of the attraction of both the paternal fitness test and the maternal deference standard is that each of these provides a fixed criterion for determining an unwed biological father's custodial claim. Unfortunately, however, the efficiency and clarity of each of these criteria are purchased at the cost of reducing legal discourse about family relationships to an assertion of either fathers' or mothers' rights.

My proposal that an unwed biological father have an opportunity to establish his intention to parent his offspring through his behavior tries to minimize the legal effects of biological asymmetry without ignoring altogether the relevance of sexual difference. I assume that an unwed biological mother has demonstrated a parental relationship with her newborn by virtue of having carried the fetus to term, while an unwed biological father may be required to show actual involvement with prenatal life if he wishes to have custody of the child. The model or norm of "parent" in this case, therefore, is established not by the male who awaits the appearance of the child after birth, but by the pregnant woman. . . .

The different biological roles of men and women in human reproduction make it imperative that law and public policy "recognize that a father and mother must be permitted to demonstrate commitment to their child in different ways." How might the law do this? What actions might it accept as indications that an unwed biological father had made every effort to act as a parent to the child? Recent court decisions in New York show that this question is not easily answered. In 1990, in *In re Raquel Marie X.*, the New York Court of Appeals struck down a statute that stipulated that only a father who had established a home with the mother for six months prior to her relinquishment of the child for adoption could veto the mother's adoption decision. The court held that the provision imposed "an absolute condition . . . only tangentially related to the parental relationship" and allowed a woman who would not live with a man the power unilaterally to cut off his constitutionally protected interest in parenting his child. It instructed the legislature to find some other way to gauge a father's commitment to his unborn child's welfare. In the meantime, courts were to follow certain standards when judging an unwed father's parental commitment. According to the Court of Appeals, "[T]he father must be willing to assume full custody, not merely attempt to prevent the adoption, and he must promptly manifest parental responsibility both before and after the child's birth." In assessing the father's demonstration of responsibility, judges should look at such matters as "public acknowledgment of paternity, payment of pregnancy and birth expenses, steps taken to establish legal responsibility for the child, and other factors evincing a commitment to the child." Three recent bills introduced to the legislature (two in the Assembly, one in the Senate) have differed strikingly in their underlying approaches to unwed fathers' rights, and reflect a widely shared uncertainty over what considerations are relevant in determining the nature and extent of an unwed biological father's custodial rights.

The weakest requirements for an unwed biological father to establish his right to consent to his offspring's adoption are contained in a bill, A. 8028, introduced in the Assembly during the 1993 and 1994 legislative sessions. This bill listed a number of actions an unwed biological father of an infant under six months might take to establish his right to consent to the adoption. The bill would make his consent necessary if he openly lived with the child or the child's mother prior to the placement of the child for adoption; *or* held himself out to be the father of such child during such period; *or* paid or offered to pay a reasonable sum, consistent with his means, for the medical expenses of pregnancy and childbirth; *or* initiated judicial proceedings to obtain custody of the child; *or* married the child's mother. Since the bill requires the unwed biological father to have taken only one of these actions, he might obtain the right to consent to the adoption simply by initiating legal proceedings *after* the child was born.

By contrast with these minimal stipulations, S. 3776, introduced in the Senate during the 1991 and 1992 legislative sessions, requires that an unwed biological father have demonstrated his commitment to his offspring in a number of ways, and have done so both prior to and after the birth of the child. It does so by replacing most "or"s in A. 8028 with the conjunctive "and," thus insisting that a biological father have supported the mother or baby financially, *and* held himself out as the father, *and* taken steps to initiate legal proceedings to assume custody of the child.

Even stronger provisions are contained in a second Assembly bill, A. 8319, introduced in the 1993 and 1994 legislative sessions. A. 8319 stipulates that the father must have paid or offered to pay a reasonable part of the medical expenses of pregnancy and childbirth and the child's living expenses, and that he must have initiated judicial proceedings to establish paternity and to obtain sole custody of the child within clearly specified time limits. The bill further states that "'ability to assume sole custody' shall mean ability to assume guardianship and custody of the child and become the primary caretaker of the child for the foreseeable future." This bill clearly means to grant the right to consent to an adoption only to unwed fathers who demonstrate that they have been and will be actively engaged in the care and upbringing of their offspring; the stipulations rest on an image of father as caretaker and nurturer, not simply as progenitor.

Although A. 8319 reflects in some respects the spirit of the principles set forth in this chapter, it might preclude legitimate custodial claims of a man without the economic resources to pay medical expenses or support for a child when he is not living with the mother. It might also disadvantage men not familiar with the workings of the legal system and who do not know of the existence of a putative fathers' registry. A satisfactory bill would need to minimize the effects of class on someone's ability to put forward a parental claim. It is also not clear what the requirement that the father become the "primary caretaker of the child" would mean in practice. Insofar as it would prevent a man from turning over full care of his child to someone else (usually a female relative), this provision rightly stresses the importance of direct parental involvement to establishing parental rights. Yet it should not be interpreted to isolate an unwed biological father from family and community relationships that might sustain his childrearing.

A. 8319 goes a long way to enact the spirit of the principles set forth in this essay, but a fully adequate statute would need to go further in protecting an unwed mother's right to be heard concerning her child. The mother's relinquishment of the child for adoption should be viewed as the last in a series of actions meant to provide care for the child, not as an act of abandonment that gives her no interest in the child's placement. Because the disputes between biological mother and father involve their relationship to one another and to the child, it is not sufficient that a court know that the mother has consented to adoption and that the father has acted promptly to assume parental responsibility; it must consider the *reasons* the biological mother opposes placing the child in the biological father's custody. Because parental rights must be grounded in the provision of care and the assumption of responsibility, any biological father seeking custody would have to show that the pregnancy was not a result of force, coercion, deception, or intercourse with a girl under the age of consent. He would have to demonstrate further that he had not harassed the mother, prevented her exercise of the right to abortion, abused her or the child, or performed any other act which would demonstrate lack of care for her or the child. Any such act would be grounds for declaring the father "unfit." This still might not meet the possibility that a man who desired children might impregnate a woman whom he knew would neither abort nor raise a child, provide care and financial support throughout the pregnancy, and petition for paternity and custody—a kind of inexpensive "surrogacy." I am convinced that such intentional instrumental use of any woman's body is morally abhorrent, but I am not certain how to insure that such a man could not assume custody of the offspring.

Finally, a pregnant woman who wishes to make plans for her child should be able to ascertain early in the pregnancy whether or not the genetic father will step forward later to oppose the adoption. The law should provide that she be able to notify him in writing of the pregnancy and preclude him from a veto if he fails to act soon after receipt of such notification. Similarly, if a genetic father is found to be entitled to veto an adoption, a mother should be able to negate her consent to the child's adoption and be put back in the same position she was in prior to her consent, that is, as one of two unwed parents each of whom seeks custody.

For a court to ascertain whether an unwed genetic father has taken the necessary steps to provide care, take responsibility, and establish his intention to assume custody of a newborn will obviously require a hearing. A hearing will, of course, take more time than assigning custody based on a rule that any "fit" biological father prevail or that a mother be able to make the decision to place her child for adoption unimpeded by the biological father. But a hearing to ascertain whether an unwed biological father has grasped the opportunity to parent his offspring should not cause more delay than a best interest hearing. Such a hearing would be to ascertain facts about the unwed father's behavior and the mother's considered opinion concerning custody, not to try to project what custodial arrangement might be in the child's best interest. Moreover, if the biological father is required to enter his name in a putative father's registry prior to the child's birth, the court and the mother will be on notice that a hearing will likely be required. This provision not only signals the man's desire to be recognized as the legal father, but facilitates meeting the need of the infant to be placed in a permanent home as soon as possible after birth.

These considerations leave unresolved the thorny issue of how the law should deal with cases in which a biological mother lies to the biological father about his paternity or otherwise hides her pregnancy, making it impossible for him to take any action to signal his willingness to take care of his offspring. In 1992 the New York Court of Appeals addressed the question of what effect a lack of knowledge of a woman's pregnancy should have on a biological father's right to seek custody after learning of the child's existence. In *Matter of Robert O. v. Russell K.*, an unwed biological father sought to overturn the adoption of his son on the grounds that either the mother or the State had a duty to ensure that he knew of the child's birth, and that their failure to inform him denied him his constitutional rights. The New York Court acknowledged that "the unwed father of an infant placed for adoption immediately at birth faces a unique dilemma should he desire to establish his parental rights." His opportunity to "shoulder the responsibility of parenthood may disappear before he has a chance to grasp it." But although the biological father, Robert O., acted as soon as he knew of the child's existence, the adoption had been finalized ten months previously. "Promptness," said the Court, "is measured in terms of the child's life, not by the onset of the father's awareness." Robert O., having failed to determine in a timely fashion whether the woman with whom he had lived was pregnant, lost the right he would have had to an opportunity to manifest his "willingness to be a parent." The responsibility to know of a child's existence should fall on the man who would assume responsibility for raising the child. By contrast, one defender of unwed fathers' rights proposes a jail sentence of up to two years for a woman who refuses to name the father of her child when surrendering the infant for adoption! A biological father aware of a woman's pregnancy should be required to act prior to birth and soon after he suspects his paternity; a biological father who is actively kept ignorant might be allowed to step forward for some specified period after birth (probably not less than six weeks nor longer than six months), but thereafter the importance of establishing a firm parent-child relationship would preclude his advancing a parental claim.

While these reflections suggest various reforms in the laws governing the custody of nonmarital children, they do not answer the question of whether the case of *Baby Girl Clausen* was decided correctly. I find that very hard to do because neither side grounded its position in the kinds of principles I have put forward here. The Iowa statute which Daniel Schmidt invoked to claim that the adoption could not be finalized required the biological father's consent, but no showing that he demonstrate his commitment to the child prior to (or even subsequent to) birth. The father's mere opposition to the adoption was a sufficient basis upon which to grant him custody. The DeBoers, for their part, based their claim that they should be allowed to adopt Jessica on the best interest standard. Placing the child with the Schmidts reinforced the notion that a biological tie between man and child automatically creates a custodial claim, while a decision favoring the DeBoers would not only have reinforced the best interest standard but might have been viewed as rewarding them for prolonging legal proceedings after Schmidt raised his claim. The outcome consonant with the principles advanced here would have granted a hearing to Schmidt, recognizing that while his biological tie alone did not guarantee him custodial rights, the fact that he acted immediately after learning that he was Jessica's biological father and within four weeks after her birth provided grounds for a hearing. That hearing would not have attempted to determine whether the child's best interest would be better served by granting custody to Schmidt or the DeBoers, but whether Schmidt's actions established a claim to custody.

The main lesson to be drawn from the case of *Baby Girl Clausen* is that it is imperative that states formulate adoption laws that will reflect the principle that parental rights are established in the first instance by a combination of biology and the provision of care, a principle already articulated by the Supreme Court. Another lesson may be that in certain instances it would make sense to allow some form of legal recognition to the fact that a child may have multiple "parents": genetic parents (sperm and egg donors), a gestational mother, step-parents, adoptive parents, social parents (that is, those that actually provide care), and legal guardians. The possibility of some such recognition might avoid some cases in which unwed biological fathers seek to block the adoption of their offspring. Some of these cases seem motivated not so much by the man's desire to raise the child as by his fear of losing all opportunity to know the child he has sired. There may be ways of dealing with this fear short of blocking the adoption. Adoption registries that allow adopted children and birth parents to contact one another by mutual consent when the child has reached his or her majority seem to have been helpful to biological parents, adoptive parents, and children alike. They allow for the simultaneous recognition of the importance of both biological and social parenting, and in doing so undercut the suggestion that something about adoption is shameful and is best kept hidden. Such registries also take into account the perspective of children who want to know their biological forebears, without weakening either the legal rights and responsibilities of the social (adopting) parents or the primacy of the emotional bonds between adopting parents and children. Beyond these legal changes, the *Baby Girl Clausen* case should also lead us to try to understand the circumstances that might lead an unwed mother to lie about or conceal the paternity of her child, such as fear of violence or harassment, or shame over an unwanted sexual relationship. Working toward justice in family relationships requires struggling to eliminate the social conditions that give rise to such fear and shame, and also requires making sure that all citizens have access to the resources that allow family relationships to survive and flourish, so that no biological parent will be forced by economic factors to relinquish custody of children they would prefer to raise themselves had they the resources to do so. This analysis of disputes over paternal custody of nonmarital newborns makes it abundantly clear that the language of individual rights, so central to liberal political theory and to the due process and equal protection guarantees of the U.S. Constitution, is not well suited to dealing with complex issues of parent-child relationships. While notions of maternal or paternal rights are not useless (for example, they allow us to think about limits to state intervention), they tend to focus attention on an adult *individual*, whereas parental issues involve at least two adults and a child, and the relationships among them. Legal and social discourse alike must put the lived relationship between parents and between parent and child, not the rights of individuals alone, at the center of the analysis of parental claims. In particular the language of a father's "right" to custody of his infant child based on his genetic tie obscures the complexity of the relationships involved in human reproductive activity.

Because parenting involves being in a relationship with another dependent person, a parental "right" cannot properly be conceived of as something independent of the relationship. An individual can exercise a parental right, but the existence or the nature of the right cannot be explained by reference to that individual alone. Only by taking account of the interpersonal dependency, reciprocity, and responsibility involved in family relationships will we be able to approach a world dedicated to achieving both lived equality between men and women and committed parents for every child.

CHAPTER 5

Is It Ever Right to Lie?

Have you told a lie in the past year? If you answer no, you are probably lying (or at the very least engaged in self-deception!). Although it is surely less than clear exactly what constitutes a lie, it is likely that sometime during the past year you deliberately deceived or misled someone by misrepresenting the truth in some way. A very few people may make it a practice never to lie. Depending on the perspective from which we judge their behavior, and perhaps depending on their motivations for adhering so strictly to truthfulness, we may consider them to be either saintly or just plain obnoxious.

Two things about lying are quite clear. On the one hand, lying is viewed as suspect; it is something that we are taught not to do as children and generally feel qualms about doing as adults. On the other, lying is a common human practice; most of us lie, in one way or another, quite often. We think of some of our lies as harmless ("I overslept because my alarm clock is broken.") or even kind ("Your hair looks really nice today."). Other lies seem designed to postpone the inevitable truth for some self-serving but in no way malicious reason ("The stork brought you."). Other lies are so commonplace that we hardly take them seriously ("With new Futz toothpaste, you'll never spend another Friday night alone."). Other lies appear plainly to be wrong ("There are no explosives in my luggage."). The range of assertions that can plausibly count as lying, together with the range of reasons people have for lying, makes it extremely difficult for the philosopher to figure out just what is wrong with lying. Why is it that such a common practice has such a bad reputation? Why is truth-telling so important? What exactly *is* a lie? Is it *always* wrong to lie? What *makes* lying wrong? If some lies are justified, then what excuses them?

In this chapter, you will discover that there is considerable disagreement among philosophers, first, as to whether lying is indeed wrong and, second, as to why it is wrong, if it is. Immanual Kant argues the most extreme position on the wrongness of lying. According to him, lying is simply and absolutely wrong. Kant believed that telling an untruth to another is always injurious. Indeed, Kant defends the view that, for example, lying to a would-be murderer as to the whereabouts of his intended victim is wrong. Charles Fried, whose sympathy lies with Kant's position, provides a carefully articulated argument for what he is even willing to call the "evil" of lying. For Fried, lying is a breach of common trust. When I lie to someone, according to Fried, I act in such a way as to appropriate for myself another person's mind. Though Fried himself does not invoke the analogy of rape, he does claim that a person who lies violate the "moral personality" of the one lied to. For both Kant and Fried, there is something about the very nature of being human, and being a member of the human community, that demands truth-telling. Although their positions may strike you as somewhat extreme (especially Kant's), you might want to think about what it would be like to try to get from one day to another if lying were the predominant practice. Try spending an hour systematically misleading and being misled and see how you and your companions fare. We begin to see how truth and honesty are necessary conditions for human communication.

Many of our lies are told because we believe that, by lying, we are in fact protecting someone from the hurtfulness of a particular truth. Lies that are told with the intention of doing good for another are benevolent lies. In his essay, Thomas E. Hill, Jr., questions whether benevolent lies are morally appropriate. He is particularly concerned with the sorts of lies that people in close or significant relationships tell one another. Should, for example, a doctor lie to a patient about her condition on the grounds that her final days will be happier if she does not know the truth? Hill's position is that even if the lie brings about greater happiness, it is morally wrong because it undermines the patient's autonomy.

In considering the merits of Hill's argument, you will be faced with the question of whether the wrongness of lying is attributable to the negative consequences of particular lies or whether it is attributable to the very nature of lying itself. Kant, Fried, and Hill differ by degrees on this question. Sidgwick, on the other hand, is a consequentialist and therefore argues that lying in and of itself is not wrong. Rather, we must judge the consequences of any particular lie. In fact, according to him, some lies are required precisely because they have superior consequences to truth-telling. For Sidgwick, there is nothing intrinsically great about the truth. Following in somewhat the same vein, Annette Baier asks us to consider whether trust itself is a virtue. She provides an account of the conditions under which it is beneficial to place one's trust in another, taking into consideration the variety of ways in which entrustment can serve as a basis for exploitation and abuse.

Mark Twain, famous for his wry sense of humor, provides an engaging defense of what he calls the "art of lying." For Twain, the problem is not that people lie, but that they lie badly. Perhaps it is no surprise that such a master of fabrication should see little value in a blind adherence to the literal truth. Though it is clear that we must read Twain's essay with a raised eyebrow, the essay does bring up important questions about how precisely we draw the lines between truth and falsehood in the multiple contexts within which human communication takes place. It is precisely this issue that Harry Frankfurt takes up in his reflections on bullshit. According to Frankfurt, what distinguishes bullshit from lying is its programmatic nature. Unlike the liar, the bullshitter constructs a whole world at the center of which is a misrepresentation of what the bullshitter is up to. Both Twain and Frankfurt leave us wondering whether we have just been made victims of their own imaginative misrepresentations.

IMMANUEL KANT

On a Supposed Right to Tell Lies from Benevolent Motives

IMMANUEL KANT (1724–1804), the great German philosopher, wrote his short *Foundations of the Metaphysics of Morals* as a summary of the more elaborate arguments in his *Critique of Practical Reason* (1788). In these books, he defends morality and moral principle as the product of practical reason, not feelings or "inclinations."

In the work called *France,* for the year 1797, Part VI. No. 1, on Political Reactions, by *Benjamin Constant,* the following passage occurs, p. 123:—

"The moral principle that it is one's duty to speak the truth, if it were taken singly and unconditionally, would make all society impossible. We have the proof of this in the very direct consequences which have been drawn from this principle by a German philosopher, who goes so far as to affirm that to tell a falsehood to a murderer who asked us whether our friend, of whom he was in pursuit, had not taken refuge in our house, would be a crime."

The French philosopher opposes this principle in the following manner, p. 124:—"It is a duty to tell the truth. The notion of duty is inseparable from the notion of right. A duty is what in one being corresponds to the right of another. Where there are no rights there are no duties. To tell the truth then is a duty, but only towards him who has a right to the truth. But no man has a right to a truth that injures others." The πρωτον ψευδος [false beginning] here lies in the statement that *"To tell the truth is a duty, but only towards him who has a right to the truth."*

It is to be remarked, first, that the expression "to have a right to the truth" is unmeaning. We should rather say, a man has a right to his own *truthfulness* (*veracitas*), that is, to subjective truth in his own person. For to have a right objectively to truth would mean that, as in *meum* and *tuum* generally, it depends on his *will* whether a given statement shall be true or false, which would produce a singular logic.

Now, the *first* question is whether a man—in cases where he cannot avoid answering Yes or No—has the *right* to be untruthful. The *second* question is whether, in order to prevent a misdeed that threatens him or some one else, he is not actually bound to be untruthful in a certain statement to which an unjust compulsion forces him.

Truth in utterances that cannot be avoided is the formal duty of a man to everyone, however great the disadvantage that may arise from it to him or any other, and although by making a false statement I do no wrong to him who unjustly compels me to speak, yet I do wrong to men in general in the most essential point of duty, so that it may be called a lie (though not in the jurist's sense), that is, so far as in me lies I cause that declarations in general find no credit, and hence that all rights founded on contract should lose their force; and this is a wrong which is done to mankind.

If, then, we define a lie merely as an intentionally false declaration towards another man, we need not add that it must injure another; as the jurists think proper to put in their definition (*mendacium est falsiloquium in praejudicium alterius*). For it always injures another; if not another individual, yet mankind generally, since it vitiates the source of justice. This benevolent lie *may*, however, by *accident* (*casus*) become punishable even by civil laws; and that which escapes liability to punishment only by accident may be condemned as a wrong even by external laws. For instance, if you have *by a lie* hindered a man who is even now planning a murder, you are legally responsible for all the consequences. But if you have strictly adhered to the truth, public justice can find no fault with you, be the unforeseen consequence what it may. It is possible that whilst you have honestly answered Yes to the murderer's question, whether his intended victim is in the house, the latter may have gone out unobserved, and so not have come in the way of the murderer, and the deed therefore have not been done: whereas, if you lied and said he was not in the house, and he had really gone out (though unknown to you), so that the murderer met him as he went, and executed his purpose on him, then you might with justice be accused as the cause of his death. For, if you had spoken the truth as well as you knew it, perhaps the murderer while seeking for his enemy in the house might have been caught by neighbours coming up and the deed been prevented. Whoever then *tells a lie*, however good his intentions may be, must answer for the consequences of it, even before the civil tribunal, and must pay the penalty for them, however unforeseen they may have been; because truthfulness is a duty that must be regarded as the basis of all duties founded on contract, the laws of which would be rendered uncertain and useless if even the least exception to them were admitted.

To be *truthful* (honest) in all declarations is therefore a sacred unconditional command of reason, and not to be limited to any expediency.

M. Constant makes a thoughtful and sound remark on the decrying of such strict principles, which it is alleged lose themselves in impracticable ideas, and are therefore to be rejected (p. 123):—"In every case in which a principle proved be true seems to be inapplicable, it is because we do not know the *middle principle* which contains the medium of its application." He adduces (p. 121) the doctrine of *equality* as the first link forming the social chain (p. 121): "namely, that no man can be bound by any laws except those to the formation of which he has contributed. In a very contracted society this principle may be directly applied and become the ordinary rule without requiring any middle principle. But in a very numerous society we must add a new principle to that which we here state. This middle principle is, that the individuals may contribute to the formation of the laws either in their own person or by *representatives*. Whoever would try to apply the first principle to a numerous society without taking in the middle principle would infallibly bring about its destruction. But this circumstance, which would only show the ignorance or incompetence of the lawgiver, would prove nothing against the principle itself." He concludes (p. 125) thus: "A principle recognized as truth must, therefore, never be abandoned, however obviously danger may seem to be involved in it." (And yet the good man himself abandoned the unconditional principle of veracity on account of the danger to society, because he could not discover any middle principle which would serve to prevent this danger; and, in fact, no such principle is to be interpolated here.)

Retaining the names of the persons as they have been here brought forward, "the French philosopher" confounds the action by which one does harm (*nocet*) to another by telling the truth, the admission of which he cannot avoid, with the action by which he does him *wrong* (*lædit*). It was merely an *accident* (*casus*) that the truth of the statement did harm to the inhabitant of the house; it was not a free *deed* (in the juridical sense). For to admit his right to require another to tell a lie for his benefit would be to admit a claim opposed to all law. Every man has not only a right, but the strictest duty to truthfulness in statements which he cannot avoid, whether they do harm to himself or others. He himself, properly speaking, does not *do* harm to him who suffers thereby; but this harm is *caused* by accident. For the man is not free to choose, since (if he must speak at all) veracity is an unconditional duty. The "German philosopher" will therefore not adopt as his principle the proposition (p. 124): "It is a duty to speak the truth, but only to him who has *a right to the truth*," first on account of the obscurity of the expression, for truth is not a possession the right to which can be granted to one, and refused to another; and next and chiefly, because the duty of veracity (of which alone we are speaking here) makes no distinction between persons towards whom we have this duty, and towards whom we may be free when it; but is an *unconditional duty* which holds in all circumstances.

Now, in order to proceed from a *metaphysic* of Right (which abstracts from all conditions of experience) to a principle of *politics* (which applies these notions to cases of experience), and by means of this to the solution of a problem of the latter in accordance with the general principle of right, the philosopher will enunciate:—1. An *Axiom*, that is, an apodictically certain proposition, which follows directly from the definition of external right (harmony of the *freedom* of each with the freedom of all by a universal law). 2. A *Postulate* of external public *law* as the united will of all on the principle of *equality*, without which there could not exist the freedom of all. 3. A *Problem*: how it is to be arranged that harmony may be maintained in a society, however large, on principles of freedom and equality (namely, by means of a representative system); and this will then become a principle of the *political system*, the establishment and arrangement of which will contain enactments which, drawn from practical knowledge of men, have in view only the mechanism of administration of justice, and how this is to be suitably carried out. Justice must never be accommodated to the political system, but always the political system to justice.

"A principle recognized as true (I add, recognized *à priori*, and therefore apodictic) must never be abandoned, however obviously danger may seem to be involved in it," says the author. Only here we must not understand the danger of *doing harm* (accidentally), but of *doing wrong*; and this would happen if the duty of veracity, which is quite unconditional, and constitutes the supreme condition of justice in utterances, were made conditional and subordinate to other considerations; and although by a certain lie I in fact do no wrong to any person, yet I infringe the principle of justice in regard to all indispensably necessary statements *generally* (I do wrong formally, though not materially); and this is much worse than to commit an injustice to any individual, because such a deed does not presuppose any principle leading to it in the subject. The man who, when asked whether in the statement he is about to make he intends to speak truth or not, does not receive the question with indignation at the suspicion thus expressed towards him that he might be a liar, but who asks permission first to consider possible exceptions, is already a liar (*in potentia*), since he shows that he does not recognize veracity as a duty in itself, but reserves exceptions from a rule which in its nature does not admit of exceptions, since to do so would be self-contradictory.

All practical principles of justice must contain strict truths, and the principles here called middle principles can only contain the closer definition of their application to actual cases (according to the rules of politics), and never exceptions from them, since exceptions destroy the universality, on account of which alone they bear the name of principles.

CHARLES FRIED

The Evil of Lying

CHARLES FRIED teaches at the Harvard University School of Law. He has written several books and articles on ethics.

The evil of lying is as hard to pin down as it is strongly felt. Is lying wrong or is it merely something bad? If it is bad, why is it bad—is it bad in itself or because of some tendency associated with it? Compare lying to physical harm. Harm is a state of the world and so it can only be classified as bad: the wrong I argued for was the *intentional doing* of harm. Lying, on the other hand, can be wrong, since it is an action. But the fact that lying is an action does not mean that it *must* be wrong rather than bad. It might be that the action of lying should be judged as just another state of the world—a time-extended state, to be sure, but there is no problem about that—and as such it would count as a negative element in any set of circumstances in which it occurred. Furthermore, if lying is judged to be bad it can be bad in itself, like something ugly or painful, or it can be bad only because of its tendency to produce results that are bad in themselves.

If lying were bad, not wrong, this would mean only that, other things being equal, we should avoid lies. And if lying were bad not in itself but merely because of its tendencies, we would have to avoid lies only when those tendencies were in fact likely to be realized. In either case lying would be permissible to produce a net benefit, including the prevention of more or worse lies. By contrast the categorical norm "Do not lie" does not evaluate states of affairs but is addressed to moral agents, forbidding lies. Now if lying is wrong it is also bad in itself, for the category of the intrinsically bad is weaker and more inclusive than the category of the wrong. And accordingly, many states of the world are intrinsically bad (such as destruction of valuable property) but intentional acts bringing them about are not necessarily wrong.

Bentham plainly believed that lying is neither wrong nor even intrinsically bad: "Falsehood, take it by itself, consider it as not being accompanied by any other material circumstances, nor therefore productive of any material effects, can never, upon the principle of utility, constitute any offense at all." By contrast, Kant and Augustine argued at length that lying is wrong. Indeed, they held that lying is not only wrong *unless* excuse or justified in defined ways (which is my view) but that lying is always wrong. Augustine sees lying as a kind of defilement, the liar being tainted by the lie, quite apart from any consequences of the lie. Kant's views are more complex. He argues at one point that lying undermines confidence and trust among men generally: "Although by making a false statement I do no wrong to him who unjustly compels me to speak, yet I do wrong to men in general. . . . I cause that declarations in general find no credit, and hence all rights founded on contract should lose their force; and this is a wrong to mankind." This would seem to be a consequentialist argument, according to which lying is bad only insofar as it produces these bad results. But elsewhere he makes plain that he believes these bad consequences to be necessarily, perhaps even conceptually linked to lying. In this more rigoristic vein, he asserts that lying is a perversion of one's uniquely human capacities irrespective of any consequences of the lie, and thus lying is not only intrinsically bad but wrong.

Finally, a number of writers have taken what looks like an intermediate position: the evil of lying is indeed identified with its consequences, but the connection between lying and those consequences, while not a necessary connection, is close and persistent, and the consequences themselves are pervasive and profound. Consider this passage from a recent work by G. F. Warnock:

> I do not necessarily do you any harm at all by deed or word if I induce you to believe what is not in fact the case: I may even do you good, possibly by way, for example, of consolation or flattery. Nevertheless, though deception is not thus necessarily directly damaging it is easy to see how crucially important it is that the natural inclination to have recourse to it should be counteracted. It is, one might say, not the implanting of false beliefs that is damaging, but rather the generation of the suspicion that they may be being implanted. For this undermines trust; and, to the extent that trust is undermined, all cooperative undertakings, in which what one person can do or has reason to do is dependent on what others have done, are doing, or are going to do, must tend to break down. . . . There is no sense in my asking you for your opinion on some point, if I do not suppose that your answer will actually express your opinion (verbal communication is doubtless the most important of all our co-operative undertakings).

Warnock does not quite say that truth-telling is good in itself or that lying is wrong, yet the moral quality of truth-telling and lying is not so simply instrumental as it is, for instance, for Bentham. Rather, truth-telling seems to bear a fundamental, pervasive relation to the human enterprise, just by lying appears to be fundamentally subversive of that enterprise. What exactly is the nature of this relation? How does truth-telling bear to human goods a relation which is more than instrumental but less than necessary?

The very definition of lying makes plain that consequences are crucial, for lying is intentional and the intent is an intent to produce a consequence: false belief. But how can I then resist the consequentialist analysis of lying? Lying is an attempt to produce a certain effect on another, and if that effect (consequence) is not bad, how can lying be wrong? I shall have to argue, therefore, that to lie is to intend to produce an effect which always has something bad about it, an effect moreover of the special sort that it is wrong to produce it intentionally. To lay that groundwork for my argument about lying, I must consider first the moral value of truth.

TRUTH AND RATIONALITY

A statement is true when the world is the way the statement says it is. Utilitarians insist (as in the quotation from Bentham above) that truth, like everything else, has value just exactly as it produces value—pleasure, pain, the satisfaction or frustration of desire. And of course it is easy to show that truth (like keeping faith, not harming the innocent, respecting rights) does not always lead to the net satisfactions of desire, to the production of utility. It may *tend* to do so, but that tendency explains only why we should discriminate between occasions when truth does and when it does not have value—an old story. It is an old story, for truth—like justice, respect, and self-respect—has a value which consequentialist analyses (utilitarian or any other) do not capture. Truth, like respect, is a foundational value.

The morality of right and wrong does not count the satisfaction of desire as the overriding value. Rather, the integrity of persons, as agents and as the objects of the intentional agency of others, has priority over the attainment of the goals which agents choose to attain. I have sought to show how respect for physical integrity is related to respect for the person. The person, I argued, is not just a locus of potential pleasure and pain but an entity with determinate characteristics. The person is, among other things, necessarily an incorporated, a physical, not an abstract entity. In relation to truth we touch another necessary aspect of moral personality: the capacity for judgment, and thus for choice. It is that aspect which Kant used to ground his moral theory, arguing that freedom and rationality are the basis for moral personality. John Rawls makes the same point, arguing that "moral personality and not the capacity for pleasure and pain . . . [is] the fundamental aspect of the self. . . . The essential unity of the self is . . . provided by the concept of right." The concept of the self is prior to the goods which the self chooses, and these goods gather their moral significance from the fact that they have been chosen by moral beings—beings capable of understanding and acting on moral principles.

In this view freedom and rationality are complementary capacities, or aspects of the same capacity, which is moral capacity. A man is free insofar as he is able to act on a judgment because he perceives it to be correct; he is free insofar as he may be moved to action by the judgments his reason offers to him. This is the very opposite of the Humean conception of reason as the slave of the passions. There is no slavery here. The man who follows the steps of a mathematical argument to its conclusion because he judges them to be correct is free indeed. To the extent that we choose our ends we are free; and as to objectively valuable ends which we choose because we see their value, we are still free.

Now, rational judgment is true judgment, and so the moral capacity for rational choice implies the capacity to recognize the matter on which choice is to act and to recognize the kind of result our choices will produce. This applies to judgments about other selves and to judgments in which one locates himself as a person among persons, a self among selves. These judgments are not just arbitrary suppositions: *they are judged to be true of the world.* For consider what the self would be like if these judgments were not supposed to be true. Maybe one might be content to be happy in the manner of the fool of Athens who believed all the ships in the harbor to be his. But what of our perceptions of other people? Would we be content to have those whom we love and trust the mere figments of our imaginations? The foundational values of freedom and rationality imply the foundational value of truth, for the rational man is the one who judges aright, that is, truly. Truth is not the same as judgment, as rationality; it is rather the proper subject of judgment. If we did not seek to judge truly, and if we did not believe we could judge truly, the act of judgment would not be what we know it to be at all.

Judgment and thus truth are *part* of a structure which as a whole makes up the concept of self. A person's relation to his body and the fact of being an incorporated self are another part of that structure. These two parts are related. The bodily senses provide matter for judgments of truth, and the body includes the physical organs of judgment.

THE WRONG OF LYING

So our capacity for judgment is foundational and truth is the proper object of that capacity, but how do we get to the badness of lying, much less its categorical wrongness?

The crucial step to be supplied has to do not with the value of truth but with the evil of lying. We must show that to lie to someone is to injure him in a way that particularly touches his moral personality. From that, the passage is indeed easy to the conclusion that to inflict such injury intentionally (remember that all lying is by hypothesis intentional) is not only bad but wrong. It is this first, crucial step which is difficult. After all, a person's capacity for true judgment is not necessarily impaired by inducing in him a particular false belief. Nor would it seem that a person suffers a greater injury in respect to that capacity when he is induced to believe a falsity than when we intentionally prevent him from discovering the truth, yet only in the first case do we lie. Do we really do injury to a person's moral personality when we persuade him falsely that it rained yesterday in Bangkok—a fact in which he has no interest? And do we do him more injury than when we fail to answer his request for yesterday's football scores, in which he is mildly interested? Must we not calculate the injury by the *other* harm it does: disappointed expectations, lost property, missed opportunities, physical harm? In this view, lying would be a way of injuring a person in his various substantive interests— a way of stealing from him, hurting his feelings, perhaps poisoning him—but then the evil of lying would be purely instrumental, not wrong at all.

All truth, however irrelevant or trivial, has value, even though we may cheerfully ignore most truths, forget them, erase them as encumbrances from our memories. The value of every truth is shown just in the judgment that the only thing we must not do is falsify truth. Truths are like other people's property, which we can care nothing about but may not use for our own purposes. It is as if the truth were not ours (even truth we have discovered and which is known only to us), and so we may not exercise an unlimited dominion over it. Our relations to other people have a similar structure: we may perhaps have no duty to them, we may be free to put them out of our minds to make room for others whom we care about more, but we may not harm them. And so we may not falsify truth. But enough of metaphors—what does it mean to say that the truth is not ours?

The capacity for true judgment is the capacity to arrive at judgments which are in fact true of the world as it exists apart from out desires, our choices, our values. It is the world presented to us by true judgments—including true judgments about ourselves— which we then make the subject of our choices, our valuation. Now, if we treat the truth as our own, it must be according to desire or valuation. But for rational beings these activities are supposed to depend on truth; we are supposed to desire and choose according to the world as it is. To choose that something not be the case when it is in fact the case is very nearly self-contradictory—for choice is not *of* truth but *on the basis of* truth. To deliberate about whether to believe a truth (not whether it is indeed true— another story altogether) is like deciding whether to cheat at solitaire. All this is obvious. In fact I suppose one cannot even coherently talk about choosing to believe something one believes to be false. And this holds equally for all truths—bit and little, useful, useless, and downright inconvenient. But we do and must calculate *about* (and not just *with*) truths all the time as we decide what truths to acquire, what to forget. We decide all the time not to pursue some inquiry because it is not worth it. Such calculations surely must go forward on the basis of what truths are useful, given one's plans and desires. Even when we pursue truth for its own sake, we distinguish between interesting and boring truths.

Considering what truth to acquire or retain differs, however, from deliberately acquiring false beliefs. All truths are acquired as propositions correctly (truly) corresponding to the world, and in this respect, all truths are equal. A lie, however, has the form and occupies the role of truth in that it too purports to be a proposition about the world; only the world does not correspond to it. So the choice of a lie is not like a choice among truths, for the choice of a lie is a choice to affirm as the basis for judgment a proposition which does not correspond to the world. So, when I say that truth is foundational, that truth precedes choice, what I mean is *not* that this or that truth his foundational but that judging according to the facts is foundational to judging at all. A scientist may deliberate about which subject to study and, having chosen his subject, about the data worth acquiring, but he cannot even deliberate as a scientist about whether to acquire false data. Clearly, then, there is something funny (wrong?) about lying to oneself, but how do we go from there to the proposition that it is wrong to lie to someone else? After all, much of the peculiarity about lying to oneself consists in the fact that it seems not so much bad as downright self-contradictory, logically impossible, but that does not support the judgment that it is wrong to lie to another. I cannot marry myself, but that hardly makes it wrong to marry someone else.

Let us imagine a case in which you come as close as you can to lying to yourself: You arrange some operation, some fiddling with your brain that has no effect other than to cause you to believe a proposition you know to be false and also to forget entirely the prior history of how you came to believe that proposition. It seems to me that you do indeed harm yourself in such an operation. This is because a free and rational person wishes to have a certain relation to reality: as nearly perfect as possible. He wishes to build his conception of himself and the world and his conception of good on the basis of truth. Now if he affirms that the truth is available for fiddling in order to accommodate either his picture of the world or his conception of the good, then this affirms that reality is dependent on what one wants, rather than what one wants being fundamentally constrained by what there is. Rationality is the respect for this fundamental constraint of truth. This is just another way of saying that the truth is prior to our plans and prospects and must be respected whatever our plans might be. What if the truth we "destroy" by this operation is a very trivial and irrelevant truth—the state of the weather in Bangkok on some particular day? There is still an injury to self, because the fiddler must have some purpose in his fiddling. If it is a substantive purpose, then the truth is in fact relevant to that purpose, and my argument holds. If it is just to show it can be done, then he is only trying to show he can do violence to his rationality—a kind of moral blasphemy. Well, what if it is a very *little* truth? Why, then, it is a very little injury he does himself—but that does not undermine my point.

Now, when I lie to you, I do to you what you cannot actually do to yourself—brain-fiddling being only an approximation. The nature of the injury I would do to myself, if I could, explains why lying to you is to do you harm, indeed why it is wrong. The lie is an injury because it produces an effect (or seeks to) which a person as a moral agent should not wish to have produced in him, and thus it is as much an injury as any other effect which a moral agent would not wish to have produced upon his person. To be sure, some people may want to be lied to. That is a special problem; they are like people who want to suffer (not just are willing to risk) physical injury. In general, then, I do not want you to lie to me in the same way that as a rational man I would not lie to myself if I could. But why does this make lying wrong and not merely bad?

Lying is wrong because when I lie I set up a relation which is essentially exploitative. It violates the principle of respect, for I must affirm that the mind of another person is available to me in a way in which I cannot agree my mind would be available to him—for if I do so agree, then I would not expect my lie to be believed. When I lie, I am like a counterfeiter: I do not want the market flooded with counterfeit currency; I do not want to get back my own counterfeit bill. Moreover, in lying to you, I affirm such an unfairly unilateral principle in respect to an interest and capacity which is crucial, as crucial as physical integrity: your freedom and your rationality. When I do intentional physical harm, I say that your body, your person, is available for my purposes. When I lie, I lay claim to your mind.

Lying violates respect and is wrong, as is any breach of trust. Every lie is a broken promise, and the only reason this seems strained is that in lying the promise is made and broken at the same moment. Every lie necessarily implies—as does every assertion—an assurance, a warranty of its truth. The fact that the breach accompanies the making should, however, only strengthen the conclusion that this is wrong. If promise-breaking is wrong, then a lie must be wrong, since there cannot be the supervening factor of changed circumstances which may excuse breaches of promises to perform in the future.

The final one of the convergent strands that make up the wrong of lying is the shared, communal nature of language. This is what I think Kant had in mind when he argued that lie does wrong "to men in general." If whether people stood behind their statements depended wholly on the particular circumstances of the utterance, then the whole point of communication would be undermined. For every utterance would simply be the occasion for an analysis of the total circumstances (speaker's and hearer's) in order to determine what, if anything, to make of the utterance. And though we do often wonder and calculate whether a person is telling the truth, we do so from a baseline, a presumption that people do stand behind their statements. After all, the speaker surely depends on such a baseline. He wants us to think that he is telling the truth. Speech is a paradigm of communication, and all human relations are based on some form of communication. Our very ability to think, to conceptualize, is related to speech. Speech allows the social to penetrate the intimately personal. Perhaps that is why Kant's dicta seem to vacillate between two positions: lying as a social offense, and lying as an offense against oneself; the requirement of an intent to deceive another, and the insistence that the essence of the wrong is not injury to another but to humanity. Every lie violates the basic commitment to truth which stands behind the social fact of language.

I have already argued that bodily integrity bears a necessary relation to moral integrity, so that an attack upon bodily integrity is wrong, not just bad. The intimate *and* social nature of truth make the argument about lying stronger. For not only is the target aspect of the victim crucial to him as a moral agent but, by lying, we attack that target by a means which itself offends his moral nature; the means of attack are social means which can be said to belong as much to the victim as to his assailant. There is not only the attack at his moral vitals, but an attack with a weapon which belongs to him. Lying is, thus, a kind of treachery. (*Kind of* treachery? Why not treachery pure and simple?) It is as if we not only robbed a man of his treasure but in doing so used his own servants or family as our agents. That speech is our *common* property, that it belongs to the liar, his victim and all of us makes the matter if anything far worse.

So this is why lying is not only bad (a hurt), but wrong, why lying is wrong apart from or in addition to any other injury it does, and why lying seems at once an offense against the victim and against mankind in general, an offense against the liar himself, and against the abstract entity, truth. Whom do you injure when you pass a counterfeit bill?

What about little pointless lies? Do I really mean they are wrong? Well, yes, even a little lie is wrong, *if* it is a true piece of communication, an assertion of its own truth and not just a conventional way of asserting nothing at all or something else (as in the case of polite or diplomatic formulas). A little lie is a little wrong, but it is still something you must not do.

THOMAS E. HILL, JR.

Autonomy and
Benevolent Lies

THOMAS E. HILL, JR., teaches philosophy at the University of North Carolina at Chapel Hill. He is well known for his work in ethics and the philosophy of Kant.

A former teacher related to me the following true story (which I have modified slightly). He had a student who showed in tutorial conversations signs of deep, suicidal depression. The student was later found dead, and the circumstances were such that others could easily have seen his death as accidental. The professor helped to gather up the boy's belongings to return to his mother, and no suicide note was found. But the mother, a devout Roman Catholic, was deeply worried about her son's soul, and she asked the professor point blank whether he had any reason to suspect suicide. The professor, an atheist, wanted to comfort her and so, by a quite deliberate lie, assured her that, as far as he knew, the boy had been in good spirits.

Another true story concerns a doctor who discovered that his mother, a very elderly but happy woman, had extremely advanced atherosclerosis. Her doctor had apparently chosen to treat the problem as best he could without informing the woman how near death she was. The son had no objection to the medical treatment or her doctor's decision to withhold information. Though he thought his mother psychologically and physically capable of handling the truth, he believed that her last days would be happier if she did not know. The problem arose when she asked her son directly, "Do you think the doctor is telling me everything?" The son lied; but since the question concerned his opinion and he had learned of her condition in ways she did not suspect and without anyone else knowing that he knew, he felt confident that she would never discover his lie. He lied to make her more comfortable, and she was in fact happy until her death.

Consider, lastly, a dilemma which could occur even if it has not. Mary has made a painful break from her ex-lover, John, and though pulled towards him, is on the mend. Her roommate is pleased for her, as she knows that John and Mary were, and will remain, painfully incompatible. She is fearful, though, that John and Mary will get together again, causing both unnecessary misery before the inevitable final separation. Overhearing John talking with a friend, she learns that John is ready to "start over" if only he receives an encouraging sign; and she expects that Mary, ever the optimist, would give the sign. Later Mary asks the roommate, "Do you think he would want to try again if I asked him?" As an act of kindness, the roommate replies, "No, I am sure he knows it would never work."

These examples illustrate the special sort of benevolent lies I want to consider. The lies are benevolent because they are intended to benefit the person deceived, for no ulterior motives, and they actually succeed in giving comfort without causing pain. Despite the benevolent motives, there is no denying that deliberate lies were told. We are not dealing with examples of mere silence, evasion, ambiguous response, and the like. The lies, moreover, are not designed to protect incompetents from truths beyond their capacities to handle sanely and responsibly. In our sample cases a lie will protect someone from avoidable pain, but it is not needed to prevent serious physical or psychological damage, violent outbursts, gross misperception of reality, and so on.

· Our examples also fall outside a range of special problem situations. Some lies, for example, are told in a context where the liar has rather little chance of being believed; but in our cases there is sufficient credibility to make the deception effective. Other lies concern matters which are, intuitively, "none of the business" of the questioner: for example, a lie told to a curious student who asked his teacher about his private sex life. But the questions in our examples are clearly not "out of bounds" in this way. What is asked for is information or opinion about what deeply concerns the questioner's own life. Also the lies in our stories cannot be deemed trivial. Unlike "little white lies," they are about matters of the utmost importance to the deceived: heaven or hell, life or death, reunion or separation from a loved one. Further, our examples concern lies between individuals, not lies from public officials or to institutions, and so certain questions of public responsibility are left aside. Finally, let us imagine that the deceived has not forfeited a right to know, for example, by his own repeated lying or by having a plain intent to misuse the truth.

Lies are often wrong at least in part because they are breaches of a promise to be truthful, but, to simplify matters, let us suppose that there were no such promises in our examples. It is easy to imagine that the professor, the dying woman's son, and the roommate never made an *explicit* promise to tell the truth as, for example, one is required to do before testifying in court. The more difficult matter is to remove the suspicion that they made a tacit or implicit promise to be truthful. Ross maintained that we make such an implicit promise every time we make an assertion, and so he viewed all lies as breaches of promise. But this position, surely, is implausible. Suppose, for example, two enemies distrust each other, have no desire to be honest with each other, and both know this. As seems to be common in international relations, they tell the truth to each other only when they expect that lying will not give them an advantage. In this situation when one asserts to the other, say, that he has documents damaging to the other's political ambitions, we cannot reasonably interpret this as a promise. Neither person believes that the speaker intends to put himself under obligation. Given their mutual understanding, the speaker cannot seriously intend to lead the other to believe that he is making it a matter of conscience to convey the truth. Furthermore if every assertion amounted to a promise to say what is true, we would not think, as in fact we do, that a lie preceded by an explicit promise to be truthful is usually worse than a lie not preceded by such a promise. There are, of course, implicit promises but it requires more than mere assertion to make one. Suppose, for example, Mary and her roommate had often discussed how they valued each other's honesty and frankness, and each had on other occasions insisted that the other tell the truth, however painful, and neither gave any hint of reservations about giving and counting on complete truthfulness between them. With this special background we might want to say that they had made implicit promises to tell each other the truth. However, to focus attention away from promises, let us suppose that in our examples there were no such special conditions to create implicit promises to be truthful.

Our examples are also meant to minimize the force of utilitarian considerations that so often tell against lying. Most importantly, the lies in our stories are extremely unlikely to be discovered. It is a moralist's fiction that lies can never remain hidden: perhaps a useful fiction, but untrue nonetheless. In each of our examples a person is asked about what he knows or believes, and if he is determined to stand by his response there is no practical way others can find out that he is lying. Even if the student's mother learns that her son committed suicide, she cannot know that the professor lied; the elderly woman can find out that she is seriously ill, but not that her son lied about his opinion; Mary may learn that John is still available, but she has no way of discovering that her roommate knew. There is, of course, always *some* chance, however remote, that those who lie will give themselves away; for example, they may talk in their sleep. If the discovery of the lie would be an utter disaster, then from a utilitarian point of view even this very small risk might not be warranted. But to simplify, let us suppose that in our cases discovery would not be disastrous. The persons deceived, let us say, have an unusually forgiving and trusting nature. If they realized the special circumstances and benevolent intent, they would forgive the lie; and, though disappointed, they would not become unreasonably suspicious and distrustful. Again, typical lies tend to multiply, one lie calling for another and each lie making successive ones easier; but we can imagine this not to be so in our example. Our professor, doctor/son, and roommate, let us suppose, are of firm character and would lie only in the special circumstances we have defined, and they do not need an entangled web of further deception to hide the first.

Lies of the sort pictured here are no doubt rare; but, by minimizing the usual considerations of utility and promises, they enable us to focus on other relevant considerations, which may be important in more typical cases as well. In particular, we can reflect on how lies can fail to respect persons' autonomy. . . .

. . . Let us say that persons have autonomy, or live autonomously, . . . if the following is true: (1) They have the psychological capacities for rational decision making . . . ; (2) they actually use these capacities when they face important choice situations; (3) they have the right . . . to make morally and legally permissible decisions about matters deeply affecting their own lives free from threats and manipulation by others; (4) other people actually respect this right as well as their other rights; (5) they are able and disposed to have distinctly human values; (6) others respect this capacity by not presuming that they value only good experiences for themselves and by not counting their comfort more important than their declared values; and, finally, (7) they have ample opportunities to make use of these conditions in living a life over which they have a high degree of control. . . .

The ideal of developing the psychological capacities associated with autonomy may give some reason to hesitate to tell lies to protect people from painful realities, but not a reason that applies in all cases. Probably, as a rule, having to face unpleasant truths about matters deeply affecting one's life helps one to develop the capacity for mature, reflective decision making. If so, there would be a general presumption against benevolent lies, even if it would not always be persuasive as, for example, when we are dealing with the very elderly whose capacities have presumably already been developed as much as they will be.

If we believe in the *right* of autonomy, however, we have more reason to object to benevolent lies. This is most obvious in our example of the roommate lying to keep her friend from re-uniting with her ex-lover. The roommate manipulates her friend's decision (to call or not to call her "ex") by actively concealing pertinent information. If we accept the right of autonomy, this could only be justified if the reunion would have been so great a disaster that the right is over-ridden. In other cases the right of autonomy may be violated but in a less obvious way. The professor and the doctor/son, for example, did not lie in order to control the decisions of the people they deceived; they only wanted to spare them avoidable pain. Nevertheless, there were important life-altering decisions which the deceived might have made if they had not been deprived of relevant information; and surely the professor and the doctor/son knew this. They knowingly prevented certain options presented by the real situation from ever being faced by the people they deceived; to pray or not, and, if so, how; to continue life as usual or to re-order one's priorities; to face death and tragedy stoically or to be open in a new way with friends.

Someone may object as follows: "Sometimes benevolent lies interfere with life-altering decisions, but not always; often benevolent lies merely keep people from suffering unnecessarily because of something which they can do nothing about. When, for example, a widow demands to know whether her husband suffered when he was killed in the war, there is little she can *do* if she is told truthfully that he died in horrible agony. And similarly, if the suicide's mother had been bedridden and terminally ill, the professors lie would not have interfered with any important decisions."

The appropriate response, I think, is this: Benevolent lies do not necessarily or always violate the right of autonomy, but we should not be hasty in concluding that a particular lie does not concern any significant decisions. Good novelists and biographers know what philosophers too easily forget, namely, that the most important decisions in life are not always about external behavior, about what to *do* in the public world. How we face death, family tragedy, our own successes and failures, and the way others treat us, is partly a matter of decision, as Sartreans knew but exaggerated. Even *whether* to see a situation as success or failure, tragic or routine, is not simply a matter of perception of fact. We can also interfere with these life-altering decisions or prevent a person from facing them, by keeping certain truths from him—even if he is immobile for the rest of his life.

Consider next the principles associated with autonomy as a capacity for distinctly human values. Their implications for benevolent lies depend upon what we know about the preferences of the person to be deceived. Suppose, first, that we have no reason to doubt that the questioner wants an honest answer. His question is in effect an expression of a desire to know the truth. To give him less because we want to spare him pain would be to count his comfort more important than what he himself professes to value more and so would be contrary to our principles.

Sometimes, of course, people ask questions wanting to be reassured rather than to learn the truth. What should we do if we have indirect evidence that the questioner does not really want to know? Much depends, I think, on the nature and strength of the evidence. Suppose, for example, the evidence is rather evenly mixed: the person often shrinks from painful realities but, on the other hand, he asked in a serious tone, he never said in advance not to reveal the sort of fact in question, and the truth is not outside the range of answers he could anticipate. Often when we are in doubt whether a person really prefers what he professes, we can remove the uncertainty by asking further questions; but the peculiarity of the dilemma of the would-be benevolent liar is that he cannot resolve the uncertainty this way. To ask, "Would you *really* prefer the truth even though it will hurt?" is in effect to give away the answer. When faced with such mixed evidence and unresolvable uncertainty, one guided by our principles of autonomy would, I believe, again be disposed to tell the truth; for respecting a person's capacity for distinctly human values implies that, other things equal, it is worse to presume that someone prefers comfort to some other declared value than to presume the opposite.

If there were definitive evidence that the questioner preferred not to learn the painful truth, then autonomy as a capacity for distinctly human values would not be relevant. This would be the case if, for example, the questioner had explicitly requested in advance not to be told the truth in specified circumstances, and then, later, those circumstances arose and ample evidence indicated that he had not changed his mind.

Such cases, however, are probably rare. Normally even if a person has previously asked not to be told the truth, his subsequent question raises legitimate doubts about his current preferences. Suppose the earlier request was not made in anticipation of a period of incompetence—like Ulysses' request to his crew before facing the sirens ("Don't listen to what I say later"). Then the would-be liar is apparently faced with two conflicting requests; an earlier request for deception, and a later request for truth. Unless there are independent reasons for discounting the latter, or for not treating the later question as a request for truth, then one might argue that respect for autonomy gives precedence to the more recent request. Other things equal, we respect a person's autonomy more by allowing changes of mind, honoring what he *does* profess to value over what he *did* profess to value.

The many-sided *ideal* of autonomous living will usually give further reason for hesitating to tell benevolent lies. Even if benevolent lies do not violate a *right*, they still deprive people of a realistic picture of their situation. Insofar as having such a realistic picture is needed for genuine rational control over one's life, to that extent the benevolent liar fails to promote an ideal end.

It may be objected that this argument supports the desirability of volunteering the truth just as much as it supports the desirability of not actively depriving someone of the truth; and yet, it might be said, it is counter-intuitive to suppose that we have as much reason to volunteer painful truths as to tell them when directly asked. The ideal does give reason to volunteer the truth, I think, but there are also reasons why lying in response to a direct question is worse than merely not volunteering the truth. There is a general presumption that one should not cause avoidable pain to others, but this presumption is at least partially set aside when the person requests the painful treatment for the sake of something he wants: e.g. painful medical tests. Thus, although there is a general presumption against expressing truths which cause pain, this presumption is at least partially set aside when a competent person asks for truth; but the presumption is not set aside when one simply volunteers the truth without being asked. Thus, though the ideal of autonomy gives some reason for volunteering painful information about someone's life, the case for volunteering is not as strong as the case for telling the truth when asked.

Another objection might be that "Sometimes we need to lie in order to increase the chances that a person will make his own decisions (and so live autonomously). For example, when my son asked me where I wanted him to go to college, I lied, telling him that I did not care. Actually I wanted very much for him to go where I went; but I figured that he could make up his own mind better if I kept my preference to myself."

The objection points to a practical problem difficult to resolve in real cases, but it does not, I think, show that the ideal of autonomy unequivocally recommends lying even in the example just presented. *One* aspect of ideal, to be sure, was encouraging people to make their important decisions in a rational way free from inner psychological obstacles such as neurotic need for a father's approval. Thus, if the son in our example was so dominated by his father's opinions that he could not make a rational choice once his father expressed his desires, then one aspect of the ideal of autonomy would urge the father to hide his opinion. But let us suppose, as in our previous examples, the person deceived is rationally competent with respect to his choice problem and so is not a slave to his father's wishes. In this case another aspect of the ideal of autonomy would urge the father to express his wishes: he should make clear both that he prefers his son to go to his old college and also that he wants his son to decide on the basis of what he, the son, most wants. This puts the pertinent facts on the table, giving the son an opportunity he would have otherwise lacked, namely, to choose whether to give weight to his father's wishes or not and, if so, which wish to count more important. By lying, the father would have helped the son make a self-interested choice; but, as we have seen, one's autonomous choice is not always self-interested. To "make up one's own mind" is not necessarily to decide without regard for others' wishes but to decide maturely in the light of the facts about the situation.

So far we have considered ways in which principles and ideals of autonomy help to explain why we view even benevolent lies as to some degree objectionable; but we also have intuitive opinions about which sort of lies (or deceptions) are worse than others. Let us consider, then, whether considerations of autonomy help to explain these intuitions as well.

To consider several factors together, I suppose it is commonly accepted that deceptive responses to questions are worse, other things equal, when (a) the response is a direct lie rather than a merely evasive, misleading, or deceptively ambiguous response, (b) the person deceived trusts the deceiver and was encouraged to do so, and (c) the lie concerns the life of the deceived rather than matters only remotely touching him. The lies of the roommate and the doctor/son described earlier exemplify the first sort. An example of the second, less significant sort of deception might be this: A person asks me, simply from curiosity, "Do you know whether so-and-so is gay?", and, though I know, I answer, "How would I know?"

Now utilitarians will have familiar explanations why the first sort of lie is regarded as more serious than the second; but it is worth nothing that our principles and ideals of autonomy provide an alternative, or additional, explanation. In brief, one's opportunity to live in rational control of one's life is increased when there are people one can unmistakably identify as prepared to give straight, honest answers to direct pointed questions. If one does not want to know, one can refrain from asking; if the first answer is evasive or ambiguous, suggesting a reluctance on the other's part to reveal the truth, then one can choose to put the question again more pointedly or to back off; and if one does insist ("I want a straight, honest answer!"), then, while allowing for honest errors, one can make important decisions with more confidence that one understands the real situation. To live in a world without people we can rely on in this way would be to live in a world in which we have less control over our lives. Utilitarians often stress the unpleasantness that results when lies which violate trust become discovered, and for this reason our examples were designed to minimize the risk of discovery. But now it emerges that ideals of autonomy not only oppose undiscoverable benevolent lies; they also oppose lies which risk discovery of a breach of trust for discovery of such lies encourages us to be distrustful and suspicious and so less able to make use of even the honest answers trustworthy persons give us; and this limits our opportunities for rational control over our lives.

●   ●   ●

These conclusions, of course, are both hypothetical and intuitive: that is, the argument has been that if one accepts certain principles of autonomy, then one has reasons to refrain from benevolent lies. But imagine now an objection from a normative hedonist unwilling to rest the issue on intuitive principles. He argues that, intuitions aside, it is *irrational* to prefer truth to comfort, unless having the truth would maximize one's pleasure in the long run. Thus, he continues, when one aims to be benevolent towards another, it is *irrational* to give him the truth if a lie will contribute more to his total satisfaction.

The objection rests on the common, but mistaken, assumption that, at least when free from moral constraints, a fully rational person would always aim for his most favorable pleasure/pain ratio. But why so? As we have seen, people do in fact have (non-moral) concerns independent of any anticipated good experiences. Some, perhaps, make maximum pleasure their goal; and others do not. What determines whether one is rational is not, by itself, the content of one's aims, but how they are arrived at, how they fit into one's life plan, etc. More plausible than the hedonist's conception of rationality, I think, is that of John Rawls, who defines ideal rationality, roughly, as satisfying certain "counting principles" (means–end efficiency, inclusion, etc.) and then deciding in light of full information about one's desires, circumstances, etc. Given this conception and the falsity of *psychological* hedonism (i.e. that all seek only to maximize their pleasure), then the rational life will be different for different people. For some, maybe, it will be predominantly pursuit of pleasure; but, unless we suppose that all non-hedonistic desires would extinguish when exposed to more information, for many the rational life will include pursuit of other values, such as truth, independently of their pay-off in personal satisfaction.

The principles of autonomy which we have considered, though still un-unified in a general theory, point toward a conception of morality quite different in spirit from familiar forms of utilitarianism, hedonistic and otherwise. The latter start with views about what is intrinsically valuable as an end, and then define morality, in one way or another, as what promotes this end. A theory of autonomy, following Kant, Rawls, and others, would first define principles for moral institutions and personal interactions, leaving each person, within these constraints, the freedom to choose and pursue whatever ends they will. Such a theory would not oppose benevolent lies on the ground that truth-telling will maximize some intrinsic value other than pleasure (e.g., self-awareness); rather, it would encourage truthfulness as, in general, a way of respecting people as free to choose their own ends.

HENRY SIDGWICK

The Duty of Veracity

HENRY SIDGWICK (1828–1900) was an English philosopher who taught at the University of Cambridge. He was a founding member and the first president of the Society for Psychical Research. Sidgwick's most noted work is his book *The Method of Ethics* (1874).

•   •   •

1. It may easily seem that when we have discussed Benevolence, Justice, and the observance of Law and Contract, we have included in our view the whole sphere of social duty, and that whatever other maxims we find accepted by Common Sense must be subordinate to the principles which we have been trying to define.

For whatever we owe definitely to our fellow-men, besides the observance of special contracts, and of positive laws, seems—at least by a slight extension of common usage—to be naturally included under Justice: while the more indefinite obligations which we recognise seem to correspond to the goodwill which we think ought to exist among all members of the human family, together with the stronger affections appropriate to special relations and circumstances. And hence it may be thought that the best way of treating the subject would have been to divide Duty generally into Social and Self-regarding, and again to subdivide the former branch into heads which I have discussed one by one; afterwards adding such minor details of duty as have obtained special names and distinct recognition. And this is perhaps the proper place to explain why I did not adopt this course. The division of duties into Social and Self-regarding, though obvious, and acceptable enough as a rough *prima facie* classification, does not on closer examination seem exactly appropriate to the Intuitional Method. For these titles naturally suggest that the happiness or well-being, of the agent or of others, is always the end and final determinant of right action: whereas the Intuitional doctrine is, that at least certain kinds of conduct are prescribed absolutely, without reference to their ulterior consequences. And if a more general meaning be given to the terms, and by Social duties we understand those which consist in the production of certain effects upon others, while in the Self-regarding we aim at producing certain effects upon ourselves, the division is still an unsuitable one. For these consequences are not clearly recognised in the enunciation of common rules of morality: and in many cases we produce marked effects both on ourselves and on others, and it is not easy to say which (in the view of Common Sense) are most important: and again, this principle of division would sometimes make it necessary to cut in two the class of duties prescribed under some common notion; as the same rule may govern both our social and our solitary conduct. Take, for example, the acts morally prescribed under the head of Courage. It seems clear that the prominence given to this Virtue in historic systems of morality has been due to the great social importance that must always attach to it, so long as communities of men are continually called upon to fight for their existence and well-being: but still the quality of bravery is the same essentially, whether it be exhibited for selfish or social ends.

It is no doubt true that when we examine with a view to definition the kinds of conduct commended or prescribed in any list of Virtues commonly recognised, we find, to a great extent, that the maxims we obtain are clearly not absolute and independent; that the quality denoted by our term is admittedly only praiseworthy in so far as it promotes individual or general welfare, and becomes blameworthy—though remaining in other respects the same—when it operates adversely to these ends. We have already noticed this result in one or two instances, and it will be illustrated at length in the following chapters. But though this is the case to a great extent, it is, for our present purpose, of special importance to note the—real or apparent—exceptions to the rule; because they are specially characteristic of the method that we call Institutionism.

One of the most important of these exceptions is Veracity: and the affinity in certain respects of this duty—in spite of fundamental differences—to the duty of Good Faith or Fidelity to Promises renders it convenient to examine the two in immediate succession. Under either head a certain correspondence between words and facts is prescribed: and hence the questions that arise when we try to make the maxims precise are somewhat similar in both cases. For example, just as the duty of Good Faith did not lie in conforming out acts to the *admissible* meaning of certain words, but to the meaning which we knew to be put on them by the promisee; so the duty of Truthspeaking is not to utter words which *might*, according to common usage, produce in other minds beliefs corresponding to our own, but words which we believe will have this effect on the persons whom we address. And this is usually a very simple matter, as the natural effect of language is to convey our beliefs to other men, and we commonly know quite well whether we are doing this or not. A certain difficulty arises, as in the case of promises, from the use of set forms imposed either by law or by custom. . . . In the case of formulæ imposed by law—such (*e.g.*) as declarations of religious belief—it is doubtful whether we may understand the terms in any sense which they commonly bear, or are to take them in the sense intended by the Legislature that imposed them; and again, a difficulty is created by the gradual degradation or perversion of their meaning, which results from the strong inducements offered for their general acceptance; for thus they are continually strained and stretched until a new general understanding seems gradually to grow up as to the meaning of certain phrases; and it is continually disputed whether we may veraciously use the phrases in this new signification. A similar process continually alters the meaning of conventional expressions current in polite society. When a man declares that he 'has great pleasure in accepting' a vexatious invitation, or is 'the obedient servant' of one whom he regards as an inferior, he uses phrases which were probably once deceptive. If they are so no longer, Common Sense condemns as over-scrupulous the refusal to use them where it is customary to do so. But Common Sense seems doubtful and perplexed where the process of degradation is incomplete, and there are still persons who may be deceived: as in the use of the reply that one is 'not at home' to an inconvenient visitor from the country.

However, apart from the use of conventional phrases, the rule 'to speak the truth' is not generally difficult of application in conduct. And many moralists have regarded this, from its simplicity and definiteness, as a quite unexceptional instance of an ethical axiom. I think, however, that patient reflection will show that this view is not really confirmed by the Common Sense of mankind.

• • •

2. In the first place, it does not seem clearly agreed whether Veracity is an absolute and independent duty, or a special application of some higher principle. We find (*e.g.*) that Kant regards it as a duty owed to oneself to speak the truth, because 'a lie is an abandonment or, as it were, annihilation of the dignity of man.' And this seems to be the view in which lying is prohibited by the code of honour, except that it is not thought (by men of honour as such) that the dignity of man is impaired by *any* lying: but only that lying for selfish ends, especially under the influence of fear, is mean and base. In fact there seems to be circumstances under which the code of honour prescribes lying. Here, however, it may be said to be plainly divergent from the morality of Common Sense. Still, the latter does not seem to decide clearly whether truth-speaking is absolutely a duty, needing no further justification: or whether it is merely a general right of each man to have truth spoken to him by his fellows, which right however may be forfeited or suspended under certain circumstances. Just as each man is thought to have a natural right to personal security generally, but not if he is himself attempting to injure others in life and property: so if we may even kill in defence of ourselves and others, it seems strange if we may not lie, if lying will defend us better against a palpable invasion of our rights: and Common Sense does not seem to prohibit this decisively. And again, just as the orderly and systematic slaughter which we call war is thought perfectly right under certain circumstances, though painful and revolting: so in the word-contests of the law-courts, the lawyer is commonly held to be justified in untruthfulness within strict rules and limits: for an advocate is thought to be over-scrupulous who refuses to say what he knows to be false, if he is instructed to say it. Again, where deception is designed to benefit the person deceived, Common Sense seems to concede that it may sometimes be right: for example, most persons would not hesitate to speak falsely to an invalid, if this seemed the only way of concealing facts that might produce a dangerous shock: nor do I perceive that any one shrinks from telling fictions to children, on matters upon which it is thought well that they should not know the truth. But if the lawfulness of benevolent deception in any case be admitted, I do not see how we can decide when and how far it is admissible, except by considerations of expediency; that is, by weighing the gain of any particular deception against the imperilment of mutual confidence involved in all violation of truth.

The much argued question of religious deception ('pious fraud') naturally suggests itself here. It seems clear, however, that Common Sense now pronounces against the broad rule, that falsehoods may rightly be told in the interests of religion. But there is a subtler form in which the same principle is still maintained by moral persons. It is sometimes said that the most important truths of religion cannot be conveyed into the minds of ordinary men, except by being enclosed, as it were, in a shell of fiction; so that by relating such fictions as if they were facts, we are really performing an act of substantial veracity. Reflecting upon this argument, we see that it is not after all so clear wherein Veracity consists. For from the beliefs immediately communicated by any set of affirmations inferences are naturally drawn, and we may clearly foresee that they will be drawn. And though commonly we intend that both the beliefs immediately communicated and the inferences drawn from them should be true, and a person who always aims at this is praised as candid and sincere: still we find relaxation of the rule prescribing this intention claimed in two different ways by at least respectable sections of opinion. For first, as was just now observed, it is sometimes held that if a conclusion is true and important, and cannot be satisfactorily communicated otherwise, we may lead the mind of the hearer to it by means of fictitious premises. But the exact reverse of this is perhaps a commoner view: viz. that it is only an absolute duty to make our actual affirmations true; for it is said that though the ideal condition of human converse involves perfect sincerity and candour, and we ought to rejoice in exhibiting these virtues where we can, still in our actual world concealment is frequently necessary to the well-being of society, and may be legitimately effected by any means short of actual falsehood. Thus it is not uncommonly said that in defence of a secret we may not indeed *lie*, *i.e.* produce directly beliefs contrary to fact; but we may "turn a question aside," *i.e.* produce indirectly, by natural inference from our answer, a negatively false belief; or "throw the inquirer on a wrong scent," *i.e.* produce similarly a positively false belief. These two methods of concealment are known respectively as *suppressio veri* and *suggestio falsi*, and many think them legitimate under certain circumstances: while others say that if deception is to be practised at all, it is mere formalism to object to any one mode of effecting it more than another.

On the whole, then, reflection seems to show that the rule of Veracity, as commonly accepted, cannot be elevated into a definite moral axiom: for there is no real agreement as to how far we are bound to impart true beliefs to others: and while it is contrary to Common Sense to exact absolute candour under all circumstances, we yet find no self-evident secondary principle, clearly defining when it is not to be exacted.

● ● ●

3. There is, however, one method of exhibiting *a priori* the absolute duty of Truth, which we must not overlook; as, if it be valid, it would seem that the exceptions and qualifications above mentioned have been only admitted by Common Sense from inadvertence and shallowness of thought.

It is said that if it were once generally understood that lies were justifiable under certain circumstances, it would immediately become quite useless to tell the lies, because no one would believe them; and that the moralist cannot lay down a rule which, if generally accepted, would be suicidal. To this there seem to be three answers. In the first place it is not necessarily an evil that men's confidence in each other's assertions should, *under certain peculiar circumstances*, be impaired or destroyed: it may even be the very result which we should most desire to produce: *e.g.* it is obviously a most effective protection for legitimate secrets that it should be universally understood and expected that those who ask questions which they have no right to ask will have lies told them: nor, again, should we be restrained from pronouncing it lawful to meet deceit with deceit, merely by the fear of impairing the security which rogues now derive from the veracity of honest men. No doubt the ultimate result of general unveracity under the circumstances would be a state of things in which such falsehoods would no longer be told: but unless this ultimate result is undesirable, the prospect of it does not constitute a reason why the falsehoods should not be told so long as they are useful. But, secondly, since the beliefs of men in general are not formed purely on rational grounds, experience shows that unveracity may long remain partially effective under circumstances where it is generally understood to be legitimate. We see this in the case of the law-courts. For though jurymen are perfectly aware that it is considered the duty of an advocate to state as plausibly as possible whatever he has been instructed to say on behalf of any criminal he may defend, still a skillful pleader may often produce an impression that he sincerely believes his client to be innocent: and it remains a question

of casuistry how far this kind of hypocrisy is justifiable. But, finally, it cannot be assumed as certain that it is never right to act upon a maxim of which the universal application would be an undoubted evil. This assumption may seem to be involved in
what was previously admitted as an ethical axiom, that what is right for me must be
right for 'all persons under similar conditions.' But reflection will show that there is a
special case within the range of the axiom in which its application is necessarily self-
limiting, and excludes the practical universality which the axiom appears to suggest:
i.e. where the agent's conditions include (1) the knowledge that his maxim is not universally accepted, and (2) a reasoned conviction that his act will not tend to make it so,
to any important extent. For in this case the axiom will practically only mean that it
will be right for all persons to do as the agent does, if they are sincerely convinced that
the act will not be widely imitated; and this conviction must vanish if it *is* widely imitated. It can hardly be said that these conditions are impossible: and if they are possible,
the axiom that we are discussing can only serve, in its present application, to direct our
attention to an important danger of unveracity, which constitutes a strong—but not
formally conclusive—utilitarian ground for speaking the truth.

ANNETTE BAIER

Trust and Anti-Trust

ANNETTE BAIER taught for many years at the University of Pittsburgh. She has published widely in moral philosophy. Her most recent book is *Moral Prejudices* (1995), from which the following selection is taken.

The few discussions of trust that I have found in the literature of moral philosophy assume that trust is a good and that disappointing known trust is always prima facie wrong, meeting it always prima facie right. But what is a trust-tied community without justice but a group of mutual blackmailers and exploiters? When the trust relationship itself is corrupt and perpetuates brutality, tyranny, or injustice, trusting may be silly self-exposure, and disappointing and betraying trust, including encouraged trust, may be not merely morally permissible but morally praiseworthy. Women, proletarians, and ex-slaves cannot ignore the virtues of watchful distrust and of judicious untrustworthiness. Only if we had reason to believe that most familiar types of trust relationship were morally sound would breaking trust be any more prima facie wrong than breaking silence. I turn to the question of when a given form of trust is morally decent, so properly preserved by trustfulness and trustworthiness, and when it fails in moral decency. . . . I shall take as the form of trust to test for moral decency the trust which one spouse has in the other, in particular as concerns their children's care.

. . . A child has reason to trust the parents when both child and parents care about the same good—the child's happiness—although the child may not see eye to eye with those trusted parents about how that is best taken care of. When one parent, say the old-style father, entrusts the main care of his young child's needs to the old-style mother, there, too, there can be agreement on the good they both want cared for but disagreement about how best it is cared for. The lord and master who entrusts such care to his good wife, the mother, and so gives her discretionary power in making moment-by-moment decisions about what is to be done, will have done so sensibly if these disagreements are not major ones, or if he has reason to think that she knows better than he does about such matters. He should defer to her judgment, as the child is encouraged to do to the parents' and as I do to my plumber's. He sensibly trusts if he has reason to think that the discretionary powers given, even when used in ways he does not fully understand or approve of, are still used to care for the goods he wants cared for. He would be foolish to trust if he had evidence that she had other ends in view in her treatment of the child or had a radically different version of what, say, the child's healthy development and proper relation to his father consisted in. Once he suspects that she, the trusted nurse of his sons and daughters, is deliberately rearing the daughters to be patriarch-toppling Amazons, the sons to be subverters of the father's values, he will sensibly withdraw his trust and dispatch his children to suitably chosen female relatives or boarding schools. What would properly undermine his trust would be beliefs he came to hold about the formerly trusted person's motives and purposes in her care of what was entrusted to her. The disturbing and trust-undermining suspicion is not necessarily that she doesn't care about the children's good, or cares only about her own—it is the suspicion that what she cares about conflicts with rather than harmonizes with what he cares about and that she is willing to sacrifice his concerns to what she sees as the children's and her own. Trusting is rational, then, in the absence of any reason to suspect in the trusted strong and operative motives which conflict with the demands of trustworthiness as the truster sees them.

But trusting can continue to be rational, even when there are such unwelcome suspicions, as long as the truster is confident that in the conflict of motives within the trusted the subversive motives will lose to the conformist motives. Should the wife face economic hardship and loss of her children if she fails to meet the husband's trust or incurs too much of his suspicion, then she will sensibly continue as the dutiful wife, until her power position alters—sensibly, that is, given what she cares about. The husband in a position to be sure that the costs to the wife of discovered untrustworthiness are a sufficient deterrent will sensibly continue in trusting her while increasing his vigilance. Nor is he relying only on her fear, since, by hypothesis, her motives are conflicting and so she is not without some goodwill and some sympathy for his goals. Should he conclude that *only* fear of sanctions keeps her at her wifely duties, then the situation will have deteriorated from trust to mere reliance on his threat advantage. In such a case he will, if he has any sense, shrink the scope of her discretionary powers to virtually zero, since it is under cover of those that she cannot merely thwart his purposes for his children but work to change the power relations in her own favor. As long as he gives her any discretion in looking after what is entrusted to her, he must trust her, and not rely solely on her fear of threatened penalties for disappointing his expectations.

The trusted wife (who usually, of course, also trusts her husband with many things that matter to her) is sensible to try to keep his trust, as long as she judges that the goods which would be endangered should she fail to meet his trust matter more to her than those she could best look after only by breaking or abusing his trust. The goods for the sake of whose thriving she sensibly remains trustworthy might include the loving relation between them and their mutual trust for its own sake as well as their agreed version of their children's good; or it might be some vestiges of these plus her own economic support or even physical safety, which are vulnerable to his punitive rage should she be found guilty of breach of trust. She will sensibly continue to meet trust, even when the goods with whose case she is trusted are no longer clearly common goods, as long as she cares a lot about anything his punitive wrath can and is likely to harm.

Sensible trust could persist, then, in conditions where truster and trusted suspect each other of willingness to harm the other if they could get away with it, the one by breach of trust, the other by vengeful response to that. The stability of the relationship will depend on the trusted's skill in cover-up activities, on the truster's evident threat advantage, or on a combination of these. Should the untrustworthy trusted person have not merely skill in concealment of her breaches of trust but skill in directing them toward increasing her own power and increasing her ability to evade or protect herself against the truster's attempted vengeance, then that will destabilize the relation, as also would frequent recourse by the truster to punitive measures against the trusted.

Where the truster relies on his threat advantage to keep the trust relation going or where the trusted relies on concealment, something is morally rotten in the trust relationship. The truster who in part relies on his whip or his control of the purse is sensible but not necessarily within his moral rights in continuing to expect trustworthiness;

and the trusted who sensibly relies on concealment to escape the penalty for untrust-worthiness may or may not be within her moral rights. I tentatively propose a test for the moral decency of a trust relationship, namely, that its continuation need not rely on successful threats held over the trusted or on her successful cover-up of breaches of trust. . . . Knowledge of what the other party is relying on for the continuance of the trust relationship would, in the above cases of concealment and of threat advantage, it-self destabilize the relation. Knowledge of the other's reliance on concealment does so fairly automatically, and knowledge of the other's partial reliance on one's fear of his revenge would tend, in a person of normal pride and self-assertiveness, to prompt her to look for ways of exploiting her discretionary powers so as to minimize her vulnera-bility to that threat. More generally, to the extent that what the truster relies on for the continuance of the trust relation is something which, once realized by the truster, is likely to lead to (increased) abuse of trust and eventually to destabilization and destruc-tion of that relation, the trust is morally corrupt. Should the wife come to realize that the husband relies on her fear of his revenge, on her stupidity in not realizing her ex-ploitation, or on her servile devotion to him to keep her more or less trustworthy, or on her servile devotion to him to keep her more or less trustworthy, that knowledge should be enough to begin to cure these weaknesses and to motivate untrustworthiness. Similarly, should the truster come to realize that the trusted relies on her skill at cover-ing up or on her ability to charm him into forgiveness for breaches of trust, that is, re-lies on *his* blindness or gullibility, that realization will help cure that blindness and gullibility. A trust relationship is morally bad to the extent that either party relies on qualities in the other which would be weakened by the knowledge that the other relies on them. Where each relies on the other's love, concern for some common good, or pro-fessional pride in competent discharge of responsibility, knowledge of what the other is relying on in one need not undermine but will more likely strengthen those relied-on features. They survive exposure as what others rely on in one in a way that some forms of stupidity, fear, blindness, ignorance, and gullibility normally do not. There are other mental states whose sensitivity to exposure as relied on by others seems more variable: good nature, detachment, inattention, generosity, forgivingness, and sexual bondage to the other party to the trust may not be weakened by knowledge that others count on their presence in one to sustain some wanted relationship, especially if they are found equally in both parties. But the knowledge that others are counting on one's nonreciprocated generosity or good nature or forgiveness can have the power of the negative, can destroy trust.

I assume that in some forms of trust the healthy and desired state will be mere self-maintenance, while in others it will be change and growth. Alteration of the trust re-lationship need not take the form of destruction of the old form and its replacement by a new form, but of continuous growth, of slight shifts in scope of discretionary powers, ad-ditions or alterations in scope of goods entrusted, and so on. Of course some excitement-addicted persons may cultivate a form of trust in part for the opportunity it provides for dramatic disruption. Trust is the atmosphere necessary for exhilarating disruptions of trust and satisfyingly spectacular transfers of trust, as well as for other goods we value. For persons with such tastes, immoral forms of trust may be preferable to what, ac-cording to my test, are moral forms of trust. . . .

Since I have . . . oversimplified the problem of morally evaluating trust relation-ships by confining my attention to relationships one by one, my account of trusting as acceptance of having as it were entrusted and my consequent expansion of trusting from a two-place into a three-place predicate will seem forced and wrong. For there are some people whom one would not trust with anything, and that is not because one has considered each good one might entrust to that one and rejected that possibility. We want then to say that unless we first trust them we will not trust them *with anything*. I think that there is some truth in this, which my account has not captured. For some kinds of enemy (perhaps class enemies?) one will not trust even with one's bodily safety as one raises a white flag, but one will find it "safer" to fight to the death. With some sorts of enemies, a contract may be too intimate a relation. If the network of relationships is systematically unjust or systematically coercive, then it may be that one's status within that network will make it unwise of one to entrust anything to those persons whose interests, given their status, are systematically opposed to one's own. In most such corrupt systems there will be limited opportunity for such beleaguered persons to "rescue" their goods from the power of their enemies—they usually will have no choice but to leave them exposed and so to act as if they trusted, although they feel proper distrust. In such conditions it may take fortitude to display distrust and heroism to disappoint the trust of the powerful. Courageous (if unwise) untrustworthiness and stoic withdrawal of trust may then be morally laudable. But since it usually will take such heroic disruptions of inherited trust relationships for persons to distance themselves from those the system makes their enemies, my test will at least be usable to justify such disruptions. In an earlier version of this essay I said that the ghost of plain trust and plain distrust haunted my account of goods-relativized or "fancy" trust. I think that I now see that ghost for what it is and see why it ought to continue to haunt. Still, such total oppositions of interest are rare, and one satisfactory thing about my account is that it enables us to see how we can salvage some respects in which we may trust even those whose interests are to some extent opposed to our own.

. . . Trust, I have claimed, is reliance on others' competence and willingness to look after, rather than harm, things one cares about which are entrusted to their care. The moral test of such trust relationships which I have proposed is that they be able to survive awareness by each party to the relationship of *what* the other relies on in the first to ensure their continued trustworthiness or trustingness. This test elevates to a special place one form of trust, namely, trusting others with knowledge of what it is about them which enables one to trust them as one does or to expect them to be trustworthy. The test could be restated this way: trust is morally decent only if, in addition to whatever else is entrusted, knowledge of each party's reasons for confident reliance on the other to continue the relationship could in principle also be entrusted—since such mutual knowledge would be itself a good, not a threat to other goods. To the extent that mutual reliance can be accompanied by mutual knowledge of the conditions for that reliance, trust is above suspicion, and trustworthiness a nonsuspect virtue. . . .

MARK TWAIN

On the Decay of the Art
of Lying

MARK TWAIN (BORN SAMUEL LANGHORNE CLEMENS IN 1835) was a noted humorist and novelist. He is especially known for his highly autobiographical stories of boyhood on the Mississippi: *The Adventures of Tom Sawyer* (1876) and *The Adventures of Huckleberry Finn* (1884).

Observe, I do not mean to suggest that the *custom* of lying has suffered any decay or interruption—no, for the Lie, as a Virtue, a Principle, is eternal; the Lie, as a recreation, a solace, a refuge in time of need, the fourth Grace, the tenth Muse, man's best and surest friend, is immortal, and cannot perish from the earth while this Club remains. My complaint simply concerns the decay of the *art* of lying. No high-minded man, no man of right feeling, can contemplate the lumbering and slovenly lying of the present day without grieving to see a noble art so prostituted. In this veteran presence I naturally enter upon this scheme with diffidence; it is like an old maid trying to teach nursery matters to the mothers in Israel. It would not become me to criticise you, gentlemen, who are nearly all my elders—and my superiors, in this thing—and so, if I should here and there *seem* to do it, I trust it will in most cases be more in a spirit of admiration than of fault-finding; indeed, if this finest of the fine arts had everywhere received the attention, encouragement, and conscientious practice and development which this Club has devoted to it, I should not need to utter this lament, or shed a single tear. I do not say this to flatter: I say it in a spirit of just and appreciative recognition.

[It had been my intention, at this point, to mention names and give illustrative specimens, but indications observable about me admonished me to beware of particulars and confine myself to generalities.]

No fact is more firmly established than that lying is a necessity of our circumstances—the deduction that it is then a Virtue goes without saying. No virtue can reach its highest usefulness without careful and diligent cultivation—therefore, it goes without saying, that this one ought to be taught in the public schools—at the fireside—even in the newspapers. What chance has the ignorant, uncultivated liar against the educated expert? What chance have I against Mr. Per—against a lawyer? *Judicious* lying is what the world needs. I sometimes think it were even better and safer not to lie at all than to lie injudiciously. An awkward, unscientific lie is often as ineffectual as the truth.

Now let us see what the philosophers say. Note that venerable proverb: Children and fools *always* speak the truth. The deduction is plain—adults and wise persons *never* speak it. Parkman, the historian, says, "The principle of truth may itself be carried into an absurdity." In another place in the same chapter he says, "The saying is old that truth should not be spoken at all times; and those whom a sick conscience worries into habitual violation of the maxim are imbeciles and nuisances." It is strong language, but true. None of us could *live* with an habitual truth-teller; but, thank goodness, none of us has to. An habitual truth-teller is simply an impossible creature; he does not exist; he never has existed. Of course there are people who *think* they never lie, but it is not so—and this ignorance is one of the very things that shame our so-called civilization. Everybody lies—every day; every hour; awake; asleep; in his dreams; in his joy; in his mourning; if he keeps his tongue still, his hands, his feet, his eyes, his attitude, will convey deception—and purposely. Even in sermons—but that is a platitude.

In a far country where I once lived the ladies used to go around paying calls, under the humane and kindly pretense of wanting to see each other; and when they returned home, they would cry out with a glad voice, saying, "We made sixteen calls and found fourteen of them out"—not meaning that they found out anything against the fourteen—not, that was only a colloquial phrase to signify that they were not at home—and their manner of saying it expressed their lively satisfaction in that fact. Now their pretense of wanting to see the fourteen—and the other two whom they had been less lucky with—was that commonest and mildest form of lying which is sufficiently described as a deflection from the truth. Is it justifiable? Most certainly. It is beautiful, it is noble; for its object is, *not* to reap profit, but to convey a pleasure to the sixteen. The iron-souled truth-monger would plainly manifest, or even utter the fact that he didn't want to see those people—and he would be an ass, and inflict a totally unnecessary pain. And next, those ladies in that far country—but never mind, they had a thousand pleasant ways of lying, that grew out of gentle impulses, and were a credit to their intelligence and an honor to their hearts. Let the particulars go.

The men in that far country were liars, every one. Their mere howdy-do was a lie, because *they* didn't care how you did, except they were undertakers. To the ordinary inquirer you lied in return; for you made no conscientious diagnosis of your case, but answered at random, and usually missed it considerably. You lied to the undertaker, and said your health was failing—a wholly commendable lie, since it cost you nothing and pleased the other man. If a stranger called and interrupted you, you said with your hearty tongue, "I'm glad to see you," and said with your heartier soul, "I wish you were with the cannibals and it was dinner-time." When he went, you said regretfully, "*Must* you go?" and followed it with a "Call again;" but you did no harm, for you did not deceive anybody nor inflict any hurt, whereas the truth would have made you both unhappy.

I think that all this courteous lying is a sweet and loving art, and should be cultivated. The highest perfection of politeness is only a beautiful edifice, built, from the base to the dome, of graceful and gilded forms of charitable and unselfish lying.

What I bemoan is the growing prevalence of the brutal truth. Let us do what we can to eradicate it. An injurious truth has no merit over an injurious lie. Neither should ever be uttered. The man who speaks an injurious truth, lest his soul be not saved if he do otherwise, should reflect that that sort of a soul is not strictly worth saving. The man who tells a lie to help a poor devil out of trouble, is one of whom the angels doubtless say, "Lo, here is an heroic soul who casts his own welfare into jeopardy to succor his neighbor's; let us exalt this magnanimous liar."

An injurious lie is an uncommendable thing; and so, also, and in the same degree, is an injurious truth—a fact which is recognizable by the law of libel.

Among other common lies, we have the *silent* lie—the deception which one conveys by simply keeping still and concealing the truth. Many obstinate truthmongers indulge in this dissipation, imagining that if they *speak* no lie, they lie not at all. In that far country where I once lived, there was a lively spirit, a lady whose impulses were always high and pure, and whose character answered to them. One day I was there at dinner, and remarked in a general way, that we are all liars. She was amazed, and said, "Not *all*?" It was before "Pinafore's" time, so I did not make the response which would naturally follow in our day, but frankly said, "Yes, *all*—we are all liars; there are no exceptions." She looked almost offended, and said, "Why, do you include *me*?" "Certainly," I said, "I think you even rank as an expert." She said, "'Sh—'sh! the children!" So the subject was changed in deference to the children's presence, and we went on talking about other things. But as soon as the young people were out of the way, the lady came warmly back to the matter and said, "I have made it the rule of my life to never tell a lie; and I have never departed from it in a single instance." I said, "I don't mean the least harm or disrespect, but really you have been lying like smoke ever since I've been sitting here. It has caused me a good deal of pain, because I am not used to it." She required of me an instance—just a single instance. So I said:

"Well, here is the unfilled duplicate of the blank which the Oakland hospital people sent to you by the hand of the sick-nurse when she came here to nurse your little nephew through his dángerous illness. This blank asks all manner of questions as to the conduct of that sick-nurse: 'Did she ever sleep on her watch? Did she ever forget to give the medicine?' and so forth and so on. You are warned to be very careful and explicit in your answers, for the welfare of the service requires that the nurses be promptly fined or otherwise punished for derelictions. You told me you were perfectly delighted with that nurse—that she had a thousand perfections and only one fault; you found you never could depend on her wrapping Johnny up half sufficiently while he waited in a chilly chair for her to rearrange the warm bed. You filled up the duplicate of this paper, and sent it back to the hospital by the hand of the nurse. How did you answer this question—'Was the nurse at any time guilty of a negligence which was likely to result in the patient's taking cold?' Come—everything is decided by a bet here in California: ten dollars to ten cents you lied when you answered that question." She said, "I didn't; *I left it blank!*" "Just so—you have told a *silent* lie; you have left it to be inferred that you had no fault to find in that matter." She said, "Oh, was that a lie? And how *could* I mention her one single fault, and she so good?—it would have been cruel," I said, "One ought always to lie, when one can do good by it; your impulse was right, but your judgment was crude; this comes of unintelligent practice. Now observe the result of this inexpert deflection of yours. You know Mr. Jones's Willie is lying very low with scarlet fever: well, your recommendation was so enthusiastic that that girl is there nursing him, and the worn-out family have all been trustingly sound asleep for the last fourteen hours, leaving their darling with full confidence in those fatal hands, because you, like young George Washington, have a reputa—However, if you are not going to have anything to do, I will come around to-morrow and we'll attend the funeral together, for, of course, you'll naturally feel a peculiar interest in Willie's case—as personal a one, in fact, as the undertaker."

But that was all lost. Before I was half-way through she was in a carriage and making thirty miles an hour toward the Jones mansion to save what was left of Willie and tell all she knew about the deadly nurse. All of which was unnecessary, as Willie wasn't sick; I had been lying myself. But that same day, all the same, she sent a line to the hospital which filled up the neglected blank, and stated the *facts*, too, in the squarest possible manner.

Now, you see, this lady's fault was *not* in lying, but only in lying injudiciously. She should have told the truth, *there*, and made it up to the nurse with a fraudulent compliment further along in the paper. She could have said, "In one respect the sick-nurse is perfection—when she is on watch, she never snores." Almost any little pleasant lie would have taken the sting out of that troublesome but necessary expression of the truth.

Lying is universal—we *all* do it; we all *must* do it. Therefore, the wise thing is for us diligently to train ourselves to lie thoughtfully, judiciously; to lie with a good object, and not an evil one; to lie for others' advantage, and not our own; to lie healingly, charitably, humanely, not cruelly, hurtfully, maliciously; to lie gracefully and graciously, not awkwardly and clumsily; to lie firmly, frankly, squarely, with head erect, not haltingly, tortuously, with pusillanimous mien, as being ashamed of our high calling. Then shall we be rid of the rank and pestilent truth that is rotting the land; then shall we be great and good and beautiful, and worthy dwellers in a world where even benign Nature habitually lies, except when she promises execrable weather. Then—But I am but a new and feeble student in this gracious art; I cannot instruct *this* Club.

Joking aside, I think there is much need of wise examination into what sorts of lies are best and wholesomest to be indulged, seeing we *must* all lie and *do* all lie, and what sorts it may be best to avoid—and this is a thing which I feel I can confidently put into the hands of this experienced Club—a ripe body, who may be termed, in this regard, and without undue flattery, Old Masters.

HARRY FRANKFURT

Reflections on Bullshit

HARRY FRANKFURT teaches philosophy at Princeton University. He is author of *The Importance of What We Care About* (1988).

One of the most salient features of our culture is that there is so much bullshit. Everyone knows this. Each of us contributes his share. But we tend to take the situation for granted. Most people are rather confident of their ability to recognize bullshit and to avoid being taken in by it. So the phenomenon has not aroused much deliberate concern, nor attracted much sustained inquiry.

In consequence, we have no clear understanding of what bullshit is, why there is so much of it, or what functions it serves. And we lack a conscientiously developed appreciation of what it means to us. In other words, we have no theory. I propose to begin the development of a theoretical understanding of bullshit, mainly by providing some tentative and exploratory philosophical analysis. I shall not consider the rhetorical uses and misuses of bullshit. My aim is simply to give a rough account of what bullshit is and how it differs from what it is not. . . .

Bullshitting involves a kind of bluff. It is closer to bluffing, surely, than to telling a lie. But what is implied concerning its nature by the fact that it is more like the former than it is like the latter? Just what is the relevant difference here between a bluff and a lie?

Lying and bluffing are both modes of misrepresentation or deception. Now the concept most central to the distinctive nature of a lie is that of falsity: the liar is essentially someone who deliberately promulgates a falsehood. Bluffing too is typically devoted to conveying something false. Unlike plain lying, however, it is more specifically a matter not of falsity but of fakery. This is what account for its nearness to bullshit. For the essence of bullshit is not that it is *false* but that it is *phony*. In order to appreciate this distinction, one must recognize that a fake or a phony need not be in any respect (apart from authenticity itself) inferior to the real thing. What is not genuine need not also be defective in some other way. It may be, after all, an exact copy. What is wrong with a counterfeit is not what it is like, but how it was made. This points to a similar and fundamental aspect of the essential nature of bullshit: although it is produced without concern with the truth, it need not be false. The bullshitter is faking things. But this does not mean that he necessarily gets them wrong.

In Eric Ambler's novel *Dirty Story*, a character named Arthur Abdel Simpson recalls advice that he received as a child from his father:

> Although I was only seven when my father was killed, I still remember him very well and some of the things he used to say. . . . One of the first things he taught me was, *"Never tell a lie when you can bullshit your way through."* . . .

The elder Simpson identifies the alternative to telling a lie as "bullshitting one's way through." This involves not merely producing one instance of bullshit; it involves a *program* of producing bullshit to whatever extent the circumstances require. This is a key, perhaps, to his preference. Telling a lie is an act with a sharp focus. It is designed to insert a particular falsehood at a specific point in a set or system of beliefs, in order to avoid the consequences of having that point occupied by the truth. This requires a degree of craftsmanship, in which the teller of the lie submits to objective constraints imposed by what he takes to be the truth. The liar is inescapably concerned with truth-values. In order to invent a lie at all, he must think he knows what is true. And in order to invent an effective life, he must design his falsehood under the guidance of that truth.

On the other hand, a person who undertakes to bullshit his way through has much more freedom. His focus is panoramic rather than particular. He does not limit himself to inserting a certain falsehood at a specific point, and thus he is not constrained by the truths surrounding that point or intersecting it. He is prepared to fake the context as well, so far as need requires. This freedom from the constraints to which the liar must submit does not necessarily mean, of course, that his task is easier than the task of the liar. But the mode of creativity upon which he relies is less analytical and less deliberative than that which is mobilized in lying. It is more expansive and independent, with more spacious opportunities for improvisation, color, and imaginative play. This is less a matter of craft than of art. Hence the familiar notion of the "bullshit artist.". . .

What bullshit essentially misrepresents is neither the state of affairs to which it refers nor the beliefs of the speaker concerning that state of affairs. Those are what lies misrepresent, by virtue of being false. Since bullshit need not be false, it differs from lies in its misrepresentational intent. The bullshitter may not deceive us or even intend to do so, either about the facts or about what he takes the facts to be. What he does necessarily attempt to deceive us about is his enterprise. His only indispensably distinctive characteristic is that in a certain way he misrepresents what he is up to.

This is the crux of the distinction between him and the liar. Both he and the liar represent themselves falsely as endeavoring to communicate the truth. The success of each depends upon deceiving us about that. But the fact about himself that the liar hides is that he is attempting to lead us away from a correct apprehension of reality; we are not to know that he wants us to believe something he supposes to be false. The fact about himself that the bullshitter hides, on the other hand, is that the truth-values of his statements are of no central interest to him; what we are not to understand is that his intention is neither to report the truth nor to conceal it. This does not mean that his speech is anarchically impulsive, but that the motive guiding and controlling it is unconcerned with how the things about which he speaks truly are.

It is impossible for someone to lie unless he thinks he knows the truth. Producing bullshit requires no such conviction. A person who lies is thereby responding to the truth, and he is to that extent respectful of it. . . . For the bullshitter, however, all these bets are off: he is neither on the side of the true nor on the side of the false. His eye is not on the facts at all, as the eyes of the honest man and of the liar are, except insofar as they may be pertinent to his interest in getting away with what he says. . . .

For this reason, telling lies does not tend to unfit a person for telling the truth in the same way that bullshitting tends to. Through excessive indulgence in the latter activity, which involves making assertions without paying attention to anything except what it suits one to say, a person's normal habit of attending to the ways things are may become attenuated or lost. Someone who lies and someone who tells the truth are playing on opposite sides, so to speak, in the same game. Each responds to the facts as he understands them, although the response of the one is guided by the authority of the truth, while the response of the other defies that authority and refuses to meet its demands. The bullshitter ignores these demands altogether. He does not reject the authority of the truth, as the liar does, and oppose himself to it. He pays no attention to it at all. By virtue of this, bullshit is a greater enemy of the truth than lies are.

One who is concerned to report or to conceal the facts assumes that there are indeed facts that are in some way both determinate and knowable. His interest in telling the truth or in lying presupposes that there is a difference between getting things wrong and getting them right, and that it is at least occasionally possible to tell the difference. Someone who ceases to believe in the possibility of identifying certain statements as true and others as false can have only two alternatives. The first is to desist both from efforts to tell the truth and from efforts to deceive. This would mean refraining from making any assertion whatever about the facts. The second alternative is to continue making assertions that purport to describe the way things are but cannot be anything except bullshit.

Why is there so much bullshit? . . . Bullshit is unavoidable whenever circumstances require someone to talk without knowing what he is talking about. Thus the production of bullshit is stimulated whenever a person's obligations or opportunities to speak about some topic are more extensive than his knowledge of the facts that are relevant to that topic. This discrepancy is common in public life, where people are frequently impelled—whether by their own propensities or by the demands of others—to speak extensively about matters of which they are to some degree ignorant. Bullshit also arises from the widespread conviction that it is the responsibility of a citizen in a democracy to have opinions about everything, or at least everything that pertains to the conduct of his country's affairs.

The contemporary proliferation of bullshit also has deeper sources, in various forms of skepticism which deny that we can have any reliable access to an objective reality and which therefore reject the possibility of knowing how things truly are. These "anti-realist" doctrines undermine confidence in the value of disinterested efforts to determine what is true and what is false, and even in the intelligibility of the notion of objective inquiry. One response to this loss of confidence has been a retreat from the discipline required by dedication to the ideal of *correctness* to a quite different sort of discipline, which is imposed by pursuit of an alternative ideal of *sincerity*. Rather than seeking primarily to arrive at accurate representations of a common world, the individual turns toward trying to provide honest representations of himself. Convinced that reality has no inherent nature, which he might hope to identify as the truth about things, he devotes himself to being true to his own nature. It is as though he decides that since it makes no sense to try to be true to the facts, he must therefore try instead to be true to himself.

But it is preposterous to imagine that we ourselves are determinate, and hence susceptible both to correct and to incorrect descriptions, while supposing that the ascription of determinacy to anything else has been exposed as a mistake. As conscious beings, we exist only in response to other things, and we cannot know ourselves at all without knowing them. Moreover, there is nothing in theory, and certainly nothing in experience, to support the extraordinary judgment that it is the truth about himself that is the easiest for a person to know. Facts about ourselves are not peculiarly solid and resistant to skeptical dissolution. Our natures are, indeed, elusively insubstantial—notoriously less stable and less inherent than the natures of other things. And insofar as this is the case, sincerity itself is bullshit.

CHAPTER 6

How Should I
Make Money?

Everyday life in America brings each of us into contact with many kinds of businesses: grocery stores, gasoline stations, convenience stores, the companies that provide the goods that stores sell, restaurants, newspapers, broadcasting networks, and countless advertisers, among others. Most of the time, you probably hardly notice the various businesses and companies with whom you interact. But occasionally you do, and once in a while you might even have a moral response to the interaction: offense at a particular advertisement, perhaps, or pleasure at observing that a fast food restaurant has stopped using styrofoam.

The ethics of the business world have an impact on all our lives, whether or not we personally have a career in business. As consumers, we expect and demand honesty in advertising, fair pricing, and reliable goods and services. The fact that these demands have not been met in notorious cases has led some people to question whether "business ethics" is not a contradiction in terms. But the reactions of both the American public and the American legal system to such incidents as the insider-trading scandal on Wall Street in the 1980s and the *Valdez* oil spill disaster indicate that ethical behavior is still considered to be among the basic responsibilities of those engaged in business.

Such incidents have led some to question our basic way of doing business. Perhaps the pressures of the business world encourage questionable ethical practices. Some have argued that the profit motive, which is essential to the American form of capitalism, works as an incentive to low moral standards. If profits can be increased by selling goods of lesser quality or by laying off workers in American factories in order to exploit cheap labor in Third World countries, doesn't the profit motive encourage such strategies? In "Profits and Liberty," John Hospers makes the case for the profit motive. He argues that the right to profit from our labor is among the essential individual rights that government is not entitled to abridge. Moreover, he contends that utilitarian considerations support the protection of an individual's right to profits, for the pursuit of profit has effects that benefit society as a whole.

Karl Marx, a nineteenth-century German philosopher, has a less sanguine view of profit and the capitalist system that pursues it. He argues that capitalism rests on the idea that someone can own the product of someone else's labor, and the result is that labor becomes "alienated." According to Marx, work is the basic way in which human beings participate and express themselves in communities with other human beings. Under capitalism, the worker does not feel connected to the activity of working; work becomes a mere means for staying alive, not something in which one can take personal satisfaction. The product of work does not belong to the worker, but to the owner of the business; similarly, one's work is not his or her own, but the property of someone else. The more the worker works, the poorer he or she becomes, because the worker adds value to materials by working on them. In this way the worker contributes to the expense of the resulting goods, so much so that these goods are often unattainable on the worker's own salary. Because Marx sees work as intimately connected with a person's sense of self, he considers the lack of satisfaction in work to be an impoverishment of the worker's sense of being human and a participant in a community.

Enrique Dussell contends that alienation of labor remains a serious problem in the contemporary world, especially in so-called developing nations. These countries stand in relation to wealthier nations much as the workers Marx described stood in relation to their companies' owners. The raw materials of developing nations are purchased cheaply by European countries and the United States, where they are converted into expensive products that people in the countries of origin cannot easily afford. Poorer countries become further impoverished through their transactions with richer ones. Dussell calls for a rethinking of economic life to develop a way to focus on service to human beings instead of on profits. He thinks that everyone stands to gain from this transformation. Dussell observes that contemporary capitalism is motivated to mistreat nature, due to the perception that environmental responsibility cuts into profit margins. Less developed nations might well be the source of ecologically sustainable conceptions of our relationship to nature, he suggests, once they are allowed a more equitable role in world trade.

Manuel Velasquez also considers the impact of international business on the global common good in the contemporary world. He does not object to capitalism as a system, but he does contend that international businesses will not, on their own, pursue the well-being of the global community. Indeed, he argues that such businesses do not even have the obligation to do so, given that this would often result in severe competitive disadvantages for them. We also cannot expect individual nations to force multinational corporations to pursue the common good, because these governments often do not have the jurisdiction to be effective in such efforts. Velasquez concludes that to address issues like environmental protection on a global scale, we need to establish an international authority that can force multinational corporations to do their part toward establishing global well-being.

The insider trading scandal provoked questions about the role that secret information has been allowed to play in American business. Joanne B. Ciulla believes that precisely because confidential information has a vital role in the conduct of business, the temptation to exploit information to unfair personal advantage is ever present. She suggests that business education in America makes students more vulnerable to the temptation to use secret information unethically by fostering the attitude that business is mere game playing. This attitude emphasizes technical excellence without considering the effects one's maneuvers may have on the complex social reality in which business operates. Business education, in Ciulla's view, should emphasize the impact of business on societal life.

Robert C. Solomon urges those in business to adopt what he calls an "Aristotelean approach" to ethics. Like Aristotle, businesspeople should be suspect of the idea that profit alone is the purpose of business. Business, instead, should be seen as integral to the basic human pursuit of living well within a community. Ideally, business enables both individuals and society as a whole to flourish. Aristotle referred to those traits that are effective in helping a person to flourish as virtues. The Aristotelean approach emphasizes the role of virtue in business. Every business depends on developing cooperative relationships within the company and within the community in which it operates. Integrity encourages trust and cooperation; it is not only a virtue within business—it is good business. So, Solomon argues, are other business virtues. A business and its community both thrive when business is conceived as a practice that can be conducted virtuously, with concern for excellence in its practices, as well as in the products and services it provides to the larger society.

The Aristotelean approach focuses on the daily practices of business; but sometimes businesses face extraordinary problems. A case in point is the accident at a Union Carbide plant in Bhopal, India, in 1984, in which deadly gas was released into the atmosphere, killing thousands of people. Ethically, a business involved in such a catastrophe behaves appropriately only if it acknowledges its responsibility. But what, exactly, is its responsibility? John Ladd explores the questions about responsibility that the Bhopal accident raises. Ladd points out that the circumstances that made this accident possible were complex, and that some responsibility should be assigned to a number of causes. It is a mistake, he thinks, to look for a single, evil person or group of persons that is completely blameworthy. In this case, as in many others, a big problem arose systemically as a result of many small, commonplace decisions. Ladd suggests that a particular kind of virtue—civic virtue, the virtue required of everyone as a citizen—is crucial for avoiding such systemic disasters. He suggests that responsibility should be recognized not only by company leadership, but by ordinary citizens, both within and outside a company.

Although new technologies have sometimes been implicated in major accidents, they have also created new opportunities for business. Mark Alfino considers the growing role that possession and control of information plays in the contemporary business world as a result of computerization. He suggests that the impact of this development should encourage us to rethink the nature of business structures. Popular thinking habits tend to characterize the corporate organization as an authoritative, hierarchical structure. Alfino suggests, however, that a more appropriate model is suggested by the importance of the flow of information. Those in higher managerial positions should consider themselves responsible for maintaining the vitality of the information network and ensuring that appropriate information reaches those who are in the best position to use it.

JOHN HOSPERS

Profits and Liberty

JOHN HOSPERS taught philosophy at the University of Southern California. He is editor of *The Monist* and author of *Libertarianism*. His publications span many areas of philosophy, including esthetics, ethics, and political philosophy.

"He's earning too much—take it away from him!" "A hundred thousand a year while some people in the world are hungry? Nobody ought to be allowed to earn that much!" Such remarks are made, and they have a "humanitarian" sound. Yet, as I shall try to show, they result from ignorance of the functions of profits in an economy: and to the extent that the suggestion is followed, the result is poverty for everyone.

In a free economy—one in which wages, costs, and prices are left to the competitive market—profits have a very important function: they help to decide what products shall be made, of what kinds, and in what amounts. It is the hope of profits that leads people to make the products (or provide the services): if little or nothing can be made from producing them, or not enough to justify the risk of investing the capital, the product will not be made; but the more one hopes to make from it, the more people will bend over backwards to produce it. The hope of profits channels the factors of production, causing products to be made in whatever quantities the public demands. In a state-controlled economy, controlled by bureaucrats, nothing at all may be made of a certain product much in demand, because the ruling decision-makers have decided simply not to make it; and at the same time, millions of other things that nobody wants may be produced, again because of a bureaucratic decision. And the bureaucracy need not respond to public demand. But in a free-enterprise economy, the producer who does not respond to public demand will soon find his warehouse full of unsalable products and his business bankrupt.

The hope of profits also makes for an enormous increase in the efficiency of production, for, other things being equal, the most efficient producer—the one who can cut out waste and motivate his workers to produce the most and best products—will earn the highest profits. And is there any reason why these profits should not be applauded? To the consumer, these profits mean that the industry producing the goods he wants is healthy and nicely functioning—one that can continue to deliver the goods, and probably for at least as low a price as its competitors, since otherwise more customers would have turned to the competitor. To the workers, profits of their employer mean that the employer is doing a good job for his customers—good enough so that they keep buying his product—and thus that they the employees, are more secure in their jobs, and are more likely to receive higher wages in the future than are the employees of a company that is just barely making it. And as for the enterprisers, who can honestly say that they do not deserve the profits they received? First, they are risk-takers: they risked their capital to start the business, and had they lost no one would have helped them. Second, they spent not only their money (and borrowed money) on the enterprise, but, in most cases, years of their lives, involving planning, down to the last detail of production, the solution of intractable problems having to do with materials, supplies, and availability of trained help. Third, they anticipated the market, and did so more expertly than their competitors, for in order to make profits they had to have the right amount of merchandise at the right places for sale at the right time. Fourth, they provided the consumer a product or service (they could not *force* the consumer to buy from them; the consumer voluntarily elected to buy), in quantity—for a price, of course (after all his time and effort, should the enterpriser give it away, or sell it without receiving a return on it?), but nevertheless they provided it at a price which the consumer was willing to pay.

But the public, or a large segment of it, becomes envious and bitter, seeing that the man makes a profit. Perhaps the envious man has tried to start a business himself and lost it; or perhaps he just lost his job or can't pay some of his bills, and sees the employer living in a large luxurious house; in any case, he doesn't understand what side his bread is buttered on, for he doesn't realize that if the employer couldn't keep going, he himself would have no job. For whatever reason, he curses the employer because the man has a larger annual income than he does. Never mind that the employer took the risks, made the innumerable decisions (any one of which could have wrecked the business), and made *his* job possible in the first place: he, the employer, must be brought down to the worker's level. So he curses him, envies him, and votes for higher taxes for his employer, which, if passed, will mean that the employer won't expand his business and hire extra employees, and in fact may even have to cut it down some, even including his (the worker's) job. Officially, his line is that the employer's profits are ill-got. And yet when one examines it carefully, the complaint is groundless and absurd.

Suppose that an enterprise can make a thousand dollars in profits by a certain amount of capital investment; let us call this amount of investment C. Suppose also there is a second enterprise, less efficiently run than the first, which can only make that same amount of profit by investing twice the capital—2C. People will then say that the first, the efficient, manager, is reaping an excessive profit. For on the same investment of capital he can make twice the profits as his sloppy competitor; and for this his profits are branded as "excessive." But this is absurd: the efficient producer who gets more profits has more money to convert into plant expansion, more reserve for research so that he can improve his product, more wherewithal to reduce consumer prices and still make a healthy profit, thus benefiting the consumer with lower costs. The consumer ought to be anxious to have the most efficient producer possible; for only in that way can he be sure of getting the best possible product at the lowest possible price. By producing efficiently, the producer can undercut his competitors and thus benefit the consumer, while at the same time earning larger profits by capturing a larger share of the market for himself. We should applaud, not condemn, efficient production.

Add to this the fact that our present insane tax laws penalize the producer for his profits, and thus penalize efficiency. "Taxing profits is tantamount to taxing success in best serving the public. . . . The smaller the input (of money) required for the production of an article becomes, the more of the scarce factors of production is left for the production of other articles. But the better an entrepreneur succeeds in this regard, the more he is vilified, and the more he is soaked by taxation. Increasing costs per unit of output, that is, waste, is praised as a virtue, [remarks Ludwig von Mises]."

> There would not be any profits but for the eagerness of the public to acquire the merchandise offered for sale by the successful entrepreneur. But the same people who scramble for these articles vilify the businessman and call his profit ill-got.

One of the main functions of profits is to shift the control of capital to those who know how to employ it in the best possible way for the satisfaction of the public. The more profits a man earns, the greater his wealth consequently becomes, the more influential does he become in the conduct of business affairs. Profit and loss are the instruments by means of which the consumers pass the direction of production activities into the hands of those who are best fit to serve them. Whatever is undertaken to curtail or to confiscate profits, impairs this function. The result of such measures is to loosen the grip the consumers hold over the course of production. The economic machine becomes, from the point of view of the people, less efficient and less responsive.

Many people are so envious of, and bitter against, the man who earns a large salary or makes large profits, that they are unable to stand back impartially and try to understand what the role of profit is in an economy, and how it tends to increase everyone's income, not merely that of the man who receives it.

• • •

Instead of resenting it when individuals or companies make a million dollars, we should be happy. That million dollars means that there is a prosperous enterpriser who has created many jobs for people and bought equipment and so on (which in turn requires jobs to produce) to keep the product going. A million dollars made on the free market means that a great deal of money has filtered down to a very large number of people in the economy—and that a product is available at a competitive price, else the consumers would not have bought it in sufficient quantity to make our company its million. By contrast, a million dollars earned in government jobs means a million dollars milked from the taxpayer, which he could have spent in other ways. [Dean Russell:]

The future prosperity of everyone—including the needy—depends on *encouraging* persons to become millionaires; to build railroads, houses, and power plants; to develop television, plastics, and new uses for atomic power. The reason is simple: *No man in a free country can make a million dollars through the machinery of production without producing something that we common men want at prices we are willing to pay.* And no man will continue to produce something we want at a price we are willing to pay unless he has the *chance* to make a profit, to become rich—yes, even to become a millionaire.

There is an old saying, "No one should have caviar until everyone has bread." This is, when one examines it, one of the most confused statements ever made, though it is easily mouthed and chanted and is useful for political campaigns. If the enterpriser were not permitted to have his caviar, he would have far less incentive (perhaps no incentive at all) to produce anything, with the result that in the end fewer people would have even bread. The correct slogan would be, "If no one were permitted to have caviar, finally not many people would have bread."

One of the prevailing impressions, which underlies many arguments in this area but seldom itself surfaces to the level of explicit argument, is that the riches of the rich are the cause of the poverty of the poor. The impression is one of a certain fixed quantity of wealth, and that if some persons have more, this must inevitably mean that others have less.

A little reflection is enough to refute this assertion. If there were only a fixed quantity of wealth, how is it that we have many hundreds of millionaires now, hundreds and even thousands of men with elaborate houses, cars, lands, and other possessions, whereas only a few kings and noblemen had anything like this in bygone ages? Where long ago only a comparative handful of people could live, at the borderline between existence and extinction, in a given area of land, today a thousand times that number live, and live so well that they need spend only 10 to 15 percent of their income on food and all the rest goes for other things, most of which were inconceivable to the population of centuries past.

What people do not comprehend is that wealth is not static, but *grows* as long as people are free to use their ingenuity to improve the quality of their life. Here are deposits of iron, lying in the ground century after century; they do no good to anyone as long as they are just lying there. Now someone devises an economical process for removing the iron from the ground; another devises a means for smelting it, and another for combining it with manganese and other metals to produce steel that can be used in buildings, railroad tracks, and countless other things. When all these factors of production are functioning and the steel is produced, the world's wealth has been increased. Consumers have something to use that they didn't have before, and workers have jobs that didn't exist before. Every party to the transaction is a gainer.

• • •

No, the world is not like a lifeboat. Wealth does increase, and it increases for all as a result of the efforts of a few creative men. The riches of the rich are not the cause of the poverty of the poor: the rich in a free enterprise society can become rich only (1) by hiring workers to produce something and (2) because these consumers on a free market choose to buy what the entrepreneur has offered. They are rich precisely *because* innumerable consumers have, through their purchases, voted for whatever product or service they have to offer. Not one penny of their income on the free market came from the taxed income of anyone else.

• • •

But perhaps the most telling argument for profits is that the hope of profit is the surest way to get increased production. Whenever the chance of profit is removed, production lags or ceases. And production is a basic human need: man must produce in order to live—that is an inescapable fact of man's situation on this planet. If some men do not produce, others must produce that much more if they are all to remain alive. A considerable amount of productive labor is required for the bare necessities of life; and if one desires more of life's goods than those required for subsistence, still more production is required.

When, in a free-enterprise economy, many thousands of kinds of items are produced, consumers scramble to buy them—if they didn't buy them, of course, they would not long continue to be produced. In practice, then, people do value the fruits of the productive process. But the moral code to which they give allegiance in their day-to-day talk puts no premium on production at all. According to popular morality, it is charity that is the supreme virtue. Presumably the production of the goods needed to sustain life is not considered virtuous because people produce to enhance their own lives and to make profits—all of which is selfish. And what is selfish, according to the popular morality, cannot be virtuous.

Yet charity is possible only from the surplus of production. Without production, there would be nothing for anyone to be charitable with. In a society on a bare subsistence level, charity would be near zero, for one could give food to another only by consigning oneself to starvation.

• • •

The producer, however, produces primarily for himself, and for his profit. Because of this fact, his activity—the supreme virtue of productivity—is not included on the popular list of virtues at all. Whatever his motives are, however, let us consider his deeds. His deeds, surely, are quite clear.

The man who perfects a method for taking materials out of the earth, and starts a factory to produce them, spends years of his time and thousands or millions in money, hoping quite properly to have a financial reward for his pains; and in the process he provides work for large numbers of people. Nevertheless, popular morality considers him an evil exploiter who deserves only to be taxed out of existence for the sake of the rest of us. And yet this man has, in all candor, probably done more good than any other kind of person in our society. The entrepreneur may not *want* to pay out money to get a product or hire workers; he would rather get the income without any effort, let us say: but he cannot get a product mass-produced without doing these things, so perforce he does them. And when he is left free to do these things, the economy of the nation flourishes; the system of free enterprise, that is economic freedom, has provided the highest standard of living ever known in the world to the degree to which nations have permitted economic freedom. In the nations which do not permit economic freedom, production stagnates, constant shortages appear, and the majority of the population fall well below the poverty level. Economic freedom, and the fruits of it, are perhaps the principal positive *moral* force in the history of America; to take just one example, the American supermarket, selling thousands of items at marginal profits per item, and making available thousands of items to thousands of people otherwise unable to buy them, has probably done more good than all the charitable schemes of the last two thousand years put together. And yet the professional do-gooders castigate and condemn the producer on whom they are dependent for the handouts they wish to give, and they praise their fellow do-gooders who, having taken it away from the producer, then undertakes to distribute these bounties to the needy—and what he is distributing isn't even his own money, but money taken by force from the men who produced the goods. Was there ever such a total inversion of moral values?

KARL MARX

Alienated Labor

KARL MARX (1818–1883) was a German philosopher and economist. Influenced by the philosophical account of G. W. F. Hegel, who interpreted history as the drama of the gradual development of human consciousness, Marx argued that the progress of history depended on the changing configurations of economic forces and the distribution of material goods. He predicted that the capitalism of his era was doomed because its structure ensured the discontent of the workers on whom it depended. The workers would revolt, and capitalism would eventually be replaced by communism. The following reading, taken from one of Marx's early essays, indicates why he believed that it was in the workers' interests to overthrow capitalism.

What, then, constitutes the alienation of labor?

First, the fact that labor is *external* to the worker, i.e., it does not belong to his essential being; that in his work, therefore, he does not affirm himself but denies himself, does not feel content but unhappy, does not develop freely his physical and mental energy but mortifies his body and ruins his mind. The worker therefore only feels himself outside his work, and in his work feels outside himself. He is at home when he is not working, and when he is working he is not at home. His labor is therefore not voluntary, but coerced; it is *forced labor*. It is therefore not the satisfaction of a need; it is merely a *means* to satisfy needs external to it. Its alien character emerges clearly in the fact that as soon as no physical or other compulsion exists, labor is shunned like the plague. External labor, labor in which man alienates himself, is a labor of self-sacrifice, of mortification. Lastly, the external character of labor for the worker appears in the fact that it is not his own, but someone else's, that it does not belong to him, that in it he belongs, not to himself, but to another. Just as in religion the spontaneous activity of the human imagination, of the human brain and the human heart, operates independently of the individual—that is, operates on him as an alien, divine or diabolical activity—so is the worker's activity not his spontaneous activity. It belongs to another; it is the loss of his self.

As a result, therefore, man (the worker) only feels himself freely active in his animal functions—eating, drinking, procreating, or at most in his dwelling and in dressing-up, etc.; and in his human functions he no longer feels himself to be anything but an animal. What is animal becomes human and what is human becomes animal.

Certainly eating, drinking, procreating, etc., are also genuinely human functions. But abstractly taken, separated from the sphere of all other human activity and turned into sole and ultimate ends, they are animal functions.

We have considered the act of estranging practical human activity, labor, in two of its aspects. (1) The relation of the worker to the *product of labor* as an alien object exercising power over him. This relation is at the same time the relation to the sensuous external world, to the objects of nature, as an alien world inimically opposed to him. (2) The relation of labor to the *act of production* within the *labor* process. This relation is the relation of the worker to his own activity as an alien activity not belonging to him; it is activity as suffering, strength as weakness, begetting as emasculating, the worker's *own* physical and mental energy, his personal life indeed, what is life but activity?—as an activity which is turned against him, independent of him and not belonging to him. Here we have *self-estrangement*, as previously we had the estrangement of the *thing*.

We have still a third aspect of *estranged labor* to deduce from the two already considered.

Man is a species being, not only because in practice and in theory he adopts the species as his object (his own as well as those of other things), but—and this is only another way of expressing it—also because he treats himself as the actual, living species; because he treats himself as a *universal* and therefore a free being.

The life of the species, both in man and in animals, consists physically in the fact that man (like the animal) lives on inorganic nature; and the more universal man is compared with an animal, the more universal is the sphere of inorganic nature on which he lives. Just as plants, animals, stones, air, light, etc., constitute theoretically a part of human consciousness, partly as objects of natural science, partly as objects of art—his spiritual inorganic nature, spiritual nourishment which he must first prepare to make palatable and digestible—so also in the realm of practice they constitute a part of human life and human activity. Physically man lives only on these products of nature, whether they appear in the form of food, heating, clothes, a dwelling, etc. The universality of man appears in practice precisely in the universality which makes all nature his *inorganic* body—both inasmuch as nature is (1) his direct means of life, and (2) the material, the object, and the instrument of his life activity. Nature is man's *inorganic body*—nature, that is, in so far as it is not itself the human body. Man *lives* on nature—means that nature is his *body*, with which he must remain in continuous interchange if he is not to die. That man's physical and spiritual life is linked to nature means simply that nature is linked to itself, for man is a part of nature.

In estranging from man (1) nature, and (2) himself, his own active functions, his life activity, estranged labor estranges the *species* from man. It changes for him the *life of the species* into a means of individual life. First it estranges the life of the species and individual life, and secondly it makes individual life in its abstract form the purpose of the life of the species, likewise in its abstract and estranged form.

Indeed, labor, *life-activity, productive life* itself, appears in the first place merely as a *means* of satisfying a need—the need to maintain physical existence. Yet the productive life is the life of the species. It is life-engendering life. The whole character of a species—its species character—is contained in the character of its life activity; and free, conscious activity is man's species character. Life itself appears only as a *means to life*.

The animal is immediately one with its life activity. It does not distinguish itself from it. It is *its life activity*. Man makes his life activity itself the object of his will and of his consciousness. He has conscious life activity. It is not a determination with which he directly merges. Conscious life activity distinguishes man immediately from animal life activity. It is just because of this that he is a species being. Or rather, it is only because he is a species being that he is a conscious being, i.e., that his own life is an object for him. Only because of that is his activity free activity. Estranged labor reverses this relationship, so that it is just because man is a conscious being that he makes his life activity, his *essential* being, a mere means to his *existence*.

In creating a *world of objects* by his practical activity, in *his work upon* inorganic nature, man proves himself a conscious species being, i.e., as a being that treats the species as its own essential being, or that treats itself as a species being. Admittedly animals also produce. They build themselves nests, dwellings, like the bees, beavers, ants, etc. But an animal only produces what it immediately needs for itself or its young. It produces one-sidedly, whilst man produces universally. It produces only under the dominion of immediate physical need, whilst man produces even when he is free from physical need and only truly produces in freedom therefrom. An animal produces only itself, whilst man reproduces the whole of nature. An animal's product belongs immediately to its physical body, whilst man freely confronts his product. An animal forms things in accordance with the standard and the need of the species to which it belongs, whilst man knows how to produce in accordance with the standard of every species, and knows how to apply everywhere the inherent standard to the object. Man therefore also forms things in accordance with the laws of beauty.

It is just in his work upon the objective world, therefore, that man first really proves himself to be a *species being*. This production is his active species life. Through and because of this production, nature appears as *his* work and his reality. The object of labor is, therefore, the *objectification of man's species life:* for his duplicates himself not only, as in consciousness, intellectually, but also actively, in reality, and therefore he contemplates himself in a world that he has created. In tearing away from man the object of his production, therefore, estranged labor tears from him his *species life,* his real objectivity as a member of the species and transforms his advantage over animals into the disadvantage that his inorganic body, nature, is taken away from him.

Similarly, in degrading spontaneous, free, activity, to a means, estranged labor makes man's species life a means to his physical existence.

The consciousness which man has of his species is thus transformed by estrangement in such a way that species life becomes for him a means.

Estranged labor turns thus:

(3) *Man's species being,* both nature and his spiritual species property, into a being *alien* to him, into a *means* to his *individual existence.* It estranges from man his own body, as well as external nature and his spiritual essence, his *human* being.

(4) An immediate consequence of the fact that man is estranged from the product of his labor, from his life activity, from his species being is the *estrangement of man* from *man.* When man confronts himself, he confronts the *other* man. What applies to a man's relation to his work, to the product of his labor and to himself, also holds of a man's relation to the other man, and to the other man's labor and object of labor.

In fact, the proposition that man's species nature is estranged from him means that one man is estranged from the other, as each of them is from man's essential nature.

The estrangement of man, and in fact every relationship in which man stands to himself, is first realized and expressed in the relationship in which a man stands to other men.

Hence within the relationship of estranged labor each man views the other in accordance with the standard and the relationship in which he finds himself as a worker. . . .

• • •

The *alien* being, to whom labor and the product of labor belongs, in whose service labor is done and for whose benefit the product of labor is provided, can only be *man* himself.

If the product of labor does not belong to the worker, if it confronts him as an alien power, then this can only be because it belongs to some *other man than the worker*. . . .

We must bear in mind the previous proposition that man's relation to himself only becomes for him *objective* and *actual* through his relation to the other man. Thus, if the product of his labor, his labor *objectified,* is for him an *alien,* hostile, powerful object independent of him, then his position towards it is such that someone else is master of this object, someone who is alien, hostile, powerful, and independent of him. If his own activity is to him related as an unfree activity, then he is related to it as an activity performed in the service, under the dominion, the coercion, and the yoke of another man. . . .

Through *estranged, alienated labor,* then, the worker produces the relationship to this labor of a man alien to labor and standing outside it. The relationship of the worker to labor creates the relation to it of the capitalist (or whatever one chooses to call the master of labor). *Private property* is thus the product, the result, the necessary consequence, of *alienated labor,* of the external relation of the worker to nature and to himself.

Private property, thus results by analysis from the concept of alienated labor, i.e., of *alienated man,* of estranged labor, of estranged life, of *estranged* man.

ENRIQUE DUSSELL

The Economics of Liberation

ENRIQUE DUSSELL is an Argentinian philosopher. He is perhaps the most prominent spokesperson for the philosophy of liberation, which is a Latin American philosophical movement that takes the position of the poor as its starting point. He is the author of *The Philosophy of Liberation*, from which the following selection is taken.

Nature as landscape, as a place in which to reside, dress, eat, as a horizon still without frontiers—an aggressive, savage, chaotic nature—is the erotic nature where humankind will make its house; it is ecologic (both "ecology" and "economy" come from the Greek stem "house": *oikia*). In this manner there originates the person-cosmos dialectic, the emergence of nature as habitat.

From nature persons take, for example, wood, which—after the domestication of fire—is warmth, security, and light. . . . In that nature they discover the cavern as house, the stone as door, the fruits of the earth as nourishment, and the animals that one day they will shepherd in order to replenish their supply of protein. Nature is nourishing, sheltering, protective, and maternal. It is the beautiful nature of the splendor of dawn and of twilight, of the rivulets of the mountains, of the song of the nightingale, of the fierceness of the oceans, of the perfume of the rose.

NATURE AND IMPERIALISM

Gardenlike nature has now been transformed by the human species into an immense dunghill. Humankind, which once lived in respect for the *terra mater* and even rendered worship to it, now transforms it into pure matter of labor—though there are romantics who plead for a "return to nature" as did the hippies. The divine nature of the Greeks, the "sister earth" of Francis of Assisi, is now interpreted in terms of sheer exploitability: *homo naturae lupus*. Wolf? Infinitely worse than the wolf, which has in no way destroyed nature.

In effect, nature as exploitable matter, destructible without limit, a cache of profits, a source of capital gains, a time-projected extension of the dominative attitude of the slave driver (who made the slave work that nature), is obviously the interpretation adhered to by the center (Europe first, but now equally the United States). This change of person-to-nature attitude started in the Industrial Revolution, and it reaches a hallucinating peak in the present state of monopolistic imperialist capitalism, the society of superconsumption and aggressive destruction of nature as a mere mediation (a "logical corollary" of the previous destruction of oppressed peoples of the periphery). The goddess nature is now industrial raw material: iron ore, petroleum, coffee, wheat, livestock, wood.

The industrial conglomerates transform the garden into a dunghill. Factory effluents kill the fish and the vegetation of the seas; they rarefy the atmosphere with asphyxiating gasses; they destroy the natural sources of oxygen (the United States robs the periphery of its oxygen because it consumes more than it produces). The Club of Rome has pointed out that there are natural resources that are nonrenewable, that pollution is on the increase, that the human species is multiplying itself irresponsibly, that food supplies are on the decline, and that we are approaching a gigantic ecological collapse. Nature could exterminate this species that has turned irrational because of its economic system. Nature, which seemingly would remain patiently passive, responds with a threat that brooks no opposition: they who destroy me destroy themselves!

But the technologico-economic system of the capitalist social formation seems unwilling to change. Launched by its own logic to the maximization of profits, and hence of consumption-production and vice versa, imperialism continues its devastating course. Until when? To what limit?

ECOLOGY AND LIBERATION OF THE PERIPHERY

Nature, earth, its biosphere and its atmosphere, have been mortally wounded. The second report of the Club of Rome says that growth is not linear but organic (that is, the regions of the center will resist crises better; those of the periphery will die sooner). But crises are global now and will affect all residents of all regions. Those responsible for the destruction of nature are the developed powers of the center: they account for more than 90 percent of the contamination of the earth (even though they count less than 30 percent of the world population). That industrial center will never make the decision to reduce its own growth: its economy is founded on the (irrational) principle of ever accelerated profit. Will some technological miracles regenerate ecological equilibrium? Or will the romantic and moralistic advice of the Club of Rome convert the wolves into lambs? It does not seem likely. A solution, if there is to be one, will come from other sources. . . .

Can it be that a new person-to-nature attitude is impossible for capitalism, given the phase it is in now? Can it be that person-to-nature relationships that are less extravagant, less destructive, less consumptive, more economical, more patient, and more respectful of nature, can emerge only in peoples that have not arrived at the contradictory degree of technology within capitalism? Can it be that the destructive system will come to an end only when person-to-person relationships are redefined?

It would seem that at the moment when the peoples of the periphery demand a just price for their raw materials (nature worked on by the servant, the oppressed, the dominated), as has been somewhat fictitiously determined in the case of petroleum—at the moment the whole system will explode. Of course, before that moment comes, the powers of the center will have been able to transfer their more pollutive industries to the periphery and assure themselves of control of the less destructive and more complex operations. And before that moment comes their imperialist armies will continue to invade, repress, and assassinate. But, in the end, the hour will come. It is only in the periphery—in Asia, Africa, and Latin America—that a regeneration of the person-to-nature relationship can begin to take place—if it is not already too late.

The political liberation of the periphery seems to be the essential condition for the possibility of the restoration of natural ecological equilibrium—if true liberation, affirmation of the cultural exteriority, is undertaken, and not simply imitation of the economic process and destructive technology of the center. It would be the authentic humanization of nature, the development of culture in justice.

It is time to search for a metaphysical foundation for the peace movements in Europe and the United States, and for the liberation movements in the Third World. This foundation cannot be anything other than *life*—the human life, as Being, that is threatened by the arms race in the geopolitical center and by injustice in the periphery. The capitalistic system, unable to distribute overproduction, cannot make use of its mammoth productive capacity. It instead produces unemployment; unemployment reduces buying potential; fewer sales further reduce production. To make up for the profit loss by reason of reduced production and consumption, recourse is had to the arms industry. Armaments (means of death, not of production or consumption) bring with them the threat of the total extinction of life in the center, and they are used to repress and exterminate liberation movements in the periphery. This life—threatened in the center by atomic missiles and in the periphery by hunger and injustice—confronts the logic of profit, and struggles—with pacifism in the center and machine guns in El Salvador. . . .

•   •   •

ECONOMIC SYSTEMS

Human exchanges (in productive and practical systems) gradually increased across the millennia; they became systematized, reproducing and sometimes destroying themselves, some imposing their dominion over others. The practico-productive totality guaranteed survival (modes of production of human life). The distinct manner in which their terms related, the distinct content of the relationship itself, kept on generating in history diverse modes of practico-productive totality; in some cases they retained their primitive simplicity (nomadic clans or tribes of hunters, fishers, gatherers), and others began to be planters until, some eight millennia before Christ, some groups developed agriculture as such; others subsisted on shepherding; others improved hunting techniques and transformed them into war methods. Thus began the era of complex practico-productive totalities or Neolithic modes of production.

Because they excelled in the techniques of warfare (for example, in the domestication of the horse and the use of steel), the Indo-Europeans dominated politically (practically) the agricultural peoples of the valley of the Indus, of Mesopotamia, of what is today Turkey, Greece, Italy, and Europe in general. Some persons dominated others (practical domination) and appropriated for themselves the product of the other's work. They did this in two ways: because they defined themselves as proprietor of the very being of the other (slavery) and thus possessed the other's life, work, and the fruit of that work; or because they demanded that part of the product of the other's work be given to them (tributary system). All the group economies practico-productive totalities or modes of production up to the fifteenth century can be reduced to these two.

On account of the crisis of the fourteenth century, Europe underwent the collapse of feudalism (recessive tributary system); this nearly coincided with the founding of overseas colonies. Thanks to revenue from rural areas and from the colonies, Europe witnessed the birth of a new practico-productive system, capitalism. During the eighteenth century, mercantilism became industrialized. Product as merchandise began to predominate.

The being of the capitalist economy is merchandise, the product that bears an exchange value. Merchandise or exchange value are not an absolute moment; they are relative to a totality that explains and sustains them: capitalist social formation. An economic system always tends toward a projected goal (within capitalism, "to-be-in-wealth"), toward the foundation whence come the possibilities or mediations that are like bridges that permit their realization. In economics such mediations are the products or fruits of human labor. . . .

The simplest is nourishment (by cultivation of the soil) in order to satiate hunger. In capitalism, however, products are produced not primarily to fulfill necessities but to be a mediation of profit; merchandise, not need. Merchandise, then, as mediation, lets us view the economic system as a totality. All economic reality takes place in a concrete system, be it microeconomic (e.g., the level of erotic economy or the industrial enterprise), or national, regional, or global macroeconomics. Small systems are only subsystems of the global economic system, which today is dominated by imperialist management of capital and the planetary dimensions of the transnational corporations. The controlling system is the capitalist, central mode of production. . . .

NATIONAL AND INTERNATIONAL ECONOMIC ALIENATION

. . . European expansion, beginning with the sixteenth century, and later American expansion have alienated the economies of the peoples that are now their neocolonies (in Latin America, the Arab world, black Africa, India, Southeast Asia, with the exception of China, Vietnam, and a few other countries). Peripheral social formations (dependent nations) are dominated by the imperialist system. Its domination results in enormous profits from manipulation of the low price of raw materials and the high price of manufactured goods. Samir Amin has demonstrated that 80 percent of the benefits that the center realizes in its commercial interchanges come from the periphery. The work of the laborer and farmer and even the capital of dominated nations are continuously exploited. Part of the labor of the periphery is paid to the center in the form of licenses, insurance, exorbitant interest rates on loans, technology (inadequate), false sales reports of the products of transnational corporations in peripheral countries, and so forth. The theft of the surplus value achieved in the periphery accounts for the structured dissymmetry in the world of today. . . . It is on this level that the most devastating human alienation in our time takes place, the alienation of alienations, the one that conditions all the others. . . .

A more developed country gains "extra profit" in the sale of its products, whereas a less developed country "transfers" (surrenders) its surplus value in the sale of its products.

In terms of the "organic composition of capital," a more developed country can produce merchandise at a lower market value than that of a less developed country because the peripheral country has a lower productivity due to less advanced technology.

In the sale of its products to a less developed country, a more developed country can offer a sale price equal to what it sells for domestically. On the contrary, the peripheral country must sell its products at a lower price than if sold domestically, in order to compete. It thus transfers its surplus value to the more developed country (surplus value robbed from peripheral labor). This type of profit and transfer constitutes the *life* of the poor of the Third World, who feed the economy of the more developed countries. . . .

The alienation that reigns at the global level (discovered by the "theory of dependence") is doubled on the national peripheral level by internal geopolitical domination and dependence. Spatially, certain regions (populous capital cities: São Paulo, Buenos Aires, Mexico City, Cairo, Bombay, etc.; or more affluent regions because of industry, mining, etc.) wield power over others, achieving a fictitious appearance of high development (e.g., the bureaucracies of neocolonial African states), which contrasts with the level of extreme poverty of the majority of the population. External dissymmetry (imperialist center vs. neocolonies) is reproduced internally (neocolonial center vs. urban and rural poverty). It is evident that privileged regions are geopolitical mediations of the center.

Developmentalist models of economy are intended to make the world believe that the origin of underdevelopment is the fact that backward countries do not imitate the models of the developed countries. The solution would be to bring capital and technology to the poor countries (substitution of imports). This developmentalist ideology does not understand or admit that the origin of underdevelopment is theft—international structural injustice that dates back five centuries: the exploitation of the periphery because of the low prices paid for its exports. There will not be any true development without cessation of dependence, without liberation of national economies, without transforming the capitalist imperialist social formation of the center, its very mode of production. . . .

•   •   •

Liberative economy is service in justice, mediation that ministers to the other, technical innovation and technology for the other—for the other's growth, development, happiness. Without economy everything is an illusion, anarchy, or utopia (in the sense of flightiness: proclaiming the impossible because the mediations necessary for its realization are not worked on). Liberation does not imply only one *proyecto* and one enthusiasm, but planned, effectuated, viable mediations that are technologically efficient. Without economic liberation—which implies inspiration from popular, traditional, national institutions—there is no real liberation. If it is true that political revolution produces an opening in the previous system, only with the mediation of technological design and labor can a new system be organized in justice today. Without work, efficacious work with scientific mediation, there is no bread. Without bread a people is not liberated. It dreams of the fleshpots of Egypt, where at least there was bread. But without just distribution, bread is kept in the granary by the oppressor; the poor have no access to it.

Economy as service to the other, to the oppressed, builds the house—the home of the liberated family—the factory, and the assembly of the community where all forge their own destiny in political economy. It provides schooling, radio, and television. It constructs the cultural world and history—in justice!

MANUEL VELASQUEZ

International Business, Morality, and the Common Good

MANUEL VELASQUEZ teaches philosophy at Santa Clara University. He specializes in business ethics, general ethics, and political philosophy.

During the last few years an increasing number of voices have urged that we pay more attention to ethics in international business, on the grounds that not only are all large corporations now internationally structured and thus engaging in international transactions, but that even the smallest domestic firm is increasingly buffeted by the pressures of international competition. This call for increased attention to international business ethics has been answered by a slowly growing collection of ethicists who have begun to address issues in this field. The most comprehensive work on this subject to date is the recent book *The Ethics of International Business* by Thomas Donaldson.

I want in this article to discuss certain realist objections to bringing ethics to bear on international transactions, an issue that, I believe, has not yet been either sufficiently acknowledged nor adequately addressed but that must be resolved if the topic of international business ethics is to proceed on solid foundations. Even so careful a writer as Thomas Donaldson fails to address this issue in its proper complexity. Oddly enough, in the first chapter where one would expect him to argue that, in spite of realist objections, *businesses* have international moral obligations, Donaldson argues only for the less pertinent claim that, in spite of realist objections, *states* have international moral obligations. But international business organizations, I will argue, have special features that render objections quite compelling. The question I want to address, here, then, is a particular aspect of the question Donaldson and others have ignored: Can we say that businesses operating in a competitive international environment have any moral obligations to contribute to the international common good, particularly in light of realist objections? Unfortunately, my answer to this question will be in the negative.

My subject, then, is international business and the common good. What I will do is the following. I will begin by explaining what I mean by the common good, and what I mean by international business. Then I will turn directly to the question whether the views of the realist allow us to claim that international businesses have a moral obligation to contribute to the common good. I will first lay out the traditional realist treatment of this question and then revise the traditional realist view so that it can deal with certain shortcomings embedded in the traditional version of realism. I will then bring these revisions to bear on the question of whether international businesses have any obligations toward the common good, a question that I will answer in the negative. My hope is that I have identified some extremely problematic issues that are both critical and disturbing and that, I believe, need to be more widely discussed than they have been because they challenge our easy attribution of moral obligation to international business organizations.

I should note that what follows is quite tentative. I am attempting to work out the implications of certain arguments that have reappeared recently in the literature on morality in international affairs. I am not entirely convinced of the correctness of my conclusions, and offer them here as a way of trying to get clearer about their status. I should also note that although I have elsewhere argued that it is improper to attribute *moral responsibility* to corporate entities, I here set these arguments aside in order to show that even if we ignore the issue of moral responsibility, it is still questionable whether international businesses have obligations toward the common good.

I. THE COMMON GOOD

Let me begin by distinguishing a weak from a strong conception of the common good, so that I might clarify what I have in mind when I refer to the common good.

What I have in mind by a weak conception of the common good is essentially the utilitarian notion of the common good. It is a notion that is quite clearly stated by Jeremy Bentham:

> The interest of the community then is—what? The sum of the interests of the several members who compose it. . . . It is vain to talk of the interest of the community, without understanding what is the interest of the individual. A thing is said to promote the interest or to be for the interest of an individual, when it tends to add to the sum total of his pleasure; or what comes to the same thing, to diminish the sum total of his pains.

On the utilitarian notion of the common good, the common good is nothing more than the sum of the utilities of each individual. The reason why I call this the "weak" conception of the common good will become clear, I believe, once it is contrasted with another, quite different notion of the common good.

Let me describe, therefore, what I will call a strong conception of the common good, the conception on which I want to focus in this essay. It is a conception that has been elaborated in the Catholic tradition, and so I will refer to it as the Catholic conception of the common good. Here is how one writer, William A. Wallace, O.P., characterizes the conception:

> A common good is clearly distinct from a *private* good, the latter being the good of one person only, to the exclusion of its being possessed by any other. A common good is distinct also from a *collective* good, which, though possessed by all of a group, is not really participated in by the members of the group; divided up, a collective good becomes respectively the private goods of the members. A true *common* good is universal, not singular or collective, and is distributive in character, being communicable to many without becoming anyone's private good. Moreover, each person participates in the whole common good, not merely in a part of it, nor can any one person possess it wholly. . . .

•   •   •

. . . We can think of the common good on two different levels. We can think of the common good on a national and on an international level. On a national level, the common good is that set of conditions within a certain nation that are necessary for the citizens of that nation to achieve their individual fulfillment and so in which all the citizens have an interest.

On an international level, we can speak of the global common good as that set of conditions that are necessary for the citizens of all or of most nations to achieve their individual fulfillment, and so those goods in which all the peoples of the world have an interest. In what follows, I will be speaking primarily about the global common good.

Now it is obvious that identifying the global common good is extremely difficult because cultures differ on their views of what conditions are necessary for humans to flourish. These differences are particularly acute between the cultures of the lesser developed third world nations who have demanded a "new economic order," and the cultures of the wealthier first world nations who have resisted this demand. Nevertheless, we can identify at least some elements of the global common good. Maintaining a congenial global climate, for example is certainly part of the global common good. Maintaining safe transportation routes for the international flow of goods is also part of the global common good. Maintaining clean oceans is another aspect of the global common good, as is the avoidance of a global nuclear war. In spite of the difficulties involved in trying to compile a list of the goods that qualify as part of the global common good, then, it is nevertheless possible to identify at least some of the items that belong on the list.

II. INTERNATIONAL BUSINESS

Now let me turn to the other term in my title: international business. When speaking of international business, I have in mind a particular kind of organization: the multinational corporation. Multinational corporations have a number of well known features, but let me briefly summarize a few of them. First, multinational corporations are businesses and as such they are organized primarily to increase their profits within a competitive environment. Virtually all of the activities of a multinational corporation can be explained as more or less rational attempts to achieve this dominant end. Secondly, multinational corporations are bureaucratic organizations. The implication of this is that the identity, the fundamental structure, and the dominant objectives of the corporation endure while the many individual human beings who fill the various offices and positions within the corporation come and go. As a consequence, the particular values and aspirations of individual members of the corporation have a relatively minimal and transitory impact on the organization as a whole. Thirdly, and most characteristically, multinational corporations operate in several nations. This has several implications. First, because the multinational is not confined to a single nation, it can easily escape the reach of the laws of any particular nation by simply moving its resources or operations out of one nation and transferring them to another nation. Second, because the multinational is not confined to a single nation, its interests are not aligned with the interests of any single nation. The ability of the multinational to achieve its profit objectives does not depend upon the ability of any particular nation to achieve its own domestic objectives.

In saying that I want to discuss international business and the common good, I am saying that I want to discuss the relationship between the global common good and multinational corporations, that is, organizations that have the features I have just identified.

The general question I want to discuss is straightforward: I want to ask whether it is possible for us to say that multinational corporations with the features I have just described have an obligation to contribute toward the global common good. But I want to discuss only one particular aspect of this general question. I want to discuss this question in light of the realist objection.

III. THE TRADITIONAL REALIST OBJECTION IN HOBBES

The realist objection, of course, is the standard objection to the view that agents— whether corporations, governments, or individuals—have moral obligations on the international level. Generally, the realist holds that it is a mistake to apply moral concepts to international activities: morality has no place in international affairs. The classical statement of this view, which I am calling the "traditional" version of realism, is generally attributed to Thomas Hobbes. I will assume that this customary attribution is correct; my aim is to identify some of the implications of this traditional version of realism even if it is not quite historically accurate to attribute it to Hobbes.

In its Hobbesian form, as traditionally interpreted, the realist objection holds that moral concepts have no meaning in the absence of an agency powerful enough to guarantee that other agents generally adhere to the tenets of morality. Hobbes held, first, that in the absence of a sovereign power capable of forcing men to behave civilly with each other, men are in "the state of nature," a state he characterizes as a "war . . . of every man, against every man." Secondly, Hobbes claimed, in such a state of war, moral concepts have no meaning:

> To this war of every man against every man, this also is consequent; that nothing can be unjust. The notions of right and wrong, justice and injustice have there no place. Where there is no common power, there is no law: where no law, no injustice.

Moral concepts are meaningless, then, when applied to state of nature situations. And, Hobbes held, the international arena is a state of nature, since there is no international sovereign that can force agents to adhere to the tenets of morality.

The Hobbesian objection to talking about morality in international affairs, then, is based on two premises: (1) an ethical premise about the applicability of moral terms and (2) an apparently empirical premise about how agents behave under certain conditions. The ethical premise, at least in its Hobbesian form, holds that there is a connection between the meaningfulness of moral terms and the extent to which agents adhere to the tenets of morality: If in a given situation agents do not adhere to the tenets of morality, then in that situation moral terms have no meaning. The apparently empirical premise holds that in the absence of a sovereign, agents will not adhere to the tenets of morality: they will be in a state of war. This appears to be an empirical generalization about the extent to which agents adhere to the tenets of morality in the absence of a third-party enforcer. Taken together, the two premises imply that in situations that lack a sovereign authority, such as one finds in many international exchanges, moral terms have no meaning and so moral obligations are nonexistent.

However, there are a number of reasons for thinking that the two Hobbesian premises are deficient as they stand. . . .

IV. REVISING THE REALIST OBJECTION: THE FIRST PREMISE

The ethical premise concerning the meaning of moral terms, is, in its original Hobbesian form, extremely difficult to defend. If one is in a situation in which others do not adhere to any moral restraints, it simply does not logically follow that in that situation one's actions are no longer subject to moral evaluation. At most what follows is that since such an extreme situation is different from the more normal situations in which we usually act, the moral requirements placed on us in such extreme situations are different from the moral requirements that obtain in more normal circumstances. For example, morality requires that in normal circumstances I am not to attack or kill my fellow citizens. But when one of those citizens is attacking me in a dark alley, morality allows me to defend myself by counterattacking or even killing that citizen. It is a truism that what moral principles require in one set of circumstances is different from what they require in other circumstances. And in extreme circumstances, the requirements of morality may become correspondingly extreme. But there is no reason to think that they vanish altogether.

Nevertheless, the realist can relinquish the Hobbesian premise about the meaning of moral terms, replace it with a weaker and more plausible premise, and still retain much of Hobbes' conclusion. . . . The ethical premise of the Hobbesian or realist argument, then, can be restated as follows:

> In situations in which other agents do not adhere to certain tenets of morality, it is not immoral for one to do likewise when one would otherwise be putting oneself at a significant competitive disadvantage.

In what follows, I will refer to this restatement as the ethical premise of the argument. I am not altogether convinced that this premise is correct. But it appears to me to have a great deal of plausibility, and it is, I believe, a premise that underlies the feelings of many that in a competitive international environment where others do not embrace the restraints of morality, one is under no obligation to be moral.

V. REVISING THE REALIST OBJECTION: THE SECOND PREMISE

Let us turn, then, to the other premise in the Hobbesian argument, the assertion that in the absence of a sovereign, agents will be in a state of war. As I mentioned, this is an apparently empirical claim about the extent to which agents will adhere to the tenets of morality in the absence of a third-party enforcer. . . . Numerous empirical counterexamples can be cited of people living in peace in the absence of a third-party enforcer, so it is difficult to accept Hobbes' claim as an empirical generalization.

Recently, the Hobbesian claim, however, has been defended on the basis of some of the theoretical claims of game theory, particularly of the prisoner's dilemma. Hobbes' state of nature, the defense goes, is an instance of a prisoner's dilemma, and *rational* agents in a Prisoner's Dilemma necessarily would choose not to adhere to a set of moral norms. Rationality is here construed in the sense that is standard in social theory: having a coherent set of preferences among the objects of choice, and selecting the one(s) that has the greatest probability of satisfying more of one's preferences rather than fewer. Or, more simply, always choosing so as to maximize one's interests.

A Prisoner's Dilemma is a situation involving at least two individuals. Each individual is faced with two choices: he can cooperate with the other individual or he can choose not to cooperate. If he cooperates and the other individual also cooperates, then he gets a certain payoff. If, however, he chooses not to cooperate, while the other individual trustingly cooperates, the noncooperator gets a larger payoff while the cooperator suffers a loss. And if both choose not to cooperate, then both get nothing.

It is a commonplace now that in a Prisoner's Dilemma situation, the most rational strategy for a participant is to choose not to cooperate. For the other party will either cooperate or not cooperate. If the other party cooperates, then it is better for one not to cooperate and thereby get the larger payoff. On the other hand, if the other party does not cooperate, then it is also better for one not to cooperate and thereby avoid a loss. In either case, it is better for one to not cooperate.

Now Hobbes' state of nature, the neo-Hobbesian realist can argue, is in fact a prisoner's dilemma situation. . . . The Hobbesian claim is not an empirical claim about how most humans actually behave when they are put at a competitive disadvantage. It is a claim about whether agents that are *rational* (in the sense defined earlier) will adopt certain behaviors when doing otherwise would put them at a serious competitive disadvantage. For our purposes, this is significant since, as I claimed above, all, most, or at least significant number of multinationals are rational agents in the required sense: all or most of their activities are rational means for achieving the dominant end of increasing profits. Multinationals, therefore, are precisely the kind of rational agents envisaged by the realist.

But this reading of the realist claim is also significant, I think, because it reveals certain limits inherent in the Hobbesian claim, and requires revising the claim so as to take these limits into account.

As more than one person has pointed out, moral interactions among agents are often quite unlike Prisoner's Dilemmas situations. The most important difference is that a Prisoner's Dilemma is a single meeting between agents who do not meet again, whereas human persons in the real world tend to have repeated dealings with each other. If two people meet each other in a Prisoner's Dilemma situation, and never have anything to do with each other again, then it is rational (in the sense under discussion) from each individual's point of view to choose not to cooperate. However, if individuals meet each other in repeated Prisoner's Dilemma situations, then they are able to punish each other for failures to cooperate, and the cumulative costs of noncooperation can make cooperation the more rational strategy. . . .

There is a second important way in which the Prisoner's Dilemma is defective as a characterization of real world interactions. Not only do agents repeatedly interact with each other, but, as Robert Frank has recently pointed out, human agents signal to each other the extent to which they can be relied on to behave morally in future interactions. . . . Moreover, based on these appraisals of each other's reliability, we then choose to interact with those who are reliable and choose not to interact with those who are not reliable. That is, we choose to enter prisoner's dilemmas situations with those who are reliable, and choose to avoid entering such situations with those who are not reliable. As Robert Frank has shown, given such conditions it is, under quite ordinary circumstances, rational to habitually be reliable since reliable persons tend to have mutually beneficial interactions with other reliable persons, while unreliable persons will tend to have mutually destructive interactions with other unreliable persons.

The implication again is that since signaling makes it rational to habitually cooperate in the rules of morality, even in the absence of a third-party enforcer, we can expect that rational humans, who can send and receive fairly reliable signals between each other, will tend to behave morally even, presumably, when doing so raises the prospect of competitive disadvantage.

These considerations should lead the realist to revise the tentative statement of the second premise of his argument that we laid out above. In its revised form, the second premise would have to read as follows:

> In the absence of an international sovereign, all rational agents will choose not to comply with the tenets of ordinary morality, when doing so will put one at a serious competitive disadvantage, provided that interactions are not repeated and that agents are not able to signal their reliability to each other.

This, I believe, is a persuasive and defensible version of the second premise in the Hobbsian argument. It is the one I will exploit in what follows.

VI. REVISED REALISM, MULTINATIONALS, AND THE COMMON GOOD

Now how does this apply to multinationals and the common good? Can we claim that it is clear that multinationals have a moral obligation to pursue the global common good in spite of the objections of the realist?

I do not believe that this claim can be made. We can conclude from the discussion of the realist objection that the Hobbesian claim about the pervasiveness of amorality in the international sphere is false when (1) interactions among international agents are repetitive in such a way that agents can retaliate against those who fail to cooperate, and (2) agents can determine the trustworthiness of other international agents.

But unfortunately, multinational activities often take place in a highly competitive arena in which these two conditions do not obtain. Moreover, these conditions are noticeably absent in the arena of activities that concern the global common good.

. . . It is not clear that governments can or will do anything effective to force multinationals to do their part to maintain the global common good. For the governments of individual nations can themselves be free riders, and can join forces with willing multinationals seeking competitive advantages over others. Let me suggest an example. It is clear that a livable global environment is part of the global common good, and it is clear that the manufacture and use of chlorofluorocarbons is destroying that good. Some nations have responded by requiring their domestic companies to cease manufacturing or using chlorofluorocarbons. But other nations have refused to do the same, since they will share in any benefits that accrue from the restraint others practice, and they can also reap the benefits of continuing to manufacture and use chlorofluorocarbons. Less developed nations, in particular, have advanced the position that since their development depends heavily on exploiting the industrial benefits of chlorofluorocarbons, they cannot afford to curtail their use of these substances. Given this situation, it is open to multinationals to shift their operations to those countries that continue to allow the manufacture and use of chlorofluorocarbons. For multinationals, too, will reason that they will share in any benefits that accrue from the restraint others practice, and that they can meanwhile reap the profits of continuing to manufacture and use chlorofluorocarbons in a world where other companies are forced to use more expensive technologies. Moreover, those nations that practice restraint cannot force all such multinationals to discontinue the manufacture or use of chlorofluorocarbons because many multinationals can escape the reach of their laws. An exactly parallel, but perhaps even more compelling, set of considerations can be advanced to show that at least some multinationals will join forces with some developing countries to circumvent any global efforts made to control the global warming trends (the so-called "greenhouse effect") caused by the heavy use of fossil fuels. . . .

Moreover, global common goods often create interactions that are not iterated. This is particularly the case where the global environment is concerned. As I have already noted, preservation of a favorable global climate is clearly part of the global common good. Now the failure of the global climate will be a one-time affair. The breakdown of the ozone layer, for example, will happen once, with catastrophic consequences for us all; and the heating up of the global climate as a result of the infusion of carbon dioxide will happen once, with catastrophic consequences for us all. Because these environmental disasters are a one-time affair, they represent a non-iterated prisoner's dilemma for multinationals. It is irrational from an individual point of view for a multinational to choose to refrain from polluting the environment in such cases. Either others will refrain, and then one can enjoy the benefits of their refraining; or others will not refrain, and then it will be better to have also not refrained since refraining would have made little difference and would have entailed heavy losses.

Finally, we must also note that although natural persons may signal their reliability to other natural persons, it is not at all obvious that multinationals can do the same. As noted above, multinationals are bureaucratic organizations whose members are continually changing and shifting. The natural persons who make up an organization can signal their reliability to others, but such persons are soon replaced by others, and they in turn are replaced by others. What endures is each organization's single-minded pursuit of increasing its profits in a competitive environment. And an enduring commitment to the pursuit of profit in a competitive environment is not a signal of an enduring commitment to morality.

VII. CONCLUSIONS

The upshot of these considerations is that it is not obvious that we can say that multinationals have an obligation to contribute to the global common good in a competitive environment in the absence of an international authority that can force all agents to contribute to the global common good. Where other rational agents can be expected to shirk the burden of contributing to the common good and where carrying such a burden will put one at a serious competitive disadvantage, the realist argument that it is not immoral for one to also fail to contribute is a powerful argument.

I have not argued, of course, nor do I find it persuasive to claim that competitive pressures automatically relieve agents of their moral obligations, although my arguments here may be wrongly misinterpreted as making that claim. All that I have tried to do is to lay out a justification for the very narrow claim that *certain very special kinds of agents, under certain very limited and very special conditions, seem to have no obligations with respect to certain very special kinds of goods.*

This is not an argument, however, for complete despair. What the argument points to is the need to establish an effective international authority capable of forcing all agents to contribute their part toward the global common good. Perhaps several of the more powerful autonomous governments of the world, for example, will be prompted to establish such an international agency by relinquishing their autonomy and joining together into a coherently unified group that can exert consistent economic, political, or military pressures on any companies or smaller countries that do not contribute to the global common good. Such an international police group, of course, would transform the present world order, and would be much different from present world organizations such as the United Nations. Once such an international force exists, of course, then both Hobbes and the neo-realist would say that moral obligations can legitimately be attributed to all affected international organizations.

Of course, it is remotely possible but highly unlikely that multinationals themselves will be the source of such promptings for a transformed world order. For whereas governments are concerned with the well being of their citizens, multinationals are bureaucratically structured for the rational pursuit of profit in a competitive environment, not the pursuit of citizen well-being. Here and there we occasionally may see one or even several multinationals whose current cadre of leadership is enlightened enough to regularly steer the organization toward the global common good. But given time, the cadre will be replaced and profit objectives will reassert themselves as the enduring end built into the on-going structure of the multinational corporation.

JOANNE B. CIULLA

Insider Trading
The Secret Seduction

JOANNE B. CIULLA teaches business ethics at the University of Richmond. She is the author of *Honest Work* (1998).

Ben Franklin once remarked, "Three may keep a secret if two of them are dead." If this were true, just think of how many dead people it would take to keep a secret on Wall Street. Consider, for example, the multiservice nature of the modern brokerage or banking firm. Underwriting, merger and acquisition advisory services, investment management, research, arbitrage, proprietary trading, program trading, broker and retail sales, and service on boards of director all potentially provide broker dealers with inside information on the firm's clients. And, while the Glass-Steagall Act prohibits banking institutions from corporate underwriting activities, banks are, nonetheless, involved in a variety of securities industry functions, such as financial consulting, municipal bond underwriting, and corporate finance. Inside information from these activities can easily come in conflict with a bank's commercial lending and trust department activities. A list of institutions supplied with inside information could go on from insurance companies to law firms to newspapers. In this environment, the practice of trading on inside or secret information is not as surprising as its absence.

The current dialogue on insider trading generally focuses on the adequacy of current regulations and self-policing policies (such as "Chinese Walls"), and the ethics of individuals. Among these concerns, the moral flaws of people like Ivan Boesky and Dennis Levine capture the public's imagination most dramatically. Playing to the public, the media have put business ethics in the limelight and given the subject its fifteen minutes of fame. The publicity link between insider trading and business ethics courses has led some people to believe that our classes are nothing but discussions of the demonic Boesky and the greedy Levine. Those who blame business schools for producing amoral or immoral MBAs are often the same ones who oppose more government regulations of the securities industry—in other words, the system's ok, it's the people who are rotten.

As one who believes that research in business ethics should be more than just a rehash of the latest scandal, I begin by looking at the role of secrecy in business and the social impact of insider trading. I then argue that if one views secrecy as an attitude toward knowledge, then there are ways in which business schools might better prepare students to deal with the temptations of Wall Street.

SECRETS AND THE PRIVACY OF PROPERTY

Adam Smith recognized the utility of concealing information about prices, if only for a short period of time. In *The Wealth of Nations,* he tells us that when the market price of a commodity goes up substantially above the natural price, it is wise for those who supply the market with that commodity to conceal price change. According to Smith, if this change in price became known, rivals would enter the market, satiate demand, and knock the price down to its natural level. He says, "Secrets of this kind, however, it must be acknowledged, can seldom be long kept; and the extraordinary profit can last very little longer than they are kept." While, on the other hand, Smith notes that secrets in manufacturers last longer than secrets in trade and can give a businessperson the competitive edge. Richard Posner, one of the many Smith clones around today, similarly argues that "some measure of privacy is necessary to enable people, by concealing their ideas from other people, to appropriate the social benefits of their discoveries and inventions."

Early on, Smith noticed that it is not just private use, but private knowledge that made property valuable. He saw that success in business can rest on the ability to keep some information secret, even while competing in a public market system. Ironically, the owner's prerogative to keep information private [militates] against the ability of the market to function according to Smith's rational ideal—making trade a bit more like gambling, because information is either uncertain or incomplete.

The privacy of private property troubled Karl Marx. In his early writings, he named private property as the root of alienation. Ownership of property gave a person the right to exclude others from it and do with it what he or she pleased. Factories could be moved, wages cut, people fired, work processes altered—all without mention to those affected. One ramification of alienation was that workers did not have control over their lives and well-being. The privacy of ownership and business decisions denied workers important knowledge of the future. This is especially true today. When a company faces a hostile takeover, employees suffer enormous stress because they are not given up-to-date information on the future of their jobs.

Writing at the turn of the century, German sociologist Georg Simmel argued that money, not property, allowed exchanges to become secret and silent transactions. But, the concealability of money is, according to Simmel, "the symptom, or the extreme form of its relationship to private ownership." In his book *The Philosophy of Money*, Simmel says, "Money's formlessness and abstractness makes it possible to invest in the most varied and most remote value and thereby to remove it from the gaze of neighbors. Its anonymity and colorlessness does not reveal the source from which it came to the present owner." Simmel goes on to say that money hides many secrets as long as it is not transformed into property.

Investigators who work on Wall Street are well aware of the invisible properties of money. For example, Wall Street private investigator Jules B. Kroll has noted that Martin Siegel and Ivan Boesky were involved in cash transactions of which there was no record or system in the corporate structure to detect. As a result of this, he believes that when you are suspicious of employees, you need to look at their life-styles, not their bank books. Money itself is abstract and secretive; it only becomes public when it's transformed into goods and services.

To combat the dangers inherent in money, such as concealment, misleading estimates, and illegitimate use, Simmel points to laws that require public disclosure of the financial policies of the government and corporations. However, Simmel does not believe that the requirement for public disclosure really addresses the dangers of money. Rather, what the legal requirement for public disclosure actually does, according to him, is further differentiate public knowledge from private knowledge.

Smith, Marx, and Simmel present some interesting insights into the uses and problems of secrecy in business. Smith appreciates the usefulness of secrets as part of a business' competitive strategy, but also realizes that the lifetime of a secret in a market setting is short-lived. Although I doubt that Marx would see it this way, in his early writings I see the worry that the secrecy allowed to private property under the capitalist system can and does lead to social irresponsibility. Simmel tells us openness (required by law) is one way to combat the danger of secrecy in business. However, he says that in its effect, mandatory disclosure actually creates even more secrets, by making a sharp distinction between the public and the private realms of knowledge.

These insights raise some provocative questions. For example, "Would more regulation concerning disclosure on Wall Street have the adverse effect of increasing stakes and making insider trading an even greater temptation?" If the question seems too far-fetched we might ask, "Given the short life of a secret, such as one concerning a takeover, would regulations eliminate secrets or simply shorten their lives?"

Sissela Bok's distinction between privacy and private property sheds some light on these two questions. She defines 'secrecy' as intentional concealment and 'privacy' as "the condition of being protected from unwanted access by others—either physical access, personal information, or attention." So, according to Bok, a privately owned company is not a secretly owned one, and the privacy of this kind of private property is the right to limit access. The question that we have to ask today is, "What kind of privacy does a corporation have?"

Bok says secrecy and privacy do overlap in cases where secrecy must be used to guard against unwanted access. Hence, secrets can guard access to the private lives of individuals and corporations that are threatened by raiders. Secrets, then, tend to proliferate and become even more valuable in a dangerous environment. Corporations today live under the threat of a hostile takeover. Do their secrets protect them from unwanted access? Since corporations are not privately owned, do they have a right to protect themselves from unwanted access with a cloak of secrecy? Or are they up for grabs by anyone who can pay the price of admission? These questions are outside the scope of this chapter, but are not unrelated to the ethical issues related to insider trading.

SECRETS AND CHINESE WALLS

If regulating secrecy from the outside is paradoxical, then consider how secrets are managed internally. In a *National Law Journal* article, Edward D. Herlihy argues that the internal self-policing systems that brokerage firms have used for the past fifty years, called "Chinese Walls," are effective. Herlihy defines a Chinese Wall as "a set of internal written policies designed to control and prevent the dissemination of non-public information acquired by one department to other separate departments of the organization."

In 1980 the SEC adopted Rule 14e-3, which prohibits insider trading while in possession of material information; however, Paragraph b of the rule provides for a safe-harbor exclusion of "the disclose or abstain from trading" proscription for multiservice firms who adopt a Chinese Wall and can show that individuals making investments have had no knowledge of inside information. Rule 17j-1, also adopted in 1980, requires every registered investment company and each investment advisor of, or principal underwriter for, such a company to adopt a written code of ethics.

Segregating people and information into departments has some obvious limitations, as do codes of ethics. Because of their bureaucratic nature, modern organizations all run the risk of, as Hannah Arendt once said, "looking like they're ruled by nobody," and this greatly obscures individual responsibility. Unless you literally lock your employees up every night and put Big Brother in the bathrooms, businesses are left depending on the morals of their employees.

Hence, in our world of fancy management systems, expensive consultants, behavioral psychologists and economists, pious CEOs, and complex rules and regulations, we still do not have complete control. In the end we are left hanging by the fragile threads of trust. These threads are crucial for the maintenance of social order in organizations and society. Since professionals are supposed to represent the height of trustworthiness with respect to technically competent performance and fiduciary obligation and responsibility, it was not unreasonable for the public eye to critically scrutinize the training ground for MBAs.

ETHICS AS AN ATTITUDE TOWARD KNOWLEDGE

Many different motifs have been used to explain insider training. Some of the more common ones are: poor moral upbringing, ethical relativism or lack of shared moral values, amoral business schools, greed, lust for power, the Reagan era, deregulation, rapid growth in the securities industries, inadequate supervision, cracks in the Chinese Wall, and, just to round things out, secular humanism. In some ways, the publicity and concern over insider trading, although distant from most people's lives, has been a catalyst for moral, social, and legal soul searching.

The question that has intrigued me is, "Is there anything about the way that business schools train MBAs that makes them more prone to do something like trade on inside information?" Several press reports about Dennis Levine have said that for him money had become "a way of keeping score." Game theory and game analogies are often used in business schools to formulate strategies. But problems arise when people come to think of themselves as players. Viewing business as a game allows people to distance themselves from their actions and the effect of their actions on others. Game-playing engenders a delight in manipulation and technical expertise that is disjointed from responsibilities that one has to others and the organization. In particular, the game attitude fosters the development of technical excellence in isolation from any notion of moral excellence.

By compartmentalizing learning in business schools, teachers often fail to integrate how the "hard" areas like finance relate to the "soft" areas of management. For example, if, after two years at a top business school, the only way that a student can tell if a business is mismanaged is if its stock is undervalued, then I think that we've failed. What's at stake here is not just a matter of teaching values—it's a failure to give students an integrated understanding of business.

Some of our students who go on to work in the financial industry take with them a rationalist view of knowledge. They believe that quantitative methods and information (deductive knowledge) are superior to information collected through observation (inductive knowledge). Systems and models allow for deductive reasoning and yield information that has the sound ring of certainty and truth. I call this view "knowledge in a box." The problem with knowledge in a box is that it's not always clear whether what is true in the box is true in the world. So, for example, hostile takeovers might be shown to be good for the economy in one box, even if they don't appear to be good for the messy society in which the box sits.

If you look at insider trading from the perspective of finance, it may be hard to show that it does any harm; hence, so the argument goes, it may not be unethical. It is also difficult to demonstrate how insider trading violates current laws and regulations. But ethical thinking (and philosophical thinking in general) forces one to look at a far broader picture. For example, one might reasonably ask a transcendental question like "What are the ethical understandings that make business possible?" Here the harm is somewhat clearer. Business transactions cannot take place without trust. By betraying this trust, the inside trader causes social chaos. He or she is like a terrorist who sends the message that institutions do not have control. This shakes public confidence, not only in financial institutions, but in the ideals of fairness that underlie the market system.

Hence, an ethical attitude toward business requires that you clearly understand how your actions affect other people, your employer, the economic system, and society in general. Trading on inside information is a private action based on one area of expertise. There doesn't seem to be any harm or victim. It's an anonymous crime, if you haven't been trained to integrate what you know so as to understand the ramifications. Acts that "don't hurt anyone" are much easier to perform and rationalize than those that do.

One striking difference between graduate education in business and education in the liberal arts is the uncritical way in which information is presented and absorbed by students. With classes, cases to prepare, resumes to write, and the quest for the perfect job, students rarely take the time to reflect on or question what they've learned. The arrogance of some MBAs is often derived from the mistaken belief that they possess certain knowledge about how to get things done in the world. This special knowledge sets them apart from organizations and sometimes leads them to believe that they can outsmart everyone else. These unfortunate few have come to view knowledge only as a tool, not a guide.

CONCLUSION

As we have seen, secrets are seductive forms of knowledge that serve to hide, protect, and corrupt through unfair advantage. The law and Chinese Walls separate knowledge insofar as it is possible. These laws and policies need to be reassessed and refreshed; however, due to the privacy of secrets, not even more or tougher rules can completely control betrayal by insiders. Businesses will always have their secrets, and Wall Street will continue to offer new unethical schemes. Many will be tempted. However, one weapon against temptation is the ability to look it critically in the eye and have a clear picture of the impact of one's actions on others. Knowledge is an important part of conscience—it doesn't guarantee that a person will resist temptation, it just makes it tougher for a rational person to give in. When it comes to the building and development of character, moral struggle is almost as important as moral victory.

We don't really need to teach students that insider trading is wrong—they know that—it's yesterday's news. We won't be able to transform demons into saints. Courses in ethics and in social responsibility can be helpful, but students need to take away more than a bag full of case discussions. We need to give them the skills to think critically and philosophically about their work, their lives, and what they have learned.

ROBERT C. SOLOMON

The Aristotelean Approach to Business Ethics

ROBERT C. SOLOMON is the Quincy Lee Centennial Professor of philosophy and business at the University of Texas at Austin. He is author of numerous books and articles on business ethics and other fields in philosophy, including *Ethics and Excellence* (1991), *The New World of Business* (1994), and *A Passion for Justice* (1990).

We can no longer accept the amoral idea that "business is business" (not really a tautology but an excuse for being socially irresponsible and personally insensitive). According to Aristotle, one has to think of oneself as a member of the larger community—the *polis* for him, the corporation, the neighborhood, the city or the country (and the world) for us—and strive to excel, to bring out what is best in ourselves and our shared enterprise. What is best in us involves our virtues, which are in turn defined by that larger community, and there is therefore no ultimate split or antagonism between international self-interest and the greater public good. Of course, there were no corporations in those days, but Aristotle would certainly know what I mean when I say that most people in business now identify themselves, if tenuously, in terms of their companies, and corporate policies, much less corporate codes of ethics, are not by themselves enough to constitute an ethics. But corporations are not isolated city-states, not even the biggest and most powerful of the multinationals. "The sovereign state of ITT" may indicate power and political autonomy, but it is, nevertheless, part and parcel of a larger global community. The people that work for them are thus citizens of (at least) two communities at once, and one might think of business ethics as getting straight about that dual citizenship. What we need to cultivate is a certain way of thinking about ourselves in and out of the corporate context, and this is the aim of ethical theory in business, as I understand it. It is not, let me insist, anti-individualistic in any sense of "individualism" that is worth defending. The Aristotelean approach to business ethics rather begins with the two-pronged idea that it is individual virtue and integrity that counts, but good corporate and social policies encourage and nourish individual virtue and integrity.

The Aristotelean approach, as I want to construe it here, begins by agreeing with Aristotle in his suspicion of purely financial thinking and dealing, what we call "the profit motive." Michael Lewis's traders seem to me to be the perfect equivalent of the sort of marginal characters that made respectable Athenians hide their wallets and their daughters at home. They too were not doing anything illegal, but their mercantile activities were (unlike the activities of Lewis's traders) not respectable. They did not seem to contribute anything to the society. The seemingly obvious place and purpose of "finance" in society needs to be reconsidered, and the problem is to define "finance" and "profits" in such a way that not all of business suffers from Aristotle's indictment.

Second, to call the approach "Aristotelean" is to emphasize the importance of community, the business community as such (I want to consider corporations as, first of all, communities) but also the larger community, even all of humanity and, perhaps, much of nature too. This emphasis on community, however, should not be taken to eclipse the importance of the individual and individual responsibility. In fact, the contrary is true; it is only within the context of community that individuality is developed and defined, and our all-important sense of individual integrity is dependent upon and not opposed to the community in which integrity gets both its meaning and its chance to prove itself.

One of the most important aspects of the "Aristotelean" approach is the emphasis on the purposiveness (or "teleology") that defines every human enterprise, including business. But that purposiveness transcends the realm of business and defines its place in the larger society, though the popular term "social responsibility" makes this sound too much like an extraneous concern rather than the purpose of business as such. On both an individual and the corporate level, the importance of the concept of *excellence* is intricately tied to this overall teleology, for what counts as excellence is defined both by its superiority in the practice and its role in serving larger social purposes. "Aristotelean" too is a strong emphasis on individual character and the virtues (where "virtue" is all-round personal excellence), embedded in and in service to the larger community. It is the role of the individual in the corporation (and of the corporation in society) that concerns me, not the individual alone, not the structure of the corporation abstracted from the individuals that are its members (and not the nature of "capitalism," abstracted from the character of particular corporations and the communities they serve). That is why the idea of business as a practice is absolutely central to this approach: it views business as a human institution in service to humans and not as a marvelous machine or in terms of the mysterious "magic" of the market.

Finally, it may be theoretically least interesting but it is perhaps nevertheless most important, but I prefer the name "Aristotelean" just because it makes no pretensions of presenting something very new, the latest "cutting-edge" theory or technique of management, but rather reminds us of something very old, a perspective and a debate that go all the way back to ancient times. What the Aristotelean approach promises is not something novel and scientific but an approach that is very staid and established and above all very human. The idea is not to infuse corporate life with one more excuse for brutal changes, a new wave of experts and seminars and yet another downsizing bloodbath. It is to emphasize the importance of continuity and stability, clearness of vision and constancy of purpose, corporate loyalty and individual integrity.

The bottom line of the Aristotelean approach to business ethics is that we have to get away from "bottom line" thinking and conceive of business as an essential part of the good life, living well, getting along with others, having a sense of self-respect, and being part of something one can be proud of. Aristotle argued that what I have called "abstract greed" ("the profit motive") was a kind of pathology, a defect of character, an "unnatural" and antisocial vice. Not that he was against wealth and comfort (no ascetics, those Athenians), but in the quest for the good life money wasn't worth worrying about. To which one might well reply, of course, that aristocrats in an aristocratic society (and their favorite philosophers) didn't have to worry about such merely material matters, but we do. But the point is not that we should stop thinking about money or trying to make a living or that we can or should discourage our students from their current career paths. It is a question of perspective, and a question of what that living, those career paths, amount to. Are they, in fact, just a means to make money? Or are they, as they should be, worthwhile activities that provide the meaningful substance of half of our adult waking lives, the source of our sense of self-worth and many of our friends? Is the community we work for a white-collar version of hell, or is it a community where (despite the early hour) we are glad to see our colleagues and get on with the work of the day? We talk about "making a living" as if it is primarily a matter of income, but the truth is that the living we make has as much to do with life and meaning as it does with paying the rent. Unhappy middle managers will testify that there seems to be nothing more demeaning and more contrary to the good life than giving years of your life to a company that ignores your every effort and continually reminds you of your expendability. Students and job hoppers (and, let me say, even professors of the humanities) who accept a position on the basis of salary alone and then hate their job miss the obvious: what makes for happiness is not money to spend but a full and meaningful life and a decent and prosperous community.

Part of the problem is the way we tend to separate—or pretend to separate—our business from our personal lives, as if these were unrelated and independent, as if one "left one's values at the office door." But of course, not only do we spend an enormous amount of our waking lives "in the office"; our values are not divided up into two (or more) categories, like outfits in the closet separated into "business" and "leisure." With only small variations, the values we were raised with as children are the essential values of our professional as well as our personal lives. But this false separation of business and personal values has another, even more depressing consequence. Since we tend to identify the personal part of our lives as pleasurable (whether or not it is), we characterize the business part of our lives as "work," meaning not just effort and energy but a burden, defined by duties and obligations and responsibility. The very suggestion, therefore, is that business is distasteful, unpleasant, deleterious to one's own better self, and in one's interests only by virtue of its outcome: the salary or wealth that one manages to accumulate. There is too little sense of business as itself enjoyable (the main virtue of the "game" metaphor), that business is not a matter of vulgar self-interest but of vital community interest, that the virtues on which one prides oneself in "personal" life are essentially the same as those essential to good business—honesty, dependability, courage, loyalty, integrity. Aristotle's central ethical concept, accordingly, is a unified, all-embracing notion of "happiness" (or, more accurately, *eudaimonia*, perhaps better translated as "flourishing" or "doing well"). The point is to view one's life as a whole and not separate the personal and the public or professional, or duty and pleasure. The point is that doing what one ought—doing one's duty, fulfilling one's responsibilities and obligations—is not counter but conducive to the good life, to becoming the sort of person one wants to become. Conversely, becoming the sort of person one wants to become—which presumably includes to a very large extent what one does "for a living"—is what happiness is all about. Happiness is "flourishing," and this means fitting into a world of other people and sharing the good life, including "a good job," with them. A good job, accordingly, is not just one that pays well or is relatively easy but one that means something, one that has (more or less) tangible and clearly beneficial results, one that (despite inevitable periods of frustration) one enjoys doing. Happiness (for us as well as for Aristotle) is an all-inclusive, holistic concept. It is ultimately one's character, one's integrity, that determines happiness, not the bottom line. And this is just as true of giant corporations as it is of the individuals who work for them.

There is no room in this picture for the false antagonism between "selfishness" on the one hand and what is called "altruism" on the other. For the properly constituted social self, the distinction between self-interest and social-mindedness is all but unintelligible, and what we call selfishness is guaranteed to be self-destructive as well. And "altruism" is too easily turned into self-sacrifice—for instance, by that self-appointed champion of selfishness, Ayn Rand. But altruism isn't self-sacrifice; it's just a more reasonable conception of self, as tied up intimately with community, with friends and family who may, indeed, count (even to us) more than we do. What the Aristotelean approach to business ethics demands isn't self-sacrifice or submerging oneself to the interests of the corporation, much less voluntary unhappiness. What it does demand is the recognition that the distinctions and oppositions between self and society that give rise to these wrongheaded conceptions are themselves the problem, and the cause of so much unhappiness and dissatisfaction. So, too, the most serious single problem in business ethics is the false antagonism between profits and social responsibility. There is an academic prejudice, for example, against clever profit-making solutions—the obviously optimal solution to "social responsibility" problems. It is as if moralists have a vested interest in the nobility of self-sacrifice (that is, self-sacrifice by others). This is the same problem, philosophy students will recognize, once raised by the theory of egoism in ethics, for example, in the famous exchange between Thomas Hobbes and Bishop Butler. According to all such views, either an action is selfish or it is selfless, and the Aristotelean synthesis of self-interested, noble behavior is eliminated from view. Once one introduces such artificial oppositions between self-interest and shared interest, between profits and social responsibility, the debate becomes a "lose-lose" proposition, either wealth and irresponsibility or integrity and failure. The Aristotelean approach is first of all a "win-win" proposition, a framework for mutually interested action.

The Aristotelean approach to business ethics begins with the concept of the individual embedded in the community and the ultimate importance of happiness as the sole criterion for success. But "happiness" is a large, ill-defined notion. What makes one person happy may not be the same as for another. One middle-aged manager will be content only when she finally makes senior vice-president and is happy to invest most of her time and energy to do so; another is perfectly happy with his middle-manager status, his congenial colleagues, and his comparatively ample time with his family. But this is not to say that any form of satisfaction or contentment counts as happiness. We have all seen friends who have just endured a traumatic separation go through periods of what is easily recognizable (to everyone but them) as "false happiness," a subjective sense of well-being that has far more to do with the repression and rationalization of awful thoughts than it does with contentment or a sense of well-being. The same sense of "false happiness" can occupy a major portion of a person's life, though only with difficulty and continuous psychological effort. It can more easily pervade an entire community's life, when people continuously encourage the wrong values and the wrong goals in one another (for example, promoting competitive, even ruthless behavior toward one another in pursuit of some merely emblematic prize, demeaning family life and treating all things domestic and affectionate as inferior). What is happening in contemporary society, it has often been argued, is very much a version of this "false happiness," when money becomes the emblematic prize and competition for money the test of "manhood" and when family life suffers from neglect, or worse.

Whatever happiness may be, and however it differs from person to person, there are certain essential if variable personal ingredients that are required. We can summarize them in a single word, in the concept of the *virtues*.

The concept of the virtues provides the conceptual linkage between the individual and his or her society. A virtue is a pervasive trait of character that allows one to "fit into" a particular society and to excel in it. Aristotle analyzed the virtues as the basic constituents of happiness, and these virtues included, we should add right away, not only such "moral" virtues as honesty but also many "nonmoral" virtues such as wittiness, generosity, and loyalty. (Aristotle, in fact, did not even bother distinguishing between what we would call the moral and the nonmoral virtues. He considered them all important.) The virtues were, on the one hand, essential aspects of the individual. On the other hand, they were precisely the "excellences" that a certain society required. The underlying assumption was that a person is who he or she is by virtue of his or her place and role in the community, by virtue of his or her actions and sense of judgment, by virtue of how his or her virtues all "hang together" to form what we might blandly call "a good person."

A virtue, to be very brief for now, is an excellent and admirable characteristic to have, not just in some narrowly defined context (as it is a virtue to be ugly in an "ugliest man contest") but in the larger social scheme as well. A virtue is a trait that helps one to fit into and contribute to society. Honesty is obviously a virtue. If everyone lied—to begin with one of the oldest and most evident philosophical insights—no one would believe anyone. There will always be liars, and there are practices that encourage and even require less than forthright disclosure, but there could not be a society of liars, even in Hollywood or on Wall Street. Courage is a virtue. There will always be cowards but most of us at some time or other have to stand up for our convictions and our freedom. Otherwise, we have no convictions and there is no freedom. But in addition to these rather general virtues, there are also virtues specific to particular institutions, activities, and practices. Spontaneous creativity and unpredictable behavior may be applauded in an artist or an intellectual but it is (usually) disastrous in a linebacker. Loyalty is almost always a virtue within a relationship or an organization, but it is a virtue that has its obvious limits. ("My company, right or wrong," displays the importance of such limits, even in their denial.) Virtues may be specific to particular institutions, activities, and practices, but they will always be measured in a larger arena. A virtue is an individual excellence that is defined in part by its contribution to the public good, even or especially in those exceptional circumstances in which it seems to run counter to corporate or public policies. Extreme examples are provided by whistleblowers and Henry David Thoreau-type protesters, by every honest man or woman who is ready and willing to speak out against waste or corruption exemplifies such virtues as well.

In certain aspects of business (as in the military), what is called "ruthlessness" can be a virtue, but it would surely be a mistake to generalize this as an essential virtue for everyone in every circumstance and it is usually a mistake to give it much value even in the most "ruthless" business. It is all too evident that even in the appropriate context this virtue (like most virtues, even honesty and courage) can be excessive and turn into a vice. Thus the virtue of a virtue (a phrase I borrow from Nietzsche) always depends on some larger context, a context in which the practice itself (art, football, business) is evaluated for its social value. Many contextual virtues thus betray their limits and some supposed virtues turn out (from a larger perspective) not to be virtues at all. In the business world, in particular, we should be on the lookout for those macho, mock virtues that in any civilized context would and should be subject to ridicule and contempt. When Lewis describes the ideal of the trading floor as "that most revered of all species: a Big Swinging Dick," we have demeaned the very idea of the virtues in favor of an adolescent, unproductive, and indefensible conception of business.

What is worth defending in business is the sense of virtue that stresses cooperative joint effort and concern for consumers and colleagues alike. Aristotelean ethics is an ethics of virtue, an ethics in which personal and corporate integrity occupies the place of central concern and focus. But virtue and integrity are not to be found in a vacuum. They do not appear miraculously in the atomistic individual, they cannot be contracted or commissioned, nor are they the special province of saints. They are not (except cynically) the result of a cost/benefit calculation of utility, and they cannot be dictated according to abstract rules or principles (thus the nagging vacuity of such principles as "Be courageous!" or "Be generous!"). A virtue has a place in a social context, in a human practice, and accordingly it is essentially part of a fabric that goes beyond the individual and binds him or her to a larger human network. Integrity—literally "wholeness"— also has to be understood (in part) in the context of a community and, in business life, the corporation. It consists not just of individual autonomy and "togetherness" but of such company virtues as loyalty and congeniality, cooperation and trustworthiness. Of course, this also means that the corporation itself must be viewed as a morally and socially responsible agent, a view that does not, however, compromise the ultimate importance of the responsibility and integrity of the individuals who work within it. Nothing is more damaging to business ethics (or to ethics in business) than the glib dismissal of corporations as agents because they are "legal fictions" or the equally fatuous if familiar insistence that the sole purpose of corporations (and, therefore, the sole responsibility of their managers) is to turn a profit and fulfill their "fiduciary obligation to the stockholders." The pursuit of integrity is determined from the start, I have argued, by such dangerous myths and metaphors about business, corporations, and the people who work for them. Corporations are neither legal fictions nor financial juggernauts but communities, people working together for common goals. That seemingly simple realization, which so much of corporate life has seemingly rejected in recent years, is the first principle of Aristotelean business ethics. And with that emphasis on integrity and community comes not only the fulfillment of obligations to stockholders (not all of them "fiduciary") but the production of quality and the earning of pride in one's products, providing good jobs and well-deserved rewards for employees, and the enrichment of a whole community and not just a select group of (possibly short-term) contracted "owners."

The Aristotelean approach to business presupposes an ideal, an ultimate purpose, but the ideal of business in general is not, as my undergraduates so smartly insist, "to make money." It is to serve society's demands and the public good and be rewarded for doing so. This ideal in turn defines the mission of the corporation and provides the criteria according to which corporations and everyone in business can be praised or criticized. "Better living through chemistry," "Quality at a good price," "Productivity through people," "Progress is our most important product"—these are not mere advertising slogans but reasons for working and for living. Without a mission, a company is just a bunch of people organized to make money while making up something to do (for example, "beating the competition"). Such activities may, unintentionally, contribute to the public good, but Adam Smith's "invisible hand" never was a very reliable social strategy, and the difference between intending to do good and doing good unintentionally is not just the special sense of satisfaction that comes from the former. Contrary to the utterly irresponsible and obviously implausible argument that those ("do-gooders") who try to do good in fact do more harm than good, the simple, self-evident truth is that most of the good in this world comes about through good intentions. Meaningful human activity is that which intends the good rather than stumbling over it on the way to merely competitive or selfish goals. . . .

In terms of explicitly ethical thinking, too much of business ethics today is focused on questions of policy—those large questions about government regulation and the propriety of government intervention, such as in failing industries and affirmative action programs, and in very general business practices and problems, such as pollution control, opacity and lying in advertising, employee due process, and the social responsibilities of companies to their surrounding communities. All of this, of course, is perfectly proper for philosophers and other social observers who have the luxury of standing outside of the pressures of the business world to survey and possibly control through legislation the larger scenery. But what gets left out of these well-plumbed studies and arguments is an adequate sense of personal values and integrity. What is missing from much of business ethics is an adequate account of the personal dimension in ethics, the dimension of everyday individual decision making. Accordingly, I want to defend business ethics as a more personally oriented ethics rather than as public policy, "applied" abstract philosophy, or a by-product of the social sciences. But business ethics so conceived is not "personal" in the sense of "private" or "subjective"; it is rather social and institutional self-awareness, a sense of oneself as an intimate (but not inseparable) part of the business world with a keen sense of the virtues and values of that world. It is an Aristotelean approach to business ethics.

JOHN LADD

Bhopal: An Essay on Moral Responsibility and Civic Virtue

JOHN LADD teaches philosophy at Brown University. He specializes in ethics and the philosophy of law.

On December 3, 1984 the greatest industrial accident ever recorded took place in Bhopal, India. The accidental release of deadly methyl isocyanate gas in a Union Carbide chemical plant resulted in the deaths of enormous numbers of people, variously estimated from 2000 to 5000, and in injuries to many others, estimated at 100,000 to 200,000, as well as the deaths of large numbers of cattle and other animals.

The tragedy at Bhopal provides a concrete, spectacular and instructive illustration of a particular set of moral problems that are a peculiar product of our time, namely, problems relating to individual and social responsibility for catastrophic accidents connected with high technology. In fact, Bhopal may provide the model for analyzing our responsibilities for preventing an even greater catastrophe, an accidental nuclear explosion....

When disasters like Bhopal occur, it is natural to ask: why did it happen? Who or what is to blame for this calamity? Who, if anyone, is responsible? Or, as the *New York Times* succinctly put it: "Where does the main responsibility for Bhopal lie?"

Responsibility, Litigation and Blame

Ever since the disaster took place there has been a great deal of soul-searching as well as a flood of "blame rhetoric" in newspapers and magazines: charges and countercharges, the Americans blaming the Indians and the Indians blaming the Americans; the company blaming the government and the government blaming the company, groups with vested interests and ideologies blaming other groups with vested interests and ideologies, and so on. All this blame rhetoric has been accompanied by wholesale denials of responsibility and attempts to shift responsibility onto others; for these purposes, there have also been cover-ups and suppression of information. In addition to those more directly involved in the accident itself, lawyers, politicians, editorial writers and pundits like William F. Buckley have jumped into the game of placing responsibility and blame.

On reflection, it is obvious that the adversarial approach to questions about responsibility blinds us to the serious and deep underlying moral issues and makes a forthright and thoroughgoing discussion of these issues, general as well as particular, difficult if not impossible. Furthermore, the approach itself is founded on what I shall argue is a basic misconception: first, that it is both necessary and possible to identify one specific person or set of persons as morally responsible for the accident and, second, that those so identified can or should be *blamed* for it. It will become evident very soon that this two-fold assumption, which underlies what I shall call *blame-responsibility,* raises more questions than it answers. This entire essay might be regarded as an attack on the notion of blame-responsibility.

The blame approach towards responsibility, along with its adversarial posture, is part and parcel of what I call *legalism,* an approach reflected in the American fondness for turning moral problems into legal ones. "Legalism" may be defined as the whole-sale use of legal or quasi-legal concepts, arguments and models as a framework for the analysis of moral issues.

Legalism reduces questions of moral responsibility to questions of legal liability, which themselves amount in the end, in crass terms, to questions of who is to pay for the damages and for the costs. (Being blamed or punished might be regarded as a kind of payment.) I shall try to show as we go along that nothing but moral confusion results from the reduction of responsibility as a moral category to the legal concepts of responsibility and liability.

The simple point about legal responsibility is that it would be a mistake to conclude that if and when it is decided by the courts after litigation that, say, UC as a corporate entity is legally responsible, i.e. liable, that is the end to the matter of moral responsibility. To put it bluntly, moral issues about responsibility cannot be resolved through litigation. I shall return to the distinction between legal and moral responsibility later in this essay when I discuss different uses of the concept of responsibility. . . .

Normal Accidents and the Problem of Responsibility

The moral problem posed by Bhopal presents a challenge of some urgency because the accident is a typical example of a new kind of catastrophe due to high technology that Charles Perrow calls *normal accidents.* Perrow's important book on the subject brings up a whole set of issues that need to be addressed by moral philosophers. He describes in detail a number of accidents of this type, including Three Mile Island. Drawing on many examples from different kinds of high technology, he shows how normal accidents are characteristically catastrophic, unpredictable and, in a sense, unavoidable. The theme of Perrow's book is that these accidents take place where there are complex interactive systems and where the systems are also tightly coupled, "that is, processes happen very fast and can't be turned off, the failed parts cannot be isolated from other parts, or there is no other way to keep the production going safely . . . recovery from the initial disturbance is not possible; it will spread quickly and irretrievably for at least some time, etc." The coincidence of a number of small and in themselves insignificant failures lead to breakdowns with enormous ramifications, where no one at the time understands what is happening, partly because the antecedent probability of these failures occurring together is so low. His conclusion is that high technology is statistically bound to produce more normal accidents, unpredictable catastrophes due to technological complexities and the tight coupling of complex systems. . . .

If there is no single cause, then, as I have already pointed out, it seems patently insufficient ethically, if not downright foolish, to try to fix the blame on one or more individuals and even sillier to put one such an individual in prison, as the Indian authorities did to Mr. Warren Anderson, the CEO of Union Carbide, when he arrived from the US to make an on the spot survey of the situation. The point should be obvious: that simple blame fixing of this kind, whether it be by the Indian government or by Union Carbide, is ethical nonsense. . . .

Instead of using an abstract theoretical approach such as utilitarianism or cost-benefit analysis to sort out the moral problems connected with Bhopal, we will find that the concept of moral responsibility is a much more appropriate tool of analysis for this purpose. To begin with, it provides the specificity lacking in utilitarianism and explains why there is a greater moral burden on certain individuals and sets of individuals like Mr. Warren Anderson, CEO of Union Carbide, to concern themselves with the misfortunes of the victims of Bhopal than there is on others, say, ordinary American citizens who have no special personal relationship to the people in Bhopal or to the disaster. It also explains why the lack of solicitude on the part of the chief actors for the health and safety of the people in Bhopal, both prior to the accident and subsequent to it, is morally so outrageous. I shall argue that the advantage of the concept of moral responsibility as a moral category for analyzing moral aspects of tragedies like Bhopal is that it is at once consequentialist, person-specific (=agent-relative) and, as a moral virtue, intrinsically motivational. . . .

Let us begin our inquiry into the concept of moral responsibility by comparing and contrasting normal accidents like Bhopal with two other sorts of disaster: first, humanly initiated calamities, and, second, natural disasters. . . .

Generally speaking, humanly initiated calamities like the Nazi holocaust and My Lai, and, of course, wars, are causally linked to human purposes, motives and goals of one sort or another, which, however objectionable, provide at least a partial explanation of their occurrence or at least their "initiation." Normal accidents, on the other hand, have no such link, at least, no direct link. It is inconceivable, for example that anyone, however evil, would intentionally and deliberately initiate a disaster like Bhopal, Chernobyl or the explosion of *Challenger*, in the way that SS guards intentionally and deliberately participated in bringing about the deaths in the gas chambers and Calley and other soldiers engaged in the massacres of My Lai.

The participation and *mens rea* of the latter raises the frightful question of complicity that does not exist in normal accidents. In some ways, from the moral point of view, the unquestioned complicity of individuals and groups in these enterprises and the condoning of them by others makes it easier to accept the attribution of responsibility than where there is no complicity or condonation. Complicity and condonation, then, provide us with a useful way of distinguishing morally between humanly initiated calamities and accidental catastrophes due to the failures of high technology.

The lack of complicity and condonation as well as the accompanying sense of helplessness on the part of the people involved, suggests that industrial catastrophes might be fruitfully compared to natural disasters such as earthquakes, floods and hurricanes. For like natural disasters, industrial accidents are calamities for everyone and are wanted by no one. They are simply misfortunes and as such might even, in the quaint expression, be called "acts of God." Does it make sense to place normal accidents in the same moral category as natural disasters? . . .

Perhaps the key to the difference is this. The occurrence of natural disasters is *completely* beyond human control and in that sense such disasters are absolutely unpreventable. Large-scale industrial disasters, on the other hand, are preventable in the sense that they might have been prevented by human intervention. . . . A normal accident is a case, not where there is no human control, but where *human control has broken down.* That, in turn, simply means that there was no control where there ought to have been control. . . .

· · ·

BHOPAL

In this part, I shall give a brief synopsis of salient facts about the Bhopal tragedy that bear on to the issue of moral responsibility. . . .

Background

(1) *MIC:* The chemical agent that was the source of the devastation was methyl isocyanate (MIC), an unusually dangerous substance, both to store and to handle. It is reactive, toxic, volatile and flammable.

Absence of information about MIC: Very little information was given by the UCC to the Indian managers, operators and employees about the chemical properties of MIC. The company to advance its own interests appears to have exploited the fact that the Indian government and the Indian populace were ignorant of the hazardous character of the technology. As a result of this lack of information, measures that might have been taken to avoid or to mitigate the disaster were unknown to those involved, including the doctors.

(2) *Economic:* The plant was not making money. For that reason, the company had cut back on personnel, including managers and operators. Safety and modernization of equipment were sacrificed to save money. Managers were untrained and unfamiliar with the technology and its hazards.

(3) *Demographic:* Contrary to official governmental policy, the UCI was permitted to locate in a highly populated area near the railway station, bus station, hospitals, etc. Consequently, the dimensions of the disaster were much greater than they would have been in a less densely populated area.

(4) *Organizational and political:* The organizational structure consisted of a complicated relationship between the UCC of Danbury, CT and the Indian unit, UCI, which was mostly under the supervision of Indian managers carrying out general directives issued from the parent company. The Indian governmental inspection agencies were themselves badly understaffed and uninformed about the safety problems relating to MIC. Safety was given a low priority by all the parties involved.

(5) *Educational:* There is no question that the operators and minor managers were not well educated nor adequately trained to deal with complicated technology. In this regard, blame has often been placed on *indigenization* by writers who claim that only those technologies that can be safely handled ought to be exported to Third World countries and that multinationals should not turn over control to local units.

To be fair to the Indians, however, the use of untrained personnel is not limited to Third World operation of high technology. Accidents at Browns Ferry and Three Mile Island also involved untrained personnel.

The Accident

The immediate cause of the accident has not yet been determined, but apparently water leaked into the MIC storage tank, causing a buildup of temperature and pressure leading to an explosion that could not be contained or controlled. It was ascertained that the MIC had already been in a dangerous state, long before the accident.

Failure of Safety Procedures

There is a long list of failures in the safety system including such items as the following: (a) The refrigeration unit had been out of operation for several months. (b) The scrubber did not have enough caustic soda to neutralize the MIC; its capacity was too small. (c) The spare tank was not empty. (d) The flare for burning off escaping gas was too short, and so on.

Operating Personnel

Essentially the operators did not realize what was going on when the leak first started. Either the instrumental temperature and pressure gauges were not working or else the operators did not trust them, owing to previous failures. The narrative of the discovery by the operators of the pressure buildup and of the subsequent events reveals that it began with nonchalance, then bewilderment, and finally panic.

No Preparation for Emergencies

There was lack of preparation for an emergency, a lack of information about the properties of MIC and little training in the handling of MIC of the local management, operators, medical staff, and the populace, a lack of reliable instrumentation and a lack of trained personnel to operate a plant that was technologically sophisticated and complex.

When the accident occurred, it was discovered that there was a shortage of oxygen masks. The siren was not turned on at once nor were the police notified, because it was company policy not to report minor accidents or leaks. If the surrounding population had been alerted and provided with information and equipment to deal with the emergency, many lives would have been saved.

General Factors

Other more general factors might be mentioned as contributory to the disaster. First, there was a striking discrepancy between directives and policies issued from on high by the UCC and even by the Indian government and the actual practices and everyday operations of plant operators, managers and governmental bureaucrats. This fact raises interesting questions about control and responsibility within a bureaucratic structure. The same sort of discrepancy has been noted in Three Mile Island.

Another general factor that needs to be mentioned is the *bureaucratic mentality*. The bureaucratic role often requires officials to be devious and irresponsible. Bureaucrats tend to sacrifice long-term considerations for short-term goals. There are numerous instances in Bhopal (as in the U.S. Nuclear Power industry) of withholding information and of cover-ups, both before and after the accident. (A number of these have already been mentioned.)

Finally, one factor that should be mentioned is the functional racism among the Americans who conducted the operations and who commented on the accident after it happened. Many agreed implicitly with what one distinguished gentleman said to me in discussing Bhopal: "After all, the Indians do not place as much value on life as we do!" Q.E.D.

Who Was to Blame?

After the survey of a number of different kinds of factors contributing to the disaster of Bhopal, it is clear that any and all of them, as well as many others not mentioned, could with some plausibility be used as a reason for blaming or for ascribing responsibility for the outcome to someone or other or to something (e.g. the system). With so many candidates and of such different kinds it seems pointless if not arbitrary to identify any single one of them as "ultimate" in the sense assumed in the question posed by the *NY Times:* "Who was ultimately responsible for the tragedy?" Anyone who tries to offer a simple answer to this ambiguous question must have an axe to grind, such as the defense of an ideological position or narrow self-interest.

The obvious lesson is that where normal accidents are concerned the kind of unilinear causation presupposed by most common conceptions of responsibility is inappropriate if not meaningless. If we reject this presupposition, which is a presupposition of what I call the standard concept of responsibility, then we have one more reason for rejecting the standard concept of responsibility and the negative concept of responsibility that it implies. . . .

MORAL RESPONSIBILITY: A LARGER VIEW

The Three Components of Responsibility

The easiest way to describe the structure of moral responsibility is to compare and contrast it with the standard concept of responsibility. According to that concept, when applied, for example, to past conduct (as in tort liability), responsibility consists of three basic components: (a) an untoward outcome (harm or injury) to the victim, (b) an agent at fault, and (c) a causal relation of some kind between the agent's conduct and the outcome. Although we must be circumspect in arguing from the legal concept of responsibility, since it is in many respects a misleading model of moral responsibility, the threefold breakdown that it suggests can be used to bring out the principal features of the enlarged concept of moral responsibility. In using this schema, we must, of course, bear in mind the qualifications that have already been mentioned earlier in the critical discussions of the standard concept of responsibility, such as the rejection of exclusivity and of secondary consequences, e.g. blame, as essential ingredients in the concept of moral responsibility. . . .

First, with respect to (a), the outcome, many people are tempted to downplay the enormity of the disaster at Bhopal (or anywhere else, for that matter). Even Mother

Teresa said that she found the disaster "to be a beautiful thing because it brought out the best in everybody," and Mr. Warren Anderson said that he regretted having "over-reacted" when he first heard of the tragedy. In reply, I hope that it suffices to point out that Stoicism over the misery of others is hardly a moral virtue!

Second, as far as causality (c) is concerned, it must be recognized that moral responsibility for an accident like Bhopal involves many different kinds of causal complexities, complexities that may be due, for example, to multiple causes, to multiple causal levels, to multiple dimensions of causality, as well as to multiple agents acting in multiple capacities and, of course, to the multiplicity of victims. Where the causation embraces large numbers of agents, we find some sense in the notion of "collective responsibility," and where an untoward outcome is ostensibly due to complex technological and social structures, we feel that we can blame the "system" and say that it is responsible. In the final analysis, however, moral responsibility always boils down to a relationship of individuals to other individuals. Neither collective responsibility nor system responsibility provides an excuse relieving specific individuals from their responsibility for outcomes.

With regard to causality, it must also be pointed out that responsibility like causality can be indirect as well as direct. Accordingly, a large number of individuals can be held indirectly responsible for Bhopal. More important, the causality involved comprises negative causes (e.g. omissions) as well as positive causes (e.g. actions). For our purposes negative causes are important, for most technological accidents are breakdowns that are due to negative causes, such as the failure of a piece of machinery to operate properly or the failure of personnel to do something like closing or opening a valve or warning others about a danger. The fallacy of supposing one is responsible only for one's positive actions and not for omissions is nicely illustrated by Mr. Warren Anderson's smug comment that "The corporation (i.e. UC) did nothing that either caused or contributed to the accident. . . ." Since omissions are, according to my analysis, also actions, the term "action" will henceforth be used to refer to both.

Fault and Moral Deficiency

Let us now turn to (b), the subjective side of responsibility, and to the question of fault. According to most versions of the standard concept of responsibility, in order to be responsible for an untoward outcome, the agent must have had what is variously described as a culpable intention, a blameworthy mental set, a fault of character, or a "weak or defective will," which explains or gives rise to his action (or non-action). . . .

The requirement of fault, a blameworthy mental set or bad intention, appears to provide a stumbling block to the use of the concept of responsibility for accidents like Bhopal. For it is indeed difficult to pinpoint any single person or set of persons who was clearly at fault in the strict sense, e.g. a person who was careless or grossly negligent. A closer look at the notion of fault will show why it is inappropriate in this context. . . .

It is clearly absurd, however, to attribute fault in the sense of a reprovable mental quality to any of the people that were involved in the Bhopal case: operators, managers and officials. They were just ordinary people doing their job and trying to earn a living. Furthermore, the actual failures on the part of specific individuals or groups to act were in themselves relatively insignificant and commonplace. The accident was not due *per se* to the individual acts or omissions of a few persons but to the accidental coincidence of a large number of failures, no one of which would have been fatal by itself. This is the typical configuration of a normal accident.

For this reason, to say that any or all of those involved were negligent, except after the fact, is to make a claim that under different circumstances would be unjustified. It is true that we can say that the managers ought to have instructed their employees more adequately about safety conditions and safety measures and that the operators ought to have taken the rise in pressure in the MIC tank more seriously and should not have gone off for tea. There are lots of *ought to haves,* but none of them amount to negligence, much less criminal negligence. . . . In order to save the concept of moral responsibility for application, e.g. to Bhopal, we need to break the connection between responsibility and blame. If we do that we can hold a large number of individuals responsible without holding any of them blamable. Earlier in this essay, I tried to show how the connection can be broken by distinguishing between the primary and the secondary consequences of responsibility. I argued that blame and blameworthiness, blamability, are only secondary consequences of responsibility. The primary consequences, the oughts still remain, however, and pertain to the conduct of all the various individuals whose acts or omissions made the accident at Bhopal possible: there are lots of things that they ought to have done, but did not do.

Reflecting further on what lies behind the subjective requirement of fault, we find that we cannot help feeling that there is something missing in the attitudes of persons whose actions have or might have a calamitous effect on the safety, health and welfare of others, and yet who have no prior or subsequent concern for the actual or possible effect of their actions on others. After all, people are supposed to care about these things; an attitude of nonchalance or indifference may not be blameworthy, but surely it is deplorable.

In the case of Bhopal we note a general lack of concern, especially on the part of the management and the government, for the safety of those around them. Safety was a low priority for almost everyone who was in any way connected with the disaster in Bhopal; other things came first, notably, jobs, positions, and careers. This lack of concern, almost indifference, for safety was manifested at all levels: the publication of and compliance with safety regulations relating to MIC from UC on down was pro forma rather than realistic and in day to day plant operations safety was sacrificed for the sake of cutting costs. Even at the lowest level, among the workers, concern for safety was less important than holding down a job. . . .

The move from fault to deficiency, . . . from the presence of an evil to the absence of a good, and, in general, to an orientation towards humanity or lack thereof, broadens our perspective on the role of responsibility in our interpersonal and public life by bringing in a subjective condition of larger dimensions than blameworthiness. At the same time, it extends the scope of responsibility by reaching out to a wider range of people and to many more different sorts of causal contributions of individual conduct to outcomes affecting the welfare of others. . . .

● ● ●

Civic Virtue and the Banality of Evil

I borrow the phrase "banality of evil" from Hannah Arendt, who uses it to describe the crimes of Eichmann. The paradox of Eichmann is that he was in almost every respect entirely "normal" and yet had no appreciation of the fact that what he had done was wrong; he portrayed himself as an idealist bureaucrat who just did his duty. The point of the reference in the present context is that the evil of irresponsibility, the nonchalance that we observe in Bhopal, both before and after the accident, is not due to some egregiously neglectful attitude on the part of various people whose actions or omissions contributed causally in one way or another to the outcome or on the part of the general public, including the stockholders of UC, who failed to concern themselves with safety. Instead, the moral deficiency of everyone who was or might have been involved was banal; it reflected a perfectly commonplace and "normal" preoccupation with matters of self-interest and of self-advancement to the exclusion of any consideration of the wider implications of their actions or non-actions and of their absence of concern for the safety and the welfare of others.

It should be obvious to all of us that the moral deficiency I have pointed out is not uncommon in our culture; it is not limited to a few miscreants. Rather it is something that we observe everywhere in our society, everywhere where a concern for the welfare of others, including particularly a concern for their safety, takes second place to other concerns, such as material self-advancement. This is part of our culture. It is reflected in our institutions and fostered by them. The effect is aggravated by the dangerous technology that we have accepted unreflectively and by the bureaucratic machinery that organizes how we use the technology and that determines how we treat each other. At the bottom of these institutions is the prevailing ideology that has aptly been called "utilitarian individualism." This ideology gives legitimacy to the priority given to self over others and to the material social values of self-advancement. It also teaches that commitment and concern for others is supererogatory, that is, it is a matter of individual preference ("expressive individualism").

Virtue, according to the ideology, is optional; it is reserved for "saints and heroes."

Our attitude towards whistleblowing illustrates how far we have gone in turning our values upside down: the concern for safety, which should motivate all of us, has been relegated to the private realm of heroes, troublemakers and nuts. Our society assumes that it is a matter of individual choice (and risk) to decide whether or not to call attention to hazards and risks instead of being, as it should be, a duty incumbent on all citizens as responsible members of society.

This is where virtue comes in, or what in the present context I shall call *civic virtue.* Civic virtue is a virtue required of all citizens as citizens. It is not just something optional—for saints and heroes. A virtuous citizen, and that should include everybody, should have a concern for the common good and for the long-range welfare of other people in the society, even where this concern demands individual sacrifices of one sort or another or simply giving less priority to one's own private interests and to one's advancement on the escalator to worldly success.

Civic virtue on the part of its citizens is what holds a society together. Once it is lost, a society rapidly degenerates into violence and, in Hobbes's terms, into a war of all against all. Only a resurgence of civic virtue, or of what Bellah calls the "republican virtues," among the citizenry can save our society from self-destruction, brought on, say, through the irresponsible use of dangerous technology (nuclear armaments) and the irresponsible exploitation by bureaucracies of fellow citizens for the sake of various narrow short-term goals.

MARK ALFINO

Information Rights and the Information Manager

MARK ALFINO teaches philosophy at Gonzaga University. In addition to business ethics, he specializes in philosophy of language and twentieth-century philosophy.

The idea that people have a right to certain kinds of information is, in one sense, a relatively new one. But there are good reasons for talking about information rights in contrast to related rights like due process and informed consent. Within organizational life, a variety of information rights are widely, if informally, recognized, such as the right to receive regular information about one's performance. Also, most professional employment settings observe "just cause" dismissal policies. In addition to these informal rights, one should also identify "information virtues," specific ways in which workers can pursue excellence by adopting sophisticated information skills. . . .

I will explicate the idea and justification of information rights and information virtues. . . .

From a conceptual standpoint, it only makes sense to talk about information rights once one can distinguish between *accessing* information and *possessing* it. The classic historical example of the emergence of this distinction is our thinking about copyright. With the development of the printing press, possession of a physical copy of written information was no longer considered an adequate protection of the printer's or author's property interest in it. Copyrights are a kind of property right, but they are also usefully described as information rights because they involve claims about the legitimate access to information, not merely about the possession of objects. Like copyrights, information rights are interesting in part because they can be granted without dispossessing someone of an object. However, to grant someone a right to access information (or restrict access by others) we do need to make a significant moral claim about that role the information plays in a person's (or organization's) life. Before looking at those justifications, it may help to articulate a more concrete idea of what an information right is.

During the past few decades, information rights have been associated less with a right to restrict access to information than with a right to gain it. Instructive examples of this domain of information rights include the Freedom of Information Act, the recently created right to legal counsel, and the right to be informed of one's rights (the Miranda rule). Although these examples are primarily concerned with the information rights governing our relationship with the government, it is not surprising that a variety of changes in the workplace have raised questions about the kinds of information rights workers should have in their relationship with their employers. Due process rights were originally thought of as rights protecting citizens from the enormous power of the state to act arbitrarily against them. T. M. Scanlon has argued persuasively that the moral goal of protecting citizens against arbitrary harm from powerful organizations like the government justifies the extension of some due process rights into the workplace, at least in large corporations.

A similar argument may justify the extension of information rights into the workplace. If, as citizens, we need access to information the government holds as a check against the abuse of government power, then as consumers and workers we may need rights both to gain information from private organizations and to control the flow of information about us among private organizations that might abuse the power that that information gives them. Such information rights in the consumer/producer relationship include product labeling and credit information. In the workplace, information rights claims are invoked at all stages of the employee appraisal process and in the conventions governing the communication of information about employees to other firms and other agencies (such as health insurers). If we apply this schema for justifying due process rights to the idea of information rights then we can see that the *question* of whether someone in the workplace has a right to some information arises whenever the absence of providing the information might increase the likelihood of arbitrary harm being done to the individual at the hands of the more powerful organization.

So far we have discussed information rights as analogous to such political rights as due process. To bring out their ethical character, however, it may be helpful to think about the role that information plays in our decision making. Virtually every major ethical theory places great emphasis on the process of rational deliberation in the formulation of claims about what we ought to do. Whether I am to deliberate about the promotion of happiness (as in utilitarian and other hedonic ethics), the comportment of my conduct with quintessential human enterprises (as in teleological and character ethics), or the conformity of my intentions with principles of rationality (as in contractarian models), I can only succeed in my deliberations if I have adequate information at my disposal.

To bring this point about the centrality of information into sharp focus, consider the case of an employee's job performance being appraised. Suppose she has, in addition to her obligations as a worker, obligations to her family, duties to make prudent decisions about financial commitments and future opportunities. If our goal, in assessing a social process such as her performance appraisal procedure, is to maximize every person's ability to lead a rational and moral life, then the appraisal process cannot merely be seen as a prerogative of the employer for the maximization of productivity. In addition to satisfying the employer's "information right" to find out about the success of the employment contract, the process serves as the basis for a whole host of ethically charged deliberative acts by the employee. When we talk of "information rights" in an exclusively moral sense, we mean the relevance of information to the pursuit of the good life, a life in which our basic duties are satisfied and our opportunities to pursue excellence are maximized. In this ethical context, the employer's property rights and the contract rights flowing from the employment contract are given weight because they are ethically relevant to the employer's ability to plan rationally. Information rights must impose obligations and duties which satisfy the mutual needs of all affected parties.

Before discussing information virtues, we should note another relationship between information rights and due process rights. Most organizational processes that give all parties "their due," do so by giving them ample opportunity to receive, communicate, and evaluate information. In the legal setting, the rules for discovery of evidence, deposing witnesses, and making arguments before a tribunal all fundamentally have to do with access to information and communication. Although the concept of "information rights" may initially seem odd or derivative in relation to due process rights, we should not lose sight of the fact that our dominant conceptual framework for justice is fundamentally an "information processing" model. In promoting information rights in the workplace, we need to ask ourselves how we are helping or hindering others in their ability to process information relevant to their pursuit of the good life.

What are information virtues? Since virtues are excellences of human character, an "information virtue" would have to treat our approach to information as a kind of character trait that promotes human excellence in the bearer. Again, it is helpful to keep in mind the close proximity of information and deliberation and the centrality of deliberation to the pursuit of the good life. With this in mind, it should not seem odd to say that one feature of our character concerns our desire to gain access to information and make information available to others. The excellence of this character trait has little to do with the *quantity* of information sought or made available. The moral value of information has more to do with the relevance of the information to deliberation. The "information virtuous" are people who ask not what they *have* to tell others or what they *have* to read, look up, or find out, but what information they *should* seek to promote their own and others' deliberation. Management theorist Peter Drucker has called this "information responsibility," and he thinks it is exercised when workers ask, "Who depends on me for information? And on whom do I depend?" Drucker is one of a number of theorists who are speculating today about the rapid evolution of work organizations into "information organizations." . . .

In the general formulation given above, information virtues come out looking like one of the core values of the Western tradition, like rational deliberation or wisdom. Indeed, when we start to look at our co-workers, supervisors, and our entire organization in terms of its information habits, virtues, and vices, we can correlate virtuous information practices to the kind of atmosphere in which philosophical ideals such as critical reflection and justified authority are pursued. In the information virtuous organization, authority and power are not conferred upon those who enjoy privileged access to information. In most fields of work, the information virtuous will make significant use of information technology. . . .

THE VIRTUE OF THE INFORMATION MANAGER

. . . The moral judgements we make about the way people handle information are based . . . upon the centrality of information to a human being's ability to pursue the good life and to make rational judgements necessary for that pursuit. In the workplace, this means that we have a general right to information when the withholding of that information might lead to arbitrary harm to us. This is the ethical basis for most due process requirements. They exist to bring information and judgement to bear on situations in which arbitrary harm is probable and avoidable. When we speak, therefore, of information rights, we are reframing a category of moral rights by showing that they are protections based on an understanding of the role of information in the moral life of the person.

Beyond this information right, I think there are information virtues, ways of handling information that we might not be justified in demanding of others, but that show a virtue or excellence of character on their part. In the workplace, the "information virtuous" are people who handle information in a way that helps their co-workers, whether they are subordinates, peers, or superiors in the traditional hierarchy, excel in their jobs and develop as productive employees. Since, in the traditional work organization, managers often have greater access to organizational information than the employees they manage, it may be helpful to develop the idea of information virtue by discussing some of the roles and behaviors of the virtuous information manager.

Another reason for focusing on the managerial role is that in the area of management and organizational theory there is not settled opinion on the nature of the managerial function. Most contemporary analyses of organizational productivity, and most popular views about how organizations ought to be restructured, involve altering the role and status of the traditional manager. Although so much of our thinking about the profession of management is open to discussion, it may be interesting to see how the manager's information values can help clarify managerial roles.

Peter Drucker, the well known theorist, provides a helpful starting point for our discussion in his article, "The Coming of the New Organization." Like other commentators in organizational dynamics and economics, Drucker believes that technological changes in the global marketplace are rendering the traditional "command and control" organization obsolete. He believes that dynamic workplaces of the present and future will be organizations that integrate expert knowledge and the wealth of information available in the marketplace as it has been altered by information technology. The new organization is an "information organization" first. Its other functions, such as production and marketing, will depend for their success upon the ability of so-called "knowledge workers" to gather, share, and analyze information.

One might object that this has always been the case, but Drucker's argument, which parallels arguments by economists such as Robert Reich, is really about the relative importance of information in a world in which the availability of information has changed such basic market variables as the rate of technology transfer and the speed with which production facilities can be established, relocated, and adapted. Perhaps it seems ironic that the more accessible information about technology, products, and markets becomes, the less an organization can base its competitive advantage upon the mere possession of information. However, there is no reason to be surprised that as the supply of information in the market system increases, the relative value of that information to any one holder decreases.

What are the chief virtues of workers in the information organization? In a command and control organization, the virtuous worker is one who reliably implements his or her part of the organizational plan as it is disseminated from a central base of knowledge residing with management. Since the new organization is essentially an organization of expertise, people with expert knowledge who are also sophisticated in acquiring knowledge and information, the virtuous worker is one who demonstrates "information responsibility." The central questions for this worker are, according to Drucker, "Who depends on me for information? And on whom do I depend?" Thus, in the new organization the worker is more of a nexus in an information network. Managers, then, are people who organize and maintain the vitality of this network.

Drucker's views are somewhat speculative and far broader than our focus, which is the virtuous information manager. In a traditional organization, managers often interpret their roles as guardians and gatekeepers of information and judgment. Indeed, much proprietary information is entrusted to managers and it is often a manager's job to maintain confidential information from many sources. However, I want to argue that in the information organization managers need to shift their thinking about how to share and distribute information from a criterion that emphasizes proprietary rights and values the conservation of information in a command and control hierarchy, to one that emphasizes the value of information to the end users of the information, the workers who ultimately have responsibility for the success of the organization and, in many cases, the customers who are well situated to "feed back" information about the organization's effectiveness.

I am suggesting that we think of managers as people who maintain the vitality of an information network and not as people who organize a competition of workers trying to ascend an organizational hierarchy. The authority of the virtuous information manager is not based on the mere *possession* of proprietary information or the proximity to the center of organizational decision-making, but on our confidence in his or her ability to maximize both organizational and professional excellence through the handling and distribution of information. To confer status and authority upon someone because of the mere possession of information, rather than the responsible use of it, is like valuing storeroom clerks because they have keys to the supply cabinets, rather than because they are effective and responsible in the handling of supplies.

This approach involves a good deal of self-criticism on the part of managers to determine whether they are using information to conserve their own authority or using their authority to optimize the flow of information. The manager is an information "gate keeper" and although it would be foolish to suggest that the gate always be left open, it is also reasonable to observe that the gate is often closed for reasons that have more to do with the maintenance of the manager's power or the conservation of authority in the organization's hierarchy, than the accomplishment of organizational objectives and the development of worker responsibility and personal or professional expertise.

The virtue of the information manager will often be shown through the ability to distribute decision-making and organizational news in a way that promotes the self-responsibility and development of workers. This is both a prudential and moral skill. Through most of the 20th century, corporations built organizational efficiency by increasingly complex divisions of labor. The new organizational structures being tried by many corporations, and advocated on a theoretical level by experts like Drucker, involve revitalizing the workers' stake in the enterprise by reintegrating various kinds of decision making into their jobs. The virtuous information manager promotes the goals of the organization by developing expertise not merely by selecting for it.

So far the rather idealistic picture I have painted makes the virtuous information manager a hero of both the staff and the rest of the organization's major stakeholders. But there is at least one potential problem with the image of managerial function I am promoting. First, on my account, the virtuous information manager is primarily a "service worker" to subordinates. I am asking managers to think of themselves as peers (and in some cases subordinates) of the workers they manage. And yet, in order to manage, there will still be situations in which we want the manager to at least diagnose and possibly prescribe remedies for human resource problems. In this function the manager traditionally holds a superior authority. Can managers coherently communicate and act effectively with a mixture of subordinate and superior roles?

The answer to this question lies in the field of organizational dynamics, but it should be clear what ethical stake we have in the information management habits of our managers and co-workers. It is crucial to both the organization and the development of the worker that we maximize opportunities for decision making, responsibility and personal challenge in the workplace. We can maximize these opportunities while preserving the benefits of a complex division of labor if we use information creatively. Clearly, the virtuous information manager plays a key part in this process.

CHAPTER 7

What Are
My Rights?

Suppose you are taking a course in which you think you are doing particularly well. You study hard for your final exam, and when you see the exam questions you are certain that your study has paid off. You are confident that in this class you have earned an A. But when your grades arrive in the mail, you discover that your grade has been reported as a C. You telephone the professor, who tells you that this reflects a new grading policy—Cs for everyone, because everyone is equal. You are furious. This is an absurd sense of equality, you think. You feel that your rights have been violated. Have they?

The concept of individual rights has been central to much political debate in America for the past several decades. Issues regarding such diverse matters as gun control, school prayer, racial integration, and abortion have been articulated in terms of rights. Rights have been the focus of both idealistic and cynical campaigns. Moreover, some alleged rights are trivial. An advertising slogan some time back even claimed that we have a right to chicken prepared a certain way.

Probably few of us take such a slogan as a serious statement of our rights. But some claims to rights that are current in America are historically as novel as the right to well-prepared chicken. During the last few decades we have heard clamors that individuals should have the right to dress as they like in certain contexts, to control the way in which their bodies are used, even to die when they want to. Many social and political activists also suggest that our society should do more to guarantee all citizens the rights to things that other societies have considered rights but that ours traditionally has not, for example, medical care and higher education. Obviously, such guarantees depend on monetary resources—and some insist that taxation for the purpose of funding such programs deprives those taxed of a different kind of right—the right to keep the profits that stem from their own labor.

In the face of such various and controversial interpretations of our rights, how can we determine what our rights are? Many of us probably have intuitions that converge with those of the framers of the U.S. Constitution, who held that all human beings, just by virtue of being human, are entitled to "certain unalienable rights." In the words of the Declaration of Independence, these include the rights to "life, liberty, and the pursuit of happiness." Whether or not the laws that our governments established actually protected the unalienable rights of all its citizens (and clearly, during the times of slavery, at least, they did not), the presumption in our society is that certain human rights are basic and self-evident. The United States Bill of Rights articulates those rights that the government is not allowed to curtail. Significantly, the Bill of Rights focuses on what are sometimes called **negative rights,** which protect individuals from interference with their pursuits, in this case by the government. Similar rights are proclaimed in the United Nations Universal Declaration of Human Rights, which articulates the human freedoms that no person or government, in the view of the United Nations, has the right to violate. However, the United Nations declaration also articulates a number of **positive rights** as well, such as the right to work, to health care, and to education. Philosophical debate continues to be waged over which kind of right should take priority in case of a conflict between the two.

The notion that government, in particular, should be prevented from interfering with personal rights is a fundamental premise of classical **liberalism.** John Stuart Mill, in one of the basic defenses of this position, argues that the government has no right to curtail human freedom except in cases in which such freedom impinges on another person's or other persons' rights. Even if a person engages in behavior that is harmful to him or herself, the government has no right to interfere unless harm to other persons also results. This argument has been used to defend a wide range of alleged civil liberties, including rights to engage in sexual activity, to use recreational drugs, to opt not to use seatbelts or motorcycle helmets, or to sell and display pornography. Often, when the legitimacy of such alleged rights is debated, both sides of the argument accept Mill's notion that only harm to other persons justifies government interference. In such cases, the debate often revolves around the question of whether any harmful effects of the behavior in question actually are limited to the perpetrator.

In a book titled *Anarchy, State, and Utopia,* Robert Nozick espouses **libertarianism,** and those who uphold this position often take inspiration from Mill. Libertarians defend a broad range of civil liberties, including the individual's right to do whatever he or she wants with his or her possessions. Libertarians also favor an extremely limited role for government (essentially, the role of "protector of liberties") and restrictions on what types of endeavors the government may tax its citizens to support. Because the libertarian position involves strong views about the individual's freedom regarding possessions, it requires a clear conception of what establishes legitimate possession. Nozick develops an "entitlement theory" to establish what we are entitled to as individuals. He argues that the legitimacy of a claim to possession depends on how the possession was acquired. Nozick is not concerned that possessions are distributed in any particular way, for example, to ensure a particular level of material comfort for everyone. Governments all too often, in such efforts, meddle with people's rights to control their property, according to Nozick. If people's rights to do what they want to with legitimately acquired possessions are respected, governments cannot ensure that a particular "fair" distribution will result.

On the other hand, John Rawls contends that distribution *must* be considered if one is to construct a government in which individuals are treated fairly. In "Justice as Fairness," Rawls argues that justice depends on two principles, one asserting each individual an equal right to as much liberty as is compatible with the same degree of liberty for others, and the other requiring that inequalities be arbitrarily distributed except in cases in which it is reasonable to expect that some other arrangement will work to everyone's advantage. Rawls also contends that rational persons would agree on these principles if they were in a position to set the basic rules for fairness without any personal knowledge of which particular advantages and disadvantages they would have in their own lives. He sees this sense of fairness as being preeminently rational.

The fact that more and more sectors of society have been claiming more and more rights has led some moral thinkers to question whether "rights" talk is still useful. Some have argued that framing our ethical discussions in terms of "duties" and "obligations" is more suitable for discussing many issues, because people who assert rights are effectively claiming that someone, perhaps the government, owes them certain things. Amitai Etzioni argues that American society has lost its perspective on rights and duties. Too many people feel entitled to claim all sorts of rights without acknowledging any kind of responsibility. Etzioni defends the **communitarian** position, which urges that we reconfigure our institutions in ways that emphasize our interconnections and interdependence. Communitarians call for a societal shift toward recognizing that every individual has responsibilities as a member of a community. Finding solutions to our social problems depends on our individual efforts to be good citizens, acknowledging the duties that go with citizenship.

This chapter closes with three readings pertaining to some of the specific debates about rights that Etzioni mentions. Amartya Sen's "The Right to Take Personal Risks" considers Mill's claim that one has the right to harm oneself so long as no one else is harmed. Sen accepts that right but questions how important such a right is by comparison with other, conflicting objectives. He proposes that in establishing laws that pertain to personal risks (for example, laws regarding the use of seatbelts), we evaluate the importance of the right to take risks in light of other goals. Public decisions must take the whole picture into account; and while rights are important, they are only part of the picture.

Most Americans feel strongly about the individual's right to be protected from government surveillance. Our law respects many other rights of the individual to withhold information: consider, for instance, the Fifth Amendment in the Bill of Rights. Sissela Bok contends that our sense of the right to secrecy and privacy is intimately linked with our sense of identity and freedom. She concludes that balancing our various intuitions about secrecy is necessarily complicated and requires sensitivity to the full range of intuitions we have on the subject.

The AIDS epidemic presents a particular case of contradictory intuitions regarding secrecy. Although most of us probably agree that confidentiality between patient and doctor should be maintained, the public health risk raises questions about whether this right should be maintained in AIDS cases. Do those who have been intimate with a person diagnosed with AIDS have the right to know that they may have been infected? Certainly their health and the health of any of their other sexual partners may depend on their awareness of the risks involved in their behavior. On the other hand, the cruel and prejudicial reactions against people known to have AIDS in many communities suggest that perhaps people with AIDS, in particular, should have their rights to privacy protected. Grant Gillett, arguing that the right to confidentiality in the doctor-patient relationship must be weighed against the duties and responsibilities required of the physician, concludes that occasionally the obligation to protect others from potential harm may require the physician to breach confidentiality. But he contends that most often, the doctor's obligation can be fulfilled by encouraging AIDS patients themselves to reveal their condition to those who need to know.

The United States Bill of Rights

THE UNITED STATES BILL OF RIGHTS is the first ten amendments to the Constitution, which outline the individual's freedoms that cannot be infringed upon by governmental power. The document was ratified on December 15, 1791.

AMENDMENT I

Congress shall make no law respecting an establishment of religion, or prohibiting the free exercise thereof; or abridging the freedom of speech, or of the press; or the right of the people peaceably to assemble, and to petition the Government for a redress of grievances.

AMENDMENT II

A well regulated Militia, being necessary to the security of a free State, the right of the people to keep and bear Arms, shall not be infringed.

AMENDMENT III

No Soldier shall, in time of peace be quartered in any house, without the consent of the Owner, nor in time of war, but in a manner to be prescribed by law.

AMENDMENT IV

The right of the people to be secure in their persons, houses, papers, and effects, against unreasonable searches and seizures, shall not be violated, and no Warrants shall issue, but upon probable cause, supported by Oath or affirmation, and particularly describing the place to be searched, and the persons or things to be seized.

AMENDMENT V

No person shall be held to answer for a capital, or otherwise infamous crime, unless on a presentment or indictment of a Grand Jury, except in cases arising in the land or naval forces, or in the Militia, when in actual service in time of War or public danger; nor shall any person be subject for the same offence to be twice put in jeopardy of life or limb; nor shall be compelled in any criminal case to be a witness against himself, nor be deprived of life, liberty, or property, without due process of law; nor shall private property be taken for public use, without just compensation.

AMENDMENT VI

In all criminal prosecutions, the accused shall enjoy the right to a speedy and public trial, by an impartial jury of the State and district wherein the crime shall have been committed, which district shall have been previously ascertained by law, and to be informed of the nature and cause of the accusation; to be confronted with the witnesses against him; to have compulsory process for obtaining witnesses in his favor, and to have the Assistance of Counsel for his defence.

AMENDMENT VII

In suits at common law, where the value in controversy shall exceed twenty dollars, the right of trial by jury shall be preserved, and no fact tried by a jury, shall be otherwise reexamined in any Court of the United States, than according to the rules of the common law.

AMENDMENT VIII

Excessive bail shall not be required, nor excessive fines imposed, nor cruel and unusual punishments inflicted.

AMENDMENT IX

The enumeration in the Constitution, of certain rights, shall not be construed to deny or disparage others retained by the people.

AMENDMENT X

The powers not delegated to the United States by the Constitution, nor prohibited by it to the States, are reserved to the States respectively, or to the people.

The United Nations Universal Declaration of Human Rights

THE UNIVERSAL DECLARATION OF HUMAN RIGHTS was adopted by the United Nations General Assembly on December 10, 1948.

Whereas recognition of the inherent dignity and of the equal and inalienable rights of all members of the human family is the foundation of freedom, justice and peace in the world,

Whereas disregard and contempt for human rights have resulted in barbarous acts which have outraged the conscience of mankind, and the advent of a world in which human beings shall enjoy freedom of speech and belief and freedom from fear and want has been proclaimed as the highest aspiration of the common people,

Whereas it is essential, if man is not to be compelled to have recourse, as a last resort, to rebellion against tyranny and oppression, that human rights should be protected by the rule of law,

Whereas it is essential to promote the development of friendly relations between nations,

Whereas the peoples of the United Nations have in the Charter reaffirmed their faith in fundamental human rights, in the dignity and worth of the human person and in the equal rights of men and women and have determined to promote social progress and better standards of life in larger freedom,

Whereas Member States have pledged themselves to achieve, in co-operation with the United Nations, the promotion of universal respect for and observance of human rights and fundamental freedoms,

Whereas a common understanding of these rights and freedoms is of the greatest importance for the full realization of this pledge,

Now, therefore, **the General Assembly** *proclaims* **this Universal Declaration of Human Rights** as a common standard of achievement for all peoples and all nations, to the end that every individual and every organ of society, keeping this Declaration constantly in mind, shall strive by teaching and education to promote respect for these rights and freedoms and by progressive measures, national and international, to secure their universal and effective recognition and observance, both among the peoples of Member States themselves and among the peoples of territories under their jurisdiction.

ARTICLE 1

All human beings are born free and equal in dignity and rights. They are endowed with reason and conscience and should act towards one another in a spirit of brotherhood.

ARTICLE 2

Everyone is entitled to all the rights and freedoms set forth in this Declaration, without distinction of any kind, such as race, colour, sex, language, religion, political or other opinion, national or social origin, property, birth or other status.

Furthermore, no distinction shall be made on the basis of the political, jurisdictional or international status of the country or territory to which a person belongs, whether it be independent, trust, non-selfgoverning or under any other limitation of sovereignty.

ARTICLE 3

Everyone has the right to life, liberty and security of person.

ARTICLE 4

No one shall be held in slavery or servitude; slavery and the slave trade shall be prohibited in all their forms.

ARTICLE 5

No one shall be subjected to torture or to cruel, inhuman or degrading treatment or punishment.

ARTICLE 6

Everyone has the right to recognition everywhere as a person before the law.

ARTICLE 7

All are equal before the law and are entitled without any discrimination to equal protection of the law. All are entitled to equal protection against any discrimination in violation of this Declaration and against any incitement to such discrimination.

ARTICLE 8

Everyone has the right to an effective remedy by the competent national tribunals for acts violating the fundamental rights granted him by the constitution or by law.

ARTICLE 9

No one shall be subjected to arbitrary arrest, detention or exile.

ARTICLE 10

Everyone is entitled in full equality to a fair and public hearing by an independent and impartial tribunal, in the determination of his rights and obligations and of any criminal charge against him.

ARTICLE 11

(1) Everyone charged with a penal offence has the right to be presumed innocent until proved guilty according to law in a public trial at which he has had all the guarantees necessary for his defence.
(2) No one shall be held guilty of any penal offence on account of any act or omission which did not constitute a penal offence, under national or international law, at the time when it was committed. Nor shall a heavier penalty be imposed than the one that was applicable at the time the penal offence was committed.

ARTICLE 12

No one shall be subjected to arbitrary interference with his privacy, family, home or correspondence, nor to attacks upon his honour and reputation. Everyone has the right to the protection of the law against such interference or attacks.

ARTICLE 13

(1) Everyone has the right to freedom of movement and residence within the borders of each State.
(2) Everyone has the right to leave any country, including his own, and to return to his country.

ARTICLE 14

(1) Everyone has the right to seek and to enjoy in other countries asylum from persecution.
(2) This right may not be invoked in the case of prosecutions genuinely arising from non-political crimes or from acts contrary to the purposes and principles of the United Nations.

ARTICLE 15

(1) Everyone has the right to a nationality.
(2) No one shall be arbitrarily deprived of his nationality nor denied the right to change his nationality.

ARTICLE 16

(1) Men and women of full age, without any limitation due to race, nationality or religion, have the right to marry and to found a family. They are entitled to equal rights as to marriage, during marriage and at its dissolution.
(2) Marriage shall be entered into only with the free and full consent of the intending spouses.
(3) The family is the natural and fundamental group unit of society and is entitled to protection by society and the State.

ARTICLE 17

(1) Everyone has the right to own property alone as well as in association with others.
(2) No one shall be arbitrarily deprived of his property.

ARTICLE 18

Everyone has the right to freedom of thought, conscience and religion; this right includes freedom to change his religion or belief, and freedom, either alone or in community with others and in public or private, to manifest his religion or belief in teaching, practice, worship and observance.

ARTICLE 19

Everyone has the right to freedom of opinion and expression; this right includes freedom to hold opinions without interference and to seek, receive and impart information and ideas through any media and regardless of frontiers.

ARTICLE 20

(1) Everyone has the right to freedom of peaceful assembly and association.
(2) No one may be compelled to belong to an association.

ARTICLE 21

(1) Everyone has the right to take part in the government of his country, directly or through freely chosen representatives.
(2) Everyone has the right of equal access to public service in his country.
(3) The will of the people shall be the basis of the authority of government; this will shall be expressed in periodic and genuine elections which shall be by universal and equal suffrage and shall be held by secret vote or by equivalent free voting procedures.

ARTICLE 22

Everyone, as a member of society, has the right to social security and is entitled to realization, through national effort and international co-operation and in accordance with the organization and resources of each State, of the economic, social and cultural rights indispensible for his dignity and the free development of his personality.

ARTICLE 23

(1) Everyone has the right to work, to free choice of employment, to just and favourable conditions of work and to protection against unemployment.
(2) Everyone, without any discrimination, has the right to equal pay for equal work.
(3) Everyone has the right to just and favourable remuneration ensuring for himself and his family and existence worthy of human dignity, and supplemented, if necessary, by other means of social protection.
(4) Everyone has the right to form and to join trade unions for the protection of his interests.

ARTICLE 24

Everyone has the right to rest and leisure, including reasonable limitation of working hours and periodic holidays with pay.

ARTICLE 25

(1) Everyone has the right to a standard of living adequate for the health and well-being of himself and of his family, including food, clothing, housing and medical care and necessary social services, and the right to security in the event of unemployment, sickness, disability, widowhood, old age or other lack of livelihood in circumstances beyond his control.
(2) Motherhood and childhood are entitled to special care and assistance. All children, whether born in or out of wedlock, shall enjoy the same social protection.

ARTICLE 26

(1) Everyone has the right to education. Education shall be free, at least in the elementary and fundamental stages. Elementary education shall be compulsory. Technical and professional education shall be made generally available and higher education shall be equally accessible to all on the basis of merit.
(2) Education shall be directed to the full development of the human personality and to the strengthening of respect for human rights and fundamental freedoms. It shall promote understanding, tolerance and friendship among all nations, racial or religious groups, and shall further the activities of the United Nations for the maintenance of peace.
(3) Parents have a prior right to choose the kind of education that shall be given to their children.

ARTICLE 27

(1) Everyone has the right to freely participate in the cultural life of the community, to enjoy the arts and to share in scientific advancement and its benefits.
(2) Everyone has the right to the protection of the moral and material interests resulting from any scientific, literary or artistic production of which he is the author.

ARTICLE 28

Everyone is entitled to a social and international order in which the rights and freedoms set forth in this Declaration can be fully realized.

ARTICLE 29

(1) Everyone has duties to the community in which alone the free and full development of his personality is possible.
(2) In the exercise of his rights and freedoms, everyone shall be subject only to such limitations as are determined by law solely for the purpose of securing due recognition and respect for the rights and freedoms of others and of meeting the just requirements of morality, public order and the general welfare in a democratic society.
(3) These rights and freedoms may in no case be exercised contrary to the purposes and principles of the United Nations.

ARTICLE 30

Nothing in this Declaration may be interpreted as implying for any State, group or person any right to engage in any activity or to perform any act aimed at the destruction of any of the rights and freedoms set forth herein.

JOHN STUART MILL

The Authority of Society over the Individual

JOHN STUART MILL (1806–1873) was one of the documented geniuses of modern history. By the age of ten, he had accomplished more than most scholars do in a lifetime. He is best known for his moral and political writings, particularly *On Liberty* (1859) and *Utilitarianism* (1863).

What, then, is the rightful limit to the sovereignty of the individual over himself? Where does the authority of society begin? How much of human life should be assigned to individuality, and how much to society?

Each will receive its proper share, if each has that which more particularly concerns it. To individuality should belong the part of life in which it is chiefly the individual that is interested; to society, the part which chiefly interests society.

Though society is not founded on a contract, and though no good purpose is answered by inventing a contract in order to deduce social obligations from it, every one who receives the protection of society owes a return for the benefit, and the fact of living in society renders it indispensable that each should be bound to observe a certain line of conduct towards the rest. This conduct consists, first, in not injuring the interests of one another; or rather certain interests, which, either by express legal provision or by tacit understanding, ought to be considered as rights; and secondly, in each person's bearing his share (to be fixed on some equitable principle) of the labors and sacrifices incurred for defending the society or its members from injury and molestation. These conditions society is justified in enforcing at all costs to those who endeavor to withhold fulfilment. Nor is this all that society may do. The acts of an individual may be hurtful to others, or wanting in due consideration for their welfare, without going the length of violating any of their constituted rights. The offender may then be justly punished by opinion, though not by law. As soon as any part of a person's conduct affects prejudicially the interests of others, society has jurisdiction over it, and the question whether the general welfare will or will not be promoted by interfering with it, becomes open to discussion. But there is no room for entertaining any such question when a person's conduct affects the interests of no persons besides himself, or needs not affect them unless they like (all the persons concerned being of full age, and the ordinary amount of understanding). In all such cases there should be perfect freedom, legal and social, to do the action and stand the consequences.

It would be a great misunderstanding of this doctrine to suppose that it is one of selfish indifference, which pretends that human beings have no business with each other's conduct in life, and that they should not concern themselves about the well-doing or well-being of one another, unless their own interest is involved. Instead of any diminution, there is need of a great increase of disinterested exertion to promote the good of others. But disinterested benevolence can find other instruments to persuade people to their good, than whips and scourges, either of the literal or the metaphorical sort. I am the last person to undervalue the self-regarding virtues; they are only second in importance, if even second, to the social. It is equally the business of education to cultivate both. But even education works by conviction and persuasion as well as by compulsion, and it is by the former only that, when the period of education is past, the self-regarding virtues should be inculcated. Human beings owe to each other help to distinguish the better from the worse, and encouragement to choose the former and avoid the latter. They should be for ever stimulating each other to increased exercise of their higher faculties, and increased direction of their feelings and aims towards wise instead of foolish, elevating instead of degrading, objects and contemplations. But neither one person, nor any number of persons, is warranted in saying to another human creature of ripe years, that he shall not do with his life for his own benefit what he chooses to do with it. He is the person most interested in his own well-being: the interest which any other person, except in cases of strong personal attachment, can have in it, is trifling, compared with that which he himself has; the interest which society has in him individually (except as to his conduct to others) is fractional, and altogether indirect: while, with respect to his own feelings and circumstances, the most ordinary man or woman has means of knowledge immeasurably surpassing those that can be possessed by any one else. The interference of society to overrule his judgment and purposes in what only regards himself, must be grounded on general presumptions; which may be altogether wrong, and even if right, are as likely as not to be misapplied to individual cases, by persons no better acquainted with the circumstances of such cases than those are who look at them merely from without. In this department, therefore, of human affairs, Individuality has its proper field of action. In the conduct of human beings towards one another, it is necessary that general rules should for the most part be observed, in order that people may know what they have to expect; but in each person's own concerns, his individual spontaneity is entitled to free exercise. Considerations to aid his judgment, exhortations to strengthen his will, may be offered to him, even obtruded on him, by others; but he himself is the final judge. All errors which he is likely to commit against advice and warning, are far outweighed by the evil of allowing others to constrain him to what they deem his good.

I do not mean that the feelings with which a person is regarded by others, ought not to be in any way affected by his self-regarding qualities or deficiencies. This is neither possible nor desirable. If he is eminent in any of the qualities which conduce to his own good, he is, so far, a proper object of admiration. He is so much the nearer to the ideal perfection of human nature. If he is grossly deficient in those qualities, a sentiment the opposite of admiration will follow. There is a degree of folly, and a degree of what may be called (though the phrase is not unobjectionable) lowness or depravation of taste, which, though it cannot justify doing harm to the person who manifests it, renders him necessarily and properly a subject of distaste, or, in extreme cases, even of contempt: a person could not have the opposite qualities in due strength without entertaining these feelings. Though doing no wrong to any one, a person may so act as to compel us to judge him, and feel to him, as a fool, or as a being of an inferior order: and since this judgment and feeling are a fact which he would prefer to avoid, it is doing him a service to warn him of it beforehand, as of any other disagreeable consequence to which he exposes himself. It would be well, indeed, if this good office were much more freely rendered than the common notions of politeness at present permit, and if one person could honestly point out to another that he thinks him in fault, without being considered unmannerly or presuming. We have a right, also, in various ways, to act upon our unfavorable opinion of any one, not to the oppression of his individuality, but in the exercise of ours. We are not bound, for example, to seek his society; we have a right to avoid it (though not to parade the avoidance), for we have a right to choose the society most acceptable to us. We have a right, and it may be our duty, to caution others against him, if we think his example or conversation likely to have a pernicious effect on those with whom he associates. We may give others a preference over him in optional good offices, except those which tend to his improvement. In these various modes a person may suffer very severe penalties at the hands of others, for faults which directly concern only himself; but he suffers these penalties only in so far as they are the natural, and, as it were, the spontaneous consequences of the faults themselves, not because they are purposely inflicted on him for the sake of punishment. A person who shows rashness, obstinacy, self-conceit—who cannot live within moderate means—who cannot restrain himself from hurtful indulgences—who pursues animal pleasures at the expense of those of feeling and intellect—must expect to be lowered in the opinion of others, and to have a less share of their favorable sentiments; but of this he has no right to complain, unless he had merited their favor by special excellence in his social relations, and has thus established a title to their good offices, which is not affected by his demerits towards himself.

What I contend for is, that the inconveniences which are strictly inseparable from the unfavorable judgment of others, are the only ones to which a person should ever be subjected for that portion of his conduct and character which concerns his own good, but which does not affect the interests of others in their relations with him. Acts injurious to others require a totally different treatment. Encroachment on their rights; infliction on them of any loss or damage not justified by his own rights; falsehood or duplicity in dealing with them; unfair or ungenerous use of advantages over them; even selfish abstinence from defending them against injury—these are fit objects of moral reprobation, and, in grave cases, of moral retribution and punishment. And not only these acts, but the dispositions which lead to them, are properly immoral, and fit subjects of disapprobation which may rise to abhorrence. Cruelty of disposition; malice and ill nature; that most anti-social and odious of all passions, envy; dissimulation and insincerity; irascibility on insufficient cause, and resentment disproportioned to the provocation; the love of domineering over others; the desire to engross more than one's share of advantages . . . ; the pride which derives gratification from the abasement of others; the egotism which thinks self and its concerns more important than everything else, and decides all doubtful questions in its own favor;—these are moral vices, and constitute a bad and odious moral character: unlike the self-regarding faults previously mentioned, which are not properly immoralities, and to whatever pitch they may be carried, do not constitute wickedness. They may be proofs of any amount of folly, or want of personal dignity and self-respect; but they are only a subject of moral reprobation when they involve a breach of duty to others, for whose sake the individual is bound to have care for himself. . . .

The distinction between the loss of consideration which a person may rightly incur by defect of prudence or of personal dignity, and the reprobation which is due to him for an offense against the rights of others, is not a merely nominal distinction. It makes a vast difference both in our feelings and in our conduct towards him, whether he displeases us in things in which we think we have a right to control him, or in things in which we know that we have not. If he displeases us, we may express our distaste, and we may stand aloof from a person as well as from a thing that displeases us; but we shall not therefore feel called on to make his life uncomfortable. We shall reflect that he already bears, or will bear, the whole penalty of his error; if he spoils his life by mismanagement, we shall not, for that reason, desire to spoil it still further: instead of wishing to punish him, we shall rather endeavor to alleviate his punishment, by showing him how he may avoid or cure the evils his conduct tends to bring upon him. He may be to us an object of pity, perhaps of dislike, but not of anger or resentment; we shall not treat him like an enemy of society: the worst we shall think ourselves justified in doing is leaving him to himself, if we do not interfere benevolently by showing interest or concern for him. . . .

The distinction here pointed out between the part of a person's life which concerns only himself, and that which concerns others, many persons will refuse to admit. How (it may be asked) can any part of the conduct of a member of society be a matter of indifference to the other members? No person is an entirely isolated being; it is impossible for a person to do anything seriously or permanently hurtful to himself, without mischief reaching at least to his near connections, and often far beyond them. If he injures his property, he does harm to those who directly or indirectly derived support from it, and usually diminishes, by a greater or less amount, the general resource of the community. If he deteriorates his bodily or mental faculties, he not only brings evil upon all who depended on him for any portion of their happiness, but disqualifies himself for rendering the services which he owes to his fellow creatures generally; perhaps becomes a burthen on their affection or benevolence; and if such conduct were very frequent, hardly any offense that is committed would detract more from the general sum of good. Finally, if by his vices or follies a person does no direct harm to others, he is nevertheless (it may be said) injurious by his example; and ought to be compelled to control himself, for the sake of those whom the sight or knowledge of his conduct might corrupt or mislead.

And even (it will be added) if the consequences of misconduct could be confined to the vicious or thoughtless individual, ought society to abandon to their own guidance those who are manifestly unfit for it? If protection against themselves is confessedly due to children and persons under age, is not society equally bound to afford it to persons of mature years who are equally incapable of self-government? If gambling, or drunkenness, or incontinence, or idleness, or uncleanliness, are as injurious to happiness, and as great a hindrance to improvement, as many or most of the acts prohibited by law, why (it may be asked) should not law, so far as is consistent with practicability and social convenience, endeavor to repress these also? And as a supplement to the unavoidable imperfections of law, ought not opinion at least to organize a powerful police against these vices, and visit rigidly with social penalties those who are known to practice them? There is no question here (it may be said) about restricting individuality, or impeding the trial of new and original experiments in living. The only things it is sought to prevent are things which have been tried and condemned from the beginning of the world until now; things which experience has shown not to be useful or suitable to any person's individuality. There must be some length of time and amount of experience, after which a moral or prudential truth may be regarded as established: and it is merely desired to prevent generation after generation from falling over the same precipice which has been fatal to their predecessors.

I fully admit that the mischief which a person does to himself may seriously affect, both through their sympathies and their interests, those nearly connected with him, and in a minor degree, society at large. When, by conduct of this sort, a person is led to violate a distinct and assignable obligation to any other person or persons, the case is taken out of the self-regarding class, and becomes amenable to moral disapproval in the proper sense of the term. If, for example, a man, through intemperance or extravagance, becomes unable to pay his debts, or, having undertaken the moral responsibility of a family, becomes from the same cause incapable of supporting or educating them, he is deservedly reprobated, and might be justly punished; but it is for the breach of duty to his family or creditors, not for the extravagance. . . .

But with regard to the merely contingent, or, as it may be called, constructive injury which a person causes to society, by conduct which neither violates any specific duty to the public, nor occasions perceptible hurt to any assignable individual except himself; the inconvenience is one which society can afford to bear, for the sake of the greater good of human freedom. If grown persons are to be punished for not taking proper care of themselves, I would rather it were for their own sake, than under pretense of preventing them from impairing their capacity of rendering to society benefits which society does not pretend it has a right to exact. But I cannot consent to argue the point as if society had no means of bringing its weaker members up to its ordinary standard of rational conduct, except waiting till they do something irrational, and then punishing them, legally or morally, for it. Society has had absolute power over them during all the early portion of their existence; it has had the whole period of childhood and nonage in which to try whether it could make them capable of rational conduct in life. The existing generation is master both of the training and the entire circumstances of the generation to come; it cannot indeed make them perfectly wise and good, because it is itself so lamentably deficient in goodness and wisdom; and its best efforts are not always, in individual cases, its most successful ones; but it is perfectly well able to make the rising generation, as a whole, as good as, and a little better than, itself. If society lets any considerable number of its members grow up mere children, incapable of being acted on by rational consideration of distant motives, society has itself to blame for the consequences. . . .

But the strongest of all the arguments against the interference of the public with purely personal conduct, is that when it does interfere, the odds are that it interferes wrongly, and in the wrong place. On questions of social morality, of duty to others, the opinion of the public, that is, of an overruling majority, though often wrong, is likely to be still oftener right; because on such questions they are only required to judge their own interests; of the manner in which some mode of conduct, if allowed to be practiced, would affect themselves. But the opinion of a similar majority, imposed as a law on the minority, on questions of self-regarding conduct, is quite as likely to be wrong as right; for in these cases public opinion means, at the best, some people's opinion of what is good or bad for other people; while very often it does not even mean that; the public, with the most perfect indifference, passing over the pleasure or convenience of those whose conduct they censure, and considering only their own preference. There are many who consider as an injury to themselves any conduct which they have a distaste for, and resent it as an outrage to their feelings; as a religious bigot, when charged with disregarding the religious feelings of others, has been known to retort that they disregard his feelings, by persisting in their abominable worship or creed. But there is no parity between the feeling of a person for his own opinion, and the feeling of another who is offended at his holding it; no more than between the desire of a thief to take a purse, and the desire of the right owner to keep it. And a person's taste is as much his own peculiar concern as his opinion or his purse.

JOHN RAWLS

Justice as Fairness

JOHN RAWLS teaches philosophy at Harvard University and is the author of
A Theory of Justice (1971).

The conception of justice which I want to develop may be stated in the form of two principles as follows: first, each person participating in a practice, or affected by it, has an
equal right to the most extensive liberty compatible with a like liberty for all; and second, inequalities are arbitrary unless it is reasonable to expect that they will work out
for everyone's advantage, and provided the positions and offices to which they attach,
or from which they may be gained, are open to all. These principles express justice as
a complex of three ideas: liberty, equality, and reward for services contributing to the
common good.

The term "person" is to be construed variously depending on the circumstances. On
some occasions it will mean human individuals, but in others it may refer to nations,
provinces, business firms, churches, teams, and so on. The principles of justice apply in
all these instances, although there is a certain logical priority to the case of human individuals. As I shall use the term "person," it will be ambiguous in the manner indicated.

The first principle holds, of course, only if other things are equal: that is, while there
must always be a justification for departing from the initial position of equal liberty
(which is defined by the pattern of rights and duties, powers and liabilities, established
by a practice), and the burden of proof is placed on him who would depart from it, nevertheless, there can be, and often there is, a justification for doing so. Now, that similar
particular cases, as defined by a practice, should be treated similarly as they arise, is part
of the very concept of a practice; it is involved in the notion of an activity in accordance
with rules. The first principle expresses an analogous conception, but as applied to the
structure of practices themselves. It holds, for example, that there is a presumption
against the distinctions and classifications made by legal systems and other practices
to the extent that they infringe on the original and equal liberty of the persons participating in them. The second principle defines how this presumption may be rebutted.

It might be argued at this point that justice requires only an equal liberty. If, however,
a greater liberty were possible for all without loss or conflict, then it would be irrational
to settle on a lesser liberty. There is no reason for circumscribing rights unless their exercise would be incompatible, or would render the practice defining them less effective.
Therefore no serious distortion of the concept of justice is likely to follow from including within it the concept of the greatest equal liberty.

The second principle defines what sorts of inequalities are permissible; it specifies
how the presumption laid down by the principle may be put aside. Now by inequalities
it is best to understand not *any* differences between offices and positions, but differences in the benefits and burdens attached to them either directly or indirectly, such as
prestige and wealth, or liability to taxation and compulsory services. Players in a game
do not protest against there being different positions, such as batter, pitcher, catcher,
and the like, nor to there being various privileges and powers as specified by the rules;
nor do the citizens of a country object to there being the different offices of government

such as president, senator, governor, judge, and so on, each with their special rights and duties. It is not differences of this kind that are normally thought of as inequalities, but differences in the resulting distribution established by a practice, or made possible by it, of the things men strive to attain or avoid. Thus they may complain about the pattern of honors and rewards set up by a practice (e.g., the privileges and salaries of government officials) or they may object to the distribution of power and wealth which results from the various ways in which men avail themselves of the opportunities allowed by it (e.g., the concentration of wealth which may develop in a free price system allowing large entrepreneurial or speculative gains).

It should be noted that the second principle holds that an inequality is allowed only if there is reason to believe that the practice with the inequality, or resulting in it, will work for the advantage of *every* party engaging in it. Here it is important to stress that *every* party must gain from the inequality. Since the principle applies to practices, it implies that the representative man in every office or position defined by a practice, when he views it as a going concern, must find it reasonable to prefer his condition and prospects with the inequality to what they would be under the practice without it. The principle excludes, therefore, the justification of inequalities on the grounds that the disadvantages of those in one position are outweighed by the greater advantages of those in another position. This rather simple restriction is the main modification I wish to make in the utilitarian principle as usually understood. . . .

Further, it is also necessary that the various offices to which special benefits or burdens attach are open to all. It may be, for example, to the common advantage, as just defined, to attach special benefits to certain offices. Perhaps by doing so the requisite talent can be attracted to them and encouraged to give its best efforts. But any offices having special benefits must be won in a fair competition in which contestants are judged on their merits. If some offices were not open, those excluded would normally be justified in feeling unjustly treated, even if they benefited from the greater efforts of those who were allowed to compete for them. Now if one can assume that offices are open, it is necessary only to consider the design of practices themselves and how they jointly, as a system, work together. It will be a mistake to focus attention on the varying relative positions of particular persons, who may be known to us by their proper names, and to require that each such change, as a once for all transaction viewed in isolation, must be in itself just. It is the system of practices which is to be judged, and judged from the general point of view: unless one is prepared to criticize it from the standpoint of a representative man holding some particular office, one has no complaint against it.

• • •

Imagine a society of persons amongst whom a certain system of practices is *already* well established. Now suppose that by and large they are mutually self-interested; their allegiance to their established practices is normally founded on the prospect of self-advantage. One need not assume that, in all senses of the term "person," the persons in this society are mutually self-interested. If the characterization as mutually self-interested applies when the line of division is the family, it may still be true that members of families are bound by ties of sentiment and affection and willingly acknowledge duties in contradiction to self-interest. Mutual self-interestedness in the relations between families, nations, churches, and the like, is commonly associated with intense loyalty and devotion on the part of individual members. Therefore, one can form a more realistic conception of this society if one thinks of it as consisting of mutually self-interested families, or some other association. Further, it is not necessary to suppose that these persons are mutually self-interested under all circumstances, but only in the usual situations in which they participate in their common practices.

Now suppose also that these persons are rational: they know their own interests more or less accurately; they are capable of tracing out the likely consequences of adopting one practice rather than another; they are capable of adhering to a course of action once they have decided upon it; they can resist present temptations and the enticements of immediate gain; and the bare knowledge or perception of the difference between their condition and that of others is not, within certain limits and in itself, a source of great dissatisfaction. Only the last point adds anything to the usual definition of rationality. This definition should allow, I think, for the idea that a rational man would not be greatly downcast from knowing, or seeing, that others are in a better position than himself, unless he thought their being so was the result of injustice, or the consequence of letting chance work itself out for no useful common purpose, and so on. So if these persons strike us as unpleasantly egoistic, they are at least free in some degree from the fault of envy.

Finally, assume that these persons have roughly similar needs and interests, or needs and interests in various ways complementary, so that fruitful cooperation amongst them is possible; and suppose that they are sufficiently equal in power and ability to guarantee that in normal circumstances none is able to dominate the others. This condition (as well as the others) may seem excessively vague; but in view of the conception of justice to which the argument leads, there seems no reason for making it more exact here.

Since these persons are conceived as engaging in their common practices, which are already established, there is no question of our supposing them to come together to deliberate as to how they will set these practices up for the first time. Yet we can imagine that from time to time they discuss with one another whether any of them has a legitimate complaint against their established institutions. Such discussions are perfectly natural in any normal society. Now suppose that they have settled on doing this in the following way. They first try to arrive at the principles by which complaints, and so practices themselves, are to be judged. Their procedure for this is to let each person propose the principles upon which he wishes his complaints to be tried with the understanding that, if acknowledged, the complaints of others will be similarly tried, and that no complaints will be heard at all until everyone is roughly of one mind as to how complaints are to be judged. They each understand further that the principles proposed and acknowledged on this occasion are binding on future occasions. Thus each will be wary of proposing a principle which would give him a peculiar advantage, in his present circumstances, supposing it to be accepted. Each person knows that he will be bound by it in future circumstances the peculiarities of which cannot be known, and which might well be such that the principle is then to his disadvantage. The idea is that everyone should be required to make in advance a firm commitment, which others also may reasonably be expected to make, and that no one be given the opportunity to tailor the canons of a legitimate complaint to fit his own special condition, and then to discard them when they no longer suit his purpose. Hence each person will propose principles of a general kind which will, to a large degree, gain their sense from the various applications to be made of them, the particular circumstances of which being as yet unknown. These principles will express the conditions in accordance with which each is the least unwilling to have his interests limited in the design of practices, given the competing interests of the others, on the supposition that the interests of others will be limited likewise. The restrictions which would so arise might be thought of as those a person would keep in mind if he were designing a practice in which his enemy were to assign him his place.

• • •

The two parts of the foregoing account are intended to mirror the kinds of circumstances in which questions of justice arise and the constraints which having a morality would impose upon persons so situated. In this way one can see how the acceptance of the principles of justice might come about, for given all these conditions as described, it would be natural if the two principles of justice were to be acknowledged. Since there is no way for anyone to win special advantages for himself, each might consider it reasonable to acknowledge equality as an initial principle. There is, however, no reason why they should regard this position as final, for if there are inequalities which satisfy the second principle, the immediate gain which equality would allow can be considered as intelligently invested in view of its future return. If, as is quite likely, these inequalities work as incentives to draw out better efforts, the members of this society may look upon them as concessions to human nature: they, like us, may think that people ideally should want to serve one another. But as they are mutually self-interested, their acceptance of these inequalities is merely the acceptance of the relations in which they actually stand, and a recognition of the motives which lead them to engage in their common practices. *They* have no title to complain of one another. And so provided that the conditions of the principle are met, there is no reason why they should not allow such inequalities. Indeed, it would be short-sighted of them to do so, and could result, in most cases, only from their being dejected by the bare knowledge, or perception, that others are better situated. Each person will, however, insist on an advantage to himself, and so on a common advantage, for none is willing to sacrifice anything for the others.

These remarks are not offered as a proof that persons so conceived and circumstanced would settle on the two principles, but only to show that these principles could have such a background, and so can be viewed as those principles which mutually self-interested and rational persons, when similarly situated and required to make in advance a firm commitment, could acknowledge as restrictions governing the assignment of rights and duties in their common practices, and thereby accept as limiting their rights against one another. The principles of justice may, then, be regarded as those principles which arise when the constraints of having a morality are imposed upon parties in the typical circumstances of justice.

• • •

A practice is just or fair, then, when it satisfies the principles which those who participate in it could propose to one another for mutual acceptance under the aforementioned circumstances. Persons engaged in a just, or fair, practice can face one another openly and support their respective positions, should they appear questionable, by reference to principles which it is reasonable to expect each to accept.

It is this notion of the possibility of mutual acknowledgment of principles by free persons who have no authority over one another which makes the concept of fairness fundamental to justice. Only if such acknowledgment is possible can there be true community between persons in their common practices; otherwise their relations will appear to them as founded to some extent on force.

• • •

Now if the participants in a practice accept its rules as fair, and so have no complaint to lodge against it, there arises a prima facie duty (and a corresponding prima facie right) of the parties to each other to act in accordance with the practice when it falls upon them to comply. When any number of persons engage in a practice, or conduct a joint undertaking according to rules, and thus restrict their liberty, those who have submitted to these restrictions when required have the right to a similar acquiescence on the part of those who have benefited by their submission. These conditions will obtain if a practice is correctly acknowledged to be fair, for in this case all who participate in it will benefit from it. The rights and duties so arising are special rights and duties in that they depend on previous actions voluntarily undertaken, in this case on the parties having engaged in a common practice and knowingly accepted its benefits. It is not, however, an obligation which presupposes a deliberate performative act in the sense of a promise, or contract, and the like. . . .

It is sufficient that one has knowingly participated in and accepted the benefits of a practice acknowledged to be fair. This prima facie obligation may, of course, be overridden: it may happen, when it comes one's turn to follow a rule, that other considerations will justify not doing so. But one cannot, in general, be released from this obligation by denying the justice of the practice only when it falls on one to obey. If a person rejects a practice, he should, so far as possible, declare his intention in advance, and avoid participating in it or enjoying its benefits.

This duty I have called that of fair play, but it should be admitted that to refer to it in this way is, perhaps, to extend the ordinary notion of fairness. Usually acting unfairly is not so much the breaking of any particular rule, even if the infraction is difficult to detect (cheating), but taking advantage of loop-holes or ambiguities in rules, availing oneself of unexpected or special circumstances which make it impossible to enforce them, insisting that rules be enforced to one's advantage when they should be suspended, and more generally, acting contrary to the intention of a practice. It is for this reason that one speaks of the sense of fair play: acting fairly requires more than simply being able to follow rules; what is fair must often be felt, or perceived, one wants to say. It is not, however, an unnatural extension of the duty of fair play to have it include the obligation which participants who have knowingly accepted the benefits of their common practice owe to each other to act in accordance with it when their performance falls due; for it is usually considered unfair if someone accepts the benefits of a practice but refuses to do his part in maintaining it. Thus one might say of the tax-dodger that he violates the duty of fair play: he accepts the benefits of government but will not do his part in releasing resources to it; and members of labor unions often say that fellow workers who refuse to join are being unfair: they refer to them as "free riders," as persons who enjoy what are the supposed benefits of unionism, higher wages, shorter hours, job security, and the like, but who refuse to share in its burdens in the form of paying dues, and so on.

ROBERT NOZICK

The Entitlement Theory

ROBERT NOZICK teaches philosophy at Harvard University.

The subject of justice in holdings consists of three major topics. The first is the *original acquisition of holdings,* the appropriation of unheld things. This includes the issues of how unheld things may come to be held, the process, or processes, by which unheld things may come to be held, the things that may come to be held by these processes, the extent of what comes to be held by a particular process, and so on. We shall refer to the complicated truth about this topic, which we shall not formulate here, as the principle of justice in acquisition. The second topic concerns the *transfer of holdings* from one person to another. By what processes may a person transfer holdings to another? How may a person acquire a holding from another who holds it? Under this topic come general descriptions of voluntary exchange, and gift and (on the other hand) fraud, as well as reference to particular conventional details fixed upon in a given society. The complicated truth about this subject (with placeholders for conventional details) we shall call the principle of justice in transfer. (And we shall suppose it also includes principles governing how a person may divest himself of a holding, passing it into an unheld state.)

If the world were wholly just, the following inductive definition would exhaustively cover the subject of justice in holdings.

1. A person who acquires a holding in accordance with the principle of justice in acquisition is entitled to that holding.
2. A person who acquires a holding in accordance with the principle of justice in transfer, from someone else entitled to the holding, is entitled to the holding.
3. No one is entitled to a holding except by (repeated) applications of 1 and 2.

The complete principle of distributive justice would say simply that a distribution is just if everyone is entitled to the holdings they possess under the distribution.

A distribution is just if it arises from another just distribution by legitimate means. The legitimate means of moving from one distribution to another are specified by the principle of justice in transfer. The legitimate first "moves" are specified by the principle of justice in acquisition. Whatever arises from a just situation by just steps is itself just. The means of change specified by the principle of justice in transfer preserve justice. As correct rules of inference are truth-preserving, and any conclusion deduced via repeated application of such rules from only true premises is itself true, so the means of transition from one situation to another specified by the principle of justice in transfer are justice-preserving, and any situation actually arising from repeated transitions in accordance with the principle from a just situation is itself just. The parallel between justice-preserving transformations and truth-preserving transformations illuminates where it fails as well as where it holds. That a conclusion could have been deduced by truth-preserving means from premises that are true suffices to show its truth. That from a just situation a situation *could* have arisen via justice-preserving means does *not* suffice to show its justice. The fact that a thief's victims voluntarily *could* have presented him with gifts does not entitle the thief to his ill-gotten gains. Justice in holdings is historical; it depends upon what actually has happened. We shall return to this point later.

Not all actual situations are generated in accordance with the two principles of justice in holdings: the principle of justice in acquisition and the principle of justice in transfer. Some people steal from others, or defraud them, or enslave them, seizing their product and preventing them from living as they choose, or forcibly exclude others from competing in exchanges. None of these are permissible modes of transition from one situation to another. And some persons acquire holdings by means not sanctioned by the principle of justice in acquisition. The existence of past injustice (previous violations of the first two principles of justice in holdings) raises the third major topic under justice in holdings: the rectification of injustice in holdings. If past injustice has shaped present holdings in various ways, some identifiable and some not, what now, if anything, ought to be done to rectify these injustices? What obligations do the performers of injustice have toward those whose position is worse than it would have been had the injustice not been done? Or, than it would have been had compensation been paid promptly? How, if at all, do things change if the beneficiaries and those made worse off are not the direct parties in the act of injustice, but, for example, their descendants? Is an injustice done to someone whose holding was itself based upon an unrectified injustice? How far back must one go in wiping clean the historical slate of injustices? What may victims of injustice permissibly do in order to rectify the injustices being done to them, including the many injustices done by persons acting through their government? I do not know of a thorough or theoretically sophisticated treatment of such issues. Idealizing greatly, let us suppose theoretical investigation will produce a principle of rectification. This principle uses historical information about previous situations and injustices done in them (as defined by the first two principles of justice and rights against interference), and information about the actual course of events that flowed from these injustices, until the present, and it yields a description (or descriptions) of holdings in the society. The principle of rectification presumably will make use of its best estimate of subjunctive information about what would have occurred (or a probability distribution over what might have occurred, using the expected value) if the injustice had not taken place. If the actual description of holdings turns out not to be one of the descriptions yielded by the principle, then one of the descriptions yielded must be realized.

The general outlines of the theory of justice in holdings are that the holdings of a person are just if he is entitled to them by the principles of justice in acquisition and transfer, or by the principle of rectification of injustice (as specified by the first two principles). If each person's holdings are just, then the total set (distribution) of holdings is just.

HISTORICAL PRINCIPLES AND END-RESULT PRINCIPLES

The general outlines of the entitlement theory illuminate the nature and defects of other conceptions of distributive justice. The entitlement theory of justice in distribution is *historical;* whether a distribution is just depends upon how it came about. In contrast, *current time-slice principles* of justice hold that the justice of a distribution is determined by how things are distributed (who has what) as judged by some *structural* principle(s) of just distribution. A utilitarian who judges between any two distributions by seeing which has the greater sum of utility and, if the sums tie, applies some fixed equality criterion to choose the more equal distribution, would hold a current time-slice principle of justice. As would someone who had a fixed schedule of trade-offs between the sum of happiness and equality. According to a current time-slice principle, all that needs to be looked at, in judging the justice of a distribution, is who ends up with what; in comparing any two distributions one need look only at the matrix presenting the distributions. No further information need be fed into a principle of justice. It is a consequence of such principles of justice that any two structurally identical distributions are equally just. (Two distributions are structurally identical if they present the same profile, but perhaps have different persons occupying the particular slots. My having ten and your having five, and my having five and your having ten are structurally identical distributions.) Welfare economics is the theory of current time-slice principles of justice. The subject is conceived as operating on matrices representing only current information about distribution. This, as well as some of the usual conditions (for example, the choice of distribution is invariant under relabeling of columns), guarantees that welfare economics will be a current time-slice theory, with all of its inadequacies.

Most persons do not accept current time-slice principles as constituting the whole story about distributive shares. They think it relevant in assessing the justice of a situation to consider not only the distribution it embodies, but also how that distribution came about. If some persons are in prison for murder or war crimes, we do not say that to assess the justice of the distribution in the society we must look only at what this person has, and that person has, and that person has, . . . at the current time. We think it relevant to ask whether someone did something so that he *deserved* to be punished, deserved to have a lower share. Most will agree to the relevance of further information with regard to punishments and penalties. Consider also desired things. One traditional socialist view is that workers are entitled to the product and full fruits of their labor; they have earned it; a distribution is unjust if it does not give the workers what they are entitled to. Such entitlements are based upon some past history. No socialist holding this view would find it comforting to be told that because the actual distribution *A* happens to coincide structurally with the one he desires *D*, *A* therefore is no less just than *D*; it differs only in that the "parasitic" owners of capital receive under *A* what the workers are entitled to under *D*, and the workers receive under *A* what the owners are entitled to under *D*, namely very little. This socialist rightly, in my view, holds onto the notions of earning, producing, entitlement, desert, and so forth, and he rejects current time-slice principles that look only to the structure of the resulting set of holdings. (The set of holdings resulting from what? Isn't it implausible that how holdings are produced and come to exist has no effect at all on who should hold what?) His mistake lies in his view of what entitlements arise out of what sorts of productive processes.

We construe the position we discuss too narrowly by speaking of *current* time-slice principles. Nothing is changed if structural principles operate upon a time sequence of current time-slice profiles and, for example, give someone more now to counterbalance the less he has had earlier. A utilitarian or an egalitarian or any mixture of the two over time will inherit the difficulties of his more myopic comrades. He is not helped by the fact that *some* of the information others consider relevant in assessing a distribution is reflected, unrecoverably, in past matrices. Henceforth, we shall refer to such unhistorical principles of distributive justice, including the current time-slice principles, as *end-result principles* or *end-state principles*.

In contrast to end-result principles of justice, *historical principles* of justice hold that past circumstances or actions of people can create differential entitlements or differential deserts to things. As injustice can be worked by moving from one distribution to another structurally identical one, for the second, in profile the same, may violate people's entitlements or deserts; it may not fit the actual history. . . .

To think that the task of a theory of distributive justice is to fill in the blank in "to each according to his _____" is to be predisposed to search for a pattern; and the separate treatment of "from each according to his _____" treats production and distribution as two separate and independent issues. On an entitlement view these are *not* two separate questions. Whoever makes something, having bought or contracted for all other held resources used in the process (transferring some of his holdings for these cooperating factors), is entitled to it. The situation is *not* one of something's getting made, and there being an open question of who is to get it. Things come into the world already attached to people having entitlements over them. From the point of view of the historical entitlement conception of justice in holdings, those who start afresh to complete "to each according to his _____" treat objects as if they appeared from nowhere, out of nothing. A complete theory of justice might cover this limit case as well; perhaps here is a use for the usual conceptions of distributive justice.

So entrenched are maxims of the usual form that perhaps we should present the entitlement conception as a competitor. Ignoring acquisition and rectification, we might say:

> From each according to what he chooses to do, to each according to what he makes for himself (perhaps with the contracted aid of others) and what others choose to do for him and choose to give him of what they've been given previously (under this maxim) and haven't yet expended or transferred.

This, the discerning reader will have noticed, has its defects as a slogan. So as a summary and great simplification (and not as a maxim with any independent meaning) we have:

> *From each as they choose, to each as they are chosen.*

AMITAI ETZIONI

Too Many Rights, Too Few Responsibilities

AMITAI ETZIONI is a professor at George Washington University and editor of *The Responsive Community*. He is the author of *The Active Society* (1968) and *The Spirit of Community: Rights, Responsibilities, and the Communitarian Agenda* (1994).

A sociological prize of sorts ought to be given to the member of the television audience who, during a show about the savings-and-loan mess, exclaimed, "The taxpayers shouldn't pay for this, the government should!" He reflected quite well a major theme in American civic culture: a strong sense of entitlement that demands the community give more services and strongly uphold rights coupled with a relatively weak sense of obligation of serving the commons and without a feeling of responsibility for the country. Hence Americans recently called for more governmental services but showed great opposition to new taxes; they express their willingness to show the flag anywhere from Central America to the Gulf but a great reluctance to serve in the armed forces; and they even have a firm sense that one has the right to be tried before a jury of one's peers but use a variety of maneuvers to evade serving on such juries.

Although the imbalance of rights and responsibilities may well have existed for a long time—some may argue it is a basic trait of the American character—in recent years leadership has exacerbated this tendency. Thus, while John F. Kennedy was still able to generate a tremendous response, including thousands of volunteers to serve in the Peace Corps, when he stated, "Ask not what your country can do for you. Ask what you can do for your country," within recent years, Reagan and Bush preferred the less challenging course of suggesting to the citizenry that it could have its cake and eat it too, gaining ever more economic growth to pay for governmental services while paying ever less for them via tax cuts.

In many other areas, from public education to the war on drugs, facile nontaxing "solutions" have been offered. For example, it has been suggested that we may improve our system of education without additional expenditures by simply increasing parental choice among schools and thus, it is said, "drive the bad schools out of business." And to deal with the illicit demands for drugs, we are told to "just say no." Radical individualists, from the ACLU to libertarians, have effectively blocked most steps to increase public responsibilities, from drug-testing, even of people directly involved in public safety (such as engineers who drive trains), to dealing with those engaged in public health (e.g., requiring disclosure of sexual contacts by those who are carriers of the AIDS virus). Last but not least, in both state legislatures and in Congress the role of special-interest groups has grown so much, especially through campaign contributions, that the public interest is very often woefully neglected. Suggestions for reform have so far found only a rather small constituency.

A new communitarian movement is now taking on this set of issues, making restoration of civility and commitment to the commons its core theme. The young movement is in part social philosophy and sociology, in part a moral call, and in part a matter of adopting a different attitude toward public policies.

Communitarians point out the illogicality of demanding the right to be tried before a jury of one's peers without being willing to serve on that jury. Aside from being a selfish, indecent position (asking to be given but not willing to give), it is absurd to expect that most of us can be tried before our peers if most of us are not willing to be one of the peers. Communitarians show that in the longer run it is not possible to have ever more governmental services and at the same time pay less for them (and the longer run comes nearer every day). They point out that a government that is trying to make do by serving numerous special interests neglects the other important matters for which there are no powerful pressure groups, from public education to public safety and health. And communitarians are showing that the Constitution, being a living document rather than a dead letter the Founding Fathers left behind, can be adapted to meeting the changing challenges of the time.

A discussion of specific measures communitarians are considering follows. Before these are outlined, it is necessary to stress two points to avoid common misunderstandings. Although several of these measures involve legal matters and governmental actions, that is, matters of the state, the core of the communitarian position is moral- and community-based rather than statist. What is needed most is a change in the moral climate of the country: a greater willingness to shoulder community responsibilities and a greater readiness to curb one's own demands. Without such change the required shifts in public service and the definition of rights will not be acceptable. Most important, the more the called-for changes are made morally acceptable and are *socially* enforced, the less need there will be for governmental actions—from policing to using courts and jails. One example: To enhance public safety, we need fewer drunken drivers. To combat drunken driving, we need, among other things, the moral commitment of individuals to the notion of a designated driver (as in Scandinavia), that is, one person per car who will not consume alcohol during an outing, party, etc. This is best done on a moral-social base. For example, those couples who come to parties and both drink would be subject to social criticism (unless, of course, they car-pool); the people who proudly state (as if saying, "look how responsible we are!") that they are not drinking tonight because they are designated drivers would gain social approval accordingly, and so on. Similarly, we need to support sobriety check points . . . to help enforce the new social-moral dictum. The changed moral orientation ensures that drunken driving will be significantly reduced with very little state action and that whatever limited state action will be needed will merely round off new social pressures (e.g., in the form of designated drivers rather than drinking to excess being tolerated) and will be supported by the electorate.

. . . What is yet to come is a major social movement, a kind of neoprogressive movement that would shore up the commons, making its main agenda the curbing of special interests and the serving of the public interests. Unfortunately, the recent public frustration with politicians has focused on attempts to "throw out the rascals" and impose term limitations, which will only lead to a new set of politicians committed to special interests replacing the other. Until elected officials' need for private money to win elections, the main mechanism by which they become obligated to special interests, is systematically reduced by various campaign-reform laws and public financing of elections, that part of the communitarian movement will lag. Finally, suggestions for creating a year of mandatory national service are meant to further enhance education and encourage the practice of service for and to the public.

Another misunderstanding that must be avoided is that the call for enhanced civic responsibilities and a greater measure of community service entails majoritarianism or even a measure of authoritarianism. To suggest that young Americans (or all citizens) ought to volunteer more often to serve the commons is not to say that those who refuse for reasons of conscience are to be disciplined. It is not to imply that the civic "religion" or set of values will replace the religious or secular values people uphold. Nor does the call for more sobriety check points, drug tests, and disclosure of sexual contacts by carriers of the AIDS virus legitimate the beginning of a police state. Communitarians are careful to craft suggested changes in public mores and regulation to allow for greater public safety, health, and education without falling into the opposite trap of radical communitarianism: authoritarianism.

The thrust of responsive communitarianism is illustrated by the following examples: to curb drug abuse it has been suggested that the government should conduct drug tests on all school kids, governmental employees, and corporate workers. This would entail massive violations of privacy both because a historically private function (urination) would have to be performed under controlled conditions and because the tests would often reveal private, off-the-job behavior. Persuasion not to use drugs seems more appropriate and keeps the door to a police state shut. On the other hand, drug testing of select groups of people whose drug violation directly endangers the public, e.g., pilots, seems justified on communitarian grounds. This is especially the case if they are informed when hired that their jobs will entail such tests; and that workers will be expected to give their consent to be tested when they sign their contracts.

Concerning matters of the rights of criminals versus those of their victims and public order, a wholesale removal of Miranda rights, as has been suggested by the Reagan administration, may well return us to more authoritarian days. At the same time, it seems reasonable and prudent not to throw out evidence when the Miranda rules were violated on technical grounds and clearly in good faith. Thus, for instance, one can fully support the Supreme Court's decision stipulating that when people confess before being read their rights and then again after hearing their rights that the second confession be allowed to stand.

In the same vein, sobriety check points, especially when they are announced so that those who enter public highways in effect consent to be subject to them, should be viewed more as a way to secure the right to drive freely than a curb on that right. Nor are airport screens, used to deter terrorist bombs, to be viewed as an unreasonable search and seizure. . . . The intrusion is minimal, and the contribution to public safety, including the freedom to travel, is considerable.

The debate over the rights of students provides still another example of a reasonable communitarian position between according students full-fledged Fifth Amendment rights, in effect deterring teachers and principals from suspending them, and declaring students fair game to any capricious school authority. It seems reasonable that students who are subject to expulsion and suspension should be granted due process to the extent that they are notified of the nature of their misconduct and given an opportunity to respond; both actions must occur before the expulsion takes place. Still, expulsion need not guarantee students the right of counsel or call for cross examination and the calling of witnesses because this would unduly encumber the ability of schools to maintain a satisfactory educational environment. In addition, schools need to be allowed to maintain for internal purposes further restrictions and simplified procedures for the reason that they are meant to be small communities, rather than adversarial environments. Far from a novel approach, several state courts are already modifying school policies in the directions we suggest.

Regarding the rights of people with AIDS, if to protect the public's health we choose to trace contacts, then we should also take pains to reduce deleterious offshoots of that policy. For example, AIDS testing and contact-tracing can lead to people losing jobs and health insurance if confidentiality is not maintained. Hence, any introduction of such a program should be accompanied by a thorough review of control of access to lists of names of those tested, procedures used in contacting sexual partners, professional-education programs on the need for confidentiality, and penalties for unauthorized disclosure and especially for those who discriminate against AIDS patients or HIV carriers. All this may seem quite cumbersome, but in view of the great dangers AIDS poses for individuals and its high cost to society, these measures are clearly appropriate.

One may, and ought to, argue about the details involved in such policies. Indeed, the changes should be carefully crafted. We need to reset a legal thermostat to afford a climate more supportive of public concerns, without melting away any of the basic safeguards of individual liberties. Those who argue that the various present interpretations of the Bill of Rights are untouchable, that any modification will push us down the slippery slope toward authoritarianism, must come to realize that the great danger to the Constitution arises out of a refusal to recognize that the Constitution is a living document that can and does adapt to the changing social situation. Without such adaptation, without some measure of increased communitarian, the mounting frustrations of the American people over politics being governed by special interests and over unsafe cities and spreading epidemics, will lead to much more extreme adjustments. Legitimate public needs are often not attended to, in part because such reasonable adaptations as selective drug testing, sobriety check points, and other such measures are disallowed. Basically the issue is not one of legal measures but a change of orientation to a stronger voice for the commons and less room for me-ism and special interests. At this stage of American history, the danger of excessive communitarianism, theoretically always present, seems quite remote.

AMARTYA SEN

The Right to Take Personal Risks

AMARTYA SEN teaches economics at Harvard University. His publications include *Commodities and Capabilities* (1985), *The Standard of Living* (1987), and *On Ethics and Economics* (1987). Sen has also conducted research on the role of rationality in social behavior.

What, then, are moral rights? These are rights that are intrinsically valuable, irrespective of whether they also have instrumental justification. There are at least two different ways of seeing moral rights. The constraint-based deontological way asserts that a person's moral rights impose constraints on what others may or may not do. If a person has a moral right to take a particular personal risk, then it would be morally wrong for anyone to stop him or her from taking that risk, no matter how good the consequences of stopping might be. "Individuals," as Robert Nozick puts it, "have rights, and there are things no person may do to them (without violating their rights)." Such "deontological rights" directly rule out certain actions, rather than being taken into account in the evaluation of states of affairs and then affecting actions through consequential links. In contrast, in the goal-based consequential view, moral rights *are* reflected in the evaluation of states of affairs—a right-fulfillment being favorable and a right-violation being unfavorable to the value of the state of affairs. Such "goal rights" influence actions through consequence-sensitive assessment. . . .

Goal rights can be characterized in several different ways. One particular view, which I have tried to explore elsewhere, is to see rights as "capabilities"—the capability to *do* this or that, or *be* this or that (such as free from hunger or free to move about). The failure to have such a capability, whether or not this is caused by the interference of others, makes the state of affairs worse, other things given. This fits into the general approach of valuing freedom *positively*. It contrasts with focusing on "negative freedom"—the right not to be prevented by others from doing things one can do. Negative freedom has been traditionally seen as imposing deontological constraints on others (stopping them from interfering), but if negative freedom, in the form of absence of interference, is *valued*, then it is natural to incorporate such freedom in a goal-rights system. This would imply attaching "disvalue" to interferences violating negative freedom. In assessing states of affairs, each agent should then have to consider the negative value of such interferences, and this applies not only to a person who may himself be interfering, but also to others whose actions could possibly prevent, or otherwise affect, such interferences.

Perhaps an example will help to bring out the contrasts involved. Consider the case in which person A bashes up person B. In the *deontological constraint formulation of negative freedom*, person A is asked not to do this, but other people, such as person C, are not asked to do anything at all in this context. In the *goal-rights formulation of negative freedom*, not only should A (the basher) take note of the disvalue of such violation of negative freedom, but so should others, such as C. A's violation of B's negative freedom in this view is a bad thing, and C may be required to consider what he can do to help stop this bad thing. . . .

SEAT BELTS AND OTHER PEOPLE

Take the issue of seat belts. A person, call him Hero, decides not to wear seat belts when driving and takes the additional risk of injury or death resulting from this courageous act. We have two immediate questions: (1) how important is this freedom for Hero's personal life and way of living? and (2) how are others affected?

On the first question, there is obviously quite a bit of person-to-person variation, but in most cases it probably is neither in itself a central concern nor a part of an important feature of one's life style. There are exceptions (I have heard some people—all Italian males, it so happens—claim that going unbelted is indeed a matter of great personal importance), but they are relatively rare. Certainly, it will be difficult in this respect to compare the taking of risk involved in going unbelted with the taking of risk that a dedicated mountain climber deliberately chooses.

Insofar as most beltless drivers are beltless "simply to avoid bother," it is not clear that a moral right based on personal liberty is involved. But in refusing to accept the status of something as a moral right for members of a group, it is not enough to be sure that a majority of that group does not see anything of moment involved in the activity in question. The passionate involvement of a minority of the group cannot be ignored just because the majority sees things differently. It is possible that a minority group values a life style that includes going unbelted. In the decisions regarding regulations and rules, the numbers won't be irrelevant, but at this stage let us concede that possibly for a group, perhaps a relatively small group, going unbelted is important as a part of a life style, and that this makes it plausible to consider that a serious moral right might well be involved.

How are others affected? There are at least five different types of effects on others.

(1) *Injury effects:* It has been argued that a driver is in a better position to drive his car safely in case of minor accidents if he is wearing a seat belt, and thus the passengers benefit directly from the belting of the driver. Also, the belted passengers do not land on others, causing them injury. This may not be a common problem, but it obviously is of some relevance.

(2) *Psychological effects:* Other persons may possibly suffer from Hero's demise or injury, and the suffering might arise not only from sympathy for Hero but also from other causes: people might be badly shocked and shaken by seeing a car crash and the resulting gore.

(3) *Opinion-offending effects:* Others, of more sedate temperament might disapprove of Hero's habit of going around without buckling his seat belt, and Hero's actions might well be offensive to them.

(4) *Medical effects:* Hero may need treatment when injured, and others may have to bear a part of the medical costs. Sometimes these might well be enormous.

(5) *Economic and social effects:* Hero's injury may affect his earning power and productivity, and a number of others might well be affected by these changes: members of

Hero's family, the business in which Hero works, the public at large through the need to pay Hero Social Security benefits. Similarly, some people may be affected by social rather than economic links: friends losing someone to talk to, the local community losing a socially active member, children losing a loving parent.

Other possible effects are easy to think of, but let us confine ourselves to these. In the list of five different types of effects, only the third, the "opinion-offending effects," would involve an intrinsic conflict with Hero's moral rights to go beltless as a part of his life style, since it is precisely that life style to which the others in question object. This is of course John Stuart Mill country. I have other issues to deal with, and so I choose not to pursue this particular question. I accept instead Mill's argument that the right to lead a particular type of life is not compromised by the existence of others who object to that life. I have pursued this issue elsewhere in essentially Millian lines, and the focus on risk in the pursuit of one's personal life does not alter the argument substantially.

It might be tempting to think that for similar reasons we must also ignore "psychological effects" in evaluating states of affairs. But this analogy does not hold. In asserting that one should ignore adverse opinion about a particular life style (in determining whether leading such a life can be a moral right), it was *not* also asserted that the suffering of those with an adverse opinion is morally irrelevant to the evaluation of states of affairs. It is indeed possible and plausible to take the view that given other things any suffering, no matter how caused, makes a state of affairs worse. The adverse opinion in question is intrinsically in conflict with the assertion of the right to lead such a life, and the Millian argument is primarily concerned with asserting the right despite that conflict. But when it comes to evaluating actions and rules by taking into account consequential links, the issue of whether or not to weigh the sufferings of others remains a separate question, requiring a treatment of its own. If all sufferings are accepted as disvaluable, then even the sufferings of the moral prig will come inter alia into the general evaluation.

This might look like a defeatist concession, through which authoritarianism might deeply compromise the exercise of liberty. In a system with trade-offs that possibility cannot indeed be fully ruled out, but three clarifying remarks are in order here. First, the alleged force of the position of "the guardians of public morality" does not rest on their personal disutilities (indeed, our "guardians" seem often enough to find much pleasure in fighting obscenity and such), but on the claim that the actions in question are intrinsically objectionable, or will in fact offend others "with good reason." The acceptance of the moral disvalue of any suffering thus does not amount at all to a concession to the authoritarian argument.

Second, to accept that any suffering is disvaluable (or that any pleasure is valuable) is not to limit all evaluations to computations of quantities of pleasure and pain. The latter is the prerogative of the utilitarian, and I am happy to leave him as the sole owner of that approach. What relative weights can be attached to suffering (and happiness) vis-à-vis other qualities of states of affairs remains an open question.

Third, even in weighing utilities vis-à-vis one another, one is not obliged to value them according to quantities only, and one can use differential weighting depending on the nonutility features associated with each case. Even Mill's utilitarianism—admittedly of a rather unusual kind—did not stop him from asserting that "there is no parity between the feeling of a person for his own opinion, and the feeling of another who is offended at his holding it."

The psychological effects on others might well be serious, and it would then be absurd to assert that the fulfillment of the moral right of an individual to take personal risks should invariably be judged more important than any suffering it might cause. The shocking experience of those who see someone's arm being chewed up by a tiger as he puts his hand into the cage might well be judged to be of greater disvalue than the violation of the person's right to put his hand in (if that is seen as a right in the first place). In other cases the balance may be seen as going the other way. One would certainly hesitate to give greater importance to the satisfaction of the "Jewish mother" than to the right of the adult son to diet if he so chooses.

The injury effects, the medical effects, and the economic and social effects typically arouse less suspicion than the psychological effects. If my driving without seat belts exposes you to greater danger of injury or death, or reduces your opportunities of getting medical attention, or harms you economically or socially, then it seems natural that these adverse effects must be weighed in the goal-rights system.

The sources of worry lie elsewhere. Three in particular may be taken up here. First, there is the problem of *robustness* of the right to take personal risks. This is a general worry about the nature of goal-rights systems. Since the acceptance of a moral right does not necessarily imply that the person having that right can do the thing he has a right to do, does this make moral rights terribly flimsy? Do they have any bite at all? What sense does it make to say that we have a moral right to take personal risks, such as not to wear seat belts, and at the same time assert that it is morally appropriate to curb the exercise of that right, such as through seat-belt regulations? Hasn't the baby been thrown away with the bath water?

Second, there is the problem of *interactivity consistency.* If seat-belt wearing is made compulsory because of, say, the medical effects, then does this not threaten the right to undertake such activities as mountaineering? Might it not even compromise the right to drive a car (with or without seat belts), since driving also increases the chances of being injured and being in need of medical services?

Third, there is the problem of *interindividual sensitivity.* While the compulsory wearing of seat belts might be accepted to be more beneficial than harmful in most cases (taking into account all the effects, including the disvalue of violating a person's right to lead the kind of life he would like to lead), this would not be so in some cases, as when someone drives alone, has no dependents, and has private medical attention. Such a person's right might seem to require that he be exempted from the seat-belt regulations. And if no such concession can be made, then should one not see, on grounds of liberty, the seat-belt regulations as unacceptable? . . .

The constraint-based deontological formulation of moral rights has the great merit of simplicity: Either others are prohibited from doing certain things, or they are entirely free to do those things. Those who tend to think of rights in such all-or-nothing terms might feel that the framework of goal-rights does not give the robustness that is expected of rights. One should be able, it might be argued, to insist on one's rights come what may. Indeed, the familiar view of rights seems to demand an overwhelming, possibly irresistible, force, at least in some circumstances. The absence of such force might be seen as undermining the entire goal-rights approach and specifically the application of that approach to the right to take personal risks.

In taking up this question, I begin with a purely formal point. If irresistible force is sought, then that can be provided even *within* the goal-rights system by giving the fulfillment of the rights in question lexicographic priority over other goals. While goal-rights systems allow trade-offs, they also permit evaluations without trade-offs. I do not, however, intend to pursue this line further; one of the chief reasons for adopting the goal-rights approach is precisely the scope that it gives to the possibility of trade-offs.

Is it reasonable to expect that all moral rights must have irresistible force? Such a point of view immediately produces a problem of consistency, since conflicting rights cannot each have irresistible force. Your right not to be forced to wear seat belts might conflict with my right not to have you land on my shoulders at the touch of a brake. The problem is avoided either by formulating rights in such a way that they cannot possibly conflict (such as in terms of abstention from certain conscious actions), or by taking rights in the "everything considered" form, so that a right is not established until it wins, as it were, over all conflicting claims. The former procedure is very restrictive and permits only a narrow class of rights. The latter, if pursued fully, would make rights no more than "outputs" of moral arguments rather than being able to *influence* such arguments. Neither procedure is satisfactory. . . .

The apparent puzzles involving interactivity consistency in the right to take risks arise from taking a nondiscriminating view of the role of rights in moral arguments. In the goal rights approach, which balances the pros and cons of restricting freedoms of different types, there is no general presumption that all cases with formal similarity would be assessed in the same way, since the assessment must go ultimately into the balancing of the relative weights of conflicting considerations. In terms of what is involved, seat-belt regulations are hardly comparable to prohibiting mountaineering or banning driving. . . .

What about Mahahero, the recluse millionaire whose taking of personal risks in not wearing seat belts would have little adverse effect on others and who, we assume, is bent on pursuing a life style involving beltless travel? Let us conceded that to force him to be belted would involve a greater loss than gain from the moral point of view. Not only, like others, does he have the right to take personal risks, but that right in his case, unlike in those of others, is important when applied to beltless driving; and the adverse effects in his case, again unlike in those of others, are relatively tiny. There is a good case, then, for letting him go unbelted, if that can be done without the difference itself causing some adverse effects.

The rub, of course, is precisely there. It might be politically impossible to let our heroic recluse millionaire go unbelted while others are forced to belt up. Even if it is possible, it may be socially costly in terms causing resentment, misunderstanding, and *perceived* discrimination.

Suppose that a separate arrangement for Mahahero is not possible. What should be done then? In a "zero-one" system the barrier of Mahahero's personal right is of course hard to cross. But the goal-rights system permits trade-offs, and it is a question of inter-individual balancing. The net disadvantage of violating Mahahero's right—a "winning" right if separate rules *were* costlessly possible—has to be compared with the net advantages, related to others, from enforcing seat-belt regulations.

So it is possible that *general* seat-belt regulations, applicable to all, are judged to be morally appropriate, and at the same time (1) everyone is acknowledged to have the moral right to take risks in these matters, and (2), furthermore, some people, such as Mahahero, have a moral right in this respect that outweighs the adverse effects of their not wearing seat belts. There is no real puzzle in this apparent oddity.

CONCLUDING REMARKS

Moral rights must be distinguished from rights with moral justification. If individual moral rights are admitted, it is difficult not to concede that people do have the moral right to take personal risks. The real issue, then, is not whether such rights exist, but how important they are vis-à-vis conflicting objectives.

The constraint-based deontological approach admits only all-conquering rights, although even there ad hoc compromises are made for the sake of plausibility. Such all-conquering rights lead to moral dilemmas that can be resolved only in a consequence-sensitive system with trade-offs. The framework of goal-rights systems can provide systematic accounting of conflicting objectives to arrive at informed moral judgment.

In the goal-rights systems the fulfillment of the right to take personal risks can compete with other goals. Personal risks can rarely be taken without other important consequences. This fact does not in any way "cancel" the right to take personal risks, but it does make that right compete with other objectives. Much of this paper has been concerned with issues involved in the balancing of competing claims. The importance of the right to take risks varies with the nature of the activity involved. It also varies from person to person. Public decisions, such as seat-belt regulations, call for integrated assessment of pros and cons. In this calculus, rights do figure, but they are not irresistible: They win some and they lose some.

There are of course many apparent puzzles in attitudes toward the right to take personal risks, such as those involving interactivity consistency (between, say, beltless travel and mountaineering) or interindividual variation (between different roles of the same activity in the lives of different persons). These puzzles seem to arise from attempts to fit the right to take personal risks into a nondiscriminating framework. More room has to be made for sensitivity to different types of information. The notion of moral rights should help us to conduct informed moral arguments, rather than getting us tied up in knots in moral maneuvers in partial darkness. There is no escape from discriminating consequential calculation in assessing the implications of rights. The right to take personal risks is no exception.

SISSELA BOK

Secrecy and Moral Choice

SISSELA BOK teaches philosophy at Brandeis University in Massachusetts.

A THOUGHT-EXPERIMENT

Imagine four different societies: two of them familiar from religious and mythological thinking, the other two closer to science fiction. To the extent that each reflects aspects of our own world, it will arouse the ambivalence and unease characteristic of conflicts over secrecy.

- In the first of the four imaginary societies, you and I cannot keep anything secret; but others, or at least someone, perhaps a deity, can. We are transparent to them, either because we are incapable of concealment or because they have means of penetrating all our defenses.

- In the second society, all is reversed. You and I can pierce all secrets. A magic ring and a coat of invisibility give us access to these secrets, unbeknownst to those on whom we focus our attention.

- In the third society, no one can keep secrets from anyone who desires to know them. Plans, actions, fears, and hopes are all transparent. Surprise and concealment are out of the question.

- In the fourth society, finally, everyone can keep secrets impenetrable at will. All can conceal innocuous as well as lethal plans, the noblest as well as the most shameful acts, and hatreds and conspiracies as much as generosity and self-sacrifice. Faces reveal nothing out of turn; secret codes remain unbroken. . . .

THE NEED FOR SECRECY

Secrecy is as indispensable to human beings as fire, and as greatly feared. Both enhance and protect life, yet both can stifle, lay waste, spread out of all control. Both may be used to guard intimacy or to invade it, to nurture or to consume. And each can be turned against itself; barriers of secrecy are set up to guard against secret plots and surreptitious prying, just as fire is used to fight fire. . . .

Control over secrecy provides a safety valve for individuals in the midst of communal life—some influence over transactions between the world of personal experience and the world shared with others. With no control over such exchanges, human beings would be unable to exercise choice about their lives. To restrain some secrets and to allow others freer play; to keep some hidden and to let others be known; to offer knowledge to some but not to all comers; to give and receive confidences and to guess at far more; these efforts at control permeate all human contact.

Those who lose all control over these relations cannot flourish in either the personal or the shared world, nor retain their sanity. If experience in the shared world becomes too overwhelming, the sense of identity suffers. Psychosis has been described as the breaking down of the delineation between the self and the outside world: the person going mad "flows out onto the world as through a broken dam." Conversely, experience limited to the inside world stunts the individual: at best it may lead to the aching self-exploration evoked by Nietzsche: "I am solitude become man—That no word ever reached me forced me to reach myself."

In seeking some control over secrecy and openness, and the power it makes possible, human beings attempt to guard and to promote not only their autonomy but ultimately their sanity and survival itself. The claims in defense of this control, however, are not always articulated. Some take them to be so self-evident as to need no articulation; others subsume them under more general arguments about liberty or privacy. But it is important for the purposes of considering the ethics of secrecy to set forth these claims. Otherwise it will not be possible to ask, in particular cases, to what extent they should apply and what restraints they might require. Nor will it be possible to study the extrapolations made from them in support of collective practices of secrecy.

The claims in defense of some control over secrecy and openness invoke four different, though in practice inseparable, elements of human autonomy: identity, plans, action, and property. They concern protection of what we are, what we intend, what we do, and what we own.

The first of these claims holds that some control over secrecy and openness is needed in order to protect identify: the sense of what we identify ourselves as, through, and with. Such control may be needed to guard solitude, privacy, intimacy, and friendship. It protects vulnerable beliefs or feelings, inwardness, and the sense of being set apart; of having or belonging to regions not fully penetrable to scrutiny, including those of memory and dream; of being someone who is more, has become more, has more possibilities for the future than can ever meet the eyes of observers. Secrecy guards, therefore, not merely isolated secrets about the self but access to the underlying experience *of* secrecy.

Human beings can be subjected to every scrutiny, and reveal much about themselves; but they can never be entirely understood, simultaneously exposed from every perspective, completely transparent either to themselves or to other persons. They are not only unique but unfathomable. The experience of such uniqueness and depth underlies self-respect and what social theorists have called the sense of "the sacredness of the self." This sense also draws on group, familial, and societal experience of intimacy and sacredness, and may attach to individual as well as to collective identity. The growing stress in the last centuries on human dignity and on rights such as the right to privacy echoes in it secular and individualized language.

Without perceiving some sacredness in human identity, individuals are out of touch with the depth they might feel in themselves and respond to in others. Given such a sense, however, certain intrusions are felt as violations—a few even as desecrations. It is in order to guard against such encroachments that we recoil from those who would tap our telephones, read our letters, bug our rooms: no matter how little we have to hide, no matter how benevolent their intentions, we take such intrusions to be demeaning.

Not only does control over secrecy and openness preserve central aspects of identity; it also guards their *changes*, their growth or decay, their progress or backsliding, their sharing and transformation of every kind. Here as elsewhere, while secrecy can be destructive, some of it is indispensable in human lives. Birth, sexual intimacy, death, mourning, experiences of conversion or of efforts to transcend the purely personal are often surrounded by special protections, and with rituals that combine secrecy and openness in set proportions. . . .

The second and third claims to control over secrecy presuppose the first. Given the need to guard identity, they invoke, in addition, the need for such control in order to protect certain plans and actions.

Choice is future-oriented, and never fully expressed in present action. It requires what is most distinctive about human reasoning: intention—the capacity to envisage and to compare future possibilities, to make estimates, sometimes to take indirect routes to a goal or to wait. What is fragile, unpopular, perhaps threatened, such as Winston Smith's plan to express his views freely in his diary, seeks additional layers of secrecy. To the extent that it is possible to strip people of their capacity for secrecy about their intentions and their actions, their lives become more transparent and predictable; they can then the more easily be subjected to pressure and defeated.

Secrecy for plans is needed, not only to protect their formulation but also to develop them, perhaps to change them, at times to execute them, even to give them up. Imagine, for example, the pointlessness of the game of chess without secrecy on the part of the players. Secrecy guards projects that require creativity and prolonged work: the tentative and the fragile, unfinished tasks, probes and bargaining of all kinds. An elopement or a peace initiative may be foiled if prematurely suspected; a symphony, scientific experiment, or an invention falters if exposed too soon. In speaking of creativity, Carlyle stressed the need for silence and secrecy, calling them "the element in which great things fashion themselves together."

Joint undertakings as well as personal ones may require secrecy for the sharing and working out of certain plans and for cooperative action. Lack of secrecy would, for instance, thwart many negotiations, in which all plans cannot easily be revealed from the outset. Once projects are safely under way, however, large portions of secrecy are often given up voluntarily, or dispelled with a flourish. Surprises are sprung and jokes explained. The result of the jury trial can be announced, the statue unveiled, the secretly negotiated treaty submitted for ratification, the desire to marry proclaimed. Here again, what is at issue is not secrecy alone, but rather the control over secrecy and openness. Many projects need both gestation and emergence, both confinement and publicity. Still others, such as certain fantasies and daydreams and hopes, may be too ephemeral or intimate at times too discreditable, ever to see the light of day.

Secrecy about plans and their execution, therefore, allows unpredictability and surprise. These are often feared; yet without them human existence would not only be unfree but also monotonous and stifling. Secrecy heightens the value of revelations; it is essential for arousing suspense, whether through stories told, surprises prepared, or waiting times imposed. It can lend the joy of concentration and solemnity to the smallest matters. Secrecy may also lower intensity and provide relief, so that when a revelation is finally made—as after the death of those most intimately connected with events described in an author's private diaries—the anguish of exposure is lessened. In all these ways, secrecy is the carrier of texture and variety. Without it, and without the suspense and wit and unexpectedness it allows, communication would be oppressively dull—lifeless in its own right.

The fourth claim to control over secrecy concerns property. At its root, it is closely linked to identity, in that people take some secrets, such as hidden love letters, to *belong* to them more than to others, to be *proper* to them. We link such secrets with our identity, and resist intrusions into them. But the claim to own secrets about oneself is often far-fetched. Thus the school-bus driver who has a severe heart condition cannot rightfully claim to *own* this medical information, even though it concerns him intimately. Even when outsiders have less need to share the information than in such a case, the question who owns a secret may be hard to answer. Should one include only those "about whom" it is a secret, those who claim a right to decide whether or not to disclose it, or all who know it?

In addition to such questions of owning secrets, secrecy is invoked to protect what one owns. We take for granted the legitimacy of hiding silver from burglars and personal documents from snoopers and busybodies. Here, too, the link to identity is close, as is that to plans and their execution. For had we no belongings whatsoever, our identity and our capacity to plan would themselves be threatened, and in turn survival itself. As H. L. A. Hart points out, life depends on the respect for at least "some minimal form of the institution of property (though not necessarily individual property) and the distinctive kind of rule which requires respect for it." At the most basic level, if crops are to be grown, land must be secure from indiscriminate entry, and food must be safe from being taken by others.

THE DANGERS OF SECRECY

Against every claim to secrecy stands, however, the awareness of its dangers. It is the experience of these dangers that has led so many to view secrecy negatively, and that underlies statements such as that by Lord Acton, that "every thing secret degenerates." Such categorical dismissals are too sweeping, but they do point to the harm that secrets can do both to those who keep them and to those from whom they are kept— harm that often thwarts and debilitates the very needs for which I have argued that control over secrecy is indispensable.

Secrecy can harm those who make use of it in several ways. I can debilitate judgment, first of all, whenever it shuts out criticism and feedback, leading people to become mired down in stereotyped, unexamined, often erroneous beliefs and ways of thinking. Neither their perception of a problem nor their reasoning about it then receives the benefit of challenge and exposure. Scientists working under conditions of intense secrecy have testified to its stifling effect on their judgment and creativity. And those who have written about their undercover work as journalists, police agents, and spies, or about living incognito for political reasons, have described similar effects of prolonged concealment on their capacity to plan and to choose, at times on their sense of identity.

Secrecy can affect character and moral choice in similar ways. It allows people to maintain façades that conceal traits such as callousness or vindictiveness—traits which can, in the absence of criticism or challenge from without, prove debilitating. And guilty or deeply embarrassing secrets can corrode from within before outsiders have a chance to respond or to be of help. This deterioration from within is the danger Acton referred to in his statement, and is at the root of the common view that secrecy, like other exercises of power, can corrupt.

These risks of secrecy multiply because of its tendency to spread. Aware of the importance of exercising control over secrecy and openness, people seek more control whenever they can, and rarely give up portions of it voluntarily. In imitation and in self-protection, others then seek more as well. The control shifts in the direction of secrecy whenever there is negligence or abuse to cover up; as a result, as Weber pointed out, bureaucracies and other organizations surround themselves with ever greater secrecy to the extent that circumstances permit.

As secrecy debilitates character and judgment, it can also lower resistance to the irrational and the pathological. It then poses great difficulties for individuals whose controls go awry. We know all the stifling rigidity that hampers those who become obsessed with secrecy. For them, secrecy no longer serves sanity and free choice. It shuts off the safety valve between the inner and the shared worlds. We know, too, the pathologies of prying into the private spheres of others, and of losing all protection for one's own: voyeurism and the corresponding hunger for self-exposure that destroy the capacity to discriminate and to choose.

The danger of secrecy, however, obviously goes far beyond risks to those who *keep* secrets. If they alone were at risk, we would have fewer reasons to try to learn about, and sometimes interfere with, their secret practices. Our attitude changes radically as soon as we suspect that these practices also hurt others. And because secrecy can debilitate judgment and choice, spread, and become obsessive, it often affects others even when it is not intended to. This helps explain why, in the absence of clear criteria for when secrecy is and is not injurious, many people have chosen to regard all secrecy as potentially harmful.

When the freedom of choice that secrecy gives one person limits or destroys that of others, it affects not only his own claims to respect for identity, plans, action, and property, but theirs. The power of such secrecy can be immense. Because it bypasses inspection and eludes interference, secrecy is central to the planning of every form of injury to human beings. It cloaks the execution of these plans and wipes out all traces afterward. It enters into all prying and intrusion that cannot be carried out openly. While not all that is secret is meant to deceive—as jury deliberations, for instance, are not— all deceit does rely on keeping something secret. And while not all secrets are discreditable, all that is discreditable and all wrongdoing seek out secrecy (unless they can be carried out openly without interference, as when they are pursued by coercive means).

Such secrecy can hamper the exercise of rational choice at every step: by preventing people from adequately understanding a threatening situation, from seeing the relevant alternatives clearly, from assessing the consequences of each, and from arriving at preferences with respect to them. Those who have been hurt in such a way by the secrecy of others may in turn seek greater control over secrecy, and thus in turn experience its impairment of choice, its tendency to spread, its capacity to corrupt and to invite abuse.

MORAL CONSIDERATIONS

I . . . rely on two presumptions that flow from the needs and dangers of secrecy that I have set forth. The first is one of *equality*. Whatever control over secrecy and openness we conclude is legitimate for some individuals should, in the absence of special considerations, be legitimate for all. If we look back at the four imaginary societies as illustrations, I can see no reason why some individuals should lack all such control, as in the first and second societies, and not others: no reason why, as in the first society, only you and I should be unable to keep anything secret or, as in the second, be able to penetrate all secrets. No just society would, if it had the choice, allocate controls so unequally. This is not to say that some people might not be granted limited powers for certain of those purposes under constraints that minimize the risks—in journalism, for instance, or government; but they would have to advance reasons sufficient to overcome the initial presumption favoring equality. On the basis of this presumption, I reject both the first and the second of the imaginary societies, and any others that come close to them even in part.

My second presumption is in favor of *partial individual control* over the degree of secrecy or openness about personal matters—those most indisputably in the private realm. (I shall leave for later consideration the question of large-scale collective control over secrecy and openness regarding personal matters, as well as individual *or* collective control over less personal matters, such as professional, business, or government secrets.) Without a premise supporting a measure of individual control over personal matters, it would be impossible to preserve the indispensable respect for identity, plans, action, and belonging that all of us need and should legitimately be able to claim.

Such individual control should extend, moreover, to what people choose to share with one another about themselves—in families, for example, or with friends and colleagues. Without the intimacy that such sharing makes possible, human relationships would be impossible, and identity and plans would themselves suffer. For these reasons, I reject also the third imaginary society, in which all is openness, and where people have no choice between such openness and secrecy, even in personal and intimate matters.

At the same time, however, it is important to avoid any presumption in favor of *full* control over such matters for individuals. Such full control is not necessary for the needs that I have discussed, and would aggravate the dangers. It would force us to disregard the legitimate claims of those persons who might be injured, betrayed, or ignored as a result of secrets inappropriately kept or revealed. I must therefore also reject the fourth imaginary society, in which all have such control and can exercise it at will.

Given these two presumptions, in favor of equal control over secrecy and openness among all individuals, and in favor of partial individual control over personal matters, exercised singly or shared with other individuals, I shall go on to ask: *What considerations override these presumptions?* This will require us to look at the reasons advanced in favor of unusual secrecy, probing, or revelation by some, and to ask when even the partial control exercised by an individual in personal matters must be overridden. It will also require us to examine the role of loyalty and promises in countering such reasons to override personal control; and the crucial difference it makes if it is one's own secret or that of another that one wonders whether to reveal. . . .

Such questions about the ethics of secrecy . . . mirror and shed light on aspects of ethics more generally. But these questions also create special difficulties; for no matter what moral principles one takes to be important in moral reasoning, they have a near-paradoxical relationship with secrecy. Thus secrecy both promotes and endangers what we think beneficial, even necessary for survival. It may prevent harm, but it follows maleficence like a shadow. Every misdeed cloaks itself in secrecy unless accompanied by such power that it can be performed openly. And while secrecy may heighten a sense of equality and brotherhood among persons sharing the secret, it can fuel gross intolerance and hatred toward outsiders. At the heart of secrecy lies discrimination of some form, since its essence is sifting, setting apart, drawing lines. Secrecy, moreover, preserves liberty, yet this very liberty allows the invasion of that of others.

GRANT GILLETT

AIDS and Confidentiality

GRANT GILLETT is both a doctor of philosophy and a surgeon. He teaches medicine and medical ethics at Otago University in Dunedin, New Zealand.

Does a doctor confronted by a patient with AIDS have a duty to maintain absolute confidentiality or could that doctor be considered to have some overriding duty to the sexual contacts of the AIDS sufferer? AIDS or Acquired Immune Deficiency Disease is a viral disease transmitted for the most part by sexual contact. It is fatal in the short or long term (i.e. nine months to six years) in those infected people who go on to develop the full-blown form of the disease.

Let us say that a 39 year old man goes to his family doctor with a dry persistent cough which has lasted three or four weeks and a 10 day history of night sweats. He admits that he is bisexually active. He is tested and found to have antibodies to HIV virus (indicating that he is infected with the virus that causes AIDS). In the setting of this clinical picture he must be considered to have the disease. He is told of his condition and also, in the course of a prolonged interview, of the risk to his wife and of the distinct possibility of his children aged one and three years old being left without parents should she contract the disease. He refuses to allow her to be told of his condition. The doctor finally accedes to his demand for absolute confidentiality. After one or two initial illnesses which are successfully combatted he dies some 18 months later. Over the last few weeks of his life he relents on his former demands and allows his wife to be informed of his problem. She is tested and, though asymptomatic, is found to be antibody positive. A year later she goes to the doctor with fever, dry cough and loss of appetite. Distraught on behalf of her children, she bitterly accuses the doctor of having failed her and them by allowing her husband to infect her when steps could have been taken to diminish the risk had she only known the truth.

In this case there is a powerful inclination to say that the wife is justified in her grievance. It seems just plain wrong for her doctor to sit back and allow her to fall victim to a fatal disease because of the wish of her husband. Against this intuition we can mobilise two powerful arguments—one deontological and the other utilitarian (of a rule or restricted utilitarian type).

(i) On a deontological view the practice of medicine will be guided by certain inviolate or absolute rules (not to harm, not to neglect the welfare of one's patients, etc.). Among these will be respect for confidentiality. Faced with this inviolable principle the deontologically inclined physician will not disclose what he has been told in confidence—he will regard the tacit agreement not to disclose his patient's affairs to others as tantamount to a substantive promise which he cannot break. Against this, in the present case, we might urge his *prima facie* duty not to neglect the welfare of his other patient, the young man's wife. His inaction has contributed to her death. In response to this he could both defend the absolute duty to respect confidentiality in general and urge some version of the doctrine of double effect, claiming that his clear duty was to honour his implicit vow of confidentiality but it had the unfortunate effect, which he had foreseen as possible but not intended, that it caused the death of his other patient. One is inclined to offer an intuitive response such as 'No moral duty is so binding that you can hazard another person's life in this manner'. It is a notorious feature of deontological systems that they involve conflicts of duties for which there exists no principled method of resolution.

(ii) A rule-utilitarian doctor can mount a more convincing case. He can observe that confidentiality is a cornerstone of a successful AIDS practice. Lack of confidentiality can cause the irrational victimisation of sufferers by a poorly educated public who are prone to witch-hunts of all kinds. The detection and treatment of AIDS, and the consequent protection of that large group of people who have contacts with the patients being treated depends on the patients who seek medical advice believing that medical confidentiality is inviolate. If confidentiality were seen as a relative duty only, suspended or breached at the discretion of the doctor, then far fewer cases would present for detection and crucial guidance about diminishing risks of spread would not be obtained. This would lead to more people suffering and dying. It may be hard on a few, unfortunate enough to be involved with people like the recalcitrant young husband, but the general welfare can only be served by a compassionate but resolute refusal to abandon sound principles in the face of such cases. Many find this a convincing argument but I will argue that it is superficial in the understanding of moral issues that it espouses.

• • •

Imagine, in order to soften the way for a rather less neatly argued position, a doctor confronted by a young man who has a scratched face and blood on his shirt and who wants to be checked for VD. In the course of the doctor's taking his history it emerges that he has forcibly raped two women and is worried that the second was a prostitute. He says to the doctor "Of course, I am telling you this in confidence, doc, because I know that you won't rat on me." Producing a knife, he then says, "See, this is the blade that I get them going with." Rather troubled, the doctor takes samples and tells the young man that there is no evidence of VD. He tries to talk his patient into giving himself up for some kind of psychiatric treatment but the young man is adamant. It becomes clear that he has certain delusional and persecutional ideas. Two days later the doctor reads that his patient has been arrested because after leaving the surgery he raped and savagely mutilated a young woman who, as a result, required emergency surgery for multiple wounds and remains in critical condition.

Here we might well feel that any principle which dictates that it is the moral duty of the doctor to keep silent is wrong—but as yet no principles conflicting with or supplementing those above have been introduced. A possible loophole is introduced by the rapist's sadomasochism and probable psychosis but we need to spell out why this is relevant. In such a case we suspend our normal moral obligations to respect the avowed interests of the patient and claim that he is incompetent to make a responsible and informed assessment of his own interests and so we assume the right to make certain decisions on his behalf. In this case it would probably mean arranging for him to be given psychiatric help and society to be protected from him in the meantime. Notice that he may have demonstrated a 'lucid' and 'intelligent' grasp of his predicament, vis-à-vis his own wish to avoid detection but we discern that his instrumental rationality is deployed in service of a deep or moral insanity. His lack of awareness of the enormity of what he is doing to others counts as a sufficient basis to diagnose madness even in the face of astute inferential thought. He is insane because a normal person would never begin from the moral position he occupies and so his rights, including that to medical confidentiality, are suspended. He has moved outside the community of trust, mutual concern and non-malificence in which moral considerations for the preferences of others have their proper place. It is not that one 'contracts in' to such a community, nor that one in any sense volunteers, but rather one is a *de facto* member of it by virtue of possessing those human sensitivities and vulnerabilities which give moral predicates their meaning and importance. Such weight as one claims for one's own personal privileges and moral principles—such as the demand for confidentiality—is derived from a 'form of life' where the interpersonal transactions which define trust, respect, harm, and so on, are in play (it is important that no particular ideological overlay has been grafted on to these). Of the insane rapist we can say that he has excluded himself from that moral community by the very fact of his violation of certain of its most basic tenets and assumptions. He has no right to demand a full place in that structure where morally significant human exchanges are operative because his behaviour and attitudes do not fit the place to which he pretends. We are, of course, not released from a *prima facie* duty to try and help him in his odious predicament but we cannot be expected to accord him the full privileges of a member of the moral community as he persists, for whatever reason, in callously turning his back on the constraints normally operative there (albeit, perhaps, without reflective malevolence in its more usual forms). So, in this case, confidentiality can be suspended for legitimate moral reasons. The mad rapist has moved beyond the pale in terms of normal moral interactions and though we may have a duty to try and restore him to full participation within that order we are also entitled to protect ourselves in the interim at the expense of those considerations that would apply to a normal person. Notice again that the boundaries of our attitudes are not arbitrary or merely conventional but involve our most basic human feelings and reactions to one another.

●   ●   ●

We can now move from a case where insanity weights the decision in a certain direction to a case where the issues are more purely moral. Imagine that a 45-year-old man goes to see his family doctor and is also worried about a sexually transmitted disease. On being questioned he admits, in confidence, not only to intercourse with a series of prostitutes but also to forced sexual intercourse with his daughter. He is confident that she will not tell anyone what is happening because she is too ashamed and scared. After counselling he gives no sign of a wish to change his ways but rather continues to justify himself because of his wife's behaviour. The doctor later hears from the school psychological service that the daughter is showing some potentially serious emotional problems.

Here, it seems to me, we have few compunctions about setting in motion that machinery to deal with child abuse, even though the sole source of our information is what was said, in medical confidence, by the father. The justification we might give for the doctor's actions is illuminating. We are concerned for the actual harm being done to the child, both physical and psychological, and we overturn the father's injunction to confidence in order to prevent further harm being done. In so doing we class the situation as one in which a *prima facie* moral claim can be suspended because of the actions and attitudes involved. I believe that we do so because we implicitly realise that here also the agent has acted in such a way as to put himself beyond the full play of moral consideration and to justify our withholding certain of his moral 'dues'. Confidentiality functions to allow the patient to be honest with the doctor and to put trust in him. Trust is (at least in part) a two-way thing and can only exist between morally sensitive human beings (this, of course, blurs a vast range of distinctions between degrees of sensitivity). A basic element of such moral attitudes is the responsiveness of the agents concerned to the moral features of human interactions. The legitimate expectation that a doctor be trustworthy and faithful to his patient's wishes regardless of the behaviour of that patient is undermined when the patient abuses the relationship so formed in ways which show a lack of these basic human reactions because it is just these reactions which ground the importance of confidentiality in general. Therefore, if the father in this example refuses to accept the enormity of what he is doing to his daughter, he thereby casts doubt upon his standing as a moral agent. Stated baldly, that sounds like an open warrant for moralistic medical paternalism, but I do not think it need be. In asking that his affairs be concealed from others, a person is demanding *either* the right to preserve himself from the harms that might befall him if the facts about his life were generally known, *or* that his sensitivity as an individual be respected and protected. On either count it is inconsistent for him to claim some moral justification for that demand when it is made solely with the aim of allowing him to inflict comparable disregard or harm upon another. By this implicit intention to use a position, which only remains tenable with the collusion of the doctor, callously to harm another individual, the father undermines the moral force of his own appeal. His case is only worsened by the fact that from any moral perspective he would be considered to have a special and protective obligation toward his own offspring.

● ● ●

Implicit within what I have said is a reappraisal of the nature of medical confidentiality. I have argued that it is not to be treated as an absolute duty but is rather to rank among other *prima facie* duties and responsibilities of the doctor-patient relationship. Just as the performance of a lifesaving procedure can be vetoed by the patient's choice to forgo treatment, even though it is a doctor's duty to strive for his patient's life, so each of these duties can be negated by certain considerations. One generally attempts to prevent a fatal illness overtaking a patient but in the case of a deformed neonate or an elderly and demented patient often the attempt is not made. In the case of confidentiality, I have claimed that we recognise the right of a patient to preserve his own personal life as inviolate. We accept that patients can and should share with a doctor details which it would not be right to disclose to other people. But we must also recognise that implicit within this recognition is the assumption that the patient is one of us, morally speaking. Our attitude to him and his rights assumes that he is one of or a participant in a community of beings who matter (or are morally interacting individuals like himself to whom the same considerations apply). We could offer a superficial and rather gross systematisation of this assumption in the universalisability test. The patient in the last two cases applies a standard to his own human concerns which he is not prepared to extend to others involved with him in relevant situations. We must therefore regard his moral demands as spurious; we are not at liberty to harm him but we are bound to see that his cynical abuse of the moral code within which he lives does not harm others. At this point it might be objected that we are on a 'slippery slope'.

Will any moral transgression suffice to undermine the moral privileges of the patient? I do not think that this extreme conclusion can be supported from what I have said. Williams, remarking on the tendency to slide down 'slippery slopes', observes, "that requires that there should be some motive to move from one step to the next" and "Possible cases are not enough, and the situation must have some other feature which means that those cases have to be confronted." Here we are not in such a position. Doctors in general have a strong tendency to protect their patients and keep their confidences. They require strong moral pressures to contemplate doing otherwise. All I have sought to do is to make explicit the moral justification upon which these exceptions can be seen to rest. I have not spelled out any formal decision-making procedure whereby the right answer will be yielded in each case. Indeed it is possible that whereas grounds and reasons recommending a certain course of action are the lifeblood of moral philosophy, such clearcut principles and derivations are a 'will o' the wisp'.

Now we can return to the AIDS patient. From what I have said it becomes clear that it is only the moral intransigent who forces us to breach confidentiality. In most cases it will be possible to guide the patient into telling those who need to know or allowing them to be told (and where it is possible to so guide him it will be mandatory to involve him in an informed way). In the face of an expressed disregard for the harm being caused to those others concerned, we will be morally correct in abandoning what would otherwise be a binding obligation. We should and do feel the need to preserve and protect the already affected life of the potential victim of his deception and in this feeling we exhibit a sensitivity to moral rectitude. Of course, it is only the active sexual partners of the patient who are at risk and thus it is only to them that we and the patient have a moral duty (in this respect talk of 'society at large' is just rhetoric). If it is the case that sexual activity, as Nagel claims, involves a mutual openness in those who have intercourse, one could plausibly argue that the cynical moral and interpersonal attitudes here evinced undermined the patient's sexual rights (assuming that people have such). The sexual activity of this individual is aberrant or perverted in the important respect that it involves a harmful duplicity toward or deception of his sexual partner. Whereas people may have a right to sexual fulfilment in general, they can hardly be said to have a right to perverted sexual fulfilment; but both Nagel's contentions and this talk of rights are contentious and it is outside my present brief to discuss them.

The doctor's obligation to inform, in the face of an enjoinder to keep his confidence, even if I am right, be seen to be restricted to those in actual danger and would in no wise extend to employers, friends or non-sexually interacting relatives of the patient or any other person with an even more peripheral interest. His duty extends only so far as to avert the actual harm that he can reasonably expect to arise from his keeping confidence.

Given the intransigent case, one further desideratum presents itself. I believe that doctors should be open with their patients and that therefore the doctor is bound to share his moral dilemma with the patient and inform him of his intention to breach confidentiality. I think he can legitimately claim a pre-emptive duty to prevent harm befalling his patients and should do so in the case of the abuse of others which the patient intends. It may be the case, with the insane rapist for instance, that the doctor will need to deceive in order to carry out his prevailing duty but this will hardly ever be so, and should, I believe, be regarded as unacceptable in general.

One thorny problem remains—the possible deleterious effect on the detection and treatment of AIDS if confidentiality is seen as only a relative principle in medical practice. Clearly, if the attitude were ever to take root that the medical profession could not be trusted to 'keep their mouths shut' then the feared effect would occur. I believe that where agencies and informal groups were told of the *only* grounds on which confidentiality would be breached and the *only* people who would be informed then this effect would not occur.

It seems to me that the remarkable intensification of one's sensitivity to personal and ethical values that is produced by contact with life-threatening or 'abyss' situations means that the cynical abuse of confidentiality by the patient which I have sought to address is likely to be both rare and transient. The greatest resource available to any of us in 'the valley of the shadow' is the closeness of those who will walk alongside us, and for many that will be a close spiritual and sexual partner. Confidentiality within the mutuality of that relationship rather than interpersonal dishonesty would thus seem to be vital to the welfare not only of the co-respondent but also of the patient himself as he struggles to cope with the disease that has him in its grip. To foster that welfare seems to me to be as close as a doctor can ever come to an absolute duty.

PART THREE

Social
Ethics

PART THREE

Social
Ethics

CHAPTER 8

How Does Racism Affect My Life?

While you were growing up, your parents probably reminded you again and again that you should not talk to strangers or accept rides from them. For your safety, you were taught to trust people you know and to mistrust people you don't know. This simplistic distinction was useful for making you less vulnerable as a small child. Your parents were no doubt confident that in time you would outgrow it and achieve a more subtle understanding of circumstances in which it is or is not appropriate to extend trust.

Racism is built on the unsophisticated distinction between those who are familiar and those who are not. It is a defensive and immature approach to humanity, which divides the trustworthy from the untrustworthy on the basis of simple and unreasonable criteria. Racism is morally objectionable by definition. Yet if the basic point of normative ethics is to guide our actions, it is not always obvious what this observation about racism implies in specific cases. Often racism constitutes a motive for action. But motives are not always transparent. That racism is wrong implies that actions motivated by racism—perhaps with the intent of accomplishing racist goals—are wrong. But determining whether our motivations are racist requires considerable self-awareness.

Kant points out that it is not always easy for the individual to know his or her own intentions, and this fact complicates ethical reflection on racism. It also explains why many moral thinkers who are concerned with racism focus on the importance of consciousness-raising, of becoming more aware of the obvious racism that may affect one's own orientation.

Investigations of the psychological mechanisms involved in racism can assist our awareness of the nature of the problem. Jean-Paul Sartre considered anti-Semitism. He explains it as a guiding passion that organizes the anti-Semite's life. Sartre suggests that the passionate hatred involved in anti-Semitism allows the anti-Semite to fortify his or her own self-perception. Sartre claims that the anti-Semite is able to take pleasure in his or her own sense of mediocrity, enhancing self-esteem through hatred of Jews.

Jorge Valadez considers the psychology of more subtle kinds of racism. Valadez suggests that many Americans, perhaps unwittingly, take the perspective that the American way of life—often understood in terms of economic, technological, and military advantages—is superior to that of their Latin American neighbors, and conclude that the United States can boast a superior worldview in all respects. Valadez observes that this amounts to metaphysical imperialism. He proposes that philosophical reflection can help overcome the patterns of oppression that such imperialism has encouraged by helping us to develop a "multi-cultural perspective," a perspective that values the contributions that various particular cultures can make to our understanding of reality in a global society.

Elizabeth V. Spelman argues that the dominant tradition of philosophy in the West has also subtly assisted the formation of racist attitudes. Spelman argues that Western philosophy has encouraged simplistic dualisms in our basic evaluations of human beings. It is particularly easy, Spelman argues, to distinguish groups of people on the basis of the kind of bodies they have. She believes that because the white male has been taken as the standard, those whose bodies are noticeably different from those of white males—women and nonwhite groups—are frequently seen an inferior or deviant. Spelman argues that this perspective has even invaded philosophical feminism, and she suggests that the feminist agenda should reassert the value of female and nonwhite bodies.

Unlike Kant, who emphasizes intention alone in his moral theory, utilitarians approach moral questions connected with racism—and all other moral questions—in terms of consequences. Utilitarians stress the impact that racism has on society and contend that our moral response to racism should focus on actions that will actually do some good.

What is the impact of racism on society? Clearly, racism has harmful effects on the individuals who are its targets. The opening of Ralph Ellison's *The Invisible Man* portrays in striking metaphors the damage that racism does to its victims' self-concepts and sense of participation in society.

It is valuable for nonvictims to empathize with victims of racism, but bell hooks reminds everyone of the dangers of relying on customary metaphors to interpret the relationship between the powerful and the powerless. She observes that the American feminist movement has taken the experiences of the middle-class white woman as paradigm, and as a consequence has reproduced the perspective of relatively privileged women, even in the movement's efforts to counter oppressive patterns in society. Hooks insists on the importance of voices from "the margins," as well as from the center of power, for the creation of a less oppressive world.

Shelby Steele, Michael Lind, and Roger Wilkins each consider the effectiveness and appropriateness of policies of reverse discrimination—practices that give preferred status to members of groups that have been victims of previous discrimination. Steele is skeptical of affirmative action programs. He questions the assumption on which they are based—that groups of citizens can be entitled to something collectively. Indeed, Steele argues, this is precisely the assumption on which racist institutions before the Civil Rights movement used to depend. Affirmative action programs only change the identity of the group that is given entitlements that are denied to other groups. The Civil Rights movement of the 1960s sought to ensure that each citizen was guaranteed the same rights as every other. Affirmative action programs, Steele contends, are not consistent with that goal.

Lind observes that a small class of elite, wealthy whites runs all of the major institutions in the United States. This "overclass," he contends, is America's social and political oligarchy, which maintains dominance through denying that it exists. It promotes the belief that American society is classless and the myth that those who run the country reached their position by means of individual merit. These myths encourage the view that groups not represented in the overclass must be inherently inferior and, indeed, the "underclass." Lind thinks that affirmative action programs have been less than effective in evening the playing field. Such programs, he contends, have been offered to minority group leaders as a kind of bribe, and in practice they have amounted to a kind of tokenism. Lind suggests, however, that the largest and most entrenched affirmative action program is the most problematic—the one that gives special preference, with little regard to merit, to the children of elite alumni.

Roger Wilkins defends affirmative action programs on the ground that they are necessary to provide equal opportunities in American society, given the long history of policies that have treated white males preferentially. The United States has never been a meritocracy, but affirmative action programs have helped to move the nation in that direction, Wilkins argues. Such programs have already extended the availability of opportunities and education to a broader portion of the American population.

American society as a whole benefits from greater integration and interaction among people of different backgrounds. Wilkins sees affirmative action as a necessary means toward this end. Without it, he contends, the entrenched assumption of white privilege will continue to dominate and damage our institutions and our lives.

JEAN-PAUL SARTRE

Anti-Semite and Jew

JEAN-PAUL SARTRE (1905–1980) was a French novelist, playwright, and philosopher. He is closely associated with the twentieth-century existentialist movement and was a Communist Party supporter until 1956. His works examine philosophical notions of freedom, political philosophy, and philosophy of the mind. His publications include *Being and Nothingness* (1948) and *Nausea* (1949), and he founded the philosophical periodical *Les Temps Modernes*.

If the Jew did not exist, the anti-Semite would invent him. . . .

Anti-Semitism is a free and total choice of oneself, a comprehensive attitude that one adopts not only toward Jews but toward men in general, toward history and society; it is at one and the same time a passion and a conception of the world. . . .

Ordinarily hate and anger have a *provocation*: I hate someone who has made me suffer, someone who condemns or insults me. . . .

Anti-Semitic passion could not have such a character. It precedes the facts that are supposed to call it forth: it seeks them out to nourish itself upon them; it must even interpret them in a special way so that they may become truly offensive. Indeed, if you so much as mention a Jew to an anti-Semite, he will show all the signs of a lively irritation. If we recall that we must always *consent* to anger before it can manifest itself and that, as is indicated so accurately by the French idiom, we "put ourselves" into anger, we shall have to agree that the anti-Semite has *chosen* to live on the plane of passion. It is not unusual for people to elect to live a life of passion rather than one of reason. But ordinarily they love the *objects* of passion: women, glory, power, money. Since the anti-Semite has chosen hate, we are forced to conclude that it is the *state* of passion that he loves. . . .

How can one choose to reason falsely? It is because of a longing for impenetrability. The rational man groans as he gropes for the truth; he knows that his reasoning is no more than tentative, that other considerations may supervene to cast doubt on it. He never sees very clearly where he is going; he is "open"; he may even appear to be hesitant. But there are people who are attracted by the durability of a stone. They wish to be massive and impenetrable; they wish not to change. Where, indeed, would change take them? We have here a basic fear of oneself and of truth. What frightens them is not the content of truth, of which they have no conception, but the form itself of truth, that thing of indefinite approximation. It is as if their own existence were in continual suspension. But they wish to exist all at once and right away. They do not want any acquired opinions: they want them to be innate. Since they are afraid of reasoning, they wish to lead the kind of life wherein reasoning and research play only a subordinate role, wherein one seeks only what he has already found, wherein one becomes only what he already was. This is nothing but passion. . . .

If then, as we have been able to observe, the anti-Semite is impervious to reason and to experience, it is not because his conviction is strong. Rather his conviction is strong because he has chosen first of all to be impervious.

He has chosen also to be terrifying. People are afraid of irritating him. No one knows to what lengths the aberrations of his passion will carry him—but he knows, for this passion is not provoked by something external. He has it well in hand; it is obedient to his will: now he lets go the reins and now he pulls back on them. He is not afraid of himself, but he sees in the eyes of others a disquieting image—his own—and he makes his words and gestures conform to it. Having this external model, he is under no necessity to look for his personality within himself. He has chosen to find his being entirely outside himself, never to look within, to be nothing save the fear he inspires in others. What he flees even more than Reason is his intimate awareness of himself. . . .

The anti-Semite has no illusions about what he is. He considers himself an average man, modestly average, basically mediocre. There is no example of an anti-Semite's claiming individual superiority over the Jews. But you must not think that he is ashamed of his mediocrity; he takes pleasure in it: I will even assert that he has chosen it. This man fears every kind of solitariness, that of the genius as much as that of the murderer; he is the man of the crowd. However small his stature, he takes every precaution to make it smaller, lest he stand out from the herd and find himself face to face with himself. He has made himself an anti-Semite because that is something one cannot be alone. The phrase, "I hate the Jews," is one that is uttered in chorus; in pronouncing it, one attaches himself to a tradition and to a community—the tradition and community of the mediocre.

We must remember that a man is not necessarily humble or even modest because he has consented to mediocrity. On the contrary, there is a passionate pride among the mediocre, and anti-Semitism is an attempt to give value to mediocrity as such, to create an elite of the ordinary. To the anti-Semite, intelligence is Jewish; he can thus disdain it in all tranquility, like all the other virtues which the Jew possesses. They are so many ersatz attributes that the Jew cultivates in place of that balanced mediocrity which he will never have. . . .

Thus I would call anti-Semitism a poor man's snobbery. . . . Anti-Semitism is not merely the joy of hating; it brings positive pleasures too. By treating the Jew as an inferior and pernicious being, I affirm at the same time that I belong to the elite. This elite, in contrast to those of modern times which are based on merit or labor, closely resembles an aristocracy of birth. There is nothing I have to do to merit my superiority, and neither can I lose it. It is given once and for all. It is a *thing*. . . .

We begin to perceive the meaning of the anti-Semite's choice of himself. He chooses the irremediable out of fear of being free; he chooses mediocrity out of fear of being alone, and out of pride he makes of this irremediable mediocrity a rigid aristocracy. To this end he finds the existence of the Jew absolutely necessary. Otherwise to whom would he be superior? Indeed, it is vis-à-vis the Jew and the Jew alone that the anti-Semite realizes that he has rights. If by some miracle all the Jews were exterminated as he wishes, he would find himself nothing but a concierge or a shopkeeper in a strongly hierarchical society in which the quality of "true Frenchman" would be at a low valuation, because everyone would possess it. He would lose his sense of rights over the country because no one would any longer contest them, and that profound equality which brings him close to the nobleman and the man of wealth would disappear all of a sudden, for it is primarily negative. His frustrations, which he has attributed to the disloyal competition of the Jew, would have to be imputed to some other cause, lest he be forced to look within himself. He would run the risk of falling into bitterness, into a melancholy hatred of the privileged classes. Thus the anti-Semite is in the unhappy position of having a vital need for the very enemy he wishes to destroy.

JORGE VALADEZ

The Metaphysics of Oppression

JORGE VALADEZ teaches philosophy at Marquette University. He has written on ontology and Latin American philosophy. This essay was written in 1989.

Consuelo had been living at a frantic pace for months. She was deeply involved in an organization of mothers who were demanding that the Guatemalan government account for their sons and daughters who had disappeared. Many of the mothers believed that their sons or daughters had probably already been killed by the government security forces, but they continued to hope that perhaps they might be alive and jailed with other political prisoners. The crimes of their loved ones consisted of their having protested and opposed the policies of the militarily controlled government. In Guatemala the degree of poverty and human suffering is staggering and many of the people from the poor and disenfranchised classes had finally decided that it was necessary to speak up against the government, even if it meant placing themselves and others close to them in danger.

Consuelo knew all of this, and she also knew that the bloated bodies of some of the disappeared were sometimes found floating in a river or buried in shallow graves. But despite it all she felt that it was preferable for her to know what had happened to her twenty year old son. Even the knowledge that he was dead was better than this insufferable uncertainty that weighed down her waking hours and haunted her dreams. At least the body could then receive a proper burial.

Early on in her life Consuelo had learned about responsibility and about hardship, and the latter she had come to accept as an inevitable aspect of her existence. She was the eldest child, and by age twelve she had assumed the duties of an adult. She had married while still an adolescent. Later, in her tenth year of marriage her husband left to seek work in the U.S. Whether he actually ever made it across the border she never knew, since she had not heard from him since. Through the years, she had convinced herself that it was best to think of him only as part of those joyful scenes that she stored in her memory like precious secret jewels.

Nothing in her life, however, had prepared her for what occurred that warm Sunday evening when the four armed men broke into her house. The organization of mothers which she headed had been particularly vocal during the last few months and the government wanted to set an example. While two of the men held her, the others grabbed her six year old child. On of them took out a pointed pair of pliers and in a savagely methodical motion pulled out the fingernail from one of the horrified child's fingers. The image of her son's contorted face and the sound of his uncontrolled screams pierced and bored into her brain. The child kicked and twisted his whole body in a crazed effort to get free, but the butchers had had practice. One of them put his knee on the boy's chest and pinned him against the floor, while holding down the other small flailing arm. His partner then completed the gruesome task.

The event just described actually occurred, and incidents of this degree of brutality are not rare in Guatemala and other Central American countries. In recent years the United States had provided tens of millions of dollars in military aid to the Guatemalan government. Even though that government has an elected civilian president, the real power is in the hands of the military, for the most powerful appointed officials in the government are military officers. Death squads and special security forces play a crucial role in the maintenance of power by the military. In Guatemala approximately two percent of the population own about 75 percent of the country's land and resources. It is a country where great inequalities of wealth exist between the privileged few and the mostly poor Indian population. About 73 percent of all children under the age of five are malnourished and, for every 1,000 births, 270 will die before reaching the age of five. The national illiteracy rate is 65 percent. Government violence has been responsible for more than 100,000 deaths in the last 30 years.

The problems faced by the Guatemalan people are not unique; they are shared by people in many other Third World countries. These problems could no doubt be analyzed from a variety of perspectives, including the sociological, political, epidemiological, etc. A question which I want to consider here is whether there are certain insights which a distinctively philosophical perspective could give us into the problem of oppression. Are there some elements of this problem which could be elucidated by taking the peculiarly general and abstract position of the philosopher? I believe the answer is yes. In what follows, I will try to show that certain of our philosophical orientations restrict and limit our understanding of Third World oppression.

In attempting to establish the need for our changing the way in which we understand oppression in underdeveloped countries, especially in Latin America, I will first discuss some pragmatic or instrumental considerations that should be taken into account and then I will discuss those issues which are of a more properly philosophical nature. Drawing the connection between the pragmatic and the philosophical reasons for reorienting our perspectives should enable us to make a more compelling case for our position, especially if it can be shown that these two types of reasons ultimately coalesce and reinforce one another.

One of the important factors to consider in analyzing the situation from an instrumental viewpoint is the economic factor. Countries like Guatemala, Mexico, Brazil, Peru, and Argentina have collective foreign debts that total in the hundreds of billions of dollars. These foreign debts are primarily the result of an inequitable system of international trade. Third World countries sell their raw materials and cash crops to industrialized countries at prices which are often determined by these industrialized countries themselves—in fact, in some cases foreign companies control the production process in Third World countries. In turn, the industrialized countries like the U.S. sell them manufactured goods (tractors, factory machinery, etc.) at a relatively higher price. The profit margin for manufactured goods is greater than that of raw or unprocessed goods. The manufactured/raw goods exchange creates an economic imbalance which is getting worse for Third World countries. In 1960 it took 165 one hundred pound bags of coffee for a country like Costa Rica to buy a tractor, and by 1977 it took 400 bags of coffee to buy that same tractor. In order to obtain the needed manufactured goods, Third World countries had to borrow from the industrialized countries. They had to pay interest on these loans, but the inequitable terms of international trade made it practically impossible for them to keep up the interest payments without borrowing more to do so. In 1973 the trade deficit of Third World countries was about nine billion dollars. In 1989 it is well over three hundred billion.

The result of this degree of indebtedness is that much needed resources that could be used for health care, education, etc. are channeled into the payments of the foreign debt. This in turn creates more misery and poverty for the majority of the population, who remain undernourished, illiterate, and with inadequate medical care. And it gets worse. The dire conditions under which the people are forced to live create an atmosphere of political instability which is exacerbated by the realization that the wealth in their countries is concentrated in a few hands. The wealthy classes and the high ranking military and government officials who benefit from the unjust distribution of resources want to maintain the status quo. In order to suppress the demands of the populace for better wages, improved working conditions, etc., the governments of many of these countries use a significant portion of their economic resources to strengthen the military and to create specialized security forces trained in intelligence and internal security operations (intimidation techniques, torture, etc.). Thus more of these countries' funds are used in areas that do not improve the living conditions of the people. The vicious cycle of poverty and oppression is reinforced—the demands of the poor for the alleviation of their misery lead to their political oppression, and the mechanisms that implement this oppression in turn increase their poverty.

In addition, the inability of these countries to pay back the money that they owe presents a serious problem for the lending institutions, many of which are American banks. And the possibility that the economies of these countries, after being declared bankrupt, may be taken over by American banks is politically, socially, and ethically unsettling. This possible scenario could be seen as the modern day equivalent of colonialism. It would validate in a frighteningly concrete way many of the fears and resentments that Latin Americans share toward the U.S. This scenario would be a clear and undeniable manifestation of the economic control that the industrialized nations have over the Third World.

Two questions which Americans should pose for themselves are these: First, at a time when our own social problems demand a wise and effective use of our economic resources, can we afford to spend many hundreds of millions of dollars in military aid to countries where the ruling classes seek to perpetuate their positions of privilege, to the detriment of the rest of the population? Second, what can be done to lessen the oppression in these countries and to strengthen their economies?

It is highly instructive to analyze the usual or official answers to these questions, i.e., the answers given by the government officials responsible for formulating our foreign policies. In regard to the first question, the position taken by the U.S. administration over the last decade is that we must keep the armies of the "democratically" elected governments of Latin America strong so that they can repel externally instigated communist threats. The idea here is that the demands which the people of El Salvador or Guatemala, for example, make of their governments for better living conditions and respect of their human rights are the result of external, communist interference and not the result of the poverty and oppression which they suffer. Democracy is so far superior to a communist system of government, so the argument goes, that almost no price is too high to pay to keep communism away from this hemisphere. This position is bolstered by the alleged threat posed by communism to our own national security. Finally, our continued support of these military regimes is justified by either denying or de-emphasizing the human rights abuses which they perpetrate.

I will now provide a philosophical analysis of these questions in order to identify certain tacit metaphysical assumptions which affect the way in which we conceptualize the issues under consideration. Several orientations and perspectives can be seen as underlying the answer to our first question. In the first place, the assumption is made that Americans have the right to interfere with and determine the internal politics of Latin American countries. The last century provides us with numerous examples of such interference, including the overthrow of established, elected governments (e.g., Chile under Allende) and the invasion of countries like Nicaragua and Mexico. What is important to note here is that this assumption of the right of interference is an expression of our supposed right to impose our visions of reality on Latin America. It is *our* perception of the world that counts. It is Americans who should determine how other people are to live, how they are to organize their governments, and how they are to choose their values and priorities. This perspective is in effect a kind of metaphysical imperialism, i.e., an imperialism that involves the force imposition of a dominant culture's vision of reality on another culture.

Most Americans are so convinced of the metaphysical imperialist perspective that it is almost impossible for us to question the basis of this perspective or to think of entering into a real and equal dialogue with the people of Latin America. Instead of engaging in an egalitarian effort to understand the world from their point of view, our attitude is that we have the right to impose our own visions of reality (through armed invasion if necessary). When dealing with under-developed countries, the notion that political truth is something that emerges as the result of a negotiated, open interchange of perspectives and ideas is foreign to most of us. And the belief that we have the right to impose our way of looking at the world on others is based on an even more deeply rooted philosophical view, namely, that those who are economically, technologically, and militarily superior, and are assumed to be intellectually and morally superior, have the right to control those who are inferior in these same respects. The history of Latin America can be seen as example of the concrete implementation of this philosophical principle, first at the hands of Western European countries and then at the hands of the United States.

It is difficult to overemphasize the importance and influence of this last philosophical principle for understanding the historical relationships between Latin America and Western Europe, and in contemporary times, between Latin America and the United States. America has, to a large extent, inherited its intellectual and philosophical traditions from Western Europe, including its attitudes towards underdeveloped or Third World nations. A common thread running through these attitudes is not only the metaphysical imperialist appropriation of the "truth" but also the above mentioned principle that those who are in possession of this "truth" have the moral right, and in some cases (like that of Christianity), even the moral obligation to impose their vision of reality on others. This principle works by assigning an inferior status to those who fail to meet our criteria of intellectual and moral worth. And once they have been categorized as inferior, it is an easy step towards the attitude that it is the task of their "superiors" either to subjugate them or to transform their perspectives of reality to conform with the ideals of their "superiors." We find an example of this in the attitudes of Anglo-Americans towards the Mexicans living in south Texas during the late 1800s and the early 1900s. According to Carey McWilliams, "To the early American settlers, the Mexicans were lazy, shiftless, jealous, cowardly, bigoted, superstitious, backward, and immoral." It is important to note that, as pointed out by McWilliams, the inferior status of the Mexicans made it easier for the American settlers to accept the practice of killing Mexicans with impunity and without due process of law.

Other examples of the oppression of cultures, and of the forced imposition of a view of reality on them, can be readily acknowledged: the conquest of Mexico, which involved not only a military conquest, but also the destruction of an indigenous metaphysical and religious worldview; the long and well-documented history of racial subjugation of blacks and Native Americans in the United States; the oppression of women and their categorization as secondary and marginal beings, etc. We can elaborate briefly on one of these cases. The refusal to recognize that women have a status equal to that of men is a phenomenon that is deeply entrenched within our historical and cultural traditions. Aristotle, one of the most influential thinkers in Western intellectual history, thought that "the slave has absolutely no deliberative faculty; the woman has but its authority is imperfect; so has the child, but in this case it is immature." The implication here is that women's rational capacity is not on an equal par with that of men, i.e., that it lacks full legitimacy or authority.

It can be said without fear of exaggeration that understanding the phenomenon of oppression is crucial for an adequate understanding of Western history and civilization. Unfortunately, such an analysis is usually neglected, especially at the metaphysical level. A philosophical approach to the phenomenon of oppression helps us to see its scope as well as its deep roots within our intellectual traditions.

Probably all cultures are, to some degree or another, ethnocentric and even predisposed to believe that others see the world as they do. But what makes the Western European culture distinctive is its excessive emphasis on control and its systematic attempts to prove the alleged inferiority of various oppressed groups. Even though in most of these attempts there may have been no conscious intention to justify oppression, nevertheless the actual impact of several prominent Western theoretical traditions has been to reinforce attitudes which make oppressive behavior toward these groups appear reasonable and justifiable. The [above mentioned] Aristotelian view of women, the early views of some Spanish conquistadores that Indians did not possess souls, and the pseudoscientific attempts throughout history to establish the "natural" inferiority of blacks are all examples of theories which have complemented and sometimes justified the control, subjugation, and/or indoctrination of these groups.

Even today there are widespread misconceptions regarding discrimination and oppression of minority groups. One of the most disturbing experiences I have had [teaching college students] dealt with the dogmatic refusal of white students to recognize that racism exists in American society. There is a commonly held perception that racism and discrimination are problems that were resolved in the 1960s. In fact, some students feel that too much is being done for minorities, i.e., that minorities are getting a "free ride" and that they "have it made." There is resentment that whites are being treated unfairly when minorities are given preferential consideration. What is so ironic about this situation is that most of these white students are almost totally ignorant of the mass of statistical facts that show that economically, socially, and educationally things are worse for minorities, in relation to whites, than they were ten years ago. A larger percentage of black women and children are living in poverty today than a decade ago. Between 1969 and 1979 the expected life-time earnings of black men was about 57 percent that of white men, and in 1984 that percentage had actually decreased to 56 percent. Also, a proportionately lower number of black men are attending college today than ten years ago. The high school drop-out rate is almost fifty percent for Hispanics nationwide and more Hispanics are living in poverty than ever before. A recent study showed that blacks were widely discriminated against when applying for housing loans.

It is an interesting fact that when discussing racism some of those Anglo students who do recognize that racism is a significant factor in society quickly exempt themselves by saying or implying "some Anglos are racist, but not me." Even though there are surely some Anglo students who can truthfully say this about themselves, I suspect that for some others this statement simply represents a refusal to reflect on racist attitudes which they might have. Students usually get very defensive when issues of racism are discussed. Perhaps this is because feelings of resentment or guilt emerge during such discussions. It is unfortunate that most students do not realize that recognizing prejudiced attitudes that one may have is not a sign of weakness or moral deficiency, but is rather a sign of an emerging intellectual and emotional maturity. It is the first step towards dealing with and eliminating such attitudes. By refusing to reflect openly and honestly on their own prejudices students miss an important opportunity to grow and develop as human beings.

The second question I proposed we Americans ask ourselves was, What should be done to alleviate the problems of poverty, oppression, and underdevelopment in Latin America? The conventional answer is also very revealing of the ontocentrism* that is so characteristic of our culture. Secretary of State James Baker recently gave succinct expression to the present administration's solution to these problems. According to Baker, the solution is greater foreign investment and ownership of businesses in Latin America and the lifting of trade restrictions. No mention was made of encouraging economic self-sufficiency, of dismantling the military units that help perpetuate corruption and oppression, of a more equitable distribution of resources, or of the need to respect human rights.

In proposing solutions to the problems of poverty and oppression, Americans ignore the need of Latin Americans to live in a manner that respects their values and traditions: instead, our solutions call for their becoming more like us; i.e., more technocratic, more modern, more socially mobile, etc., even if this entails a weakening of their cultural heritage and values. To be sure, there are some technological advances that all Third World countries would benefit from, especially regarding medical care and education, but Third World nations can enjoy these advances without having to transform their value system into one which prizes materialism, depersonalization, hierarchical rigidity, efficiency, and egocentrism over community relationships, rootedness in history and cultural tradition, economic decentralization and self-sufficiency, and an integrative approach to life. The assumption that people of a different culture can deal with the problems of poverty and economic underdevelopment only by adopting our values and way of life once again betrays the ontocentrism of our conceptual framework.

Just as the philosophical point of view has deepened our understanding of oppression, can it now offer us some insights that can serve as a starting point for resolving the problem of oppression in the Third World and in Latin America? Even though

---

* *Ontocentrism* can be defined as the conviction held by a group that its conception of reality is superior to all others.

philosophical reflection by itself will certainly not resolve this problem, philosophy can nevertheless help us to formulate a useful approach to dealing with this issue. The approach which I want to propose can be called the multi-cultural perspective. According to this perspective, an adequate understanding of reality is one which emerges as the result of an open, mutually liberated dialogue between the participants of different cultural traditions. This multi-cultural context of dialogue and interaction would make possible the recognition and removal of the cultural blinders of each of the participants. Thus, one of the first goals of this dialogue would be for the participants to understand and appreciate the perspectives from which the others perceive reality. The articulation and negotiation of their different needs and concerns would them be based on this prior understanding. None of the perspectives would have an initial or *a priori* privileged status, nor would there be an initial hierarchical differentiation between perspectives or between the elements of the perspectives.

It is important to note that there would be certain normative principles implicit in the adoption of this multi-cultural perspective. The liberated dialogue would in essence be free from ideological distortions; its participants would have an equal access to information (and would have developed the critical understanding necessary for evaluating that information); and there would be a lack of hierarchical controls in the exchange of information, etc. The practical and political implications of these principles are profound and wide-ranging. Consider the second of the conditions just mentioned. If the participants in the dialogue are to have an equal access to as well as a critical understanding of any information that may be relevant for the negotiation of a case at hand, then this implies at least an approximate parity in the educational preparation of the participants, as well as an elimination of economic restrictions that would impose arbitrary limitations on the use of available information. Furthermore, a critical understanding of this information presupposes an absence of sexist, racist, classist, and other ideological factors that may distort its meaning and interpretation. It is important to note that putting these normative principles into practice will take work and effort, and that we should not be discouraged by the realization that these principles will not be implemented simply by adopting the multi-cultural perspective. Attaining educational parity, for example, or developing modes of communication that are free of ideological distortions and biases, will take strong efforts to achieve.

The satisfaction of these conditions for liberated dialogue implies the elimination of substantial differences in the economic and educational status of the participants. In the multi-cultural perspective the connection between the socioeconomic position of the participants of a political community and their capacity to participate meaningfully in the decision making process of that community are emphasized. This perspective thus avoids the naive viewpoint of classical liberal political theory that severs the connection between political and economic power and the capacity to equally exercise one's civil rights in a real political setting.

Finally, I want to clarify the multi-cultural perspective by saying what it is not. It is not a relativistic or perspectival approach according to which all cultural perspectives are "equally valid." It is entirely possible that the participants in the open liberated dialogue may determine that certain cultural practices are oppressive or unethical (traditional views of women are a case in point). Thus we do not naively idealize or romanticize other cultures. This perspective does not tell us ahead of time which practices of what culture are oppressive or not. Instead, what it does is to give us a methodology by which the identification of such practices is to be achieved. Also, the multi-cultural perspective is not a Marxist perspective, because, although it recognizes the important role of economic factors in oppression, it leaves it as an open question whether it is in the best interests of the members of a community (either local, national, or international) to adopt a capitalist, socialist, communist, or mixed economic system. It is certainly logically possible that one or another of these systems may be more effective and desirable to different communities at different points in time.

It is unlikely that we will be able to deal adequately with the issues of poverty and oppression in the Third World until we recognize the philosophical assumptions which shape the way in which we understand these issues. In our dealings with the Third World and in our own domestic policies we should have the moral courage to strive for economic and social justice, for this is the ethically correct thing to do. But in addition to this compelling moral reason, we have strong practical reasons to do so. We can no longer afford not to. The facts that the population of the U.S. is becoming increasingly multi-cultural and that we live in an increasingly interdependent world make it necessary for us to adopt the multi-cultural perspective in order to function effectively, at a political and economic level, in the future. We must reevaluate the philosophy of egoism and ontocentrism which is so central to our conceptual orientations. And, most importantly, we must realize that refusing to deal with oppression involves an alienation from our own humanity and compassion. The struggle with the problem of oppression is not to be taken lightly, for ultimately the battle is to reclaim our own souls.

ELIZABETH V. SPELMAN

The Erasure of Black Women

ELIZABETH V. SPELMAN teaches philosophy at Smith College and has written extensively on issues of feminist theory. Her book *Inessential Woman: Problems of Exclusion in Feminist Thought* was published in 1988.

Recent feminist theory has not totally ignored white racism, though white feminists have paid much less attention to it than have black feminists. Nor have white feminists explicitly enunciated and espoused positions of white superiority. Yet much of feminist theory has reflected and contributed to what Adrienne Rich has called "white solipsism":

> to think, imagine, and speak as if whiteness described the world.
>
> not the consciously held belief that one race is inherently superior to all others, but a tunnel-vision which simply does not see nonwhite experience or existence as precious or significant, unless in spasmodic, impotent guilt-reflexes, which have little or no long-term, continuing momentum or political usefulness.

In this essay, I shall focus on what I take to be instances and sustaining sources of such solipsism in recent theoretical works by, or of interest to, feminists—in particular, certain ways of comparing sexism and racism, and some well-ingrained habits of thought about the source of women's oppression and the possibility of our liberation. . . . To begin, I will examine some recent prominent claims to the effect that sexism is more fundamental than racism. . . . Before turning to the evidence that has been given in behalf of that claim, we need to ask what it means to say that sexism is more fundamental than racism. It has meant or might mean several different though related things:

- It is harder to eradicate sexism than it is to eradicate racism.
- There might be sexism without racism but not racism without sexism: any social and political changes which eradicate sexism will have eradicated racism, but social and political changes which eradicate racism will not have eradicated sexism.
- Sexism is the first form of oppression learned by children.
- Sexism is historically prior to racism.
- Sexism is the cause of racism.
- Sexism is used to justify racism.

In the process of comparing racism and sexism, Richard Wasserstrom describes ways in which women and blacks have been stereotypically conceived of as less fully developed than white men. "Men and women are taught to see men as independent, capable, and powerful; men and women are taught to see women as dependent, limited in abilities, and passive. . . ." But who is taught to see black men as "independent, capable, and powerful," and by whom are they taught? Are black men taught that? Black women? White men? White women? Similarly, who is taught to see black women as "dependent, limited in abilities, and passive"? If this stereotype is so prevalent, why then have black women had to defend themselves against the images of matriarch and whore?

Wasserstrom continues:

> As is true for race, it is also a significant social fact that to be a female is to be an entity or creature viewed as different from the standard, fully developed person who is male as well as white. *But to be female, as opposed to being black,* is not to be conceived of as simply a creature of less worth. That is one important thing that differentiates sexism from racism; the ideology of sex, as opposed to the ideology of race, is a good deal more complex and confusing. *Women are both put on a pedestal* and deemed not fully developed persons. (emphasis mine)

In this brief for the view that sexism is a "deeper phenomenon" than racism, Wasserstrom leaves no room for the black woman. For a black woman cannot be "female, as opposed to being black"; she is female *and* black. Since Wasserstrom's argument proceeds from the assumption that one is either female or black, it cannot be an argument that applies to black women. Moreover, we cannot generate a composite image of the black women from the above, since the description of women as being put on a pedestal, or being dependent, never generally applied to black women in the United States and was never meant to apply to them.

Wasserstrom's argument about the priority of sexism over racism has an odd result, which stems from the erasure of black women in his analysis. He wishes to claim that in this society sex is a more fundamental fact about people than race. Yet his description of woman does not apply to the black woman, which implies that being black is a more fundamental fact about her than being a woman. I am not saying that Wasserstrom actually believes this is true, but that paradoxically the terms of his theory force him into that position. . . .

ADDITIVE ANALYSES

Sexism and racism do not have different "objects" in the case of black women. Moreover, it is highly misleading to say, without further explanation, that black women experience sexism and racism. For to say *merely* that suggests that black women experience one form of oppression, *as blacks*—the same thing black men experience—and that they experience another form of oppression, *as women*—the same thing white women experience. But this way of describing and analyzing black women's experience seems to me to be inadequate. For while it is true that images and institutions that are described as sexist affect both black and white women, they are affected in different ways, depending upon the extent to which they are affected by other forms of oppression.

For example. . . . it will not do to say that women are oppressed by the image of the "feminine" woman as fair, delicate, and in need of support and protection by men. While all women are oppressed by the use of that image, we are not oppressed in the same ways. As Linda Brent puts it so succinctly, "That which commands admiration in the white woman only hastens the degradation of the female slave." More specifically, as Angela Davis reminds us, "the alleged benefits of the ideology of femininity did not accrue" to the black female slave—she was expected to toil in the fields for just as long and hard as the black male was.

Reflection on the experience of black women also shows that it is not as if one form of oppression is merely piled upon another. As Barbara Smith has remarked, the effect of multiple oppression "is not merely arithmetic." Such an "additive" analysis informs, for example, Gerda Lerner's remark about the nature of the oppression of black women under slavery: "Their work and duties were the same as that of the men, while childbearing and rearing fell upon them as an added burden." But, as Angela Davis has pointed out, the mother/housewife role (even the words seem inappropriate) doesn't have the same *meaning* for women who experience racism as it does for those who are not so oppressed:

> . . . In the infinite anguish of ministering to the needs of the men and children around her (who were not necessarily members of her immediate family), she was performing the *only* labor of the slave community which could not be directly and immediately claimed by the oppressor. . . . Even as she was suffering from her unique oppression as female, she was thrust by the force of circumstances into the center of the slave community.

The meaning and the oppressive nature of the "housewife" role has to be understood in relation to the roles against which it is contrasted. The work of mate/mother/nurturer has a different meaning depending on whether it is contrasted to work which has high social value and ensures economic independence, or to labor which is forced, degrading and unpaid. All of these factors are left out in a simple additive analysis. How one form of oppression (e.g., sexism) is experienced, is influenced by and influences how another form (i.e., racism) is experienced. So it would be quite misleading to say simply that black women and white women both are oppressed *as women*, and that a black women's oppression as a black is thus separable from her oppression as a woman because she shares the latter but not the former with the white woman. An additive analysis treats the oppression of a black woman in a sexist and racist society as if it were a *further* burden than her oppression in a sexist but non-racist society, when, in fact, it is a *different* burden. As the article by Davis, among others, shows, to ignore the difference is to deny or obscure the particular reality of the black woman's experience.

If sexism and racism must be seen as interlocking, and not as piled upon each other, serious problems arise for the claim that one of them is more fundamental than the other. As we saw, one meaning of the claim that sexism is more fundamental than racism is that sexism causes racism: racism would not exist if sexism did not, while sexism could and would continue to exist even in the absence of racism. In this connection, racism is sometimes seen as something which is both derivative from sexism and in the service of it: racism keeps women from uniting in alliance against sexism. This view has been articulated by Mary Daly in *Beyond God the Father*. According to Daly, sexism is "root and paradigm" of other forms of oppression such as racism. Racism is a "deformity *within* patriarchy. . . . It is most unlikely that racism will be eradicated as long as sexism prevails."

Daly's theory relies on an additive analysis, and we can see again why such an analysis fails to describe adequately black women's experience. Daly's analysis makes it look simply as if both black and white women experience sexism, while black women also experience racism. Black women should realize, Daly says, that they must see what they have in common with white women—shared sexist oppression—and see that black and white women are "pawns in the racial struggle, which is basically not the struggle that will set them free as *women*." The additive analysis obscures the differences between black and white women's struggles. Insofar as she is oppressed by racism in a sexist context and sexism in a racist context, the black woman's struggle cannot be compartmentalized into two struggles—one *as a black* and one *as a woman*. But that way of speaking about her struggle is required by a theory which insists not only that sexism and racism are distinct but that one might be eradicated before the other. Daly rightly points out that the black woman's struggle can easily be, and has usually been, subordinated to the black man's struggle in anti-racist organizations. But she does not point out that the black woman's struggle can easily be, and usually has been, subordinated to the white woman's struggle in anti-sexist organizations.

Daly's line of thought also promotes the idea that, were it not for racism, there would be no important differences between black and white women. Since sexism is the fundamental form of oppression, and racism works in its service, the only significant differences between black and white women are differences which men have created and which are the source of antagonism between women. What is really crucial about us is our sex; racial distinctions are one of the many products of sexism, of patriarchy's attempt to keep women from uniting. It is through our shared sexual identity that we are oppressed together; it is through our shared sexual identity that we shall be liberated together.

A serious problem in thinking or speaking this way, however, is that it seems to deny or ignore the positive aspects of "racial" identities. It ignores the fact that being black is a source of pride, as well as an occasion for being oppressed. It suggests that once racism is eliminated (!), black women no longer need be concerned about or interested in their blackness—as if the only reason for paying attention to one's blackness is that it is the source of pain and sorrow and agony. But that is racism pure and simple, if it assumes that there is nothing positive about having a black history and identity. . . .

RACISM AND SOMATOPHOBIA

Feminist theorists as politically diverse as Simone de Beauvoir, Betty Friedan and Shulamith Firestone have described the conditions of women's liberation in terms which suggest that the identification of woman with her body has been the source of our oppression, and that, hence, the source of our liberation lies in sundering that connection. For example, de Beauvoir introduces *The Second Sex* with the comment that woman has been regarded as "womb"; woman is thought of as planted firmly in the world of "immanence," that is, the physical world of nature, her life defined by the dictates of her "biologic fate." In contrast, men live in the world of "transcendence," actively using their minds, to create "values, mores, religions," the world of culture as opposed to the world of nature. Among Friedan's central messages is that women should be allowed and encouraged to be "culturally" as well as "biologically" creative, because the former activities, which are "mental," are of "highest value to society" in comparison to childbearing and rearing—"mastering the secrets of atoms, or the stars, composing symphonies, pioneering a new concept in government or society." . . .

I bring up the presence of somatophobia in the work of Firestone and others because I think it is a force that contributes to white solipsism in feminist thought, in at least three related ways.

First, insofar as feminists do not examine somatophobia, but actually accept it and embrace it in prescriptions for women's liberation, we will not be examining what often has been an important element in racist thinking. For the superiority of men to women is not the only hierarchical relationship that has been linked to the superiority of the mind to the body. Certain kinds, or "races," of people have been held to be more body-like than others, and this has been meant as more animal-like and less god-like.

For example, in *The White Man's Burden*, Winthrop Jordan describes ways in which white Englishmen portrayed black Africans as beastly, dirty, highly sexed beings. Lillian Smith tells us in *Killers of the Dream* how closely run together were her lessons about the evil of the body and the evil of blacks.

Derogatory stereotypes of blacks versus whites (as well as of manual workers versus intellectuals) have been very similar to the derogatory stereotypes of women versus men. Indeed, the grounds on which Plato ridiculed women were so similar to those on which he ridiculed slaves, beasts and children that he typically ridiculed them in one breath. He also thought it sufficient ridicule of one such group to accuse it of being like another (women are like slaves, slaves are like children, etc.). Aristotle's defense of his claim about the inferiority of women to men in the *Politics* is almost the same as his defense of the view that some people are meant to be slaves (Aristotle did not identify what he called the natural class of slaves by skin color, but he says that identifying that class would be much easier if there were readily available physical characteristics by which one could do that.) Neither in women nor in slaves does the rational element work the way it ought to. Hence women and slaves are, though in different ways, to attend to the physical needs of the men/masters/intellectuals. . . .

So we need to examine and understand somatophobia and look for it in our own thinking, for the idea that the work of the body and for the body has no part in real human dignity has been part of racist as well as sexist ideology. That is, oppressive stereotypes of "inferior races" and of women have typically involved images of their lives as determined by basic bodily functions (sex, reproduction, appetite, secretions and excretions) and as given over to attending to the bodily functions of others (feeding, washing, cleaning, doing the "dirty work"). Superior groups, we have been told from Plato on down, have better things to do with their lives. As Hannah Arendt has pointed out, the position of women and slaves has been directly tied to the notion that their lives are to be devoted to taking care of bodily functions. It certainly does not follow from the presence of somatophobia in a person's writings that she or he is a racist or a sexist. But somatophobia historically has been symptomatic of sexist and racist (as well as classist) attitudes.

Human groups know that the work of the body and for the body is necessary for human existence, and they make provisions for that fact. And so even when a group views its liberation in terms of being free of association with, or responsibility for, bodily tasks, explicitly or implicitly, its own liberation may be predicated on the oppression of other groups—those assigned to do the body work. For example, if feminists decide that women are not going to be relegated to doing such work, who do we think is going to do it? Have we attended to the role that racism (and classism) historically has played in settling that question?

Finally, if one thinks—as de Beauvoir, Friedan and Firestone do—that the liberation of women requires abstracting the notion of woman from the notion of woman's body, then one perhaps also will think that the liberation of blacks requires abstracting the notion of a black person from the notion of a black body. Since the body is thought to be the culprit (or anyway certain aspects of the body are thought to be the culprits), the solution may seem to be: keep the person and leave the occasion for oppression behind. Keep the woman, somehow, but leave behind her woman's body; keep the black person but leave the blackness behind. . . .

Once the concept of woman is divorced from the concept of woman's body, conceptual room is made for the idea of a woman who is no particular historical woman—she has no color, no accent, no particular characteristics that require having a body. She is somehow all and only woman; that is her only identifying feature. And so it will seem inappropriate or beside the point to think of women in terms of any physical characteristics, especially if it has been in the name of such characteristics that oppression has been rationalized. . . .

RICH ON EMBODIMENT

Adrienne Rich is perhaps the only well-known white feminist to have noted "white solipsism" in feminist theorizing and activity. I think it is no coincidence that she also noticed and attended to the strong strain of somatophobia in feminist theory. . . .

Both de Beauvoir and Firestone wanted to break it by insisting that women need be no more connected—in thought or deed—with the body than men have been. De Beauvoir and Firestone more or less are in agreement, with the patriarchal cultural history they otherwise question, that embodiment is a drag. Rich, however, insists that the negative connection between woman and body be broken along other lines. She asks us to think about whether what she calls "flesh-loathing" is the only attitude it is possible to have toward our bodies. Just as she explicitly distinguishes between motherhood as experience and motherhood as institution, so she implicitly asks us to distinguish between embodiment as experience and embodiment as institution. Flesh-loathing is part of the well-entrenched beliefs, habits and practices epitomized in the treatment of pregnancy as a disease. But we need not experience our flesh, our body, as loathsome. . . .

I think it is not a psychological or historical accident that having reflected so thoroughly on flesh-loathing, Rich focused on the failure of white women to see black women's experiences as different from their own. For looking at embodiment is one way (though not the only one) of coming to note and understand the *particularity* of experience. Without bodies we could not have personal histories, for without them we would not live at a particular time nor in a particular place. Moreover, without them we could not be identified as woman or man, black or white. This is not to say that reference to publicly observable bodily characteristics settles the question of whether someone is woman or man, black or white; nor is it to say that being woman or man, black or white, just means having certain bodily characteristics. But different meanings are attached to having those characteristics, in different places and at different times and by different people, and those differences make a huge difference in the kinds of lives we lead or experiences we have. Women's oppression has been linked to the meanings assigned to having a woman's body by male oppressors. Blacks' oppression has been linked to the meanings assigned to having a black body by white oppressors. We cannot hope to understand the meaning of a person's experiences, including her experiences of oppression, without first thinking of her as embodied, and second thinking about the particular meanings assigned to that embodiment. If, because of somatophobia, we think and write as if we are not embodied, or as if we would be better off if we were not embodied, we are likely to ignore the ways in which different forms of embodiment are correlated with different kinds of experience. . . .

Rich does not run away from the fact that women have bodies, nor does she wish that women's bodies were not so different from men's. That healthy regard for the ground of our differences from men is logically connected—though of course does not ensure— to a healthy regard for the ground of the differences between black women and white women.

RALPH ELLISON

The Invisible Man

RALPH ELLISON (1914–1994), originally from Oklahoma, taught at the University of Chicago and New York University. He is the author of *The Invisible Man* (1952), which won the National Book Award.

I am an invisible man. No, I am not a spook like those who haunted Edgar Allan Poe; nor am I one of your Hollywood-movie ectoplasms. I am a man of substance, of flesh and bone, fiber and liquids—and I might even be said to possess a mind. I am invisible, understand, simply because people refuse to see me. Like the bodiless heads you see sometimes in circus sideshows, it is as though I have been surrounded by mirrors of hard, distorting glass. When they approach me they see only my surroundings, themselves, or figments of their imagination—indeed, everything and anything except me.

Nor is my invisibility exactly a matter of a biochemical accident to my epidermis. That invisibility to which I refer occurs because of a peculiar disposition of the eyes of those with whom I come in contact. A matter of the construction of their *inner* eyes, those eyes with which they look through their physical eyes upon reality. I am not complaining, nor am I protesting either. It is sometimes advantageous to be unseen, although it is most often rather wearing on the nerves. Then too, you're constantly being bumped against by those of poor vision. Or again, you often doubt if you really exist. You wonder whether you aren't simply a phantom in other people's minds. Say, a figure in a nightmare which the sleeper tries with all his strength to destroy. It's when you feel like this that, out of resentment, you begin to bump people back. And, let me confess, you feel that way most of the time. You ache with the need to convince yourself that you do exist in the real world, that you're a part of all the sound and anguish, and you strike out with your fists, you curse and you swear to make them recognize you. And, alas, it's seldom successful.

One night I accidentally bumped into a man, and perhaps because of the near darkness he saw me and called me an insulting name. I sprang at him, seized his coat lapels and demanded that he apologize. He was a tall blond man, and as my face came close to his he looked insolently out of his blue eyes and cursed me, his breath hot in my face as he struggled. I pulled his chin down sharp upon the crown of my head, butting him as I had seen the West Indians do, and I felt his flesh tear and blood gush out, and I yelled, "Apologize! Apologize!" But he continued to curse and struggle, and I butted him again and again until he went down heavily, on his knees, profusely bleeding. I kicked him repeatedly, in a frenzy because he still uttered insults though his lips were frothy with blood. Oh, yes, I kicked him! And in my outrage I got out my knife and prepared to slit his throat, right there beneath the lamplight in the deserted street, holding him in the collar with one hand, and opening the knife with my teeth—when it occurred to me that the man had not *seen* me, actually; that he, as far as he knew, was in the midst of a walking nightmare! And I stopped the blade, slicing the air as I pushed him away, letting him fall back to the street. I stared at him hard as the lights of a car stabbed through the darkness. He lay there, moaning on the asphalt: a man almost killed by a phantom. It unnerved me. I was both disgusted and ashamed. I was like a drunken man myself, wavering about on weakened legs. Then I was amused: Something in this man's thick head had sprung out and beaten him with an inch of his life. I began to laugh at this crazy discovery. Would he have awakened at the point of death? Would Death himself have freed him for wakeful living? But I didn't linger. I ran away into the dark, laughing so hard I feared I might rupture myself. The next day I saw his picture in the *Daily News*, beneath a caption stating that he had been "mugged." Poor fool, poor blind fool, I thought with sincere compassion, mugged by an invisible man!

Most of the time (although I do not choose as I once did to deny the violence of my days by ignoring it) I am not so overtly violent. I remember that I am invisible and walk softly so as not to awaken the sleeping ones. Sometimes it is best not to awaken them: there are few things in the world as dangerous as sleepwalkers. I learned in time though that it is possible to carry on a fight against them without their realizing it. For instance, I have been carrying on a fight with Monopolated Light & Power for some time now. I use their service and pay them nothing at all, and they don't know it. Oh, they suspect that power is being drained off, but they don't know where. All they know is that according to the master meter back there in their power station a hell of a lot of free current is disappearing somewhere into the jungle of Harlem. The joke, of course, is that I don't live in Harlem but in a border area. Several years ago (before I discovered the advantages of being invisible) I went through the routine process of buying service and paying their outrageous rates. But no more. I gave up all that, along with my apartment, and my old way of life: That way based upon the fallacious assumption that I, like other men, was visible. Now, aware of my invisibility, I live rent-free in a building rented strictly to whites, in a section of the basement that was shut off and forgotten during the nineteenth century. . . .

The point now is that I found a home—or a hole in the ground, as you will. Now don't jump to the conclusion that because I call my home a "hole" it is damp and cold like a grave; there are cold holes and warm holes. Mine is a warm hole. And remember, a bear retires to his hole for the winter and lives until spring; then he comes strolling out like the Easter chick breaking from its shell. I say all this to assure that it is incorrect to assume that, because I'm invisible and live in a hole, I am dead. I am neither dead nor in a state of suspended animation. Call me Jack-the-Bear, for I am in a state of hibernation.

My hole is warm and full of light. Yes, *full* of light. I doubt if there is a brighter spot in all New York than this hole of mine, and I do not exclude Broadway. Or the Empire State Building on a photographer's dream night. But that is taking advantage of you. Those two spots are among the darkest of our whole civilization—pardon me, our whole *culture* (an important distinction, I've heard)—which might sound like a hoax, or a contradiction, but that (by contradiction, I mean) is how the world moves: Not like an arrow, but a boomerang. (Beware of those who speak of the *spiral* of history; they are preparing a boomerang. Keep a steel helmet handy.) I know; I have been boomeranged across my head so much that I now can see the darkness of lightness. And I love light. Perhaps you'll think it strange that an invisible man should need light, desire light, love light. But maybe it is exactly because I *am* invisible. Light confirms my reality, gives birth to my form. A beautiful girl once told me of a recurring nightmare in which she lay in the center of a large dark room and felt her face expand until it filled the whole room, becoming a formless mass while her eyes ran in bilious jelly up the chimney. And so it is with me. Without light I am not only invisible, but formless as well; and to be unaware of one's form is to live a death. I myself, after existing some twenty years, did not become alive until I discovered my invisibility.

That is why I fight my battle with Monopolated Light & Power. The deeper reason, I mean: It allows me to feel my vital aliveness. I also fight them for taking so much of my money before I learned to protect myself. In my hole in the basement there are exactly 1,369 lights. I've wired the entire ceiling, every inch of it. And not with fluorescent bulbs, but with the older, more-expensive-to-operate kind, the filament type. An act of sabotage, you know. I've already begun to wire the wall. A junk man I know, a man of vision, has supplied me with wire and sockets. Nothing, storm or flood, must get in the way of our need for light and ever more and brighter light. The truth is the light and light is the truth. When I finish all four walls, then I'll start on the floor. Just how that will go, I don't know. Yet when you have lived invisible as long as I have you develop a certain ingenuity. I'll solve the problem. And maybe I'll invent a gadget to place my coffee pot on the fire while I lie in bed, and even invent a gadget to warm my bed—like the fellow I saw in one of the picture magazines who made himself a gadget to warm his shoes! Though invisible, I am in the great American tradition of tinkers. That makes me kin to Ford, Edison and Franklin. Call me, since I have a theory and a concept, a "thinker-tinker." Yes, I'll warm my shoes; they need it, they're usually full of holes. I'll do that and more. . . .

Please, a definition: A hibernation is a covert preparation for a more overt action. . . .

Meanwhile I enjoy my life with the compliments of Monopolated Light & Power. Since you never recognize me even when in closest contact with me, and since, no doubt, you'll hardly believe that I exist, it won't matter if you know that I tapped a power line leading into the building and ran it into my hole in the ground. Before that I lived in the darkness into which I was chased, but now I see. I've illuminated the blackness of my invisibility—and vice versa. And so I play the invisible music of my isolation. The last statement doesn't seem just right, does it? But it is; you hear this music simply because music is heard and seldom seen, except by musicians. Could this compulsion to put invisibility down in black and white be thus an urge to make music of invisibility? But I am an orator, a rabble rouser—Am? I *was*, and perhaps shall be again. Who knows? All sickness is not unto death, neither is invisibility.

I can hear you say, "What a horrible, irresponsible bastard!" And you're right. I leap to agree with you. I am one of the most irresponsible beings that ever lived. Irresponsibility is part of my invisibility; any way you face it, it is a denial. But to whom can I be responsible, and why should I be, when you refuse to see me? And wait until I reveal how truly irresponsible I am. Responsibility rests upon recognition, and recognition is a form of agreement. Take the man whom I almost killed: Who was responsible for that near murder—I? I don't think so, and I refuse it. I won't buy it. You can't give it to me. *He* bumped *me, he* insulted *me.* Shouldn't he, for his own personal safety, have recognized my hysteria, my "danger potential"? He, let us say, was lost in a dream world. But didn't *he* control that dream world—which, alas, is only too real!—and didn't *he* rule me out of it? And if he had yelled for a policeman, wouldn't *I* have been taken for the offending one? Yes, yes, yes! Let me agree with you, I was the irresponsible one; for I should have used my knife to protect the higher interests of society. Some day that kind of foolishness will cause us tragic trouble. All dreamers and sleepwalkers must pay the price, and even the invisible victim is responsible for the fate of all. But I shirked that responsibility; I became too snarled in the incompatible notions that buzzed within my brain. I was a coward . . .

Black Women
Shaping Feminist Theory

BELL HOOKS teaches at Yale University. She has published several books on black women and feminism, including *Bone Black: Memories of Girlhood* (1997).

Feminism in the United States has never emerged from the women who are most victimized by sexist oppression; women who are daily beaten down, mentally, physically, and spiritually—women who are powerless to change their condition in life. They are a silent majority. A mark of their victimization is that they accept their lot in life without visible question, without organized protest, without collective anger or rage. Betty Friedan's *The Feminine Mystique* is still heralded as having paved the way for contemporary feminist movement—it was written as if these women did not exist. Friedan's famous phrase, "the problem that has no name," often quoted to describe the condition of women in this society, actually referred to the plight of a select group of college-educated, middle and upper class, married white women—housewives bored with leisure, with the home, with children, with buying products, who wanted more out of life. Friedan concludes her first chapter by stating: "We can no longer ignore that voice within women that says: 'I want something more than my husband and my children and my house.'" That "more" she defined as careers. She did not discuss who would be called in to take care of the children and maintain the home if more women like herself were freed from their house labor and given equal access with white men to the professions. She did not speak of the needs of women without men, without children, without homes. She ignored the existence of all non-white women and poor white women. She did not tell readers whether it was more fulfilling to be a maid, a babysitter, a factory worker, a clerk, or a prostitute, than to be a leisure class housewife.

She made her plight and the plight of white women like herself synonymous with a condition affecting all American women. In so doing, she deflected attention away from her classism, her racism, her sexist attitudes towards the masses of American women. In the context of her book, Friedan makes clear that the women she saw as victimized by sexism were college-educated, white women who were compelled by sexist conditioning to remain in the home. She contends:

> It is urgent to understand how the very condition of being a housewife can create a sense of emptiness, non-existence, nothingness in women. There are aspects of the housewife role that make it almost impossible for a woman of adult intelligence to retain a sense of human identity, the firm core of self or "I" without which a human being, man or woman, is not truly alive. For women of ability, in America today, I am convinced that there is something about the housewife state itself that is dangerous.

Specific problems and dilemmas of leisure class white housewives were real concerns that merited consideration and change but they were not the pressing political concerns of masses of women. Masses of women were concerned about economic survival, ethnic and racial discrimination, etc. When Friedan wrote *The Feminine Mystique*, more than one third of all women were in the work force. Although many women longed to be housewives, only women with leisure time and money could actually shape their identities on the model of the feminine mystique. They were women who, in Friedan's words, were "told by the most advanced thinkers of our time to go back and live their lives as if they were Noras, restricted to the doll's house by Victorian prejudices."

From her early writing, it appears that Friedan never wondered whether or not the plight of college-educated, white housewives was an adequate reference point by which to gauge the impact of sexism or sexist oppression on the lives of women in American society. Nor did she move beyond her own life experience to acquire an expanded perspective on the lives of women in the United States. I say this not to discredit her work. It remains a useful discussion of the impact of sexist discrimination on a select group of women. Examined from a different perspective, it can also be seen as a case study of narcissism, insensitivity, sentimentality, and self-indulgence which reaches its peak when Friedan, in a chapter titled "Progressive Dehumanization," makes a comparison between the psychological effects of isolation on white housewives and the impact of confinement on the self-concept of prisoners in Nazi concentration camps.

Friedan was a principal shaper of contemporary feminist thought. Significantly, the one-dimensional perspective on women's reality presented in her book became a marked feature of the contemporary feminist movement. Like Friedan before them, white women who dominate feminist discourse today rarely question whether or not their perspective on women's reality is true to the lived experiences of women as a collective group. Nor are they aware of the extent to which their perspectives reflect race and class biases, although there has been a greater awareness of biases in recent years. Racism abounds in the writings of white feminists, reinforcing white supremacy and negating the possibility that women will bond politically across ethnic and racial boundaries. Past feminist refusal to draw attention to and attack racial hierarchies suppressed the link between race and class. Yet class structure in American society has been shaped by the racial politic of white supremacy; it is only by analyzing racism and its function in capitalist society that a thorough understanding of class relationships can emerge. Class struggle is inextricably bound to the struggle to end racism. Urging women to explore the full implication of class in an early essay, "The Last Straw," Rita Mae Brown explained:

> Class is much more than Marx's definition of relationship to the means of production. Class involves your behavior, your basic assumptions about life. Your experience (determined by your class) validates those assumptions, how you are taught to behave, what you expect from yourself and from others, your concept of a future, how you understand problems and solve them, how you think, feel, act. It is these behavioral patterns that middle class women resist recognizing although they may be perfectly willing to accept class in Marxist terms, a neat trick that helps them avoid really dealing with class behavior and changing that behavior in themselves. It is these behavioral patterns which must be recognized, understood, and changed.

White women who dominate feminist discourse, who for the most part make and articulate feminist theory, have little or no understanding of white supremacy as a racial politic, of the psychological impact of class, of their political status within a racist, sexist, capitalist state.

• • •

A central tenet of modern feminist thought has been the assertion that "all women are oppressed." This assertion implies that women share a common lot, that factors like class, race, religion, sexual preference, etc. do not create a diversity of experience that determines the extent to which sexism will be an oppressive force in the lives of individual women. Sexism as a system of domination is institutionalized but it has never determined in an absolute way the fate of all women in this society. Being oppressed means the *absence of choices*. It is the primary point of contact between the oppressed and the oppressor. Many women in this society do have choices (as inadequate as they are), therefore exploitation and discrimination are words that more accurately describe the lot of women collectively in the United States. Many women do not join organized resistance against sexism precisely because sexism has not meant an absolute lack of choices. They may know they are discriminated against on the basis of sex, but they do not equate this with oppression. Under capitalism, patriarchy is structured so that sexism restricts women's behavior in some realms even as freedom from limitations is allowed in other spheres. The absence of extreme restrictions leads many women to ignore the areas in which they are exploited or discriminated against; it may even lead them to imagine that no women are oppressed.

There are oppressed women in the United States, and it is both appropriate and necessary that we speak against such oppression. French feminist Christine Delphy makes the point in her essay, "For a Materialist Feminism," that the use of the term oppression is important because it places feminist struggle in a radical political framework:

> The rebirth of feminism coincided with the use of the term "oppression." The ruling ideology, i.e. common sense, daily speech, does not speak about oppression but about a "feminine condition." It refers back to a naturalist explanation; to a constraint of nature, exterior reality out of reach and not modifiable by human action. The term "oppression," on the contrary, refers back to a choice, an explanation, a situation that is political. "Oppression" and "social oppression" are therefore synonyms or rather social oppression is a redundance: the notion of a political origin, i.e. social, is an integral part of the concept of oppression.

However, feminist emphasis on "common oppression" in the United States was less a strategy for politicization than an appropriation by conservative and liberal women of a radical political vocabulary that masked the extent to which they shaped the movement so that it addressed and promoted their class interests.

Although the impulse towards unity and empathy that informed the notion of common oppression was directed at building solidarity, slogans like "organize around your own oppression" provided the excuse many privileged women needed to ignore the differences between their social status and the status of masses of women. It was a mark of race and class privilege, as well as the expression of freedom from the many constraints sexism places on working class women, that middle class white women were able to make their interests the primary focus of feminist movement and employ a rhetoric of commonality that made their condition synonymous with "oppression." Who was there to demand a change in vocabulary? What other group of women in the United States had the same access to universities, publishing houses, mass media, money? Had middle class black women begun a movement in which they had labeled themselves "oppressed," no one would have taken them seriously. Had they established public forums and given speeches about their "oppression," they would have been criticized and attacked from all sides. This was not the case with white bourgeois feminists for they could appeal to a large audience of women, like themselves, who were eager to change their lot in life. Their isolation from women of other class and race groups provided no immediate comparative base by which to test their assumptions of common oppression.

• • •

The ideology of "competitive, atomistic liberal individualism" has permeated feminist thought to such an extent that it undermines the potential radicalism of feminist struggle. The usurpation of feminism by bourgeois women to support their class interests has been to a very grave extent justified by feminist theory as it has so far been conceived. (For example, the ideology of "common oppression.") Any movement to resist the cooptation of feminist struggle must begin by introducing a different feminist perspective—a new theory—one that is not informed by the ideology of liberal individualism.

The exclusionary practices of women who dominate feminist discourse have made it practically impossible for new and varied theories to emerge. Feminism has its party line and women who feel a need for a different strategy, a different foundation, often find themselves ostracized and silenced. Criticisms of or alternatives to established feminist ideas are not encouraged, e.g. recent controversies about expanding feminist discussions of sexuality. Yet groups of women who feel excluded from feminist discourse and praxis can make a place for themselves only if they first create, via critiques, an awareness of the factors that alienate them. Many individual white women found in the women's movement a liberatory solution to personal dilemmas. Having directly benefited from the movement, they are less inclined to criticize it or to engage in rigorous examination of its structure than those who feel it has not had a revolutionary impact on their lives or the lives of masses of women in our society. Nonwhite women who feel affirmed within the current structure of feminist movement (even though they may form autonomous groups) seem to also feel that their definitions of the party line, whether on the issue of black feminism or on other issues, is the only legitimate discourse. . . .

• • •

We resist hegemonic dominance of feminist thought by insisting that it is a theory in the making, that we must necessarily criticize, question, re-examine, and explore new possibilities. My persistent critique has been informed by my status as a member of an oppressed group, experience of sexist exploitation and discrimination, and the sense that prevailing feminist analysis has not been the force shaping my feminist consciousness. This is true for many women. There are white women who had never considered resisting male dominance until the feminist movement created an awareness that they could and should. My awareness of feminist struggle was stimulated by social circumstance. Growing up in a Southern, black, father-dominated, working class household, I experienced (as did my mother, my sisters, and my brother) varying degrees of patriarchal tyranny and it made me angry—it made us all angry. Anger led me to question the politics of male dominance and enabled me to resist sexist socialization. Frequently, white feminists act as if black women did not know sexist oppression existed until they voiced feminist sentiment. They believe they are providing black women with "the" analysis and "the" program for liberation. They do not understand, cannot even imagine, that black women, as well as other groups of women who live daily in oppressive situations, often acquire an awareness of patriarchal politics from their lived experience just as they develop strategies of resistance (even though they may not resist on a sustained or organized basis).

These black women observed white feminist focus on male tyranny and women's oppression as if it were a "new" revelation and felt such a focus had little impact on their lives. To them it was just another indication of the privileged living conditions of middle and upper class white women that they would need a theory to inform them that they were "oppressed." The implication being that people who are truly oppressed know it even though they may not be engaged in organized resistance or are unable to articulate in written form the nature of their oppression. These black women saw nothing liberatory in party line analysis of women's oppression. Neither the fact that black women have not organized collectively in huge numbers around the issues of "feminism" (many of us do not know or use the term) nor the fact that we have not had access to the machinery of power that would allow us to share our analyses or theories about gender with the American public negate its presence in our lives or place us in a position of dependency in relationship to those white and non-white feminists who address a larger audience.

The understanding I had by age thirteen of patriarchal politics created in me expectations of the feminist movement that were quite different from those of young, middle class, white women. When I entered my first women's studies class at Stanford University in the early 1970s, white women were revelling in the joy of being together—to them it was an important, momentous occasion. I had not known a life where women had not been together, where women had not helped, protected, and loved one another deeply. I had not known white women who were ignorant of the impact of race and class on their social status and consciousness. (Southern white women often have a more realistic perspective on racism and classism than white women in other areas of the United States.) I did not feel sympathetic to white peers who maintained that I could not expect them to have knowledge of or understand the life experiences of black women. Despite my background (living in racially segregated communities) I knew about the lives of white women, and certainly no white women lived in our neighborhood, attended our schools, or worked in our homes.

When I participated in feminist groups, I found that white women adopted a condescending attitude towards me and other non-white participants. The condescension they directed at black women was one of the means they employed to remind us that the women's movement was "theirs"—that we were able to participate because they allowed it, even encouraged it; after all, we were needed to legitimate the process. They did not see us as equals. They did not treat us as equals. And though they expected us to provide first hand accounts of black experience, they felt it was their role to decide if these experiences were authentic. Frequently, college-educated black women (even those from poor and working class backgrounds) were dismissed as mere imitators. Our presence in movement activities did not count, as white women were convinced that "real" blackness meant speaking the patois of poor black people, being uneducated, streetwise, and a variety of other stereotypes. If we dared to criticize the movement or to assume responsibility for reshaping feminist ideas and introducing new ideas, our voices were tuned out, dismissed, silenced. We could be heard only if our statements echoed the sentiments of the dominant discourse.

Attempts by white feminists to silence black women are rarely written about. All too often they have taken place in conference rooms, classrooms, or the privacy of cozy living room settings, where one lone black woman faces the racist hostility of a group of white women. From the time the women's liberation movement began, individual black women went to groups. Many never returned after a first meeting. Anita Cornwall is correct in "Three for the Price of One: Notes from a Gay Black Feminist," when she states, ". . . sadly enough, fear of encountering racism seems to be one of the main reasons that so many black women refuse to join the women's movement." Recent focus on the issue of racism has generated discourse but has had little impact on the behavior of white feminists towards black women. Often the white women who are busy publishing papers and books on "unlearning racism" remain patronizing and condescending when they relate to black women. This is not surprising given that frequently their discourse is aimed solely in the direction of a white audience and the focus solely on changing attitudes rather than addressing racism in a historical and political context. They make us the "objects" of their privileged discourse on race. As "objects," we remain unequals, inferiors. Even though they may be sincerely concerned about racism, their methodology suggests they are not yet free of the type of paternalism endemic to white supremacist ideology. Some of these women place themselves in the position of "authorities" who must mediate communication between racist white women (naturally they see themselves as having come to terms with their racism) and angry black women whom they believe are incapable of rational discourse. Of course, the system of racism, classism, and educational elitism remain intact if they are to maintain their authoritative positions.

•   •   •

Racist stereotypes of the strong, superhuman black woman are operative myths in the minds of many white women, allowing them to ignore the extent to which black women are likely to be victimized in this society and the role white women may play in the maintenance and perpetuation of that victimization. In Lillian Hellman's autobiographical work *Pentimento*, she writes, "All my life, beginning at birth, I have taken orders from black women, wanting them and resenting them, being superstitious the few times I disobeyed." The black women Hellman describes worked in her household as family servants and their status was never that of an equal. Even as a child, she was always in the dominant position as they questioned, advised, or guided her; they were free to exercise these rights because she or another white authority figure allowed it. Hellman places power in the hands of these black women rather than acknowledge her own power over them; hence she mystifies the true nature of their relationship. By projecting onto black women a mythical power and strength, white women both promote a false image of themselves as powerless, passive victims and deflect attention away from their aggressiveness, their power, (however limited in a white supremacist, male-dominated state) their willingness to dominate and control others. These unacknowledged aspects of the social status of many white women prevent them from transcending racism and limit the scope of their understanding of women's overall social status in the United States.

Privileged feminists have largely been unable to speak to, with, and for diverse groups of women because they either do not understand fully the inter-relatedness of sex, race, and class oppression or refuse to take this inter-relatedness seriously. Feminist analyses of woman's lot tend to focus exclusively on gender and do not provide a solid foundation on which to construct feminist theory. They reflect the dominant tendency in Western patriarchal minds to mystify women's reality by insisting that gender is the sole determinant of woman's fate. Certainly it has been easier for women who do not experience race or class oppression to focus exclusively on gender. Although socialist feminists focus on class and gender, they tend to dismiss race or they make a point of acknowledging that race is important and then proceed to offer an analysis in which race is not considered.

As a group, black women are in an unusual position in this society, for not only are we collectively at the bottom of the occupational ladder, but our overall social status is lower than that of any other group. Occupying such a position, we bear the brunt of sexist, racist, and classist oppression. At the same time, we are the group that has not been socialized to assume the role of exploiter/oppressor in that we are allowed no institutionalized "other" that we can exploit or oppress. (Children do not represent an institutionalized other even though they may be oppressed by parents.) White women and black men have it both ways. They can act as oppressor or be oppressed. Black men may be victimized by racism, but sexism allows them to act as exploiters and oppressors of women. White women may be victimized by sexism, but racism enables them to act as exploiters and oppressors of black people. Both groups have led liberation movements that favor their interests and support the continued oppression of other groups. Black male sexism has undermined struggles to eradicate racism just as white female racism undermines feminist struggle. As long as these two groups or any group defines liberation as gaining social equality with ruling class white men, they have a vested interest in the continued exploitation and oppression of others.

Black women with no institutionalized "other" that we may discriminate against, exploit, or oppress often have a lived experience that directly challenges the prevailing classist, sexist, racist social structure and its concomitant ideology. This lived experience may shape our consciousness in such a way that our world view differs from those who have a degree of privilege (however relative within the existing system). It is essential for continued feminist struggle that black women recognize the special vantage point our marginality gives us and make use of this perspective to criticize the dominant racist, classist, sexist hegemony as well as to envision and create a counterhegemony. I am suggesting that we have a central role to play in the making of feminist theory and a contribution to offer that is unique and valuable. The formation of a liberatory feminist theory and praxis is a collective responsibility, one that must be shared. Though I criticize aspects of feminist movement as we have known it so far, a critique which is sometimes harsh and unrelenting, I do so not in an attempt to diminish feminist struggle but to enrich, to share in the work of making a liberatory ideology and a liberatory movement.

SHELBY STEELE

The New Sovereignty

SHELBY STEELE teaches history at San Jose State University. He is author of *The Content of Our Character: A New Vision of Race in America* (1990), which was awarded a National Book Critics Circle Award.

In *The True Believer*, Eric Hoffer wrote presciently of this phenomenon I have come to call the New Sovereignty:

> When a mass movement begins to attract people who are interested in their individual careers, it is a sign that it has passed its vigorous stage; that it is no longer engaged in molding a new world but in possessing and preserving the present. It ceases then to be a movement and becomes an enterprise.

If it is true that great mass movements begin as spontaneous eruptions of long-smoldering discontent, it is also true that after significant reform is achieved they do not like to pass away or even modify their grievance posture. The redressing of the movement's grievances wins legitimacy for the movement. Reform, in this way, also means recognition for those who struggled for it. The movement's leaders are quoted in the papers, appear on TV, meet with elected officials, write books—they come to embody the movement. Over time, they and they alone speak for the aggrieved; and, of course, they continue to speak *of* the aggrieved, adding fresh grievances to the original complaint. It is their vocation now, and their means to status and power. The idealistic reformers thus become professional spokespersons for the seemingly permanently aggrieved. In the civil rights movement, suits and briefcases replaced the sharecropper's denim of the early years, and $500-a-plate fund-raisers for the National Association for the Advancement of Colored People replaced volunteers and picket signs. The raucous bra burning of late-Sixties feminism gave way to women's-studies departments and direct-mail campaigns by the National Organization of Women.

This sort of evolution, however natural it may appear, is not without problems for the new grievance-group executive class. The winning of reform will have dissipated much of the explosive urgency that started the movement; yet the new institutionalized movement cannot justify its existence without this urgency. The problem becomes one of maintaining a reformist organization after considerable reforms have been won.

To keep alive the urgency needed to justify itself, the grievance organization will do three things. First, it will work to inspire a perpetual sense of grievance in its constituency so that grievance becomes the very centerpiece of the group itself. To be black, or a woman, or gay, is, in the eyes of the NAACP, NOW, or Act Up, to be essentially threatened, victimized, apart from the rest of America. Second, these organizations will up the ante on what constitutes a grievance by making support of sovereignty itself the new test of grievance. If the women's-studies program has not been made autonomous, this constitutes a grievance. If the National Council of La Raza hasn't been consulted, Hispanics have been ignored. The third strategy of grievance organizations is to arrange

365

their priorities in a way that will maximize their grievance profile. Often their agendas will be established more for their grievance potential than for the actual betterment of the group. Those points at which there is resistance in the larger society to the group's entitlement demands will usually be made into top-priority issues, thereby emphasizing the status of victim and outsider necessary to sustain the sovereign organization.

Thus, at its 1989 convention, the NAACP put affirmative action at the very top of its agenda. Never mind the fact that studies conducted by both proponents and opponents of affirmative action indicate the practice has very little real impact on the employment and advancement of blacks. Never mind, too, that surveys show most black Americans do not consider racial preferences *their* priority. In its wisdom the NAACP thought (and continues to think) that the national mood against affirmative-action programs is a bigger problem for black men and women than teen pregnancy, or the disintegrating black family, or black-on-black crime. Why? Because the very resistance affirmative action meets from the larger society makes it an issue of high grievance potential. Affirmative action can generate the urgency that justifies black sovereignty far more than issues like teen pregnancy or high dropout rates, which carry no load of collective entitlement and which the *entire* society sees as serious problems. . . .

• • •

How did America evolve its now rather formalized notion that groups of its citizens could be entitled collectively? I think it goes back to the most fundamental contradiction in American life. From the beginning America has been a pluralistic society, and one drawn to a radical form of democracy—emphasizing the freedom and equality of *individuals*—that could meld such diversity into a coherent nation. In this new nation no group would lord it over any other. But, of course, beneath this America of its ideals there was from the start a much meaner reality, one whose very existence mocked the notion of a nation made singular by the equality of its individuals. By limiting democracy to their own kind—white, male landowners—the Founding Fathers collectively entitled themselves and banished all others to the edges and underside of American life. There, individual entitlement was either curtailed or—in the case of slavery—extinguished.

The genius of the civil rights movement that changed the fabric of American life in the late 1950s and early 1960s was its profound understanding that the enemy of black Americans was not the ideal America but the unspoken principle of collective entitlement that had always put the lie to true democracy. This movement, which came to center stage from America's underside and margins, had as its single, overriding goal the eradication of white entitlement. And, correspondingly, it exhibited a belief in democratic principles at least as strong as that of the Founding Fathers, who themselves had emerged from the (less harsh) margins of English society. In this sense the civil rights movement re-enacted the American Revolution, and its paramount leader, Martin Luther King, spoke as twentieth-century America's greatest democratic voice.

All of this was made clear to me for the umpteenth time by my father on a very cold Saturday afternoon in 1959. There was a national campaign under way to integrate the lunch counters at Woolworth stores, and my father, who was more a persuader than an intimidator, had made it a point of honor that I join him on the picket line, civil rights being nothing less than the religion of our household. By this time, age twelve or so, I was sick of it. I'd had enough of watching my parents heading off to still another meeting or march; I'd heard too many tedious discussions on everything from the philosophy of passive resistance to the symbolism of going to jail. Added to this, my own experience of picket lines and peace marches had impressed upon me what so many people who've partaken of these activities know: that in themselves they can be crushingly boring—around and around and around holding a sign, watching one's own feet fall, feeling the minutes like hours. All that Saturday morning I hid from my father and tried to convince myself of what I longed for—that he would get so busy that if he didn't forget the march he would at least forget me.

He forgot nothing. I did my time on the picket line, but not without building up enough resentment to start a fight on the way home. What was so important about integration? We had never even wanted to eat at Woolworth's. I told him the truth, that he never took us to *any* restaurants anyway, claiming always that they charged too much money for bad food. But he said calmly that he was proud of me for marching and that he knew *I* knew food wasn't the point.

My father—forty years a truck driver, with the urges of an intellectual—went on to use my little rebellion as the occasion for a discourse, in this case on the concept of integration. Integration had little to do with merely rubbing shoulders with white people, eating bad food beside them. It was about the right to go absolutely anywhere white people could go being the test of freedom and equality. To be anywhere they could be and do anything they could do was the point. Like it or not, white people defined the horizon of freedom in America, and if you couldn't touch their shoulder you weren't free. For him integration was the *evidence* of freedom and equality.

My father was a product of America's margins, as were all the blacks in the early civil rights movement, leaders and foot soldiers alike. For them integration was a way of moving from the margins into the mainstream. Today there is considerable ambivalence about integration, but in that day it was nothing less than democracy itself. Integration is also certainly about racial harmony, but it is more fundamentally about the ultimate extension of democracy—beyond the racial entitlements that contradict it. The idea of racial integration is quite simply the most democratic principle America has evolved, since all other such principles depend on its reality and are diminished by its absence.

But the civil rights movement did not account for one thing: the tremendous release of black anger that would follow its victories. The 1964 Civil Rights Act and the 1965 Voting Rights Act were, on one level, admissions of guilt by American society that it had practiced white entitlement at the expense of all others. When the oppressors admit their crimes, the oppressed can give full vent to their long repressed rage because now there is a moral consensus between oppressor and oppressed that a wrong was done. This consensus gave blacks the license to release a rage that was three centuries deep, a rage that is still today everywhere visible, a rage that—in the wake of the Rodney King verdict, a verdict a vast majority of all Americans thought unfair—fueled the worst rioting in recent American history.

By the mid-Sixties, the democratic goal of integration was no longer enough to appease black anger. Suddenly for blacks there was a sense that far more was owed, that a huge bill was due. And for many whites there was also the feeling that some kind of repayment was truly in order. This was the moral logic that followed inevitably from the new consensus. But it led to an even simpler logic: if blacks had been oppressed collectively, that oppression would now be redressed by entitling them collectively. So here we were again, in the name of a thousand good intentions, falling away from the hard challenge of a democracy of individuals and embracing the principle of collective entitlement that had so corrupted the American ideal in the first place. Now this old sin would be applied in the name of uplift. And this made an easy sort of sense. If it was good enough for whites for three hundred years, why not let blacks have a little of it to get ahead? In the context of the Sixties—black outrage and white guilt—a principle we had just decided was evil for whites was redefined as a social good for blacks. And once the formula was in place for blacks, it could be applied to other groups with similar grievances. By the 1970s more than 60 percent of the American population—not only blacks but Hispanics, women, Asians—would come under the collective entitlement of affirmative action.

• • •

In the early days of the civil rights movement, the concept of solidarity was essentially a moral one. That is, all people who believed in human freedom, fairness, and equality were asked to form a solid front against white entitlement. But after the collaboration of black rage and white guilt made collective entitlement a social remedy, the nature of solidarity changed. It was no longer the rallying of diverse peoples to breach an oppressive group entitlement. It was the very opposite: a rallying of people within a grievance group to pursue their own group entitlement. As early as the mid-Sixties, whites were made unwelcome in the civil rights movement, just as, by the mid-Seventies, men were no longer welcome in the women's movement. Eventually, collective entitlement *always* requires separatism. And the irony is obvious: those who once had been the victims of separatism, who had sacrificed so dearly to overcome their being at the margins, would later create an ethos of their own separatism. After the Sixties, solidarity became essentially a separatist concept, an exclusionary principle. One no longer heard words like "integration" or "harmony"; one heard about "anger" and "power." Integration is anathema to grievance groups for precisely the same reason it was anathema to racist whites in the civil rights era: because it threatens their collective entitlement by insisting that no group be entitled over another. Power is where it's at today— power to set up the organization, attract the following, run the fiefdom.

But it must also be said that this could not have come to pass without the cooperation of the society at large and its institutions. Why did the government, the public and private institutions, the corporations and foundations, end up supporting principles that had the effect of turning causes into sovereign fiefdoms? I think the answer is that those in charge of America's institutions saw the institutionalization and bureaucratization of the protest movements as ultimately desirable, at least in the short term, and the funding of group entitlements as ultimately a less costly way to redress grievances. The leaders of the newly sovereign fiefdoms were backing off from earlier demands that America live up to its ideals. Gone was the moral indictment. Gone was the call for difficult, soulful transformation. The language of entitlements is essentially the old, comforting language of power politics, and in the halls of power it went down easily enough.

With regard to civil rights, the moral voice of Dr. King gave way to the demands and cajolings of poverty-program moguls, class-action lawyers, and community organizers. The compromise that satisfied both political parties was to shift the focus from democracy, integration, and developmental uplift to collective entitlements. This satisfied the institutions because entitlements were cheaper in every way than real change. Better to set up black studies and women's studies departments than to have wrenching debates within existing departments. Better to fund these new institutions clamoring for money because who knows what kind of fuss they'll make if we turn down their proposals. Better to pass laws permitting Hispanic students to get preferred treatment in college admission—it costs less than improving kindergartens in East Los Angeles.

And this way to uplift satisfied the grievance-group "experts" because it laid the ground for their sovereignty and permanency: You negotiated with *us*. You funded *us*. You shared power, at least a bit of it, with *us*.

This negotiation was carried out in a kind of quasi-secrecy. Quotas, set-asides, and other entitlements were not debated in Congress or on the campaign trail. They were implemented by executive orders and Equal Employment Opportunity Commission guidelines without much public scrutiny. Also the courts played a quiet but persistent role in supporting these orders and guidelines and in further spelling out their application. Universities, corporations, and foundations implemented their own grievance entitlements, the workings of which are often kept from the public.

Now, it should surprise no one that all this entitlement has most helped those who least need it—white middle-class women and the black middle class. Poor blacks do not guide the black grievance groups. Working-class women do not set NOW's agenda. Poor Hispanics do not clamor for bilingualism. Perhaps there is nothing wrong with middle-class people being helped, but their demands for entitlements are most often in the name of those less well off than themselves. The negotiations that settled on entitlements as the primary form of redress after the Sixties have generated a legalistic grievance industry that argues the interstices of entitlements and does very little to help those truly in need.

• • •

In a liberal democracy, collective entitlements based upon race, gender, ethnicity, or some other group grievance are always undemocratic expedients. Integration, on the other hand, is the most difficult and inexpedient expansion of the democratic ideal; for in opting for integration, a citizen denies his or her impulse to use our most arbitrary characteristics—race, ethnicity, gender, sexual preference—as the basis for identity, as a key to status, or for claims to entitlement. Integration is twentieth-century America's elaboration of democracy. It eliminates such things as race and gender as oppressive barriers to freedom, as democrats of an earlier epoch eliminated religion and property. Our mistake has been to think of integration only as a utopian vision of perfect racial harmony. I think it is better to see integration as the inclusion of all citizens into the same sphere of rights, the same range of opportunities and possibilities that our Founding Fathers themselves enjoyed. Integration is not social engineering or group entitlements; it is a fundamental *absence* of arbitrary barriers to freedom.

If we can understand integration as an absence of barriers that has the effect of integrating all citizens into the same sphere of rights, then it can serve as a principle of democratic conduct. Anything that pushes anybody out of this sphere is undemocratic and must be checked, no matter the good intentions that seem to justify it. Understood in this light, collective entitlements are as undemocratic as racial and gender discrimination, and a group grievance is no more a justification for entitlement than the notion of white supremacy was at an earlier time. We are wrong to think of democracy as a gift of freedom; it is really a kind of discipline that avails freedom. Sometimes its enemy is racism and sexism; other times the enemy is our expedient attempts to correct these ills.

I think it is time for those who seek identity and power through grievance groups to fashion identities apart from grievance, to grant themselves the widest range of freedom, and to assume responsibility for that freedom. Victimhood lasts only as long as it is accepted, and to exploit it for an empty sovereignty is to accept it. The New Sovereignty is ultimately about vanity. It is the narcissism of victims, and it brings only a negligible power at the exorbitant price of continued victimhood. And all the while integration remains the real work.

MICHAEL LIND

To Have and Have Not

MICHAEL LIND is a senior editor of *Harper's*. He is author of *Up from Conservatism: Why the Right Is Wrong for America* (1996) and *The Next American Nation: The New Nationalism and the Fourth American Revolution* (1995), from which the following essay is adapted.

The American oligarchy spares no pains in promoting the belief that it does not exist, but the success of its disappearing act depends on equally strenuous efforts on the part of an American public anxious to believe in egalitarian fictions and unwilling to see what is hidden in plain sight. Anybody choosing to see the oligarchy in its native habitat need do nothing else but walk down the street of any big city to an office tower housing a major bank, a corporate headquarters or law firm, or a national television station. Enter the building and the multiracial diversity of the street vanishes as abruptly as the sound of the traffic. Step off the elevator at the top of the tower and apart from the clerical and maintenance staff hardly anybody is nonwhite. The contrast between the street and the tower is the contrast between the grass roots and the national headquarters, the field office and the home office. No matter what your starting point, the closer you come to the centers of American politics and society, the more everyone begins to look the same. Though corporate executives, shop stewards, and graduate student lecturers could not be more different, the people who run big business bear a remarkable resemblance to the people who run big labor, who in turn might be mistaken for the people in charge of the media and the universities. *They are the same people.* They differ in their opinions—and in almost no other way. Almost exclusively white, disproportionately mainline Protestant or Jewish, most of the members of the American elites went to one of a dozen Ivy League colleges or top state universities. Not only do they have advanced professional or graduate degrees—J.D.'s, M.B.A.'s, Ph.D.'s, M.D.'s—but usually at least one of their parents (and sometimes both) has advanced professional or graduate degrees. They dress the same. They talk the same. They walk the same. They have the same body language, the same gestures. They eat the same food, drink the same drinks, and play the same sports. They read the same publications. They . . . but I should say *we*. As a second-generation professional with an Ivy League diploma, having worked for liberal Democrats and conservative Republicans, business lobbyists and pro-labor intellectuals, among professors and journalists and lawyers and Foreign Service officers, I am a card-carrying member of the overclass. So, in all likelihood, reader, are you.

Amounting, with their dependents, to about 20 percent of the population,[1] this relatively new and still evolving political and social oligarchy is not identified with any

---

[1] Defined as individuals with professional or graduate education (which is roughly correlated with high income), and without counting dependents, the members of the overclass account for no more than 5 percent of the U.S. population.

particular region of the country. Homogeneous and nomadic, the overclass is the first truly national upper class in American history. In a managerial capitalist society like our own, the essential distinction is not between the "bourgeoisie" (the factory owners) and the "proletariat" (the factory workers) but between the credentialed minority (making a living from fees or wages supplemented by stock options) and the salaried majority. The salaried class—at-will employees, lacking a four-year college education, paid by the hour, who can be fired at any time—constitutes the real "middle class," accounting, as it does, for three-quarters of the population.

The white overclass, then, properly perceived, is neither a middle class nor a high bourgeoisie but a sort of guild oligarchy, like those that ran early modern Italian and Dutch city-states. Our latter-day oligarchs (lawyers, bankers, publishers, anchorpersons) are the contemporary equivalents of the plump and goateed syndics, haloed by starched collars, who gaze smugly back at us through honey veils of impasto from the paintings of Rembrandt and Hals. The precedent for our class war can't be found in the slapstick melee pitting thick-necked proles against top-hatted, umbrella-wielding bourgeois that enlivens Sergei Eisenstein's *Ten Days That Shook The World*. We should think, instead, of the civic discord between great guilds and lesser guilds—the bankers and merchants versus the artisans—that troubled cities like Florence and Milan in the Renaissance, and that resembled the struggle over universal health care between the insurance lobby and the AFL-CIO.

At least the syndics of Amsterdam and the Venetian families in the Golden Book did not add insult to injury by insisting that they were not "elites." The most remarkable thing about our own American oligarchy is the pretense that it doesn't constitute anything as definite as a social class. We prefer to assign good fortune to our individual merit, saying that we owe our perches in the upper percentiles of income and education not to our connections but solely to our own I.Q., virtue, brio, genius, *sprezzatura*, chutzpah, gumption. Had we been switched at birth by accident, had we grown up in a ghetto or barrio or trailer park, we would have arrived at our offices at ABC News or the Republican National Committee or the ACLU in more or less the same amount of time. The absence of black and Hispanic Americans in our schools and our offices and our clubs can only be explained, we tell ourselves, not by *our* extrinsic advantages but by *their* intrinsic defects. Compared with us (and perhaps with middle-class East Asian immigrants), most blacks and Hispanics must be disproportionately lazy, even (if Charles Murray and the late Richard Herrnstein are to be believed) disproportionately retarded. What other explanation for their failure to rise can there be? America, after all, is a classless society.

Or rather a two-class society. The belated acknowledgement of an "underclass" as a distinct group represents the only exception to the polite fiction that everyone in the United States, from a garage mechanic to a rich attorney (particularly the rich attorney), belongs to the "middle class." Over the past decade the ghetto poor have been the topic of conversation at more candlelight-and-wine dinner parties than I can recall, but without looking at the program or the wine list it is impossible to tell whether one is among nominal liberals or nominal conservatives. The same kind of people in the same kind of suits go on about "the blacks" as though a minority within a 12 percent minority were taking over the country, as if Washington were Pretoria and New York a suburb of Johannesburg. Not only do the comfortable members of the overclass single out the weakest and least influential of their fellow citizens as the cause of all their sorrows but they routinely, and preposterously, treat the genuine pathologies of the ghetto—high levels of violence and illegitimacy—as the major problems facing a country with uncontrollable trade and fiscal deficits, a low savings rate, an obsolete military strategy, an anachronistic and corrupt electoral system, the worst system of primary education in the First World, and the bulk of its population facing long-term economic decline.

To be sure, upper classes in other societies have often fretted, sometimes to the point of panic, about the lower orders, and in Japan, as in Britain and France (to an even greater degree than in the United States), the people in charge tend to go to the same schools, not a dozen but one or two. But in those countries people at least acknowledge the existence of an upper stratum, and the public-school old-boy network or the *énarquate* retains some tradition of responsibility for the less fortunate, some sense of noblesse oblige based on self-preservation if not on superior morality. (As Disraeli observed in 1848, "The palace is not safe when the cottage is not happy.") Among all the industrial democracies, only in the United States do the members of the oligarchy absolve themselves with the comforting notion that their class does not exist. Willing to pursue collective economic interests but lacking any sense of a political commonwealth, the American overclass at the end of the twentieth century takes as its own what Adam Smith identified as "the vile maxim of the masters of mankind. . . . All for ourselves, and nothing for other people." The sentiment is heartfelt and bipartisan. . . .

•   •   •

Unified along the lines of economic interest, the wealthy American minority hold the fragmented majority at bay by pitting blacks against whites in zero-sum struggles for government patronage and by bribing potential black and Hispanic leaders, who might otherwise propose something other than rhetorical rebellion, with the gifts of affirmative action. The policy was promoted by Richard Nixon, who, as much as any American politician, deserves to be acknowledged as the father of racial preferences.

"What most militants want," Nixon explained in 1968, using the language of gangsterism to support his proposal for minority contracting preferences, "is not separation, but to be included in . . . to have a share of the wealth, and a piece of the action." Racial-preference policies give middle-class and wealthy blacks and Hispanics "a share of the wealth and a piece of the action." The ritual that symbolizes civil-rights "progress" in today's oligarchic America is the "integration" of an all-white country club, which invariably means admitting one of the wealthiest black citizens who can be found in the local community. Similarly, in the matter of presidential Cabinet posts, diversity means appointing rich professionals educated in the Ivy League who happen to belong to different races and sexes.

The Ivy League, in its turn, rigs its admissions policies to disproportionately benefit well-off black and Hispanic Americans (at Harvard, for example, 70 percent of black undergraduates are the children of parents in managerial or professional fields, while at Cornell twice as many minority students, in some years, come from the suburbs as from the cities). In order not to lose accreditation, most colleges and universities try to have approximately as many black students as there are black Americans in the general population, around 12 percent. These goals and timetables can be met only by

drastically lowering admissions standards for black students, who for obvious historical reasons are far less academically prepared than many of their white competitors.

●   ●   ●

"To get past racism, we must here take account of race," McGeorge Bundy, the former aide to Presidents Kennedy and Johnson, declared magisterially in "The Issue
Before the Court: Who Gets Ahead in America?", an article in *The Atlantic Monthly* that
appeared in November 1977 during the formative period of affirmative action in college admissions. Bundy could afford to be generous in redistributing opportunities
from middle-class whites to middle-class blacks and Hispanics because so many members of his class are safely insulated from the effects of racial preference by the largest
affirmative-action program in the United States: legacy preference.

Legacies, or children of alumni, are three times more likely to be accepted to Harvard
than other high school graduates with the same (sometimes better) scores (at Harvard,
the dean of admissions reads legacy applications—but not those of non-legacies). Children of Yale graduates are two and a half times more likely than non-alumni kin to be
admitted to Yale. According to a former Princeton dean of admissions, legacies at "one
Ivy League university" had average SAT scores of 1,280, compared with the average of
1,350 out of a possible 1,600 for the total freshman class.

As the number of black and Hispanic students at selective universities and partners
in prestigious law firms is artificially maintained, the average wages of black and Hispanic workers, along with those of white workers, continue to stagnate or decline. The
tokenism embodied in racial preference and multiculturalism is thus about as threatening to the American elite as an avant-garde sculpture in the lobby of a bank.

ROGER WILKINS

The Case for
Affirmative Action
Racism Has Its Privileges

ROGER WILKINS teaches history at George Mason University and is an editorial
board member of *The Nation*.

Some years ago, after watching me teach as a visiting professor for two semesters, members of the history department at George Mason University invited me to compete for a
full professorship and endowed chair. Mason, like other institutions in Virginia's higher
education system, was under a court order to desegregate. I went through the appropriate application and review process and, in due course, was appointed. A few years
later, not long after I had been honored as one of the university's distinguished professors, I was shown an article by a white historian asserting that he had been a candidate
for that chair but that at the last moment the job had been whisked away and handed
to an unqualified black. I checked the story and discovered that this fellow had, in fact,
applied but had not even passed the first threshold. But his "reverse discrimination"
story is out there polluting the atmosphere in which this debate is taking place.

Affirmative action, as I understand it, was not designed to punish anyone; it was,
rather—as a result of a clear-eyed look at how America actually works—an attempt to
enlarge opportunity for *everybody*. As amply documented in the 1968 Kerner Commission report on racial disorders, when left to their own devices, American institutions
in such areas as college admissions, hiring decisions and loan approvals had been
making choices that discriminated against blacks. That discrimination, which flowed
from doing what came naturally, hurt more than blacks: It hurt the entire nation, as the
riots of the late 1960s demonstrated. Though the Kerner report focused on blacks, similar findings could have been made about other minorities and women.

Affirmative action required institutions to develop plans enabling them to go beyond business as usual and search for qualified people in places where they did not ordinarily conduct their searches or their business. Affirmative action programs generally
require some proof that there has been a good-faith effort to follow the plan and numerical guidelines against which to judge the sincerity and the success of the effort.
The idea of affirmative action is *not* to force people into positions for which they are
unqualified but to encourage institutions to develop realistic criteria for the enterprise
at hand and then to find a reasonably diverse mix of people qualified to be engaged in
it. Without the requirements calling for plans, good-faith efforts and the setting of broad
numerical goals, many institutions would do what they had always done: assert that
they had looked but "couldn't find anyone qualified," and then go out and hire the
white man they wanted to hire in the first place.

Affirmative action has done wonderful things for the United States by enlarging opportunity and developing and utilizing a far broader array of the skills available in the

American population than in the past. It has not outlived its usefulness. It was never designed to be a program to eliminate poverty. It has not always been used wisely, and some of its permutations do have to be reconsidered, refined or, in some cases, abandoned. It is not a quota program, and those cases where rigid numbers are used (except under a court or administrative order after a specific finding of discrimination) are a bastardization of an otherwise highly beneficial set of public policies.

President Clinton is right to review what is being done under present laws and to express a willingness to eliminate activities that either don't work or are unfair. Any program that has been in place for thirty years should be reviewed. Getting rid of what doesn't work is both good government and good politics. Gross abuses of affirmative action provide ammunition for its opponents and undercut the moral authority of the entire effort. But the President should retain—and strengthen where required—those programs necessary to enlarge social justice.

What makes the affirmative action issue so difficult is that it engages blacks and whites exactly at those points where they differ the most. There are some areas, such as rooting for the local football team, where their experiences and views are virtually identical. There are others—sometimes including work and school—where their experiences and views both overlap and diverge. And finally, there are areas such as affirmative action and inextricably related notions about the presence of racism in society, where the divergences draw out almost all the points of difference between the races.

THIS LAND IS MY LAND

Blacks and whites experience America very differently. Though we often inhabit the same space, we operate in very disparate psychic spheres.

Whites have an easy sense of ownership of the country; they feel they are entitled to receive all that is best in it. Many of them believe that their country—though it may have some faults—is superior to all others and that, as Americans, they are superior as well. Many of them think of this as a white country and some of them even experience it that way. They think of it as a land of opportunity—a good place with a lot of good people in it. Some suspect (others *know*) that the presence of blacks messes everything up.

To blacks there's nothing very easy about life in America, and any sense of ownership comes hard because we encounter so much resistance in making our way through the ordinary occurrences of life. And I'm not even talking here about overt acts of discrimination but simply about the way whites intrude on and disturb our psychic space without even thinking about it.

A telling example of this was given to me by a black college student in Oklahoma. He said whites give him looks that say: "What are *you* doing here?"

"When do they give you that look?" I asked.

"Every time I walk in a door," he replied.

When he said that, every black person in the room nodded and smiled in a way that indicated recognition based on thousands of such moments in their own lives.

For most blacks, America is either a land of denied opportunity or one in which the opportunities are still grudgingly extended and extremely limited. For some—that one-third who are mired in poverty, many of them isolated in dangerous ghettos—America is a land of desperadoes and desperation. In places where whites see a lot of idealism, blacks see, at best, idealism mixed heavily with hypocrisy. Blacks accept America's greatness, but are unable to ignore ugly warts that many whites seem to need not to see. I am reminded here of James Baldwin's searing observation from *The Fire Next Time*:

> The American Negro has the great advantage of having never believed that collection of myths to which white Americans cling: that their ancestors were all freedom-loving heroes, that they were born in the greatest country the world has ever seen, or that Americans are invincible in battle and wise in peace, that Americans have always dealt honorably with Mexicans and Indians and all other neighbors or inferiors, that American men are the world's most direct and virile, that American women are pure.

It goes without saying, then, that blacks and whites remember America differently. The past is hugely important since we argue a lot about who we are on the basis of who we think we have been, and we derive much of our sense of the future from how we think we've done in the past. In a nation in which few people know much history these are perilous arguments, because in such a vacuum, people tend to weave historical fables tailored to their political or psychic needs.

Blacks are still recovering the story of their role in America, which so many white historians simply ignored or told in ways that made black people ashamed. But in a culture that batters us, learning the real history is vital in helping blacks feel fully human. It also helps us understand just how deeply American we are, how richly we have given, how much has been taken from us and how much has yet to be restored. Supporters of affirmative action believe that broad and deep damage has been done to American culture by racism and sexism over the whole course of American history and that they are still powerful forces today. We believe that minorities and women are still disadvantaged in our highly competitive society and that affirmative action is absolutely necessary to level the playing field.

Not all white Americans oppose this view and not all black Americans support it. There are a substantial number of whites in this country who have been able to escape our racist and sexist past and to enter fully into the quest for equal justice. There are other white Americans who are not racists but who more or less passively accept the powerful suggestions coming at them from all points in the culture that whites are entitled to privilege and to freedom from competition with blacks. And then there are racists who just don't like blacks or who actively despise us. There are still others who may or may not feel deep antipathy, but who know how to manipulate racism and white anxiety for their own ends. Virtually all the people in the last category oppose affirmative action and some of them make a practice of preying upon those in the second category who are not paying attention or who, like the *Post*'s Richard Cohen, are simply confused.

THE POLITICS OF DENIAL

... The fact is that the successful public relations assault on affirmative action flows on a river of racism that is as broad, powerful and American as the Mississippi. And, like the Mississippi, racism can be violent and deadly and is a permanent feature of American life. But while nobody who is sane denies the reality of the Mississippi, millions of

Americans who are deemed sane—some of whom are powerful and some even thought wise—deny, wholly or in part, that racism exists.

It is critical to understand the workings of denial in this debate because it is used to obliterate the facts that created the need for the remedy in the first place. . . . [B]lacks have been on this North American continent for 375 years and . . . for 245 the country permitted slavery. . . . [F]or the next hundred years we had legalized subordination of blacks, under a suffocating blanket of condescension and frequently enforced by night-riding terrorists. We've had only thirty years of something else.

That something else is a nation trying to lift its ideals out of a thick, often impenetrable slough of racism. Racism is a hard word for what over the centuries became second nature in America—preferences across the board for white men and, following in their wake, white women. Many of these men seem to feel that it is un-American to ask them to share anything with blacks—particularly their work, their neighborhoods, or "their" women. To protect these things—apparently essential to their identity—they engage in all forms of denial. . . .

Denial of racism is much like the denials that accompany addictions to alcohol, drugs or gambling. It is probably not stretching the analogy too much to suggest that many racist whites are so addicted to their unwarranted privileges and so threatened by the prospect of losing them that all kinds of defenses become acceptable, including insistent distortions of reality in the form of hypocrisy, lying or the most outrageous political demagogy.

'THOSE PEOPLE' DON'T DESERVE HELP

The demagogues have reverted to a new version of quite an old trick. Before the 1950s, whites who were busy denying that the nation was unfair to blacks would simply assert that we didn't deserve equal treatment because we were *inferior*. These days it is not permissible in most public circles to say that blacks are inferior, but it is perfectly acceptable to target the *behavior* of blacks, specifically poor blacks. The argument then follows a fairly predictable line: The behavior of poor blacks requires a severe rethinking of national social policy, it is said. Advantaged blacks really don't need affirmative action anymore, and when they are the objects of such programs, some qualified white person (unqualified white people don't show up in these arguments) is . . . "punished." While it is possible that color-blind affirmative action programs benefitting all disadvantaged Americans are needed, those (i.e., blacks) whose behavior is so distressing must be punished by restricting welfare, shriveling the safety net and expanding the prison opportunity. All of that would presumably give us, in William Bennett's words, "what we want—a color-blind society," for which the white American psyche is presumably fully prepared.

There are at least three layers of unreality in these precepts. The first is that the United States is not now and probably never will be a color-blind society. It is the most color-conscious society on earth. Over the course of 375 years, whites have given blacks absolutely no reason to believe that they can behave in a color-blind manner. In many areas of our lives—particularly in employment, housing and education—affirmative action is required to counter deeply ingrained racist patterns of behavior.

Second, while I don't hold the view that all blacks who behave badly are blameless victims of a brutal system, I do believe that many poor blacks have, indeed, been brutalized by our culture, and I know of *no* blacks, rich or poor, who haven't been hurt in some measure by the racism in this country. The current mood (and, in some cases like the Speaker's, the cultivated ignorance) completely ignores the fact that some blacks never escaped the straight line of oppression that ran from slavery through the semi-slavery of sharecropping to the late mid-century migration from Southern farms into isolated pockets of urban poverty. Their families have always been excluded, poor and without skills, and so they were utterly defenseless when the enormous American economic dislocations that began in the mid-1970s slammed into their communities, followed closely by deadly waves of crack cocaine. One would think that the double-digit unemployment suffered consistently over the past two decades by blacks who were *looking for work* would be a permanent feature of the discussions about race, responsibility, welfare and rights.

But a discussion of the huge numbers of black workers who are becoming economically redundant would raise difficult questions about the efficiency of the economy at a time when millions of white men feel insecure. Any honest appraisal of unemployment would reveal that millions of low-skilled white men were being severely damaged by corporate and Federal Reserve decisions; it might also refocus the anger of those whites in the middle ranks whose careers have been shattered by the corporate downsizing fad.

But people's attention is kept trained on the behavior of some poor blacks by politicians and television news shows, reinforcing the stereotypes of blacks as dangerous, as threats, as unqualified. Frightened whites direct their rage at pushy blacks rather than at the corporations that export manufacturing operations to low-wage countries, or at the Federal Reserve, which imposes interest rate hikes that slow down the economy.

WHO BENEFITS? WE ALL DO

There is one final denial that blankets all the rest. It is that only society's "victims"— blacks, other minorities and women (who should, for God's sake, renounce their victimological outlooks)—have been injured by white male supremacy. Viewed in this light, affirmative action remedies are a kind of zero-sum game in which only the "victims" benefit. But racist and sexist whites who are not able to accept the full humanity of other people are themselves badly damaged—morally stunted—people. The principal product of a racist and sexist society is damaged people and institutions—victims and victimizers alike. Journalism and education, two enterprises with which I am familiar, provide two good examples.

Journalistic institutions often view the nation through a lens that bends reality to support white privilege. A recent issue of *U.S. News & World Report* introduced a package of articles on these issues with a question on its cover: "Does affirmative action mean NO WHITE MEN NEED APPLY?" The words "No white men need apply" were printed in red against a white background and were at least four times larger than the other words in the question. Inside, the lead story was illustrated by a painting that carries out the cover theme, with a wan white man separated from the opportunity ladders eagerly being scaled by women and dark men. And the story yielded up the following sentence: "Affirmative action poses a conflict between two cherished American principles: the belief that all Americans deserve equal opportunities and the idea that hard work and merit, not race or religion or gender or birthright, should determine who prospers and who does not."

Whoever wrote that sentence was in the thrall of one of the myths that Baldwin was talking about. The sentence suggests—as many people do when talking about affirmative action—that America is a meritocratic society. But what kind of meritocracy excludes women and blacks and other minorities from all meaningful competition? And even in the competition among white men, money, family and connections often count for much more than merit, test results (for whatever they're worth) and hard work.

The *U.S. News* story perpetuates and strengthens the view that many of my white students absorb from their parents: that white men now have few chances in this society. The fact is that white men still control virtually everything in America except the wealth held by widows. According to the Urban Institute, 53 percent of black men aged 25–34 are either unemployed or earn too little to lift a family of four from poverty.

Educational institutions that don't teach accurately about why America looks the way it does and why the distribution of winners and losers is as it is also injure our society. Here is another anecdote.

A warm, brilliant young white male student of mine came in just before he was to graduate and said that my course in race, law and culture, which he had just finished, had been the most valuable and the most disturbing he had ever taken. I asked how it had been disturbing.

"I learned that my two heroes are racists," he said.

"Who are your heroes and how are they racists?" I asked.

"My mom and dad," he said. "After thinking about what I was learning, I understood that they had spent all my life making me into the same kind of racists they were."

Affirmative action had brought me together with him when he was 22. Affirmative action puts people together in ways that make that kind of revelation possible. Nobody is a loser when that happens. The country gains.

And that, in the end, is the case for affirmative action. The arguments supporting it should be made on the basis of its broad contributions to the entire American community. It is insufficient to vilify white males and to skewer them as the whiners that journalism of the kind practiced by *U.S. News* invites us to do. These are people who, from the beginning of the Republic, have been taught that skin color is destiny and that whiteness is to be revered. Listen to Jefferson, writing in the year the Constitution was drafted:

> The first difference that strikes us is that of colour. . . . And is the difference of no importance? Is it not the foundation of a greater or less share of beauty in the two races? Are not the fine mixtures of red and white . . . in the one, preferable to that eternal monotony, which reigns in the countenances, that immoveable veil of black which covers all the emotions of the other race? Add to these, flowing hair, a more elegant symmetry of form, their own judgment in favor of the whites, declared by their preference for them, as uniformly as is the preference of the Oran-ootan for the black women over those of his own species. The circumstance of superior beauty, is thought worthy attention in the propagation of our horses, dogs, and other domestic animals; why not in that of man?

In a society so conceived and so dedicated, it is understandable that white males would take their preferences as a matter of natural right and consider any alteration of that a primal offense. But a nation that operates in that way abandons its soul and its economic strength, and will remain mired in ugliness and moral squalor because so many people are excluded from the possibility of decent lives and from forming any sense of community with the rest of society. . . .

. . . [W]hite skin has made some citizens—particularly white males—*the special favorites of the culture.* It may be that we will need affirmative action until most white males are really ready for a color-blind society—that is, when they are ready to assume 'the rank of a mere citizen." As a nation we took a hard look at that special favoritism thirty years ago. Though the centuries of cultural preference enjoyed by white males still overwhelmingly skew power and wealth their way, we have in fact achieved a more meritocratic society as a result of affirmative action than we have ever previously enjoyed in this country.

If we want to continue making things better in this society, we'd better figure out ways to protect and defend affirmative action against the confused, the frightened, the manipulators and, yes, the liars in politics, journalism, education and wherever else they may be found. In the name of longstanding American prejudice and myths and in the service of their own narrow interests, power-lusts or blindness, they are truly victimizing the rest of us, perverting the ideals they claim to stand for and destroying the nation they pretend to serve.

CHAPTER 9

Can There Be Equality between Men and Women?

Story 1: Driving the truck to work one day, Sandy noticed somebody by the side of the road with a flat tire. Sandy stopped and got out to help fix the flat. Because neither of them had a jack, Sandy had to hold up the rear end of the car while the owner replaced the tire. When they were done, Sandy reminded herself to buy a new jack on her way home.

Story 2: Lee was putting the finishing touches on the pie when the kids rushed in the door. "What's for dinner? We're starved." "Wash your hands, kids, and set the table," Lee replied. "We'll be eating as soon as Mom gets home from work."

It is a rare person indeed who would read either of these stories without experiencing a "gender jolt" at the end of them. No matter what your views about sexual equality, it is nevertheless true that we tend to make certain associations when it comes to gender. Even if your father does the cooking every night, you probably assumed that the person putting the finishing touches on the pie was a woman. Similarly, even if your mother is a body builder who drives a Harley, you probably assumed that the person holding up the rear of the car was a man.

Although we do make such characteristic gender associations, it is far from clear whether they are rooted in fundamental, irreversible differences between men and women or whether they are a function of changeable social practices. Look around the world. How many women are steamroller operators? Heads of state? CIA agents? Garage mechanics? Nuclear physicists? How many men are elementary schoolteachers? Stay-at-home dads? Secretaries? Nurses? It is important to notice two things. First, men and women tend to occupy different roles in our culture. Second, the roles that women occupy tend to be subordinate, or considered subordinate, to those of men.

These facts often lead people to conclude that gender differences are "natural," that they are part of the order of things and hence cannot be changed in any significant way. John Stuart Mill argues that the conceptions we have of the alleged "natures" of men and women are the result of equating facts about the way things *are* with the way things *must be.* Suppose that you are in the hospital for a week, and during that time you never encounter a male nurse. Are you entitled to conclude that men cannot, by their very nature, be nurses? Or that women, by their very nature, are suited to nursing? Mill provides us with reasons for being cautious about making inferences like these.

Writing a hundred years after John Stuart Mill, Simone de Beauvoir sought to provide a more complete account of the causes and effects of the oppression of women. Beauvoir argues that men have constructed women as what she calls "the Other" in order to establish the superiority of their own characteristics. The human tendency toward self-importance takes the form, in men, of casting feminine characteristics in a negative light. The feminine becomes the negative, that which is not male. By denying women the capacity to make sound judgments, men ensure that whatever resistance women might show to this negative assessment of their abilities is itself dismissed as yet another error in judgment. Left with no other resources, women come to see themselves as men want them to be seen. They expect to be weak, silly, emotional, powerless, and dependent. They, too, see themselves as the Other.

The remaining essays in this chapter take up in various ways the challenge posed by Beauvoir's original, illuminating, though rather dismal, depiction of woman's consciousness of herself as inferior to men. If Beauvoir is correct in her assertion that woman's consciousness is constructed by men, then it looks as though women have no feelings, thoughts, or desires that are truly their own. In her essay, Jean Grimshaw explores the differences between the Beauvoirian view and that of other feminists who have argued that, lying underneath the encrustations of male dominance, there is an authentic female self waiting to be discovered. She finds both views to be inadequate and proposes a way of thinking about the self that avoids what she takes to be the philosophical and political dangers of each.

Marilyn Frye provides a rigorous analysis of the term "sexism" in order to render sexist institutions, people, and actions more visible. The fact that sexism is not always apparent—either to those who suffer from it or to those who perpetrate it—is, she wants to claim, part of what allows sexism to prosper. According to Frye, sexism results from a particular system of "sex-marking." She asks us to think about the various ways that sex differences are reinforced by clothing and by manners of walking and speaking. The reinforcement of sex differences maintains a system in which one group of people is subordinate to another. By continuing, as a culture, to emphasize the importance of sex differences, we further reinforce the relationship of domination and subordination whose purpose it serves. Caryl Rivers, a contemporary media critic, looks at how the mass media representations of gender differences support age-old myths about the "definitive" characteristics of men and women. She argues that women are positioned in contradictory ways: as weak and helpless on the one hand, and as conniving and emasculating on the other hand.

Jacob Joshua Ross and Linda Bell each critique feminist efforts to define and defend sexual equality, but they do so from very different perspectives. Ross focuses on the traditional sexual division of labor, according to which women do reproductive work, and men do economically productive work. Ross takes issue with those he labels "radical feminists" (you might want to think about how this label itself suggests a negative view of feminism) who, he claims, consider the "naturalization" of women's reproductive work to be a principal cause of their inequality. Although he is inclined to think that women are naturally more suited to "mothering" tasks, he does not rest his commitment to the sexual division of labor on nature alone. He argues that custom itself can be seen as a justification for maintaining particular practices. Bell, on the other hand, asks us to consider sexual inequality in relation to other forms of oppressive domination, for example, racist practices and institutions. She argues that we need to focus on the way that the family (the setting within which children are informed about values) perpetuates a misunderstanding of power as domination, a perspective that, in turn, infects social and personal relationships more generally. She argues for an account of power that avoids a feminist tendency to cast as victims those dominated by oppressive power relations.

JOHN STUART MILL

The Subjection of Women

JOHN STUART MILL (1806–1873) was one of the documented geniuses of modern history. By the age of ten, he had accomplished more than most scholars do in a lifetime. He is best known for his moral and political writings, particularly *On Liberty* (1859) and *Utilitarianism* (1863).

Neither does it avail anything to say that the *nature* of the two sexes adapts them to their present functions and position, and renders these appropriate to them. Standing on the ground of common sense and the constitution of the human mind, I deny that any one knows, or can know, the nature of the two sexes, as long as they have only been seen in their present relation to one another. If men had ever been found in society without women, or women without men, or if there had been a society of men and women in which the women were not under the control of the men, something might have been positively known about the mental and moral differences which may be inherent in the nature of each. What is now called the nature of women is an eminently artificial thing — the result of forced repression in some directions, unnatural stimulation in others. It may be asserted without scruple, that no other class of dependents have had their character so entirely distorted from its natural proportions by their relation with their masters; for, if conquered and slave races have been, in some respects, more forcibly repressed, whatever in them has not been crushed down by an iron heel has generally been let alone, and if left with any liberty of development, it has developed itself according to its own laws; but in the case of women, a hot-house and stove cultivation has always been carried on of some of the capabilities of their nature, for the benefit and pleasure of their masters. Then, because certain products of the general vital force sprout luxuriantly and reach a great development in this heated atmosphere and under this active nurture and watering, while other shoots from the same root, which are left outside in the wintry air, with ice purposely heaped all around them, have a stunted growth, and some are burnt off with fire and disappear; men, with that inability to recognize their own work which distinguishes the unanalytic mind, indolently believe that the tree grows of itself in the way they have made it grow, and that it would die if one half of it were not kept in a vapour bath and the other half in the snow.

Of all difficulties which impede the progress of thought, and the formation of well-grounded opinions on life and social arrangements, the greatest is now the unspeakable ignorance and inattention of mankind in respect to the influences which form human character. Whatever any portion of the human species now are, or seem to be, such, it is supposed, they have a natural tendency to be: even when the most elementary knowledge of the circumstances in which they have been placed, clearly points out the causes that made them what they are. . . . Because the Greeks cheated the Turks, and the Turks only plundered the Greeks, there are persons who think that the Turks are naturally more sincere: and because women, as is often said, care nothing about politics except their personalities, it is supposed that the general good is naturally less interesting to women than to men. History, which is now so much better understood than formerly, teaches another lesson: if only by showing the extraordinary susceptibility of human nature to external influences, and the extreme variableness of those of its manifestations which are supposed to be most universal and uniform. But in history, as in travelling, men usually see only what they already had in their own minds; and few learn much from history, who do not bring much with them to its study.

Hence, in regard to that most difficult question, what are the natural differences between the two sexes—a subject on which it is impossible in the present state of society to obtain complete and correct knowledge—while almost everybody dogmatizes upon it, almost all neglect and make light of the only means by which any partial insight can be obtained into it. This is, an analytic study of the most important department of psychology, the laws of the influence of circumstances on character. For, however great and apparently ineradicable the moral and intellectual differences between men and women might be, the evidence of there being natural differences could only be negative. Those only could be inferred to be natural which could not possibly be artificial—the residuum, after deducting every characteristic of either sex which can admit of being explained from education or external circumstances. The profoundest knowledge of the laws of the formation of character is indispensable to entitle any one to affirm even that there is any difference, much more what the difference is, between the two sexes considered as moral and rational beings; and since no one, as yet, has that knowledge (for there is hardly any subject which, in proportion to its importance, has been so little studied), no one is thus far entitled to any positive opinion on the subject. Conjectures are all that can at present be made; conjectures more or less probable, according as more or less authorized by such knowledge as we yet have of the laws of psychology, as applied to the formation of character.

Even the preliminary knowledge, what the differences between the sexes now are, apart from all question as to how they are made what they are, is still in the crudest and most incomplete state. Medical practitioners and physiologists have ascertained, to some extent, the differences in bodily constitution; and this is an important element to the psychologist: but hardly any medical practitioner is a psychologist. Respecting the mental characteristics of women; their observations are of no more worth than those of common men. It is a subject on which nothing final can be known, so long as those who alone can really know it, women themselves, have given but little testimony, and that little, mostly suborned. It is easy to know stupid women. Stupidity is much the same all the world over. A stupid person's notions and feelings may confidently be inferred from those which prevail in the circle by which the person is surrounded. Not so with those whose opinions and feelings are an emanation from their own nature and faculties. It is only a man here and there who has any tolerable knowledge of the character even of the women of his own family. I do not mean, of their capabilities; these nobody knows, not even themselves, because most of them have never been called out. I mean their actually existing thoughts and feelings. Many a man thinks he perfectly understands women, because he has had amatory relations with several, perhaps with many of them. If he is a good observer, and his experience extends to quality as well as quantity, he may have learnt something of one narrow department of their nature—an important department, no doubt. But of all the rest of it, few persons are generally more ignorant, because there are few from whom it is so carefully hidden. The most favorable case which a man can generally have for studying the character of a woman, is that of his own wife: for the opportunities are greater, and the cases of complete sympathy not so unspeakably rare. And in fact, this is the source from which any knowledge worth having on the subject has, I believe, generally come. But most men have not had the opportunity of studying in this way more than a single case: accordingly one can, to an almost laughable degree, infer what a man's wife is like, from his opinions about women in general. To make even this one case yield any results, the woman must be worth knowing, and the man not only a competent judge, but of a character so sympathetic in itself, and so well adapted to hers, that he can either read her mind by sympathetic intuition, or has nothing in himself which makes her shy of disclosing it. Hardly anything, I believe, can be more rare than this conjunction. It often happens that there is the most complete unity of feeling and community of interests as to all external things, yet the one has as little admission into the internal life of the other as if they were common acquaintance. Even with true affection, authority on the one side and subordination on the other prevent perfect confidence. Though nothing may be intentionally withheld, much is not shown. In the analogous relation of parent and child, the corresponding phenomenon must have been in the observation of every one. As between father and son, how many are the cases in which the father, in spite of real affection on both sides, obviously to all the world does not know, nor suspect, parts of the son's character familiar to his companions and equals. The truth is, that the position of looking up to another is extremely unpropitious to complete sincerity and openness with him. The fear of losing ground in his opinion or in his feelings is so strong, that even in an upright character, there is an unconscious tendency to show only the best side, or the side which, though not the best, is that which he most likes to see: and it may be confidently said that thorough knowledge of one another hardly ever exists, but between persons who, besides being intimates, are equals. How much more true, then, must all this be, when the one is not only under the authority of the other, but has it inculcated on her as a duty to reckon everything else subordinate to his comfort and pleasure, and to let him neither see nor feel anything coming from her, except what is agreeable to him. All these difficulties stand in the way of a man's obtaining any thorough knowledge even of the one woman whom alone, in general, he has sufficient opportunity of studying. When we further consider that to understand one woman is not necessary to understand any other woman; that even if he could study many women of one rank or of one country, he would not thereby understand women of other ranks or countries; and even if he did, they are still only the women of a single period of history; we may safely assert that the knowledge which men can acquire of women, even as they have been and are, without reference to what they might be, is wretchedly imperfect and superficial, and always will be so, until women themselves have told all that they have to tell.

And this time has not come; nor will be come otherwise than gradually. It is but of yesterday that women have either been qualified by literary accomplishments, or permitted by society, to tell anything to the general public. As yet very few of them dare tell anything, which men, on whom their literary success depends, are unwilling to hear. Let us remember in which manner, up to a very recent time, the expression, even by a male author, of uncustomary opinions, or what are deemed eccentric feelings, usually was, and in some degree still is, received; and we may form some faint conception under what impediments a woman, who is brought up to think custom and opinion her sovereign rule, attempts to express in books anything drawn from the depths of her own nature. The greatest woman who has left writings behind her sufficient to give her an eminent rank in the literature of her country, thought it necessary to prefix as a motto to her boldest work, 'A man dares to have an opinion; a woman must submit to it.' The greater part of what women write about women is mere sycophancy to men. In the case of unmarried women, much of it seems only intended to increase their chance of a husband. Many, both married and unmarried, overstep the mark, and inculcate a servility beyond what is desired or relished by any man, except the very vulgarest. But this not so often the case as, even at a quite late period, it still was. Literary women are becoming more freespoken, and more willing to express their real sentiments. Unfortunately, in this country especially, they are themselves such artificial products, that their sentiments are compounded of a small element of individual observation and consciousness, and a very large one of acquired associations. This will be less and less the case, but it will remain true to a great extent, as long as social institutions do not admit the same free development of originality in women which is possible to men. When that time comes, and not before, we shall see, and not merely hear, as much as it is necessary to know of the nature of women, and the adaptation of other things to it.

I have dwelt so much on the difficulties which at present obstruct any real knowledge by men of the true nature of women, because in this as in so many other things 'opinio copiae inter maximas causas inopiae est'; and there is little chance of reasonable thinking on the matter, while people flatter themselves that they perfectly understand a subject of which most men know absolutely nothing, and of which it is at present impossible that any man, or all men taken together, should have knowledge which can qualify them to lay down the law to women as to what is, or is not, their vocation. Happily, no such knowledge is necessary for any practical purpose connected with the position of women in relation to society and life. For, according to all the principles involved in modern society, the question rests with women themselves—to be decided by their own experience, and by the use of their own faculties. There are no means of finding what either one person or many can do, but by trying—and no means by which any one else can discover for them what it is for their happiness to do or leave undone.

One thing we may be certain of—that what is contrary to women's nature to do, they never will be made to do by simply giving their nature free play. The anxiety of mankind to interfere in behalf of nature, for fear lest nature should not succeed in effecting its purpose, is an altogether unnecessary solicitude. What women by nature cannot do, it is quite superfluous to forbid them from doing. What they can do, but not so well as the men who are their competitors, competition suffices to exclude them from; since nobody asks for protective duties and bounties in favour of women; it is only asked that the present bounties and protective duties in favour of men should be recalled. If women have a greater natural inclination for some things than for others, there is no need of laws or social inculcation to make the majority of them do the former in preference to the latter. Whatever women's services are most wanted for, the free play of competition will hold out the strongest inducements to them to undertake. And, as the words imply, they are most wanted for the things for which they are most fit; by the apportionment of which to them, the collective faculties of the two sexes can be applied on the whole with the greatest sum of valuable result.

The general opinion of men is supposed to be, that the natural vocation of a woman is that of a wife and mother. I say, is supposed to be, because, judging from acts—from the whole of the present constitution of society—one might infer that their opinion was the direct contrary. They might be supposed to think that the alleged natural vocation of women was of all things the most repugnant to their nature; insomuch that if they are free to do anything else—if any other means of living, or occupation of their time and faculties, is open, which has any chance of appearing desirable to them—there will not be enough of them who will be willing to accept the condition said to be natural to them. If this is the real opinion of men in general, it would be well that it should be spoken out. I should like to hear somebody openly enunciating the doctrine (it is already implied in much that is written on the subject)—'It is necessary to society that women should marry and produce children. They will not do so unless they are compelled. Therefore it is necessary to compel them.' The merits of the case would then be clearly defined. It would be exactly that of the slaveholders of South Carolina and Louisiana. 'It is necessary that cotton and sugar should be grown. White men cannot produce them. Negroes will not, for any wages which we choose to give. *Ergo* they must be compelled.' An illustration still closer to the point is that of impressment. Sailors must absolutely be had to defend the country. It often happens that they will not voluntarily enlist. Therefore there must be the power of forcing them. How often has this logic been used! and, but for one flaw in it, without doubt it would have been successful up to this day. But it is open to the retort—First pay the sailors the honest value of their labour. When you have made it as well worth their while to serve you, as to work for other employers, you will have no more difficulty than others have in obtaining their services. To this there is no logical answer except 'I will not': and as people are now not only ashamed, but are not desirous, to rob the labourer of his hire, impressment is no longer advocated. Those who attempt to force women into marriage by closing all other doors against them, lay themselves open to a similar retort. If they mean what they say, their opinion must evidently be, that men do not render the married condition so desirable to women, as to induce them to accept it for its own recommendations. It is not a sign of one's thinking the boon one offers very attractive, when one allows only Hobson's choice, 'that or none.' And here, I believe, is the clue to the feelings of those men, who have a real antipathy to the equal freedom of women. I believe they are afraid, not lest women should be unwilling to marry, for I do not think that any one in reality has that apprehension; but lest they should insist that marriage should be on equal conditions: lest all women of spirit and capacity should prefer doing almost anything else, not in their own eyes degrading, rather than marry, when marrying is giving themselves a master, and a master too of all their earthly possessions. And truly, if this consequence were necessarily incident to marriage, I think that the apprehension would be very well founded. I agree in thinking it probable that few women, capable of anything else, would, unless under an irresistible *entraînement*, rendering them for the time insensible to anything but itself, choose such a lot, when any other means were open to them of filling a conventionally honourable place in life: and if men are determined that the law of marriage shall be a law of despotism, they are quite right, in point of mere policy, in leaving to women only Hobson's choice. But, in that case, all that has been done in the modern world to relax the chain on the minds of women, has been a mistake. They never should have been allowed to receive a literary education. Women who read, much more women who write, are, in the existing constitution of things, a contradiction and a disturbing element: and it was wrong to bring women up with any acquirements but those of an odalisque, or of a domestic servant. . . .

When we consider how vast is the number of men, in any great country, who are little higher than brutes, and that this never prevents them from being able, through the law of marriage, to obtain a victim, the breadth and depth of human misery caused in this shape alone by the abuse of the institution swells to something appalling. Yet these are only the extreme cases. They are the lowest abysses, but there is a sad succession of depth after depth before reaching them. In domestic as in political tyranny, the case of absolute monsters chiefly illustrates the institution by showing that there is scarcely any horror which may not occur under it if the despot pleases, and thus setting in a strong light what must be the terrible frequency of things only a little less atrocious. Absolute fiends are as rare as angels, perhaps rarer: ferocious savages, with occasional touches of humanity, are, however, very frequent: and in the wide interval which separates these from any worthy representatives of the human species, how many are the forms and gradations of animalism and selfishness, often under an outward varnish of civilization and even cultivation, living at peace with the law, maintaining a creditable appearance to all who are not under their power, yet sufficient often to make the lives of all who are so, a torment and a burthen to them! It would be tiresome to repeat the commonplaces about the unfitness of men in general for power, which, after the political discussions of centuries, every one knows by heart, were it not that hardly any one thinks of applying these maxims to the case in which above all others they are applicable, that of power, not placed in the hands of a man here and there, but offered to every adult male, down to the basest and most ferocious. . . . I know that there is another side to the question. I grant that the wife, if she cannot effectually resist, can at least retaliate; she, too, can make the man's life extremely uncomfortable, and by that power is able to carry many points which she ought, and many which she ought not, to prevail in. But this instrument of self-protection—which may be called the power of the scold, or the shrewish sanction—has the fatal defect, that it avails most against the least tyrannical superiors, and in favor of the least deserving dependants. It is the weapon of irritable and self-willed women; of those who would make the worst use of power if they themselves had it, and who generally turn this power to a bad use. The amiable cannot use such an instrument, the high-minded disdain it. And on the other hand, the husbands against who it is used most effectively are the gentler and more inoffensive; those who cannot be induced, even by provocation, to resort to any very harsh exercise of authority. The wife's power of being disagreeable generally only establishes a counter-tyranny, and makes victims in their turn chiefly of those husbands who are least inclined to be tyrants. . . .

With regard to the fitness of women, not only to participate in elections, but themselves to hold offices or practise professions involving important public responsibilities; I have already observed that this consideration is not essential to the practical question in dispute: since any woman, who succeeds in an open profession, proves by that very fact that she is qualified for it. And in the case of public offices, if the political system of the country is such as to exclude unfit men, it will equally exclude unfit women: while if it is not, there is no additional evil in the fact that the unfit persons whom it admits may be either women or men. As long therefore as it is acknowledged that even a few women may be fit for these duties, the laws which shut the door on those exceptions cannot be justified by any opinion which can be held respecting the capacities of women in general. But, though this last consideration is not essential, it is far from being irrelevant. An unprejudiced view of it gives additional strength to the arguments against the disabilities of women, and reinforces them by high consideration of practical utility.

Let us at first make entire abstraction of all psychological considerations tending to show, that any of the mental differences supposed to exist between women and men are but the natural effect of the differences in their education and circumstances, and indicate no radical difference, far less radical inferiority, of nature. Let us consider women only as they already are, or as they are known to have been; and the capacities which they have already practically shown. What they have done, that at least, if nothing else, it is proved that they can do. When we consider how sedulously they are all trained away from, instead of being trained towards, any of the occupations or objects reserved for men, it is evident that I am taking a very humble ground for them, when I rest their case on what they have actually achieved. For, in this case, negative evidence is worth little, while any positive evidence is conclusive. It cannot be inferred to be impossible that a woman should be a Homer, or an Aristotle, or a Michelangelo, or a Beethoven, because no woman has yet actually produced works comparable to theirs in any of those lines of excellence. This negative fact at most leaves the question uncertain, and open to psychological discussion. But it is quite certain that a woman can be a Queen Elizabeth, or a Deborah, or a Joan of Arc, since this is not inference, but fact. Now it is a curious consideration, that the only things which the existing law excludes women from doing, are the things which they have proved that they are able to do. There is no law to prevent a woman from having written all the plays of Shakespeare, or composed all the operas of Mozart. But Queen Elizabeth or Queen Victoria, had they not inherited the throne, could not have been entrusted with the smallest of the political duties, of which the former showed herself equal to the greatest.

If anything conclusive could be inferred from experience, without psychological analysis, it would be that the things which women are not allowed to do are the very ones for which they are peculiarly qualified; since their vocation for government has made its way, and become conspicuous, through the very few opportunities which have been given; while in the lines of distinction which apparently were freely open to them, they have by no means so eminently distinguished themselves. We know how small a number of reigning queens history presents, in comparison with that of kings. Of this smaller number a far larger proportion have shown talents for rule; though many of them have occupied the throne in difficult periods. It is remarkable, too, that they have, in a great number of instances, been distinguished by merits the most opposite to the imaginary and conventional character of women: they have been as much remarked for the firmness and vigour of their rule, as for its intelligence. When, to queens and empresses, we add regents, and viceroys of provinces, the list of women who have been eminent rulers of mankind swells to a great length. . . .

Exactly where and in proportion as women's capacities for government have been tried, in that proportion have they been found adequate.

This fact is in accordance with the best general conclusions which the world's imperfect experience seems as yet to suggest, concerning the peculiar tendencies and aptitudes characteristic of women, as women have hitherto been. I do not say, as they will continue to be; for, as I have already said more than once, I consider it presumption in any one to pretend to decide what women are or are not, can or cannot be, by natural constitution. They have always hitherto been kept, as far as regards spontaneous development, in so unnatural a state, that their nature cannot but have been greatly distorted and disguised; and no one can safely pronounce that if women's nature were left to choose its direction as freely as men's, and if no artificial bent were attempted to be given to it except that required by the conditions of human society, and given to both sexes alike, there would be any material difference, or perhaps any difference at all, in the character and capacities which would unfold themselves. . . . Even the least contestable of the differences which now exist, are such as may very well have been produced merely by circumstances, without any difference of natural capacity.

SIMONE DE BEAUVOIR

The Second Sex

SIMONE DE BEAUVOIR (1908–1986) was a French philosopher best known for her extensive contributions to the development of feminist thought. A lifelong companion of Jean-Paul Sartre, her philosophical roots are in the existentialist tradition. Her book *The Second Sex* (1952) is a classic of feminist philosophy.

For a long time I have hesitated to write a book on woman. The subject is irritating, especially to women; and it is not new. Enough ink has been spilled in the quarreling over feminism, now practically over, and perhaps we should say no more about it. It is still talked about, however, for the voluminous nonsense uttered during the last century seems to have done little to illuminate the problem. After all, is there a problem? And if so, what is it? Are there women, really? Most assuredly the theory of the eternal feminine still has its adherents who will whisper in your ear: "Even in Russia women still are *women*"; and other erudite persons—sometimes the very same—say with a sigh: "Woman is losing her way, woman is lost." One wonders if women still exist, if they will always exist, whether or not it is desirable that they should, what place they occupy in this world, what their place should be. "What has become of women?" was asked recently in an ephemeral magazine.

But first we must ask: what is a woman"? *"Tota mulier in utero,"* says one, "woman is a womb." But in speaking of certain women, connoisseurs declare that they are not women, although they are equipped with a uterus like the rest. All agree in recognizing the fact that females exist in the human species; today as always they make up about one half of humanity. And yet we are told that femininity is in danger; we are exhorted to be women, remain women, become women. It would appear, then, that every female human being is not necessarily a woman; to be so considered she must share in that mysterious and threatened reality known as femininity. Is this attribute something secreted by the ovaries? Or is it a Platonic essence, a product of the philosophic imagination? Is a rustling petticoat enough to bring it down to earth? Although some women try zealously to incarnate this essence, it is hardly patentable. It is frequently described in vague and dazzling terms that seem to have been borrowed from the vocabulary of the seers, and indeed in the times of St. Thomas it was considered an essence as certainly defined as the somniferous virtue of the poppy.

But conceptualism has lost ground. The biological and social sciences no longer admit the existence of unchangeable fixed entities that determine given characteristics, such as those ascribed to woman, the Jew, or the Negro. Science regards any characteristic as a reaction dependent in part upon a *situation*. If today femininity no longer exists, then it never existed. But does the word *woman*, then, have no specific content? This is stoutly affirmed by those who hold to the philosophy of the enlightenment, of rationalism, of nominalism; women, to them, are merely the human beings arbitrarily designated by the word *woman*. Many American women particularly are prepared to think that there is no longer any place for woman as such; if a backward individual still takes herself for a woman, her friends advise her to be psychoanalyzed and thus get rid of this obsession. In regard to a work, *Modern Woman: The Lost Sex,* which in other respects has its irritating features, Dorothy Parker has written: "I cannot be just to books which treat of woman as woman. . . . My idea is that all of us, men as well as women, should be regarded as human beings." But nominalism is a rather inadequate doctrine, and the antifeminists have had no trouble in showing that woman simply *are not* men. Surely woman is, like man, a human being; but such a declaration is abstract. The fact is that every concrete human being is always a singular, separate individual. To decline to accept such notions as the eternal feminine, the black soul, the Jewish character, is not to deny that Jews, Negroes, women exist today—this denial does not represent a liberation for those concerned, but rather a flight from reality. Some years ago a well-known woman writer refused to permit her portrait to appear in a series of photographs especially devoted to women writers; she wished to be counted among the men. But in order to gain this privilege she made use of her husband's influence! Women who assert that they are men lay claim none the less to masculine consideration and respect. I recall also a young Trotskyite standing on a platform at a boisterous meeting and getting ready to use her fists, in spite of her evident fragility. She was denying her feminine weakness; but it was for love of a militant male whose equal she wished to be. The attitude of defiance of many American women proves that they are haunted by a sense of their femininity. In truth, to go for a walk with one's eyes open is enough to demonstrate that humanity is divided into two classes of individuals whose clothes, faces, bodies, smiles, gaits, interests, and occupations are manifestly different. Perhaps these differences are superficial, perhaps they are destined to disappear. What is certain is that right now they do most obviously exist.

If her functioning as a female is not enough to define woman, if we decline also to explain her through "the eternal feminine," and if nevertheless we admit, provisionally, that women do exist, then we must face the question: what is a woman?

To state the question is, to me, to suggest, at once, a preliminary answer. The fact that I ask it is in itself significant. A man would never get the notion of writing a book on the peculiar situation of the human male. But if I wish to define myself, I must first of all say: "I am a woman"; on this truth must be based all further discussion. A man never begins by presenting himself as an individual of a certain sex; it goes without saying that he is a man. The terms *masculine* and *feminine* are used symmetrically only as a matter of form, as on legal papers. In actuality the relation of the two sexes is not quite like that of two electrical poles, for man represents both the positive and the neutral, as is indicated by the common use of *man* to designate human beings in general; whereas woman represents only the negative, defined by limiting criteria, without reciprocity. In the midst of an abstract discussion it is vexing to hear a man say: "You think thus and so because you are a woman"; but I know that my only defense is to reply: "I think thus and so because it is true," thereby removing my subjective self from the argument. It would be out of the question to reply: "And you think the contrary because you are a man," for it is understood that the fact of being a man is no peculiarity. A man is in the right in being a man; it is the woman who is in the wrong. It amounts to this: just as for the ancients there was an absolute vertical with reference to which the oblique was defined, so there is an absolute human type, the masculine. Woman has ovaries, a uterus; these peculiarities imprison her in her subjectivity, circumscribe her within the limits of her own nature. It is often said that she thinks with her glands. Man superbly ignores the fact that his anatomy also includes glands, such as the testicles, and that they secrete hormones. He thinks of his body as a direct and normal connection with the world, which he believes he apprehends objectively, whereas he regards the body of woman as a hindrance, a prison, weighed down by everything peculiar to it. "The female is a female by virtue of a certain *lack* of qualities," said Aristotle; "we should regard the female nature as afflicted with a natural defectiveness." And St. Thomas for his part pronounced woman to be an "imperfect man," an "incidental" being. This is symbolized in Genesis where Eve is depicted as made from what Bossuet called "a supernumerary bone" of Adam.

Thus humanity is male and man defines woman not in herself but as relative to him; she is not regarded as an autonomous being. Michelet writes: "Woman, the relative being. . . ." And Benda is most positive in his *Rapport d'Uriel*: "The body of man makes sense in itself quite apart from that of woman, whereas the latter seems wanting in significance by itself. . . . Man can think of himself without woman. She cannot think of herself without man." And she is simply what man decrees; thus she is called "the sex," by which is meant that she appears essentially to the male as a sexual being. For him she is sex—absolute sex, no less. She is defined and differentiated with reference to man and not he with reference to her; she is the incidental, the inessential as opposed to the essential. He is the subject, he is the Absolute—she is the Other.

The category of the *Other* is as primordial as consciousness itself. In the most primitive societies, in the most ancient mythologies, one finds the expression of a duality—that of the Self and the Other. This duality was not originally attached to the division of the sexes; it was not dependent upon any empirical facts. It is revealed in such works as that of Granet on Chinese thought and those of Dumézil on the East Indies and Rome. The feminine element was at first no more involved in such pairs as Varuna-Mitra, Uranus-Zeus, Sun-Moon, and Day-Night than it was in the contrasts between Good and Evil, lucky and unlucky auspices, right and left, God and Lucifer. Otherness is a fundamental category of human thought.

Thus it is that no group ever sets itself up as the One without at once setting up the Other over against itself. If three travelers chance to occupy the same compartment, that is enough to make vaguely hostile "others" out of all the rest of the passengers on the train. In small-town eyes all persons not belonging to the village are "strangers" and suspect; to the native of a country all who inhabit other countries are "foreigners"; Jews are "different" for the anti-Semite, Negroes are "inferior" for American racists, aborigines are "natives" for colonists, proletarians are the "lower class" for the privileged. . . .

The native traveling abroad is shocked to find himself in turn regarded as a "stranger" by the natives of neighboring countries. As a matter of fact, wars, festivals, trading, treaties, and contests among tribes, nations, and classes tend to deprive the concept *Other* of its absolute sense and to make manifest its relativity; willy-nilly, individuals and groups are forced to realize the reciprocity of their relations. How is it, then, that this reciprocity has not been recognized between the sexes, that one of the contrasting terms is set up as the sole essential, denying any relativity in regard to its correlative and defining the latter as pure otherness? Why is it that women do not dispute male sovereignty? No subject will readily volunteer to become the object, the inessential; it is not the Other who, in defining himself as the Other, establishes the One. The Other is posed as such by the One in defining himself as the One. But if the Other is not to regain the status of being the One, he must be submissive enough to accept this alien point of view. Whence comes this submission in the case of woman? . . .

History has shown us that men have always kept in their hands all concrete powers; since the earliest days of the patriarchate they have thought best to keep woman in a state of dependence; their codes of law have been set up against her; and thus she has been definitely established as the Other. This arrangement suited the economic interests of the males; but it conformed also to their ontological and moral pretensions. Once the subject seeks to assert himself, the Other, who limits and denies him, is none the less a necessity to him: he attains himself only through that reality which he is not, which is something other than himself. That is why man's life is never abundance and quietude; it is dearth and activity, it is struggle. Before him, man encounters Nature; he has some hold upon her, he endeavors to mold her to his desire. But she cannot fill his needs. Either she appears simply as a purely impersonal opposition, she is an obstacle and remains a stranger; or she submits passively to man's will and permits assimilation, so that he takes possession of her only through consuming her—that is, through destroying her. In both cases he remains alone; he is alone when he touches a stone, alone when he devours a fruit. There can be no presence of an other unless the other is also present in and for himself: which is to say that true alterity—otherness—is that of a consciousness separate from mine and substantially identical with mine.

It is the existence of other men that tears each man out of his immanence and enables him to fulfill the truth of his being, to complete himself through transcendence, through escape toward some objective, through enterprise. But this liberty not my own, while assuring mine, also conflicts with it: there is the tragedy of the unfortunate human consciousness; each separate conscious being aspires to set himself up alone as sovereign subject. Each tries to fulfill himself by reducing the other to slavery. But the slave, though he works and fears, senses himself somehow as the essential; and, by a dialectical inversion, it is the master who seems to be the inessential. It is possible to rise above this conflict if each individual freely recognizes the other, each regarding himself and the other simultaneously as object and as subject in a reciprocal manner. But friendship and generosity, which alone permit in actuality this recognition of free beings, are not facile virtues; they are assuredly man's highest achievement, and through that achievement he is to be found in his true nature. But this true nature is that of a struggle unceasingly begun, unceasingly abolished; it requires man to outdo himself at every moment. We might put it in other words and say that man attains an authentically moral attitude when he renounces *mere being* to assume his position as an existent; through this transformation also he renounces all possession, for possession is one way of seeking mere being; but the transformation through which he attains true wisdom is never done, it is necessary to make it without ceasing, it demands a constant tension. And so, quite unable to fulfill himself in solitude, man is incessantly in danger in his relations with his fellows: his life is a difficult enterprise with success never assured.

But he does not like difficulty; he is afraid of danger. He aspires in contradictory fashion both to life and to repose, to existence and to merely being; he knows full well that "trouble of spirit" is the price of development, that his distance from the object is the price of his nearness to himself; but he dreams of quiet in disquiet and of an opaque plentitude that nevertheless would be endowed with consciousness. This dream incarnated is precisely woman; she is the wished-for intermediary between nature, the stranger to man, and the fellow being who is too closely identical. She opposes him with neither the hostile silence of nature nor the hard requirement of a reciprocal relation; through a unique privilege she is a conscious being and yet it seems possible to possess her in the flesh. Thanks to her, there is a means for escaping that implacable dialectic of master and slave which has its source in the reciprocity that exists between free beings.

We have seen that there were not at first free women whom the males had enslaved nor were there even castes based on sex. To regard woman simply as a slave is a mistake; there were women among the slaves, to be sure, but there have always been free women—that is, women of religious and social dignity. They accepted man's sovereignty and he did not feel menaced by a revolt that could make of him in turn the object. Woman thus seems to be the inessential who never goes back to being the essential, to be the absolute Other, without reciprocity. This conviction is dear to the male, and every creation myth has expressed it, among others the legend of Genesis, which, through Christianity, has been kept alive in Western civilization. Eve was not fashioned at the same time as the man; she was not fabricated from a different substance, nor of the same clay as was used to model Adam: she was taken from the flank of the first male. Not even her birth was independent; God did not spontaneously choose to create her as an end in herself and in order to be worshipped directly by her in return for it. She was destined by Him for man; it was to rescue Adam from loneliness that He gave her to him, in her mate was her origin and her purpose; she was his complement on the order of the inessential. Thus she appeared in the guise of privileged prey. She was nature elevated to transparency of consciousness; she was a conscious being, but naturally submissive. And therein lies the wondrous hope that man has often put in woman: he hopes to fulfill himself as a being by carnally possessing a being, but at the same time confirming his sense of freedom through the docility of a free person. No man would consent to be a woman, but every man wants women to exist. "Thank God for having created woman." "Nature is good since she has given women to men." In such expressions man once more asserts with naïve arrogance that his presence in this world is an ineluctable fact and a right, that of woman a mere accident—but a very happy accident. Appearing as the Other, woman appears at the same time as an abundance of being in contrast to that existence the nothingness of which man senses in himself; the Other, being regarded as the object in the eyes of the subject, is regarded as *en soi*; therefore as a being. In woman is incarnated in positive form the lack that the existent carries in his heart, and it is in seeking to be made whole through her that man hopes to attain self-realization. . . .

Perhaps the myth of woman will some day be extinguished; the more women assert themselves as human beings, the more the marvelous quality of the Other will die out in them. But today it still exists in the heart of every man.

A myth always implies a subject who projects his hopes and his fears toward a sky of transcendence. Women do not set themselves up as Subject and hence have erected no virile myth in which their projects are reflected; they have no religion or poetry of their own; they still dream through the dreams of men. Gods made by males are the gods they worship. Men have shaped for their own exaltation great virile figures: Hercules, Prometheus, Parsifal; woman has only a secondary part to play in the destiny of these heroes. No doubt there are conventional figures of man caught in his relations to woman: the father, the seducer, the husband, the jealous lover, the good son, the wayward son; but they have all been established by men, and they lack the dignity of myth, being hardly more than clichés. Whereas woman is defined exclusively in her relation to man. The asymmetry of the categories—male and female—is made manifest in the unilateral form of sexual myths. We sometimes say "the sex" to designate woman; she is the flesh, its delights and dangers. The truth that for woman man is sex and carnality has never been proclaimed because there is no one to proclaim it. Representation of the world, like the world itself, is the work of men; they describe it from their own point of view, which they confuse with absolute truth.

It is always difficult to describe a myth; it cannot be grasped or encompassed; it haunts the human consciousness without ever appearing before it in fixed form. The myth is so various, so contradictory, that at first its unity is not discerned: Delilah and Judith, Aspasia and Lucretia, Pandora and Athena—woman is at once Eve and the Virgin Mary. She is an idol, a servant, the source of life, a power of darkness; she is the elemental silence of truth, she is artifice, gossip, and falsehood; she is healing presence and sorceress; she is man's prey, his downfall, she is everything that he is not and that he longs for, his negation and his *raison d'être*. . . .

Man seeks in woman the Other as Nature and as his fellow being. But we know what ambivalent feelings Nature inspires in man. He exploits her, but she crushes him, he is born of her and dies in her; she is the source of his being and the realm that he subjugates to his will; Nature is a vein of gross material in which the soul is imprisoned, and she is the supreme reality; she is contingence and Idea, the finite and the whole; she is what opposes the Spirit, and the Spirit itself. Now ally, now enemy, she appears as the dark chaos from whence life wells up, as this life itself, and as the over-yonder toward which life tends. Woman sums up nature as Mother, Wife and Idea; these forms now mingle and now conflict, and each of them wears a double visage. . . .

This, then, is the reason why woman has a double and deceptive visage; she is all that man desires and all that he does not attain. She is the good mediatrix between propitious Nature and man; and she is the temptation of unconquered Nature, counter to all goodness. She incarnates all moral values, from good to evil, and their opposites; she is the substance of action and whatever is an obstacle to it, she is man's grasp on the world and his frustration; as such she is the source and origin of all man's reflection on his existence and of whatever expression he is able to give to it; and yet she works to divert him from himself, to make him sink down in silence and in death. She is servant and companion, but he expects her also to be his audience and critic and to confirm him in his sense of being; but she opposes him with her indifference, even with her mockery and laughter. He projects upon her what he desires and what he fears, what he loves and what he hates. And if it is so difficult to say anything specific about her, that is because man seeks the whole of himself in her and because she is All. She is All, that is, on the plane of the inessential; she is all the Other. And, as the other, she is other than herself, other than what is expected of her. Being all, she is never quite *this* which she should be; she is everlasting deception, the very deception of that existence which is never successfully attained nor fully reconciled with the totality of existents.

JEAN GRIMSHAW

Autonomy and Identity in Feminist Thinking

JEAN GRIMSHAW teaches philosophy and cultural studies at Bristol Polytechnic in England. She is the author of *Feminist Philosophers: Women's Perspectives on Philosophical Traditions* (1986).

Issues about women's autonomy have been central to feminist thinking and action. Women have so often been in situations of powerlessness and dependence that any system of belief or programme of action that could count as 'feminist' must in some way see this as a central concern. But what is meant by 'autonomy' and under what conditions is it possible? This has been an important and contentious question in philosophy. But questions about autonomy, and related questions about self and identity have also been important to feminism, and within feminist thinking it is possible to find radically different ways of thinking about these things. In this paper, I want to look at one kind of way in which some feminists have tried to conceptualize what it is for a woman to be 'autonomous', and at the implications this has for ways of thinking about the human self. I shall argue that this conception is not only philosophically problematic, but also has an implicit politics which is potentially damaging. And I shall try to suggest some ways of beginning to think about 'autonomy' which seem to me to be more fruitful and adequate, and to draw on different traditions of thinking about the self which have become influential in some recent feminist thinking.

Feminist thinking does not, of course, exist in a vacuum, and in thinking about women's autonomy, feminists have drawn on different (and conflicting) approaches to questions about the human self, some of which have a long history. I want to begin by going back to an argument that Aristotle put forward in the *Ethics*, since I think that the point at which his argument breaks down can illuminate the nature of the problem some feminist thinking has faced.

Aristotle's argument concerns the question of what it is that makes an action 'voluntary', done of a person's own free will, and in order to answer this question, he distinguished between actions whose origin was 'inside' a person, and those whose origin was 'outside', which resulted from external influences or pressure or compulsion. He discussed at some length the problems that arise over trying to define ideas such as 'compulsion', and in estimating the degree of severity of pressure that could make an action not voluntary. But in this sort of model of autonomy, what defines an action as autonomous is seen as its point of *origin*; it must have an 'immaculate conception', as it were, from *within* the self.

Now ultimately I think that it is this definition of 'autonomy' in terms of origin, and the associated distinction between an 'inner' self which can in some way spontaneously generate its 'own' actions, and 'external' influences which are not 'part' of the self, that will need challenging. But I think it is possible to defend the Aristotelian version of autonomy up to a point, provided notions of 'inside' and 'outside' the self are defined in a certain way. If a person is prevented from doing what they would otherwise intend or desire to do, or if they are coerced into doing what they would *not* otherwise want or desire to do, they are not acting autonomously. Under this interpretation, actions which originate from 'inside' the self are those which are seen as in accordance with conscious desires or intentions, and those which originate from 'outside' the self are those which one would not do if one were not coerced. The pressure here is to consider the sorts of circumstances which do, in fact, coerce people in these sorts of ways. And, of course, a central concern of feminism has been to identify and fight against the kinds of coercion to which women have been subjected, including things like physical violence and economic dependence.

But it is at this point that an Aristotelian-type argument fails to be able to deal with the most difficult questions about autonomy. The Aristotelian view, as I have interpreted it, 'works' only to the extent that it is assumed that there is no problem about what I shall call 'the autonomy of desires'. Autonomy is defined as acting in accordance with desire (or intention). But what of the desires themselves? Are there *desires* (or intentions) which are not 'autonomous', which do not originate from 'within' the self, which are not authentic, not really 'one's own'?

Feminist writers have wanted, of course, to indict the various forms of brutality and coercion from which women have suffered. But this brutality and coercion has been seen not merely as a question of physical or 'external' coercion or constraint; the force of subjection has also been seen as a psychic one, invading women's very selves. The language of 'conditioning', 'brainwashing', 'indoctrination', and so forth, has been used to describe this force. The female self, under male domination, is riddled through and through with false or conditioned desires. But set against this conditioned, non-autonomous female self are various images of a female self that would be authentic, that would transcend or shatter this conditioning. I want now to look at some of these images of the female self in feminist discourse: my particular examples are from the work of Mary Daly, Marilyn Frye and Kate Millett.

Daly, Frye and Millett all stress the way in which women have been subject to the *power* of men. Much of Daly's book, *Gyn/Ecology* (1979), is an account of the barbarities inflicted on women such as suttee, clitorectomy, foot-binding and other forms of mutilation. Millett, in *Sexual Politics* (1977), sees patriarchal power as something so historically all-embracing that it has totally dominated women's lives. Frye, in *The Politics of Reality* (1983), uses the situation of a young girl sold into sexual slavery and then systematically brutalized and brainwashed into a life of service to her captors as an analogy for the situation of all women. And all three writers stress the way in which they see the female self as 'invaded' by patriarchal conditioning. Millett writes:

> When, in any group of persons, the ego is subjected to such invidious versions of itself through social beliefs, ideology and tradition, the effect is bound to be pernicious. This should make it no very special cause for surprise that women develop group characteristics common to those who suffer minority status and a marginal existence.

Women, she argues, are deprived of all but the most trivial sources of dignity or self-respect. In her discussion of Lawrence's depiction of Connie in *Lady Chatterley's Lover*, what she sees Connie as relinquishing is 'self, ego, will, individuality', all those things which, Millett argues, women had but recently achieved, (and for which Lawrence had a profound distaste).

Mary Daly's picture of the way in which women's selves are invaded by patriarchal conditioning is even more striking. She describes women, for example, as 'moronised', 'robotised', 'lobotomised', as 'the puppets of Papa'. At times she seems to see women as so 'brainwashed' that they are scarcely human; thus she describes them as 'fembots', even as 'mutants'. In Millett, Daly and Frye, women are seen primarily as victims: the monolithic brutality and psychological pressures of male power have reduced women almost to the state of being 'non-persons'. And indeed, as Daly sees women as having become 'mutants' or 'fembots', so Millett sees them as not having been allowed to participate in fully 'human' activities (which she characterises as those that are most remote from the biological contingencies of life), and Frye sees them as simply 'broken' and then 'remade' in the way that suits their masters.

But behind this victimised female self, whose actions and desires are assumed to be not truly 'her own', since they derive from processes of force, conditioning or psychological manipulation, there is seen to be an authentic female self, whose recovery or discovery it is one of the aims of feminism to achieve. The spatial metaphor implicit in the word 'behind' is not accidental, since this model of self is premised on the possibility of making a distinction between an 'inner' and an 'outer' self. . . . In *Gyn/Ecology*, discovering or recovering one's own self is seen as akin to a process of salvation or religious rebirth, and Daly writes of what she calls the unveiling or unwinding of the 'shrouds' of patriarchy to reveal the authentic female Spirit-Self underneath. And this Self is seen as a unitary and harmonious one. Splits and barriers within the psyche, she argues, as well as those between Selves, are the result of patriarchal conditioning. In the unitary and harmonious female Spirit-Self there will be no such splits.

Millett's picture of the authentic female self is rather different from that of Daly. It does not draw, as Daly's does, on religious metaphors of salvation and rebirth. It derives, rather, from a picture of the self as fundamentally a unitary, conscious and rational thing, a picture which, in Western philosophy, can be traced back to Descartes. It emerges most clearly in her discussion of Freud. She describes Freud's theory of the Unconscious as a major contribution to human understanding, but her account of the self owes, in fact, scarcely anything to Freud. She is scathingly critical of Freud's theory of penis envy: Freud, she argued, 'did not accept his patient's symptoms as evidence of a justified dissatisfaction with the limiting circumstances imposed on them by society, but as symptomatic of an independent and universal feminine tendency'. He made a major (and foolish) confusion between biology and culture. Girls, Millett argues, are fully cognisant of male supremacy long before they see their brother's penis: and what they envy is not the penis, but the things to which having a penis gives the boy access—power, status and rewards. Freud ignored the more likely 'social' hypothesis for feminine dissatisfaction, preferring to ascribe it to a biologically based female nature. What we should be studying, Millett argues, are the effects of male-supremacist culture on the female ego. And what will undo these effects, she writes in the Postscript, is altered consciousness, and a process of 'human growth and true re-education'.

The 'social' factors of which Millett writes are here seen as pressures which are 'external' to the self, and which have the effect of thwarting the conscious and unitary rationality of female individuality, or the female ego. And the task is that of *removing* their influence. . . .

The paradigm of coercion, writes Frye, is *not* the direct application of physical force. Rather, it is a situation in which choice and action *do* take place, and in which the victim acts under her own perception and judgement. Hence, what the exploiter needs is that

> the will and intelligence of the victim be disengaged from the projects of resistance and escape but that they not be simply broken or destroyed. Ideally, the disintegration and misintegration of the victim should accomplish the detachment of the victim's will and intelligence from the victim's own interests and their attachment to the interests of the exploiter. This will effect a displacement or dissolution of self-respect and will undermine the victim's intolerance of coercion. With that, the situation transcends the initial paradigmatic form or structure or coercion; for if people don't mind doing what you want them to do, you can't really be *making* them do it.

And, she writes:

> The health and integrity of an organism is a matter of its being organised largely towards its own interests and welfare. *She* is healthy and 'working right' when her substance is organised primarily on principles which align it to *her* interests and welfare. Co-operation is essential of course, but it will not do that I arrange everything so that *you* get enough exercise; for me to be healthy, *I* must get enough exercise. My being adequately exercised is logically independent of your being so.

Frye is writing here as if it were possible to distinguish the interests of one self sharply from those of another, and as if, were the effects of male domination to be undone, it would not be too much of a problem for the self to know what its interests were.

In various ways then, underlying much of the work of these three writers is a set of assumptions about the self. First, that it is, at least potentially, a unitary, rational thing, aware of its interests. Second, that 'splits' within the psyche should be seen as resulting from the interference of patriarchal or male-dominated socialisation or conditioning. Third, that the task of undoing this conditioning is one that can be achieved solely by a rational process of learning to understand and fight against the social and institutional effects of male domination. And implicit in these assumptions about the self, I think, is a conception of autonomy. Frye writes that 'left to themselves' women would not want to serve men. Daly writes of unveiling or unwinding the 'shrouds' of patriarchy. Millett writes of the individuality and ego that women can discover in themselves once they recognise the effects of their patriarchal socialisation. And in all three, what is autonomous (or authentic) is what is seen as originating in some way from *within* the self; what is in some way *untainted* by the conditioning or manipulation to which a woman has previously been subjected.

Before I come to discuss the philosophical problems that are raised by this sort of account of self and autonomy, I want to look at what I have called its implicit politics; and what I mean by this primarily is its possible consequences for the way in which women might think about their relationships to each other, and the way in which they might think about themselves. The first consequence seems to me to be this. Any view which see self-affirmation in terms of an 'authentic' inner self arising from the smashing of a socially conditioned 'false self', or which sees autonomy as a question of the origin of actions from 'inside' rather than 'outside', is almost bound to adopt, however implicitly, a derogatory attitude towards those who are not yet 'authentic'. The precise nature and tone of this attitude may vary. But Mary Daly, for example, in *Gyn/Ecology*, sometimes writes as if most women were really little more than the programmed, robotic puppets. . . . And this is related, for example, to Daly's scorn for 'tokenism'—for those women who participate in what are seen as patriarchal institutions. Kate Millett's language is less obviously extreme. But the picture she paints of women is nevertheless often a derogatory one. She describes them, for example, as 'infantilised'; she accepts without question research which purported to show that most women despised each other; she sees women as having little 'self-respect', and as devoting almost all their time and attention to pleasing and flattering men.

This implicitly derogatory attitude to women is linked both to an overmonolithic account of male power, and to a failure to give much attention to the ways in which women have, in fact, often spent much of their lives, and to the activities which have been particularly theirs (such as the rearing of children, for example). Sometimes women are depicted almost as a caricature of a male stereotype of themselves—they *are* servile, weak, powerless etc.

Mary Daly's indictment of male power and brutality similarly allows little space for a consideration of the patterns of women's lives, or the strengths and capacities that these might have enabled them to develop. Her female Spirit-Self simply seems to rise mysteriously like a phoenix from the ashes of patriarchal conditioning. And Frye is sceptical about the possibility of women looking to their foremothers as a source of inspiration; of seeing some women, at least, as having led lives that were not wholly male-mediated. Feminist vision or imagination has no real resource to turn to.

Now these kinds of accounts (or perhaps one might say *failures* to give an adequate account?) of women's lives are implicitly divisive and threatening. They are divisive because they have a tendency to divide women into two camps; those who have and those who have not shaken the dust of patriarchal conditioning from their feet. And they are threatening, because it is offensive and undermining to be told that the life one has led has merely been one of servility, that it has not been of truly 'human' value, that one has been a 'fembot' or a 'puppet'. I think that one important strand in the rejection of feminism by many women has been a feeling that feminists are saying that their lives have been of no value, and that their activities and concerns have been trivial.

But this image of autonomy and of the self can be threatening, too, to women who *do* have a strong allegiance to feminism; and the threat intersects with assumptions that have been made in some feminist discourse about who is or is not 'really' a feminist. The threat arises because this account of autonomy is in fact often a strongly *normative* one; it presents an image of what a 'feminist self' should be like. To be autonomous or authentic one should be strong, independent, rational, coherent or consistent, able to distinguish clearly those aspects of one's previous self which derive from male-dominated conditioning and reject them. If one is ambivalent, conflicted, uncertain, confused, unwilling to make wholesale rejections, one stands to be accused, whether by oneself or by others, of bad faith, of lack of courage, of 'selling out', of tokenism.

I am here giving an account of just one (influential) strand in feminist discourse. There are other strands which have rejected this account of self and autonomy. As I have said before, a picture of the self as conscious, unitary and rational can be traced back, in Western philosophy, to Descartes. . . .

Now any adequate account of self needs to be able, I think, to encompass and try to make intelligible the ways in which women and men experience themselves. And the central reasons for rejecting the 'humanist' paradigm of the self—as I have outlined it above—are, firstly, that there may be aspects of the development of self which are not easily accessible to consciousness, and secondly, that there are conscious experiences which are not easy to make intelligible within the humanist paradigm. I want now to look at some aspects of self-experience that I think should be central to any theory of self, and hence to any discussion of women's autonomy. . . .

There is a type of feminist criticism, both in literature and other media (and in fields such as education), which has been called 'Images of Women' criticism. This has supposed that feminist effort should be devoted, first, to showing how the 'images' in question oppress or denigrate women, and second, to offering positive images of women to replace these. One problem with this kind of criticism is that the 'images' in question have often been misinterpreted, since they have been discussed without reference to the context or narrative structure in which they may appear. But there are two other problems with this type of criticism which I want to focus on here. First, what this approach often fails to recognise is the importance of understanding the *appeal* of the 'images' that are criticised; the relations they may have to women's pleasures, desires, fantasies, fears and conceptions of themselves. Second, it fails to recognise what is signally obvious in the experience of many women, myself of course included, namely that it is perfectly possible to agree 'in one's head' that certain images of women might be reactionary or damaging or oppressive, while remaining committed to them in emotion and desire. I suspect that this 'split' happens at times in all women, and perhaps particularly in those who have some commitment to feminism. And what it suggests is that structures of desire, emotion and fantasy have deep roots of some sort in the self which are not necessarily amenable in any simple way to processes of conscious rational argument. An adequate theory of subjectivity has to recognise and try to understand these roots. . . .

In his *Introductory Lectures on Psychoanalysis* (1973), Freud discussed the way in which symptoms are experienced in certain forms of obsessional neurosis. He wrote:

> Obsessional neurosis is shown in the patient's being occupied with thoughts in which he is in fact not interested, in his being aware of impulses which appear very strange to him and his being led to actions the performance of which give him no enjoyment, but which it is quite impossible for him to omit. The thoughts (obsessions) may be senseless in themselves, or merely a matter of indifference to the subject; often they are completely silly, and invariably they are the starting-point of a strenuous mental activity, which exhausts the patient and to which he only surrenders himself most unwillingly.

Obsessional neurosis is characterized, Freud argued, by the fact that the symptoms are not only debilitating, but are experienced by the person as *alien;* they do not seem 'part' of him or her, and they seem discrepant with an everyday or normal sense of the self. In the case of many of Freud's patients the disruption and debilitation caused by the symptoms was so extreme that they were scarcely able to carry on their lives adequately at all. But Freud insisted that there was no sharp dividing line between 'normal' and 'neurotic' people, and would have argued that similar, though less extreme, obsessions and apparently inexplicable compulsions can be found in all of us. In these cases, the self is, as it were, split against itself, subject to desires and impulses that seem 'out of character'.

But one cannot assume that an everyday 'coherent' sense of self is readily available. One reason for this is that women (and men, of course) are often faced with the problem of negotiating contradictory or conflicting conceptions of themselves. Women may, for example, be required to be *both* sexually exciting and available, *and* modest and chaste. And gender relationships may be subject to the problems that can arise from conflicting discourses about femininity or masculinity. Men may, for example, *both* see themselves as 'stronger' than women and tend to see women as more weak and passive, but *also* see women as having a power over them that can seem to engulf the man in forms of emotional dependence by which he may feel threatened. Discourse about femininity and masculinity is by no means a homogeneous or stable thing.

In the twentieth century, the advent of a 'consumer culture' and of mass communications has given questions about self and identity a peculiar intensity and difficulty in some repects. They have led, for example, to a focus on appearance and 'style', and the way in which these may 'express' one's individuality, that is historically novel. The clothes one wears, the 'room of one's own' in the Sunday Supplements: one may, apparently, how 'try on' identities as if they really were clothes. And women have often tended to be the main target of fashion and 'lifestyle' talk. For all the rejection of what was sometimes called 'woman garbage' by American feminists, the issue of appearance is something that no woman can wholly avoid. Feminists too, of course, have used style of dress and demeanour to express a sense of self and of political commitment. . . .

The concept of self-deception is one that has constantly puzzled philosophers. How can one both know and yet not know something about oneself. I do not have space here to discuss the question of self-deception in detail. But an important thing to recognise at the outset is that knowing about oneself can never be a matter of 'mere information'. One cannot be distanced from or emotionally neutral about issues of self-knowledge. (Freud stressed this in his account of the transference in the analytic situation.) Herbert Fingarette uses the concept of 'avowal' to give an account of the concept of self-deception. We do not see everything that we think or do or fantasise or desire as equally 'central' to ourselves. It is quite common, in everyday discourse, to say things like 'I wasn't really myself' or 'It wasn't like *me* to do that'. Sometimes this process of rejection, of not avowing, is quite conscious. At other times it may be barely admitted to consciousness, if whatever it was is seen as threatening to the self. And sometimes it is, I think, not conscious at all. Psychoanalysts have talked, for example, about the process of 'projection', in which aspects of oneself of which one is fearful may be projected on to other people. (A number of writers have seen 'projection' as involved in the problem of masculinity, and have suggested that men may sometimes project their own fears of such things as emotional intimacy on to women, who are then seen as 'bad' because they cause these problems.)

Self-knowledge can never be a matter of easy or immediate introspection. This is partly because aspects of oneself may be disavowed, sometimes unconsciously, and partly because the 'meaning' of the deliverances of introspection is always dependent on an interpretation. One may be *aware* of feelings, sexual ones for example, that one is not able to conceptualize *as* sexual at the time. Freud believed that at the root of all neuroses lay repressed sexual desires, but even if one does not follow him in this, it would be hard to resist the conclusion that this was true of some of his patients. Sometimes his patients lacked the kind of knowledge that would have enabled them to interpret the experience as 'sexual' at all. Sometimes they possessed knowledge about sex, but could not admit that *this* was sexual, or that *they* had those sorts of desires.

•   •   •

I have outlined above some of the experiences and the problems about subjectivity that any adequate theory of self must be able to encompass, in a way that the 'humanist' paradigm is, I think, unable to do. There are approaches to understanding and theorizing self which depart radically from the humanist paradigm. I shall not attempt to enumerate them all here, nor do I think that feminism should accept any of them uncritically. What they share, despite their differences, is an insistence that there is no 'original' wholeness or unity in the self, nor a 'real self' which can be thought of as in some way *underlying* the self of everyday life. The self is *always* a more or less precarious and conflictual construction out of, and compromise between, conflicting and not always conscious desires and experiences, which are born out of the ambivalences and contradictions in human experience and relationships with others. . . .

Feminism, as I have said, needs to preserve a critical distance from all theories of self. But it needs also to engage with those theories which deconstruct the distinction between the 'individual' and the 'social', which recognise the power of desire and fantasy and the problems of supposing any 'original' unity in the self, while at the same time preserving its concern with lived experience and the practical and material struggles of women to achieve more autonomy and control over their lives.

MARILYN FRYE

Sexism

MARILYN FRYE teaches feminist philosophy at Michigan State University. Some of her extensive contributions to feminist thought are collected in her book *The Politics of Reality* (1983).

The first philosophical project I undertook as a feminist was that of trying to say carefully and persuasively what sexism is, and what it is for someone, some institution or some act to be sexist. This project was pressed on me with considerable urgency because, like most women coming to a feminist perception of themselves and the world, I was seeing sexism everywhere and trying to make it perceptible to others. I would point out, complain and criticize, but most frequently my friends and colleagues would not see that what I declared to be sexist was sexist, or at all objectionable.

As the critic and as the initiator of the topic, I was the one on whom the burden of proof fell—it was I who had to explain and convince. Teaching philosophy had already taught me that people cannot be persuaded of things they are not ready to be persuaded of; there are certain complexes of will and prior experience which will inevitably block persuasion, no matter the merits of the case presented. I knew that even if I could explain fully and clearly what I was saying when I called something sexist, I would not necessarily be able to convince various others of the correctness of this claim. But what troubled me enormously was that I could not explain it in any way which satisfied *me*. It is this sort of moral and intellectual frustration which, in my case at least, always generates philosophy.

The following was the produce of my first attempt to state clearly and explicitly what sexism is:

> The term 'sexist' in its core and perhaps most fundamental meaning is a term which characterizes anything whatever which creates, constitutes, promotes or exploits any irrelevant or impertinent marking of the distinction between the sexes.

When I composed this statement, I was thinking of the myriads of instances in which persons of the two sexes are treated differently, or behave differently, but where nothing in the real differences between females and males justifies or explains the difference of treatment or behavior. I was thinking, for instance, of the tracking of boys into Shop and girls into Home Ec, where one can see nothing about boys or girls considered in themselves which seems to connect essentially with the distinction between wrenches and eggbeaters. I was thinking also of sex discrimination in employment—cases where someone otherwise apparently qualified for a job is not hired because she is a woman. But when I tried to put this definition of 'sexist' to use, it did not stand the test.

Consider this case: If a company is hiring a supervisor who will supervise a group of male workers who have always worked for male supervisors, it can scarcely be denied that the sex of a candidate for the job is relevant to the candidate's prospects of moving smoothly and successfully into an effective working relationship with the supervisees (though the point is usually exaggerated by those looking for excuses not to hire women). Relevance is an intra-systematic thing. The patterns of behavior, attitude and custom within which a process goes on determine what is relevant to what in matters of describing, predicting or evaluating. In the case at hand, the workers' attitudes and the surrounding customs of the culture make a difference to how they interact with their supervisor and, in particular, *make* the sex of the supervisor a relevant factor in predicting how things will work out. So then, if the company hires a man, in preference to a more experienced and knowledgeable woman, can we explain our objection to the decision by saying it involved distinguishing on the basis of sex when sex is irrelevant to the ability to do the job? No: sex is relevant here.

So, what did I mean to say about 'sexist'? I was thinking that in a case of a candidate for a supervisory job, the reproductive capacity of the candidate has nothing to do with that person's knowing what needs to be done and being able to give properly timed, clear and correct directions. What I was picturing was a situation purified of all sexist perception and reaction. But, of course, *If* the whole context were not sexist, sex would not be an issue in such a job situation; indeed, it might go entirely unnoticed. It is precisely the fact that the sex of the candidate *is* relevant that is the salient symptom of the sexism of the situation.

I had failed, in that first essay, fully to grasp or understand that the locus of sexism is primarily in the system or framework, not in the particular act. It is not accurate to say that what is going on in cases of sexism is that distinctions are made on the basis of sex when sex is irrelevant; what is wrong in cases of sexism is, in the first place, that sex *is* relevant; and then that the making of distinctions on the basis of sex reinforces the patterns which make it relevant.

In sexist cultural/economic systems, sex is always relevant. To understand what sexism is, then, we have to step back and take a larger view.

● ● ●

Sex-identification intrudes into every moment of our lives and discourse, no matter what the supposedly primary focus or topic of the moment is. Elaborate, systematic, ubiquitous and redundant marking of a distinction between the two sexes of humans and most animals is customary and obligatory. One *never* can ignore it.

Examples of sex-marking behavior patterns abound. A couple enters a restaurant; the headwaiter or hostess addresses the man and does not address the woman. The physician addresses the man by surname and honorific (Mr. Baxter, Rev. Jones) and addresses the woman by given name (Nancy, Gloria). You congratulate your friend—a hug, a slap on the back, shaking hands, kissing; one of the things which determines which of these you do is your friend's sex. In everything one does one has two complete repertoires of behavior, one for interactions with women and one for interactions with men. Greeting, storytelling, order-giving and order-receiving, negotiating, gesturing deference or dominance, encouraging, challenging, asking for information: one does all of these things differently depending upon whether the relevant others are male or female.

That this is so has been confirmed in sociological and socio-linguistic research, but it is just as easily confirmed in one's own experience. To discover the differences in how you greet a woman and how you greet a man, for instance, just observe yourself, paying attention to the folowing sorts of things: frequency and duration of eye contact, frequency and type of touch, tone and pitch of voice, physical distance maintained between bodies, how and whether you smile, use of slang or swear words, whether your body dips into a shadow curtsy or bow. That I have two repertoires for handling introductions to people was vividly confirmed for me when a student introduced me to his friend, Pat, and I really could not tell what sex Pat was. For a moment I was stopped cold, completely incapable of action. I felt myself helplessly caught between two paths—the one I would take if Pat were female and the one I would take if Pat were male. Of course the paralysis does not last. One is rescued by one's ingenuity and good will; one can invent a way to behave as one says "How do you do?" to a human being. But the habitual ways are not for humans: they are one way for women and another for men. . . .

In order to behave "appropriately" toward women and men, we have to know which of the people we encounter are women and which are men. But if you strip humans of most of their cultural trappings, it is not always that easy to tell without close inspection which are female, which are male. The tangible and visible physical differences between the sexes are not particularly sharp or numerous and in the physical dimensions we associate with "sex differences," the range of individual variation is very great. The differences between the sexes could easily be, and sometimes are, obscured by bodily decoration, hair removal and the like. So the requirement of knowing everyone's sex in every situation and under almost all observational conditions generates a requirement that we all let others know our sex in every situation. And we do. We announce our sexes in a thousand ways. We deck ourselves from head to toe with garments and decorations which serve like badges and buttons to announce our sexes. For every type of occasion there are distinct clothes, gear and accessories, hairdos, cosmetics and scents, labeled as "ladies'" or "men's" and labeling us as females or males, and most of the time most of us choose, use, wear or bear the paraphernalia associated with our sex. It goes below the skin as well. There are different styles of gait, gesture, posture, speech, humor, taste and even of perception, interest and attention that we learn as we grow up to be women or to be men and that label and announce us as women or as men. It begins early in life: even infants in arms are color coded.

That we wear and bear signs of our sexes, and that this is absolutely compulsory, is made clearest in the relatively rare cases when we do not do so, or not enough. Responses ranging from critical to indignant to hostile meet mothers whose babies are not adequately coded; one of the most agitated criticisms of the sixties' hippies was that "you can't tell the boys from the girls." The requirement of sex-announcement is laden, indeed, with all the urgency of the taboo against homosexuality. One appears heterosexual by informing people of one's sex *very* emphatically and *very* unambiguously, and lesbians and homosexuals who wish *not* to pass as heterosexual generally can accomplish this just by cultivating ambiguous sex-indicators in clothes, behavior and style. The power of this ambiguity to generate unease and punitive responses in others mirrors and demonstrates the rigidity and urgency of this strange social rule that we all be and assertively act "feminine" or "masculine" (and not both)—that we flap a full array of sex-signals at all times.

The intense demand for marking and for asserting what sex each person is adds up to a strenuous requirement that there *be* two distinct and sharply dimorphic sexes. But, in reality, there are not. There are people who fit on a biological spectrum between two not-so-sharply defined poles. In about 5 percent of live births, possibly more, the babies are in some degree and way not perfect exemplars of male and female. There are individuals with chromosome patterns other than XX or YY and individuals whose external genitalia at birth exhibit some degree of ambiguity. There are people who are chromosomally "normal" who are at the far ends of the normal spectra of secondary sex characteristics—height, musculature, hairiness, body density, distribution of fat, breast size, etc.—whose overall appearance fits the norm of people whose chromosomal sex is the opposite of theirs.

These variations not withstanding, persons (mainly men, of course) with the power to do so actually *construct* a world in which men are men and women are women and there is nothing in between and nothing ambiguous; they do it by chemically and/or surgically altering people whose bodies are indeterminate or ambiguous with respect to sex. Newborns with "imperfectly formed" genitals are immediately "corrected" by chemical or surgical means, children and adolescents are given hormone "therapies" if their bodies seem not to be developing according to what physicians and others declare to be the norm for what has been declared to be that individual's sex. Persons with authority recommend and supply cosmetics and cosmetic regimens, diets, exercises and all manner of clothing to revise or disguise the too-hairy lip, the too-large breast, the too-slender shoulders, the too-large feet, the too-great or too-slight stature. Individuals whose bodies do not fit the picture of exactly two sharply dimorphic sexes are often enough quite willing to be altered or veiled for the obvious reason that the world punishes them severely for their failure to be the "facts" which would verify the doctrine of two sexes. The demand that the world be a world in which there are exactly two sexes is inexorable, and we are all compelled to answer to it emphatically, unconditionally, repetitiously and unambiguously.

Even being physically "normal" for one's assigned sex is not enough. One must be female or male, actively. Again, the costumes and performances. Pressed to acting feminine or masculine, one colludes (co-lude: play along) with the doctors and counselors in the creation of a world in which the apparent dimorphism of the sexes is so extreme that one can only think there is a great gulf between female and male, that the two are, essentially and fundamentally and naturally, utterly different. One helps to create a world in which it seems to us that we *could* never mistake a woman for a man or a man for a woman. We never need worry.

• • •

Along with all the making, marking and announcing of sex-distinction goes a strong and visceral feeling or attitude to the effect that sex-distinction is the most important thing in the world: that it would be the end of the world if it were not maintained, clear and sharp and rigid; that a sex-dualism which is rooted in the nature of the beast is absolutely crucial and fundamental to all aspects of human life, human society and human economy. . . .

It is a general and obvious principle of information theory that when it is very, very important that certain information be conveyed, the suitable strategy is redundancy. If a message *must* get through, one sends it repeatedly and by as many means or media as one has at one's command. On the other end, as a receiver of information, if one receives the same information over and over, conveyed by every medium one knows, another message comes through as well, and implicitly: the message that this information is very, very important. The enormous frequency with which information about people's sexes is conveyed conveys implicitly the message that this topic is enormously important. I suspect that this is the single topic on which we most frequently receive information from others throughout our entire lives. If I am right, it would go part way to explaining why we end up with an almost irresistible impression, unarticulated, that the matter of people's sexes is the most important and most fundamental topic in the world.

We exchange sex-identification information, along with the implicit message that it is very important, in a variety of circumstances in which there really is no concrete or experientially obvious point in having the information. There are reasons, as this discussion has shown, why you should want to know whether the person filling your water glass or your tooth is male or female and why that person wants to know what you are, but those reasons are woven invisibly into the fabric of social structure and they do not have to do with the bare mechanics of things being filled. Furthermore, the same culture which drives us to this constant information exchange also simultaneously enforces a strong blanket rule requiring that the simplest and most nearly definitive physical manifestations of sex difference be hidden from view in all but the most private and intimate circumstances. The double message of sex-distinction and its preeminent importance is conveyed, in fact, in part *by* devices which systematically and deliberately cover up and hide from view the few physical things which do (to a fair extent) distinguish two sexes of humans. The messages are overwhelmingly dissociated from the concrete facts they supposedly pertain to, and from matrices of concrete and sensible reasons and consequences. . . .

If one is made to feel that a thing is of prime importance, but common sensory experience does not connect it with things of obvious concrete and practical importance, then there is mystery, and with that a strong tendency to the construction of mystical or metaphysical conceptions of its importance. If it is important, but not of mundane importance, it must be of transcendent importance. All the more so if it is *very* important.

This matter of our sexes must be very profound indeed if it must, on pain of shame and ostracism, be covered up and must, on pain of shame and ostracism, be boldly advertised by every means and medium one can devise.

There is one more point about redundancy that is worth making here. If there is one thing more effective in making one believe a thing than receiving the message repetitively, it is rehearsing it repetitively. Advertisers, preachers, teachers, all of us in the brainwashing professions, make use of this apparently physical fact of human psychology routinely. The redundancy of sex-marking and sex-announcing serves not only to make the topic seem transcendently important, but to make the sex-duality it advertises seem transcendently and unquestionably *true*. . . .

Sex-marking and sex-announcing are equally compulsory for males and females; but that is as far as equality goes in this matter. The meaning and import of this behavior is profoundly different for women and for men.

Whatever features an individual male person has which tend to his social and economic disadvantage (his age, race, class, height, etc.), one feature which never tends to his disadvantage in the society at large is his maleness. The case for females is the mirror image of this. Whatever features an individual female person has which tend to her social and economic advantage (her age, race, etc.), one feature which always tends to her disadvantage is her femaleness. Therefore, when a male's sex-category is the thing about him that gets first and most repeated notice, the thing about him that is being framed and emphasized and given primacy is a feature which in general is an asset to him. When a female's sex-category is the thing about her that gets first and most repeated notice, the thing about her that is being framed and emphasized and given primacy is a feature which in general is a liability to her. Manifestations of this divergence in the meaning and consequences of sex-announcement can be very concrete.

Walking down the street in the evening in a town or city exposes one to some risk of assault. For males the risk is less; for females the risk is greater. If one announces oneself male, one is presumed by potential assailants to be more rather than less likely to defend oneself or be able to evade the assault and, if the male-announcement is strong and unambiguous, to be a noncandidate for sexual assault. If one announces oneself female, one is presumed by potential assailants to be less rather than more likely to defend oneself or to evade the assault and, if the female-announcement is strong and unambiguous, to be a prime candidate for sexual assault. Both the man and the woman "announce" their sex through style of gait, clothing, hair style, etc., but they are not equally or identically affected by announcing their sex. The male's announcement tends toward his protection or safety, and the female's announcement tends toward her victimization. It could not be more immediate or concrete; the meaning of the sex-identification could not be more different.

The sex-marking behavioral repertoires are such that in the behavior of almost all people of both sexes addressing or responding to males (especially within their own culture/race) generally is done in a manner which suggests basic respect, while addressing or responding to females is done in a manner that suggests the females' inferiority (condescending tones, presumptions of ignorance, overfamiliarity, sexual aggression, etc.). So, when one approaches an ordinary well-socialized person in such cultures, if one is male, one's own behavioral announcement of maleness tends to evoke supportive and beneficial response and if one is female, one's own behavioral announcement of femaleness tends to evoke degrading and detrimental response.

The details of the sex-announcing behaviors also contribute to the reduction of women and the elevation of men. The case is most obvious in the matter of clothing. As feminists have been saying for two hundred years or so, ladies' clothing is generally restrictive, binding, burdening and frail; it threatens to fall apart and/or to uncover something that is supposed to be covered if you bend, reach, kick, punch or run. It typically does not protect effectively against hazards in the environment, nor permit the wearer to protect herself against the hazards of the human environment. Men's clothing is generally the opposite of all this—sturdy, suitably protective, permitting movement and locomotion. The details of feminine manners and postures also serve to bind and restrict. To be feminine is to take up little space, to defer to others, to be silent or affirming of others, etc. It is not necessary here to survey all this, for it has been done many times and in illuminating detail in feminist writings. My point here is that though both men and women must behave in sex-announcing ways, the behavior which announces femaleness is in itself both physically and socially binding and limiting as the behavior which announces maleness is not.

The sex-correlated variations in our behavior tend systematically to the benefit of males and the detriment of females. The male, announcing his sex in sex-identifying behavior and dress, is both announcing and acting on his membership in a dominant caste—dominant within his subculture and to a fair extent across subcultures as well.

The female, announcing her sex, is both announcing and acting on her membership in the subordinated caste. She is obliged to inform others constantly and in every sort of situation that she is to be treated as inferior, without authority, assaultable. She cannot move or speak within the usual cultural norms without engaging in self-deprecation. The male cannot move or speak without engaging in self-aggrandizement. Constant sex-identification both defines and maintains the caste boundary without which there could not be a dominance-subordination structure. . . .

The cultural and economic structures which create and enforce elaborate and rigid patterns of sex-marking and sex-announcing behavior, that is, create gender as we know it, mold us as dominators and subordinates (I do not say "mold our minds" or "mold our personalities"). They construct two classes of animals, the masculine and the feminine, where another constellation of forces might have constructed three or five categories, and not necessarily hierarchically related. Or such a spectrum of sorts that we would not experience them as "sorts" at all.

• • •

The term 'sexist' characterizes cultural and economic structures which create and enforce the elaborate and rigid patterns of sex-marking and sex-announcing which divide the species, along lines of sex, into dominators and subordinates. Individual act and practices are sexist which reinforce and support those structures, either as culture or as shapes taken on by the enculturated animals. Resistance to sexism is that which undermines those structures by social and political action and by projects of reconstruction and revision of ourselves.

CARYL RIVERS

Put the Blame on Eve, Boys

CARYL RIVERS teaches journalism at Boston University. She has published novels and nonfiction, and contributes regularly to major newspapers. Her most recent book is *Slick Spins and Fractured Facts: How Cultural Myths Distort the News* (1996), from which the following selection is taken.

The wonderful thing about myths is that they don't have to be logical; often two of them operate side by side, even though they are polar opposites. That's exactly what happens with two of the most potent—the Myth of Female Weakness and the Myth of Female Strength. In one, a woman is a sniveling, small-brained, hormone-wracked creature so filled with anxieties and chemical twitches it seems a miracle she can get out of bed in the morning. In the other, she's Wonder Woman and Medusa, all wrapped up in one, able to reduce men to irrational behavior, making them desert their senses and become besotted fools. And media coverage of women often bounces from one to the other like bumper cars gone mad.

Mythology about women pervades our culture, and feminist scholars have spent the last two decades trying to unravel it. Simone de Beauvoir, in her brilliant critique of women's place, *The Second Sex*, fired the first shot in the current era of what was to become a barrage of female inquiry and scholarship. Yet the myths still stand, like battlements on a hill, exerting a tremendous power over our media, our politics, our culture, our imaginations.

Beauvoir pointed out how women's physiology, which is more involved in the processes of giving birth and nurturing life than men's, is devalued by that very fact. Anthropologist Sherry Ortner says,

> Woman's body seems to doom her to mere reproduction of life; the male, in contrast, lacking natural creative functions, must (or has the opportunity to) assert his creativity externally, "artificially" through the medium of technology and symbols. In doing so he creates relatively lasting, eternal, transcendent objects, while the woman creates only perishables—human beings.
>
> This formulation opens up a number of important insights. It speaks, for example, to the great puzzle of why male activities involving the destruction of life (hunting and warfare) are often given more prestige than the female's ability to give birth, create life. Within De Beauvoir's framework, we realize it is not the killing that is the relevant and valued aspect of hunting and warfare, rather it is the transcendental (social and cultural) nature of these activities, as opposed to the naturalness of the process of birth. For it is not in giving life but in risking life that man is raised above the animal; that is why superiority has been accorded in humanity not to the sex that brings forth but that which kills.

If woman in her essence is seen as nature, in her sexuality she is seen once again through the prism of the male imagination. Vivian Gornick writes,

Deeply interwoven in the fabric of this cultural cloak is the image of woman: woman the temptress, woman the slut, woman the heartless bitch—luring men eternally towards spiritual death, making them come up against what they most fear and hate in themselves, pulling them down, down into the pit of themselves. Sensuous Circe luring Ulysses onto the rocks of his worst self, sluttish Mildred in *Of Human Bondage* mangling crippled Philip still further, heartless Marlene Dietrich casually destroying the weak, decent professor in *The Blue Angel*—the list is endless and the lesson is always the same. Woman herself is not locked in this profound struggle with the self; she is only the catalyst for the man's struggle with himself. It is never certain that the woman has any self at all. What is certain is that onto woman is projected all that is worst in man's view of himself, all that is primitive, immature and degrading.

Or, conversely, woman becomes another mirror image: the idea of goodness—the noblest, the best, the most loved. If she is not the temptress, she is the goddess, the mother, the angel of mercy, the pure golden-haired heroine of Victorian fiction. Norman Mailer once said that women were either sloppy beasts or goddesses—quite a choice. Can you imagine those as the only choices given to men—gods or slobs? Either way, woman is not whole, a true complex person.

"I am not real to my civilization," Gornick writes, "I am not real to the culture that has spawned me and made use of me. I am only a collection of myths. I am an existential stand-in. The *idea* of me is real: the temptress, the goddess, the child, the mother—but *I* am not real. The mythic proportions of women are recognizable and real; it is only the human dimensions that are patently false and will be denied to the death; our death."

To be denied humanity, to be reassembled as a collection of myths, also means to be silenced. As scholar Deborah Cameron has pointed out, "The silence of woman is above all an absence of female voices and concerns from high culture." Women have always been allowed to talk to their children, to gossip, to tell stories, to write in their diaries—but these are only private means of communication. Women's public speech has been silenced by laws, by tradition, and by taboo. The strictures against women's speech in public go back to primitive societies that had rules forbidding women to speak outside the house—in the tribal council, in the town meeting—and are seen as well in the long-standing tradition in Western culture that women be barred from universities; they linger today in a ban on women in the priesthood and the absence of women in legislative bodies. In 1992 it was still considered an unusual event when two women won Senate seats from the state of California.

Feminist scholars have pointed out that women throughout history have been defined as mad when they were overtly sexual or assertive, that they were burned at the stake as witches when they threatened the social status quo or gained too much wealth, that at the same time that they were worshiped as sexless ministering angels in upper-class society in the Victorian era, they were physically mutilated when they displayed what was seen as excessive sexuality. Weak or strong, woman is to be feared. And when journalists take up their pens or march to their word processors, these myths linger in their subconscious, and *woman weak/woman strong* are two archetypes that resonate still.

The news media sensation of the decade, the Clarence Thomas–Anita Hill duel that took place before the eyes of millions of viewers, exemplified this mythological paradox with stunning clarity. Watching Anita Hill, many people saw a poised, coolly professional black woman talk about the sexual invitations and suggestive talk of a man who was her employer in the federal government. But if you stayed tuned, as the Senate Republicans came down like a wolf on the fold and the news media watched it all, you would have seen sketches of two separate portraits of Professor Hill, two myths in operation:

The Myth of Female Weakness: Alas, poor Anita. Perhaps she was simply a pawn in the scheming designs of those (read: liberal Democrats) who wanted to see Clarence Thomas defeated for the Supreme Court. Naïve, foolish, willing to be used as a pawn in the plans of powerful men, she was a silly woman embroiled in something she could not understand. (Or perhaps she was simply a prisoner of her hormones. Judge Thomas's wife—picking up the lead of the senators—suggested in a *People* magazine cover piece that Hill was a poor, love-besotted girl, a pathetic creature who fantasized a relationship with a powerful man.) *Poor thing*, clucked some of the Senate Republicans, seduced by Democrats or bewitched by her fantasies, she should be an object of pity.

Unless. . .

Unless she was the embodiment of the *Myth of Female Strength*, that witch, that temptress, that Medusa whose pleasure lies in destroying men. In this reincarnation she was, Senator Arlen Specter suggested again and again in his prosecutorial tones, the scorned woman, lying in wait for revenge, and hell hath no fury et cetera, et cetera. According to Specter, Hill apparently spent her time prowling through old copies of *The Exorcist*, looking for obscure references to pubic hairs, or doing a little light reading of Oklahoma obscenity cases to come across the porno star Long Dong Silver. (Just what a woman from a Baptist family does on her weekends.) Or maybe she was just a pathological liar, like the heroine of *Fatal Attraction*, a career woman whose barren life and biological clock led her to terrible dark deeds. Or perhaps she was a steely-eyed Joan of Arc eager to become a feminist martyr.

. . . The Myth of Female Weakness may have begun as far back as Eve, who, according to Scripture, couldn't resist taking a bite out of the apple and thus got the First Couple kicked out of Eden. I was a parochial school student and remember that—as soon as we were old enough to understand kissing—the nuns interpreted Eve's noshing as having to do with lust. But long before sex reared its ugly head, I found myself identifying with Eve. Biting into the apple seemed to me to be the first example of intellectual curiosity in recorded history. Adam, the lout, just wanted to sit around Paradise, fat, dumb and happy, but Eve, an achiever, wanted to know something of what God knew.

Male biblical sages did not render this interpretation, however. They often wailed about how all afflictions were the curse of Eve; her weakness brought on everything from the Babylonian captivity to the pains of childbirth, a punishment for her curiosity. In medieval times church fathers seriously discussed whether women had a soul. The preponderance of evidence was negative, as I recall.

As we move closer to our own time, the tradition of blaming Eve does not abate. The debate over the soul shifts to a more easily located place: her brain. Oh, she has one, but how big is it? Women and blacks seem to be the subjects of most brain-size inquiries. In the early nineteenth century Louis Agassiz, a well-respected Harvard zoologist, declaimed that the brain casing of blacks was smaller than that of whites, and too much education would expand the brain size beyond the capacity of the skull, causing serious brain damage or death. (Kids have tried to use a similar argument as an excuse to avoid homework, but it rarely works.) Later on, as biologist Stephen Jay Gould has pointed out in his book *The Mismeasure of Man*, such measurement "dominated the human sciences for much of the 19th century and remained popular until intelligence testing replaced skull measurement as a favorite device for making invidious comparisons among classes, races and sexes."

Craniologist Paul Broca suggested that women could never reach the intellectual heights of men, because their brains were smaller. And one of Broca's disciples suggested that giving women equal education with men would be a "dangerous chimera."

If tiny weak brains weren't enough to keep women away from the halls of learning, some people decided to focus on a lower area of the anatomy. It was accepted medical belief in much of the nineteenth century that women's brains and reproductive organs could not develop at the same time. That's why women's education consisted of a little knitting, a little French, nothing too heavy; those all-important ovaries needed all of a woman's energy.

"Woman is less under the influence of the brain than the uterine system," Dr. J. G. Mulligan, a prominent physician, wrote in 1848. And G. Stanley Hall, president of Clark University, warned in 1906 that "overactivity of the brain during the critical period of the middle and late teens will interfere with the full development of mammary power and of the functions essential for the full transmission of life generally."

Early in the century surgical removal of the clitoris was a favored remedy for all forms of mental illness, including depression, and later medical science turned to lobotomies. Even when nineteenth-century science found that women did something better than men did, it managed to turn that information into further proof of women's weakness. When one researcher found that women could read faster and more accurately than men, two esteemed scientists of the era decreed that the ability to read well is linked with the ability to lie, and women are better liars than men.

Another theory—proposed by none other than Charles Darwin himself—was that of morphological infantilism—the notion that women, being smaller than men, are *morphologically*—that is, physically—more like babies or children than men. As psychologists Paula Caplan and Jeremy Caplan explain,

> Some Victorian theorists speculated that, therefore, women are less intelligent than men but more intelligent than infants and children. This is equivalent to saying that men must be more like gorillas than are women, because men are hairier. It might even be valid, but what reason is there to believe it? . . . The Social Darwinists who promoted morphological infantilism as applied to women used the same notion to keep whites in power over blacks. Black people, they argued, are more similar to apes than are white people and are therefore, less intelligent.

But this is ancient history—is it not?—the stuff of Gothic novels or history courses but having nothing to do with today. Would that that were true. In intellectual—and family—history, 1906 was only yesterday. Our grandparents or great-grandparents lived in a world that accepted these beliefs.

Many deep-seated cultural myths have the abilities of chameleons—they shed the Victorian garb of yesteryear and emerge in wash-and-wear Spandex: the same old thing, decked in modern dress. Women's brains are still regarded with suspicion. Anita Hill may have been a graduate of Yale Law, but that did not stop the esteemed gentlemen of the Senate from picturing her as the embodiment of female irrationality or the media from echoing that scenario. No matter what women achieve, that fatal flaw—located someplace in the cerebellum or the ovaries—is going to crop up sooner or later.

Women's strengths rarely become the focus of media attention, except in a distorted way—as when women are seen as *too* strong. When tests show that on average women are better than men at something, this fact is mentioned sotto voce. Footnote, page 242, women have generally tested better than men on verbal ability. Do we get headlines like ARE MEN BORN TO BE ILLITERATE? or DO WOMEN HAVE A WRITING GENE MISSING IN MEN? You see those about as often as you see a unicorn in your driveway. But let a test apparently show that men do something better than women do, and it's bring out the banners.

MATH AND SEX; ARE GIRLS BORN WITH LESS ABILITY? headlined *Science* magazine, on a story in the early eighties about a study done by two Johns Hopkins University psychologists of Scholastic Aptitude Tests (SATs) of 9,927 gifted seventh- and eighth-grade boys and girls. The girls did less well than the boys on the math test, especially in mathematical reasoning. The researchers concluded—in the most controversial section of their report—that the difference could not be explained by environmental factors, so it had to be genetic. The most chilling aspect of their report was the suggestion that maybe girls just shouldn't *try* to be good at math. One researcher likened the girls' situation to that of a short boy's thinking he should make the basketball team.

Voilà! the math gene leapt into the headlines.

DO MALES HAVE A MATH GENE? asked *Newsweek,* and the story wondered, "Can girls do math as well as boys? All sorts of recent tests have shown that they cannot." The *Washington Post* headlined, AT MATHEMATICAL THINKING, BOYS OUTPERFORM GIRLS. *Time* looked at THE GENDER FACTOR IN MATH. The *New York Times* asked, ARE BOYS BETTER AT MATH?

Why were the media so eager to believe in the math gene? Why did this particular piece of scientific research—from among the veritable torrent of such studies that researchers produce every year—receive such widespread attention? Because it was a modern incarnation of the idea that something is wrong with women's brains. But how conclusive was the research? Not very, said a lot of critics. For one thing the researchers invited ten thousand junior-high-school-aged children to take the SAT. "But what does it mean to give a seventh or eighth grader college level tests?" asked mathematician Edith H. Luchins. "How are we to interpret the results? We scarcely know what the test scores mean when they are made by high school students. Many educators now question the ability of the SAT to test mathematical reasoning, problem-solving and spatial ability."

But the main problem was that the researchers, Camilla Benbow and Julian Stanley, had made a whopping assumption when they said that these boys and girls at their stage of schooling probably had the same training in—and attitudes about—math. Their entire thesis rested on the assumption that because boys and girls often shared classrooms, their experiences were the same. Had they forgotten that they were talking about children in the seventh grade?

The Seventh Grade. You were considered a dork if you had even half a brain. You fell in love with rock stars and scribbled their names across your algebra texts. In the seventh grade, if everybody else had pink hair and green lipstick, *you* had pink hair and green lipstick. And math? That's for the geeky boys who haven't hit puberty yet, whose skin is the shade of flounder bellies because they sit in their basement rec rooms all day hacking with their computers. Math. Ugh. Will guys make out in the back seat with a girl who likes *math*? Peer pressure at this age is at its most intense, and it is also the age, as Harvard's Carol Gilligan found in her studies of girls at puberty, that sturdy independent little girls begin to suffer a loss of self-esteem as they first encounter the tremendous pressure to please males above all else. Boys generally do not suffer the same loss of self-esteem as they hit puberty. To assume that girls and boys at this age have the same experiences is to ignore the reality of adolescence in America.

As Professor Alice Schafer of Wellesley College, chair of the Women in Math Committee of the American Mathematical Society, says, "Just because seventh-grade boys and girls sat the same number of hours in the same classroom doesn't mean they get the same mathematical education."

Research showed she was right, in particular about the youngsters who were part of the Hopkins test. Another Hopkins scientist, Lynn Fox, interviewed the kids who took part in the test. She found that boys' parents noticed their sons' talents at an early age, encouraged them by buying math books, and talked about math careers. Girls' parents generally didn't notice. Studies have shown that nearly half of girls interested in math careers have reported being discouraged by high-school guidance counselors from taking advanced math courses. And when Edith Luchins gave a talk at a local high school career day, a guidance counselor told her, "I'll be honest with you; I don't encourage girls to go into math. They wouldn't be good at it, and in any case, what would they do with it?" Sadly, that is an attitude reflected in many American schools.

Science writer K. C. Cole, whose specialty is physics, writes about a friend who won a Bronx-wide mathematics competition in the second grade: "Her friends—both boys and girls—warned her that she shouldn't be good in math. 'You'll never find a boy who likes you.' The girl nevertheless went on to win a number of awards at Bronx High School of Science, but after a year as a science major at Harvard, she switched her major to English. She had been discouraged, she said, by the macho mores of science, and besides, what was the payoff for sticking with it? 'You'd be considered a freak.'"

It's exactly this sort of experience the Hopkins researchers ignored. The math gene argument doesn't account for the sudden precipitous drop in girls' math ability at puberty—exactly when stereotypes about correct female behavior kick in. A number of studies show that girls score evenly with boys until about the first year of high school—and that only 18 percent of girls—compared with 64 percent of boys—taking high school physics and calculus classes plan to major in science or engineering in college.

Could the math gene just disappear in girls when they get their first bra? "Unless nature selected for smart girls and dumb women, something goes very wrong at the middle school level," writes critic Barbara Ehrenreich. "Maybe it's teachers who call on and encourage boys more. Or maybe it's high school politics that equate good grades with terminal geekdom. Even more important than teachers, though, is girls' growing realization that straight A's aren't necessarily the fastest way to point B (for boyfriend)."

Ehrenreich's hunches were borne out by research. The girls who took part in the tests told researchers that they didn't want to take part in accelerated math classes. They thought that other kids would regard them as "different," and they thought that the classes were dull and the boys in them "little creeps."

Evelyn Fox Keller, the author of *Reflections on Gender and Science*, notes that the roots of viewing science as male go deep into our cultural soil. "The linguistic rooting of this stereotype is not lost among children. . . . From strikingly early ages, even in the presence of non-stereotypic role models, children learn to identify mathematics as male. 'Science,' my five-year-old son declared, confidently bypassing that fact that his mother was a scientist, 'is for men!'"

Researchers also say that instructors tend to teach to the learning style of boys—which favors getting the right answer, whereas girls enjoy the *process* as much as they enjoy getting the answer—and girls do better in cooperative situations. And studies of children in the United States, Japan, and China show that when girls are in the first grade, they and their mothers assume that boys are better at math. The result of that self-fulfilling prophecy starts to show up around the third grade.

But none of this got into the headlines. MATH GENE swept the national media. Anne Fausto-Sterling, a Brown University biologist, writes of an urgent call from a friend whose ten-year-old daughter had read that girls simply shouldn't try to do higher math and was devastated.

"Daddy," she said, "I always wanted to be a math professor just like you. Does that mean I can't do it?"

Fausto-Sterling remembered the cartoon she had seen in *Time* a few days earlier. A puzzled little girl and a toothy smiling boy stood in front of a blackboard with a multiplication problem on it. Obviously, the little girl didn't know the answer, and the boy did. "Interpreting the image does not require a degree in art history, and the aftershocks from the *Science* article and subsequent press coverage still rumble beneath our feet," she says.

The father who made the panicked phone call was not alone. Psychologist Jackie Eccles, in a longitudinal study, found that mothers who read the news reports had lower expectations of their daughters' math abilities than they did before. Here then was an example of the media's reporting uncritically a questionable scientific assumption and the mass media coverage's reinforcing the low expectations that could keep girls from doing well in math. Another exercise in self-fulfilling prophecy.

Wading further into muddy waters, Camilla Benbow and her husband Robert Benbow claimed that hormones accounted for boys' "greater" ability in math. Hormones are really sexy these days. Psychologists Paula and Jeremy Caplan say,

> Naturally, the media eagerly reported the story. What they did not mention was that hormonal levels of the students in their study were never measured, thus making the Benbows' claim entirely unjustified. This is a particularly important issue, since, when there is, or seems to be, a biologically based and innate difference such as a hormonal one, people are likely to assume that little or nothing can be done to reduce the supposed inferiority of one sex.

The Caplans explain that the hormonal argument is convoluted and presents problems every step of the way. Two researchers had previously reported that left-handed people are more likely than righties to suffer from immune disorders, learning disabilities, and migraines, hypothesizing that this was the result of high levels of the male hormone testosterone. (This claim was vigorously criticized and not supported by other research.) If testosterone slows down the development of the left hemisphere of the brain so that the right side compensates by growing stronger, the mathematical abilities *might* improve in the possessor of this brain. So good math students ought to be left-handed and have more immune problems than the rest of the population. Indeed good math students include more left-handers and more people who have allergies than the general population. "However," the Caplans point out, "as every introductory psychology student learns, left-handers are more common in a wide range of unusual populations, including prisoners and students at Harvard University. Math genius may be rampant in Harvard Yard, but is it at Sing Sing?"

If you are still following this complex and convoluted reasoning, the Benbows went on to speculate that some good math students might have been exposed before birth to high testosterone levels. They had no proof of this, but they claimed that these students were more likely than other students to have been born during months that have more than twelve hours a day of light, and "daylight affects pineal gland secretion, altering the level of melanin, which in turn has an inhibitory effect on reproductive hormones."

The Caplans say,

> Aside from the sheer length of this unproved explanation about how top math students might have been exposed to high levels of testosterone, their reasoning is simply wrong. If more daylight is supposed to reduce the reproductive hormones, then these students should have had less testosterone, not more, than most students. And according to the Benbows' own (unsupported) line of reasoning, lower testosterone levels should lead to *poorer* mathematical abilities.

If all this makes the old how-many-angels-can-you-fit-on-the-head-of-a-pin argument seem positively straightforward, it is but an example of the complex realm of hormones, genes, and behavior. In this case a tortured train of highly questionable assumptions led to the math gene stories. The Caplans note, "If you look at the headlines . . . it may seem surprising that the public could be presented such claims when they are based on highly speculative theories, research on extreme groups of people and just plain poor reasoning. However, such presentation is not uncommon. When some journalists hear what seems to be a 'hot' story, they do not stop to learn whether or not there is any scientific basis for it."

Of course, most people are not fascinated with the intricate details of left-brain, right-brain functions and daylight actions of hormones, and all they remember is the headline. The Caplans note that "many scientists and lay people, and today, the media, become intensely interested in an issue, believe in a report of some bit of research about the issue, and then lose interest in it. If, later on, the research they had read about is discredited, they may have become so accustomed to believing in the early research they do not invest the mental and emotional energy necessary to revise that belief."

In other words, many people do not want the facts to confuse them.

Add to that the tendency for the media to repeat old information even after it is moribund, and you understand why the math gene might well be immortal.

But since the math gene was trumpeted in the early eighties, a surprising thing has happened: gender differences in math and verbal abilities on tests have begun to disappear. In recent years all the things that used to show up on the standardized tests, and that we have come to believe—such as girls' superior verbal abilities and boys' math superiority—have been knocked into a cocked hat. When researcher Alan Feingold studied national tests given since 1947, he noted that girls' edge in verbal ability had become tiny, and boys' edge in spatial relations had shrunk by half. In 1989 Berkeley psychologist Marcia C. Linn reported that she had looked at results of the SATS and the PSATS and differences had virtually disappeared. Recent meta-analyses—very sophisticated studies—confirm this.

Girls outperform boys on language and spelling tests only by a small margin. (Why are boys doing better than they used to with verbal skills? Perhaps old notions about writing and literature being "sissified" have declined in a competitive society in which only the brightest and best-prepared student will get ahead. The "gentleman's C" is a thing of the past.)

On math tests, in verbal reasoning, using analogies, abstract reasoning, and numerical ability, the girls have caught up with the boys. Boys still do better in spatial relations—the ability to manipulate objects in three dimensions, although the girls are gaining here as well. Feingold told *Newsweek*, "Biological imperatives do not change in the space of a generation." He notes, "As women's roles change, so have the abilities encouraged by parents and teachers. . . . In a more egalitarian society, the sexes develop more similarly."

The boys' edge in manipulating objects in three-dimensional space may be the result of boys' early games involving such skills as throwing and kicking balls. Games such as baseball and football give a player a feeling for relationships of time, speed, and distance. As more girls play Little League baseball and soccer, perhaps that gap will close more rapidly.

However, these findings will probably not make a dent in the conviction—thanks to the media—that a math gene really does exist. ABC's John Stossel completely missed the new science in a 1995 hour-long, primetime TV special, "Boys and Girls Are Different." He simply failed to report the shrinking sex differences in math and verbal abilities, giving the impression that huge gaps still exist. Not only was the show bad science, but it clearly implied that girls should be discouraged from entering such fields as architecture.

•   •   •

The media also love simple solutions to complex problems. A math gene fits neatly in a headline, and it seems easy to understand. But as Evelyn Fox Keller says, behavior is a complex phenomenon. You wouldn't look at your car and say that the carburetor makes it run, but that's the sort of reductionist thinking that too often goes on where women are concerned. There is a vast difference, Keller says, between genetic information and complex traits, be they physical or behavioral. Not only do genetically coded contributions act on each other, but "for human behavioral traits. . .the influence of the external, including cultural, environment becomes critical." In other words, just as in a car's engine, it takes a number of parts, acting together, to produce the final result. However, this sort of complexity does not produce neat Bodoni bold, 48–point headlines.

Another intriguing thing about the math gene controversy was not what the media chose to put under their microscope but what they did *not* examine.

Professor Mary Gray, who heads the math department at American University, notes that the same SAT scores also showed that Asian-American males outscored white males. Where, she wonders, was the *Science* magazine headline that reported, ASIANS INNATELY SUPERIOR TO WHITES AT MATH? Why was this finding not trumpeted in headlines across the nation? It came from the same study. Why was it a nonstory, whereas the female "weakness" shot into the headlines?

After all, Asian-American students often walk away with top math and science prizes, they are disproportionately represented in graduate programs, and the stereotype of today's MIT student is an Asian-American with a calculator. But where is the demand to study the brains of Asian-Americans to find the biological root of Asian superiority? Why aren't people suggesting that white guys just accept fate and not try to make the math team?

And, of course, if it turns out to be true that more males have superior math ability than females, so what? There will be lots of women math whizzes out there. The fact that women for many years scored significantly higher than men on verbal abilities did not mean that Shakespeare, Faulkner, and even Stephen King did not exist. But massive coverage of real or perceived sex differences in which women come out the losers reinforces—and to some justifies—their second-class status. The coverage that created the math gene notion was not followed by the same bold headlines for the critics who carefully and convincingly deconstructed the idea. A good indicator of how deeply entrenched in the culture the math gene has become is that in 1992, a "talking Barbie" came onto the market, and one of the things she said was that she didn't like math.

From *Science* headlines to Barbie Dolls: the line of cultural transmission of a wrongheaded idea is complete.

JACOB JOSHUA ROSS

Gender Differences

JACOB JOSHUA ROSS teaches philosophy at Tel-Aviv University in Israel. He is author of *The Virtues of the Family* (1994), from which the following selection is taken.

A revolutionary thesis currently being mooted by the radical wing of the feminist movement holds that the subjugation and discrimination of women will cease only when the traditional family roles allocated to husbands and wives have been completely abolished. The family roles regulating the allocation of household duties (the wife in charge of cleanliness, meals, hospitality, etc.; the husband responsible for funding, supporting, etc.) and parental tasks (she in charge of nursing and feeding; he of disciplining, setting general educational goals, and seeing to it that the steps to achieving these goals are taken) have inevitably cast the wife in an inferior and more menial role. The husband is left relatively free to pursue his activities outside the family circle, while the wife, at any rate during the greater part of her childrearing years, is so bound to her household and family that she becomes relatively sequestered from the outside world. That creates a situation, it is argued, in which the wife becomes enslaved to the family and household, which come to fill her whole horizon.

Those who defend such division of labor within the family argue that it is not only inevitable but also perfectly natural. The differences between husband and wife, after all, are biologically based: she being equipped by superior constitutional strength to bear the child, to nurse and attend to it, and generally to be more sedentary; he being equipped by superior muscular strength to be more mobile and capable of seeking the means outside the family of feeding and supporting it. The Radical Feminists rebut this in three ways: (1) The customary allocation of tasks between husband and wife goes well beyond the biological basis, and the development of mankind since prehistory has changed the way of life that made the original biological equipment necessary in the first place (e.g. the average superior muscular development of the male is hardly needed in modern life—he no longer has to track and hunt for food). (2) The constant changes in our way of life and our environment have already made the traditional allocation of tasks between husband and wife problematic and unworkable (e.g. women are being forced by economic necessity to seek jobs and pursue careers outside the family, thus rendering the pious ideology that "a woman's place is in the home" otiose). (3) Finally, who says that humanity must be bound by nature? We have already overcome and controlled natural circumstances in so many fields, even within the purview of the family (e.g. birth control), that it becomes possible to contemplate even more radical changes in the future.

At this point those particular feminists put in their revolutionary claim. Simone de Beauvoir wrote many years ago:

> The tragedy of marriage is not that it fails to assure woman the promised happiness. . . but that it mutilates her; it dooms her to repetition and routine. . . . At twenty or thereabouts mistress of a home, bound permanently to a man, a child in her arms, she stands with her life virtually finished forever.

424

Beauvoir thus regarded childbearing and nurture as a form of slavery for women; she considered the loss of freedom unavoidable as long as human reproduction required the woman's womb. Her views were completely antifamily. A more contemporary feminist, Carol Gould, following a similar line of argument, advocates the abolition of marriage. She favors single parenting, co-parenting, and communal parenting. She does not share Beauvoir's pessimism about women's ever being free and equal unless they freed themselves of the womb and its use, however. Gould says it might be possible to retain normal hysteric reproduction while rectifying women's enslavement by alternative social arrangements that jettison the traditional family. It is not the womb that is at fault, then, but the institutional arrangements that govern its use, i.e., the family.

Another Radical Feminist, Alison Jaggar, apparently agreeing more with Beauvoir's pessimism, looks forward to a still more radical solution. She anticipates a possible transformation of biological functions "so that one woman could inseminate another . . . and . . . fertilized ova could be transplanted into women's or even men's bodies." She also entertains the science-fiction notion that one day there will be a situation in which "neither sex bears children, but both sexes, through hormone treatments, suckle them."

The idea common to all such strains of feminist thought seems to be a rejection of the possibility of "different but equal." In other words, if men and women are to be really equal, then they must not be differentiated from each other at all. The ideal, as Richard Wasserstrom admits, must be unisex or assimilationist. "Bisexuality, not heterosexuality or homosexuality, would be the typical intimate, sexual relationship in the ideal society that was assimilationist in respect to sex."

The supposition of the more radical of these feminists—that it will be impossible to assure women's equality so long as their biological function in reproduction continues to be different, especially as this difference has come to be hallowed in the traditional family—is far from obvious. It flies in the face of the common experience of millions of happy families in which both husbands and wives feel themselves fulfilled in their humanity. So it is well that we should consider why anyone should take it to be so obviously true that only the assimilationist ideal, which seeks to wipe out differences between husband and wife, between male and female, can bring about genuine equality between them. . . .

It seems to me that the demand for equal status for women by feminists is, philosophically speaking, simply a particular example of the more general issue of egalitarianism. The claim that all should be equal is still highly problematic, despite the fact it has been one of the most celebrated ideals and slogans in Western political thought since antiquity, having particular influence during the last few centuries. People differ one from another in all sorts of ways—skills, intelligence, strength, virtue—so in what sense can it be claimed that they are or ought to be equal? It cannot be the aim of this claim that all people should be treated alike in all circumstances, or even that they should be treated alike as much as possible. To ignore the differences between the aged and the very young or between the highly intelligent and those backward in intelligence would, for most purposes, be not only unjust but foolish.

Still, Isaiah Berlin appears to be right in supposing that many egalitarians nurse a sort of hankering for an ideal egalitarianism in which everything and everybody should be as similar as possible to everything and everybody else. Of course, Berlin himself says he doubts that anyone ever seriously desired to bring such a society into being, or even supposed it could be created. But he goes on to say:

Nevertheless, it seems to me that the demands for human equality which have been expressed both by philosophers and by men of action who have advocated or attempted to reform society, can best be represented as modifications of this absolute and perhaps absurd ideal. In the ideal egalitarian society, inequality—and this must ultimately mean disimilarity—would be reduced to a minimum.

This claim of Berlin has been disputed by many, who have belabored the "obvious" point that

... the ideal of equality has nothing to do with uniformity. To recognize that men are equally individual human beings involves no desire or need to treat them uniformly in any ways other than those in which they clearly have a moral claim to be treated alike.

Berlin's claim has been bracketed, in a recent article by Kai Nielsen, with the sort of claim usually made by conservative critics of egalitarianism and characterized as "the critics' bogeyman."

But that sort of comment misses the point. As Nielsen himself recognizes, there is a real problem in explaining what it is to be an egalitarian. Most egalitarians are nowadays also (inconsistently?) in favor of nonegalitarian reverse discrimination in order to achieve equality of opportunity for minorities. Saying that all men are equal cannot be the same as saying that all persons who are in the same situation have the same rights, for we must then be ready to explain why it is claimed that people who are manifestly different (Sikhs and Untouchables in India) are "in the same situation." The idea that egalitarianism is freighted with a desire that rules entailing identical treatment for a larger number of people always be preferred to rules ensuring identical treatment only for a smaller number is, as Nielsen points out, neither obvious nor true. It would suggest that "we never distinguish between men, women, children, the aged, mental defectives, the physically handicapped, and the like."

As Berlin makes clear, the egalitarian ideal has a historical context in which the discriminations thought to be iniquitous were related to disparities in the possession or enjoyment of such things as "property, political or social power, status, opportunities for the development of faculties or the obtaining of experiences, social and personal, liberties, and privileges of all kinds." The modified egalitarian position that came to be embodied in the liberalist tradition held that the essential equalities to be achieved or protected were "equality of political and juridical rights." When equality before the law exists, no interference in other areas of activity, such as the economic, should be permitted, for such interference would necessarily curtail people's liberty. Liberals recognized that in such a situation inequalities in the distribution of wealth and power might develop or be perpetuated, but they were regarded as the price to be paid for political liberty and legal equality.

Berlin clearly supports that sort of "old egalitarianism." He admits, however, that the more thoroughgoing egalitarians would find it not enough, objecting that extensive inequalities of power and wealth necessarily curtail the freedom of the underdogs. Hence many egalitarians, like Nielsen, will be satisfied with nothing less than the social equality of the classless society and the abolition of the wage relationship. But, Nielsen argues, even such egalitarians recognize that there are real differences in origin, circumstances, or outlook, as well as physical and psychological, between people, and no one wants to achieve a uniform society in which there is a complete equality of needs among people. It is an equality of rights to the satisfaction of basic and elementary needs that has occasioned the political ideal of egalitarianism. All differences that have no bearing on their satisfaction are irrelevant. So, Nielsen suggests, Berlin must be wrong in thinking that egalitarians cherish a secret wish that there should be much greater uniformity between people.

I think, on the contrary, that Berlin is right. It may indeed be the case that egalitarians, in practice, restrict themselves only to the rejection of *irrelevant* differences as the basis of a sharing of rights and the satisfaction of need, but it turns out that there is no foolproof and clear way for distinguishing between relevant and irrelevant differences. What may or may not be relevant is completely contingent upon the circumstances. It is idle to deny the possibility that *any* difference between people can sometimes bring about the need for unequal distribution of benefits.

Differences in pigmentation, for example, may in certain circumstances (e.g. in a very hot climate) mean that certain races (e.g. blacks) have advantages not shared by others (e.g. in weathering the heat better), so that they come to be preferred by prospective employers over others. Is this not unfair discrimination?

Similarly, differences in gender may also bring about real differences of preference in the work market, of the sort, for example, that lead many employers to hire males rather than females, since the latter may, on occasion, require maternity leave. Again, is such discrimination fair or unfair? Any difference between people may, given the right circumstances, eventuate in the sort of inequalities egalitarians have been intent on removing, so clearly it is, in practice, far more difficult than we thought to distinguish differences between people that are relevant from those which are irrelevant to the sharing of power, rights, and benefits among human beings in society. Hence Berlin seems to be quite right in saying that those who insist upon equality wherever possible, sometimes at the expense of other ends human beings regard as valuable (e.g. happiness), may well be suspected of implicitly regarding complete uniformity as an ideal, which, unfortunately, cannot be realized in human affairs.

I believe this helps us to understand the tendency of radical feminists to pursue the assimilationist ideal, rather than accept the more commonsense ideal of "equal even though different." When supporters of the Kantian view that the innate refinement and kindness of women fits them for domesticity might argue that women will naturally find their greatest happiness in their family roles as wives and mothers, the Radical Feminists will reject this as "brainwashing." Behind their attitude we may suspect them of believing that happiness has nothing to do with the point—we do not want happy slaves (à la Aristotle) but free and equal human beings. So if, as some feminists, like Beauvoir and Alison Jaggar acknowledge (differing here from the Optimistic view), innate differences between men and women exist at present because of women's biological role, and will continue so long as women continue to perform that role in the accepted way, they find themselves inclined to accept, in the name of equality and justice, the paradoxical conclusion that women's biological role must be eliminated or so altered that justice and equality can be assured.

To understand why the Radical Feminists have been drawn to adopt their far-reaching conclusions is also to understand how their position can be attacked. There are two lines of procedure. The primary line of argument is to reject their egalitarian ideal and conception of justice as exaggerated, which I shall do in the next chapter. The other line of attack, which I shall pursue in the remainder of this chapter, is to point out that to relinquish the biological roles of men and women in reproduction, as well as their nurturing roles in human society, must lead to the impoverishment of their self-identity and humanity. . . .

A legal textbook in the United States, apparently still widely in use, defines the differing functions of husband and wife within the family as follows:

> [T]he husband is to provide the family with food, clothing, shelter, and as many of the amenities of life as he can manage. . . . The wife is to be mistress of the household, maintaining the home with the resources furnished by the husband. . . . [A] reading of contemporary judicial opinions leaves the impression that these roles have not changed over the last two hundred years.

That last sentence is particularly significant. I realize that it is not quite true—in many states a change in the legal expectations from husband and wife has been brought about, by the increasing influence of state equal rights amendments—but the author's implication is that in many cases the law has lagged behind the accepted view of the respective obligations of husband and wife. Increasingly today, one finds both husband and wife holding jobs, pursuing careers outside the family, and jointly providing for the economic needs of the family. In upper-middle-class and professional families there is much more sharing of household tasks between husband and wife than previously. With the spread of a more egalitarian approach to the family and the growing acceptance of some of the feminist demands for women's emancipation from their traditional dependent status, public opinion is no longer as sure as it used to be about the husband's duty to be the provider and the wife's duty to be the mistress of the household. Nonetheless, when marriages break down, by law it is still primarily the husband who has to undertake the financial support of wives and young children, whereas the wife is usually entrusted with continuing the truncated household through the custody of the children. So the law still seems to regard the traditional family as the norm, even while recognizing that in fact couples may voluntarily adopt all sorts of alternative arrangements for allocating domestic responsibilities between them.

Whatever the state of public opinion about the allocation of economic and management responsibilities within the family, when it comes to "fathering" and "mothering," they are still commonly viewed as different and distinct activities that are the responsibility of fathers and mothers, respectively, and define their primary roles vis-à-vis their children. Mothers are expected to provide the love, warmth, and care for the children, a natural continuation of their biological function of nursing them when infants. Fathers have the obligation to provide security, discipline, and direction, duties also presumed to constitute a natural extension of their function as the protectors and providers for nursing mothers and their infants. It is precisely here that the Radical Feminists set themselves apart by challenging the obviousness and the justice of those assumptions.

Virginia Held, in a thoughtful paper offering opinions that by and large even a non-radical and liberal feminist can accept, implicitly casts doubt on or even rejects the accepted wisdom that there is a distinctive contribution to the family to be made severally by fathers and mothers. The main thesis is that while the egalitarian demand for equality of obligation need not require that both parents perform exactly the same tasks within the family, it does require

. . . a *starting presumption* that all the tasks connected with supporting and bringing up children should *each* be divided equally. Dividing the tasks equally might be done by having both parents engage in the same activities for the same periods of their lives, as when they both split their days equally between child care and outside work. Or, dividing the tasks equally might be achieved through taking somewhat longer turns, one parent working away from home for a few years for instance, while the other stayed home, and then, for the next few years, reversing the roles. These latter divisions may be especially appropriate for parents who are separated, or who must live separately at times for professional or other reasons.

The idea seems to be for husband and wife to make a budget, as it were, of all the tasks that will be involved in bringing up the child or children for the next ten to thirty years, say, and to work out an equitable arrangement between them regarding who is to do what at which period. They are to assume, initially, that each is equally responsible for every task, even though the two may not be equally competent or willing to perform each task. That being so, the equitable arrangement between them will be reached by a series of tradeoffs, which will reflect career desires, competences, abilities, constraints, and wishes.

Equality of obligation here requires that each parent perform the same tasks, and it is noteworthy that every departure from this standard must be justified in terms of relevant criteria and appropriate principles. Held says: "There must be good reasons, and not merely customs and social pressures, for such departures. Simply being male or female is not a relevant ground for such departures and cannot be the basis for justifiable differences in parental roles." She argues that we have "no reliable knowledge of any genuine differing talents and tendencies of mothers and fathers (except the dispensable and brief capacity of mothers to nurse their infants)." We should be wary of accepting any division of labor between mothers and fathers based on their differing talents at the time they become parents, she warns, as they may result from years of sex-stereotyped preparation in which little boys have been encouraged to be physically active, to perform certain tasks, and to prepare themselves for specific jobs, while little girls are expected to play with dolls, babysit, and do housework.

There is an amazing naïveté about arguments of this sort that strikes me as artificial. What the biologist regards as one of the primary characteristics of the human species, i.e., that humans are mammals, Held relegates to relative insignificance—a "dispensable and brief capacity of mothers to nurse their children." Since it is so dispensable (presumably she has in mind the possibility of bottle-feeding), it is surprising that in a later article (quoted) she found it necessary to speculate on the possibility of hormone treatments enabling husbands to nurse their infant children. Who needs such measures? Cannot both husbands and wives equally manipulate a bottle? Cannot the flow of mother's milk easily be stopped by medication? Current medical opinion seems to prefer breast-feeding to bottle-feeding, but there is no doubt that if we really regarded this as important, medical science could probably improve substitute feeding for infants enough to eliminate the difference almost completely. Then female breasts could, in the brave new world, merely retain their status as sex ornaments.

It is clear that Held is trying to cut out natural differences between men and women altogether as a possible basis for differences in their parental responsibilities. The mere fact that something is natural—as natural as breast-feeding—does not mean it has to be retained. Whenever possible, in fact, she wishes to deny that phenomena supposed to be natural differences between men and women are really natural at all, hence her claim that we have no empirical knowledge of genuinely different talents and tendencies between men and women. Anything learned from simple observation is dismissed on the grounds that such observed differences may result from training, so apparently only innate talents and tendencies that will show themselves without any training can be counted.

But this is absurd. Using similar reasoning, we must conclude that we do not know whether most (and, for all I know, *any*) species of birds have any genuine talents and tendencies to fly, because fledglings require training by their parents. Nor have we any reliable empirical knowledge that human beings have any genuine talents and tendencies to walk, because infants generally need help and training in order to be able to do so.

To put the point succinctly, the distinction between nature and nurture is not absolute in the biological world. The only way we can determine empirically what is to be expected in a given species is simply to examine what normally happens. It is not helpful to argue that if evolution of the species had taken a different turning, then what now is regarded as normal might not have been so. In the early history of the human species it seems to have been universally true that females succored their infants and led more sedentary lives, while the males protected their mates and provided for their young. That was the normal state of affairs then, and it forms the basis for what counts as the normal state of affairs today. What other empirical evidence is necessary?

But let us assume, contrary to the facts, that we were somehow able to establish that what we take to be normal now resulted from some conventional arrangement, which diverted the course of human behavior from what it might otherwise have been, giving us cause for regret that the abstract principles of justice we now maintain were not then taken into consideration in allocating the nurturing tasks between husband and wife. Let us assume, further, that the practice whereby husbands are the providers and wives the mistresses of the household reflects nothing more than custom. On what ground does Held find the justification to say, as she does, that such customs do not provide good reasons for departing from her imaginary budget of parental obligations requiring each parent to perform the same tasks? Does custom therefore constitute no reason whatsoever for doing anything?

The difference between the way men and women dress and the way they wear their hair is almost entirely a matter of custom. A parent misguided enough to decide that she must dress her little boy and her little girl (to make the case more vivid let us assume they are twins) exactly the same and cut their hair the same right through childhood and adolescence, on the ground that any departure from uniform treatment must be justified by good reasons and not custom, would soon find that she had made herself and, more important, her children into a laughingstock. She has probably caused them psychological damage as well. The fact that something is customary may itself constitute at least a *prima facie* reason for honoring it. Custom may well deserve to be laid aside because of more important considerations—and justice may be one such consideration. But it is most unwise to contrast custom with good reason as if the former constituted no reason at all.

LINDA A. BELL

Racism, Sexism, and the Ideal of Equality

LINDA A. BELL teaches philosophy at Georgia State University. She has published widely on existentialism and feminist philosophy. Her most recent book is *Ethics in the Midst of Violence: A Feminist Approach to Freedom* (1993), from which the following selection is taken.

. . . Some goals are touted by society as essential to any emancipatory movement. One such goal is equality. Given the generally unquestioning praise of equality by those who have worked against oppression and given the fact that most hostility to equality comes from those who favor oppression, this goal will no doubt continue to attract the attention of feminists. In fact, it should. Certainly, where people have been subjected to such grossly unfair treatment as refusal to consider, much less to hire or admit to important positions, regardless of qualifications, anyone from certain ethnic or racial groups or even women from the dominant group, equal treatment of all contenders may indeed go a long way toward correcting some of the worst aspects of the society.

For feminists, though, equality is double-edged. For one thing, equality is often used ideologically to mystify oppression. As Janet Radcliffe Richards recognizes, equality is praised in sentimental ways, such as when men laud the work women do "behind the scenes" while not admitting either that this was the only way the women were *allowed* to contribute or that, without the restrictions, the same women could have contributed much more to the general welfare in other and more visible ways. As she says: "Under all the assertions of equality the facts of inequality can go unexamined, to the advantage of any group which has the upper hand."

Because of its connection with ideology, equality is a tricky notion to unpack. In a society where domination along lines of gender, race, and class is taught in a variety of ways as the way things are and ought to be and where indeed this *is* largely the way things are, more likely than not "equality" will reflect this dominance. Catharine MacKinnon shows how this notion is defined so as to buttress and perpetuate the status quo and the dominance therein. In discussing pornography, she says:

> Pornography constructs what a woman is in terms of its view of what men want sexually, such that acts of rape, battery, sexual harassment, prostitution,and sexual abuse of children become acts of sexual equality. Pornography's world of equality is a harmonious and balanced place. Men and women are perfectly complementary and bipolar. Women's desire to be fucked by men is equal to men's desire to fuck women. All the ways men love to take and violate women, women love to be taken and violated.

Janice Raymond raises a different problem with equality. Her objection is that defining feminism in terms of a concern that women be equal with men "places feminism at a false starting point" by continuing to give women's relation to men paramount importance. This could be stated a bit differently and more in line with feminist theorists like MacKinnon by noting that such a definition of feminism continues, inadvertently to be sure, to acknowledge men, at least some men, as the norm.

Marilyn Frye, too, sees equality as problematic, but for yet another reason: it accepts and reinforces dominance. If liberal white feminists simply desire that white women share equality with their white brothers, then, as Frye says, "what we [white women] want is, among other things, our own firsthand participation in racial dominance rather than the secondhand ersatz dominance we get as the dominant group's women." This is clearly objectionable since it means that the woman desiring such equality "simply wants to be in there *too,* as one of the men for whom men's God made everything 'for meat.'" It is a desire simply to be allowed to become one of the dominant; it does not change the quality, degree, or wrongness of the domination. Unfortunately, according to MacKinnon, "much of what has passed for feminism in law has been the attempt to get for men what little has been reserved for women or to get for some women some of the plunder that some men have previously divided (unequally) among themselves."

Bell hooks sees that equality blurs a complex situation, in which many ambiguities need to be clarified and about which some hard questions must be answered. Existing systems of oppression, exploitation, and discrimination are complex enough to allow that the same individual may be, in different ways, both victim and oppressor. For example, white women have been and continue to be victimized by sexism; but because of racism they, too, are in a position to exploit and oppress people of color. Similarly, black men have been and continue to be victimized by racism, but sexism allows them in turn to exploit and oppress black women. Even black women, victimized by multiple oppressions, may engage in homophobia, thus, as Patricia Collins says, "maintaining 'straightness.' . . [as] our last resort." There are, as she notes, "few pure oppressors or victims."

Consequently, we must object, with bell hooks, to any group defining "liberation" in terms of "social equality with ruling class white men," since this leaves the group with "a vested interest in the continued exploitation and oppression of other." Thus, the liberal feminist demand for equality is problematic inasmuch as it leaves open the important question "—To which men do women wish to be equal?"—a question that makes apparent the domination and elitism in human relationships in the culture.

Instead of working for equality, feminists must work, with bell hooks, to eradicate domination and elitism in all human relationships. Feminism, defined as "a struggle to end sexist oppression," thus becomes "necessarily a struggle to eradicate the ideology of domination that permeates Western culture on various levels as well as a commitment to reorganizing society so that the self-development of people can take precedence over imperialism, economic expansion, and material desires."

This requires that those who join the struggle "leave behind the apolitical stance sexism decrees is . . . [women's] lot and develop political consciousness." The requisite political consciousness enables us to see that the enemy is not men, that, for example, while a lower class man may perpetuate sexism, "[t]he ruling class male power structure that promotes his sexist abuse of women reaps the real material benefits and privileges from his actions." "As long as he is attacking women and not sexism or capitalism, he helps to maintain a system that allows him few, if any, benefits or privileges."

Bell hooks concludes from all this that men victimized by oppression, even those men who in turn victimize some women, may be natural allies in the struggle—if, that is, a developed political consciousness allows feminists to see and to help such apparently antifeminist men to look beyond the personal level to the larger systems of oppression. This political awareness allows her to acknowledge those men who truly are victimized by oppression while avoiding the "meaninglessness," to which Marilyn Frye also objects, of those who stretch the word "oppression" to include "the stresses and frustration of being a man." Labeling all stresses and frustrations "oppression" leads to absurd claims, e.g., that both slaveholders and slaves were oppressed by slavery, a claim that obscures their actual relations to each other, to the system of slavery, and to its profits. To avoid such absurdities, we must follow bell hooks's lead in meticulously examining the actual workings of the systems of oppression in which we are enmeshed.

Finally, political consciousness will disclose to us, as it does to bell hooks, the "primary importance" of sexist oppression, not, as Friedrich Engels would claim, because it is the basis of all other oppression, but because "[i]t is the practice of domination most people are socialized to accept before they even know that other forms of group oppression exist." This does not mean that sexist oppression is the only form of oppression to be fought, but only that it is an extremely important one. Surely it is one that no women can afford to ignore. We simply do not need to determine which form of oppression is the most serious, important, or fundamental; indeed, it is foolish to waste our time and energy in such disputes and counterproductive to try to limit our work against oppression to any one type. With Patricia Collins, we must realize that resistance can and should take place on each of the three levels on which oppression works: "the level of personal biography; the group or community level of the cultural context created by race, class, and gender; and the systemic level of social institutions."

This does mean, however, that the traditional family and the sex roles and identities it inculcates and perpetuates must be brought under extremely critical scrutiny. Thus, as Andrea Nye indicates, feminist theory must take seriously what Freud recognized, namely, the family's role in forming masculine and feminine selves. Fundamental changes in relationships and in child-rearing practices are called for so that individuals, from the cradle on, do not learn the practice of domination and are not taught to see themselves and others in terms of those extra identities to which Sartre refers as "overdeterminations."

Legal equality also is problematic, as many men as well as women have occasion to discover. To equalize the treatment of individuals under the law is to treat unequals equally and thereby to act unjustly. Long ago, Aristotle recognized such treatment as a paradigm of injustice. Today, many are rediscovering this truth in a particularly compelling fashion as they learn first-hand how equal treatment by law of economically and socially unequal individuals results in unequal representation by lawyers and unequal chances of winning contested child custody cases or criminal cases involving accusations of child abuse, rape, battery, and even murder.

Quite apart from the social and economic inequality between various litigants and accusers and those against whom they proceed, equal treatment before the law results in injustice if individuals have radically different needs. Women have found this to be so when their medical needs are denied coverage, for example, by corporate insurance programs. It is of little comfort and certainly no help in paying the bills for women to be told by those in control of these programs and perhaps even by the courts that men and women are *both* being denied pregnancy benefits—obviously, affecting women—and are *both* being granted, for example, benefits to cover hair implants—a procedure designed primarily for men.

As Catharine MacKinnon observes, the liberal view of equality, insisting on color blindness and sex-blindness in a society that is neither color- nor sex-blind, effectively discounts color and sex differences. Since the white and at least middle-class male constitutes the standard, those who are not white and middle class and male are recognized as meriting equal treatment to the extent they are *like* the white, middle class male. For example, as Rosemarie Tong notes, as long as the test of offense is whether "a person of ordinary sensibilities" (generally—and appropriately—termed "the ordinary man") would have been offended—and as long as men find the offensiveness of sexual harassment very difficult to understand—courts are bound to find much sexual harassment problematic. After all, men frequently are encouraged to regard such behavior toward women as normal and appropriate; many even profess (mistakenly, I believe) that they would feel flattered were a woman to engage in comparable behavior toward them.

Even Tong's remedy of "a supplemental ordinary *woman* test" is not likely to work as a remedy as long as the courts, men, and women themselves find male dominance acceptable and are indoctrinated with its assumptions almost every moment of every day. Indeed, the very commonplaceness of images and activities of dominance may be used, as it was in one case cited by Catharine MacKinnon, as evidence that no offense should be taken and, consequently, that no discrimination exists. She sees this as meaning that if the abuse is pervasive enough, it is not actionable. Nor will it remove "the threat of making the sexual abuse public knowledge," a power held by perpetrators, which "functions like blackmail in silencing the victim and allowing the abuse to continue." Victims shun publicity since "[i]t is a fact that public knowledge of sexual abuse is often worse for the abused than the abuser, and victims who choose to complain have the courage to take that on."

Moreover, Tong's "ordinary *woman* test" would be inadequate as a corrective inasmuch as sexism is not the only hegemonic oppression in the legal system in need of eradication. Racism and other systematic oppressions very likely would enter into the selection of the women who are thought to be "ordinary," that is, representative, and into the judgments of those women. Fortunately or unfortunately, all women are neither treated the same nor affected in the same way and with the same consequences even by activities specifically directed at them as women. Black women like Alice Walker have noted that black and white women are not even demeaned in the same way in pornography.

When individuals who are not white and male demand that their differences receive the same attention as do those of white males, this is denounced as asking for special treatment. Thus, women find themselves caught in the legal double bind described by MacKinnon. They are "not receiving the benefits of the social change that would qualify them to assert rights on the same terms as men," while more and more they are losing the few benefits of the earlier "protection racket" in which at least some women were able to acquiesce to male prescriptions of "femininity" in exchange for so-called "benign discrimination" under the law. She points out: "Almost every sex discrimination case that has been won at the Supreme Court level has been brought by a man." Although the state's "protections" of women have not applied to all women, have been woefully inadequate, and more often than not have worked to women's disadvantage, MacKinnon sees this, not as grounds for quiescence, but rather as reason "to demand that the promise of 'equal protection of the laws' be *delivered upon* for us, as it is when real people are violated." This is why she urges "a further step," which she calls "the women's rights amendment": decreeing that "the subordination of women to men is hereby abolished."

Even when the special needs of new parents are recognized by companies and leave is granted regardless of the gender of the parent, this superficially equal treatment leaves much to be desired if hidden costs of taking such leave make it exceedingly unlikely that men will use the leave and if the women who use it are passed over for promotions, losing their competitive edge to others who do not exercise their "right" to such leave. Moreover, in this as well as in other cases of supposedly equal treatment, it is not questioned, as it should be, "whether equality before the moral or positive law may not be rendered empty because of the dominant-subordinate structures in the economic or social (e.g., family) spheres." As Friedrich Engels observed, contracts are not necessarily freely entered into just because the law has made the parties "equal on paper."

According to MacKinnon, even constitutional equality guarantees cannot correct the position of women since such guarantees can be invoked only where the state has *acted*. The state has *not acted* vis-à-vis many of the ways women are coerced, violated, and silenced; rather, much of this activity takes place in private and for the most part in areas ignored by law. Furthermore, the state does not need to act, e.g., by enacting laws giving men the right to rape women, to abuse their daughters sexually and otherwise, to batter their wives, to silence women, and to infringe the privacy of women. What she means is that such laws are totally unnecessary: given that no laws have seriously undermined men's sexual access to women and girls, there is nothing to stop men from raping, battering, and silencing women; and most women have no privacy to take from them. In summation, she says: "No law guarantees that women will forever remain the social unequals of men. This is not necessary, because the law guaranteeing sex equality requires, in an unequal society, that before one can be equal legally, one must be equal socially. . . . So long as men dominate women effectively enough in society without the support of positive law, nothing constitutional can be done about it."

Equal treatment, either by law or in the workplace, leaves unexamined and unchallenged the demands and assumptions built into both. In *Three Guineas,* Virginia Woolf observes and critiques the demands and assumptions built into the workplace, at least as far as the professions are concerned. She cautions:

[I]f you [women] are going to make the same incomes from the same professions that those men make you will have to accept the same conditions that they accept. . . . You will have to leave the house at nine and come back to it at six. . . . You will have to do this daily from the age of twenty-one or so to the age of about sixty-five. . . . You will have to perform some duties that are very arduous, others that are very barbarous. You will have to wear certain uniforms and profess certain loyalties.

Her conclusion is that, though the cash value and prestige of these professions is admittedly great, their spiritual, moral, and intellectual value is not only questionable but indeed quite negative:

They make us of the opinion that if people are highly successful in their professions they lose their senses. Sight goes. They have no time to look at pictures. Sound goes. They have no time to listen to music. Speech goes. They have no time for conversation. They lose their sense of proportion—the relations between one thing and another.

Humanity goes. Money making becomes so important that they must work by night as well as by day. Health goes. And so competitive do they become that they will not share their work with others though they have more than they can do themselves.

What remains, she says, is "[o]nly a cripple in a cave." . . .

Like "equality," "power" requires rethinking. That feminism must address issues of power is beyond dispute; less obvious is the fact that the prevailing sense of power (in bell hooks's words, "domination and control over people or things") should be examined and rejected as too hierarchical and too narrow. Not doing so leaves us stuck in oppressive power relations. As long as men and women are taught from childhood "that domination and controlling others is *the* basic expression of power," women will not substantially change things as they move into positions where they can affect political and social policies. Rather, if oppression remains part of their "model of humanity," the oppressed will, as Paulo Friere says, simply become oppressors in their turn, following the sad example of native populations, observed by Frantz Fanon, where nationalism has only meant "the transfer into native hands of those unfair advantages which are the legacy of the colonial period."

At the very least, feminist reforms will be co-opted by the ruling male groups unless these reforms incorporate "alternative value systems that would include new concepts of power." Patricia Collins is thinking along these lines when she discusses "power as energy [that] can be fostered by creative acts of resistance." Opposing such power to that of domination, she connects this creative power with "the power to self-definition and the necessity of a free mind." Rejecting the kind of strength U.S. policy has too often presupposed and contrasting that "power-over" with something quite different—"power-with"—Sharon Welch warns that eschewing the power of domination is difficult, even for those fighting to make the world safer and less oppressive: "To ask for elimination of nuclear weapons is to desire total control, a humanly impossible degree of domination. It presumes an immoral control of the actions of others now and in the future and misses a different sort of power, the influence that our disarmament might have."

Although bell hooks is quite right that feminists must work out alternatives to the power over-exemplified in domination, perhaps she is a bit hasty in dismissing the latter from feminist strategy. Feminist reforms will no doubt be co-opted by the ruling male groups, regardless of what strategies are used and what kind of power is utilized. Thus, the problem is not co-optation, since that is inevitable, but rather the use of means that undermine and render impossible the end sought. But what if the end sought can be achieved in no other way; or worse, what if not using the unacceptable kind of power would result in an even stronger system of domination and destruction? Carol Anne Douglas quotes with approval Charlotte Bunch's affirmation that patriarchal domination and destruction can be ended only through the power dynamics already at work in the domination and destruction. However true that may be, we should fear, with bell hooks, that uncritical use of the same kind of power will make impossible any move to a different and better world. If feminists are to use the kind of power they reject, they must do so by maintaining a clear sense that, though necessary in situations where all options are violent because of the violence of others, such measures are immoral as means and are clearly banned by the ideal toward which they strive. . . .

While it is important to recognize the active and vicious systems of power over others in which we live, bell hooks argues that women bonding out of shared victimization is dangerous. It is dangerous because it simply reinforces rather than challenges sexist ideology, which "teaches women that to be female is to be a victim." It is dangerous, moreover, because women cannot afford to see themselves as powerless since their very survival may depend upon their own action, hence on their "continued exercise of whatever personal powers they possess."

For women to see themselves simply as powerless is distorting and dangerous in many ways. First, because it perpetuates the myth of women's helplessness, it continues to obscure and hide from view the history of women's resistance to oppression, a history that some, like Adrienne Rich, have tried to make visible.

Second, as Sarah Hoagland recognizes, victimization "ignores a woman's choices," thereby denying women's moral agency. To acknowledge choices does not mean that women choose or are to blame for their own oppression, nor does it free oppressors from responsibility for their actions. Rather, with Patricia Collins, it affirms "that there is always choice, and power to act, no matter how bleak the situation may appear to be." Seeing themselves as victims obscures whatever control might be exerted by women over their own lives and saps the energy women have used to make significant accomplishments. Paula Giddings suggests that the Afro-American woman has been able to accomplish so much "because she had an unshakable conviction: The progress of neither *race nor womanhood* could proceed without her." Giddings adds what is no doubt at least equally important: "And she understood the relationship between the two."

Third, victimization also encourages a fear and a hiding that is dangerous. As Audrey Lorde says, whatever an individual hides out of fear can be used against her. Realizing that silence is no protection, Lorde says she has developed, as a protective mechanism for herself, the strategy of speaking first. For her, though, this is more than just "an imperfect but useful argument for honesty" since the moral agency one thus exercises reveals that "that visibility which makes us most vulnerable is that which also is the source of our greatest strength."

Fourth, to see women merely as victims obscures the ways women themselves exercise oppressive power over others, whether, for example, as women over their children or as white women over nonwhite women and men or as middle- and upper-class women over poor women and men. In discussing the "oppressor's nightmare" of realizing that those he has oppressed are not in fact so very different from himself after all, Cherríe Moraga proposes that "women have a similar nightmare, for each of us in some way has been both oppressed and the oppressor. We are afraid to look at how we have failed each other. We are afraid to see how we have taken the values of our oppressor into our hearts and turned them against ourselves and one another. We are afraid to admit how deeply 'the man's' words have been ingrained in us."

Fifth, concentrating attention on women as victims tends to divert attention away from the complex network of power relations to a simplistic "focus on particular agents or roles that have power, and on agents over whom these powerful agents or roles have power." This dyadic modeling of power, according to Iris Young, results from the atomistic bias of distributive paradigms of power and obscures the institutionalization of power, "the larger structure of agents and actions that mediates between two agents in a power relation." As she says, "One agent can have institutionalized power over another only if the actions of many third agents support and execute the will of the powerful." Thus, in three poignant instances provided by Michèle Le Doeuff, this dyadic model fails to recognize (1) that the way the French Head of State deferentially receives the Pope can encourage a village pharmacist to attempt publicly to shame and thus intimidate an unmarried woman who comes to him for birth control pills, (2) that silent and unprotesting passersby can support the continued battery of a wife whose skull is fractured even though she fled to the street hoping for protection, and (3) that a newspaper's indulgence of admitted racists who beat a Tunisian worker to death in Nice in 1987 can "sign a blank checque for the violence done by others." The network of power relations is further complicated by the ways self-oppression plays into our victimization.

Finally, seeing themselves as victims keeps women from examining, and creating alternatives to, the prevailing notion of power as power over others. It thereby accepts and helps to perpetuate a culture which, as Margaret Randall observes, makes a book like *Women Who Love Too Much* into an instant best-seller while leaving unwritten and for the most part unthought the much needed *Men Who Hit Too Much*. Bell hooks merely alludes to possibilities of power over self when she quotes Nancy Hartsock's view that power can be "understood as energy, strength, and effective interaction." This reflects the truth of Sandra Lee Bartky's acknowledgment that "[t]he consciousness of victimization is a divided consciousness," divided between the awareness of the injury and the sense of exposure and diminishment, on the one hand, and, on the other, the "joyous consciousness of one's own power, of the possibility of unprecedented person growth and of the release of energy long suppressed."

Even women's traditionally ascribed passivity can, as Virginia Woolf observes, provide possibilities for effective interaction. While working women may have more real power in the sense that their not working to make, for example, munitions could materially affect the course of a war, sometimes even those who seem totally powerless and passive—e.g., "daughters of educated men"—can make their absence felt and their presence desirable. This is possible, of course, only if those in power require in some way the attention or approval of the "outsiders," a condition that frequently limits who can in this way make their absence felt and their presence desirable to women connected with the dominant.

Woolf refers to these individuals who supposedly remain outside as the "Society of Outsiders," a characterization to which Janice Raymond objects, preferring as she does the term "inside-outsider": "because it helps to make clear the dual tension of women who see the man-made world for what it is and exist in it with worldly integrity, while at the same time seeing beyond it to something different. The term also highlights the reality of women who know that they can never really be insiders yet who recognize the liabilities of the dissociated outsider." Woolf ultimately makes the same point, however, when she observes that these "outsiders," by displaying indifference, can sometimes help to modify or even abolish institutions: "[T]his use of indifference by the daughters of educated men would help materially to prevent war. For psychology would seem to show that it is far harder for human beings to take action when other people are indifferent and allow them complete freedom of action, than when their actions are made the centre of excited emotion." But Raymond has a different explanation for those occasions where women's turning away from men's spectacles is effective: "Men prove they are agents in this world only in contrast to the passivity of those who watch and are thus acted upon. Yet women who watch are never really passive. They are active in consolidating the spectacle of male bonding. Without women watching, male activity of any sort would be recognized for what it often is—passivity."

Thus, if women define themselves as sufferers, they will not see, much less take advantage of, the possibilities open to them, and, as Raymond says, "will settle for the world as men have made it." It is necessary to understand the intricacies and fluidity of the power relations that victimize women and many men, even while implicating many of these individuals in victimization of others and of themselves. This understanding is vital to the disclosing of actual and possible points and strategies of resistance and will encourage individuals to be beyond what is demanded by traditional ethics (namely, performing or avoiding certain deliberate actions) to assume responsibility for the "unconscious reactions, habits, and stereotypes [that] reproduce the oppression of some groups." Finally, it is important so that we can be clear both about what we reject as well as alternatives for which to strive. This is especially true in a context of what Margo Adair calls "polished ignoring," in which, as in our society, "[i]t is taboo to name power." . . .

Feminists, then, armed with outrage at violence and oppression, an awareness of freedom, ambiguity, and difference, and an ideal of objectivity, will approach the development of an ethics carefully and critically and with an especially acute concern that this development not exacerbate the plight of victims of violence and oppression. At the same time, attuned to problems of co-optation by the status quo, feminists will anticipate and try to keep such problems from derailing the struggle against violence and oppression. The analysis of equality and power is especially important to this development.

CHAPTER 10

Can We
Control
Violence?

Imagine the worst day you had this semester, one of those days when everything seems to go wrong. On days like that, irritations that would be easy enough to handle on ordinary occasions (the alarm clock not ringing, hectic traffic on the way to class, running into someone who has annoyed you) seem to be insurmountable challenges. Suppose that on that worst day of the semester, someone bumps into you on the sidewalk and starts yelling at you. What do you do? Do you yell back? Do you hurl every insult you can think at the person? Do you get out of that person's way but yell later when you discover that your roommate has thrown out the leftovers you planned to eat for dinner? Would any of these scenarios make the world a more violent place in which to live?

Violence is often held up as an indicator of societal malaise. The typical list of acts that are commonly agreed to be wrong includes certain violent acts, such as murder, torture, and child molestation. In fact, "violence" is sometimes taken to be almost synonymous with "wrongdoing": one is said to "do violence to" someone or something when one has done wrong.

At the same time, much of our entertainment is seasoned with violence, so much so that the motion picture industry is compelled to indicate whether the level of violence of a given film exceeds what a young child should be permitted to see. Rock videos commonly allude to violence as part of their aesthetic. Capital punishment is legal in the majority of states. Aside from total pacifists, most people believe that violence is sometimes justified—in law enforcement, perhaps, or in waging a "moral" war.

One can reasonably ask when such measures are appropriate, and how one can best apply them. Sun-Tzu was a military adviser to the king of the Chinese state of Wu in the sixth century B.C.E., and he has become one of the most influential military theorists in history. (His influence extends far beyond Asia. In the United States alone, some of Sun-Tzu's most avid recent readers have been American military officers and Wall Street financiers.) Sun-Tzu's handbook, *The Art of War,* is more concerned with military effectiveness than with ethical propriety. Interestingly, however, he couches his recommendations for successful warfare in the context of arguing against war. Sun-Tzu insists that it is best to arrange one's circumstances so that war is not necessary. A ruler who embarks on warfare has already conceded some measure of loss. War sometimes becomes inevitable, however, and the ruler who undertakes war should seek strategic positions that will do much of the army's work. Strategically, one should operate on the best intelligence one can get, because if you know the enemy as well as you know your own strengths, *you* will not be surprised. The best tactic is to surprise *the enemy* while making oneself as invulnerable as possible. "Know oneself, know one's enemy, and in 100 battles one will not be at risk."

A politician and diplomat in Renaissance Italy, Niccolò Machiavelli was also concerned about effectiveness in military strategy. Unlike Sun-Tzu, who thought that one should go to war only when no alternative existed, Machiavelli argued that war is a normal condition of relations between nations, and that a ruler should maintain an army that was in a constant state of preparedness for battle. In contrast to Sun-Tzu's recommendation of strategic positioning as a means of avoiding battle, Machiavelli has more activist recommendations. In *The Prince,* his strategic guide for maintaining power, Machiavelli contends that the ruler should concentrate on "war and its organization and discipline" as the indispensable art for continuing control. He also argues that although it is best for a ruler to be both loved and feared, fear is preferable to love. Like

Sun-Tzu, Machiavelli insists on being attentive to what each set of circumstances de-mands. In his view this includes dispensing with traditional virtues when they impede the attainment of one's objectives. For many, Machiavelli's writing marks the break be-tween Aristotle's view, which holds that politics is continuous with ethics, and the mod-ern view, which distinguishes the two.

Most contemporary Americans believe that there is far too much violence in our country and in our world. Ethics plays a role in our reflections on violence. Moral phi-losophy ponders questions such as the following: When, if ever, is violence morally appropriate? Are human beings inherently violent? If so, can we control or limit our expressions of violence? If not, is violence dispensable? Are certain ways of thinking in-herently violent? Can we undercut violence, at least to some extent, by changing the ways we think?

Sam Keen argues that our tendency to see other groups of people as enemies is a product of habits of thought that are entrenched in our own and other societies. We have been taught to see our enemies as "inhuman" and therefore as not deserving of the respect to which human beings are entitled. Unfortunately, the means of modern war-fare have made it easier to dehumanize "the enemy." Because violent attitudes toward an enemy are not essential aspects of human beings, such thinking, and the violence it facilitates, can be eradicated. But overcoming these socially cultivated habits must be-gin within the individual's own mind.

William James, by contrast, believes that violence is based on deep-seated human needs that traditionally have been satisfied by war. War, in his view, has provided the circumstances for developing hardiness, valor, and other virtues among individuals, as well as the possibility of changing the world in decisive, dramatically satisfying ways. But James denies that war is inevitable. He proposes an alternative: a conscription of all young people to be part of an army "against Nature." This army would work to con-trol nature to serve human beings and thus to achieve desirable civic goals. Such a con-scription, James argues, would provide the benefits that war has conferred on societies without entailing the violence and horrors of war.

Writing more recently, John McMurtry similarly urges a transformation of our cul-tural assumptions about warfare. Recent military thinking has, in his opinion, focused too much on the systematic destruction of other human beings and their life supports, on killing as efficiently as possible. This kind of thinking has made the destruction of human life, even most life on the planet, a real possibility. McMurtry encourages mili-tary thinkers to focus not on killing people, but on undercutting threatening military patterns. Disabling such patterns does not necessarily require killing people. By refo-cusing in this fashion, military thought could develop humane approaches to national defense, in contrast to the current tendency that often tolerates, even encourages, the mass destruction of human lives.

War, however, is not the only kind of violence that ethical reflection should address. Although it is arguable that the violence of war might sometimes be justified, certain kinds of violence are wrong by definition; unlike war, they are domestic and personal concerns. Date rape is among these. Lois Pineau, like other authors in this chapter, be-lieves that our way of thinking has done much to perpetuate violence. Pineau believes that a whole mythology of rape has undercut legal protection for victims of date rape. In such cases, the point of view on which the legal system depends, that of "the rea-sonable man," is biased by mythological ideas—for instance, the idea that women often say no when they mean yes. For the law to protect victims of date rape adequately, Pineau concludes, it must learn to recognize criteria for consent that conform to the point of view of the "reasonable woman."

Do we have a moral obligation to prevent violence? Presumably, there are cases in which our failure to attempt to prevent violence ought to be considered a moral failure. A case in point occurred several decades ago when a New York woman was stabbed to death while more than twenty people simply looked on. But what one is morally obligated to do depends on one's ability to do something. "Ought implies can," a premise of most moral theorists, makes precisely this point.

But if ought implies can, then we need factual information if we are to know what we ought to do. On the ground that it deters further violence, some consider the death penalty to be a legitimate use of violence. The deterrence argument figures prominently in the majority opinion of the U.S. Supreme Court in the landmark case of *Gregg v. Georgia* (1976), the decision that upheld the constitutionality of the death penalty. The Court acknowledges that we are uncertain as to whether the death penalty works as a deterrent, but it nevertheless thinks we can assume that it sometimes does. The majority opinion also reasons that the death penalty, as such, does not violate a citizen's right not to be subjected to "cruel and unusual punishment." It contends that the death penalty does not necessarily involve the "unnecessary and wanton infliction of pain," nor is it out of proportion to the crime in certain cases (such as when applied as the punishment for first-degree murder). The death penalty also does not seem to conflict with societal ideas of decency, given that a majority of state legislatures have passed laws that allow for capital punishment for certain crimes. Indeed, capital punishment seems to give expression to society's ideas of decency by enabling society to express its moral outrage at particularly heinous crimes.

Albert Camus takes issue with such defenses of the death penalty. He is unpersuaded that capital punishment deters crime. Moreover, he sees the government's action in capital cases to be essentially murder—often the murder of innocents—and he observes that the way in which capital cases typically proceed involves psychological cruelty as well. It is difficult, he feels, to see how such wanton behavior on the government's part can deter potential criminals. He also worries about the broader societal effects of the government endorsing the principle of retaliation so obviously as it does in the case of capital punishment.

Terrorism presents another case in which the justification of violence is hotly debated. Many Americans concur with the view expressed by the leaders of several Western nations that terrorism is always unjustifiable—even that it is wrong to negotiate with terrorists. (The latter position often rests on utilitarian grounds, namely, that it is wrong to negotiate with terrorists because to do so would be to recognize terrorism as a legitimate strategic ploy and thereby to encourage potential terrorists in the belief that terrorism is useful to them.) On the other hand, those who think that the unequal distribution of power among nations and among ethnic groups is wrong sometimes argue that terrorism seems the only available tactic for disenfranchised groups. Bat-Ami Bar On considers this issue. Although terrorism may aim to achieve reasonable objectives, On nevertheless contends that it is morally inappropriate because it is cruel. Terrorism produces cruelty in those who inflict it and destroys the selfhood of its victims. Although terrorists may believe that they are working for a better world, On is convinced that their strategy is counterproductive.

SUN-TZU

The Art of Warfare

SUN-TZU, or "Master Sun," lived in ancient China during the Spring and Autumn period (722–481 B.C.E.), an era when warfare was common and brutal. He was a military expert who advised rulers in his home state of Wu on the most effective means of waging war.

Master Sun said:

. . . to gauge the outcome of war we must compare the two sides by assessing their relative strengths. This is to ask the following questions:

Which ruler has the way?

Which commander has the greater ability?

Which side has the advantages of climate and terrain?

Which army follows regulations and obeys orders more strictly?

Which army has superior strength?

Whose officers and men are better trained?

Which side is more strict and impartial in meting out rewards and punishments?

On the basis of this comparison I know who will win and who will lose. . . .

Warfare is the art of deceit. Therefore, when able, seem to be unable; when ready, seem unready; when nearby, seem far away; and when far away, seem near. If the enemy seeks some advantage, entice him with it. If he is in disorder, attack him and take him. If he is formidable, prepare against him. If he is strong, evade him. If he is incensed, provoke him. If he is humble, encourage his arrogance. If he is rested, wear him down. If he is internally harmonious, sow divisiveness in his ranks. Attack where he is not prepared; go by way of places where it would never occur to him you would go. These are the military strategist's calculations for victory—they cannot be settled in advance.

It is by scoring many points that one wins the war beforehand in the temple rehearsal of the battle; it is by scoring few points that one loses the war beforehand in the temple rehearsal of the battle. The side that scores many points will win; the side that scores few points will not win, let alone the side that scores no points at all. When I examine it in this way, the outcome of the war becomes apparent. . . .

● ● ●

In joining battle, seek the quick victory. If battle is protracted, your weapons will be blunted and your troops demoralized. If you lay siege to a walled city, you exhaust your strength. If your armies are kept in the field for a long time, your national reserves will not suffice. Where you have blunted your weapons, demoralized your troops, exhausted your strength and depleted all available resources, the neighboring rulers will take advantage of your adversity to strike. And even with the wisest of counsel, you will not be able to turn the ensuing consequences to the good.

Of old the expert in battle would first make himself invincible and then wait for the enemy to expose his vulnerability. Invincibility depends on oneself; vulnerability lies with the enemy. Therefore the expert in battle can make himself invincible, but cannot guarantee for certain the vulnerability of the enemy. Hence it is said:

Victory can be anticipated,
But it cannot be forced.

Being invincible lies with defense; the vulnerability of the enemy comes with the attack. If one assumes a defensive posture, it is because the enemy's strength is overwhelming; if one launches the attack, it is because the enemy's strength is deficient. The expert at defense conceals himself in the deepest recesses of the earth; the expert on the attack strikes from out of the highest reaches of the heavens. Thus he is able to both protect himself and to take the complete victory.

To anticipate the victory is not going beyond the understanding of the common run; it is not the highest excellence. To win in battle so that the whole world says "Excellent!" is not the highest excellence. Hence, to lift an autumn hair is no mark of strength; to see the sun and moon is no mark of clear-sightedness; to hear a thunder clap is no mark of keen hearing. He whom the ancients called an expert in battle gained victory where victory was easily gained. Thus the battle of the expert is never an exceptional victory, nor does it win him reputation for wisdom or credit for courage. His victories in battle are unerring. Unerring means that he acts where victory is certain, and conquers an enemy that has already lost. . . .

●　　●　　●

Generally in battle use the "straightforward" to engage the enemy and the "surprise" to win the victory. Thus the expert at delivering the surprise assault is as boundless as the heavens and earth, and as inexhaustible as the rivers and seas. Like the sun and moon, he sets only to rise again; like the four seasons, he passes only to return again. . . .

The expert at battle seeks his victory from strategic advantage (*shih*) and does not demand it from his men. He is thus able to select the right men and exploit the strategic advantage. He who exploits the strategic advantage sends his men into battle like rolling logs and boulders. It is the nature of logs and boulders that on flat ground, they are stationary, but on steep ground, they roll; the square in shape tends to stop but the round tends to roll. Thus, that the strategic advantage of the expert commander in exploiting his men in battle can be likened to rolling round boulders down a steep ravine thousands of feet high says something about his strategic advantage. . . .

●　　●　　●

The ultimate skill in taking up a strategic position is to have no form. If your position is formless, the most carefully concealed spies will not be able to get a look at it, and the wisest counsellors will not be able to lay plans against it. I present the rank and file with victories gained through strategic positioning, yet they are not able to understand them. Everyone knows the position that has won me victory, yet none fathom how I came to settle on this winning position. Thus one's victories in battle cannot be repeated—they take their form in response to inexhaustibly changing circumstances.

The positioning of troops can be likened to water: Just as the flow of water avoids high ground and rushes to the lowest point, so on the path to victory avoid the enemy's strong points and strike where he is weak. As water varies its flow according to the fall of the land, so an army varies its method of gaining victory according to the enemy.

Thus an army does not have fixed strategic advantages or an invariable position. To be able to take the victory by varying one's position according to the enemy's is called being inscrutable.

Thus, of the five phases, none is the constant victor; of the four seasons, none occupies a constant position; the days are both short and long; the moon waxes and wanes.

NICCOLÒ MACHIAVELLI

The Prince

NICCOLÒ MACHIAVELLI (1469–1527) wrote *The Prince* as a guidebook to explain the mechanisms that would enable a leader to stay in power. Although winning friends and influencing people were among his suggestions, Machiavelli recommended these only as means of maintaining political dominance. Indeed, as the following selection indicates, he contended that the leader should be concerned more that people fear him than that they love him.

THE DUTIES OF A PRINCE WITH REGARD TO THE MILITIA

A prince should . . . have no other aim or thought, nor take up any other thing for his study, but war and its organisation and discipline, for that is the only art that is necessary to one who commands, and it is of such virtue that it not only maintains those who are born princes, but often enables men of private fortune to attain to that rank. And one sees, on the other hand, that when princes think more of luxury than of arms, they lose their state. The chief cause of the loss of states, is the contempt of this art, and the way to acquire them is to be well versed in the same.

Francesco Sforza, through being well armed, became, from private status, Duke of Milan; his sons, through wishing to avoid the fatigue and hardships of war, from dukes became private persons. For among other evils caused by being disarmed, it renders you contemptible; which is one of those disgraceful things which a prince must guard against, as will be explained later. Because there is no comparison whatever between an armed and a disarmed man; it is not reasonable to suppose that one who is armed will obey willingly one who is unarmed; or that any unarmed man will remain safe among armed servants. For one being disdainful and the other suspicious, it is not possible for them to act well together. And therefore a prince who is ignorant of military matters, besides the other misfortunes already mentioned, cannot be esteemed by his soldiers, nor have confidence in them.

He ought, therefore, never to let his thoughts stray from the exercise of war; and in peace he ought to be loved more than feared, or feared more than loved. The reply is, that one ought to be both feared and loved, but as it is difficult for the two to go together, it is much safer to be feared than loved, if one of the two has to be wanting. For it may be said of men in general that they are ungrateful, voluble, dissemblers, anxious to avoid danger, and covetous of gain; as long as you benefit them, they are entirely yours; they offer you their blood, their goods, their life, and their children, as I have before said, when the necessity is remote; but when it approaches, they revolt. And the prince who has relied solely on their words, without making other preparations, is ruined; for the friendship which is gained by purchase and not through grandeur and nobility of spirit is bought but not secured, and at a pinch is not to be expended in your service. And men have less scruple in offending one who makes himself loved than one who makes himself feared; for love is held by a chain of obligation which, men being selfish, is broken whenever it serves their purpose; but fear is maintained by a dread of punishment which never fails.

Still, a prince should make himself feared in such a way that if he does not gain love, he at any rate avoids hatred; for fear and the absence of hatred may well go together, and will be always attained by one who abstains from interfering with the property of his citizens and subjects or with their women. And when he is obliged to take the life of any one, let him do so when there is a proper justification and manifest reason for it; but above all he must abstain from taking the property of others, for men forget more easily the death of their father than the loss of their patrimony. Then also pretexts for seizing property are never wanting, and one who begins to live by rapine will always find some reason for taking the goods of others, whereas causes for taking life are rarer and more fleeting.

But when the prince is with his army and has a large number of soldiers under his control, then it is extremely necessary that he should not mind being thought cruel; for without this reputation he could not keep an army united or disposed to any duty. Among the noteworthy actions of Hannibal is numbered this, that although he had an enormous army, composed of men of all nations and fighting in foreign countries, there never arose any dissension either among them or against the prince, either in good fortune or in bad. This could not be due to anything but his inhuman cruelty, which together with his infinite other virtues, made him always venerated and terrible in the sight of his soldiers, and without it his other virtues would not have sufficed to produce that effect. Thoughtless writers admire on the one hand his actions, and on the other blame the principal cause of them. . . .

I conclude, therefore, with regard to being feared and loved, that men love at their own free will, but fear at the will of the prince, and that a wise prince must rely on what is in his power and not on what is in the power of others, and he must only contrive to avoid incurring hatred, as has been explained.

OF CRUELTY AND CLEMENCY, AND WHETHER IT IS BETTER TO BE LOVED OR FEARED

Proceeding to the other qualities . . . [needed], I say that every prince must desire to be considered merciful and not cruel. He must, however, take care not to misuse this mercifulness. Cesare Borgia was considered cruel, but his cruelty had brought order to the Romagna, united it, and reduced it to peace and fealty. If this is considered well, it will be seen that he was really much more merciful than the Florentine people, who, to avoid the name of cruelty, allowed Pistoia to be destroyed. A prince, therefore, must not mind incurring the charge of cruelty for the purpose of keeping his subjects united and faithful; for, with a very few examples, he will be more merciful than those who, from excess of tenderness, allow disorders to arise, from whence spring bloodshed and rapine; for these as a rule injure the whole community, while the executions carried out by the prince injure only individuals. And of all princes, it is impossible for a new prince to escape the reputation of cruelty, new states being always full of dangers. . . .

Nevertheless, he must be cautious in believing and acting, and must not be afraid of his own shadow, and must proceed in a temperate manner with prudence and humanity, so that too much confidence does not render him incautious, and too much diffidence does not render him intolerant.

From this arises the question whether it is better to practise it more than in war, which he can do in two ways: by action and by study. As to action, he must, besides keeping his men well disciplined and exercised, engage continually in hunting, and thus accustom his body to hardships; and meanwhile learn the nature of the land, how steep the mountains are, how the valleys debouch, where the plains lie, and understand the nature of rivers and swamps. To all this he should devote great attention. This knowledge is useful in two ways. In the first place, one learns to know one's country, and can the better see how to defend it. Then by means of the knowledge and experience gained in one locality, one can easily understand any other that it may be necessary to observe; for the hills and valleys, plains and rivers of Tuscany, for instance, have a certain resemblance to those of other provinces, so that from a knowledge of the country in one province one can easily arrive at a knowledge of others. And that prince who is lacking in this skill is wanting in the first essentials of a leader; for it is this which teaches how to find the enemy, take up quarters, lead armies, plan battles and lay siege to towns with advantage.

Philopoemen, prince of the Achaei, among other praises bestowed on him by writers, is lauded because in times of peace he thought of nothing but the methods of warfare, and when he was in the country with his friends, he often stopped and asked them: If the enemy were on that hill and we found ourselves here with our army, which of us would have the advantage? How could we safely approach him maintaining our order? If we wished to retire, what ought we to do? If they retired, how should we follow them? And he put before them as they went along all the contingencies that might happen to an army, heard their opinion, gave his own, fortifying it by argument; so that thanks to these constant reflections there could never happen any incident when actually leading his armies for which he was not prepared.

But as to exercise for the mind, the prince ought to read history and study the actions of eminent men, see how they acted in warfare, examine the causes of their victories and defeats in order to imitate the former and avoid the latter, and above all, do as some men have done in the past, who have imitated some one, who has been much praised and glorified, and have always kept his deeds and actions before them, as they say Alexander the Great imitated Achilles, Caesar Alexander, and Scipio Cyrus. And whoever reads the life of Cyrus written by Xenophon, will perceive in the life of Scipio how gloriously he imitated the former, and how, in chastity, affability, humanity, and liberality Scipio conformed to those qualities of Cyrus as described by Xenophon.

A wise prince should follow similar methods and never remain idle in peaceful times, but industriously make good use of them, so that when fortune changes she may find him prepared to resist her blows, and to prevail in adversity.

SAM KEEN

The Enemy as Abstraction

SAM KEEN is a contributing editor for *Psychology Today*. He is author of *The Passionate Life* (1983), *Faces of the Enemy* (1986), and *Fire in the Belly* (1991). He lives and raises horses in Sonoma, California, and he consults with a number of corporations.

The execution of the Air-Land Battle doctrine will depend on our ability to distribute the information gained in microprocessors, embedded computers and data processing devices which are integral to the new system. The chip is the technological key to the new doctrine— the counterpart to the blitzkrieg's use of the gasoline engine.

MAJ. GEN. JOHN WOODMANSEE, JR.

Modern technological warfare is gradually changing the way we think about the enemy. Both the heroic and the vitriolic images are being replaced by sterile concepts as the long reach of our weapons no longer makes it necessary for us to respect or hate those we intend to kill. The missile technician or the bomber pilot is so far removed from his "target" that he need not confront the carnage he inflicts. As one pilot who served in Vietnam told me, "I was OK so long as I was conducting high altitude missions, but when I had to come in and strafe and I could see the faces of the people I was killing, I got very disturbed." The ancient warrior needed massive physical strength and agility, a passionate hatred, and an ability to relish killing. He was either fierce, proud, arrogant, dominating, boastful, comfortable with cruelty, or dead. The modern warrior, by contrast, must be a specialist, coolheaded and emotionally detached. He prevails only if his calculations are accurate and his mind uncluttered by any passion save the love of efficiency. It has not escaped the attention of the Army that the now and future warrior will have all the virtues of a computer expert and video game player.

The change from heroic tradition to modern warrior is from

Intimacy	to	Distance
Hot	to	Cool
Courage	to	Calculation
Hate	to	Feelinglessness
Physical fierceness	to	Intellectual accuracy
Individual initiative	to	Bureaucratic cooperation
Daring	to	Obedience

In the past when decisive victory was the point of war, a warrior needed to be aggressive, impatient, and ready for immediate action. Today stalling, posturing, rendering the threat of nuclear annihilation credible and creating stalemates is the essence of warfare. Hence another type of military personalty is needed. The National War College has a course called "Executive Skills Development" that is directed at developing

450

a personality called ISTJ (introverted, sensing, thinking, judging), and students are tested by using the Myers-Briggs Type Indicator, a test based on the work of Jung, that measures whether one is introverted or extroverted, intuitive or sensing, thinking or feeling, and judging or perceptive. The ISTJs like to look for canned answers, they want to know the right answer. This personality type is the same as the corporate executive—objective decision makers. According to psychologist Otto Kroeger, a consultant to the U.S. Army,

> This corporate personality is something fairly new in the military, and it helps explain why during war games, the students prefer deterrence to destruction. The peacetime Army does not have the George Patton type. They've been weeded out. I know a number who have early-outed in the last ten years. The action types, the hard-nosed risk-taking daredevils, said, "I didn't come to push papers, I joined the action Army and there's no action."

As the modern warrior has become increasingly disembodied and warfare an intellectual and technological matter, the enemy has been progressively reduced to an abstraction.

The process began with the introduction of the drum and the uniform. Forcing men to march to a single cadence and to dress in ways that eradicated all distinctions, removed the element of individuality that was essential to heroic warfare. Enemies and allies alike are all pretty much olive drab or dull gray. Like a unit in a society governed by mass production, the soldier has been reduced to standardized functionary. He is a part of a well-oiled war machine, and his highest virtue is to function efficiently, which involves obeying the orders of his superiors. And the enemy is merely an impediment, an obstacle to be removed.

Occasionally we use machine images to dehumanize the enemy. We suggest that he is an automaton, a mindless being who is programmed by some higher, but demonic, intelligence. The enemy as automaton is an updated version of the enemy as puppet. In both cases what is central is the notion that he has no independent will and is controlled by something beyond himself. Hence we should have no more compunction in dispatching him than we would in destroying a robot. There is no soul in the machine.

More often than lending the enemy even the slight dignity we accord to machines, we simply erase him from our field of vision and act as if he is not there. Robert Bathurst reports that in the 1970s the U.S. Naval War College got the idea "that the study of war can be abstracted from people." After Vietnam there was a feeling that the language of war and enemies was immoral and old-fashioned, and that these subjects could be made more agreeable by being denationalized and universalized. Thus all specific references to the Soviets as enemies were deleted from textbooks, and men were told that they would be fighting to defend "land areas." "With such planning armed forces tend to become transformed into enormous riot squads being sent to a neighborhood they don't know to fight an enemy difficult to recognize, an enemy with technological characteristics, but no human face."

Nowhere has the statistical, abstract concept of the enemy become more obvious than in the American practice in Vietnam of determining "progress" in war by announcing daily "body counts." Under such conditions all it took to define an enemy was a body. As the popular saying went, "If it's dead, it's Viet Cong." The enemy is only a number used in our mathematical calculations. He is one of 6 million Jews killed, 20 million Soviets, 8,000 Sandinistas, 36 Arab terrorists, 250,000 Hindus, and so forth.

One professional soldier with much combat experience, Col. Anthony Herbert, translates the pathetic language of abstraction into its tragic reality:

> To say that it had not been a very important day because the Second Battalion had but two NVA kills now seems ludicrous; it was a damned important day for those two dead men. When even just one man died or got his fingers blown off or his leg shattered or his hearing impaired or his eyes bloodied and blinded, it was one hell of a costly battle—especially if you happened to be the guy who got it that day. It's something generals and presidents can never understand—only mothers, fathers, brothers, sons and daughters, and wives. . . . If anything has happened to our country as a result of the Vietnam War, it is our national infection with the sickness of the numbers game. We reduced the blood and suffering and the death and destruction to mere ciphers, and in so doing we reduced our own souls. Numbers don't die; people do. Columns of figures don't disintegrate in the explosion of a bomb; human beings do. Statistics don't bleed, and if you can make your war a war of numbers, you have no trouble sleeping. Most generals and presidents sleep well.

> . . . To see how completely we have dehumanized and eliminated the enemy, even to the point of not dignifying him with an image we can hate, we must look at the euphemistic language of modern warfare. Our weapons have become so indiscriminate and omnicidal that we dare not look specifically at the enemy on whom they will fall. To imagine what nuclear weapons will do would require the "nice" technician, the computer specialist, the games theorist, the modern human general, to admit that he is contemplating a crime against humanity that makes Hitler's extermination camps appear small scale. To visualize the millions of Soviet or American men, women, and children who would be incinerated by even a small atomic "device" might upset our digestion. So long as we want to kill from a distance with clean hands, we must refrain from imagining the consequences of our weapons, and must completely eliminate any awareness of the enemy as human. Our new language of warfare is not accidental. The Air Force colonel who described the Titan II missile with a nine-megaton warhead as "a potentially disruptive re-entry system" (and was awarded the National Association of English Teacher's American Doublespeak Award in 1983), should have also gotten the Adolph Eichmann Memorial Prize. When a missile warhead becomes a "re-entry vehicle," when killing civilians becomes "collateral damage," when the destruction of cities becomes "countervalue," when an MX missile becomes "Peacemaker," when combat becomes "violence processing," when destroying entire areas with Agent Orange becomes "an environmental adjustment," and peace becomes "permanent pre-hostility," we have reached the end of the line of dehumanization: 100 on a scale of 100. (Incidentally, the Grenada "invasion" was changed by the U.S. State Department first to a "rescue mission" and then to "a pre-dawn vertical insertion.") When the warrior makes only technical decisions with no reference to moral considerations, the enemy is reduced to a cipher, a statistical unit. Both the warrior and the enemy have disappeared. No living, feeling, agonizing, tragic, cruel, compassionate, courageous, fearful, anxious person is left on the battlefield, which has now become the entire world. Only machines fighting other machines. Little wonder that when Army futurists speculate about the human aspects of Airland Battle 2000 they present us with the ultimate triumph and nemesis of the historical union of *Homo faber* and *Homo hostilis:*

The human aspects of Airland Battle 2000 are of genuine concern for which we have far more questions than answers. Will soldiers be able to exist on the battlefield of the year 2000? Or are we imagining such a technologically hostile environment that soldiers themselves will not be accommodated? We expect, in addition to more and worse physical wounds, more psychological stress casualties. Whole battle staffs of professional officers may collapse; commanders may have to be replaced or dual command instituted. Human engineering to immunize our soldiers against stress may be required, just as we now immunize against disease.

When war has become so terrible that we can no longer bear to think about those we destroy and when we must think of "engineering" a new breed of man to withstand the horror, it should be clear that *Homo hostilis* has reached the end of the line.

We are faced with choices so radical that any one of them will completely change the way we think about ourselves. We may resign from all hope of remaining human and alive and accept our fate as anonymous victims of "potentially dangerous re-entry systems." If we refuse this path of impotent despair, we may control our technology, run the arms race backward, and learn to fight limited wars with minimal weapons. Or we may undertake the heroic psychological, political, and spiritual task of transforming our ancient habit of enmity.

Realistically, most of what has masqueraded as practical politics and rational warfare has been mass madness, corporate schizophrenia. Rarely is warfare an effective solution to conflict. Therefore we will fall far short of investigating promising solutions to the problem of war if we limit ourselves to looking for rational, exterior, political means for adjudicating conflict. No doubt, the habit of warfare will not be ended without an effective international law and enforcement agency and the creation of new political institutions both within and between nations. But even less will it be ended without a psychological transformation of large numbers of individuals.

Healing begins when we cease playing the blame game, when we stop assigning responsibility for war to some mysterious external agency and dare to become conscious of our violent ways. . . .

If we desire peace, each of us must begin to demythologize the enemy; cease politicizing psychological events; re-own our shadows; make an intricate study of the myriad ways in which we disown, deny, and project our selfishness, cruelty, greed, and so on onto others; be conscious of how we have unconsciously created a warrior psyche and have perpetuated warfare in its many modes:

1. *The civil war within the self*—the enemy within, agonizing self-consciousness, the struggle between "I should" and "I want," the battle between "good" and "evil" parts of the self
2. *The war between the sexes*—combat in the erogenous zones, the creation of familiar enemies, the practice of seduction, rape, one-upmanship. The sadistic-masochistic element in sexual and familiar relationships, the practice of superiority–inferiority, winners and victims
3. *The political war between Us and Them*—how our psyches have been shaped by the consensual paranoia and the standard propaganda of our society and by the barrage of images of the enemy

4. *The battle against nature, life*—the measure in which we have a propensity to identify ourselves "against," to assume that we must struggle, control, dominate, in order to be safe: the mistrust of self, others, life.

It should go without saying that individuals dealing with their personal enmity will not automatically solve the problem of warfare. But it is likewise certain that the politics of the warrior will not change without a constituency of individuals who have made the solitary decision to follow the path of metanoia rather than paranoia and to begin the practice of compassion rather than competition. Or, as the matter was stated a long time ago, "Remove first the beam from your own eye and then you will see more clearly to remove the mote from your brother's eye."

I believe the initiative for world peace at this time in history rests primarily with North Americans. Our repentance will be the major factor in determining the future of enmity. To use an analogy, every family therapist knows that the healthiest person in a diseased family system bears the most responsibility for changing the conflict and pathology of the system. For various historical reasons, the Soviet Union is an exceptionally paranoid nation. The United States is slightly less paranoid. Therefore, we have a greater responsibility to introduce sanity, to be willing to repent of our mistakes, to de-escalate our propaganda, to demythologize the "communist" as enemy. Our blame for world conflict is not greater, but our psychological opportunity for resolution is greater. When it comes to the individual task of reowning the enemy, of practicing metanoia, we are all equal. The journey into the wilderness of the shadow requires a heroic and solitary effort of anyone who would make it. But Americans, at least, have a wide access to alternative media, to information, and therapeutic help which is necessary to become genuinely self-critical, to jump outside the prison of the tribal or national psyche. . . .

JOHN McMURTRY

The Military Paradigm

JOHN McMURTRY teaches at the University of Guelph. He specializes in social and political philosophy.

THE HIDDEN PREMISES OF
THE MILITARY PARADIGM

What one finds in surveying the vast philosophical and social-scientific literature on war and defence is that a particular and narrow form of both is unspokenly presupposed. This presupposed form is so reductively prescriptive in its sense that one might regard it as inconceivable to human intelligence, were its objective not so conventionally assumed: namely, national defence or war means the threat or the action of *systematically killing, maiming, and destroying the life-supports of other human beings by maximally efficient means.*

A family of prescriptions normally accompanies this unstated principle of military intention. Though these prescriptions may in principle contradict every value of democratic or progressive social order we espouse, they too are presupposed at the pre-reflective level. We need to unpack from the institutionally given what they are. Like the ruling purpose they serve, they can only be derived by a kind of transcendental deduction. The following general properties of the military programme are here abstracted from its operations over two millennia, and together they constitute its underlying regulative form: (i) social segregation of a specialist arms-monopolizing group to execute the programme's general objective; (ii) a rank-ordered command structure relying upon motivation by fear to coerce its membership into performing and risking its mass-homicidal prescription; (iii) immersion programmes of obedience conditioning, indoctrination, and life-uniformity to liquidate individuality and choice; (iv) an autonomous technological development whose *telos* is ever more efficiently homicidal and destructive weapons; (v) an enshrinement of heroic life-sacrifice as a supreme ethical good.

From this culturally universal programme of military war and defence, two main kinds of reflective or theoretical argument have arisen over two millennia of consideration: (1) arguments which specify those types of occasion when other humans are to be systematically killed and maimed with good moral reason (i.e. 'just war' theory, 'moral means' arguments, and the like); (2) arguments which specify, by game-theoretical or other rational calculation, those strategies for military killing and destruction which will by threat or enactment maximize payoffs for one side in the conflict.

Further narrowing this premiss-base of the established theory of war and defence is an invariant a priori principle regulating judgment: namely, justification from the standpoint of one side only, the side to which one is assigned by one's prescribed membership in a predefined group (what we may call the *tribal a priori*). . . .

Deriving from this premiss base, military commands have also typically assumed that the opposing sides of any military conflict will, because rationally pursuing their self-interest, inflict the worst harm they can on the other side to maximize their own side's gains. This follows necessarily from the logic of zero-sum games where payoffs and losses are exactly equal, but is an assumption which antedates its formalization in mathematical theory. This regulating logic of self-interest maximization then generates a system of hypotheses called 'worse-case scenarios', by which the worst that the other side can possibly do is posited as a given of 'hard realism'. Reasoning then proceeds from these postulates of gross violation by the adversary towards decisions of threatened or enacted social massacre and destruction.

The depth and consequence of unexamined assumption here are breathtaking, but widely assumed as requirements of 'rationality'. War's military mode has, by its historical dominance, so locked social and moral judgment into presupposing a homicidal and mass-destructive logic of war and defence that conventional reflection has closed itself to the most fundamental choices of which 'making war' or 'self defence' admit. . . .

• • •

WHO IS THE SELF OF NATIONAL SELF-DEFENCE?

At the base of our conceptual constructions of the world we must defend ourselves in is the self-other disjunction. As Hegel and Sartre have emphasized, this relationship of self to other may at bottom *be* a war, a contest to the death in some sense. But even in the restricted sense of war between human groups with homicidal weapons of attack and defence, the self-other axis at the heart of such oppositions can take many different alternative forms.

At the most primitive level, there is the Hobbesian possibility of merely individual selves, organic or national, driven by inborn appetites of power or fear to wage a *bellum omnium contra omnes*, with further differentiated conceptions of 'self' possible with these parameters: from, at one end, the self posited as a brutish shortness of existence, a mere pawn of chance in the mortal struggle, to, at the other end, a vainglorious self-concept whose negation of otherness spans across the state of nature in a projected structure of omnipotence.

By contrast, there are many other, less atavistic possibilities of the national or individual self underlying the life-and-death struggle of war: the self as free-trade contestant in a 'marketplace competition of survival and elimination'; or, as in the brahminical tradition, the self as an ego-annihilative warrior against attachment to material objects of desire; or, as in sociobiological theory, the self or population group as a vehicle of genetic reproduction in the evolutionary war for continued life. These and other conceptions of self imply radically different types of defence and war. What might be the commercial self's opportunity for exchange could be the spiritual self's deadly insult. What could be a provocation of racial impurity to the genetic self might to the cosmopolitan self be an opportunity for love. What might be a mortal provocation for any of these selves could also be, for any other, a stimulus to agreement under a different construction of thought. In short, wholly different forms of war and defence are generated from different concepts of who or what we *are*. Thus, from Homeric warriors to contemporary anti-racists, invocations of self-identity invariably accompany declarations of war.

These are some of the fundamental alternatives of self-other lines of contests to the death. Yet each in turn admits of further subtypes. The 'patriotic' self, for example, is protean in its varieties. It may be based on disguised private self-interest—commander glory, class hegemony, or envy of youth, for example. On the other hand, a nation of people might conceive of themselves in terms of their country's geographical integrity and preservation, or its heritage of civil and political institutions, or its potential contribution to human well-being, or the conceit of being 'number one' in the world. These are all options for a patriotic identity's asserting itself through projects of defence or war. The underlying choices of value here are complex and rich, and all can provide the basis from which judgment leads to *non*-homicidal war. For example, against flies, corruption, or official lies.

Let us suppose, in line with current proclamations of national identity, that 'freedom for all people' is a nation's self-defining objective in defence and war. This self-base obviously opens onto a horizon of possibilities very different from that of the self-base for which it may merely be the cloak: the self as essentially acquisitor. For example, the patriot of global freedom could not consistently adopt the plan of transferring a maximum of capital from poorer countries to its wealthiest citizens through military means. For the exploitation in such a project would contradict the declared patriotic identity. On the other hand, such a programme of choice and action would be quite consistent with the underlying self that seeks capital accumulation for its corporate citizens before all else. *Which* self a nation constitutes itself as makes all the difference to what kind of enemy that nation will face, and what sort of defence or war it will choose. The concept of 'national self-interest' does not designate a given, but an open question.

This is what is ultimately meant by the insight that 'war reveals a society's inner nature'. Through the lines of life and death it draws, war expresses what a people will sacrifice for, what they will keep, what is their ultimate self, and what is not. Almost anything at all is possible here, from nationally distributed delusion and the sovereignty of narrow class interests to the common will to make possible a comprehensive development of conscious life. The 'national interest' is not a premiss from which rational policy can be inferred, as is assumed in the literature that passes as analytic in these matters. It is a conclusion of an unexamined metaphysic of social self and other which has been epistemically foreclosed by a reductive military a priori which has become a cultural mindset.

WAR AND CLASS INTERESTS

. . . It is a well-known fact, from the vantage-point of historical hindsight or cultural opposition, that ruling groups use the goal of 'national self-defence' or 'national security' as a recurrent pretext for what is, in fact, the defence and security of their own privileged positions of office or wealth, and the capacity to attack what poses an organized challenge to these. What is represented as the nation's collective salvation from external threat is, we know from afar, a controlling class's quite private advantage—its continuance in authority in the face of domestic unrest redirected towards an external 'enemy', the extravagant profiting of its leading business members from national arms races, or the seizure of foreign lands, markets, resources, strategic sites, or labour-pools to increase its membership's own wealth and power. Though these concealed projects of appropriation are perfectly obvious to us underneath claims of the 'national interest' when pursued by rulers made objective to us by time or geopolitical division, they do not normally appear thus when pursued by the leaderships of what we suppose to be our own countries. . . .

• • •

BENEATH THE MILITARY PARADIGM: WAR AS A HUMANISM

War moves towards its pathological pole the more it destroys or is capable of destroying humans and human capacities or, more broadly, the very life of the earth. The military programme of war is plainly the historical bearer of this pathological extreme. Even those disabling wars which are apparently *non*-military in nature, for example inquisitorial wars against perceived satanic influences by religious authorities, acquire an ever closer family resemblance to the military programme of war the more life-destructive they become. The military programme of rank-ordered command and destruction by maximally efficient scientific means may undergird even industrial devastation itself, whose systematic assaults on natural ecosystems have their historical prototype in the military model of conquest. We have not yet confronted the possibility that the military form of war is a deep-structural derangement of the life of our species which has become increasingly dominant the more its destructive capacities have advanced. We are now at the stage where some decisive recognition of these poles of possibility is needed to comprehend adequately our evolutionary lot. At the present juncture of humanity's self-formation, global life itself lies between the pincers of military technology's expansion in both its anti-human and its anti-nature forms.

TOWARDS THE JUST WAR

Once we cease presupposing the military form of war, we are better able to make a distinction between the enemy we seek to destroy by war and, what ought not to be destroyed, other human lives. Just as with morally unimpeachable wars against organic diseases and other unambiguously destructive patterns, which are best waged with an ever more exact focus against enemies whose elimination entails no loss of higher life-forms, so here. War seeks only to *kill the disabling pattern.* This pattern is judged the enemy (e.g. bubonic plague), not necessarily the being that bears it (e.g. the rodent).

Applying this fundamental but overlooked distinction to national enemies, we can say that such-and-such a *pattern* of behaviour (e.g. Nazism) is an utmost evil, and that it obliges us to go to battle to the death against it. But such a value judgment may not require the death of persons bearing the pattern (e.g. even of Nazism) for it is not *persons* as such which are finally depraved (since they can and may reform), but rather the murderous pattern they choose or are forced to bear. . . .

This fundamental distinction between persons and the patterns they bear is deeper than the well-known distinction between civilians and soldiers advocated by more discriminating analysts of military war such as Elizabeth Anscombe. Under our deeper distinction, that is, it does not suffice for a right to kill T that T is militarily determined to kill you. Rather, one's war is properly to be waged against the military pattern that is imposed from above, and by a command which is normally the very last to be harmed by military attack. Entirely different consequences of rational calculation and action follow. One does not look for ways of blowing up enemy soldiers, but of fighting to the death the economic-military programme by which they are temporarily and usually coercively bound. This fight can proceed by any number of long-term or short-term strategies of non-military war—abolishing established armies themselves (as in distinctively peaceful Costa Rica or post-war Japan), state policies of demilitarization (as in current Czechoslovakia and Hungary), non-violent methods of national defence (as are advocated by a growing movement led by successful civilian uprisings in Iran, the Philippines, Palestine, and Eastern Europe), or national and international activisms of weapon-dismantling, collective boycott, co-ordinated strike, or civilian tax-revolt against military tribute. . . .

The solution to the question of whom one can rightfully kill in war will continue to evade us until we move to this deeper ground of the social structures within which participants in military war are normally constrained to act. The traditional quest to identify 'innocent' or 'guilty' intentions of individuals implementing the military programme misses the underlying structure determining their actions. The full problem will be plumbed only when analysis moves to the institutionalized substructure by which personal moral intentions are essentially *ruled out*. Until we move to this deeper level of analysis, we are without the bearings we require to understand our problem, floundering about in assessments of guilt and innocence of role-players in a prescribed killer game. It is this military game and its leading beneficiaries who preside in safety over its imposition that require moral targeting to advance inquiry beyond mere surface symptoms.

When we do begin to question the institutional a priori with which war's massacres occur, and consider in reflection the more coherent alternatives of which national security and self-defence admit, much emerges to notice. We think across the military-enemy dichotomies which confine reason within automaton presuppositions of mass homicide and destruction, and begin to comprehend a larger scheme of things. The enemy which threatens us most directly, we begin to see, is within our own borders, as it is within theirs, and it is the pathological logic of the military paradigm itself.

WILLIAM JAMES

The Moral Equivalent of War

WILLIAM JAMES (1842–1910) was one of the greatest American philosophers. He graduated from Harvard with a medical degree but decided to teach (at Harvard) rather than practice medicine. A founder of modern pragmatism, he also established himself as one of the fathers of modern psychology with his *Principles of Psychology* (1890).

Reflective apologists for war at the present day all take it religiously. It is a sort of sacrament. Its profits are to the vanquished as well as to the victor; and quite apart from any question of profit, it is an absolute good, we are told, for it is human nature at its highest dynamic. Its "horrors" are a cheap price to pay for rescue from the only alternative supposed, or a world of clerks and teachers, of co-education and zoophily, of "consumer's leagues" and "associated charities," of industrialism unlimited, and feminism unabashed. No scorn, no hardness, no valor any more! Fie upon such a cattleyard of a planet!

So far as the central essence of this feeling goes, no healthy minded person, it seems to me, can help to some degree partaking of it. Militarism is the great preserver of our ideals of hardihood, and human life with no use for hardihood would be contemptible. Without risks or prizes for the darer, history would be insipid indeed; and there is a type of military character which every one feels that the race should never cease to breed, for every one is sensitive to its superiority. The duty is incumbent on mankind, of keeping military characters in stock—of keeping them, if not for use, then as ends in themselves and as pure pieces of perfection—so that Roosevelt's weaklings and mollycoddles may not end by making everything else disappear from the face of nature.

This natural sort of feeling forms, I think, the innermost soul of army-writings. Without any exception known to me, militarist authors take a highly mystical view of their subject, and regard war as a biological or sociological necessity, uncontrolled by ordinary psychological checks and motives. When the time of development is ripe the war must come, reason or no reason, for the justifications pleaded are invariably fictitious. War is, in short, a permanent human *obligation*. . . .

Turn the fear over as I will in my mind, it all seems to lead back to two unwillingnesses of the imagination, one aesthetic, and the other moral: unwillingness, first to envisage a future in which army-life, with its many elements of charm, shall be forever impossible, and in which the destinies of peoples shall nevermore be decided quickly, thrillingly, and tragically, by force, but only gradually and insipidly by "evolution"; and, secondly, unwillingness to see the supreme theatre of human strenuousness closed, and the splendid military aptitudes of men doomed to keep always in a state of latency and never show themselves in action. These insistent unwillingnesses, no less than other esthetic and ethical insistencies have, it seems to me, to be listened to and respected. One cannot meet them effectively by mere counter-insistency on war's expensiveness and horror. The horror makes the thrill; and when the question is of getting the extremest and supremest out of human nature, talk of expense sounds ignominious. The weakness of so much merely negative criticism is evident—pacificism makes no converts from the military party. The military party denies neither the bestiality nor the horror, nor the expense; it only says that these things tell but half the story. It only says that war is *worth* them; that, taking human nature as a whole, its wars are its best protection against its weaker and more cowardly self, and that mankind cannot *afford* to adopt a peace-economy. . . .

Having said thus much in preparation, I will now confess my own utopia. I devoutly believe in the reign of peace and in the gradual advent of some sort of a socialistic equilibrium. The fatalistic view of the war-function is to me nonsense, for I know that war-making is due to definite motives and subject to prudential checks and reasonable criticisms, just like any other form of enterprise. And when whole nations are the armies, and the science of destruction vies in intellectual refinement with the sciences of production, I see that war becomes absurd and impossible from its own monstrosity. Extravagant ambitions will have to be replaced by reasonable claims, and nations must make common cause against them. I see no reason why all this should not apply to yellow as well as to white countries, and I look forward to a future when acts of war shall be formally outlawed as between civilized peoples.

All these beliefs of mine put me squarely into the anti-militarist party. But I do not believe that peace either ought to be or will be permanent on this globe, unless the states pacifically organized preserve some of the old elements of army-discipline. A permanently successful peace-economy cannot be a simple pleasure-economy. In the more or less socialistic future towards which mankind seems drifting we must still subject ourselves collectively to those severities which answer to our real position upon this only partly hospitable globe. We must make new energies and hardihoods continue the manliness to which the military mind so faithfully clings. Martial virtues must be the enduring cement; intrepidity, contempt of softness, surrender of private interest, obedience to command, must still remain the rock upon which states are built—unless, indeed, we wish for dangerous reactions against commonwealths fit only for contempt, and liable to invite attack whenever a centre of crystallization for military-minded enterprise gets formed anywhere in their neighborhood.

The war-party is assuredly right in affirming and reaffirming that the martial virtues, although originally gained by the race through war, are absolute and permanent human goods. Patriotic pride and ambition in their military form are, after all, only specifications of a more general competitive passion. They are its first form, but that is no reason for supposing them to be its last form. Men now are proud of belonging to a conquering nation, and without a murmur they lay down their persons and their wealth, if by so doing they may fend off subjection. But who can be sure that *other aspects of one's country* may not, with time and education and suggestion enough, come to be regarded with similarly effective feelings of pride and shame? Why should men not some day feel that it is worth a blood-tax to belong to a collectivity superior in *any* ideal respect? Why should they not blush with indignant shame if the community that owns them is vile in any way whatsoever? Individuals, daily more numerous, now feel this civic passion. It is only a question of blowing on the spark till the whole population gets incandescent, and on the ruins of the old morals of military honour, a stable system of morals of civic honour builds itself up. What the whole community comes to believe in grasps the individual as in a vise. The war-function has graspt us so far; but constructive interests may some day seem no less imperative, and impose on the individual a hardly lighter burden.

Let me illustrate my idea more concretely. There is nothing to make one indignant in the mere fact that life is hard, that men should toil and suffer pain. The planetary conditions once for all are such, and we can stand it. But that so many men, by mere accidents of birth and opportunity, should have a life of *nothing else* but toil and pain and hardness and inferiority imposed upon them, should have *no* vacation, while others natively no more deserving never get any taste of this campaigning life at all,—*this* is capable of arousing indignation in reflective minds. It may end by seeming shameful to all of us that some of us have nothing but campaigning, and others nothing but unmanly ease. If now—and this is my idea—there were, instead of military conscription a conscription of the whole youthful population to form for a certain number of years a part of the army enlisted against *Nature*, the injustice would tend to be evened out, and numerous other goods to the commonwealth would follow. The military ideals of hardihood and discipline would be wrought into the growing fibre of the people; no one would remain blind as the luxurious classes now are blind, to man's real relations to the globe he lives on, and to the permanently sour and hard foundations of his higher life. To coal and iron mines, to freight trains, to fishing fleets in December, to dish-washing, clothes-washing, and window-washing, to road-building and tunnel-making, to foundries and stokeholes, and to the frames of skyscrapers, would our gilded youths be drafted off, according to their choice, to get the childishness knocked out of them, and to come back into society with healthier sympathies and soberer ideas. They would have paid their blood-tax, done their own part in the immemorial human warfare against nature, they would tread the earth more proudly, the women would value them more highly, they would be better fathers and teachers of the following generation.

Such a conscription, with the state of public opinion that would have required it, and the many moral fruits it would bear, would preserve in the midst of a pacific civilization the manly virtues which the military party is so afraid of seeing disappear in peace. We should get toughness without callousness, authority with as little criminal cruelty as possible, and painful work done cheerily because the duty is temporary, and threatens not, as now, to degrade the whole remainder of one's life. I spoke of the "moral equivalent" of war. So far, war has been the only force that can discipline a whole community, and until an equivalent discipline is organized, I believe that war must have its way. But I have no serious doubt that the ordinary prides and shames of social man, once developed to a certain intensity, are capable of organizing such a moral equivalent as I have sketched, or some other just as effective for preserving manliness of type. It is but a question of time, of skillful propagandism, and of opinion-making men seizing historic opportunities.

The martial type of character can be bred without war. Strenuous honour and disinterestedness abound elsewhere. Priests and medical men are in a fashion educated to it, and we should all feel some degree of it imperative if we were conscious of our work as an obligatory service to the state. We should be *owned*, as soldiers are by the army, and our pride would rise accordingly. We could be poor, then, without humiliation, as army officers now are. The only thing needed henceforward is to inflame the civic temper as past history has inflamed the military temper. H.G. Wells, as usual, sees the centre of the situation. "In many ways," he says, "military organization is the most peaceful of activities. When the contemporary man steps from the street, of clamorous insincere advertisement, push, adulteration, underselling and intermittent employment, into the barrack-yard, he steps on to a higher social plane, into an atmosphere of service and co-operation and of infinitely more honourable emulations. Here at least men are not flung out of employment to degenerate because there is no immediate work for them to do. They are fed and drilled and trained for better services. Here at least a man is supposed to win promotion by self-forgetfulness and not by self-seeking. And beside the feeble and irregular endowment of research by commercialism, its little short-sighted snatches at profit by innovation and scientific economy, see how remarkable is the steady and rapid development of method and appliances in naval and military affairs! Nothing is more striking than to compare the progress of civil conveniences which has been left almost entirely to the trader, to the progress in military apparatus during the last few decades. The house-appliances of to-day for example, are little better than they were fifty years ago. A house of to-day is still almost as ill-ventilated, badly heated by wasteful fires, clumsily arranged and furnished as the house of 1858. Houses a couple of hundred years old are still satisfactory places of residence, so little have our standards risen. But the rifle or battleship of fifty years ago was beyond all comparison inferior to those we possess; in power, in speed, in convenience alike. No one has a use now for such superannuated things."

Wells adds that he thinks that the conceptions of order and discipline, the tradition of service and devotion, of physical fitness, unstinted exertion, and universal responsibility, which universal military duty is now teaching European nations, will remain a permanent acquisition, when the last ammunition has been used in the fireworks that celebrate the final peace. I believe as he does. It would be simply preposterous if the only force that could work ideals of honour and standards of efficiency into English or American natures should be the fear of being killed by the Germans or the Japanese. Great indeed is Fear; but it is not, as our military enthusiasts believe and try to make us believe, the only stimulus known for awakening the higher ranges of men's spiritual energy. The amount of alteration in public opinion which my utopia postulates is vastly less than the difference between the mentality of those black warriors who pursued Stanley's party on the Congo with their cannibal war-cry of "Meat! Meat!" and that of the "general-staff" of any civilized nation. History has seen the latter interval bridged over: the former one can be bridged over much more easily.

LOIS PINEAU

Date Rape
A Feminist Analysis

LOIS PINEAU teaches philosophy at Kansas State University in Manhattan, Kansas. She publishes in the areas of ethics, philosophy of language, and feminism.

Date rape is nonaggravated sexual assault, nonconsensual sex that does not involve physical injury, or the explicit threat of physical injury. But because it does not involve physical injury, and because physical injury is often the only criterion that is accepted as evidence that *actus reas* is nonconsensual, what is really sexual assault is often mistaken for seduction. The replacement of the old rape laws with the new laws on sexual assault have done nothing to resolve this problem.

Rape, defined as nonconsensual sex, usually involving penetration by a man of a woman who is not his wife, has been replaced in some criminal codes with the charge of sexual assault. This has the advantage both of extending the range of possible victims of sexual assault, the manner in which people can be assaulted, and replacing a crime which is exclusive of consent, with one for which consent is a defence. But while the consent of a woman is now consistent with the conviction of her assailant in cases of aggravated assault, nonaggravated sexual assault is still distinguished from normal sex solely by the fact that it is not consented to. Thus the question of whether someone has consented to a sexual encounter is still important, and the criteria for consent continues to be the central concern of discourse on sexual assault.

However, if a man is to be convicted, it does not suffice to establish that the *actus reas* was nonconsensual. In order to be guilty of sexual assault a man must have the requisite *mens rea*, i.e., he must either have believed that his victim did not consent or that she was probably not consenting. In many common law jurisdictions a man who sincerely believes that a woman consented to a sexual encounter is deemed to lack the required *mens rea*, even though the woman did not consent, and even though his belief is not reasonable. Recently, strong dissenting voices have been raised against the sincerity condition, and the argument made that *mens rea* be defeated only if the defendant has a reasonable belief that the plaintiff consented. The introduction of legislation which excludes 'honest belief' (unreasonable sincere belief) as a defence, will certainly help to provide women with greater protection against violence. But while this will be an important step forward, the question of what constitutes a reasonable belief, the problem of evidence when rapists lie, and the problem of the entrenched attitudes of the predominantly male police, judges, lawyers, and jurists who handle sexual assault cases, remains.

The criteria for *mens rea*, for the reasonableness of belief, and for consent are closely related. For although a man's sincere belief in the consent of his victim may be sufficient to defeat *mens rea*, the court is less likely to believe his belief is sincere if his belief is unreasonable. If his belief is reasonable, they are more likely to believe in the sincerity of his belief. But evidence of the reasonableness of his belief is also evidence that consent really did take place. For the very things that make it reasonable for *him* to believe that the defendant consented are often the very things that incline the court to believe that she consented. What is often missing is the voice of the woman herself, an account of what it would be reasonable for *her* to agree to, that is to say, an account of what is reasonable from *her* standpoint.

Thus, what is presented as reasonable has repercussions for four separate but related concerns: (1) the question of whether a man's belief in a woman's consent was reasonable; (2) the problem of whether it is reasonable to attribute *mens rea* to him; (3) the question of what could count as reasonable from the woman's point of view; (4) the question of what is reasonable from the court's point of view. These repercussions are of the utmost practical concern. In a culture which contains an incidence of sexual assault verging on epidemic, a criterion of reasonableness which regards mere submission as consent fails to offer persons vulnerable to those assaults adequate protection.

The following statements by self-confessed date rapists reveal how our lack of a solution for dealing with date rape protects rapists by failing to provide their victims with legal recourse:

> All of my rapes have been involved in a dating situation where I've been out with a woman I know. . . . I wouldn't take no for an answer. I think it had something to do with my acceptance of rejection. I had low self-esteem and not much self-confidence and when I was rejected for something which I considered to be rightly mine, I became angry and I went ahead anyway. And this was the same in any situation, whether it was rape or it was something else.

• • •

> When I did date, when I was younger, I would pick up a girl and if she didn't come across I would threaten her or slap her face then tell her she was going to fuck—that was it. But that's because I didn't want to waste time with any come-ons. It took too much time. I wasn't interested because I didn't like them as people anyway, and I just went with them just to get laid. Just to say that I laid them.

There is, at this time, nothing to protect women from this kind of unscrupulous victimization. A woman on a casual date with a virtual stranger has almost no chance of bringing a complaint of sexual assault before the courts. One reason for this is the prevailing criterion for consent. According to this criterion, consent is implied unless some emphatic episodic sign of resistance occurred, and its occurrence can be established. But if no episodic act occurred, or if it did occur, and the defendant claims that it didn't, or if the defendant threatened the plaintiff but won't admit it in court, it is almost impossible to find any evidence that would support the plaintiff's word against the defendant. This difficulty is exacerbated by suspicion on the part of the courts, police, and legal educators that even where an act of resistance occurs, this act should not be interpreted as a withholding of consent, and this suspicion is especially upheld where the accused is a man who is known to the female plaintiff.

In Glanville William's classic textbook on criminal law we are warned that where a man is unknown to a woman, she does not consent if she expresses her rejection in the form of an episodic and vigorous act at the 'vital moment'. But if the man is known to the woman she must, according to Williams, make use of "all means available to her to repel the man". Williams warns that women often welcome a 'mastery advance' and present a token resistance. He quotes Byron's couplet,

> A little still she strove, and much repented
> And whispering 'I will ne'er consent'—consented

by way of alerting law students to the difficulty of distinguishing real protest from pretence. Thus, while in principle, a firm unambiguous stand, or a healthy show of temper ought to be sufficient, if established, to show nonconsent, in practice the forceful overriding of such a stance is apt to be taken as an indication that the resistance was not seriously intended, and that the seduction had succeeded. The consequence of this is that it is almost impossible to establish the defendant's guilt beyond a reasonable doubt.

Thus, on the one hand, we have a situation in which women are vulnerable to the most exploitive tactics at the hands of men who are known to them. On the other hand, almost nothing will count as evidence of their being assaulted, including their having taken an emphatic stance in withholding their consent. The new laws have done almost nothing to change this situation. Yet clearly, some solution must be sought. Moreover, the road to that solution presents itself clearly enough as a need for a reformulation of the criterion of consent. It is patent that a criterion that collapses whenever the crime itself succeeds will not suffice. . . .

The reasoning that underlies the present criterion of consent is entangled in a number of mutually supportive mythologies which see sexual assault as masterful seduction, and silent submission as sexual enjoyment. Because the prevailing ideology has so much informed our conceptualization of sexual interaction, it is extraordinarily difficult for us to distinguish between assault and seduction, submission and enjoyment, or so we imagine. At the same time, this failure to distinguish has given rise to a network of rationalizations that support the conflation of assault which seduction, submission and enjoyment. . . .

RAPE MYTHS

The belief that the natural aggression of men and the natural reluctance of women somehow makes date rape understandable underlies a number of prevalent myths about rape and human sexuality. These beliefs maintain their force partly on account of a logical compulsion exercised by them at an unconscious level. The only way of refuting them effectively, is to excavate the logical propositions involved, and to expose their misapplication to the situations to which they have been applied. In what follows, I propose to excavate the logical support for popular attitudes that are tolerant of date rape. These myths are not just popular, however, but often emerge in the arguments of judges who acquit date rapists, and policemen who refuse to lay charges.

The claim that the victim provoked a sexual incident, that 'she asked for it,' is by far the most common defence given by men who are accused of sexual assault. Feminists, rightly incensed by this response, often treat it as beneath contempt, singling out the defence as an argument against it. On other fronts, sociologists have identified the response as part of an overall tendency of people to see the world as just, a tendency which disposes them to conclude that people for the most part deserve what they get. However, an inclination to see the world as just requires us to construct an account which yields this outcome, and it is just such an account that I wish to examine with regard to date rape.

The least sophisticated of the 'she asked for it' rationales, and in a sense, the easiest to deal with, appeals to an injunction against sexually provocative behaviour on the part of women. If women should not be sexually provocative, then, from this standpoint, a woman who is sexually provocative deserves to suffer the consequences. Now it will not do to respond that women get raped even when they are not sexually provocative, or that it is men who get to interpret (unfairly) what counts as sexually provocative. The question should be: Why shouldn't a woman be sexually provocative? Why should this behaviour warrant any kind of aggressive response whatsoever?

Attempts to explain that women have a right to behave in sexually provocative ways without suffering dire consequences still meet with surprisingly tough resistance. Even people who find nothing wrong or sinful with sex itself, in any of its forms, tend to suppose that women must not behave sexually unless they are prepared to carry through on some fuller course of sexual interaction. The logic of this response seems to be that at some point a woman's behaviour commits her to following through on the full course of a sexual encounter as it is defined by her assailant. At some point she has made an agreement, or formed a contract, and once that is done, her contractor is entitled to demand that she satisfy the terms of that contract. Thus, this view about sexual responsibility and desert is supported by other assumptions about contracts and agreement. But we do not normally suppose that casual nonverbal behaviour generates agreements. Nor do we normally grant private persons the right to enforce contracts. What rationale would support our conclusion in this case?

The rationale, I believe, comes in the form of a belief in the especially insistent nature of male sexuality, an insistence which lies at the foot of natural male aggression, and which is extremely difficult, perhaps impossible to contain. At a certain point in the arousal process, it is thought, a man's rational will gives way to the prerogatives of nature. His sexual need can and does reach a point where it is uncontrollable, and his natural masculine aggression kicks in to assure that this need is met. Women, however, are naturally more contained, and so it is their responsibility not to provoke the irrational in the male. If they do go so far as that, they have both failed in their responsibilities, and subjected themselves to the inevitable. One does not go into the lion's cage and expect not to be eaten. Natural feminine reluctance, it is thought, is no protection against a sexually aroused male.

This belief about the normal aggressiveness of male sexuality is complemented by common knowledge about female gender development. Once, women were taught to deny their sexuality and to aspire to ideals of chastity. Things have not changed so much. Women still tend to eschew conquest mentalities in favour of a combination of sex and affection. Insofar as this is thought to be merely a cultural requirement, however, there is an expectation that women will be coy about their sexual desire. The assumption that women both want to indulge sexually, and are inclined to sacrifice this desire for higher ends, gives rise to the myth that they want to be raped. After all, doesn't rape give them the sexual enjoyment they *really* want, at the same time that it relieves them of the responsibility for admitting to and acting upon what they want? And how then can we blame men, who have been socialized to be aggressively seductive precisely for the purpose of overriding female reserve? If we find fault at all, we are inclined to cast our suspicions on the motives of the woman. For it is on her that the contradictory roles of sexual desirer and sexual denier has been placed. Our awareness of the contradiction expected of her makes us suspect her honesty. In the past, she was expected to deny her complicity because of the shame and guilt she felt at having submitted. This expectation persists in many quarters today, and is carried over into a general suspicion about her character, and the fear that she might make a false accusation out of revenge, or some other low motive.

But if women really want sexual pleasure, what inclines us to think that they will get it through rape? This conclusion logically requires a theory about the dynamics of sexual pleasure that sees that pleasure as an emergent property of overwhelming male insistence. For the assumption that a raped female experiences sexual pleasure implies that the person who rapes her knows how to cause that pleasure independently of any information she might convey on that point. Since her ongoing protest is inconsistent with requests to be touched in particular ways in particular places, to have more of this and less of that, then we must believe that the person who touches her knows these particular ways and places instinctively, without any directives from her.

Thus, we find, underlying and reinforcing this belief in incommunicative male prowess, a conception of sexual pleasure that springs from wordless interchanges, and of sexual success that occurs in a place of meaningful silence. The language of seduction is accepted as a tacit language: eye contact, smiles, blushes, and faintly discernible gestures. It is, accordingly, imprecise and ambiguous. It would be easy for a man to make mistakes about the message conveyed, understandable that he should mistakenly think that a sexual invitation has been made, and a bargain struck. But honest mistakes, we think, must be excused.

In sum, the belief that women should not be sexually provocative is logically linked to several other beliefs, some normative, some empirical. The normative beliefs are that (1) people should keep the agreements they make (2) that sexually provocative behaviour, taken beyond a certain point, generates agreements (3) that the peculiar nature of male and female sexuality places such agreements in a special category, one in which the possibility of retracting an agreement is ruled out, or at least made highly unlikely, (4) that women are not to be trusted, in sexual matters at least. The empirical belief, which turns out to be false, is that male sexuality is not subject to rational and moral control.

DISPELLING THE MYTHS

The 'she asked for' justification of sexual assault incorporates a conception of a contract that would be difficult to defend in any other context and the presumptions about human sexuality which function to reinforce sympathies rooted in the contractual notion of just deserts are not supported by empirical research.

The belief that a woman generates some sort of contractual obligation whenever her behaviour is interpreted as seductive is the most indefensible part of the mythology of rape. In law, contracts are not legitimate just because a promise has been made. In particular, the use of pressure tactics to extract agreement is frowned upon. Normally, an agreement is upheld only if the contractors were clear on what they were getting into, and had sufficient time to reflect on the wisdom of their doing so. Either there must be a clear tradition in which the expectations involved in the contract are fairly well known (marriage), or there must be an explicit written agreement concerning the exact terms of the contract and the expectations of the persons involved. But whatever the terms of a contract, there is no private right to enforce it. So that if I make a contract with you on which I renege, the only permissible recourse for you is through the legal process.

Now it is not clear whether sexual contracts can be made to begin with, or if so, what sort of sexual contracts would be legitimate. But assuming that they could be made, the terms of those contracts would not be enforceable. To allow public enforcement would be to grant the State the overt right to force people to have sex, and this would clearly be unacceptable. Granting that sexual contracts are legitimate, state enforcement of such contracts would have to be limited to ordering nonsexual compensation for breaches of contract. So it makes no difference whether a sexual contract is tacit or explicit. There are no grounds whatsoever that would justify enforcement of its terms.

Thus, even if we assume that a woman has initially agreed to an encounter, her agreement does not automatically make all subsequent sexual activity to which she submits legitimate. If during coitus a woman should experience pain, be suddenly overcome with guilt or fear of pregnancy, or simply lose her initial desire, those are good reasons for her to change her mind. Having changed her mind, neither her partner nor the state has any right to force her to continue. But then if she is forced to continue she is assaulted. Thus, establishing that consent occurred at a particular point during a sexual encounter should not conclusively establish the legitimacy of the encounter. What is needed is a reading of whether she agreed throughout the encounter.

If the 'she asked for it' contractual view of sexual interchange has any validity, it is because there is a point at which there is no stopping a sexual encounter, a point at which that encounter becomes the inexorable outcome of the unfolding of natural events. If a sexual encounter is like a slide on which I cannot stop halfway down, it will be relevant whether I enter the slide of my own free will, or am pushed.

But there is no evidence that the entire sexual act is like a slide. While there may be a few seconds in the 'plateau' period just prior to orgasm in which people are 'swept' away by sexual feelings to the point where we could justifiably understand their lack of heed for the comfort of their partner, the greater part of a sexual encounter comes well within the bounds of morally responsible control of our own actions. Indeed, the available evidence shows that most of the activity involved in sex has to do with building the requisite level of desire, a task that involves the proper use of foreplay, the possibility of which implies control over the form that foreplay will take. Modern sexual therapy assumes that such control is universally accessible, and so far there has been no reason to question that assumption. Sexologists are unanimous, moreover, in holding that mutual sexual enjoyment requires an atmosphere of comfort and communication, a minimum of pressure, and an ongoing check-up on one's partner's state. They maintain that different people have different predilections, and that what is pleasurable for one person is very often anathema to another. These findings show that the way to achieve sexual pleasure, at any time at all, let alone with a casual acquaintance, decidedly does not involve overriding the other person's express reservations and providing them with just any kind of sexual stimulus. And while we do not want to allow science and technology a voice in which the voices of particular women are drowned, in this case science seems to concur with women's perception that aggressive incom-municative sex is not what they want. But if science and the voice of women concur, if aggressive seduction does not lead to good sex, if women do not like it, or want it, then it is not rational to think that they would agree to it. Where such sex takes place, it is therefore rational to presume that the sex was not consensual.

The myth that women like to be raped, is closely connected, as we have seen, to doubt about their honesty in sexual matters, and this suspicion is exploited by defence lawyers when sexual assault cases make it to the courtroom. It is an unfortunate con-sequence of the presumption of innocence that rape victims who end up in court fre-quently find that it is they who are on trial. For if the defendant is innocent, then either he did not intend to do what he was accused of, or the plaintiff is mistaken about his identity, or she is lying. Often the last alternative is the only plausible defence, and as a result, the plaintiff's word seldom goes unquestioned. Women are frequently ac-cused of having made a false accusation, either as a defensive mechanism for dealing with guilt and shame, or out of a desire for revenge.

Now there is no point in denying the possibility of false accusation, though there are probably better ways of seeking revenge on a man than accusing him of rape. However, we can now establish a logical connection between the evidence that a woman was subjected to high-pressure aggressive 'seduction' tactics, and her claim that she did not consent to that encounter. Where the kind of encounter is not the sort to which it would be reasonable to consent, there is a logical presumption that a woman who claims that she did not consent is telling the truth. Where the kind of sex involved is not the sort of sex we would expect a woman to like, the burden of proof should not be on the woman to show that she did not consent, but on the defendant to show that contrary to every reasonable expectation she did consent. The defendant should be required to convince the court that the plaintiff persuaded him to have sex with her even though there are no visible reasons why she should.

In conclusion, there are no grounds for the 'she asked for it' defence. Sexually pro-vocative behaviour does not generate sexual contracts. Even where there are sexual agreements, they cannot be legitimately enforced either by the State, or by private right, or by natural prerogative. Secondly, all the evidence suggests that neither women nor men find sexual enjoyment in rape or in any form of noncommunicative sexuality. Thirdly, male sexual desire is containable, and can be subjected to moral and rational control. Fourthly, since there is no reason why women should not be sexually provoca-tive, they do not 'deserve' any sex they do not want. This last is a welcome discovery. The taboo on sexual provocativeness in women is a taboo both on sensuality and on teasing. But sensuality is a source of delight, and teasing is playful and inspires wit. What a relief to learn that it is not sexual provocativeness, but its enemies, that consti-tutes a danger to the world. . . .

In thinking about sex we must keep in mind its sensual ends, and the facts show that aggressive high-pressure sex contradicts those ends. Consensual sex in dating sit-uations is presumed to aim at mutual enjoyment. It may not always do this, and when it does, it might not always succeed. There is no logical incompatibility between want-ing to continue a sexual encounter, and failing to derive sexual pleasure from it.

But it seems to me that there is a presumption in favour of the connection between sex and sexual enjoyment, and that if a man wants to be sure that he is not forcing himself on a woman, he has an obligation either to ensure that the encounter really is mutually enjoyable, or to know the reasons why she would want to continue the encounter in spite of her lack of enjoyment. A closer investigation of the nature of this obligation will enable us to construct a more rational and more plausible norm of sexual conduct.

Onora O'Neill has argued that in intimate situations we have an obligation to take the ends of others as our own, and to promote those ends in a non-manipulative and non-paternalistic manner. Now it seems that in honest sexual encounters just this is required. Assuming that each person enters the encounter in order to seek sexual satisfaction, each person engaging in the encounter has an obligation to help the other seek his or her ends. To do otherwise is to risk acting in opposition to what the other desires, and hence to risk acting without the other's consent.

But the obligation to promote the sexual ends of one's partner implies that obligation to know what those ends are, and also the obligation to know how those ends are attained. Thus, the problem comes down to a problem of epistemic responsibility, the responsibility to know. The solution, in my view, lies in the practice of a communicative sexuality, one which combines the appropriate knowledge of the other with respect for the dialectics of desire. . . .

CULTURAL PRESUMPTIONS

Now it may well be that we have no obligation to care for strangers, and I do not wish to claim that we do. Nonetheless, it seems that O'Neill's point about the special moral duties we have in certain intimate situations is supported by a conceptual relation between certain kinds of personal relationships and the expectation that it should be a communicative relation. Friendship is a case in point. It is a relation that is greatly underdetermined by what we usually include in our sets of rights and obligations. For the most part, rights and obligations disappear as terms by which friendship is guided. They are still there, to be called upon, in case the relationship breaks down, but insofar as the friendship is a friendship, it is concerned with fostering the quality of the interaction and not with standing on rights. Thus, because we are friends, we share our property, and property rights between us are not invoked. Because we are friends, privacy is not an issue. Because we are friends we may see to each other's needs as often as we see to our own. The same can be said for relations between lovers, parents and dependent children, and even between spouses, at least when interaction is functioning at an optimal level. When such relations break down to the point that people must stand on their rights, we can often say that the actors ought to make more of an effort, and in many instances fault them for their lack of charity, tolerance, or benevolence. Thus, although we have a right to end friendships, it may be a reflection on our lack of virtue that we do so, and while we cannot be criticized for violating other people's rights, we can be rightfully deprecated for lacking the virtue to sustain a friendship.

But is there a similar conceptual relation between the kind of activity that a date is, and the sort of moral practice that it requires? My claim is that there is, and that this connection is easily established once we recognize the cultural presumption that dating is a gesture of friendship and regard. Traditionally, the decision to date indicates that two people have an initial attraction to each other, that they are disposed to like each other, and look forward to enjoying each other's company. Dating derives its implicit meaning from this tradition. It retains this meaning unless other aims are explicitly stated, and even then it may not be possible to alienate this meaning. It is a rare woman who will not spurn a man who states explicitly, right at the onset, that he wants to go out with her solely on the condition that he have sexual intercourse with her at the end of the evening, and that he has no interest in her company apart from gaining that end, and no concern for mutual satisfaction.

Explicit protest to the contrary aside, the conventions of dating confer on it its social meaning, and this social meaning implies a relationship which is more like friendship than the cutthroat competition of opposing teams. As such, it requires that we do more than stand on our rights with regard to each other. As long as we are operating under the auspices of a dating relationship, it requires that we behave in the mode of friendship and trust. But if a date is more like a friendship than a business contract, then clearly respect for the dialectics of desire is incompatible with the sort of sexual pressure that is inclined to end in date rape. And clearly, also, a conquest mentality which exploits a situation of trust and respect for purely selfish ends is morally pernicious. Failure to respect the dialectics of desire when operating under the auspices of friendship and trust is to act in flagrant disregard of the moral requirement to avoid manipulative, coercive, and exploitive behaviour. Respect for the dialectics of desire is *prima facie* inconsistent with the satisfaction of one person at the expense of the other. The proper end of friendship relations is mutual satisfaction. But the requirement of mutuality means that we must take a communicative approach to discovering the ends of the other, and this entails that we respect the dialectics of desire.

But now that we know what communicative sexuality is, and that it is morally required, and that it is the only feasible means to mutual sexual enjoyment, why not take this model as the norm of what is reasonable in sexual interaction. The evidence of sexologists strongly indicates that women whose partners are aggressively uncommunicative have little chance of experiencing sexual pleasure. But it is not reasonable for women to consent to what they have little chance of enjoying. Hence it is not reasonable for women to consent to aggressive noncommunicative sex. Nor can we reasonably suppose that women have consented to sexual encounters which we know and they know they do not find enjoyable. With the communicative model as the norm, the aggressive contractual model should strike us as a model of deviant sexuality, and sexual encounters patterned on that model should strike us as encounters to which *prima facie* no one would reasonably agree. But if acquiescence to an encounter counts as consent only if the acquiescence is reasonable, something to which a reasonable person, in full possession of knowledge relevant to the encounter, would agree, then acquiescence to aggressive noncommunicative sex is not reasonable. Hence, acquiescence under such conditions should not count as consent.

Thus, where communicative sexuality does not occur, we lack the main ground for believing that the sex involved was consensual. Moreover, where a man does not engage in communicative sexuality, he acts either out of reckless disregard, or out of willful ignorance. For he cannot know, except through the practice of communicative sexuality, whether his partner has any sexual reason for continuing the encounter. And where she does not, he runs the risk of imposing on her what she is not willing to have. All that is needed then, in order to provide women with legal protection from 'date rape' is to make both reckless indifference and willful ignorance a sufficient condition of *mens rea* and to make communicative sexuality the accepted norm of sex to which a reasonable woman would agree. Thus, the appeal to communicative sexuality as a norm for sexual encounters accomplishes two things. It brings the aggressive sex involved in 'date rape' well within the realm of sexual assault, and it locates the guilt of date rapists in the failure to approach sexual relations on a communicative basis.

Gregg v. Georgia (1976)

Gregg v. Georgia was the 1976 decision in which the U.S. Supreme Court decided that the death penalty did not, in itself, constitute "cruel and unusual punishment," and therefore did not conflict with the Eighth Amendment. The majority opinion in this 7–2 decision contends that the death penalty satisfies the human desire for retribution and deters future crime.

MAJORITY OPINION

The issue in this case is whether the imposition of the sentence of death for the crime of murder under the law of Georgia violates the Eighth and Fourteenth Amendments.

I

The petitioner, Troy Gregg, was charged with committing armed robbery and murder. In accordance with Georgia procedure in capital cases, the trial was in two stages, a guilt stage and a sentencing stage. . . .
. . . The jury found the petitioner guilty of two counts of armed robbery and two counts of murder.
At the penalty stage, which took place before the same jury, . . . the trial judge instructed the jury that it could recommend either a death sentence or a life prison sentence on each count. . . . The jury returned verdicts of death on each count.

II

. . . The Georgia statute, as amended after our decision in *Furman v. Georgia* (1972), retains the death penalty for six categories of crime: murder, kidnaping for ransom or where the victim is harmed, armed robbery, rape, treason, and aircraft hijacking. . . .

III

We address initially the basic contention that the punishment of death for the crime of murder is, under all circumstances, "cruel and unusual" in violation of the Eighth and Fourteenth Amendments of the Constitution.
The Court on a number of occasions has both assumed and asserted the constitutionality of capital punishment. In several cases that assumption provided a necessary foundation for the decision, as the Court was asked to decide whether a particular

method of carrying out a capital sentence would be allowed to stand under the Eighth Amendment. But until *Furman v. Georgia* (1972), the Court never confronted squarely the fundamental claim that the punishment of death always, regardless of the enormity of the offense or the procedure followed in imposing the sentence, is cruel and unusual punishment in violation of the Constitution. Although this issue was presented and addressed in *Furman*, it was not resolved by the Court. Four Justices would have held that capital punishment is not unconstitutional *per se*; two Justices would have reached the opposite conclusion; and three Justices, while agreeing that the statutes then before the Court were invalid as applied, left open the question whether such punishment may ever be imposed. We now hold that the punishment of death does not invariably violate the Constitution.

A

The history of the prohibition of "cruel and unusual" punishment already has been reviewed at length. The phrase first appeared in the English Bill of Rights of 1689, which was drafted by Parliament at the accession of William and Mary. The English version appears to have been directed against punishments unauthorized by statute and beyond the jurisdiction of the sentencing court, as well as those disproportionate to the offense involved. The American draftsmen, who adopted the English phrasing in drafting the Eighth Amendment, were primarily concerned, however, with proscribing "tortures" and other "barbarous" methods of punishment.

In the earliest cases raising Eighth Amendment claims, the Court focused on particular methods of execution to determine whether they were too cruel to pass constitutional muster. The constitutionality of the sentence of death itself was not at issue, and the criterion used to evaluate the mode of execution was its similarity to "torture" and other "barbarous" methods. . . .

But the Court has not confined the prohibition embodied in the Eighth Amendment to "barbarous" methods that were generally outlawed in the 18th century. Instead, the Amendment has been interpreted in a flexible and dynamic manner. The Court early recognized that "a principle to be vital must be capable of wider application than the mischief which gave it birth." Thus the Clause forbidding "cruel and unusual" punishments "is not fastened to the obsolete but may acquire meaning as public opinion becomes enlightened by a humane justice."

But our cases also make clear that public perceptions of standards of decency with respect to criminal sanctions are not conclusive. A penalty also must accord with "the dignity of man," which is the "basic concept underlying the Eighth Amendment." This means, at least, that the punishment not be "excessive." When a form of punishment in the abstract (in this case, whether capital punishment may ever be imposed as a sanction for murder) rather than in the particular (the propriety of death as a penalty to be applied to a specific defendant for a specific crime) is under consideration, the inquiry into "excessiveness" has two aspects. First, the punishment must not involve the unnesessary and wanton infliction of pain. Second, the punishment must not be grossly out of proportion to the severity of the crime.

• • •

The imposition of the death penalty for the crime of murder has a long history of acceptance both in the United States and in England. . . .

It is apparent from the text of the Constitution itself that the existence of capital punishment was accepted by the Framers. At the time the Eighth Amendment was ratified, capital punishment was a common sanction in every State. Indeed, the First Congress of the United States enacted legislation providing death as the penalty for specified crimes. . . .

For nearly two centuries, this Court, repeatedly and often expressly, has recognized that capital punishment is not invalid *per se*. . . .

Four years ago, the petitioners in *Furman* and its companion cases predicated their argument primarily upon the asserted proposition that standards of decency had evolved to the point where capital punishment no longer could be tolerated. The petitioners in those cases said, in effect, that the evolutionary process had come to an end, and that standards of decency required that the Eighth Amendment be construed finally as prohibiting capital punishment for any crime regardless of its depravity and impact on society. This view was accepted by two Justices. Three other Justices were unwilling to go so far; focusing on the procedures by which convicted defendants were selected for the death penalty rather than on the actual punishment inflicted, they joined in the conclusion that the statutes before the Court were constitutionally invalid.

The petitioners in the capital cases before the Court today renew the "standards of decency" argument, but developments during the four years since *Furman* have undercut substantially the assumptions upon which their argument rested. Despite the continuing debate, dating back to the nineteenth century, over the morality and utility of capital punishment, it is now evident that a large proportion of American society continues to regard it as an appropriate and necessary criminal sanction.

The most marked indication of society's endorsement of the death penalty for murder is the legislative response to *Furman*. The legislatures of at least thirty-five States have enacted new statutes that provide for the death penalty for at least some crimes that result in the death of another person. And the Congress of the United States, in 1974, enacted a statute providing the death penalty for aircraft piracy that results in death. These recently adopted statutes have attempted to address the concerns expressed by the Court in *Furman* primarily (i) by specifying the factors to be weighed and the procedures to be followed in deciding when to impose a capital sentence, or (ii) by making the death penalty mandatory for specified crimes. But all of the post-*Furman* statutes make clear that capital punishment itself has not been rejected by the elected representatives of the people. . . .

The jury also is a significant and reliable objective index of contemporary values because it is so directly involved. The Court has said that "one of the most important functions any jury can perform in making . . . a selection [between life imprisonment and death for a defendant convicted in a capital case] is to maintain a link between contemporary community values and the penal system." It may be true that evolving standards have influenced juries in recent decades to be more discriminating in imposing the sentence of death. But the relative infrequency of jury verdicts imposing the death sentence does not indicate rejection of capital punishment *per se*. Rather, the reluctance of juries in many cases to impose the sentence may well reflect the humane feeling that this most irrevocable of sanctions should be reserved for a small number of extreme cases. Indeed, the actions of juries in many States since *Furman* are fully compatible with the legislative judgments, reflected in the new statutes, as to the continued utility and necessity of capital punishment in appropriate cases. At the close of

1974 at least 254 persons had been sentenced to death since *Furman,* and by the end of March 1976, more than 460 persons were subject to death sentences.

As we have seen, however, the Eighth Amendment demands more than that a challenged punishment be acceptable to contemporary society. The Court also must ask whether it comports with the basic concept of human dignity at the core of the Amendment. Although we cannot "invalidate a category of penalties because we deem less severe penalties, adequate to serve the ends of penology," the sanction imposed cannot be so totally without penological justification that it results in the gratuitous infliction of suffering.

The death penalty is said to serve two principal social purposes: retribution and deterrence of capital crimes by prospective offenders.

In part, capital punishment is an expression of society's moral outrage at particularly offensive conduct. This function may be unappealing to many, but it is essential in an ordered society that asks its citizens to rely on legal processes rather than self-help to vindicate their wrongs.

> The instinct for retribution is part of the nature of man, and channeling that instinct in the administration of criminal justice serves an important purpose in promoting the stability of a society governed by law. When people begin to believe that organized society is unwilling or unable to impose upon criminal offenders the punishment they "deserve," then there are sown the seeds of anarchy—of self-help, vigilante justice, and lynch law. *Furman v. Georgia* (Stewart, J., concurring).

"Retribution is no longer the dominant objective of the criminal law," but neither is it a forbidden objective nor one inconsistent with our respect for the dignity of men. Indeed, the decision that capital punishment may be the appropriate sanction in extreme cases is an expression of the community's belief that certain crimes are themselves so grievous an affront to humanity that the only adequate response may be the penalty of death.

Statistical attempts to evaluate the worth of the death penalty as a deterrent to crimes by potential offenders have occasioned a great deal of debate. The results simply have been inconclusive. . . .

Although some of the studies suggest that the death penalty may not function as a significantly greater deterrent than lesser penalties, there is no convincing empirical evidence either supporting or refuting this view. We may nevertheless assume safely that there are murderers, such as those who act in passion, for whom the threat of death has little or no deterrent effect. But for many others, the death penalty undoubtedly is a significant deterrent. There are carefully contemplated murders, such as murder for hire, where the possible penalty of death may well enter into the cold calculus that precedes the decision to act. And there are some categories of murder, such as murder by a life prisoner, where other sanctions may not be adequate.

The value of capital punishment as a deterrent of crime is a complex factual issue the resolution of which properly rests with the legislatures, which can evaluate the results of statistical studies in terms of their own local conditions and with a flexibility of approach that is not available to the courts. Indeed, many of the post-*Furman* statutes reflect just such a responsible effort to define those crimes and those criminals for which capital punishment is most probably an effective deterrent.

In sum, we cannot say that the judgment of the Georgia Legislature that capital punishment may be necessary in some cases is clearly wrong. Considerations of federalism, as well as respect for the ability of a legislature to evaluate, in terms of its particular State, the moral consensus concerning the death penalty and its social utility as a sanction, require us to conclude, in the absence of more convincing evidence, that the infliction of death as a punishment for murder is not without justification and thus is not unconstitutionally severe.

Finally, we must consider whether the punishment of death is disproportionate in relation to the crime for which it is imposed. There is no question that death as a punishment is unique in its severity and irrevocability. When a defendant's life is at stake, the Court has been particularly sensitive to insure that every safeguard is observed. But we are concerned here only with the imposition of capital punishment for the crime of murder, and when a life has been taken deliberately by the offender, we canot say that the punishment is invariably disproportionate to the crime. It is an extreme sanction, suitable to the most extreme of crimes.

We hold that the death penalty is not a form of punishment that may never be imposed, regardless of the circumstances of the offense, regardless of the character of the offender, and regardless of the procedure followed in reaching the decision to impose it.

ALBERT CAMUS

Reflections on the Guillotine

ALBERT CAMUS (1913–1960), a leading French intellectual, was a political activist and an associate of Jean-Paul Sartre. Awarded the Nobel Prize for Literature in 1957, Camus' philosophical concerns were often expressed in fiction.

We all know that the great argument of those who defend capital punishment is the exemplary value of the punishment. Heads are cut off not only to punish but to intimidate, by a frightening example, any who might be tempted to imitate the guilty. Society is not taking revenge; it merely wants to forestall. It waves the head in the air so that potential murderers will see their fate and recoil from it.

This argument would be impressive if we were not obliged to note:

1) that society itself does not believe in the exemplary value it talks about;
2) that there is no proof that the death penalty ever made a single murderer recoil when he had made up his mind, whereas clearly it had no effect but one of fascination on thousands of criminals;
3) that in other regards, it constitutes a repulsive example, the consequences of which cannot be foreseen.

To begin with, society does not believe in what it says. If it really believed what it says, it would exhibit the heads. Society would give executions the benefit of the publicity it generally uses for national bond issues or new brands of drinks. But we know that executions in our country, instead of taking place publicly, are now perpetrated in prison courtyards before a limited number of specialists. . . .

How can a furtive assassination committed at night in a prison courtyard be exemplary? At most, it serves the purpose of periodically informing the citizens that they will die if they happen to kill—a future that can be promised even to those who do not kill. For the penalty to be truly exemplary it must be frightening. . . .

But, after all, why should society believe in that example when it does not stop crime, when its effects, if they exist, are invisible? To begin with, capital punishment could not intimidate the man who doesn't know that he is going to kill, who makes up his mind to it in a flash and commits his crime in a state of frenzy or obsession, nor the man who, going to an appointment to have it out with someone, takes along a weapon to frighten the faithless one or the opponent and uses it although he didn't want to or didn't think he wanted to. In other words, it could not intimidate the man who is hurled into crime as if into a calamity. This is tantamount to saying that it is powerless in the majority of cases. It is only fair to point out that in our country capital punishment is rarely applied in such cases. But the word "rarely" itself makes one shudder.

Does it frighten at least that race of criminals on whom it claims to operate and who live off crime? Nothing is less certain. We can read in Koestler that at a time when pickpockets were executed in England, other pickpockets exercised their talents in the

479

crowd surrounding the scaffold where their colleague was being hanged. Statistics drawn up at the beginning of the century in England show that out of 250 who were hanged, 170 had previously attended one or more executions. And in 1886, out of 167 condemned men who had gone through the Bristol prison, 164 had witnessed at least one execution. . . .

If fear of death is, indeed, a fact, another fact is that such fear, however great it may be, has never sufficed to quell human passions. Bacon is right in saying that there is no passion so weak that it cannot confront and overpower fear of death. Revenge, love, honor, pain, another fear manage to overcome it. How could cupidity, hatred, jealousy fail to do what love of a person or a country, what a passion for freedom manage to do? For centuries the death penalty, often accompanied by barbarous refinements, has been trying to hold crime in check; yet crime persists. Why? Because the instincts that are warring in man are not, as the law claims, constant forces in a state of equilibrium. They are variable forces constantly waxing and waning, and their repeated lapses from equilibrium nourish the life of the mind as electrical oscillations, when close enough, set up a current. . . . But it may happen that one of the soul's forces breaks loose until it fills the whole field of consciousness; at such a moment no instinct, not even that of life, can oppose the tyranny of that irresistible force. For capital punishment to be really intimidating, human nature would have to be different; it would have to be as stable and serene as the law itself. But then human nature would be dead.

It is not dead. This is why, however surprising this may seem to anyone who has never observed or directly experienced human complexity, the murderer, most of the time, feels innocent when he kills. Every criminal acquits himself before he is judged. He considers himself, if not within his right, at least excused by circumstances. He does not think or foresee; when he thinks, it is to foresee that he will be forgiven altogether or in part. How could he fear what he considers highly improbable? He will fear death after the verdict but not before the crime. Hence the law, to be intimidating, should leave the murderer no chance, should be implacable in advance and particularly admit no extenuating circumstance. But who among us would dare ask this?

If anyone did, it would still be necessary to take into account another paradox of human nature. If the instinct to live is fundamental, it is no more so than another instinct of which the academic psychologists do not speak: the death instinct, which at certain moments calls for the destruction of oneself and of others. It is probable that the desire to kill often coincides with the desire to die or to annihilate oneself. Thus, the instinct for self-preservation is matched, in variable proportions, by the instinct for destruction. The latter is the only way of explaining altogether the various perversions which, from alcoholism to drugs, lead an individual to his death while he knows full well what is happening. Man wants to live, but it is useless to hope that this desire will dictate all his actions. He also wants to be nothing; he wants the irreparable, and death for its own sake. So it happens that the criminal wants not only the crime but the suffering that goes with it, even (one might say, especially) if that suffering is exceptional. When that odd desire grows and becomes dominant, the prospect of being put to death not only fails to stop the criminal, but probably even adds to the vertigo in which he swoons. Thus, in a way, he kills in order to die.

Such peculiarities suffice to explain why a penalty that seems calculated to frighten normal minds is in reality altogether unrelated to ordinary psychology. All statistics without exception, those concerning countries that have abolished execution as well as the others, show that there is no connection between the abolition of the death penalty and criminality. Criminal statistics neither increase nor decrease. The guillotine exists, and so does crime; between the two there is no other apparent connection than that of the law. . . .

"Nothing proves, indeed," say the conservatives, "that the death penalty is exemplary; as a matter of fact, it is certain that thousands of murderers have not been intimidated by it. But there is no way of knowing those it has intimidated; consequently, nothing proves that it is not exemplary." Thus, the greatest of punishments, the one that involves the last dishonor for the condemned and grants the supreme privilege to society, rests on nothing but an unverifiable possibility. Death, on the other hand, does not involve degrees or probabilities. It solidifies all things, culpability and the body, in a definitive rigidity. Yet it is administered among us in the name of chance and a calculation. Even if that calculation were reasonable, should there not be a certainty to authorize the most certain of deaths? However, the condemned is cut in two, not so much for the crime he committed but by virtue of all the crimes that might have been and were not committed, that can be and will not be committed. The most sweeping uncertainty in this case authorizes the most implacable certainty. . . .

What will be left of that power of example if it is proved that capital punishment has another power, and a very real one, which degrades men to the point of shame, madness, and murder? . . .

What can we think of those officials who call the guillotine "the shunting engine," the condemned man "the client" or "the parcel"? The priest Bela Just, who accompanied more than thirty condemned men writes: "The slang of the administrators of justice is quite as cynical and vulgar as that of the criminals." And here are the remarks of one of our assistant executioners on his journeys to the provinces: "When we would start on a trip, it was always a lark, with taxis and the best restaurants part of the spree!" The same one says, boasting of the executioner's skill in releasing the blade: "You could *allow yourself the fun* of pulling the client's hair." The dissoluteness expressed here has other, deeper aspects. The clothing of the condemned belongs in principle to the executioner. The elder Deibler used to hang all such articles of clothing in a shed and *now and then would go and look at them.* But there are more serious aspects. Here is what our assistant executioner declares: "The new executioner is batty about the guillotine. He sometimes spends days on end at home sitting on a chair, ready with hat and coat on, waiting for a summons from the Ministry." . . .

The fine and solemn example, thought up by our legislators, at least produces one sure effect—to depreciate or to destroy all humanity and reason in those who take part in it directly. But, it will be said, these are exceptional creatures who find a vocation in such dishonor. They seem less exceptional when we learn that hundreds of persons offer to serve as executioners without pay. The men of our generation, who have lived through the history of recent years, will not be astonished by this bit of information. They know that behind the most peaceful and familiar faces slumbers the impulse to torture and murder. The punishment that aims to intimidate an unknown murderer certainly confers a vocation of killer on many another monster about whom there is no doubt. And since we are busy justifying our cruelest laws with probable considerations, let there be no doubt that out of those hundreds of men whose services were declined, one at least must have satisfied otherwise the bloodthirsty instincts the guillotine excited in him.

If, therefore, there is a desire to maintain the death penalty, let us at least be spared the hypocrisy of a justification by example. Let us be frank about that penalty which can have no publicity, that intimidation which works only on respectable people, so long as they are respectable, which fascinates those who have ceased to be respectable and debases or deranges those who take part in it. It is a penalty, to be sure, a frightful torture, both physical and moral, but it provides no sure example except a demoralizing one. It punishes, but it forestalls nothing; indeed, it may even arouse the impulse to murder. It hardly seems to exist, except for the man who suffers it—in his soul for months and years, in his body during the desperate and violent hour when he is cut in two without suppressing his life. Let us call it by the name which, for lack of any other nobility, will at least give the nobility of truth, and let us recognize it for what it is essentially: a revenge. . . .

Many laws consider a premeditated crime more serious than a crime of pure violence. But what then is capital punishment but the most premeditated of murders, to which no criminal's deed, however calculated it may be, can be compared? For there to be equivalence, the death penalty would have to punish a criminal who had warned his victim of the date at which he would inflict a horrible death on him and who, from that moment onward, had confined him at his mercy for months. Such a monster is not encountered in private life.

BAT-AMI BAR ON

Why Terrorism Is Morally Problematic

BAT-AMI BAR ON teaches philosophy and is the Director of Women's Studies at the State University of New York at Binghamton. She has edited two books of critical feminist readings on the history of philosophy.

That terrorism operates psychologically in certain ways became clearest for me just after the *intifada* started. I was in Israel and talking with one of my cousins about the situation. I argued that the formation of an independent Palestinian state was the only realistic compromise solution to the Jewish-Israeli-Palestinian conflict. I was told in response that the formation of an independent Palestinian state would endanger the state of Israel with a war. When I claimed that the *intifada* together with the militarily enforced official Israeli repression constitute a war, I was told that at least this war is not happening within Israel's borders and thus does not endanger the majority of the Jewish-Israeli population.

I realized as the discussion developed that my cousin genuinely believed that for the Palestinians an independent state would be first and foremost a means to assert a destructive power against her and her family and against the Jewish-Israeli population. Motivating this belief was a deep-seated fear that also motivated a clinging to the Israeli military as the only shield against the expected destruction and a commitment to the deployment and use, including inhumane use, of the military against the Palestinians.

Since Jewish-Israeli life within the 1948 disengagement lines, which delineate what is popularly believed to form the pre-1967 Israeli borders, seemed undisturbed by the *intifada*, my cousin's fear can make sense only given the history of the Jewish-Israeli-Palestinian relationship. Looked at from the Jewish-Israeli perspective, this relationship has been colored by Palestinian terrorism ever since the beginning of Jewish settlement in the area at the end of the nineteenth century. My cousin's fear, a fear I recognize in myself, is a product of growing up under and living with the constant threat of terrorism. Although this threat was magnified by the Israeli government's official pronouncements and the official history of Israel, it was nonetheless real.

For the purpose of this essay the only salient fact about terrorism is that it is a practice of terrorization in which terror is a means to an end other than itself. The means used to terrorize, the possible distinctions among the ends, and the practitioners of terrorism are all insignificant insofar as this essay is concerned. Knowing the means, ends, and practitioners may help one to list the different kinds of terrorism, to chart it historically and culturally, to understand the relation between it and technology, or to see its place in local or global social, political, or economic structures or power relations. But knowledge of the means, ends, and practitioners of terrorism does not shed light on terrorism as a formative process.

Letting terrorism be understood as a practice of terrorization in which terror is a means to an end other than itself does not permit one to categorize as terroristic a random attack on a school by a psychotic person, no matter how violent and terrifying, since it is not a means to a further end. On the other hand, such a conception of terrorism does permit one to categorize as terroristic certain practices of nation-states—for example, the repressive actions of the Argentinian junta during the "dirty war," the nuclear strategies of the United States and the USSR, the actions of criminal organizations such as the Colombian drug cartel, and the U.S. government's tactics of intimidation against organized crime—since they do have ends other than terrorization. . . .

• • •

Suppose, then, that terrorism is a practice of terrorization in which terror is a means to an end other than itself. What can be said about it as a process through which the terrorized are formed? . . .

. . . [A]s a formative process, terrorism produces people who are afraid. Terrorized people's fear is deep and easily triggered by the slightest indication of possible danger. Yet the fear is triggered by things and movements that are not extraordinary within an ordinary day-to-day context. And the day-to-day ordinariness of the terrorized circumstances does not dissipate the fear.

Morgan does not talk about the consequences of living a life in which fear is triggered so easily under what should be ordinary circumstances. Some of the consequences are described by Leo Lowenthal in his "Terror's Atomization of Man," an essay written in 1946 about fascist state terrorism. According to Lowenthal, terrorism interrupts the causal relation between what people do and what happens to them. As a result, the terrorized's sense of a continuous experience and memory weakens and even breaks down. This in turn leads to a shrinking or breakdown of personality. . . .

A . . . way to understand terrorism as a formative process is by comparing it with torture, which, like seasoning, is also a practice in which brutalization is used as a means to break a person down. In *The Body in Pain*, Elaine Scarry analyzes several aspects of torture. Like Morgan, Scarry begins with the transformation of the ordinary. Like Lowenthal, she emphasizes the consequences of torture, which also constitute the dissolution of the ordinary world. Scarry describes the transformation of a room:

> In torture the world is reduced to a single room or set of rooms. Called "guest rooms" in Greece and "safe houses" in the Philippines, the torture rooms are often given names that acknowledge and call attention to the generous, civilizing impulse normally present in the human shelter. They call attention to the impulse only as a prelude to announcing its annihilation. The torture room is not just the setting in which the torture occurs. . . . It is itself literally converted into another weapon, into an agent of pain. All aspects of the basic structure—walls, ceiling, windows, doors—undergo this conversion.

Scarry proceeds from here to focus on the interrogation and its end—the confession—and calls attention to elements that Frye focuses on in her discussion of seasoning. Scarry writes: "Torture systematically prevents the prisoner from being the agent of anything and simultaneously pretends that he is the agent of some things. Despite the fact that in reality he has been deprived of all control over, and therefore all responsibility for, his world, his words, his body, he is to understand his confession as it will be understood by others, as an act of self-betrayal."

It is not only confession that will be experienced as self-betrayal. The torturer controls the tortured body and voice and can make the tortured act or stop acting, speak, sing, or scream or stop speaking, singing, or screaming. The torturer's control is a function of the ability to cause pain, and it is through the experience of pain that the tortured is formed into a self-betrayer, because this experience dissolves the distinction between outside and inside the body, conflates the private and the public, destroys language, and obliterates the contents of consciousness.

Like the tortured, the terrorized may come to experience themselves as self-betrayers, and the possibility of self-betrayal is one of the things they fear most, because the terrorized, like the tortured, realize very quickly once their terrorization begins that what is at issue for their tormentors is the length of time it may take for them to break down and betray themselves by accepting the terrorists' demands. Indeed, from the point of view of the terrorist, as from the point of view of the torturer, terrorization consists of a series of tests of strength that are designed to reveal the weakness of their victims to the terrorist and to the victims.

When the victims feel tested, they know that what is being tested is the strength of their will. As they become aware of their weakness, they also become aware of the erosion of their will. This is accompanied by a diminishing sense of self, since under these conditions the self becomes the will. Everything else is stripped away. When the will erodes totally or when it feels as if it has been broken, nothing is left of the self. . . .

• • •

. . . Again, much too much is claimed about terrorism in general. But even in the case of those terrorized by oppositional political terrorism—the kind of terrorism that at the outset seems just not to take place in circumstances resembling the confinement and isolation of the tortured—the situation is much more complicated. This fact is testified to by the practices states institute to control terrorism (such as careful inspection of people and luggage in airports) and the general fear that terrorism endangers the liberal democratic state.

This general fear, noted by many contemporary experts on international oppositional political terrorism, causes liberal democratic states to risk violating civil liberties because of the practices they have to institute to prevent terrorism within their borders. To be effective they have to work like a screen that does not permit infiltration by terrorists into the state. They must also facilitate tracing an infiltration if and when it occurs.

Thus in Israel, for example, roads at certain intervals have checkpoints staffed by military personnel, who stop and inspect all cars. For buses, the armed soldiers get in and inspect the luggage racks, making sure that every item has an owner among the people on the bus. To maximize security on its campus, the University of Tel-Aviv is surrounded by a fence, and at the gates, security personnel check every bag that is brought in. Security personnel check every bag brought into every public building in Israel, including movie theaters. Helicopters patrol the seashores on the hour, and a civilian militia patrols them on foot. It also patrols the streets of every town twenty-four hours a day. Children at summer camps and at schools are always accompanied by armed guards on their field trips. Everyone in Israel is expected to carry officially issued identity papers and produce them upon the demand of the police, militia, or army. Everywhere in Israel there are posters that remind the public of terrorism and of the people's obligation to be alert and vigilant, to always survey their environment for suspicious items, movement, or individuals.

These various practices instituted by states to combat terrorism confine and isolate the citizenry and put it under constant surveillance. Surveillance makes one feel simultaneously safer and more vulnerable. One feels safer because one feels protected by it. But at the same time, one feels more exposed and not only to one's own government, especially if terrorists have been successful in their attempts, because this means that they are even better at surveillance than the government. The consequences of this state of affairs are best captured by Foucault's explanation of the workings of Bentham's panopticon in *Discipline and Punish*. According to him the panoptic mechanism arranges things so that it is possible to see everyone constantly and recognize everyone immediately, and anyone can use it at anytime. The effect is to induce in those who are observed a state of conscious and permanent visibility that assures the automatic functioning of power.

Thus even in the case of terrorists who do not confine and isolate their victims, circumstances are altered in response to their terrorism. The new situation has within it the elements needed to create for the terrorized an intense experience of feeling totally at the mercy of the terrorists. This suffices to start the process of the formation of the self as the self of a terrorized person, a fearful self that contracts and is organized more and more around its experience as a certain level of strength of will. . . .

• • •

. . . Conceiving terrorism as a practice of terrorization through which a self is intentionally eroded and a will is intentionally broken implies, I believe, that *what morally problematizes terrorism is that it is cruel.*

That cruelty is the crux of what is morally problematic with terrorism becomes clearer when one thinks about the things terrorists do when they terrorize: bombing a city, shooting indiscriminately in an airport, abducting and killing people. Such events provide the occasion for a variety of possible attitudes and moral dispositions toward those who suffer as a result of these terroristic acts. Some people are motivated to help the victims of terrorism. Others are motivated to increase their suffering. The latter disposition is cruelty. One expects people who intentionally induce and increase suffering either to take pleasure in other people's pain or to be indifferent to it. . . .

• • •

Terrorists intentionally intensify the suffering of people whom they intentionally victimize. And although they may not take pleasure in this, in some important sense they have to be indifferent to the pain they cause. Sergey Nechaev and Mikhail Bakunin express this clearly in their *Revolutionary Catechism*, written in 1869 for clandestine Russian oppositional groups. In this booklet, they say:

1. The revolutionary is a lost man; he has no interests of his own, no cause of his own, no feelings, no habits, no belongings; he does not even have a name. . . .
2. In the very depths of his being, not just in words but in deed, he has broken every tie with the civil order, with the educated world and all laws, conventions, and generally accepted conditions and with the ethics of this world. . . .

• • •

6. Hard with himself, he must be hard toward others. All the tender feelings of family life, of friendship, love, gratitude, and even honour must be stifled in him by a single cold passion for the revolutionary cause. . . .

• • •

13. . . . He is not a revolutionary if he feels pity for anything in this world. If he is able to, he must face the annihilation of a situation, of a relationship, or of any person who is part of this world—everything and everyone must be equally odious to him.

Terrorists are cruel, therefore, not only because they create and worsen in an obvious way the suffering that comes through the body but also because they create the anguish that the terrorized experience as they feel their selves erode and fear they will break. . . .

●   ●   ●

. . . [M]y concern with how individuals are formed through terrorization, be it the terrorized or the terrorists, is not merely a concern with the physical damage inflicted, and I am not unconcerned with justice. Like others who have tried to argue that an ethics of care and an ethics of justice, though different, are not really in conflict, I am interested in challenging the prioritization of justice and not in its substitution by empathy. Both empathy and justice have to be accorded a serious place in moral thinking.

I am not certain how to accord both empathy and justice a serious place in moral thinking. Yet when I reflect on terrorism, I find that responses to the terrorism or organized crime or perhaps to covert right-wing state terrorism (for example, that practiced in Guatemala) are helpful in clarifying the relation between empathy and justice in the moral assessment of terrorism. As I see it, the difference between the responses to these two forms of terrorism is that though both horrify because both are cruel, the horror in the case of organized crime is not accompanied by surprise at or disillusionment with the cruelty of the criminals, whereas the horror in state terrorism is accompanied by surprise at and disillusionment with the cruelty of politicians. Unlike the terrorism of organized crime, the terrorism of a state against its citizens leaves the victims with a deep sense of betrayal.

I believe this difference in response can be accounted for by expectations from the relation between the ends and the means used to achieve them. The ends of organized crime—the accumulation of wealth and power—do not limit the means that can be used to obtain them. On the other hand, unless one is already disillusioned and corrupted by cynicism, one cannot view the means to the ends that politicians ought to have—the service and maintenance of communities for the good of their members—as independent of these ends. Organized crime can achieve its ends by all means necessary. Criminals need not be just or decent. However, politicians must be just and decent and so cannot use all means necessary to achieve their ends.

Moreover, there are means that would not fit organized crime's ends but would undermine them just as there are means that would not fit the ends that politicians ought to have but would undermine them. Terrorism is not a means that would undermine the ends of organized crime. Yet even if one could show, as the Guatemalan right-wing politicians try to, that terrorism may serve a greater communal good in the future (for example, increase the wealth available for distribution to all the members of the community, thereby making the community better and more just), it is very hard to see how this should count for more than what happens to the people who are terrorized and who terrorize. Terrorism produces fearful people with diminished selves organized around the experience of the fear of the loss of their strength of will. It also produces cruel people, people who feel no compassion or kindness and are inhospitable. Could such people enjoy the promised future goods?

If there is a promised future good whose value seems overwhelming, it is freedom from conditions in which people are formed as they are by terrorism. . . . I doubt very much that such a future can be brought about by terrorism. Fanon's patients are much more resilient than I think people really are, especially given the growing evidence on post-traumatic stress disorder. Post-traumatic stress shapes the lives not only of individuals whose experiences resulted in the stress but the young people who grow up with them as well. The children of Holocaust survivors have Holocaust nightmares.

So in the case of terrorism, it seems that one cannot fail to give precedence to empathy, to concern about what happens to people who are terrorized and to people who terrorize. Yet this concern has its foundation not merely in care for people as individuals and the possibility that they may be harmed but also in care for them as members of communities. As producers and distributors of wealth and power, communities can continue for a long time independently of the kind of people who populate them. But good communities—communities that are fairly just, that get along not only contractually but generously, that take each other concretely into consideration, and whose members are free of daily fears for their survival and physical well-being—these communities need people who care. Neither the terrorized nor the terrorists can care well enough—for themselves or for others.

CHAPTER 11

What Should We Sacrifice for Animals and the Environment?

Should we do more than we are doing to protect our natural environment? Fifty years ago most people would have been relatively unconcerned about the environment. But today we live in an age in which most people believe it is important to devote time and resources to the protection of the environment. But if most people already agree that we should do more, then what philosophical problems could we have about environmental issues? Similarly, most people would agree we shouldn't be cruel to animals—what then is philosophically perplexing about the treatment of animals?

Interestingly, both of these areas raise a host of important and perplexing philosophical issues. The most obvious of these concerns the *extent* of our obligations toward animals and the environment. Several years ago a dam project undertaken by the Tennessee Valley Authority was temporarily halted when it was discovered that some of the marshes that were to be submerged by the dam project were the only habitat of a small fish called a "snail darter." The dilemma was this: the dam would bring significant economic improvement to thousands of people, but the snail darter would become extinct as its habitat was flooded. More recently, vast tracks of forest in the Pacific Northwest have been declared off-grounds for lumbering because they provide the only habitat for the spotted owl, an endangered species. Protecting the spotted owl will put thousands of people out of work. It is arguable in both of these cases that some human lives might be lost because people will be less able to pay for food, health care, automobile maintenance, and safety measures. Is it right to save animals, or animal species, when doing so costs people their jobs, or even their lives? What is the extent of our obligation? How much must we sacrifice?

Obviously it is not possible to answer questions like these by setting some amount in dollars, pesos, or person-hours that each person must sacrifice for animals and the environment. Even to approach such a question, we need to have some idea of the basis for valuing the environment and the interests of animals. In his article, Tom Regan distinguishes three kinds of justification we might appeal to for valuing the environment. The first, a *management ethic,* holds that animals and the environment are valuable because they benefit humans. According to this view, we must protect animals and the environment to the extent that it is in our (human) interest to do so. For example, one might argue that we should not build a dam that will prevent fish migration and harm the fishing industry or that will drown scenic land that could be used for recreation. One could argue that biological diversity is important on ecological grounds, and that we ultimately are beneficiaries of such diversity. A management ethic might question whether the snail darter was valuable enough to warrant canceling a significant river project.

A second justification is a *kinship ethic,* which holds that we value things that bear a "kinship" to us. In most versions of this view, our kinship is to other creatures that are sentient (capable of thought), or to creatures that can suffer; these, in addition to ourselves, are the creatures we feel impelled to protect. Peter Singer, an influential animal-rights theorist, argues in his selection that it is wrong of us to raise animals in harsh conditions for food, but that there is no need to sacrifice a river project for the snail darter. Similarly, we have no special obligation to protect endangered *species,* so long as we do not cause the suffering of any particular members of those species.

The third justification, which Regan claims to be a true *environmental ethic,* holds that nonsentient beings—animals, plants, and even natural formations—have inherent value and moral standing independent of their value, or kinship, to humans. Just as it is racist to hold that the interests of whites count more than the interests of other races, and just as it is sexist to hold that the interests of men count more than the interests of women, it is *speciesist* of us to hold that the interests of humans (and of animals that are relevantly like humans) count for more than the interests of snail darters, plants, or deserts. In a classic statement, Aldo Leopold argues eloquently that we must stop seeing land use as a narrowly economic problem and see it rather as a problem of environmental ethics. On the other hand, Mark Sagoff claims in his article that you can't be both an environmentalist and in favor of animal rights. If he is right, then we cannot agree both with Leopold and with Singer.

One principal reason for protecting the environment is that if we do not, future generations will inherit an inhospitable, perhaps unlivable, planet. For example, plutonium waste created by nuclear power plants is deathly poisonous in even minute quantities and takes more than 20,000 years to lose even half of its toxicity. The loss of rain forests contributes to the greenhouse effect, and once a critical mass of them has been lost, they cannot be restored by replanting. But people living on the planet often feel that they need to use these resources now. Most future generations don't even exist yet. To what extent must we sacrifice our well-being to protect the interests of people who don't even exist?

In her selection, Annette Baier focuses on what has been called the *futurity problem*. Here is an example of the futurity problem in an individual case. Suppose a couple decides to have a baby. Out of concern for their future child's health, they agree to stop drinking alcohol during the entire course of the pregnancy — even before conceiving a child. Because they have stopped consuming alcohol, they go to bed at 10 P.M.—earlier than they would have if they had gone out drinking. The sperm that therefore fertilizes the egg is different from the one that would have fertilized the egg if the couple had gone to bed at 11 P.M. after drinking. It is even possible that a different egg is fertilized. Let's call the baby that *would* have been conceived at 11 P.M. *Sue* and call the baby that *was* conceived in an alcohol-free body at 10 P.M. *Mike*.

Remember that the couple decided to stop drinking out of concern for their child's health, and that the child who would have been born if they had continued drinking would have been Sue. But now that they have stopped drinking, Sue will not be born more healthy—Sue will not be born at all. Rather, Mike will be born. Mike may well be healthier than Sue would have been, but that is hardly a benefit to Sue, who will not exist. Accordingly, if the couple had *not* stopped drinking, and if Sue had been born with alcohol-related birth defects, Sue would hardly seem in a position to complain about her parents' drinking; she would not exist at all if her parents had stopped drinking. Baier tries to show how Sue could coherently complain that her or his interests had not been served, even if serving them better would have caused the person never to exist.

Marti Kheel claims that the very structures of thought that have brought us such staggering environmental problems are now being invoked in an effort to solve them. In an attempt to reframe completely the discussion of environmental issues, she argues that we must turn to a feminist conception of environmental ethics. Such a framework would offer hope of a truly holist approach toward the environment, one based less on the dualistic discussion of rights and principles that has caused the problems in the first place and that will prevent their resolution.

The chapter opens with a wry poem by Allen Ginsberg, a chronicle of environmental woes. It closes, too, on a wry note by John Stuart Mill, written well over a century ago, reminding us not to be uncritical in our glorification of nature.

ALLEN GINSBERG

Ballade of Poisons

ALLEN GINSBERG (1926–1997) was a poet, photographer, and musician associated with the Beat generation poets of the 1950s and the antiwar movement of the 1960s. He was the author of many books, including *The Fall of America: Poems of These States*, which won the 1974 National Book Award.

With oil that streaks streets a magic color,
With soot that falls on city vegetables
With basement sulfurs & coal black odor
With smog that purples suburbs' sunset hills
With Junk that feebles black & white men's wills
With plastic bubbles aeons will dissolve
With new plutoniums that only resolve
Their poison heat in quarter million years,
With pesticides that round food Chains revolve
May your soul make home, may your eyes weep tears.

With freak hormones in chicken & soft egg
With panic red dye in cow meat burger
With mummy med'cines, nitrate in sliced pig
With sugar'd cereal kids scream for murder,
With Chemic additives that cause Cancer
With bladder and mouth in your salami,
With Strontium Ninety in milks of Mommy,
With sex voices that spill beer thru your ears
With Cups of Nicotine till you vomit
May your soul make home, may your eyes weep tears.

With microwave toaster television
With Cadmium lead in leaves of fruit trees
With Trade Center's nocturnal emission
With Coney Island's shore plopped with Faeces
While blue Whales sing in high infrequent seas
With Amazon worlds with fish in ocean
Washed in Rockefellers greasy Potion
With oily toil fueled with atomic fears
With CIA tainting World emotion
May your soul make home, may your eyes weep tears.

Envoi

President, 'spite cockroach devotion,
Folk poisoned with radioactive lotion,
'Spite soulless bionic energy queers
May your world move to healthy emotion,
Make your soul at home, let your eyes weep tears.

TOM REGAN

The Nature and Possibility
of an Environmental Ethic

TOM REGAN teaches philosophy at North Carolina State University and has published widely on ethics. He is best known as a defender of animal rights.

I. INTRODUCTION

Is an environmental ethic possible? Answers to this question presuppose that we have an agreed upon understanding of the nature of an environmental ethic. Evidently we do not, and one fundamental problem for this burgeoning area of ethics is to say what such an ethic must be like. In this essay, I characterize and defend, although incompletely, a particular conception of an environmental ethic. My modest objective is to show that there is something worth thinking about completing.

II. TWO CONDITIONS OF AN
ENVIRONMENTAL ETHIC

The conception I favor accepts the following two conditions:

1. An environmental ethic must hold that there are nonhuman beings that have moral standing.
2. An environmental ethic must hold that the class of those beings that have moral standing includes but is larger than the class of conscious beings—that is, all conscious beings and some nonconscious beings must be held to have moral standing.

If both conditions are accepted, then a theory that satisfies neither of them is not a false environmental ethic; it is not an environmental ethic at all. Any theory that satisfies (1), but does not satisfy (2) might be regarded as a theory "on the way to becoming" such an ethic, in that it satisfies a necessary condition, but, since it fails to satisfy condition (2), it fails to qualify as a genuine environmental ethic. Only theories that satisfy (2), on the conception advanced here, can properly be regarded as environmental ethics, whether true, reasonable, or otherwise.

Though only a necessary condition, (1) assists us in distinguishing between (*a*) an ethic *of* the environment, and (*b*) an ethic *for the use* of the environment. Suppose we think that only the interests of human beings matter morally. Then it certainly would be possible to develop a homocentric ethic for the use of the environment. Roughly speaking, such an ethic would declare that the environment ought to be used so that the quality of human life, including possibly that of future generations, ought to be enhanced. I do not say developing such an ethic (what I shall call "a management ethic") would be simple or unimportant, but a management ethic falls short of an ethic of the environment, given the conditions stated earlier. It restricts the loci of value to the lives and interests of *human* beings, whereas an environmental ethic requires that we recognize the moral standing of nonhumans.

L. W. Sumner advances considerations that, if accepted, would lead us to an ethical theory that satisfies condition (1) and thereby takes us beyond a management ethic. Sumner argues that the lives and interests of nonhuman animals, not just those of human beings, ought to be taken into account in their own right. Recognition of this fact, he states, marks "the beginning of a genuine environmental consciousness." Other thinkers have advanced similar arguments. Despite many differences, these thinkers share the belief that only *conscious* beings can have moral standing. I refer to theories that embody this belief as *kinship theories* because they grow out of the idea that beings resembling humans in the quite fundamental way of being conscious, and thus to this extent kin to us, have moral standing. I have more to say about kinship theories below (Section IV).

Management and kinship theories are clearly distinct. Management theories direct us, for example, to preserve wildlife if this is in the interest of human beings, including (possibly) the interest of generations yet unborn. Animals in the wild are not themselves recognized as having interests or value that ought to be taken into account. Given a kinship ethic, however, wild animals, in their own right, figure in the moral arithmetic, though precisely how we are to carry out the required computations is unclear. When, for example, there is a clash between the preservation of wild animals and the economic development of the wilderness, it is unclear how conflicting interests are to be weighed. The value of survival of how many caribou, for example, equals the disvalue of how much financial loss to oil investors in Northern Canada?

Whatever difficulties may exist for management or kinship theories in weighing conflicting claims, however, these difficulties seem to be compounded if we move beyond these theories to ones that meet condition (2), for then we are required, it appears, to deal with the possibility that human and animal interests might come into conflict with the survival or flourishing of nonconscious beings, and it is extremely doubtful whether such conflicts can *in principle* admit of rational adjudication.

I do not wish to minimize the difficulties that attend the development of an environmental ethic that is consequentialist in nature (e.g., some form of utilitarianism). There are difficulties of comparison, perhaps themselves great enough to foreclose the possibility of developing a consequentialist environmental ethic. I have more to say on this matter as we proceed. First, though, a more fundamental problem requires our attention. Is it even logically possible for a theory to meet both the conditions I have recommended for an environmental ethic? The answer clearly is no if compelling reasons can be given for limiting moral standing *only* to conscious beings. In the following section I reject three arguments that attempt to establish this restriction.

III. ARGUMENTS AGAINST THE POSSIBILITY OF AN ENVIRONMENTAL ETHIC

The first argument to be considered I call the "interest argument":

The Interest Argument

1. The only beings that can have moral standing are those beings that can have interests.
2. The only beings that can have interests are those that have the capacity for consciousness.
3. Therefore, the only beings that can have moral standing are beings having the capacity for consciousness.

Now, this argument, as I have argued elsewhere against a similar argument, has apparent plausibility because it exploits an ambiguity in the concept of something having interests. To speak of A's interests in x might mean either (a) that A is interested in (wants, desires, hopes for, cares about, etc.) x, or (b) that x is in A's interest (that x will contribute to A's good, or well-being, or welfare). Clearly if the only beings that can have moral standing are those that can be interested in things (have desires, wants, etc.), then only conscious beings can have moral standing. The idea of nonconscious beings having desires, or wants, at least in any literal sense, seems plainly unintelligible. If, however, we mean beings that can be benefited or harmed by what is given or denied them, then it is an open question whether the class of beings which can have moral standing is coextensive with the class of beings having the capacity for consciousness. Perhaps other beings can have a good or value that can be advanced or retarded depending on what is done to them. The interest argument provides us with no resolution of this question, and so fails to demonstrate the impossibility of an environmental ethic.

A second argument, which I shall call the "sentience argument," closely resembles the interest argument and is vulnerable to the same type of objection:

The Sentience Argument

1. The only beings that can have moral standing are those that are sentient.
2. The only beings that are sentient are those that have the capacity for consciousness.
3. Therefore, the only beings that can have moral standing are those that have the capacity for consciousness.

I limit my critical remarks to step (1). How might it be supported? First, one might argue that only sentient beings have interests; that is, one might seek to support the sentience argument by invoking the interest argument, but since we have shown this latter argument is incomplete, at best, this defense of the sentience argument must bear the same diagnosis. A second defense consists in claiming that it is "meaningless" to think that nonconscious beings possibly have moral standing. This is unconvincing. If it is meaningless, there ought to be some way of illuminating why this is so, and this illumination is not provided by the mere charge of meaninglessness itself. Such a defense has more the aura of rhetoric than of philosophy.

A third defense consists in arguing that the only beings having moral standing are those having value in their own right, *and* that only sentient beings have value of this kind. This defense, as I argue in a moment, is a token of the argument type I call the "goodness argument." Its major liability is that by itself it provides no justification for its two central claims—namely, (*a*) that only beings that can have value in their own right can have moral standing, and (*b*) that only sentient beings have value in their own right. For reasons to which I come below, I believe (*b*) is false while (*a*) is true. Meanwhile, neither is self-evident and so each stands in need of rational defense, something not provided by the sentience argument itself.

The final argument to be considered is the goodness argument:

The Goodness Argument

1. The only beings that can have moral standing are those that can have a good of their own.
2. The only beings that can have a good of their own are those capable of consciousness.
3. Therefore, the only beings that can have moral standing are those capable of consciousness.

Premise (1) of the goodness argument seems to identify a fundamental presupposition of an environmental ethic. The importance of this premise is brought out when we ask for the grounds on which we might rest the obligation to preserve any existing *x*. Fundamentally, two types of answer are possible. First, preserving *x* is necessary to bring about future good or prevent future evil for beings other than *x*; on this account *x*'s existence has instrumental value. Second, the obligation we have might be to *x* itself, independently of *x*'s instrumental value, because *x* has a good or value in its own right. Given our conditions for an environmental ethic, not all of the values recognized in nonconscious nature can be instrumental. Only if we agree with premise (1) of the goodness argument, therefore, can we have a necessary presupposition of an environmental ethic. How inherent goodness or value can be intelligibly ascribed to nonconscious beings is a difficult question, one we shall return to later (Section V). At present, we must consider the remainder of the goodness argument, since if sound, it rules out the logical possibility of nonconscious beings having a good or value of their own.

"The only beings that have a good of their own," premise (2) states, "are those capable of consciousness." What arguments can be given to support this view? I have examined suggested answers elsewhere at length. What these arguments come to in the end, if I am right, is the thesis that consciousness is a logically necessary condition of having only *a certain kind* of good of one's own, happiness. Thus, though we may speak metaphorically of a "happy azalea" or a "contented broccoli," the only sorts of beings that literally can have happiness are conscious beings. There is no disputing this. What is disputable is the tacit assumption that this is the *only* kind of good or value a given *x* can have in its own right. Unless or until a compelling supporting argument is supplied, for limiting inherent goodness to happiness, the goodness argument falls short of limiting moral standing to just those beings capable of consciousness.

Four truths result if the argument of this section is sound. First, an environmental ethic must recognize that the class of beings having moral standing is larger than the class of conscious beings. Second, the basis on which an environmental ethic must pin this enlargement is the idea that nonconscious beings can have a good or value in their own right. Third, though it remains to be ascertained what this goodness or value is, it is not happiness; and fourth, efforts to show that nonconscious beings cannot have moral standing fail to show this. The conclusion we guardedly reach, then, is that the impossibility of an environmental ethic has not been shown.

IV. ARGUMENTS AGAINST THE NECESSITY OF AN ENVIRONMENTAL ETHIC

We turn now to a second series of objections against an environmental ethic, all of which concede that it is *possible* that nonconscious beings may have value in themselves, and thus that it is *possible* to develop an environmental ethic, but which all deny, nonetheless, that there are good enough reasons for holding that nonconscious beings *do* have a good or value in their own right. There are, these objections hold in common, alternative ways of accounting for the moral dimensions of our relationship to the environment which are rationally preferable to postulating inherent value in it. Thus, while granting the possibility of an environmental ethic, the four views about to be considered deny its necessity.

The Corruption of Character Argument

Advocates of this argument insist that it is wrong to treat nonconscious nature in certain ways—for example, unchecked strip mining—but account for this by urging that people who engage in such activities tend to become similarly ruthless in their dealings with people. Just as Kant speculated that those who act cruelly to animals develop the habit of cruelty, and so are likely to be cruel to their fellow man, so similarly those who indiscriminately destroy the natural environment will develop destructive habits that will in time wreak havoc on their neighbor. Our duties to act toward the environment in certain ways are thus explained without our having to postulate value *in* the environment.

This argument cannot be any stronger than its central empirical thesis that those who treat the environment in certain ways will be inclined to treat their fellow humans in analogous ways. I do not believe there is any hard empirical evidence at hand which supports this hypothesis. Comparing the crime rates of strip miners and accountants would probably provide much hard empirical data against it. Indeed, one cannot help wondering if the very reverse habits might not be fostered by instructing persons to do anything they want to the environment, if no person is harmed, while insisting on strict prohibitions in our dealings with persons. There would appear to be just as much (or just as little) empirical data to support this hypothesis as there is to support the hypothesis central to the corruption of character argument. On empirical grounds, the argument lacks credibility.

The Utilitarian Argument

To speak of *the* utilitarian argument is misleading. A wide variety of utilitarian arguments is possible, even including positions that hold that some nonconscious beings do have value in their own right. I restrict my attention to forms of utilitarianism that deny this, focusing mainly on hedonistic utilitarianism.

Abstractly and roughly, hedonistic utilitarianism holds that an action is right if no alternative action produces a better balance of pleasure over pain for all those affected. A theory of this type is "on the way to becoming" an environmental ethic if, as utilitarians since Bentham have argued, animals are sentient, and thus, given the utilitarian criteria, have moral standing. But hedonistic utilitarianism fails to satisfy the second condition of an environmental ethic and thus fails to qualify as an ethic of the environment. Its shortcomings are highlighted by asking, "Why not plastic trees? Why not lawns of astro-turf, or mountains of papier-mâché suitably coated with vinyl to withstand harsh weather?" Stories find their way almost daily into the popular press which illustrate that a plastic environment is increasingly within the reach of modern technology. If, as Martin Krieger argues, "the demand for rare environments is a learned one," then "conscious public choice can manipulate this learning so that the environments which people learn to use and want reflect environments which are likely to be available at low cost." Thus, as Mark Sagoff sees it, "This is the reason that the redwoods are (given Krieger's position) replaceable by plastic trees." "The advertising that created rare environments," Krieger writes, "can create plentiful (e.g., plastic) substitutes."

A hedonistic utilitarianism cannot quarrel over the *source* of environmentally based pleasures, whether they arise from real stands of redwoods or plastic replicas. Provided only that the pleasures are equal in the relevant respects (e.g., of equal duration and intensity), both are of equal value. To the suggestion that pleasures rooted in real redwoods are "higher" or "nobler" than those rooted in plastic ones, the reply must be that there is a long, untold story surrounding the idea of "higher" and "lower" pleasures, that no hedonistic utilitarian has yet succeeded in telling this story, and, indeed, that it may be inconsistent for a hedonistic utilitarian to believe this. Other things being equal, if a plastic environment can give rise to pleasures equal in value to those arising out of a natural environment, we will have just as much or as little reason to preserve the latter as to manufacture the former. Moreover, if the pleasures flowing from the manufactured environment should happen to outweigh those accompanying the natural environment, we would then have greater reason to enlarge the world of plastic trees and reduce that of living ones.

The Embodiment of Cultural Values Argument

According to this argument, the natural environment, or certain parts of it, symbolize or express certain of our culture's value. In Sagoff's words, "Our rivers, forests, and wildlife . . . serve our society as paradigms of concepts we cherish," for example, freedom, integrity, power. "A wild area may be powerful, majestic, free; an animal may express courage, innocence, purpose, and strength. As a nation we value these qualities: the obligation toward nature is an obligation toward them." Thus, we are to preserve the environment because in doing so we preserve these natural expressions of the values of our culture.

This argument is not intended to be utilitarian. The claim is not made that the consequences of natural preservation will be better, all considered, if we preserve wilderness areas, for example, than if we allow their development for commercial purposes.

Whether we ought to preserve wilderness is not to be settled by cost–benefit analysis. Rather, since our obligation is to the cultural values themselves embodied in nature, our obligation to preserve the natural environment cannot be overridden by or, for that matter, based upon calculations about the comparative value of the consequences of respecting them. The propriety of respect for cultural values is not a consequence of its being useful to respect them. . . .

What the embodiment argument has in common with the other arguments considered here is the view that environmental objects have no value in their own right. This view is perhaps not so clear in this case because the embodiment argument carries with it "objectivist" presuppositions. Advocates of this argument do hold that the environment itself has certain objective qualities—for example, majesty, power, freedom. These *qualities* are *in* nature no less than are, say, chromosomes. But the *value* these qualities have is not something else that is *in them* independently of the dominant interest of a given culture ("our cultural heritage"). On the contrary, what qualities in nature are valuable is a consequence of what qualities are essential in one's cultural heritage. For example, if freedom is a dominant cultural value, then, since animals or rivers in the wild embody this quality, they have value and ought to be preserved. What *qualities* a natural object expresses is an objective question, but the *value* a natural object has is not something it has objectively in its own right, but only as it happens to embody those qualities valued by one's culture.

The embodiment argument provides an enormously important and potentially powerful basis for a political-legal argument on behalf of the preservation of American wilderness. It is easy to see how one may use it to argue for "what is best" in American society: freedom, integrity, independence, loyalty, and so on. It is the speculative developer rather than the conservationist who seems to be running roughshod over our nation's values. On this view, Disneyland, not Yosemite, seems un-American. Moreover, by insisting that such values as freedom and integrity cannot be trumped even if the consequences of doing so are utilitarian, advocates of the embodiment argument strike a blow that helps to counter the developer's argument that the commercial development of the wilderness will bring about better consequences, more pleasure to more people, than leaving it undeveloped. The embodiment argument replies that, though this may be true, it just so happens to be irrelevant. Given the nature of values such as freedom, integrity, and the like, it is inappropriate to destroy their expression in nature in the name of utilitarian consequences. The rhetorical force of such arguments can be great, and can be a powerful practical weapon in the war for the preservation of nature.

But the embodiment argument does not have comparable philosophical strength. Two problems in particular haunt it. First, how are we to establish what our culture's values are? Sagoff states that we are to do this by consulting our artistic (cultural) history. If we do this, however, we do not hear a chorus singing the same tune; on the contrary, there is much dissonance, some of which Sagoff himself mentions (e.g., the view of wilderness as an adversary to be tamed versus the view that it is to be cherished). Moreover, even if we were to arrive at a cultural consensus, the basis that Sagoff recommends is suspiciously elitist, reminding one of Ross's reference to "the judgment of the best people" in the determination of what is valuable. Implicit in Sagoff's way of establishing what our cultural values are is an evaluative estimate of whose judgment to trust. The cards are stacked against the developer from the outset, since developers normally do not have the time or inclination to dabble in arts, history, and letters. It is not surprising, therefore, that developers take a back seat to the values of freedom and integrity. The argument is indeed potentially a powerful political weapon, but fundamental questions go begging.

A second problem is no less severe. Cultural values can be relative, both between different cultures and within the same culture at different times. Thus, even were we to concede that *our* cultural values up to now call for the preservation of nature, that would entail nothing whatever about what environmental policies ought to be pushed in *other* countries (e.g., in Kenya or India, where many species of wild animals are endangered). Nor would it guarantee even in our own country that future environmental policy should continue to be protectionist. If plastic trees are possible, our culture might evolve to prefer them over real ones, in which case the embodiment of cultural values argument would sanction replacing natural with plastic flora and fauna.

Sagoff recognizes the possibility of significant changes in a culture's dominant values. He observes that we might "change the nature of our cultural heritage" and then goes on to imagine what a changed cultural heritage might be like—for example, imagining a four-lane highway painted through *Christina's World*. But I do not believe he realizes the full significance of the issues at hand. If, as he supposes, hedonistic utilitarianism falls victim to a *reductio* by allowing that a plastic environment might be just as good or better than a living one, consistency requires that we reach the same judgment *re* the embodiment of cultural values argument. That argument, too, allows that a plastic environment might be just as good or better than a natural one, *if* the dominant values of our culture were to become plasticized.

I conclude this section, therefore, not by claiming to have shown that nonconscious natural objects do have a good or value of their own, independent of human interests. I only conclude that the principal arguments that might be advanced for thinking that we can reasonably account for our duties regarding the environment short of postulating such value in nature fail to do so. Thus, neither the possibility of, nor the need for, postulating that nonconscious natural objects have a value that is independent of human interests, has been rationally undermined.

V. INHERENT GOODNESS?

In this final section, I offer some tentative remarks about the nature of inherent goodness, emphasizing their tentativeness and incompleteness. I comment first on five different but related ideas.

1. *The presence of inherent value in a natural object is independent of any awareness, interest, or appreciation of it by any conscious being.*

   This does not tell us what objects are inherently good or why, only that *if* an object is inherently good its value must *inhere in* (*be in*) the object itself. Inherent value is not conferred upon objects in the manner of an honorary degree. Like other properties in nature, it must be discovered. . . . There is value *in* the world, if natural objects are inherently valuable.

2. *The presence of inherent value in a natural object is a consequence of its possessing those other properties that it happens to possess.*

  This follows from (1), given the further assumption that inherent goodness is a consequential or supervenient property. By insisting that inherent goodness depends on an object's *own* properties, the point made in (1), that inherent goodness is a value possessed by the object independently of any awareness, is reemphasized. *Its* goodness depends on *its* properties.

3. *The inherent value of a natural object is an objective property of that object.*

  This differs from but is related to Sagoff's objectivity of the freedom and majesty of natural objects. Certain stretches of the Colorado River, for example, are free, not subjectively, but objectively. The freedom expressed by (or in) the river is an objective fact. But this goes beyond Sagoff's position by insisting that *the value of the river's being free* also is an objective property of the river. If the river is inherently good, in the sense explained in (1), then it is a *fact about the river* that it is good inherently.

4. *The inherent value of a natural object is such that toward it the fitting attitude is one of admiring respect.*

  This brings out the appropriateness of regarding what is inherently valuable in a certain way and thus provides a way of connecting what is inherently valuable in the environment with an ideal of human nature. In part, the ideal in question bids us be appreciative of the values nature holds, not merely as a resource to be used in the name of human interests, but inherently. The ideal bids us, further, to regard what is inherently valuable with both admiration and respect. Admiration is fitting because not everything in nature is inherently valuable (what *is* is to be admired both because of its value *and* because of its comparative uniqueness). Respect is appropriate because this is a fitting attitude to have toward whatever has value in its own right. One must realize that its being valuable is not contingent on one's happening to value it, so that to treat it *merely* as a means to human ends is to mistreat it. Such treatment shows a lack of respect for its being something that has value independently of these ends. Thus, I fall short of the ideal if I gratuitously destroy what has inherent value, or even if I regard it merely as having value only relative to human desires. But half the story about ideals of human nature remains untold if we leave out the part about the value inherent in those things toward what we can act in the ideal way. So it is vital to insist that our having ideals is neither to deny nor diminish the further point that this ideal requires postulating inherent value in nature, independently of these ideals.

5. *The admiring respect of what is inherently valuable in nature gives rise to the preservation principle.*

  By the "preservation principle" I mean a principle of nondestruction, noninterference, and, generally, nonmeddling. By characterizing this terms of a principle, moreover, I am emphasizing that preservation (letting be) be regarded as a moral imperative. Thus, if I regard wild stretches of the Colorado River as inherently valuable and regard these sections with admiring respect, I also think it is wrong to destroy these sections of the river; I think one ought not to meddle in the river's affairs, as it were.

A difficult question to answer is whether the preservation principle gives us a principle of absolute or of prima facie duty. It is unclear how it can be absolute, for it appears conceivable that in some cases letting be what is at present inherently good in nature may lead to value diminution or loss in the future. For example, because of various sedimentary changes, a river that is now wild and free might in time be transformed into a small, muddy creek; thus, it might be necessary to override the preservation principle to preserve or increase what is inherently valuable in nature. Even if the preservation principle is regarded as being only prima facie, however, it is still possible to agree on at least one point with those who regard it as absolute, that is, the common rejection of the "human interests principle," which says:

> Whenever human beings can benefit more from overriding the preservation principle than if they observe it, the preservation principle ought to be overridden.

This principle *must* be rejected by anyone who accepts the preservation principle because it distorts the very conception of goodness underlying that principle. If the sort of value natural objects possess is inherent, then one fails to show a proper respect for these objects if one is willing to destroy them merely on the grounds that this would benefit human beings. Since such destruction is precisely what the human interests principle commits one to, one cannot *both* accept the preservation principle, absolute or prima facie, *and* also accept the human interests principle. The common enemies of all preservationists are those who accept the human interests principle.

This brief discussion of the preservation principle may also cast some light on the problem of making intelligible cross-species value comparisons, for example, in the case of the survival of caribou versus the economic development of wilderness. The point preservationists must keep in mind is that to ask how many caribou lives equal in value the disvalue of how much economic loss is unanswerable because it is an improper question. It confounds two incommensurable kinds of good, the inherent good of the caribou with the noninherent good of economic benefits. Indeed, because these kinds of good are incommensurable, a utilitarian or consequentialist environmental ethic, which endeavors to accommodate both kinds of goodness, is doomed to fail. The inherent value of the caribou cannot be cashed in terms of human economic benefit, and such a theory ends up providing us with no clear moral direction. For the preservationist, the proper philosophical response to those who would uproot the environment in the name of human benefit is to say that they fail to understand the very notion of something being inherently good.

Two questions that I have not endeavored to answer are: (*a*) what, if anything in general, makes something inherently good, and (*b*) how can we know, if we can, what things are inherently good? The two questions are not unrelated. If we could establish that there is something (*x*) such that, whenever any object (*y*) has *x* it is inherently good, we could then go on to try to establish how we can know that any object has *x*. Unfortunately, I now have very little to say about these questions, and what little I do have to say concerns only how not to answer them.

Two possible answers to question (*a*) merit mention. The first is that an object (*x*) is inherently good if it is good of its kind. This is a view I have assumed and argued for elsewhere, but it now appears to me to be completely muddled. The concept of inherent goodness cannot be reduced to the notion of something being good of its kind, for though I believe that we can conceive of the goodness any *x* has, if *x* is good of its kind, as a value it has in its own right, there is no reason to believe that we ought to have the attitude of admiring respect toward what is (merely) good of its kind. A good murderer is good-of-his-kind, but is not thereby a proper object of admiring respect, and similarly in the case of natural objects. The type of inherent goodness required by an environmental ethic is conceptually distinct from being good of its kind.

The second possible answer to (*a*) is that life makes something inherently good. To what extent this view is connected with Schweitzer's famous ethic of reverence for life, or with Kenneth Goodpaster's recent argument for considering life as a necessary and sufficient condition of something being "morally considerable," I do not know, and I cannot here explore these matters in detail. But limiting the class of beings that have inherent value to the class of living beings seems to be an arbitrary decision and one that does not serve well as a basis for an environmental ethic. That it appears arbitrary is perhaps best seen by considering the case of beauty, since in nature, as in art, it is not essential to the beauty of an object to insist that something living be involved.

As for question (*b*), I have even less to say and that is negative also. My one point is that we cannot find out what is inherently good merely by finding out what those things are toward which we have admiring respect. All that this tells us is facts about the people who have this attitude. It does not tell us whether it is the fitting attitude to have. To put the point differently, we can be as mistaken in our judgment that something is inherently good as we can be in our judgment about how old or how heavy it is. Our feeling one way or another does not settle matters one way or the other.

How, then, are we to settle these matters? I wish I knew. I am not even certain that they can be settled in a rationally coherent way, and hence the tentativeness of my closing remarks. But more fundamentally, there is the earlier question about the very possibility of an environmental ethic. If I am right, the development of what can properly be called an environmental ethic requires that we postulate inherent value in nature. I have tried to say something about this variety of goodness as well as something about its role in an ethic of the environment. If my remarks have been intelligible and my arguments persuasive, then, though the project is far from complete, we at least know the direction in which we must move to make headway in environmental ethics. And that is no small advantage.

PETER SINGER

Not for Humans Only
The Place of Nonhumans in Environmental Issues

PETER SINGER teaches philosophy and directs the Center for Human Bioethics at Monash University in Australia. His best-known work is *Animal Liberation* (1975). He has written widely on civil disobedience and medical ethics.

When we humans change the environment in which we live, we often harm ourselves. If we discharge cadmium into a bay and eat shellfish from that bay, we become ill and may die. When our industries and automobiles pour noxious fumes into the atmosphere, we find a displeasing smell in the air, the long-term results of which may be every bit as deadly as cadmium poisoning. The harm that humans do the environment, however, does not rebound solely, even chiefly, on humans. It is nonhumans who bear the most direct burden of human interference with nature.

By "nonhumans" I mean to refer to all living things other than human beings, though for reasons to be given later, it is with nonhuman animals, rather than plants, that I am chiefly concerned. It is also important, in the context of environmental issues, to note that living things may be regarded either collectively or as individuals. In debates about the environment the most important way of regarding living things collectively has been to regard them as species. Thus, when environmentalists worry about the future of the blue whale, they usually are thinking of the blue whale as a species, rather than of individual blue whales. But this is not, of course, the only way in which one can think of blue whales, or other animals, and one of the topics I shall discuss is whether we should be concerned about what we are doing to the environment primarily in so far as it threatens entire species of nonhumans, or primarily insofar as it affects individual nonhuman animals.

The general question, then, is how the effects of our actions on the environment of nonhuman beings should figure in our deliberations about what we ought to do. There is an unlimited variety of contexts in which this issue could arise. To take just one: Suppose that it is considered necessary to build a new power station, and there are two sites, A and B, under consideration. In most respects the sites are equally suitable, but building the power station on site A would be more expensive because the greater depth of shifting soil at that site will require deeper foundations; on the other hand to build on site B will destroy a favored breeding ground for thousands of wildfowl. Should the presence of wildfowl enter into the decision as to where to build? And if so, in what manner should it enter, and how heavily should it weigh?

In a case like this the effects of our actions on nonhuman animals could be taken into account in two quite different ways: directly, giving the lives and welfare of non-human animals an intrinsic significance which must count in any moral calculation; or indirectly, so that the effects of our actions on nonhumans are morally significant only if they have consequences for humans.

It is the latter view which has been predominant in the Western tradition. Aristotle was among the founders of this tradition. He regarded nature as a hierarchy, in which the function of the less rational and hence less perfect beings was to serve the more rational and more perfect. So, he wrote:

> Plants exist for the sake of animals, and brute beasts for the sake of man—domestic animals for his use and food, wild ones (or at any rate most of them) for food and other accessories of life, such as clothing and various tools.
>
> Since nature makes nothing purposeless or in vain, it is undeniably true that she has made all animals for the sake of man.

If one major strain of Western thought came from Greece, the other dominant influence was that of Christianity. The early Christian writers were no more ready than Aristotle to give moral weight to the lives of non-human animals. When St. Paul, in interpreting the old Mosaic law against putting a muzzle on the ox that treads out the corn, asked: "Doth God care for oxen?" it is clear that he was asking a rhetorical question, to which the answer was "No"; the law must have somehow been meant "altogether for our sakes." Augustine agreed, using as evidence for the view that there are no common rights between humans and lesser living things, the incidents in the Gospels when Jesus sent devils into a herd of swine, causing them to hurl themselves into the sea, and with a curse withered a fig tree on which he had found no fruit.

It was Thomas Aquinas, blending Aristotle and the Christian writings, who put most clearly the view that any consideration of the lives or welfare of animals must be because of the indirect consequences of such consideration for humans. Echoing Aristotle, he maintained that plants exist for the sake of animals, and animals for the sake of man. Sins can only be against God, one's human neighbors, or against oneself. Even charity does not extend to "irrational creatures," for, among other things, they are not included in "the fellowship of everlasting happiness." We can love animals only "if we regard them as the good things that we desire for others," that is, "to God's honor and man's use." Yet if this was the correct view, as Aquinas thought, there was one problem that needed explaining: Why does the Old Testament have a few scattered injunctions against cruelty to animals, such as "The just man regardeth the life of his beast, but the bowels of the wicked are cruel?" Aquinas did not overlook such passages, but he did deny that their intention was to spare animals pain. Instead, he wrote, "it is evident that if a man practices a pitiable affection for animals, he is all the more disposed to take pity on his fellow-men." So, for Aquinas, the only sound reason for avoiding cruelty to animals was that it could lead to cruelty to humans.

The influence of Aquinas has been strong in the Roman Catholic church. Not even that oft-quoted exception to the standard Christian view of nature, Francis of Assisi, really broke away from the orthodox theology of his co-religionists. Despite his legendary kindness to animals, Francis could still write: "every creature proclaims: 'God made me for your sake, O man!'" As late as the nineteenth century, Pope Pius IX gave evidence of the continuing hold of the views of Paul, Augustine, and Aquinas by refusing to allow a society for the prevention of cruelty to animals to be established in Rome because to do so would imply that humans have duties toward animals.

It is not, however, only among Roman Catholics that a view like that of Aquinas has found adherents. Calvin, for instance, had no doubt that all of nature was created specifically for its usefulness to man; and in the late eighteenth century, Immanuel Kant, in lecturing on ethics, considered the question of our duties to animals, and told his students: "So far as animals are concerned, we have no direct duties. Animals are not self-conscious and are there merely as a means to an end. That end is man." And Kant then repeated the line that cruelty to animals is to be avoided because it leads to cruelty to humans.

The view that the effects of our actions on other animals has no direct moral significance is not as likely to be openly advocated today as it was in the past; yet it is likely to be accepted implicitly and acted upon. When planners perform cost-benefit studies on new projects, the costs and benefits are costs and benefits for human beings only. This does not mean that the impact of the power station or highway on wildlife is ignored altogether, but it is included only indirectly. That a new reservoir would drown a valley teeming with wildlife is taken into account only under some such heading as the value of the facilities for recreation that the valley affords. In calculating this value, the cost-benefit study will be neutral between forms of recreation like hunting and shooting and those like bird watching and bush walking—in fact hunting and shooting are likely to contribute more to the benefit side of the calculations because larger sums of money are spent on them, and they therefore benefit manufacturers and retailers of firearms as well as the hunters and shooters themselves. The suffering experienced by the animals whose habitat is flooded is not reckoned into the costs of the operation; nor is the recreational value obtained by the hunters and shooters offset by the cost to the animals that their recreation involves.

Despite its venerable origins, the view that the effects of our actions on nonhuman animals have no intrinsic moral significance can be shown to be arbitrary and morally indefensible. If a being suffers, the fact that it is not a member of our own species cannot be a moral reason for failing to take its suffering into account. This becomes obvious if we consider the analogous attempt by white slaveowners to deny consideration to the interests of blacks. These white racists limited their moral concern to their own race, so the suffering of a black did not have the same moral significance as the suffering of a white. We now recognize that in doing so they were making an arbitrary distinction, and that the existence of suffering, rather than the race of the sufferer, is what is really morally significant. The point remains true if "species" is substituted for "race." The logic of racism and the logic of the position we have been discussing which I have elsewhere referred to as "speciesism," are indistinguishable; and if we reject the former then consistency demands that we reject the latter too.

It should be clearly understood that the rejection of speciesism does not imply that the different species are in fact equal in respect of such characteristics as intelligence, physical strength, ability to communicate, capacity to suffer, ability to damage the environment, or anything else. After all, the moral principle of human equality cannot be taken as implying that all humans are equal in these respects either—if it did, we would have to give up the idea of human equality. That one being is more intelligent than another does not entitle him to enslave, exploit, or disregard the interests of the less intelligent being. The moral basis of equality among humans is not equality in fact, but the principle of equal consideration of interests, and it is this principle that, in consistency, must be extended to any nonhumans who have interests.

There may be some doubt about whether any nonhuman beings have interests. This doubt may arise because of uncertainty about what it is to have an interest, or because of uncertainty about the nature of some nonhuman beings. So far as the concept of "interest" is the cause of doubt, I take the view that only a being with subjective experiences, such as the experience of pleasure or the experience of pain, can have interests in the full sense of the term; and that any being with such experiences does have at least one interest, namely, the interest in experiencing pleasure and avoiding pain. Thus consciousness, or the capacity for subjective experience, is both a necessary and a sufficient condition for having an interest. While there may be a loose sense of the term in which we can say that it is in the interests of a tree to be watered, this attenuated sense of the term is not the sense covered by the principle of equal consideration of interests. All we mean when we say that it is in the interests of a tree to be watered is that the tree needs water if it is to continue to live and grow normally; if we regard this as evidence that the tree has interests, we might almost as well say that it is in the interests of a car to be lubricated regularly because the car needs lubrication if it is to run properly. In neither case can we really mean (unless we impute consciousness to trees or cars) that the tree or car has any preference about the matter.

The remaining doubt about whether nonhuman beings have interests is, then, a doubt about whether nonhuman beings have subjective experiences like the experience of pain. I have argued elsewhere that the commonsense view that birds and mammals feel pain is well founded; but more serious doubt arise as we move down the evolutionary scale. Vertebrate animals have nervous systems broadly similar to our own and behave in ways that resemble our own pain behavior when subjected to stimuli that we would find painful; so the inference that vertebrates are capable of feeling pain is a reasonable one, though not as strong as it is if limited to mammals and birds. When we go beyond vertebrates to insects, crustaceans, mollusks and so on, the existence of subjective states becomes more dubious, and with very simple organisms it is difficult to believe that they could be conscious. As for plants, though there have been sensational claims that plants are not only conscious, but even psychic, there is no hard evidence that supports even the more modest claim.

The boundary of beings who may be taken as having interests is therefore not an abrupt boundary, but a broad range in which the assumption that the being has interests shifts from being so strong as to be virtually certain to being so weak as to be highly improbable. The principle of equal consideration of interests must be applied with this in mind, so that where there is a clash between a virtually certain interest and a highly doubtful one, it is the virtually certain interest that ought to prevail.

In this manner our moral concern ought to extend to all beings who have interests. Unlike race or species, this boundary does not arbitrarily exclude any being; indeed it can truly be said that it excludes nothing at all, not even "the most contemptible clod of earth" from equal consideration of interests—for full consideration of no interests still results in no weight being given to whatever was considered, just as multiplying zero by a million still results in zero.

Giving equal consideration to the interests of two different beings does not mean treating them alike or holding their lives to be of equal value. We may recognize that the interests of one being are greater than those of another, and equal consideration will then lead us to sacrifice the being with lesser interests, if one or the other must be sacrificed. For instance, if for some reason a choice has to be made between saving the life of a normal human being and that of a dog, we might well decide to save the human because he, with his greater awareness of what is going to happen, will suffer more before he dies; we may also take into account the likelihood that it is the family and friends of the human who will suffer more; and finally, it would be the human who had the greater potential for future happiness. This decision would be in accordance with the principle of equal consideration of interests, for the interests of the dog get the same consideration as those of the human, and the loss to the dog is not discounted because the dog is not a member of our species. The outcome is as it is because the balance of interests favors the human. In a different situation—say, if the human were grossly mentally defective and without family or anyone else who would grieve for it—the balance of interests might favor the nonhuman.

The more positive side of the principle of equal consideration is this: where interests are equal, they must be given equal weight. So where human and nonhuman animals share an interest—as in the case of the interest in avoiding physical pain—we must give as much weight to violations of the interest of the nonhumans as we do to similar violations of the human's interest. This does not mean, of course, that it is as bad to hit a horse with a stick as it is to hit a human being, for the same blow would cause less pain to the animal with the tougher skin. The principle holds between similar amounts of felt pain, and what this will vary from case to case.

It may be objected that we cannot tell exactly how much pain another animal is suffering, and that therefore the principle is impossible to apply. While I do not deny the difficulty and even, so far as precise measurement is concerned, the impossibility of comparing the subjective experiences of members of different species, I do not think that the problem is different in kind from the problem of comparing the subjective experiences of two members of our own species. Yet this is something we do all the time, for instance when we judge that a wealthy person will suffer less by being taxed at a higher rate than a poor person will gain from the welfare benefits paid for by the tax; or when we decide to take our two children to the beach instead of to a fair, because although the older one would prefer the fair, the younger one has a stronger preference the other way. These comparisons may be very rough, but since there is nothing better, we must use them; it would be irrational to refuse to do so simply because they are rough. Moreover, rough as they are, there are many situations in which we can be reasonably sure which way the balance of interests lies. While a difference of species may make comparisons rougher still, the basic problem is the same, and the comparisons are still often good enough to use, in the absence of anything more precise. . . .

We can now draw at least one conclusion as to how the existence of nonhuman living things should enter into our deliberations about actions affecting the environment: Where our actions are likely to make animals suffer, that suffering must count in our deliberations, and it should count equally with a like amount of suffering by human beings, insofar as rough comparisons can be made.

The difficulty of making the required comparison will mean that the application of this conclusion is controversial in many cases, but there will be some situations in which it is clear enough. Take, for instance, the wholesale poisoning of animals that is euphemistically known as "pest control." The authorities who conduct these campaigns give no consideration to the suffering they inflict on the "pests," and invariably use the method of slaughter they believe to be cheapest and most effective. The result is that hundreds of millions of rabbits have died agonizing deaths from the artificially introduced disease, myxomatosis, or from poisons like "ten-eighty"; coyotes and other wild dogs have died painfully from cyanide poisoning; and all manner of wild animals have endured days of thirst, hunger, and fear with a mangled limb caught in a leg-hold trap. Granting, for the sake of argument, the necessity for pest control—though this has rightly been questioned—the fact remains that no serious attempts have been made to introduce alternative means of control and thereby reduce the incalculable amount of suffering caused by present methods. It would not, presumably, be beyond modern science to produce a substance which, when eaten by rabbits or coyotes, produces sterility instead of a drawn-out death. Such methods might be more expensive, but can anyone doubt that if a similar amount of human suffering were at stake, the expense would be borne?

Another clear instance in which the principle of equal consideration of interests would indicate methods different from those presently used is in the timber industry. There are two basic methods of obtaining timber from forests. One is to cut only selected mature or dead trees, leaving the forest substantially intact. The other, known as clear-cutting, involves chopping down everything that grows in a given area, and then re-seeding. Obviously when a large area is clear-cut, wild animals find their whole living area destroyed in a few days, whereas selected felling makes a relatively minor disturbance. But clear-cutting is cheaper, and timber companies therefore use this method and will continue to do so unless forced to do otherwise.

This initial conclusion about how the effects of our actions on nonhuman animals should be taken into account is the only one which follows directly from the argument that I have given against the view that only actions affecting our own species have intrinsic moral significance. There are, however, other suggestions which I shall make more tentatively which are at least consistent with the preceding argument, although much more discussion would be needed to establish them.

The first of these suggestions is that while the suffering of human and nonhuman animals should, as I have said, count equally, the killing of nonhuman animals is in itself not as significant as the killing of normal human beings. Some of the reasons for this have already been discussed—the probable greater grief of the family and friends of the human, and the human's greater potential. To this can be added the fact that other animals will not be made to fear for their own lives, as humans would, by the knowledge that others of their species have been killed. There is also the fact that normal humans are beings with foresight and plans for the future, and to cut these plans off in midstream seems a greater wrong than that which is done in killing a being without the capacity for reflection on the future.

All these reasons will seem to some not to touch the heart of the matter, which is the killing itself and not the circumstances surrounding it; and it is for this reason that I have put forward this view as a suggestion rather than a firm conclusion. For it might be held that the taking of life is intrinsically wrong—and equally wrong whatever the characteristics of the life that was taken. This, perhaps, was the view that Schweitzer held and which has become famous under his memorable if less than crystal-clear phrase, "reverence for life." If this view could be supported, then of course we would have to hold that the killing of nonhuman animals, however painless, is as serious as the killing of humans. Yet I find Schweitzer's position difficult to justify. What is it that is so valuable in the life of, say, a fly, which presumably does not itself have any awareness of the value of its own life, and the death of which will not be a source of regret to any member of its own species or of any other species? . . .

For Schweitzer, life itself is sacred, not even consciousness being necessary. So the truly ethical man, he says, will not tear a leaf from a tree or break off a flower unnecessarily. Not surprisingly, given the breadth of its coverage, it is impossible for the ethic of reverence for life to be absolute in its prohibitions. We must take plant life, at least, if we are to eat and live. Schweitzer therefore accepts the taking of one form of life to preserve another form of life. Indeed, Schweitzer's whole life as a doctor in Africa makes no sense except on the assumption that the lives of the human beings he was saving are more valuable than the lives of the germs and parasites he was destroying in their bodies, not to mention the plants and probably animals that those humans would kill and eat after Schweitzer had cured them. So I suggest that the idea that all life has equal value, or is equally sacred, lacks a plausible theoretical basis and was not, in practice, adhered to even by the man whose name is most often linked with it. . . .

To this point we have been discussing the place of individual nonhuman animals in environmental issues, and we have seen that an impartial consideration of their interests provides sufficient reason to show that present human attitudes and practices involving environmental issues are morally unjustifiable. Although this conclusion is, I think, obvious enough to anyone who thinks about the issue along the lines just discussed, there is one aspect of it that is in sharp contrast to an underlying assumption of much environmental debate, an assumption accepted even by many who consider themselves for animals and against the arrogant "human chauvinism" that sees all of nature as a resource to be harvested or a pit for the disposal of wastes. This assumption is that concern for nonhuman animals is appropriate when a whole species is endangered, but not when the threat is only to individual animals. It is in accordance with this assumption that the National Wildlife Federation has sought and obtained a court injunction preventing the U.S. Department of Transportation from building an interstate highway interchange in an area frequented by the extremely rare Mississippi sandhill crane, while the same organization openly supports what it calls "the hunter-sportsman who, during legal hunting seasons, crops surplus wildlife." Similarly the National Audubon Society has fought to preserve rare birds and other animals but opposed moves to stop the annual slaughter of 40,000 seals on the Pribilof Islands of Alaska on the grounds that this "harvest" could be sustained indefinitely, and the protests were thus "without foundation from a conservation and biological viewpoint." Other "environmentalist" organizations which either actively support or refuse to oppose hunting include the Sierra Club, the Wilderness Society, and the World Wildlife Fund.

Since we have already seen that animals' interests in avoiding suffering are to be given equal weight to our own, and since it is sufficiently obvious that hunting makes animals suffer—for one thing, no hunter kills instantly every time—I shall not discuss the ethics of hunting, though I cannot resist inviting the reader to think about the assumptions behind the use of such images as the "cropping" of "surplus wildlife" or the "harvesting" of seals. The remaining ethical issue that needs to be discussed is whether it is still worse to hunt or otherwise to kill animals of endangered species than it is to kill those of species that are plentiful. In other words, suppose that groups like the National Wildlife Federation were to see the error of their prohunting views, and swing round to opposition to hunting. Would they nevertheless be justified in putting greater efforts into stopping the shooting of the Mississippi sandhill crane than into stopping duck-shooting? If so, why?

Some reasons for an affirmative answer are not hard to find. For instance, if we allow species to become extinct, we shall deprive ourselves and our descendants of the pleasures of observing all of the variety of species that we can observe today. Anyone who has ever regretted not being able to see a great auk must have some sympathy with this view. Then again, we never know what ecological role a given species plays, or may play under some unpredictable change of circumstances. Books on ecology are full of stories about how farmers/the health department/the army/the Forestry Commission decided to get rid of a particular rodent/bird/fish/insect because it was a bit of a nuisance, only to find that that particular animal was the chief restraint on the rate of increase of some much nastier and less easily eradicated pest. Even if a species has already been reduced to the point where its total extinction could not have much "environmental impact" in the sense of triggering off other changes, it is always possible that in the future conditions will change, the species will prove better adapted to the new conditions than its rivals, and will flourish, playing an important part in the new ecological balance in its area to the advantage of humans living there. Yet another reason for seeking to preserve species is that, as is often said, the removal of a species depletes the "gene pool" and thus reduces the possibility of "improving" existing domestic or otherwise useful animals by crossbreeding with related wild animals. We do now know what qualities we may want domestic animals to have in the future. It may be that existing breeds lack resistance to a build-up of toxic chemicals or to a new disease that may break out in some remote place and sweep across our planet; but by interbreeding domestic animals with rare wild varieties, we might be able to confer greater resistance on the former, or greater usefulness to humans on the latter.

These reasons for preserving animals of endangered species have something in common: They are all concerned with benefits or dangers for humans. To regard these as the only reasons for preserving species is to take a position similar to that of Aquinas and Kant, who, as we saw earlier, thought cruelty to animals wrong only because it might indirectly harm human beings. We dismissed that argument on the grounds that if human suffering is intrinsically bad, then it is arbitrary to maintain that animal suffering is of no intrinsic significance. Can we similarly dismiss the view that species should be preserved only because of the benefits of preservation to humans? It might seem that we should, but it is not easy to justify doing so. While individual animals have interests, and no morally defensible line can be drawn between human interests and the interests of nonhuman animals, species as such are not conscious entities and so do not have interests above and beyond the interests of the individual animals that are members of the species. These individual interests are certainly potent reasons against killing rare animals, but they are no more potent in the case of rare animals than in the case of common animals. The rarity of the blue whale does not cause it to suffer any more (nor any less) when harpooned than the more common sperm whale. On what basis, then, other than the indirect benefits to humans, can we justifiably give preference to the preserving of animals of endangered species rather than animals of species that are not in any danger?

One obvious answer, on the basis of the foregoing, is that we ought to give preference to preserving animals of endangered species if so doing will have indirect benefits for nonhuman animals. This may sometimes be the case, for if the extinction of a species can lead to far-reaching ecological damage, this is likely to be bad for nonhuman animals as well as for humans. Yet this answer to our question, while extending the grounds for preserving species beyond the narrow limits of human benefits, still provides no basis for attributing intrinsic value to preservation. To find such a basis we need an answer to the following modified version of the question asked above: On what basis, other than the indirect benefits to humans or other animals, can we justifiably give preference to the preserving of animals of endangered species rather than animals of species that are not in danger?

To this question I can find no satisfactory answer. The most promising suggestion, perhaps, is that the destruction of a whole species is the destruction of something akin to a great work of art; that the tiger, or any other of the "immensely complex and inimitable items produced in nature" has its own, noninstrumental value, just as a great painting or cathedral has value apart from the pleasure and inspiration it brings to human beings. On this view, to exterminate a species is to commit an act of vandalism, like setting about Michelangelo's *Pietà* with a hammer; while allowing an endangered species to die out without taking steps to save it is like allowing Angkor Wat to fall into ruins and be obliterated by the jungle.

My difficulty with this argument is a difficulty with the allegedly less controversial case on which the analogy is built. If the analogy is to succeed in persuading us that there may be intrinsic value quite independently of any benefits for sentient beings in the existence of a species, we must believe that there is this kind of intrinsic value in the existence of works of art; but how can it be shown that the *Pietà* has value independently of the appreciation of those who have seen or will see it? If, as philosophers are fond of asking, I were the last sentient being on earth, would it matter if, in a moment of boredom, I entertained myself by making a bonfire of all the paintings in the Louvre? My own view is that it would not matter—provided, of course, I really could exclude the possibility that, as I stood around the dying embers, a flying saucer would not land and disgorge a load of tourists from Alpha Centauri who had come all the way solely in order to see the Mona Lisa. But there are those who take the opposite view, and I would agree that *if* works of art have intrinsic value, then it is plausible to suppose that species have too.

I conclude, then, that unless or until better grounds are advanced, the only reasons for being more concerned about the interests of animals from endangered species than about other animals are those which relate the preservation of species to benefits for humans and other animals. The significance of these reasons will vary from case to case, depending on such factors as just how different the endangered species really is from other nonendangered species. For instance, if it takes an expert ornithologist to tell a Mississippi sandhill crane from other, more common cranes (and I have no knowledge of whether this is so), then the argument for preservation based on the pleasures of observing a variety of species cannot carry much weight in this case, for this pleasure would be available only to a few people. Similarly, the value of retaining species that perhaps will one day be usefully crossbred with domestic species will not apply to species that have no connection with any domestic animal; and the importance we place on this reason for preserving species will also depend on the importance we place on domestic animals. If, as I have argued elsewhere, it is generally both inefficient and inhumane to raise animals for food, we are not going to be greatly moved by the thought of "improving" our livestock. Finally, although the argument that the greater the variety of species, the better the chances of a smooth adjustment to environmental changes, is usually a powerful one, it has little application to endangered species that differ only marginally and in ecologically insignificant ways—like minor differences in the markings of birds—from related, nonendangered species.

This conclusion may seem unfavorable to the efforts of environmental groups to preserve endangered species. I would not wish it to be taken in that way. Often the indirect reasons for preservation will make an overwhelming case for preservation; and in any case we must remember that what we have been discussing is not whether to defend animals against those who would kill them and deprive them of their habitat but whether to give preference to defending animals of endangered species. Defending endangered species is, after all, defending individual animals too. If we are more likely to stop the cruel form of commercial hunting known as whaling by pointing out that blue whales may become extinct than by pointing out that blue whales are sentient creatures with lives of their own to lead, then by all means let us point out that blue whales may become extinct. If, however, the commercial whalers should limit their slaughter to what they call the "maximum sustainable yield" and so cease to be a threat to blue whales as a species, let us not forget that they remain a threat to thousands of individual blue whales. My aim throughout this essay has been to increase the importance we give to individual animals when discussing environmental issues, and not to decrease the importance we presently place on defending animals which are members of endangered species.

ALDO LEOPOLD

The Land Ethic

ALDO LEOPOLD (1887–1948) was a pioneer in the field of wildlife conservation. He was a scientist and author of more than 350 articles on science and wildlife management. He is best known for *A Sand County Almanac* (1948), from which this selection is taken, and for the text *Game Management,* which is still in use today. His articulation of the environmental ethic is considered by many to be the classic statement on that subject. He died of a heart attack while helping his neighbors fight a grass fire.

When god-like Odysseus returned from the wars in Troy, he hanged all on one rope a dozen slave-girls of his household whom he suspected of misbehavior during his absence.

This hanging involved no question of propriety. The girls were property. The disposal of property was then, as now, a matter of expediency, not of right and wrong.

Concepts of right and wrong were not lacking from Odysseus' Greece: witness the fidelity of his wife through the long years before at last his black-prowed galleys clove the wine-dark seas for home. The ethical structure of that day covered wives, but had not yet been extended to human chattels. During the three thousand years which have since elapsed, ethical criteria have been extended to many fields of conduct, with corresponding shrinkages in those judged by expediency only.

THE ETHICAL SEQUENCE

This extension of ethics, so far studied only by philosophers, is actually a process in ecological evolution. Its sequences may be described in ecological as well as in philosophical terms. An ethic, ecologically, is a limitation on freedom of action in the struggle for existence. An ethic, philosophically, is a differentiation of social from anti-social conduct. These are two definitions of one thing. The thing has its origin in the tendency of interdependent individuals or groups to evolve modes of co-operation. The ecologist calls these symbioses. Politics and economics are advanced symbioses in which the original free-for-all competition has been replaced, in part, by co-operative mechanisms with an ethical content.

The complexity of co-operative mechanisms has increased with population density, and with the efficiency of tools. It was simpler, for example, to define the anti-social uses of sticks and stones in the days of the mastodons than of bullets and billboards in the age of motors.

The first ethics dealt with the relation between individuals; the Mosaic Decalogue [the Ten Commandments] is an example. Later accretions dealt with the relation between the individual and society. The Golden Rule tries to integrate the individual to society; democracy to integrate social organization to the individual.

There is as yet no ethic dealing with man's relation to land and to the animals and plants which grow upon it. Land, like Odysseus' slave-girls, is still property. The land-relation is still strictly economic, entailing privileges but not obligations.

The extension of ethics to this third element in human environment is, if I read the evidence correctly, an evolutionary possibility and an ecological necessity. It is the third step in a sequence. The first two have already been taken. Individual thinkers since the days of Ezekel and Isaiah have asserted that the despoliation of land is not only inexpedient but wrong. Society, however, has not yet affirmed their belief. I regard the present conservation movement as the embryo of such an affirmation.

An ethic may be regarded as a mode of guidance for meeting ecological situations so new or intricate, or involving such deferred reactions, that the path of social expediency is not discernible to the average individual. Animal instincts are models of guidance for the individual in meeting such situations. Ethics are possibly a kind of community instinct in-the-making.

THE COMMUNITY CONCEPT

All ethics so far evolved rest upon a single premise: that the individual is a member of a community of interdependent parts. His instincts prompt him to compete for his place in that community, but his ethics prompt him also to cooperate (perhaps in order that there may be a place to compete for).

The land ethic simply enlarges the boundaries of the community to include soils, water, plants, and animals, or collectively: the land.

This sounds simple: do we not already sing our love for and obligation to the land of the free and the home of the brave? Yes, but just what and whom do we love? Certainly not the soil, which we are sending helter-skelter downriver. Certainly not the waters, which we assume have no function except to turn turbines, float barges, and carry off sewage. Certainly not the plants, of which we exterminate whole communities without batting an eye. Certainly not the animals, of which we have already extirpated many of the largest and most beautiful species. A land ethic of course cannot prevent the alteration, management, and use of these 'resources,' but it does affirm their right to continued existence, and, at least in spots, their continued existence in a natural state.

In short, a land ethic changes the role of *Homo sapiens* from conqueror of the land-community to plain member and citizen of it. It implies respect for his fellow-members, and also respect for the community as such.

In human history, we have learned (I hope) that the conqueror role is eventually self-defeating. Why? Because it is implicit in such a role that the conqueror knows, *ex cathedra*, just what makes the community clock tick, and just what and who is valuable, and what and who is worthless, in community life. It always turns out that he knows neither, and this is why his conquests eventually defeat themselves.

In the biotic community, a parallel situation exists. Abraham knew exactly what the land was for: it was to drip milk and honey into Abraham's mouth. At the present moment, the assurance with which we regard this assumption is inverse to the degree of our education.

The ordinary citizen today assumes that science knows what makes the community clock tick; the scientist is equally sure that he does not. He knows that the biotic mechanism is so complex that its workings may never be fully understood.

That man is, in fact, only a member of a biotic team is shown by an ecological interpretation of history. Many historical events, hitherto explained solely in terms of human enterprise, were actually biotic interactions between people and land. The characteristics of the land determined the facts quite as potently as the characteristics of the men who lived on it.

Consider, for example, the settlement of the Mississippi valley. In the years following the Revolution, three groups were contending for its control: the native Indian, the French and English traders, and the American settlers. Historians wonder what would have happened if the English at Detroit had thrown a little more weight into the Indian side of those tipsy scales which decided the outcome of the colonial migration into the cane-lands of Kentucky. It is time now to ponder the fact that the cane-lands, when subjected to the particular mixture of forces represented by the cow, plow, fire, and axe of the pioneer, became bluegrass. What if the plant succession inherent in this dark and bloody ground had, under the impact of these forces, given us some worthless sedge, shrub, or weed? Would Boone and Kenton have held out? Would there have been any overflow into Ohio, Indiana, Illinois, and Missouri? Any Louisiana Purchase? Any transcontinental union of new states? Any Civil War?

Kentucky was one sentence in the drama of history. We are commonly told what the human actors in this drama tried to do, but we are seldom told that their success, or the lack of it, hung in large degree on the reaction of particular soils to the impact of the particular forces exerted by their occupancy. In the case of Kentucky, we do not even know where the bluegrass came from—whether it is a native species, or a stowaway from Europe.

Contrast the cane-lands with what hindsight tells us about the Southwest, where the pioneers were equally brave, resourceful, and persevering. The impact of occupancy here brought no bluegrass, or other plant fitted to withstand the bumps and buffetings of hard use. This region, when grazed by livestock, reverted through a series of more and more worthless grasses, shrubs, and weeds to a condition of unstable equilibrium. Each recession of plant types bred erosion; each increment to erosion bred a further recession of plants. The result today is a progressive and mutual deterioration, not only of plants and soils, but of the animal community subsisting thereon. The early settlers did not expect this: on the ciénegas [marshes] of New Mexico some even cut ditches to hasten it. So subtle has been its progress that few residents of the region are aware of it. It is quite invisible to the tourist who finds this wrecked landscape colorful and charming (as indeed it is, but it bears scant resemblance to what it was in 1848). . . .

In short, the plant succession steered the course of history; the pioneer simply demonstrated, for good or ill, what successions inhered in the land. Is history taught in this spirit? It will be, once the concept of land as a community really penetrates our intellectual life.

THE ECOLOGICAL CONSCIENCE

Conservation is a state of harmony between men and land. Despite nearly a century of propaganda, conservation still proceeds at a snail's pace; progress still consists largely of letterhead pieties and convention oratory. On the back forty we still slip two steps backward for each forward stride.

The usual answer to this dilemma is 'more conservation education.' No one will debate this, but is it certain that only the *volume* of education needs stepping up? Is something lacking in the *content* as well?

It is difficult to give a fair summary of its content in brief form, but, as I understand it, the content is substantially this: obey the law, vote right, join some organizations, and practice what conservation is profitable on your own land; the government will do the rest.

Is not this formula too easy to accomplish anything worth-while? It defines no right or wrong, assigns no obligation, calls for no sacrifice, implies no change in the current philosophy of values. In respect of land-use, it urges only enlightened self-interest. Just how far will such education take us? . . .

No important change in ethics was ever accomplished without an internal change in our intellectual emphasis, loyalties, affections, and convictions. The proof that conservation has not yet touched these foundations of conduct lies in the fact that philosophy and religion have not yet heard of it. In our attempt to make conservation easy, we have made it trivial.

SUBSTITUTES FOR A LAND ETHIC

When the logic of history hungers for bread and we hand out a stone, we are at pains to explain how much the stone resembles bread. I now describe some of the stones which serve in lieu of a land ethic.

One basic weakness in a conservation system based wholly on economic motives is that most members of the land community have no economic value. Wildflowers and songbirds are examples. Of the 22,000 higher plants and animals native to Wisconsin, it is doubtful whether more than 5 per cent can be sold, fed, eaten, or otherwise put to economic use. Yet these creatures are members of the biotic community, and if (as I believe) its stability depends on its integrity, they are entitled to continuance.

When one of these non-economic categories is threatened, and if we happen to love it, we invent subterfuges to give it economic importance. At the beginning of the century songbirds were supposed to be disappearing. Ornithologists jumped to the rescue with some distinctly shaky evidence to the effect that insects would eat us up if birds failed to control them. The evidence had to be economic on order to be valid.

It is painful to read these circumlocutions today. We have no land ethic yet, but we have at least drawn nearer the point of admitting that birds should continue as a matter of biotic right, regardless of the presence or absence of economic advantage to us.

A parallel situation exists in respect of predatory mammals, raptorial birds, and fish-eating birds. Time was when biologists somewhat overworked the evidence that these creatures preserve the health of game by killing weaklings, or that they control rodents for the farmer, or that they prey only on 'worthless' species. Here again, the evidence had to be economic in order to be valid. It is only in recent years that we hear the more honest argument that predators are members of the community, and that no special interest has the right to exterminate them for the sake of a benefit, real or fancied, to itself. Unfortunately this enlightened view is still in the talk stage. In the field the extermination of predators goes merrily on: witness the impending erasure of the timber wolf by fiat of Congress, the Conservation Bureaus, and many state legislatures. . . .

When the private landowner is asked to perform some unprofitable act for the good of the community, he today assents only with outstretched palm. If the act costs him cash this is fair and proper, but when it costs only forethought, open-mindedness, or time, the issue is at least debatable. The overwhelming growth of land-use subsidies in recent years must be ascribed, in large part, to the government's own agencies for conservation education: the land bureaus, the agricultural colleges, and the extension services. As far as I can detect, no ethical obligation toward land is taught in these institutions.

To sum up: a system of conservation based solely on economic self-interest is hopelessly lopsided. It tends to ignore, and thus eventually to eliminate, many elements in the land community that lack commercial value, but that are (as far as we know) essential to its healthy functioning. It assumes, falsely, I think, that the economic parts of the biotic clock will function without the uneconomic parts. It tends to relegate to government many functions eventually too large, too complex, or too widely dispersed to be performed by government.

An ethical obligation on the part of the private owner is the only visible remedy for these situations. . . .

LAND HEALTH AND THE A–B CLEAVAGE

A land ethic, then, reflects the existence of an ecological conscience, and this in turn reflects a conviction of individual responsibility for the health of the land. Health is the capacity of the land for self-renewal. Conservation is our effort to understand and preserve this capacity.

Conservationists are notorious for their dissensions. Superficially these seem to add up to mere confusion, but a more careful scrutiny reveals a single plane of cleavage common to many specialized fields. In each field one group (A) regards the land as soil, and its function as commodity-production; another group (B) regards the land as a biota, and its function as something broader. How much broader is admittedly in a state of doubt and confusion.

In my own field, forestry, group A is quite content to grow trees like cabbages, with cellulose as the basic forest commodity. It feels no inhibition against violence; its ideology is agronomic. Group B, on the other hand, sees forestry as fundamentally different from agronomy because it employs natural species, and manages a natural environment rather than creating an artificial one. Group B prefers natural reproduction on principle. It worries on biotic as well as economic grounds about the loss of species like chestnut, and the threatened loss of the white pines. It worries about a whole series of secondary forest functions: wildlife, recreation, watersheds, wilderness areas. To my mind, Group B feels the stirrings of an ecological conscience.

In the wildlife field, a parallel cleavage exists. For Group A the basic commodities are sport and meat; the yardsticks of production are ciphers of take in pheasants and trout. Artificial propagation is acceptable as a permanent as well as a temporary recourse—if its unit costs permit. Group B, on the other hand, worries about a whole series of biotic side-issues. What is the cost in predators of producing a game crop? Should we have further recourse to exotics? How can management restore the shrinking species, like prairie grouse, already hopeless as shootable game? How can management restore the threatened rarities, like trumpeter swan and whooping crane? Can management principles be extended to wildflowers? Here again it is clear to me that we have the same A–B cleavage as in forestry. . . .

In all of these cleavages, we see repeated the same basic paradoxes; man the conqueror *versus* man the biotic citizen; science the sharpener of his sword *versus* science the searchlight on his universe; land the slave and servant *versus* land the collective organism. Robinson's injunction to Tristram may well be applied, at this juncture, to *Homo sapiens* as a species in geological time:

> Whether you will or not
> You are a king, Tristram, for you are one
> Of the time-tested few that leave the world,
> When they are gone, not the same place it was.
> Mark what you leave.

THE OUTLOOK

It is inconceivable to me that an ethical relation to land can exist without love, respect, and admiration for land, and a high regard for its value. By value, I of course mean something far broader than mere economic value; I mean value in the philosophical sense.

Perhaps the most serious obstacle impeding the evolution of a land ethic is the fact that our educational and economic system is headed away from, rather than toward, an intense consciousness of land. Your true modern is separated from the land by many middlemen, and by innumerable physical gadgets. He has no vital relation to it; to him it is the space between cities on which crops grow. Turn him loose for a day on the land, and if the spot does not happen to be a golf links or a 'scenic' area, he is bored stiff. If crops could be raised by hydroponics instead of farming, it would suit him very well. Synthetic substitutes for wood, leather, wool, and other natural land products suit him better than the originals. In short, land is something he has 'outgrown.'

Almost equally serious as an obstacle to a land ethic is the attitude of the farmer for whom the land is still an adversary, or a taskmaster that keeps him in slavery. Theoretically, the mechanization of farming ought to cut the farmer's chains, but whether it really does is debatable.

One of the requisites for an ecological comprehension of land is an understanding of ecology, and this is by no means co-extensive with 'education'; in fact, much higher education seems deliberately to avoid ecological concepts. An understanding of ecology does not necessarily originate in courses bearing ecological labels; it is quite as likely to be labeled geography, botany, agronomy, history, or economics. This is as it should be, but whatever the label, ecological training is scarce.

The case for a land ethic would appear hopeless but for the minority which is in obvious revolt against these 'modern' trends.

The 'key-log' which must be moved to release the evolutionary process for an ethic is simply this: quit thinking about decent land-use as solely an economic problem. Examine each question in terms of what is ethically and esthetically right, as well as what is economically expedient. A thing is right when it tends to preserve the integrity, stability, and beauty of the biotic community. It is wrong when it tends otherwise.

It of course goes without saying that economic feasibility limits the tether of what can or cannot be done for land. It always has and it always will. The fallacy the economic determinists have tied around our collective neck, and which we now need to cast off, is the belief that economics determines *all* land-use. This is simply not true. An innumerable host of actions and attitudes, comprising perhaps the bulk of all land relations, is determined by the land-users' tastes and predilections, rather than by his purse. The bulk of all land relations hinges on investments of time, forethought, skill, and faith rather than on investments of cash. As a land-user thinketh, so is he.

I have purposely presented the land ethic as a product of social evolution because nothing so important as an ethic is ever 'written.' Only the most superficial student of history supposes that Moses 'wrote' the Decalogue; it evolved in the minds of a thinking community, and Moses wrote a tentative summary of it for a 'seminar.' I say tentative because evolution never stops.

The evolution of a land ethic is an intellectual as well as emotional process. Conservation is paved with good intentions which prove to be futile, or even dangerous, because they are devoid of critical understanding either of the land, or of economic land-use. I think it is a truism that as the ethical frontier advances from the individual to the community, its intellectual content increases.

The mechanism of operation is the same for any ethic: social approbation for right actions: social disapproval for wrong actions.

By and large, our present problem is one of attitudes and implements. We are remodeling the Alhambra with a steamshovel, and we are proud of our yardage. We shall hardly relinquish the shovel, which after all has many good points, but we are in need of gentler and more objective criteria for its successful use.

MARK SAGOFF

Animal Liberation and Environmental Ethics
Bad Marriage, Quick Divorce

MARK SAGOFF works at the Center for Philosophy and Public Policy at the University of Maryland at College Park. He is president of the International Society for Environmental Studies.

"The land ethic," Aldo Leopold wrote in *A Sand County Almanac,* "simply enlarges the boundaries of the community to include soils, waters, plants, and animals, or collectively, the land." What kind of community does Leopold refer to? He might mean a *moral* community, a group of individuals who respect each other's right to treatment as equals or who regard one another's interests with equal respect and concern. Leopold may also mean an *ecological* community, a community tied together by biological relationships in interdependent webs of life.

Let us suppose, for a moment, that Leopold has a *moral* community in mind; he would expand our *moral* boundaries to include soils, waters, plants, and animals, as well as human beings. Leopold's view, then, might not differ in principle from that of Christopher Stone, who has suggested that animals and even trees be given legal standing, so that their interests may be represented in court. Stone sees the expansion of our moral consciousness in this way as part of a historical progress in which societies have recognized the equality of groups of oppressed people, notably blacks, women, and children.

Peter Singer, perhaps more than any other writer, has emphasized the analogy between human liberation movements (e.g., abolitionism and suffragism) and "animal liberation" or the "expansion of our moral horizons" to include members of other species in "the basic principle of equality." Singer differs from Stone in arguing that the question whether animals have *rights* is less important than it appears: "what matters is how we think animals ought to be treated, and not how we employ the concept of a right." He also confines membership in the moral community to beings with the "capacity for subjective experience, such as the experience of pleasure or the experience of pain." But Stone and Singer agree that we have a moral obligation to minimize the suffering of animals and to balance their interests against our own.

MOTHER NATURE VS. FRANK PERDUE

What practical course of action should we take once we have climbed the spiral of moral evolution high enough to recognize our obligation to value the rights, interests, or welfare of animals equally with our own? In discussing the rights of human beings,

Henry Shue describes two that are basic in the sense that "the enjoyment of them is essential to the enjoyment of all other rights." These are the right to physical security and the right to minimum subsistence. These, surely, are basic to animal rights as well. To allow animals to be killed, to permit them to die of disease or starvation, when it is within our power to prevent it, surely seems not to balance their interests with our own.

Where, then, shall we begin to provide for the basic welfare—the security and subsistence—of animals? Plainly, where they most lack this security, where their basic rights, needs, or interests are most thwarted and where their suffering is the most intense. This is in nature. Ever since Darwin, we have been aware that few organisms survive to reach sexual maturity; most are quickly annihilated in the struggle for existence.

Consider this rough but reasonable statement of the facts, given by Fred Hapgood: "All species reproduce to excess, way past the carrying capacity of their niche. In her lifetime a lioness might have 20 cubs; a pigeon, 150 chicks; a mouse, 1,000 kits; a trout, 20,000 fry; a tuna or cod, a million fry or more; an elm tree, several million seeds; and an oyster, perhaps a hundred million spat. If one assumes that the population of each of these species is, from generation to generation, roughly equal, then on the average only one offspring will survive to replace each parent. All the other thousands and millions will die, one way or another."

The way creatures in nature die are typically violent: predation, starvation, disease, parasitism, cold. If the dying animal in the wild understood his condition, what would he think? Surely, he would prefer to be raised on a farm, where his chances of survival would be good and to escape from the wild, where they are negligible. Either way, the animal will be killed; few die of old age. The path from birth to slaughter, however, is nearly always longer and less painful in the barnyard than in the woods. The misery of animals in nature beggars by comparison every other form of suffering in the world. Mother Nature is so cruel to her children she makes [chicken magnate] Frank Perdue look like a saint.

I do not know how animal liberationists, such as Singer, propose to relieve animal suffering in nature, but there are many ways we could greatly improve the situation at little cost to ourselves. It may not be beyond the reach of science to attempt a broad program of contraceptive care for animals in nature so that fewer will fall victim to an early and horrible death. One may propose, with all modesty, the conversion of our national wilderness areas, especially our national parks, into farms in order to replace violent wild areas with humane, managed environments. Animals and trees would then benefit from the same efficient and productive technology that benefits us.

My point in raising this argument is to suggest that the thesis that animals have important rights and interests that command our respect has little bearing on the policies it is supposed by some to support, in particular, policies intended to preserve and protect the natural environment. We must ask ourselves whether in fact the kind of policies environmentalists recommend would make animals better off in the long run. I see no reason at all to suppose that they would.

CAN ENVIRONMENTALISTS BE HUNTERS?

In a persuasive essay, J. Baird Callicott describes a number of differences between the idea of Aldo Leopold and those of Peter Singer—differences, which suggest Leopold's environmental ethic and Singer's humanitarianism lead in opposite directions. First, while Singer and other animal liberationists deplore the suffering of domestic animals, "Leopold manifests an attitude that can only be described as indifference." Second, while Leopold expresses an urgent concern about the disappearance of species, Singer, consistently with his premises, is concerned with the welfare of individual animals, without special regard to their status as endangered species.

Third, wilderness, according to Leopold, provides "a means of perpetuating, in sport form, the more virile and primitive skills. . . ." He had hunting in mind. Hunters, since top predators are gone, may serve an important ecological function. Leopold was himself an enthusiastic hunter and wrote unabashedly about his exploits pursuing game. The term "game" as applied to animals, Callicott wryly comments, "appears to be morally equivalent to referring to a sexually appealing young woman as a 'piece' or to a strong, young black man a 'buck'—if animal rights, that is, are to be considered on a par with women's rights and the rights of formerly enslaved races."

Hunting is what disturbs animal liberationists as much as any other human activity. Singer expresses disdain and chagrin at what he calls "'environmentalist'" organizations which actively support or refuse to oppose hunting, such as the Sierra Club and the World Wildlife Fund. I can appreciate Singer's aversion to hunting, but why does he place the word "environmentalist" in shudder quotes when he refers to organizations like the Sierra Club? Environmentalist and conservationist organizations traditionally have been concerned with ecological, not with humanitarian, issues. They make no pretense to improving the lot of individual animals; they attempt rather to maintain the diversity, integrity, beauty, and authenticity of the natural environment. These goals are ecological, not eleemosynary. They are entirely consistent with licensing hunters to shoot animals whose populations exceed the carrying capacity of their habitats.

I do not in any way mean to support the practice of hunting; nor am I advocating environmentalism at this time. I merely want to point out that groups like the Sierra Club, the Wilderness Society, and the World Wildlife Fund do not fail in their mission insofar as they devote themselves to causes other than the happiness or welfare of individual creatures; that never was their mission. These organizations, which promote a love and respect for the functioning of natural ecosystems, differ ideologically from organizations that make the suffering of animals their primary concern—groups like the Fund for Animals, the Animal Protection Institute, Friends of Animals, the American Humane Association, and various single issue groups such as Friends of the Sea Otter, Beaver Defenders, Friends of the Earthworm, and Worldwide Fair Play for Frogs.

I proposed earlier that Aldo Leopold views the community of nature as a *moral community*—one in which we, as members, have obligations to all other animals, presumably to minimize their pain. I suggested that Leopold, like Singer, may be committed to the idea that we should preserve and respect the natural environment only insofar as that promotes the welfare of the individual animals nature contains. This is plainly not Leopold's view, however. The principle of natural selection is not a humanitarian principle; the predator—prey relation does not depend on moral empathy. Nature ruthlessly limits animal populations by doing violence to virtually every individual before it reaches maturity. These conditions respect animal equality only in the darkest sense. Yet these are precisely the ecological relationships which Leopold admires; they are the conditions which he would not interfere with, but protect. Leopold, apparently, does not think that an ecological system has to be a moral system in order to deserve our love. An ecological order to deserve our love. An ecological system has a beauty and an authenticity we can admire—but not on humanitarian grounds.

ANIMAL LIBERATION AND ENVIRONMENTAL LAW

Muckraking journalists, thank God for them, who depict the horrors that all too often occur in laboratories and on farms, appeal, quite properly, to our conviction that mankind should never inflict needless pain on animals, especially for the sake of profit. When we read stories about man's cruelty to domestic animals, we respond, as we should, with moral outrage and revulsion. When we read accounts of natural history, which reveal as much suffering and slaughter, we do not respond with outrage or indignation. Why not? The reason is plain. It is not suffering per se that concerns us. What outrages us is human responsibility for that suffering.

Moral obligations to animals may arise in either of two ways. Our duties to nonhuman animals may be based on the principle that cruelty to animals is obnoxious, a principle nobody denies. These obligations, however, might rest instead on the stronger contention that we are obliged to prevent and to relieve animal suffering wherever it occurs and however it is caused; that we are obliged to protect the welfare of *all* animals just because they are sentient beings.

Animal liberationists insist, as Singer does, that moral obligations to animals are justified by their distress and by our ability to relieve that distress. Accordingly, the liberationist must ask: how can I most efficiently relieve animal suffering? The answer must be: by getting animals out of the natural environment. Starving deer in the woods might be adopted as pets; they might be fed in kennels. Birds that now kill earthworms may repair instead to birdhouses stocked with food—including textured soybean protein that looks and smells like worms. And to protect the brutes from cold, we might heat their dens or provide shelter for the all too many who freeze.

Now, whether you believe that this harangue is a *reductio ad absurdum* of Singer's position or whether you think it should be taken seriously as an ideal is no concern to me. I merely wish to point out that an environmentist must take what I have said as a *reductio* whereas an animal liberationist must regard it as stating a serious position. An environmentalist cannot be an animal liberationist; nor may animal liberationists be environmentalists. The environmentalist would sacrifice the welfare of individual creatures to preserve the authenticity, integrity, and complexity of ecological systems. The liberationist must be willing to sacrifice the authenticity, integrity, and complexity of ecosystems for the welfare of animals. A humanitarian ethic will not help us to understand or to justify an environmental ethic. It will not provide new foundations for environmental law.

ANNETTE BAIER

For the Sake of Future Generations

ANNETTE BAIER taught at the University of Pittsburgh. Her interests are the history of modern philosophy, especially Hume's philosophy, ethics, and philosophy of mind. Some of her most important essays are collected in her books, *Postures of the Mind* (1985) and *Moral Prejudices* (1994). She currently works in New Zealand.

I. INTRODUCTION

Moral philosophers have only quite recently worried over the question of what we are morally obliged to do, or not to do, for the sake of persons who will live after we are dead. Classical moral traditions give us little help with this question. Though ordinary common sense moralities have usually regarded waste as immoral, and have recognized a vague general obligation to leave our camping places as clean as we found them, such popular moral beliefs are not specific about exactly what our duties to future people are, nor about the ground of such obligations—whether for example their basis lies in the rights of our successors to a fair share in what we might squander, to a camping site no dirtier than that enjoyed by their predecessors. We do not find most older moral theorists addressing the questions of what is due to future persons, why it is due, nor how any such moral dues link up with what is due to those persons whose lives overlap with our own.

§1 Seeing into the Future

Several explanations might be offered for this recent emergence of the question of obligations to future persons. The increase in our ability or sense of our ability to foresee the long-term effects of our policies might be thought to explain it. As long as persons could not see how their actions affected later generations, they could not be expected to feel any obligation to bring about good rather than bad effects. Our recently won confidence that we do control the fate of future persons brings with it a moral burden, responsibility for what we knowingly do. As long as our ancestors did not know what they did to us, and could not reasonably be expected to have known it, they cannot be blamed for any ill effects they produced, nor praised for any good effects. We, rightly or wrongly, feel we can estimate the effects of our policies, we think we know just how our great-great-grandchildren's teeth will be set on edge by the sour grapes we eat. . . .

§2 Laws and Consequences

Consequentialist moral theories see the moral status of actions to depend on their good or bad effects. But as long as doing the right thing is equated with doing what one believes God requires, one does not need to know about the long-term consequences of one's actions to discern right and wrong. One can leave it to God to see to it that our doing the right thing does some good to someone or something, at some time or other. The immorality of, say, willful waste, will be thought to lie not in its causal link with woeful want, but in divine prohibition of wasteful policies. A belief in divine goodwill toward human beings will lead the believer to expect that there is *some* link between the content of the divinely ordained moral law and human welfare, but not a link we need to discern in order to know what is right. Then it would make sense to praise past persons for their great acts, from which we do in fact benefit, without thereby praising them *for* benefiting us. We might praise them because they did what was right or virtuous, and praise God that the consequences of their virtuous action for us are beneficial rather than harmful. For a non-consequentialist moral theory, it is possible that there are duties whose discharge does benefit future generations, yet which are not duties *to* those future generations. They might be the beneficiaries of our obligations, without being either those to whom the obligations are owed, or those for whose sake the obligatory action must be done. "Against thee only have I sinned," said David to God, not thereby denying that his sinful action (arranging the death of his ladylove's husband, [Uriah]) harmed another human, nor even that God prohibits such acts *because* they harm other humans. If our duties are to God and His law, our moral task would not be to fathom God's reasons, but to obey, trusting in the goodness of the will whose word is law. For such a religious non-consequentialist, it might be wrong to squander resources, poison air and water, and the like, not because future generations would thereby suffer (although this consequence of wrongful action is foreseen) but simply because God and His moral law forbids it. Future persons could condemn us for such wrongful action, action which in fact hurt them, but would do so not because it hurt them but because it was wrong, contrary to God's will and so to the moral law.

§3 From Religious Ethics to Secular Ethics

One does not need to equate morality with the revealed content of God's will or God's law in order to be a non-consequentialist in moral theory. The great German philosopher Immanuel Kant (1724–1804) believed that human reason could discern the moral law, and that we need know neither about God's will nor about the actual long-run consequences of individual right and wrong acts in order to recognize this law. Just as it is in the power of human reason, in its scientific employment, to discern regularities or laws which hold good in physical nature, so reason in its practical employment can recognize law—indeed can *make* law to govern human behavior. The moral lawmaker, Kant claimed, was the individual acting as if setting an example all other persons would follow. For us to know what acts to perform, what example to try to set, theoretical predictive reason often has to help practical legislative reason, in order to work out what would be involved if everyone followed a particular example. But once we are satisfied that we can will that everyone follow our example of, say, ceasing to make nuclear weapons, then we have established that policy as morally right, and are not to consider as morally relevant the *actual* consequences of this policy in the real world where others may not and often do not all follow our example. The right thing to do must be seen to have acceptable consequences *were everyone to do likewise*, but may not have good consequences when done only by some. "Let justice be done, though the earth perish," or, in this case, although the just person or just nation perishes.

This complex moral theory of Kant's both gives our power to envisage consequences of various policies an important role to play in moral reasoning, yet does not identify the right action with that which will in the actual state of things have the best consequences. Kant still needs and keeps a divine power in the background of morality, a power who is to see to it that the discrepancy between ideal and real world consequences is somehow compensated for, some day, so that obedience to the moral law does not, *in the end*, prove destructive to those who do what is right or to the world they would will into being. Kant's is a non-consequentialist moral theory where the test of moral rightness is the rational acceptability of hypothetical *universal* conformity to a policy, and of the consequences over time of such conformity. We are to do the act which we can will as universal law in "a system of nature," that is, in an ongoing world with interaction and feedback.

This ethical theory holds that some promise of applicability to the question of our duty to future persons, since any practice like dumping toxic wastes where they will poison soil, air, or water seems forbidden by Kant's test—we cannot conceive of a system of nature in which all humans regularly do this, yet survive as a species. It is not a coherently universalizable practice. Some, such as the contemporary Australian philosopher John Passmore, have seen Kant's ethics as addressing the question of our obligations to future persons, and there is no doubt that Kant's test of moral rightness can easily be applied to condemn many current practices, and also that the very form of his *test* for rightness (Can I will this as a law in a system of nature?) forces us to think about the long-term implications of policies. But, as far as I know, Kant did not himself actually draw out the consequences of his theory for this issue. He did make some claims about our *motivation*—he believed that we cannot help but care to some degree about future persons and the sort of life they will have—but he did not spell out what our duty to such persons is, or even if there are any special duties we owe them. To find out whether we do wrong if we refuse to help our contemporaries when they are in need, Kant's test forces us to consider what our world would be like, over time, if such refusal were the universal rule; so to discern our duty to anybody, we must in a sense think of everybody, future persons included, according to Kant's test. Future persons therefore come into his theory implicitly, but not as ones whose interests give rise to any *special* problems about duties on our part. Future persons themselves, and the foreseeable consequences of our actions for them, come into Kant's theory only indirectly. His theory is usable only by moral agents capable of seeing the long-run implications of policies for whole systems, natural and social, and he believed that we moral agents do in fact care about the future of the human world, but he did not spell out any particular obligations we have or, for that matter, which we fail to have, to future persons.

§4 Modern Moral Theories and the Person-Affecting Principle

Post-Kantian moral theories, both utilitarian and some *rights* theories, have focused attention very strongly on the *effects* of right and wrong actions on the good of human persons, often making this the decisive test of their rightness or wrongness. They see human moral agents, not some supervising God, as responsible for the foreseeable effects of their actions. Modern moral theorists, while agreed on seeing morality as promoting our human good, disagree over what precise effect on human (and perhaps animal) good determines the moral rightness of an action: Utilitarians see the crucial thing to be the effect of an action or policy on people's *happiness,* others emphasize the effect on *interests,* while those who hold a theory of rights (either rights arising from a hypothetical agreement, or so-called natural rights) see the crucial question to be the effect of an action on people as rights holders.

The violation of a right is, of course, a special sort of effect on a person and on his or her good. It cannot be equated with making that person unhappier, or less able to get what she in fact wants. If I don't want to vote, then the violation of my right to vote by the removal of my name from electoral rolls will not hurt me—it may not even be noticed by me. Nevertheless someone else on my behalf might correctly protest the violation of my right, and correctly say that my position is worsened by this inability to do what in fact I have no wish to do. I might even myself protest, and insist on my rights, then never exercise them. Once we see ourselves as right holders, the violation of our rights becomes an injury, even if it makes no *other* difference to our lives. The violation of my rights affects my position among right holders, even if that position is not very important to my particular goals in life. I shall return to this question of the relation between what affects our happiness and what affects our interests and our position among persons in §10. For the moment I want merely to draw attention to the agreement between most utilitarians and most of those who hold a rights theory that the moral wrongness of an act consists in some sort of bad effect it has on people.

The principle which they agree upon (but which religious moralists, or even Kantians, need not accept) has been called the *Person-Affecting Principle,* which says *that for any action to be wrong, it must affect some person or persons (usually other than the agent) for the worse.* This is a minimal requirement of wrongness—the principle does not say that all acts which have any bad effects on others are wrong, but only that, if an action has *no* bad effect on anyone, it cannot be really wrong. . . .

The *Person-Affecting Principle* directs us always to think of the consequences of our actions for other people, when making a moral decision. It is natural, if one finds the principle plausible, to think of consequences for future people as well as for our contemporaries, and to see a moral agent's responsibility as extending to the foreseeable effects of our actions on future and distant as well as present and close persons. . . .

Paradoxically enough, however, that same Person-Affecting Principle which seems to direct us to think about future persons has been invoked by some recent thinkers to reveal a problem in the very idea that future people could possibly be our victims. I turn next to that worry.

II. THE FUTURITY PROBLEM

§5 Our Knowledge of Future People

There are several features of future people, in relation to us, which can make the idea that we have duties to them seem problematic. I shall consider their *unknowability, their indeterminacy,* and their *contingency.* We do not know much about all those children who will be born during the next seven months, although their genetic makeup is now quite fixed and determinate. For people further in the future, not only *do* we not know details about them, those details are not yet fixed, so are unknowable. Such lack of knowledge, especially when due to the not-yet-determinate status of future people, does, I think, rule out our having to them one kind of duty which we can have to our contemporaries. For example, some people now living are accustomed to a particular diet, and *could* not easily adapt to a different one. There would be no point in shipping canned pork and beans off to avert a famine in a Muslim country—the people could not eat it. We know, or can find out, this sort of special need, when we are considering the effects of our policies on our contemporaries, but we cannot know this sort of fact about distant future people. Since they are not yet determinate people, their special requirements are as yet unknowable. *Some* wrongs we can do to our contemporaries, those harmings which depend upon their special needs, we cannot knowingly do to future persons. Their indeterminacy protects us against the charge of doing them that sort of wrong.

But such wrongs, although real, are only one sort of wrong we can do people, and there are plenty of other wrongs which do not depend upon the victims' special needs, but on their common human nature. However little we know about future people, however much about them is not yet fixed, as long as they are human people they can be expected to need air, water, some fruits of the earth to eat. They will be vulnerable to poisons, just as we are, and we can, it seems, affect the availability to them of the unpoisoned air, water, soil, undestroyed naturally self-renewing or self-cleansing basic physical resources, which we as a species need. By the Person-Affecting Principle then, as far as we have seen, there can be wrongs to future persons despite their indeterminacy and our ignorance of their special needs. The principle will not itself tell us how bad the effects of our action must be for future persons to have been wronged, but it allows room for the idea that we really can wrong future persons. So far so good.

There is, however, the third characteristic of future persons to consider, namely their *contingency*. Not merely is their identity now indeterminate, but what will eventually fix it are a host of causal factor is including the actions and inactions of their predecessors. It is *this* fact, the *contingency of future people on their predecessors*, which generates what has come to be seen as the worst philosophical "problem of futurity," one which might seem to cancel all duties we may have thought we had to future persons. I turn to that problem.

§6 The Ontological Precariousness of Persons

A thing is ontologically precarious, precarious in its very being, to the extent that its coming into being is dependent on other things. To appreciate just how precarious we all are, or were, we need merely think of the many possible things our parents might have done which would have led to our own nonbeing, to our total absence from the human scene. Not merely do deliberate parental actions of family planning determine which children come to exist, but all sorts of outside factors determining the precise time of conception also play their role—such things as owl hootings or train whistles which wake potential parents in the night. The English philosopher Derek Parfit, who has in the last ten years in a number of influential papers explored this problem thoroughly, asks how many of us could truly claim that we would have existed even if railways had never been invented. A recent electricity blackout in the city of New York was followed nine months later by a significantly increased number of births. As time goes on, the number of descendants of these "blackout babies" will probably become larger and larger, so that factors such as trains and blackouts come to figure in causal ancestry of a larger and larger proportion of the population.

Philosophers have long been aware of this radical contingency of particular existent things on earlier happenings, of the reverberating effects of seemingly trivial events, given a long enough time. In metaphysical discussions of causal determinism, and in theological discussions of divine predestination, the implications of this dependency of future on past realities have often been explored, and moral philosophers have often worried about the implications of this interrelatedness of things for our free will and moral responsibility for what we do or fail to do. Recently the implications for our responsibility for and to future people have been drawn out by Parfit and others.

§7 Wanting the Past to Have Been Different

If anyone's existence would have been prevented by so many thinkable changes in earlier history, it seems to follow that there are severe constraints on seriously judging that it would have been better if some earlier event, no matter how bad it may seem, had not occurred. In particular, one must consider the likelihood that, had it not occurred, one would not have existed at all to do any judging.

I am inclined to judge that the potato famine in Ireland and food shortages in Scotland in the nineteenth century were bad things, and that it would have been better if those in charge of agricultural policy in Britain had made different decisions which would have averted those hard times. Then I reflect that my great-grandparents left Britain for New Zealand because of those very hard times. Had they not done so, they would not have met one another, married, had the children they did. Had the famine been averted, their great-grandchildren, if any, would have been *other* possible people, and I would not have existed. So do I *sincerely* judge that it would have been better had the past been different, had those persons who, as things actually turned out, did have me as a great-grandchild had a less difficult life, had not been faced with famine? I will sincerely make this judgment only if I can sincerely say that it would have been better, all things considered, that I not have existed. (Alternative interpretations of this judgment are examined below, in §9.) So it is not as easy as one might have thought to judge that it would have been better for the past to have been other than it was. Even to wish that one's own parents had been richer, or more fortunate, or healthier than they were in youth becomes hard, since any change in their lives before the time of one's own conception probably would have brought with it one's own nonexistence.

§8 The No Obligation Argument

Let us now see how this presumed fact, the extreme ontological precariousness of persons (and indeed of all other particular things), and the consequent difficulty of wanting the past to have been different, can be made to yield the conclusion that we have no obligations to future persons. We need to add, to what I shall call the *precariousness* premise (P), a version of the Person-Affecting Principle which I will call the *victim* premise (V), which says that a person has not been wronged by another unless he has been made worse off by the other's act, unless, that is, he is thereby the other's victim. Now we can construct a simple argument from P and V, to give us the conclusion C that nothing which we do can wrong future persons unless what we do is so bad that future persons wish they had never been born. To spell it our more fully:

V. We do not wrong a person by our current action or policy unless it would have been better for that person had we not acted that way.

P. For any actual future person F, the outcome had we not done what we are doing would (in all likelihood) have been that F not exist at all, rather than that F exist and be better off.

C. Unless it would have been better for F not to exist at all, we are (in all likelihood) not wronging F by what we are doing.

This argument, if it works, works whatever our actions are—however wasteful, depleting, or polluting. As long as future persons are not so affected by our actions that they can make a charge of "wrongful existence" against us, they have no complaint against us, since they cannot claim to have been wronged by what we did. The only wrong, it seems, that we can do future persons is to allow them to exist in an intolerable world. As long as that world is tolerable enough for them not to regret existing, they are not wronged by our world-spoiling activities. No future person will be able to say to us (or to our ghosts), "If you had acted rightly, *I* would have had a better life."

This is a very troubling argument. What troubles most of us about it is that the conclusion seems at odds with our moral intuitions on this matter. For, once the issue has been raised, most of us do feel that we would be wronging our successors by unrestrainedly depleting and polluting the earth even if that did not render their lives intolerable. We may be unclear exactly what we must, in decency, do for the sake of future person . . . , but most of us do feel not only that it is wrong to pollute and deplete, but also that it is "future people," in some sense of that phrase, who are the ones who are wronged if we act wrongly in this regard. The contemporary American political philosopher Thomas Schwartz, when he propounded an early version of our argument above, concluded not that we were free to do what we liked, as far as the consequences for the world future people will live in goes, but rather that *we owe it to one another*, to our *contemporaries* who do happen to care about humanity's future, to restrain our earth-ravaging activities. If Schwartz is right we will have sinned only against our contemporaries, if we poison the wells of the future; we will not have sinned against the persons who suffer the poisoning.

Now although it is good to have our conviction that we are not morally free to pollute the earth endorsed and given some basis, despite the troublesome argument we are examining, I think that we still are apt to feel that Schwartz's proposed basis for our obligations is not the right one. Many of us also care about the future of various precious artworks, or other nonsentient things. If we have a duty to preserve such things, it is a duty to our fellow art lovers, not to the artworks themselves. It seems wrong to put our concern for our successors in the same moral boat as our concern for the future of anything else which happens at present to have a place in our affections. Surely it must be in some sense for future persons' sakes, not just for our own sakes, that we consider what sort of existence for them our actions entail? If Schwartz is right, then if we could make ourselves or let ourselves cease to feel concerned about the future of our human communities, then we would be rid not only of a sense of obligation not to pollute but also of the obligation itself. If it is only that "those who would like our distant descendants to enjoy a clean commodious well stocked world just may owe it to their like-minded contemporaries to contribute to these goals," then if we all cultivate indifference, cease to care, we can come to owe nothing to anyone in this regard. Can this be right? For whose sake, and for whose good, ought we conserve scarce resources and refrain from putting delayed-action poisons in our common wells—if, that is, we do have a duty to conserve and not to poison? To help us see if it can be said to be for the sake of future persons, despite the troubling argument, we need first to have a closer look at the conclusion C, and the qualification in that conclusion. When would a person judge that it would have been better, for her *own* sake, that she not have been born?

§9 Better for One Not to Have Been Born

We have already seen in §7 how one can become committed to the judgment that it would have been better if one had not been born. One is committed to this if one seriously judges that some event such as a famine (without whose occurrence one would not have been born) was a bad thing, better averted. But such a judgment (if we ever really do make it) is made from an attempted God's-eye view, so to speak, one that takes into account *all* those who are involved. It is not made from one's own self-concerned standpoint, since one might make it although one's own life was pleasant enough, or was until one starts being obsessed with what went into one's own "prehistory," the human cost of one's own existence. To make the issues clearer, we need to distinguish two "objective" judgments from two subjective judgments. The former are judgments about the comparative value of alternative "world histories," made from no particular person's point of view, while the latter are judgments about a particular life history, made from the point of view of the one whose life it is.

O_1 All things considered, the world history (after some chosen fixed point) where F comes to exist is, given the causal chains which produced F, and the nature of F's life, worse than alternative world histories in which F does not exist.

O_2 The world history containing F's life is, because of F's own dreadfully intolerable life, *thereby* a worse world history than alternative world histories in which F's existence is prevented.

We could only make this second objective judgment if we (or F) could make one of two more subjective judgments, ones made from F's own point of view:

S_1 For F's own sake, or from her own self-concerned point of view, the sooner her life ends the better.

S_2 For F's own sake, or from her own self-concerned point of view, it would have been better if her life had never started.

The qualification in C, the conclusion of the No Obligation Argument, seems to refer only to those cases where the judgment O_2 could be made, and this in turn requires us to make either S_1 or S_2. Which of them does O_2 presuppose?

I think that S_2 is what is needed to support O_2. S_1 is the judgment made by most suicides, but a person need not be driven to suicide in order to judge S_2 and to have a valid claim of wrongful existence against someone. There are powerful forces, religious, instinctive, and altruistic, which may prevent even desperately unhappy people from ending their own lives even when they judge S_2. Nor is it true that one need judge S_2 in order to judge S_1. One's life can *become* intolerable enough to make one judge S_1 although long stretches of it were good and one would not judge S_2. For one to judge S_2, one's life would have had to be continuously intolerable, or some bits so bad that they clearly outweighed the good bits, when weighed not from a momentary but from a "life's eye" point of view. One does not need to suppose that a suicide's life was as bad as that, bad enough to support S_2, in order to understand how suicide can look the best option. But it is just this very strong judgment, S_2, which F would need to make to charge her predecessors with wronging her by allowing her to exist at all.

The conclusion, C, of the No Obligation Argument then, presupposes that S_2 makes sense, that it is conceivable that a person could be wronged by having been allowed to come into existence at all. Persons who judge S_2 are victims of previous events or actions in a sense which is *wider*, or different, than that in which our contemporaries are victims of our assault or neglect. In the latter case, we can say that the victim's *life* is worse than it would have been without the assault or neglect. But the victims of earlier events who are driven to S_2 judgments about their own lives are not complaining that they don't have lives better in this or that respect, they are complaining that they are, and ever were, alive at all, given their life prospects. This means that we must interpret premise V in a fairly wide way, to include this sort of victim, if V is to be even *compatible* with giving any sense to C, the conclusion which is supposed to follow from V and P. The argument itself requires us to recognize that not all victims of policies are victims because their *lives* would have been better in some respect if someone had done something different, rather some people are victims because they are alive—period. This fact will become important in the following sections when I try to diagnose the fault of the No Obligation Argument.

§10 Varieties of Victims, Varieties of Ills

So far we have seen that there can be victims of events and policies, those who judge S_2, whose claim is not that their lives would have been better had those events not occurred. Earlier, in §4, we said that one can be affected for good or ill by a policy or action in a variety of ways. One's rights may be violated, even when one might not need to exercise those rights to further the interests one in fact has. Similarly, one's interests can be injured, say by loss of a job opportunity, or a pension scheme, even when one would not have wanted that job and does not yet care about one's old age. Normally what advances one's interests *does* help one get what one wants, and getting what one wants does make one happy, but one's interests can be injured without that affecting one's getting what one wanted, and one's wants can be frustrated, although getting what one wanted would not have made one happy. Misery, frustration, injury to one's interests, violation or denial of rights, all unfavorably affect a person's good but can do so in different ways. The good of a person is complex since persons are and usually see themselves as bearers of rights, possessors of interests, as well as goal-directed and sentient. To act for the sake of some person or group is to act to advance any of these components of their good. The good of persons, seen prospectively, includes more than what will in fact give them happiness, since they may not be aware of some of their interests, so not be unhappy at their nonadvancement, and they may neither know nor care about some violations of their rights. One needs not only to be fully self-conscious but also to have what today we call a "raised consciousness" for one's feeling of happiness to reflect the level to which one's rights and interests as well as one's purposes and tastes are respected.

As I am using the term "interests," we have an interest in the obtaining *conditions*, or *states of affairs*, such as our own good health, our prosperity, peace in our time, liberty, where these conditions are favorable for our success in satisfying a whole range of particular desires we have and expect to have in the future. The sort of things a parent or godparent wishes for a child are general goods of this sort, conditions which will enable the child to acquire and cultivate ambitions, desires, and tastes which can in those conditions be satisfied, and give pleasure when satisfied. Although it might occasionally turn out that these conditions are *not* needed or even favorable for the satisfaction of the actual desires the child comes to have, as a general rule the furthering of one's interests *does* increase the extent to which one's desires get satisfied, just as normally getting what one desired does give one the pleasure one expected it would. In acting in the interests of a person, we are trying to increase their *prospects* of satisfying their desires, and so, normally, of being happy with the outcome.

As a person grows from childhood to adulthood, and tastes and concerns become formed, these very general interests, shared with almost all persons, become specified in ways which often limit the number of other persons with whom we share them. An interest in peace in our time will become associated with an interest in the success of the political party whose plan for peace one judges the best one. One will have an interest not only in health but in the maintenance of a specific health insurance scheme, not just in prosperity but in the wise policies of certain banks and corporations, not just in liberty but in the removal of some specific threats to liberty. However specific one's interests become, they usually are still specifications of interests most people have, interests in livelihood, health, peace, in a decent community which provides scope for public participation and for private friendships, for satisfying work and for the enjoyment both of nature and of a rich, varied, and historically conscious cultural tradition.

Among the interests we share with others are interests we have only because we are cooperating with others in some project. Membership in a nation gives us this sort of interest in the nation's affairs, and gives each of us an interest in the protection of our individual roles as citizens and taxpayers. As a member of the taxpaying public my interests are injured by the tax fraud of my fellows as well as by misuse of public funds by officials. Here my interest is the same as that of any other honest taxpayer, an interest in not being ripped off. Yet this interest I share with many others can clash with more private interests I may have, if for example my employer is among those guilty to tax fraud and my job depends on his illgotten "savings." My interest as a member of the taxpaying public and my interest as an employee of this employer may be in conflict with one another. Often we need to refer to the *roles* we play, roles relating us to others and to schemes of cooperation, to specify the variety of our interests, and many of the duties and rights we have, and wrongs done to us, also depend upon these social roles. I have duties as a daughter, family member, department member, teacher, university employee, and citizen, and I have rights as all of these, as well as a member of a particular professional association, health insurance scheme, and so on. Since in most of these roles my rights and interests coincide with those of some others,

I will protest any violation of rights, and wrongful injury of interests, even if I foresee that my own goals will not be frustrated by those wrongs. For example I will protest *as university teacher*, if tenure guarantees are broken, even if I am about to retire and so will not be hurt myself.

Let us now try to apply these points about the complexity of a person's good, its inclusion of *interests* to be protected or furthered as well as desires to be satisfied and pleasures to be enjoyed, to the case of future people. Because interests are *always* future-oriented, and because we can know what they are, at least at a general level, without having much if any information about what particular tastes and desires a person has, it seems to me that future persons' *interests* can be determinate even when the persons themselves are not yet determinate, even when the *whole* of what will count as their good is not yet fixed. Of course, in being sure that, whoever they are, they will *have* an interest in clean air, we are also usually assuming that they will *want* to breathe, and be *pained* by inability to do so—some assumptions about their sensitivities and their desires will be included in our claims about their interests. A person whose interests in good health is badly injured will most probably also have frustration and pain, as "ills" which accompany the ill of ill health. We may even feel we know what *particular* desires a future person will have because of grave ill health—for example, in extreme cases the desire to end life. So in concentrating on the *interests* of future people in what follows, I shall not be supposing that in injuring interests we are not usually also frustrating and hurting. I shall, however, be relying on the *possibility* that an injury to a person's interest can (and sometimes should) be averted, although that does *not* bring that person a better life, more satisfaction and less frustration, more pleasure and less pain. Interests are important, and injury to interests is important, *whether or not* averting the injury in fact leads to less frustration and less pain for the one whose interest it is.

Future people, once actual, will come to have specific interests as well as general ones, and will have particular desires and sensitivities, as well as interests, which will need to be taken into account by anyone *then* concerned with their good. We now *cannot* consider their good "all things considered," because all the relevant things are not yet determinate. But we *can* consider some vital dimensions of what will be their good, and do so when we consider those of their interests which are general enough, or, even though specific, predictable enough, to be already fixed. (One specific interest we can be fairly sure that people a few generations after us will have is an interest in the advancement of knowledge of methods of *detoxifying* all the resources we are currently poisoning. This is not an interest people in the past have needed to have.)

What we now need to consider is whether the fact that our acts help to *determine* both the identity of future persons and some of the specific interests they will have means that *those* acts cannot at the same time damage interests of those persons. The No Obligation Argument seems to allow us to injure only one of the interests a future person might have, a rather complex interest, namely the interest in not existing at all if other vital interests, such as health, are to be very badly served. This is a conditional interest—an interest in not existing unless other unconditional interests can be tolerably well served. The No Obligation Argument in effect claims that unless a future person has *this* exceptional interest injured by us, she is not wronged by us by those policies of ours which "select" her for existence. Is it possible, contrary to what the argument claims, for us to wrong a person by injuring an interest she has even though she comes to *be* a person with that interest only because of the very actions which also injure that interest? Can that person say *both* "If you had acted differently, *my interests* would have been better served," *and* also "Had you acted differently, I would not have been one of those who exist and have such interests"? I shall try to show that such a complaint makes sense.

§11 Selecting Populations by Our Acts

Before looking at future people, let us consider present people, and sketch analogous ways in which our actions can injure their interests, perhaps violate their rights. Take a case such as a teacher who writes a course description. It is surely primarily for the sake of the students who will be in the course that such descriptions are written, with whatever care is taken. Yet *who* precisely they turn out to be depends to some degree on the course description itself, if it is an elective course. The description, and the care taken in writing it, both is for the sake of the students, and also helps to select which students are those for whose sake a course plan is produced. The teacher's actions help to fix the class population. Similar sorts of cases arise with immigration policy—the ways in which a nation encourages or discourages immigrants help to determine who comes, but once in a country an immigrant might complain, "You didn't warn me about the high unemployment. Had you done so, I probably wouldn't have come." (Note that it need *not* be claimed that they regret being there for them to have a complaint.) Have we injured and perhaps wronged the class members who suffer once in the badly described course, the immigrants who come with inadequate advance warning of conditions, even if, once in the class or nation, they do not on balance regret being there?

It is important to see that a version of the No Obligation Argument can be used to give a negative answer here too. To any complainer we can say, "If you wouldn't have been in the relevant population (class member, immigrant) had we done what you say we should have done, then you are not a wronged member of that population. You would not have been a *better-off* class member or immigrant, had we acted as you think we should have, *you* would not have been a member of that population *at all*. So you have no complaint as class member, as immigrant." Must they then reformulate their complaint, and say that it was the population of those *considering* joining the class or nation, not those actually joining it, whose interests are injured by the poor descriptions and plans? Such wider populations certainly are affected, but it would seem counterintuitive to say that when a teacher designs a course and makes the design known in a course description she is fulfilling a duty only to the wider group of all those who might consider joining, not also to the narrower group who actually join. Any class member (or immigrant) whose complaint is responded to by these moves would, if she had her wits about her, say "I *as class member* (immigrant) as well as a potential class member have been wronged by the bad advance description. You owe it to all those deciding whether to join, and in particular to those who *do* so decide, to have an adequate plan and to give adequate advance notice of it. Had you done the right thing, I would not have *been* a class member, but you didn't, and I am, and I, like all other members, have been wronged by you."

It seems to me that this response is right. The interests of ours which can be injured include those dependent on the act which does the injury, in this case the act which helped make one a class member. This may sound paradoxical, but the paradox disappears once we are clear about what interests are, and how we can possess them in virtue of roles we fill and come to fill. Sometimes we come to fill a particular role, giving rise to an interest, because of the very act of another person which injures our interest once we are in that role.

Of course the extent of the analogy between this case and the case of future persons is limited. *They* do not *decide* to become actual persons, it is "decided" for them. But we can find, among injuries to present persons, cases on nonvoluntary as well as voluntary membership in some group where the act of determining membership also injures the interests of the members, as members. An annexation of a territory subjects the inhabitants to a new rule, makes them members of a new "population," and may simultaneously make them second-class subjects, a disadvantaged minority. After the second world war, Transylvanians who had been Hungarians became subjects of Rumania, and could complain (as many of them did) that the very act which made them Rumanians also injured their interests as Rumanians. Adopted children sometimes feel that the very fact that they are adopted gives them a lower place in their adoptive parents' affections than those who are the parents' "own" children in the biological sense. The very act which made the adopted children members of their new family, some feel, injured them *as* members of that family. (They may feel this without believing that it would have been better had they never been adopted, without feeling that they are, all things considered, injured by the act of adoption.) Could future persons, as our successors, be injured by us although the injuring act selected them *as* our successors? Well, so far we can say that the fact that they didn't *choose* that status does not rule that out. Nevertheless, the fact that our acts determine who will exist, and so do not *shift* them from one "population" into another, but determines their very availability for *any* population, must not be glossed over.

This fact certainly limits the analogy between our relation to future people and our relation to students in our elective courses, to our adopted children, and to members of our annexed territories. We do not by any act literally *select* from a host of already determinate possible people the ones who will become actual, as would-be adoptive parents might survey the row of orphaned babies in a nursery, picking out the one to become their child. If there *are* fully determinate possible people, we cannot distinguish them as such. All we can do is consider similar descriptions of them such as "the next child I shall have," or "my future eldest great-great-grandchild," or "the first future person who may actually formulate a complaint beginning, 'Those Americans who had any say over policy in the 1980s are to blame for. . . .'" Although each of these titles is designed to pick out one and only one person, we have little idea what that person will be like, or what their total good will consist in. To discern injuries to people we know, we consider them, fully determinate people about whose good-all-things-considered we may have opinions, people whose full range of characteristics enables them to fit many descriptions and fill many bills, then we emphasize the role relevant to the injury we discern: "He was injured *as a parent*," or "*as an employee*." With actual people we do not know, we usually know more of the roles and bills they fill than simply the one relevant to the injury, so that although we do not know much about, say, those who are starving in the Sahara, we can say *something* about who it is whose interests in health and nourishment are so injured. With future people, there may be nothing yet fixed and known about them except the general interests we need to consider to try to avoid injuring them. All there is, yet, are those interests, not yet the actual people whose interests they will be, whose good those interests will help comprise. So we should not pretend that our relation to future persons is not significantly different from our relation to already existent persons, nor pretend that making them existent is simply moving them from the "population" of possible people into the more exclusive population of actual people. Any responses we make to the No Obligation Argument should avoid that confusion.

Nevertheless we ought also not forget that any act which injures an actual person's long-term interests is one which looks ahead to the not-yet-fixed *older person* the injured one might become. If I now lose my retirement pension rights, I am injured, even though, as far as I know, the older person of retirement age is not yet fixed in her needs or wants. There are many possible future me's. I may become rich enough not to need any pension, or become a beachcomber and not want one, or I may not live long enough to reach retirement age. All these uncertainties for the future are always there, and my interests lie in being somehow prepared for any of them. My interests are injured if I today lose my pension rights, even if I come into an unexpected inheritance or drop dead tomorrow. We must steer clear, then, not only of blurring the difference between future not-yet-actual people and actual people, but also of exaggerating it, of treating the interests it is wrong to injure as always the interests of people with determinate sets of concerns, wants, tastes. Only the dead are *fully* determinate, and the very finality, fixedness, of the nature of their wants and the character of their lives severely limits the interests they can have.

§12 Past, Present, and Future Persons

Although a past person cannot any longer suffer, nor want anything, some interests and rights of past people can still be protected or neglected. If I tell malicious lies about some dead persons, their interests in having and keeping a good name is injured. I can do things for the sake of past persons, although they neither know nor feel the effects of what I do. Once we are dead, the range of things which it is possible for others to do for our sake, or to do us ill, shrinks. But we may still, for the dead person's sake, protect his reputation, do what he wanted or would have wanted (especially with his estate), and we may even do things like putting flowers on his grave, thinking that to have some link with what pleased or would have pleased him. (If we put flowers on the grave of someone who hated flowers, it certainly is not done for that one's sake.) The very finished fixed character of the past person's life history puts him beyond most of the harms present and future persons can suffer—he cannot be hurt or frustrated, nor has he any longer many of the interests and rights living persons have. He is safe from much but not all ill.

Future persons too seem safe from being harmed by us in certain ways in which we may harm our contemporaries. We cannot deny them their marital rights, nor any contractual rights, nor libel them, nor take an unfairly large share of a good to which they too have *contributors'* rights. (But we *may* take, for ourselves, too large a share of what earlier people "bequeathed" to an indefinite run of future generations, or ruin a "bequest" which could have been enjoyed much longer but for our spoiling activities.) Just as there are many harms and wrongs we *cannot* do past people, so there are many harms and wrongs we *cannot* do future people.

Future people will, whoever they turn out to be, have a good, but only some components of that good are yet fixed. Must we say the same of the interests which help comprise that good, that they *will be* their interests, but are not yet their interests? We have seen how some interests, like that in not being spoken ill of, last longer than does the person whose interest it is. I have argued that some interests preexist the person whose interests they are. Common predictable human interests, such as the availability of unpoisoned soil as a resource, seem to depend in no way upon that combination of specific interests, concerns, wants, tastes that comprise the concrete *individuality* of persons, which possible people lack, and which future people do not yet have. Whoever becomes actual will have such common interests and we know they will, so I see nothing wrong in saying that those already existent interests are now *theirs*. We do not need to know exactly who "they" are to recognize the reality of their common human interests. Whomever we allow to become actual, those ones have the interests all people have and we can also see what specific form some of those interests will take, since it depends on our policies. Of the interests people claim as their interests, some were predictable before the person's conception or birth, others come into being only because of particular unpredictable facts about them and choices they make. It is the interests which are fixed and predictable in advance which we can say preexist the person of whose good they form a part, and usually it is other less predictable and more specific interests of theirs, such as the sources of a particular book they wrote, which last once they are dead. People cast shadows in the form of interests both before them and after them.

We can, then, speak of acting *for the sake of* a person not merely when we act to promote that one's all-things-considered good, as an actual living person, or act to prevent injuries to their *individual* and perhaps eccentric interests, but also when we protect the general interests they have, *in advance of their existence,* or do things for them *after they are dead.* We can even prevent a person's existence, for that person's sake, when we think that, if she were born, she would judge S_2. The concept of a person's sake is the most flexible and so the best concept for us to use to cover all the ways in which what we do can be *better for* a person. If, contrary to what the No Obligation Argument concluded, there *are* things we can do which are better for future persons, in addition to preventing their coming to exist to judge S_2, then they will be things we do *for their sake.*

§13 The No Obligation Argument Rejected

We can now see what is wrong with the No Obligation Argument. The Victim Premise, V, did not spell out all the ways in which a person can be a victim, and only if some of those ways, especially ways of injuring interests, are neglected or denied does the conclusion C really follow from V and P. To see this we should expand V, mentioning all the ways we have distinguished in which something can be worse or better for a person's sake.

The revised version, V_r, will read

V_r We do not wrong a person by our action or policy unless it would have been better, for that person's sake, not to have acted that way because our present actions bring

  (1) more suffering than the person would have had, had we acted differently;

or (2) more frustration than the person would have had, had we acted differently;

or (3)   greater injury to the person's interests than would have occurred had we acted differently, where such interests include the interest in not existing at all, if other interests are to be very badly injured;

or (4)   greater violation of the person's rights than would have occurred had we acted differently.

What do we get when we add the original Precariousness Premise to V_r? I think we need first to add a premise we can derive from the preceding account of the nature and variety of our interests, namely

I   Among the interests of a person which can be injured are interests which are fixed before the identity of those whose interests they are is fixed, and includes interests which a given person comes to possess only because of the very act which injures those interests.

What we add I to P and V_r, I think we can get a revised conclusion, C_r, which is very different from the No Obligation conclusion.

C_r Therefore the wrongs we can do a future person are usually restricted to injuries to interests fixed before the identity of future persons are fixed (and to such frustration and pain as is consequent upon the injury to such interests), and cannot include injury to interests not yet fixed or frustration of wants and concerns not yet fixed or hurts to sensibilities not yet fixed.

C_r is very different from C since it not merely allows the wrong of "wrongful existence," now included as injury of an already fixed conditional interest of all persons, but it also allows those *injuries to other already fixed interests* where the act which does the injury at the same time helps settle who it is whose interest it is.

We have avoided the No Obligation conclusion, C, by allowing the concept of an effect on a person to include *"effect" on interests,* including interests which come to be possessed only because of the "affecting" act. Parfit regards such interpretations of the Person-Affecting Principle as a "cheat," and himself avoids the No Obligation conclusion by renouncing the Person-Affecting Principle in favor of a vaguer principle which says, "It is bad if those who live are worse off than those who might have lived," a principle explicitly allowing comparisons between *different* possible people, not just comparisons of the possible fates of people of fixed identity. I think that once we come to see what sort of things interests are, and how indirectly injury to them is linked to worsening of the determinate life history of a person, then it is no "cheat" to allow the Person-Affecting Principle to include effect on interests, including those of the future people whose very existence to possess interests is due to the act which perhaps adversely affects those interests. So although no future person may be able to say to our ghosts, "If you had acted differently and rightly, I would have had a better life," plenty of the future people might well be able to say, "Interests which are, as it turns out, *my* interests, have been injured by what you did, and would have been less injured had you acted differently."

All we have done, so far, is to try to show that there is no good reason to think that the only wrongful injury we can do future people is to inflict "wrongful existence" upon them. We can now admit other injuries to their interests, other things we can, perhaps wrongfully, fail to do *for their sakes.* But which of these other injuries to the interests of future persons *should count as wrongs?* That is a question we have yet to consider, and different moral theories will give different answers. All would agree that our duties to future people are what can in reason be demanded of us for their sake, that wrongs to future people are neglectings of these duties, but there is no agreed way of determining *what* it is reasonable to demand of any of us for others', including our successors', sakes.

MARTI KHEEL

The Liberation of Nature
A Circular Affair

MARTI KHEEL has been active in the animal-rights movement and is cofounder of Feminists for Animal Rights. She writes about esthetics, ecology, ethics, and feminist thought and is a contributing editor of the journal *Between the Species*.

The new understanding of life must be systemic and interconnected. It cannot be linear and hierarchical, for the reality of life on earth is a whole, a circle, an interconnected system in which everything has its part to play and can be respected and accorded dignity.

ELIZABETH D. GRAY

I. INTRODUCTION

Over the last ten years feminist thought has shed a radically new light on many fields of inquiry. One of the most recent areas to receive the benefit of such illumination has been that of our society's attitudes toward nature. During this same time period, a voluminous body of literature has emerged in a new field of philosophy called "environmental ethics." The writers in this field (predominantly men) have shown little or no interest in the feminist literature. In the following, I attempt to redress this neglect and to show that feminist thought can, indeed, shed significant light on this important new area of study.

Central to feminist thought has been a critique of Western dualistic thinking. Western dualistic thoughts sees the world in terms of static polarities—"us and them," "subject and object," "superior and inferior," "mind and body," "animate and inanimate," "reason and emotion," "culture and nature." All such dualities have two characteristics in common: (1) the first half of the duality is always valued more than the other, and (2) the more valued half is always seen as "male" and the less valued half as "female." The Western dualistic world view can be traced back to early Greek philosophy and the Jewish and Christian religions, being reinforced in the 1600s by the increasingly mechanistic world view of modern science. The result of this long history of dualistic thinking has been the ruthless exploitation of women, animals, and all of nature. In place of dualistic thinking feminists have posited a holistic vision of reality in which everything is integrally interconnected and thus part of a larger "whole." Thus, whereas dualistic thought has perceived the world through a "spatial metaphor (up-and-down)," these feminists have seen diversity within a larger whole. The recent findings of quantum physics have reaffirmed this feminist vision. They have verified in the world of matter what many people have experienced in the world of spirit—namely, the oneness of the universe.

543

Thus, we learn from quantum physics that atoms instead of being hard and indestructible consist, instead, of vast regions of space in which extremely small particles move. At the subatomic level, we are told, matter consists of very abstract entities that have a dual aspect: "Depending on which way the experiments are performed, they appear sometimes as particles, sometimes as waves." The Taoist notion that everything is in flux, and that the only constant is change, turns out to have a solid grounding in the world of matter. Thus, we learn that "subatomic particles do not exist with certainty at definite places, but rather show 'tendencies to exist', and atomic events do not occur with certainty at definite times and in definite ways, but rather show 'tendencies to occur'." Consequently, we can never predict an atomic event with certainty; we can only say how likely it is to happen. As Capra puts it, "Quantum theory forces us to see the universe not as a collection of physical objects, but rather as a complicated web of relations between the various parts of a unified whole."

II. HIERARCHICAL THOUGHT WITHIN ENVIRONMENTAL ETHICS

The Dualistic Heritage

By contrast with the holistic vision set forth by both feminists and quantum physicists, the goal of much of the literature in environmental ethics has been the establishment of hierarchies of value for the different parts of nature. It is assumed that hierarchy is necessary to aid us in making moral choices in our interactions with nature. Conflict is taken for granted; it is assumed that one part of nature must always win, while another must always lose. Thus, in a real sense, the field of environmental ethics perpetuates the tradition of dualistic thought.

Holism

The concept of hierarchy finds two major forms of expression in the literature. One form is expressed through the ongoing debate over whether individual beings or the larger concept of "the whole" (or the "biotic community") should be given moral preference. Some "animal liberationists" argue that it is the individual who must be considered over the whole, whereas many "holists" argue that it is the good of the whole that must take precedence. Many holists will protest that theirs is a nonhierarchical paradigm in that everything is viewed as an integral part of an interconnected web. However, holists such as Aldo Leopold and J. Baird Callicott clearly indicate that the interconnected web does, indeed, contain its own system of ranking. Such writers have dispensed with the system of classification that assigns value to a being on the basis of its possession of certain innate characteristics, only to erect a *new* form of hierarchy in which individuals are valued on the basis of their relative contribution to the good of the whole (i.e., the biotic community.)

According to Callicott, the "good of the community as a whole, serves as a standard for the assessment of the relative value and relative ordering of its constitutive parts and therefore provides a means of adjudicating the often mutually contradictory demands of the parts considered separately for *equal* consideration." At the top of Callicott's scale are rare and endangered species: "*Specimens* of rare and endangered species, for example, have a *prima facie* claim to preferential consideration from the perspective of the land ethic." At the bottom of Callicott's hierarchy of value are domestic animals: "Environmental ethics sets a very low priority on domestic animals as they very frequently contribute to the erosion of the integrity, stability, and beauty of the biotic communities into which they have been insinuated." Callicott goes so far as to posit a mathematical equation by which the value of an individual being may be gauged: "The preciousness of individual deer, as of any other specimen, is inversely proportional to the population of the species." To eliminate any doubt concerning his views on equality, he adds that "the land ethic manifestly does not accord equal moral worth to each and every member of the biotic community." . . .

Ironically, Callicott's "holism" may be seen to have much in common with utilitarianism. In both systems, the individual is treated, in Kantian terms, as a "means" for the attainment of a greater "end." In the former case, that which is good is judged by the standard of the biotic community, whereas in the latter case, it is gauged by the happiness of the greatest number. Although the content of the hierarchy varies, the structure remains the same. Both systems of thought also share the problem inherent in any scheme that claims the ability to compare the relative value of such abstractions as "happiness" or the "biotic good"—i.e., who should establish such values and how?

Individual Rights

The other form of hierarchical thought within environmental ethics is reflected in the attempt by both "ethical humanists" and "animal liberationists" to establish the relative values of the individual parts of nature. In this endeavor various criteria are proposed such as "sentience," "consciousness," "rationality," "self-determination," "interests," etc. A being that possesses one of these characteristics is said to have "intrinsic value" or the right to "moral consideration," whereas a being without them is said to lack these. A large part of this literature consists of debating which beings possess these characteristics—i.e., arguing whether divisions should occur along the lines of species or whether some overlap may exist. Ironically, although many of these writers feel that they are arguing against notions of hierarchy, the vast majority simply remove one set of hierarchies only to establish another. Thus, many writers on the subject of animal liberation may raise the status of animals to a level that warrants our moral concern only to exclude other parts of nature, such as plants and trees. Thus, Bernard Rollins, who clearly feels that animals merit our ethical consideration, emphatically states that "in and of itself, the physical environment has no interests and life and is, therefore, not a direct object of moral concern."

Some animal liberationists have attempted to expand the notion of rights arguing for the concept of the inherent value of individual beings. Even these writers, however, often fail to overcome the concept of hierarchy. Thus, according to Tom Regan, beings are deserving of rights if they can have a life that is "better or worse for them, independently of whether they are valued by anyone else." But if we were, as Regan suggests, to accord rights or value only to those beings that can have a life that is better or worse for them, our current understanding of the word *life* would exclude from direct moral consideration such parts of nature as streams, mountains, and air.

Regan seems to show some concern over this limitation. In his words, "But limiting the class of beings that have inherent value to the class of living beings seems to be an

546   Chapter 11 | What Should We Sacrifice for Animals and the Environment?

arbitrary decision and one that does not serve well as a basis for an environmental ethic. . . . if I am right, the development of what can properly be called an environmental ethic requires that we postulate inherent value in nature."

Outside of this important reference, however, Regan has failed to argue for the inherent value of all of nature. What has, perhaps, hindered him from so doing is the belief that this notion necessarily precludes a valuing of the individual parts of nature. The holist camp, by contrast, is convinced that a valuing of the individual for itself will somehow detract from a valuing of the whole. Both schools of thought are trapped within the dualistic mind set. Neither can see that moral worth can exist *both* in the individual parts of nature *and* in the whole of which they are a part. It is reliance on reason as the sole arbiter in our dealings with nature that makes the two schools of thought appear distinct. But these positions are not polar opposites, nor even part of a "triangular affair" (each position representing one extreme of a triangle, as Callicott argues). If we allow for an element of feeling in our interactions with nature, the positions represented by these camps dissolve into different points on a circle. No point may, thus, be said to be more important than any other. The liberation of nature is, in fact, a circular affair.

A vision of nature that perceives value both in the individual and in the whole of which it is a part is a vision that entails a reclaiming of the term *holism* from those for whom it signifies a new form of hierarchy (namely, a valuing of the whole over the individual). Such a vision asks us to abandon the dualistic way of thinking that sees value as inherently exclusive (i.e., the belief that the value of the whole cannot also be the value of the individual). It invites us to see value not as a commodity to be assigned by isolated rational analysis, but rather as a living dynamic that is constantly in flux. If we can believe the findings of quantum physics, ecology, and the spiritual experiences of many individuals, we can agree with the holists that the nature of reality is, indeed, a web of interconnection, a circle or a "whole." What most holists seem to forget, however, is that the whole consists of individual beings—beings with emotions, feelings, and inclinations—and that these, too, are part of the whole. To rely on rational analysis alone to determine what the good of the whole might be is to ignore the reality of such feelings as well as their expression in particular circumstances.

The concept of holism I am advocating here does not view the "whole" as composed of discrete individual beings connected by static relationships which rational analysis can comprehend and control. Rather, I am proposing a concept of holism that perceives nature (much like the new physics perceives subatomic particles) as comprising individual beings that are part of a *dynamic* web of interconnections in which feelings, emotions, and inclinations (or energy) play an integral role. Just as quantum physics cannot predict atomic events with certainty at exact times and specific places, so too we cannot postulate that one species or one individual is of greater or lesser value than another. The attempt to formulate universal, rational rules of conduct ignores the constantly changing nature of reality. It also neglects the emotional-instinctive or spontaneous component in each particular situation, for in the end, emotion cannot be contained by boundaries and rules; in a single leap it can cross over the boundaries of space, time, and species. It is, I feel, the failure of most writers within environmental ethics to recognize the role of emotion that has perpetuated within the environmental ethics literature the dualistic thinking so characteristic of Western society.

III. REASON VERSUS EMOTION IN ENVIRONMENTAL ETHICS

The Rule of Reason

Most of the literature within the field of environmental ethics may be seen as an attempt to establish rationally both hierarchies of value and universal rules of conduct based on such values. Most such literature presumes that reason alone will tell us which beings are of greatest value and, thus, what rules of conduct should govern our interactions with them. Singer refers to this idea when he states, "Ethics requires us to go beyond 'I' and 'you' to the universal law, the universalizable judgment, the standpoint of the impartial spectator or ideal observer or whatever we choose to call it."

Interestingly, the field of environmental ethics is an outgrowth of two movements that were (and are) highly charged emotionally—i.e., the animal rights and environmental movements. Significantly, the members (mostly women) of the early animal rights movement were often labeled "animal lovers" or "sentimentalists" in an attempt to belittle their concerns. But, as James Turner points out, "animal lovers were not ashamed to admit that their campaign to protect brutes from abuse was more the result of sentiment than of reason."

With the publication of Peter Singer's *Animal Liberation*, the animal liberation movement took a new direction. It was assumed that one of the reasons for the failure of the earlier movement was its appeal to emotion, rather than hard, logical, well-reasoned arguments. The new movement for animal rights (as well as environmental ethics) proudly grounds itself in rationality. As Peter Singer states, "Nowhere in this book, however, do I appeal to the reader's emotions where they cannot be *supported by reason*." Elsewhere Singer elaborates, "Ethics does not demand that we eliminate personal relationships and partial affections, but it does demand that when we act we assess the moral claims of those affected by our actions *independently of our feelings for them*."

The appeal to reason in ethics has a long philosophical tradition. One of its most notable proponents was Kant, who felt that an action was moral only if it was derived from a rationally grounded conception of the right or morally correct course of action. Kant went so far as to maintain that no action that springs from a natural inclination can have moral worth. Although most modern-day philosophers do not elevate reason to quite such heights, most still feel that any appeal to emotion is tantamount to having no argument at all. . . .

The call to reason is also used by other writers as a means of learning our "natural place" within nature. Such writers argue that by understanding our "natural place" within nature we can learn what our moral actions should be. But, one might ask, why should *is* imply *ought*? Why should our natural place within nature dictate what it *should* be? To my knowledge, no philosopher to date has answered this question with a convincing "rational" argument, and I suspect that none will. Pragmatic arguments about how we will destroy all life on Earth unless we find our natural place within nature cannot persuade those who have no regard for life to begin with. Only those who *feel* their connection to all of nature to begin with will take an interest in its continuation. In more ways than one, the liberation of nature is a circular affair.

Dissolving the Dichotomies

What seems to be lacking in much of the literature in environmental ethics (and in ethics in general) is the open admission that we cannot even begin to talk about the issue of ethics unless we admit that we care (or feel something). And it is here that the emphasis of many feminists on personal experience and emotion has much to offer in the way of reformulating our traditional notion of ethics. Although this may appear at first to support the stereotypical divisions of our society which associate men with rationality and women with emotion, the emphasis on feeling and emotion does not imply the exclusion of reason. Rather, a kind of unity of reason and emotion is envisioned by many feminists. . . . Robin Morgan has used the term *unified sensibility* to describe this fusion of feeling and thought. In her words:

> How often have feminists called . . . for the 'peculiar blend of feeling and ratiocination' in our battles against the patriarchal dichotomization of intellect and emotion! It is the insistence on the connections, the demand for synthesis, the refusal to be narrowed into desiring less than everything—that is so much the form of metaphysical poetry and of metaphysical feminism. The unified sensibility.

How, then, are we to attain such a "unified sensibility"? The difficulty lies in conceiving of something as alien to our usual conception of hierarchy and rules as what is proposed. The problem of unifying our own nature is compounded further when we, ourselves, are removed from the rest of nature. Emotion easily divides from reason when we are divorced from the immediate impact of our moral decisions. A possible step, therefore, in striving to fuse these divisions is to experience directly the full impact of our moral decisions. If we *think*, for example, that there is nothing morally wrong with eating meat, we ought, perhaps, to visit a factory farm or slaughter house to see if we still *feel* the same way. If we, ourselves, do not want to witness, let alone participate in, the slaughter of the animals we eat, we ought, perhaps, to question the morality of indirectly paying someone else to do this on our behalf. When we are physically removed from the direct impact of our moral decisions—i.e., when we cannot see, smell, or hear their results—we deprive ourselves of important sensory stimuli which may be important in guiding us in our ethical choices.

Feminists have often emphasized the importance of personal experience in political and other seemingly impersonal matters. Its importance for ethical decisions is equally vital. This is, perhaps, the most practical implication of a feminist ethic: that we must involve ourselves as directly as possible in the *whole* process of our moral decisions. We must make our moral choices a circular affair. . . .

In her book *In a Different Voice*, Carol Gilligan has argued that the emphasis on particularity and feeling is a predominantly female mode of ethical thought. As she puts it,

> The moral imperative that emerges repeatedly in interviews with women is an injunction to care, a responsibility to discern and alleviate the real and recognizable trouble of this world . . . the reconstruction of the dilemma in its contextual particularity allows the understanding of cause and consequence which engages the compassion and tolerance repeatedly noted to distinguish the moral judgments of women.

Men, on the other hand, she states, develop a sense of morality in which "relationships are subordinated to rules (stage four) and rules to universal principles of justice (stages five and six)." According to Gilligan, "the rights conception of morality that informs [Lawrence] Kohlberg's principled level (stages five and six) is geared to arriving at an objectively fair or just resolution to moral dilemmas upon which all rational persons, could agree. . . ."

The problems entailed in implementing a female mode of ethical thought within a patriarchal society are obvious. With men building bigger and better bombs, rapidly depleting our natural resources, and torturing millions of animals in laboratories, one rightly worries what a particular individual's natural inclination might be. As Sara Ebenreck puts it, "If the answer to how to treat a tree or a field is dependent on what the person 'hears intuitively' from the field or tree, then—as John Kultgen points out—we must be open to the possibility that some people will hear a message which is 'rape us, despoil us, enslave us.' "

It needs to be said in this context that men may respond in different ways to the call to ground our ethics in practical experience. Clearly, men do have a greater propensity toward violence as can be seen by their greater involvement in such violent activities as wars, violent crime, hunting, trapping, etc. Whether this propensity is biological or environmental or a combination of both is still an unanswered question. Whatever else we may conclude from this difference, however, it is difficult to escape the conclusion that in our dealings with nature, men have much to learn from women. Indeed, many men, including Buckminster Fuller, Lionel Tiger, Lyall Watson have concluded that "the only hope may be to turn the world over to women."

Most nonhumans seem instinctively to take only what they need from the environment to survive. If humans ever had such an ability, we seem to have lost it. The further divorced human beings are from this instinct or sensibility that nonhuman animals have, the more we seem to require rationality to act as its substitute. Interestingly, Aldo Leopold suggests that "ethics are possibly a kind of community instinct in-the-making." Perhaps, then, we are fortunate in that the human capacity to destroy life, to ravage the Earth, and to otherwise wreak havoc on the world around us coexists with yet another capacity—namely, the capacity to question our right to do so.

It is only when our instincts have failed us that we turn to such concepts as rights. Thus, it is not surprising that the idea of individual rights and natural law emerged during the civil war in England, a time of great social upheaval. The notion of *rights* can, in fact, be conceived of only within an antagonistic or competitive environment. The concept of competition is inherent in the very definition of rights. As Joel Feinberg states, "To have a right is to have a claim *to* something *against* someone. . . ." The concept of rights is, thus, inherently dualistic. Unfortunately, however, we do live in a dualistic society where competition is a fact of life. The concept of rights in an expanded form to include all of nature may thus be a necessary tactical device within our current society.

CONCLUSION

Feminist spirituality has shown us how the concept of a patriarchal religion, which views God as a male figure of authority in the sky telling us how we should think or feel, does not speak to the needs of those who feel that their spirituality flows from within. In a similar vein, it may be argued, the concept of ethics as a hierarchical set of rules to be superimposed upon the individual does not address the needs of those people (perhaps, mostly women) who feel that their morality or inclinations toward nature reside within themselves.

For such people, an environmental ethic might be described in the words of Elizabeth Dodson Gray:

> Some day, perhaps, we shall have an identity that can enjoy the earth as friend, provider and home. When that happens, we will know that when the earth hurts, it will hurt us. Then, the environmental ethic will not just be in our heads but in our hearts—in the nerve endings of our sensitivity.

With such a sensitivity we could perhaps, then dispense with the rigid, hierarchical rules of the past. If guidelines were to exist at all, they might simply flow from the desire to minimize human interference with the rest of nature. . . .

How might the field of environmental ethics be changed by a recognition of the importance of feeling and emotion and personal experience in moral decision making? For one thing, writers in environmental ethics might spend less time formulating universal laws and dividing lines and spend more time using reason to show the limitations of its own thought. They might, for instance, show how seemingly "rational" rules and ideas are, in fact, based on distinct feelings. Few of us, for example, would relinquish the idea that we, as humans, are more important than a stone. Yet, by showing that such a thought is based, in fact, on a feeling and that it cannot be justified by rational thought alone, we may be able to detach from our egos long enough to see that we are, indeed, all part of a whole of which no part may rationally be said to be more important than another. Currently, those with power in our society use rationality as a means of enforcing their own morality. If it could also be shown that such rationality is, in fact, derived from particular feelings, we could then begin to genuinely assess those feelings and the morality that flows from them.

Environmental theorists also might begin to talk more openly about their experiences and feelings and their relevance to their ideas and actions. Rather than spending time trying to find a moral dividing line within nature, they might, instead, examine their own internal divisions (such as that between reason and emotion). In order to unite these dualities within themselves they might then attempt as far as possible to experience in practice the full implications of their own moral theories. In a similar vein, an appeal to their readers' emotions and sympathies might be considered more relevant in an argument for moral vegetarianism than an appeal to reason.

Finally, environmental ethics might become more willing to recognize that the most fundamental questions about nature and the universe cannot, in the end, be answered rationally. Such an admission may not leave us with the sense of resolution and control that so many of us seem to hunger for, but it may, on the other hand, bring us closer to a feeling of the wonder of the universe and, perhaps, as a consequence, a greater appreciation of all of life.

JOHN STUART MILL

Against the Glorification of Nature

JOHN STUART MILL (1806–1873) is best known for his moral and political writings (see his selections in Chapters 7 and 9), particularly *On Liberty* (1859) and *Utilitarianism* (1863).

However offensive the proposition may appear to many religious persons, they should be willing to look in the face the undeniable fact, that the order of nature, in so far as unmodified by man, is such as no being, whose attributes are justice and benevolence, would have made, with the intention that his rational creatures should follow it as an example. If made wholly by such a Being, and not partly by beings of very different qualities, it could only be as a designedly imperfect work, which man, in his limited sphere, is to exercise justice and benevolence in amending. The best persons have always held it to be the essence of religion, that the paramount duty of man upon earth is to amend himself: but all except monkish quietists have annexed to this in their inmost minds (though seldom willing to enunciate the obligation with the same clearness) the additional religious duty of amending the world, and not solely the human part of it but the material; the order of physical nature.

In considering this subject it is necessary to divest ourselves of certain preconceptions which may justly be called natural prejudices, being grounded on feelings which, in themselves natural and inevitable, intrude into matters with which they ought to have no concern. One of these feelings is the astonishment, rising into awe, which is inspired (even independently of all religious sentiment) by any of the greater natural phenomena. A hurricane; a mountain precipice; the desert; the ocean, either agitated or at rest; the solar system, and the great cosmic forces which hold it together; the boundless firmament, and to an educated mind any single star; excite feelings which make all human enterprises and powers appear so insignificant, that to a mind thus occupied it seems insufferable presumption in so puny a creature as man to look critically on things so far above him, or dare to measure himself against the grandeur of the universe. But a little interrogation of our own consciousness will suffice to convince us, that what makes these phenomena so impressive is simply their vastness. The enormous extension in space and time, or the enormous power they exemplify, constitutes their sublimity; a feeling in all cases, more allied to terror than to any moral emotion. And though the vast scale of these phenomena may well excite wonder, and sets at defiance all idea of rivalry, the feeling it inspires is of a totally different character from admiration of excellence. Those in whom awe produces admiration may be aesthetically developed, but they are morally uncultivated. It is one of the endowments of the imaginative part of our mental nature that conceptions of greatness and power, vividly realized, produce a feeling which though in its higher degrees closely bordering on pain, we prefer to most of what are accounted pleasures. But we are quite equally capable of experiencing this feeling towards maleficent power; and we never experience it so strongly towards most of the powers of the universe, as when we have most present to our consciousness a vivid sense of their capacity of inflicting evil. Because these natural powers have what we cannot imitate, enormous might, and overawe us by that one attribute, it would be a great error to infer that their other attributes are such as we ought to emulate, or that we should be justified in using our small powers after the example which Nature sets us with her vast forces. . . .

In sober truth, nearly all things which men are hanged or imprisoned for doing to one another, are nature's every day performances. Killing, the most criminal act recognized by human laws, Nature does once to every being that lives; and in a large proportion of cases, after protracted tortures such as only the greatest monsters whom we read of ever purposely inflicted on their living fellow-creatures. If, by an arbitrary reservation, we refuse to account anything murder but what abridges a certain term supposed to be allotted to human life, nature also does this to all but a small percentage of lives, and does it in all the modes, violent or insidious, in which the worst human beings take the lives of one another. Nature impales men, breaks them as if on the wheel, casts them to be devoured by wild beasts, burns them to death, crushes them with stones like the first christian martyr, starves them with hunger, freezes them with cold, poisons them by the quick or slow venom of her exhalations, and has hundreds of other hideous deaths in reserve, such as the ingenious cruelty of a Nabis or a Domitian never surpassed. All this, Nature does with the most supercilious disregard both of mercy and of justice, emptying her shafts upon the best and noblest indifferently with the meanest and worst; upon those who are engaged in the highest and worthiest enterprises, and often as the direct consequence of the noblest acts; and it might almost be imagined as a punishment for them. She mows down those on whose existence hangs the well-being of a whole people, perhaps the prospects of the human race for generations to come, with as little compunction as those whose death is a relief to themselves, or a blessing to those under their noxious influence. Such are Nature's dealings with life. Even when she does not intend to kill, she inflicts the same tortures in apparent wantonness. In the clumsy provision which she has made for that perpetual renewal of animal life, rendered necessary by the prompt termination she puts to it in every individual instance, no human being ever comes into the world but another human being is literally stretched on the rack for hours or days, not unfrequently issuing in death. Next to taking life (equal to it according to a high authority) is taking the means by which we live; and Nature does this too on the largest scale and with the most callous indifference. A single hurricane destroys the hopes of a season; a flight of locusts, or any inundation, desolates a district; a trifling chemical change in an edible root, starves a million of people. The waves of the sea, like banditti seize and appropriate the wealth of the rich and the little all of the poor with the same accompaniments of stripping, wounding, and killing as their human antitypes. Everything in short, which the worst men commit either against life or property is perpetrated on a larger scale by natural agents. . . . Even the love of "order" which is thought to be a following of the ways of Nature, is in fact a contradiction of them. All which people are accustomed to deprecate as "disorder" and its consequences, is precisely a counterpart of Nature's ways. Anarchy and the Reign of Terror are overmatched in injustice, ruin, and death, by a hurricane and a pestilence. . . .

The phrases which ascribe perfection to the course of nature can only be considered as the exaggerations of poetic or devotional feeling, not intended to stand the test of a sober examination. No one, either religious or irreligious, believes that the hurtful agencies of nature, considered as a whole, promote good purposes, in any other way than by inciting human rational creatures to rise up and struggle against them. If we believe that those agencies were appointed by a benevolent Providence as the means of accomplishing wise purposes which could not be compassed if they did not exist, then everything done by mankind which tends to chain up these natural agencies or to restrict their mischievous operation, from draining a pestilential marsh down to curing the toothache, or putting up an umbrella, ought to be accounted impious; which assuredly nobody does account them, notwithstanding an undercurrent of sentiment setting in that direction which is occasionally perceptible. On the contrary, the improvements on which the civilized part of mankind most pride themselves, consist in more successfully warding off those natural calamities which if we really believed what most people profess to believe, we should cherish as medicines provided for our earthly state by infinite wisdom. Inasmuch too as each generation greatly surpasses its predecessors in the amount of natural evil which it succeeds in averting, our condition, if the theory were true, ought by this time to have become a terrible manifestation of some tremendous calamity, against which the physical evils we have learnt to overmaster, had previously operated as a preservative. Any one, however, who acted as if he supposed this to be the case, would be more likely, I think, to be confined as a lunatic, than reverenced as a saint. . . .

This brief survey is amply sufficient to prove that the duty of man is the same in respect to his own nature as in respect to the nature of all other things; namely not to follow but to amend it. Some people however who do not attempt to deny that instinct ought to be subordinate to reason, pay deference to nature so far as to maintain that every natural inclination must have some sphere of action granted to it: some opening left for its gratification. . . .

But even if it were true that every one of the elementary impulses of human nature has its good side, and may by a sufficient amount of artificial training be made more useful than hurtful; how little would this amount to, when it must in any case be admitted that without such training all of them, even those which are necessary to our preservation, would fill the world with misery, making human life an exaggerated likeness of the odious scene of violence and tyranny which is exhibited by the rest of the animal kingdom, except in so far as tamed and disciplined by man. There, indeed, those who flatter themselves with the notion of reading the purposes of the Creator in his works, ought in consistency to have seen grounds for inferences from which they have shrunk. If there are any marks at all of special design in creation, one of the things most evidently designed is that a large proportion of all animals should pass their existence in tormenting and devouring other animals. They have been lavishly fitted out with the instruments necessary for that purpose; their strongest instinct impel them to it, and many of them seem to have been constructed incapable of supporting themselves by any other food. If a tenth part of the pains which have been expended in finding benevolent adaptations in all nature, had been employed in collecting evidence to blacken the character of the Creator, what scope for comment would not have been found in the entire existence of the lower animals, divided, with scarcely an exception, into devourers and devoured, and a prey to a thousand ills from which they are denied the faculties necessary for protecting themselves! If we are not obliged to believe the animal creation to be the work of a demon, it is because we need not suppose it to have been made by a Being of infinite power. But if imitation of the Creator's will as revealed in nature, were applied as a rule of action in this case, the most atrocious enormities of the worst men would be more than justified by the apparent intention of Providence that throughout all animated nature the strong should prey upon the weak. . . .

The scheme of Nature regarded in its whole extent, cannot have had, for its sole or even principal object, the good of human or other sentient beings. What good it brings to them, is mostly the result of their own exertions. Whatsoever, in nature, gives indication of beneficent design, proves this beneficence to be armed only with limited power; and the duty of man is to co-operate with the beneficent powers, not by imitating but by perpetually striving to amend the course of nature—and bringing that part of it over which we can exercise control, more nearly into conformity with a high standard of justice and goodness.

CHAPTER 12

How Should
I Respond
to Poverty?

The unprecedented number of homeless people in the United States over the past few decades has brought poverty to the attention of the national media. And for many of us the increased number of individuals asking for money on the street has also brought poverty to our individual attention. These days poverty cannot be seen as the exclusive problem of the Third World and the occasional unfortunate. It is a big problem in all American cities, and every time someone on the street asks you for a quarter, you are confronted with the need to respond. What should you do? Should you give money to anyone you pass who might need it? Should you refuse to give money to someone you expect will use it for drugs? Should you adopt the habit of giving to established charities in lieu of giving money to people on the streets? Is the need of someone on a street in your city really your problem at all?

When are we required to help other people? Most moral theorists—and most people in general—believe that we have an obligation to help those who need our help. According to this line of reasoning, one who could easily save a drowning child has a moral obligation to attempt the rescue. Philosophers differ in their explanations of why we have this obligation. According to Kant, for instance, we should assist others because we could not rationally live in a world in which people made it a policy to ignore those who need their help. According to Mill, we should offer help because this course of action would promote more happiness for more people than any alternative action. Even before reflecting on the basis of our obligation, most of us share the intuition that not offering help in this case would be morally offensive.

What, then, is our moral obligation toward poor people? Is it comparable to the case of a drowning child whom one is in a position to save? Or is it more similar to the case of a drowning person that one might save, but might also fail to save—and might risk one's own life in the process? We can only answer such questions by becoming more specific about what we mean by "helping those in need." Giving a quarter to a street person is not likely to put you in much risk. Becoming a doctor and treating victims of contagious infectious diseases in a poor neighborhood might involve risks. When you think of helping the poor, what strategies do you have in mind?

Welfare reform has become a political issue in the United States. Much of the discussion has emphasized the importance of fighting poverty by getting people off welfare. John D. Jones observes, however, that this strategy alone will not end poverty. The impoverished would also have to be able to get good-paying jobs when they got off welfare; but good-paying jobs are chronically scarce in our society. Assuming that we desire a society in which people of all races and backgrounds have equal opportunities, this situation is particularly unfortunate. Members of racial minority groups fall below the poverty line in disproportionate numbers; and a larger percentage earns less than a living wage, since the official poverty line is unrealistically low. Unmarried teenage mothers are only a part of the problem, Jones claims. Our society's programs to fight poverty have been half-hearted and ineffective, and they have reinforced the stigmatization of the poor, which impoverishes them further by undermining their sense of human dignity. Welfare reform will help eliminate poverty only if society makes a concentrated effort to reduce unemployment and to create jobs that pay well enough to lift poor people out of poverty on a permanent basis.

Nancy Fraser considers the condition of impoverished women in a similar light. She observes that the "feminization of poverty," the tendency for increasing numbers of women to fall below the official poverty line, has not led to the development of programs that actually pertain to women's needs or situations. Moreover, programs actually exacerbate the problems of poor women by ensuring that they assume the position of a "dependent" as opposed to that of "rights-bearing beneficiary." Fraser urges the development of programs that address women's needs and that treat them as full adults with rights.

Peter Marin agrees that sexism contributes to the plight of poor people. He observes, however, that gender assumptions also harm poor men. Although society is male dominated, only a subset of the male population actually dominates. On the other end of the spectrum are the homeless, the vast majority of whom are single men. Marin contends that society has let these men down. They have only enough education to be classed as "unskilled" laborers, yet jobs for the unskilled have largely disappeared. Moreover, households that include an able-bodied man have often been denied welfare; as a consequence, some men have become homeless so that their loved ones could get assistance. Marin thinks these arrangements reflect a societal belief that although women and children can be dependent, men cannot. Any man who is unable or unwilling to be independent is considered undeserving of help. The consequence is that homeless men often despair. Marin proposes the creation of job and educational opportunities and the development of a more extensive social net for men in trouble. Fundamentally, he contends, society needs to revise its assumptions and acknowledge that a man can need help and still be a man.

Peter Singer addresses the question of how far we are morally required to go in addressing the needs of poor people. His answer is that we are morally required to do as much as we can without sacrificing anything else "of comparable moral importance." Thus, each of us ought to give until he or she reaches the point at which further sacrifice would cause more suffering to oneself or one's dependents than giving would alleviate. Singer bases his argument on utilitarian grounds. Garrett Hardin also uses utilitarian grounds to counter Singer's view. He contends that with respect to the poor people of the world, those who are better off are like people in a lifeboat who can only rescue a limited number from drowning. The alternatives for those better off, as Hardin sees it, are to do what they can for themselves and posterity or to distribute the goods of the world so thinly that everyone suffers.

The debate between Singer and Hardin raises the question of justice in connection with the distribution of the world's goods. Some thinkers question whether wealth can be morally justified in a world in which so many people are impoverished. Andrew Carnegie offers a defense of wealth based on the advantages that competition for wealth provides to society as a whole. Carnegie, however, believes that those who are wealthy have a moral obligation to bestow charity. He thus defends the concept of *noblesse oblige*, the idea that privilege brings with it responsibilities to those who are not so privileged.

Amartya Sen considers the nature of poor people's rights. He observes that property rights have long been considered fundamental in societies with common law backgrounds, whereas the right not to be hungry has only recently been taken seriously in certain nations. He observes that "rights" can be understood as instruments to other goals, as constraints, or as goals in their own right. Rights are themselves goals, Sen is convinced, but he notes that the right to be free from hunger might be defended as both valuable in itself and as a means to other desirable social goals. He concludes that either type of defense depends on our understanding of empirical facts. Thus, our moral thinking about poverty requires that we undertake serious empirical investigations.

Frequently, discussions of possible remedies for poverty have considered the basic policy approach that government ought to take. Should government, for instance, be in the business of ensuring the material welfare of its citizens? Some would argue that this is not the proper business of government and that "welfare governments" are harmful to society at large. Many are convinced that the material and spiritual needs of citizens are best met by a government that supports free enterprise and competition. Michael Harrington analyzes the history of American capitalism and reaches different conclusions. In our current situation, as he sees it, free enterprise is not as "free" as many people imagine. Our economy is a planned economy, and it will continue to be so. The question we need to address is whether the planning will be the province of business or of government. Harrington believes that powerful business leaders currently make major decisions, affecting the lives of all Americans, without sufficient checks and balances. His solution to this problem is greater government control.

JOHN D. JONES

Multiculturalism and Welfare Reform

JOHN D. JONES teaches philosophy at Marquette University. His research is primarily in the areas of social philosophy, philosophical anthropology, and phenomenology. He is the author of numerous articles on poverty and a book titled *Poverty and the Human Condition* (1990).

There is no one simple definition of or "paradigm" for a multicultural society. At the very least, I assume that multiculturalism focuses on creating conditions for human flourishing within the context of a racially and culturally diverse society. Of course, creation of a multicultural society requires that people and communities have adequate economic wherewithal, not just for literary, artistic, or intellectual activities, but also for such daily activities as child-raising, creating of safe and aesthetically pleasant neighborhoods, securing adequate health care, and so on. Certainly, a great deal of strength, vitality and creativity may exist among economically impoverished people and cultures; nevertheless, poverty is also a basic impediment to full human realization and flourishing. This is especially true in our society where so many activities require success in the economic domain.

Given the widespread and disproportionate poverty that people of color experience, it seems to me that multiculturalism remains profoundly incomplete if it neglects issues of poverty and limits itself, even tacitly, to issues relating to the arts, education, public discourse, the media, workplace etiquette and access to better paying or more prestigious jobs. Moreover, a crucial point of my paper is that if we are to successfully discuss poverty as an issue within multiculturalism, then there must be a serious critique of the current framework of welfare reform since it perpetuates a basic stigmatization of the poor and it has little to do with the general alleviation of poverty. That is, I will argue that the current thrust of welfare reform and the manner in which it frames our discourse about poverty—both in what it allows into discussion as well as what it excludes—is a fundamental obstacle to the creation of a multicultural, non-racist society which does not rest on economic exploitation.

Let me make one additional remark before I turn to my principal argument. In the United States, poverty disproportionately affects not only people of color, but women and children of all races and cultures. Given that current welfare reform focuses principally on unmarried women with children since they are the recipients of Aid to Families with Dependent Children (AFDC), it might seem odd not to address explicitly the relation between women and poverty. Of course, poverty and welfare reform have been addressed far more directly within feminist discourse, especially in discussions on the feminization of poverty, than within multicultural discourse. However, while poverty and welfare reform should be vital issues to those interested in feminism and multiculturalism, I believe that it is a mistake to approach poverty and welfare reform as if it is principally a matter of dealing with unmarried women and their children. Current welfare reform encourages this error. As I will argue, approaching poverty and welfare reform in this way shifts our focus away from the full extent of poverty in this country and away from basic questions and presuppositions about the very ways in which we typically conceive of and grant assistance to the poor.

Consider some basic statistics concerning the status of the poor in this country. In 1992, 36.9 million people or 14.5 percent of the population lived in poverty. While the poverty rate for Whites was 11.6 percent, it was 33.3 percent and 29.3 percent for African-Americans and people of Hispanic origin respectively (US Bureau of the Census, 1993). As I have argued elsewhere, government poverty lines at best demarcate a level of minimal, basic physical subsistence. Consequently, poverty line incomes do not count as a "living wage." If we adopt relational measures of poverty that set poverty lines at thresholds which demarcate minimal levels of human flourishing (and not just basic subsistence), current poverty lines should be raised by approximately 50 percent. This increase would have a striking effect on estimating the number of poor. For example, while the official poverty rate was 11.6 percent in 1988, it would have increased to about 20–25 percent of the population under relational measures. Further, about 45 percent of all non-Whites would have been counted as poor.

For the most part, current approaches to welfare reform respond to the plight of the poor in the following manner. The social welfare programs of the War on Poverty have fundamentally failed; poverty has not been eliminated. Moreover, these programs have produced a class of welfare poor who are dependent on welfare and who are either unwilling or unable to work. The alleged solution: "end welfare as we know it" by moving able-bodied welfare recipients—principally unmarried women with dependent children (AFDC recipients)—off welfare roles and into the labor market. To be sure, various programs may offer job training, education and childcare. Yet, this "solution" seems to ignore a chronic shortage of jobs, let alone jobs with decent wages. According to David Riemer, available data on the relationship of job vacancies to eligible workers:

> . . . all points to the same conclusion: the supply of officially unemployed workers *alone* exceeds the supply of unfilled jobs. . . . [Studies] show that—depending on the official unemployment rate—the number of officially, unemployed consistently exceeds the number of unfilled jobs by ratios ranging from 10:1 to 3:1. When welfare recipients and "discouraged workers" are thrown into the mix that ratio gets worse. . . . While any individual's poverty in the United States may be the result of inadequate motivation . . . aggregate poverty in this country is the result of two simple shortcomings of the labor market: too few jobs and too many jobs that pay wages too low.

Along with a chronic shortage of jobs, we must also take into account the reality of depressed wages relative to income required to escape poverty and achieve a decent living wage. In 1989, a full-time, year-round job at the minimum wage did not even support a family of two at the poverty line. Furthermore, "according to the Census Bureau, 14.4 million year-round, full-time workers 16 years of age or older (18 percent of the total) had annual earnings below the poverty level in 1990, up from 10.3 million (14.6 percent) in 1984 and 6.6 million (12.3 percent) in 1974."

Unfortunately, despite the billions of dollars devoted to social services in this country, "welfare relief" simply does not substantially relieve the pervasiveness of poverty.

In 1983, only about 50 percent of the poor received some form of means-tested assistance such as Supplemental Security Income (SSI), AFDC or General Assistance.
According to the Census Bureau (1993):

> . . . in 1992, about 27 percent of the poor received no assistance. About 43 percent of persons below the poverty level in 1992 received means-tested cash assistance through such programs as Aid to Families with Dependent Children. The majority (56 percent) of persons in households where cash assistance was received had incomes still below the official poverty level after the assistance was counted as income in 1992.

Indeed in 1988, 38 percent of the poor (12 million persons) lived on incomes, including cash assistance, which were less than half of the poverty line.

It seems to me that such pervasive poverty in the US has significant implications for multiculturalism. Those who support multiculturalism and the goal of creating a culturally and racially inclusive society must confront the extremely serious threat posed by the high rates of poverty experienced by people of color and also by the current thrust of welfare reform. Even if one grants that many of the poor require training and other services before they can obtain decent jobs; nevertheless, while necessary, such programs are not sufficient to alleviate poverty. If Riemer's claims about job scarcity are even reasonably correct, then as Riemer argues:

> . . . there are only two practical methods of ending poverty in the United States: give the poor money—so much money that they get out of poverty. Or get the poor into jobs—and then make sure the jobs that they take or already hold (for most poor adults work in the first place) yield an "earnings related income" consisting of wages and earnings supplements higher than the poverty line.

Consequently, if we are to end the disproportionate poverty among people of color, numerous jobs and extensive supplemental income supports will have to be targeted to these people. However, the current consensus about cutting welfare benefits makes it highly unlikely that massive assistance and income supplements will be forthcoming for any poor, let alone poor people of color in particular. No evidence exists that we are prepared to create significant numbers of public works jobs. . . .

. . . [S]o far as current welfare reform focuses predominantly on unmarried mothers with children (in particular, Black teenage mothers) and the urban underclass (largely perceived as Black and Hispanic), it shifts our focus away from the pervasiveness of poverty and low wages throughout the economy. Yet, unless the full extent of US poverty is addressed in terms of a thoroughgoing critique of economic and welfare policies, I doubt that the disproportionate poverty that affects people of color will be fundamentally alleviated. Consequently, those interested in the creation of a multicultural society cannot simply critique welfare reform within its present framework.

One might argue that present attempts to diversify educational institutions, the arts, the media, and even the work force will help to alleviate the poverty of people of color by ensuring that more of them will gain wealth and, presumably, power and influence. Unfortunately, this result need not happen. For example, while the average White family has more than ten times the wealth of the average Black family, there is greater income inequality among Black and Hispanic families than among White families. Moreover, while the aggregate share of income for all families in the lowest two quintiles diminished during the period from 1967–91, the loss was much greater for Black and Hispanic families in the lowest quintile. That is, poverty among Blacks and Hispanics is generally more intense than poverty among Whites. Furthermore, from 1967–91, and mirroring the trend for White families, the percentage of Black and Hispanic families with incomes over $50,000 increased (and rather dramatically so for Black families). On the other hand, the percentage of Black and Hispanic families with incomes below $10,000 remained basically stable for Blacks, increased significantly for Hispanics, and decreased slightly for Whites (US Bureau of the Census, 1992). This evidence, at least, does not support the conjecture that the creation of larger Black and Hispanic middle and upper classes will translate into an improvement of the general economic conditions for poor and lower income Blacks and Hispanics.

Thus far, I have argued that the current thrust of welfare reform impedes the creation of multicultural society at the level of the policy enactment. Welfare reform also impedes this process at the ideological level or, what Handler and Hasenfeld call, "myth and ceremony." As they insightfully point out:

> . . . it is the overriding need to distinguish between the able-bodied and disabled poor, between the "undeserving" and the "deserving" poor, be they men or women of any racial or ethnic origin, that is the driving force behind welfare policy. It is the able-bodied poor, whatever their ascriptive status, who present the moral dilemma to the modern capitalist state because they challenge the legitimacy of its economic and civic order.

The stigma to which the poor, especially the welfare poor, are subjected has a two-fold nature. First, people are stigmatized simply by virtue of their poverty. Second, they are stigmatized if they receive welfare assistance. In a capitalist society, where human worth seems to be determined by successful participation in the economic domain, those who fail to participate successfully are deemed inferior as people, especially when their poverty is explained primarily in individualistic rather than in structural terms. Those on welfare are also stigmatized for dependency on the state since the dependency is, of itself, an indication that they lack the paramount virtue of self-sufficiency.

Furthermore, the demand to separate the poor into those who are able-bodied and those who are disabled has always been crucial in welfare policy. Those deemed able-bodied are often excluded from assistance, especially the non-elderly poor without children. People who do receive welfare are the subjects of persistent efforts to "ferret out" the able-bodied poor in order to compel them to work. As Handler and Hasenfeld assert:

> The work requirement has both symbolic and social-regulation functions. The work requirement casts welfare recipients as morally depraved because it assumes that they lack the inner motivation to work, which must, therefore, be forced upon them.

Not surprisingly, the most vicious stigmas of poverty are reserved for urban poor. Consider the following description of the "underclass" given in the popular press:

> Behind [the ghetto's] crumbling walls live a large group of people who are more intractable, more socially alien, and more hostile than anyone had imagined. They are the unreachables. . . . [They are] a second nation . . . a separate culture of have-nots drifting further apart from the values of the haves.

This stigma is not new. Compare these descriptions with a description of the poor in nineteenth-century London:

> . . . a vast heap of social refuse—the mere human street sweepings—the great living mixen that is destined, as soon as spring returns, to be strewn far and near over the land, and serve as manure for the future crime crop of the country.

It is important to distinguish stigmatization from other sorts of cognitive and affective activities. Stigmatizing people for their poverty is not a process of stereotyping which is basically a cognitive matter of hasty generalization. It is also different from the legitimate diagnosis of behavioral, personal, and familial problems or character flaws that prevent people from escaping poverty. Rather, stigmatization involves the hostile rejection of people on the basis of their imputed intrinsic degeneracy as human beings. Consequently, what is taken to be most disturbing about the poor is not the external conditions of their poverty, but an imputed inner poverty of a moral and existential character that is the basis of their external poverty. Given the alleged degradation of the poor, especially the urban welfare poor, they are viewed as a dangerous class that demands social control and rehabilitation that are likely to be futile. . . .

If multicultural discourse fails to critique the symbolic framework in which the poor are stigmatized then it implicitly legitimates that framework because it leaves unchallenged the invidious distinctions of class stratification that cut across racial, cultural and gender boundaries. If left unchallenged, the relative success of people of color benefiting from increased racial and cultural pluralism may be self-defeating in the sense that it will serve to legitimate the stigma of those who do not succeed. That is, without such a critique, multicultural discourse may indirectly perpetuate the stigmatization of poor people of color similar to the way that work requirements perpetuate the stigma of welfare mothers. As Handler and Hasenfeld observe:

> Work requirements say that dependent mothers are expected to work, but [those requirements] are designed to ensure that most welfare recipients will not be able to escape welfare through employment . . . a few will be anointed into majoritarian society . . . [i.e.,] the model welfare mother who progresses through training, gets a decent job, and is no longer dependent. Those success stories will validate majoritarian ideologies; the great majority of welfare mothers will remain deviant by failing the work expectations. . . .

• • •

To sum up: the widespread, disproportionate poverty experienced by people of color poses a substantive threat to the development of a truly inclusive and multicultural society. The present approach to poverty that is often present in welfare reform is defective on two fundamental counts. First, welfare reform seems principally designed to reduce welfare dependency by moving so-called able-bodied welfare recipients off welfare and into the labor market. However, if evidence concerning chronic scarcity of jobs, and especially decent paying jobs, is correct, then welfare-to-work programs are unlikely to succeed. Moreover, it seems likely that welfare reform functions less in interest of the poor than of the non-poor through ostensible containment or reduction of welfare assistance benefits. Second, given that many poor do not presently receive means-tested welfare assistance, such as AFDC or General Assistance, welfare reform is fundamentally incomplete as a framework to address the general problem of alleviating poverty.

Moreover, our concept of poverty and welfare is founded on an invidious distinction between the able-bodied poor (viewed as unworthy and disreputable) and the disabled poor. This distinction is rooted in the very symbolic and conceptual foundations of capitalism: the linkage of a person's worth with his or her successful participation in the marketplace; the identification of work with paid labor; the naive presumption that people can be whatever they want so long as they work hard enough; the misplaced hope that personal labor is sufficient to command the resources and opportunities required to realize human aspirations; the belief that poverty is primarily a personal and moral failure; and so on. . . .

By way of closing, I want to briefly suggest three issues that must be addressed if multicultural discourse is effectively to critique dominant thinking about poverty and welfare reform. First, it is important to rethink the entire manner in which we define poverty, especially since poverty lines are taken to indicate thresholds of minimally adequate standards of living. Current poverty lines simply do not provide such standards; at best, they indicate the point where people can meet basic physical subsistence requirements. In other words, even if we were to eliminate subsistence-level poverty in this country, there would still be widespread deprivation, especially among people of color. As I noted at the beginning of the paper, approximately 45 percent of non-Whites would have been counted as poor in 1988 under alternative poverty lines set at roughly 150 percent of current poverty lines.

Second, we must rethink the nature of peoples' obligation to work. Typically, we assume that people have a moral obligation to support themselves and their families through participation in the labor market. "Able-bodied" poor who rely on welfare are presumed to have failed this moral obligation. Yet, if our country does not (and, perhaps, cannot) generate an adequate number of jobs with decent wages for everyone who is expected to work, then this obligation has, at best, a *prima facie* status. Surely, this obligation cannot be imposed universally on all those expected to work especially if work is defined as "wage labor." Consequently, why should economic assistance to the poor be cast in a framework that automatically stigmatizes them as moral deviants?

Third, we must question the legitimacy of the economic inequality that plagues our society and, indeed, has worsened over the last decade. Certainly, individual economic mobility exists in this country. Yet, it is difficult to see how collective poverty will ever be reduced if, as has been the case since 1950, those in the lowest quintile of income distribution consistently receive less than 5 percent of aggregate income. To what extent is this inequality embedded in the very structure of a capitalist economic system? Should we agree with bell hooks that capitalism "is a system that depends upon economic exploitation for its survival?" If we suspect she is correct, then how do we conceive the realization of a multicultural society which avoids this exploitation?

The issues involved here are not just economic and political; they are also symbolic. For, I doubt that we can achieve a just multicultural society if we lack a sense of solidarity across economic class lines. Exaggerated conceptions of individualism and competition, the linkage of human well-being with constant "upward mobility," as well as the obscene glorification of "conspicuous consumption" (one of the worst legacies of the Reagan era) inevitably support the stigmatization of the poor and implicitly undergird minimalist conceptions of poverty and welfare support. In a fundamental way, our consumer society is deeply imbued with a Callicles-like cynicism about happiness: no one can ever be happy since our desires can never be adequately satisfied. How, then, can a democratic society find the political will to work for the common economic welfare of all our people if we insist on viewing our economic life as a game of "king on the mountain"?

Women, Welfare, and the Politics of Need Interpretation

NANCY FRASER teaches philosophy, comparative literature, and women's studies at Northwestern University. Since the 1960s, she has been an activist in several oppositional social movements and is the author of *Unruly Practices: Power, Discourse and Gender in Contemporary Social Philosophy* (1989).

Long before the emergence of welfare states, governments have defined legally secured arenas of societal action. In so doing, they have at the same time codified corresponding patterns of agency or social roles. Thus, early modern states defined an economic arena and the corresponding role of an economic person capable of entering into contracts. More or less at the same time, they codified the "private sphere" of the household and the role of household head with dependents. Somewhat later, governments were led to secure a sphere of political participation and the corresponding role of citizen with (limited) political rights. In each of these cases, the original and paradigmatic subject of the newly codified social role was male. Only secondarily and much later was it conceded that women, too, could occupy these subject-positions, without however entirely dispelling the association with masculinity.

Matters are different, however, with the contemporary welfare state. When this type of government defined a new arena of activity—call it "the social"—and a new societal role, the welfare client, it included women among its original and paradigmatic subjects. Today, in fact, women have become the principal subjects of the welfare state. On the one hand, they comprise the overwhelming majority both of program recipients and of paid social service workers. On the other hand, they are the wives, mothers and daughters whose unpaid activities and obligations are redefined as the welfare state increasingly oversees forms of caregiving. Since this beneficiary-social worker-caregiver nexus of roles is constitutive of the social-welfare arena, one might even call the latter as feminized terrain.

A brief statistical overview confirms women's greater involvement with and dependence on the U.S. social-welfare system. Consider first women's greater dependence as program clients and beneficiaries. In each of the major "means-tested" programs in the U.S., women and the children for whom they are responsible now comprise the overwhelming majority of clients. For example, more than 81% of households receiving Aid to Families with Dependent Children (AFDC) are headed by women; more than 60% of families receiving food stamps or Medicaid are headed by women; and 70% of all households in publicly owned or subsidized housing are headed by women. High as they are, these figures actually underestimate the representation of women. As Barbara Nelson notes, in the androcentric reporting system, households counted as female-headed by definition contain no healthy adult men. But healthy adult women live in most households counted as male-headed. Such women may directly or indirectly receive benefits going to "male-headed" households, but they are invisible in the statistics, even though they usually do the work of securing and maintaining program eligibility.

Women also predominate in the major U.S. "age-tested" programs. For example, 61.6% of all adult beneficiaries of Social Security are women; and 64% of those covered by Medicaid are women. In sum, because women as a group are significantly poorer than men—indeed they now comprise nearly two-thirds of all U.S. adults below the official poverty line—and because women tend to live longer than men, women depend more on the social-welfare system as clients and beneficiaries.

But this is not the whole story. Women also depend more on the social-welfare system as paid human service workers—a category of employment which includes education and health, as well as social work and services administration. In 1980, 70% of the 17.3 million paid jobs in this sector in the U.S. were held by women. This accounts for one-third of U.S. women's total paid employment and a full 80% of all professional jobs held by women. The figures for women of color are even higher than this average, since 37% of their total paid employment and 82.4% of their professional employment is in this sector. It is a distinctive feature of the U.S. social-welfare system, as opposed to, say, the British and Scandinavian systems, that only 3% of these jobs are in the form of direct federal government employment. The rest are in state and local government, in the "private non-profit" sector and in the "private" sector. But the more decentralized and privatized character of the U.S. system does not make paid welfare workers any less vulnerable in the face of federal program cuts. On the contrary, the level of federal social-welfare spending affects the level of human service employment in *all* sectors. State and local government jobs depend on federal and federally financed state and local government contracts; and private profit and non-profit jobs depend on federally financed transfer payments to individuals and households for the purchase of services like health care in the market. Thus, reductions in social spending mean the loss of jobs for women. Moreover, as Barbara Ehrenreich and Frances Fox Piven note, this loss is not compensated when spending is shifted to the military, since only 0.5% of the entire female paid workforce is employed in work on military contracts. In fact, one study they cite estimates that with each one billion dollar increase in military spending, 9500 jobs are lost to women.

Finally, women are subjects of and to the social-welfare system in their traditional capacity as unpaid caregivers. It is well known that the sexual division of labor assigns women primary responsibility for the care of those who cannot care for themselves. (I leave aside women's traditional obligations to provide personal services to adult males—husbands, fathers, grown sons, lovers—who can very well care for themselves.) Such responsibility includes child care, of course, but also care for sick and/or elderly relatives, often parents. For example, a 1975 British study cited by Hilary Land found that three times as many elderly people live with married daughters as with married sons, and that those without a close female relative were more likely to be institutionalized, irrespective of degree of infirmity. As unpaid caregivers, then, women are more directly affected than men by the level and character of government social services for children, the sick and the elderly.

As clients, paid human service workers and unpaid caregivers, then, women are the principal subjects of the social-welfare system. It is as if this branch of the state were in effect a "Bureau of Women's Affairs."

Of course, the welfare system does not deal with women on women's terms. On the contrary, it has its own characteristic ways of interpreting women's needs and positioning women as subjects. In order to understand these, we need to examine how gender norms and meanings are reflected in the structure of the U.S. social-welfare system.

This issue is quite complicated. On the one hand, nearly all U.S. social-welfare programs are official gender neutral. Yet the system as a whole is a dual or two-tiered one; and it has an unmistakable gender subtext. There is one set of programs oriented to *individuals* and tied to participation in the paid workforce, for example, unemployment insurance and Social Security. These programs are designed to supplement and compensate for the primary market in paid labor power. There is a second set of programs oriented to *households* and tied to combined household income, for example, AFDC, food stamps and Medicaid. These programs are designed to compensate for what are considered to be family failures, generally the absence of a male breadwinner.

What integrates the two sets of programs is a common core of assumptions, underlying both, concerning the sexual division of labor, domestic and nondomestic. It is assumed that families do or should contain one primarily breadwinner who is male and one unpaid domestic worker (homemaker and mother) who is female. It is further assumed that when a woman undertakes paid work outside the home this is or should be in order to supplement the male breadwinner's wage and so it neither does nor ought override her primary housewifely and maternal responsibilities. It is assumed, in other words, that society is divided into two separate spheres of home and outside work and that these are women's and men's spheres respectively.

These assumptions are increasingly counterfactual. At present, fewer than 15% of U.S. families conform to the normative ideal of a domicile shared by a husband who is the sole breadwinner, a wife who is a full-time homemaker and their offspring.

Nonetheless, the separate spheres norms determine the structure of the social-welfare system. They determine that it contain a primary labor market-related subsystem and a family or household-related subsystem. Moreover, they determine that these subsystems be gender-linked, that the labor market-related system be implicitly "masculine" and the family-related system be implicitly "feminine." Consequently, the normative, ideal-typical recipient of primary labor market-oriented programs is a (white) male, while the normative, ideal-typical client of household-based programs is a female.

This gender subtext of the U.S. welfare system is confirmed when we take a second look at participation figures. Consider again the figures just cited for the "feminine" or family-based programs, which I earlier referred to as "means-tested" programs: more than 81% of households receiving AFDC are female-headed, as are more than 70% of those receiving housing assistance and more than 60% of those receiving Medicaid and food stamps. Now recall that these figures do not compare female vs. male individuals, but rather female vs. male headed-*households*. They therefore confirm four things: 1) these programs have a distinctive administrative identity in that their recipients are not individualized but *familialized*; 2) they serve what are considered to be defective families, overwhelmingly families without a male breadwinner; 3) the ideal-typical (adult) client is female; and 4) she makes her claim for benefits on the basis of her status as an unpaid domestic worker, a homemaker and mother, not as a paid worker based in the labor market.

Now contrast this with the case of a typical labor market-based and thus "masculine" program, namely, unemployment insurance. Here the percentage of female claimants drops to 38%, a figure which contrasts female vs. male *individuals,* as opposed to households. As Diana Pearce notes, this drop reflects at least two different circumstances. First, and most straightforwardly, it reflects women's lower rate of participation in the paid workforce. Second, it reflects the fact that many women wage-workers are not eligible to participate in this program, for example, paid household service workers, part-time workers, pregnant workers and workers in the "irregular economy" such as prostitutes, baby-sitters and home typists. The exclusion of these predominantly female wage-workers testifies to the existence of a gender segmented labor market, divided into "primary" and "secondary" employment. It reflects the more general assumption that women's earnings are "merely supplementary," not on a par with those of the primary (male) breadwinner. Altogether, then, the figures tell us four things about programs like unemployment insurance: 1) they are administered in a way which *individualizes* rather than familiarizes recipients; 2) they are designed to compensate primary labor market effects, such as the temporary displacement of a primary breadwinner; 3) the ideal-typical recipient is male; and 4) he makes his claim on the basis of his identity as a paid worker, not as an unpaid domestic worker or parent.

One final example will round out the picture. The Social Security system of retirement insurance presents the interesting case of a hermaphrodite or androgyne. I shall soon show that this system has a number of characteristics of "masculine" programs in virtue of its link to participation in the paid workforce. However, it is also internally dualized and gendered, and thus stands as a microcosm of the entire dual-benefit welfare system. Consider that, while a majority—61.6%—of adult beneficiaries are female, only somewhat more than half of these—or 33.3% of all recipients—claim benefits on the basis of their own paid work records. The remaining female recipients claim benefits on the basis of their husbands' records, that is, as wives or unpaid domestic workers. By contrast, virtually no male recipients claim benefits as husbands. On the contrary, they claim benefits as paid workers, a labor market-located as opposed to family-located identity. So the Social Security system is hermaphroditic or androgynous; it is internally divided between family-based, "feminine" benefits, on the one hand, and labor market-based, "masculine" benefits, on the other hand. Thus, it too gets its structure from gender norms and assumptions.

So far, we have established the dualistic structure of the U.S. social-welfare system and the gender subtext of the dualism. Now, we can better tease out the system's implicit norms and tacit assumptions by examining its mode of operation. To see how welfare programs interpret women's needs, we should consider what benefits consist in. To see how programs position women as subjects, we should examine administrative practices. In general, we shall see that the "masculine" and "feminine" subsystems are not only separate but also unequal.

Consider that the "masculine" social-welfare programs are social insurance schemes. They include unemployment insurance, Social Security (retirement insurance), Medicare (age-tested health insurance) and Supplemental Social Security Insurance (disability insurance for those with paid work records). These programs are contributory; wage-workers and their employers pay into trust funds. They are administered on a national basis and benefit levels are uniform across the country. Though bureaucratically organized and administered, they require less, and less demeaning effort on the part of beneficiaries in qualifying and maintaining eligibility than do "feminine" programs.

They are far less subject to intrusive controls and in most cases lack the dimension of surveillance. They also tend to require less of beneficiaries in the way of benefit-collection efforts, with the notable exception of unemployment insurance.

In sum, "masculine" social insurance schemes position recipients primarily as *rights-bearers*. The beneficiaries of these programs are in the main not stigmatized. Neither administrative practice nor popular discourse constitutes them as "on the dole." They are constituted rather as receiving what they deserve, what they, in "partnership" with their employers, have already paid in for, what they, therefore, have a *right* to. Moreover, these beneficiaries are also positioned as *purchasing consumers*. They receive cash as opposed to "in kind" benefits and so are positioned as having "the liberty to strike the best bargain they can in purchasing services of their choice on the open market." In sum, these beneficiaries are what C. B. MacPherson calls "possessive individuals." Proprietors of their own persons who have freely contracted to sell their labor-power, they become participants in social insurance schemes and, thence, paying consumers of human services. They therefore qualify as *social citizens* in virtually the fullest sense that term can acquire within the framework of a male-dominated capitalist society.

All this stands in stark contrast to the "feminine" sector of the U.S. social-welfare system. This sector consists in relief programs, such as AFDC, food stamps, Medicaid and public housing assistance. These programs are not contributory, but are financed out of general tax revenues, usually with one-third of the funds coming from the federal government and two-thirds coming from the states. They are not administered nationally but rather by the states. As a result, benefit levels vary dramatically, though they are everywhere inadequate, deliberately pegged below the official poverty line. The relief programs are notorious for the varieties of administrative humiliation they inflict upon clients. They require considerable work in qualifying and maintaining eligibility; and they have a heavy component of surveillance.

These programs do not in any meaningful sense position their subjects as rights-bearers. Far from being considered as having a right to what they receive, recipients are defined as "beneficiaries of governmental largesse" or "clients of public charity." In the androcentric-administrative framework, "welfare mothers" are considered not to work and so are sometimes required, that is to say coerced, to work off their benefits via "workfare." They thus become inmates of what Diana Pearce calls a "workhouse without walls." Indeed, the only sense in which the category of rights is relevant to these clients' situation is the somewhat dubious one according to which they are entitled to treatment governed by the standards of formal-bureaucratic procedural rationality. But if that right is construed as protection from administrative caprice, then even it is widely and routinely disregarded. Moreover, recipients of public relief are generally not positioned as purchasing consumers. A significant portion of their benefits is "in kind" and what cash they get comes already carved up and earmarked for specific, administratively designated purposes. These recipients are therefore essentially *clients*, a subject-position which carries far less power and dignity in capitalist societies than does the alternative position of purchaser. In these societies, to be a client in the sense relevant to relief recipients is to be an abject dependent. Indeed, this sense of the term carries connotations of a fall from autonomy, as when we speak, for example, of "the client-states of empires or superpowers." As clients, then, recipients of relief are *the negatives of possessive individuals*. Largely excluded from the market, both as workers and as consumers, claiming benefits not as individuals but as members of "failed" families, these recipients are effectively denied the trappings of social citizenship as the latter are defined within male-dominated capitalist societies.

Clearly, this system creates a double-bind for women raising children without a male breadwinner. By failing to offer them day care, job training, a job that pays a "family wage" or some combination of these, it constructs them exclusively as mothers. As a consequence, it interprets their needs as maternal needs and their sphere of activity as that of "the family." Now, according to the ideology of separate spheres, this should be an honorific social identity. Yet the system does not honor these women. On the contrary, instead of providing them a guaranteed income equivalent to a family wage as a matter of right, it stigmatizes, humiliates and harasses them. In effect, it decrees that these women must be, yet cannot be, normative mothers.

Moreover, the way in which the U.S. social-welfare system interprets "maternity" and "the family" is race- and culture-specific. The bias is made plain in Carol Stack's study, *All Our Kin.* Stack analyzes domestic arrangements of very poor Black welfare recipients in a midwestern city. Where ideologues see "the disorganization of *the* [sic] black family," she finds complex, highly organized kinship structures. These include kin-based networks of resource pooling and exchange which enable those in direst poverty to survive economically and communally. The networks organize delayed exchanges or "gifts," in Mauss' (1967) sense, of prepared meals, food stamps, cooking, shopping, groceries, furniture, sleeping space, cash (including wages and AFDC allowances), transportation, clothing, child care, even children. They span several physically distinct households and so transcend the principal administrative category which organizes relief programs. It is significant that Stack took great pains to conceal the identities of her subjects, even going so far as to disguise the identity of their city. The reason, though unstated, is obvious: these people would lose their benefits if program administrators learned that they did not utilize them within the confines and boundaries of a "household."

We can summarize the separate and unequal character of the two-tiered, gender-linked, race- and culture-biased U.S. social-welfare system in the following formulae: Participants in the "masculine" subsystem are positioned as *rights-bearing beneficiaries and purchasing consumers of services.* Participants in the "feminine" subsystem, on the other hand, are positioned as *dependent clients.*

PETER MARIN

Homelessness and Welfare
The Prejudice against Men

PETER MARIN is an essayist and novelist. He has written a number of articles on homelessness, recently with the support of the Alicia Patterson Foundation.

For the past several years advocates for the homeless have sought public support and sympathy by drawing attention to the large number of homeless families on our streets. That is an understandable tactic. Americans usually respond to social issues on the basis of sympathy for "innocent" victims—those whose blamelessness touches our hearts and whom we deem unable to care for themselves. Families, and especially children, obviously fill the bill.

But the fact remains, despite the claims of advocates, that the problem of chronic homelessness is essentially a problem of *single adult men*. Far more single adults than families, and far more men than women, end up homeless on our streets. Until we understand how and why that happens, nothing we do about homelessness will have much of an impact.

Most figures pertaining to the homeless come from limited studies or educated guesses that tend, when examined, to dissolve in one's hand. The most convincing figures I know can be found in James Wright's book *Address Unknown: The Homeless in America*. According to Wright's data, out of every 1,000 homeless people in America, 120 or so will be adults with children, another hundred will be children and the rest will be single adults. Out of that total, 156 will be single women and 580 will be single men. Now break that down into percentages. Out of all single homeless adults, 78 percent are men; out of all homeless adults, more than 64 percent are single men; and out of all homeless people—adults or children—58 percent are single men.

But even those figures do not give the full story. Our federal welfare system has been designed, primarily, to aid women with children or whole families. That means that most of the families and children on the streets have either fallen through the cracks of the welfare system or have not yet entered it. They will, in the end, have access to enough aid to get them off the streets and into some form of shelter, while most men will be left permanently on their own.

I do not mean to diminish here the suffering of families or children, nor to suggest that welfare provides much more than the meanest alternative to homelessness. It is a form of indentured pauperism so grim it shames the nation. But it does in fact eventually get most families off the streets, and that leaves behind, as the chronically homeless, single adults, of whom four-fifths are men. Seen that way, homelessness emerges as a problem involving what happens to men without money, or men in trouble.

Why do so many more men than women end up on the streets? Let me begin with the simplest answers.

First, life on the streets, as dangerous as it is for men, is even more dangerous for women, who are far more vulnerable. While many men in trouble drift almost naturally onto the streets, women do almost anything to avoid it.

Second, there are far better private and public shelters and services available to women.

Third, women are accustomed to asking for help while men are not; women therefore make better use of available resources.

Fourth, poor families *in extremis* seem to practice a form of informal triage. Young men are released into the streets more readily, while young women are kept at home even in the worst circumstances.

Fifth, there are cultural and perhaps even genetic factors at work. There is some evidence that men—especially in adolescence—are more aggressive and openly rebellious than women and therefore harder to socialize. Or it may simply be that men are allowed to live out the impulses women are taught to suppress, and that they therefore end up more often in marginal roles.

More important, still, may be the question of work. Historically, the kinds of work associated with transient or marginal life have been reserved for men. They brought in crops, worked on ships and docks, built roads and railroads, logged and mined. Such labor granted them a place in the economy while allowing them to remain on society's edges—an option rarely available to women save through prostitution.

And society has always seemed, by design, to produce the men who did such work. Obviously, poverty and joblessness forced men into marginality. But there was more to it than that. Schools produced failures, dropouts and rebels; family life and its cruelties produced runaways and throwaways; wars rendered men incapable of settled or domestic life; small-town boredom and provinciality led them to look elsewhere for larger worlds.

Now, of course, the work such men did is gone. But like a mad engine that cannot be shut down, society goes right on producing them. Its institutions function as they always did: The schools hum, the families implode or collapse, the wars churn out their victims. But what is there for them to do? The low-paying service-sector jobs that have replaced manual labor in the economy go mainly to women or high school kids, not the men who once did the nation's roughest work.

Remember, too, in terms of work, that women, especially when young, have one final option denied to men. They can take on the "labor" of being wives and companions to men or of bearing children, and in return they will often be supported or "taken care of" by someone else. Yes, I know: Such roles can often constitute a form of oppression especially when assumed out of necessity. But nonetheless, the possibility is there. It is permissible (as well as often necessary) for women to become financially, if precariously, dependent on others, while such dependence is more or less forbidden to men.

Finally, there is the federal welfare system. I do not think most Americans understand how the system works, or how for decades it has actually sent men into the streets, creating at least some male homelessness while aiding women and children. Let me explain. There are two main programs that provide care for Americans in trouble. One is Social Security Disability Insurance. It goes to men or women who are unable, because of physical or mental problems, to work or take care of themselves. The other is Aid to Families with Dependent Children (A.F.D.C.). It is what we ordinarily call "welfare."

With its roots early in this century, it was established more or less in its present form during the Depression. Refined and expanded again in the 1960s, A.F.D.C. had always been a program meant mainly for women and children and limited to households headed by women. As long as an adult man remained in the household as mate, companion or father, *no aid was forthcoming.* Changes have recently been made in the system, and men may remain in the household if they have a work history satisfying certain federal guidelines. But in poor areas and for certain ethnic groups, where unemployment runs high and few men have a qualifying work history, these changes have not yet had much of an impact and men remain functionally outside the welfare system.

When it comes to single and "able-bodied," or employable, adults, there is no federal aid whatsoever. Individual states and localities sometimes provide their own aid through "general assistance" and "relief." But this is usually granted only on a temporary basis or in emergencies. And in those few places where it is available for longer periods to large numbers of single adults—California, for instance, or New York—it is often so grudging, so ringed round with capricious requirements and red tape, that it is of little use to those in need.

This combination of approaches not only systematically denies men aid as family members or single adults. It means that the aid given to women has sometimes actually deprived men of homes, even as it has provided for women and children. Given the choice between receiving aid for themselves and their children and living with men, what do you think most women do? The regulations as they stand actually force men to compete with the state for women; as a woman in New Orleans once told me: "Welfare changes even love. If a man can't make more at a job than I get from welfare, I ain't even gonna look at him. I can't afford it."

Everywhere in America poor men have been forced to become ghost-lovers and ghost-fathers, one step ahead of welfare workers ready to disqualify families for having a man around. In many ghettos throughout the country you find women and children in their deteriorating welfare apartments, and their male companions and fathers in even worse conditions: homeless in gutted apartments and abandoned cars, denied even the minimal help granted the opposite sex.

Is it surprising, in this context, that many African-Americans see welfare as an extension of slavery that destroys families, isolates women and humiliates men according to white bureaucratic whim? Or is it accidental that in poor communities family structure has collapsed and more and more children are born outside marriage at precisely the same time that disfranchised men are flooding the streets? Welfare is not the only influence at work in all of this, of course. But before judging men and their failures and difficulties, one must understand that their social roles are in no way supported or made easier by the social policies that in small ways make female roles sustainable.

Is this merely an accidental glitch in the system, something that has happened unnoticed? Or does it merely have something to do with a sort of lifeboat ethic, where our scarce resources for helping people are applied according to the ethics of a sinking ship—women and children first, men into the sea?

I do not think so. Something else is at work: deep-seated prejudices and attitudes toward men that are so pervasive, so pandemic, that we have ceased to notice or examine them.

To put it simply: Men are neither supposed nor allowed to be dependent. They are expected to take care of both others *and* themselves. And when they cannot do it, or "will not" do it, the built-in assumption at the heart of the culture is that they are *less than men* and therefore unworthy of help. An irony asserts itself: Simply by being in need of help, men forfeit the right to it.

Think here of how we say "helpless as a woman." This demeans women. But it also does violence to men. It implies that a man cannot be helpless and still be a man, or that helplessness is not a male attribute, or that a woman can be helpless through no fault of her own, but that if a man is helpless it is or must be his own fault. . . .

We are so used to thinking of ours as a male-dominated society that we tend to lose track of the ways in which some men are as oppressed, or perhaps even more oppressed, than most women. But race and class, as well as gender, play roles in oppression. And while it is true, in general, that men dominate society and women, in practice it is only *certain* men who are dominant; others, usually those from the working class and often darker skinned (at least 50 percent of homeless men are black or Latino), suffer endlessly from forms of isolation and contempt that often exceed what many women experience.

The irony at work in all of this is that what you often find among homeless men, and what seems at the heart of their troubles, is precisely what our cultural myths deny them: a helplessness they cannot overcome on their own. You find vulnerability, a sense of injury and betrayal and, in their isolation, a despair equal to what we accept without question in women.

Often this goes unadmitted. Even when in deep trouble men understand, sometimes unconsciously, that they are not to complain or ask for help. I remember several men I knew in the local hobo jungle. Most of them were vets. They had constructed a tiny village of half-caves and shelters among the trees and brush, and when stove smoke filled the clearing and they stood bare to the waist, knives at their hips, you would swear you were in an army jungle camp. They drank throughout the day, and at dusk there always came a moment when they wandered off individually to sit staring out at the mountains or sea. And you could see on their faces at such moments, if you caught them unawares, a particular and unforgettable look: pensive, troubled, somehow innocent—the look of lost children or abandoned men.

I have seen the same look multiplied hundreds of times on winter nights in huge shelters in great cities, where a thousand men at a time will sometimes gather, each encapsulated in solitude on a bare cot, coughing and turning or sometimes crying all night, lost in nightmares as terrible as a child's or as life on the street. In the mornings they returned to their masked public personas, to the styles of behavior and appearance that often frightened passers-by. But while they slept you could see past all that, and you found yourself thinking: These are still, even grown, *somebody's* children, and many fare no better on their own, as adults, than they would have as children.

I remember, too, a young man in my town who was always in trouble for beating up older drunken men. No one understood his brutality until he explained it one day to a woman he trusted: "When I was a kid my daddy ran off and my mother's drunken brothers disciplined me. Whenever I made a mistake they punished me by slicing my legs with a straight razor." And he pulled up his pant-legs to reveal on each shin a ladder of scars marking each childhood error or flaw.

This can stand for countless stories I've heard. The feeling you get, over and over, is that most men on the street have been "orphaned" in some way, deprived somewhere along the line of the kinds of connection, support and sustenance that enable people to find and keep places in the social order. Of course economics plays a part in this—I do not mean to suggest it does not. But more often than not, something else is also at work, something that cuts close to the bone of social and psychological as well as economic issues: the dissolution of family structures and the vitiation of community; subtle and overt forms of discrimination and racism; and institutions—schools, for instance—that harm or marginalize almost as many people as they help.

For decades now, sociologists have called our attention to rents in our private social fabric as well as our public "safety nets," and to the victims they produce: abused kids, battered women, isolated adults, alcoholics, addicts. Why, I wonder, is it so hard to see homeless men in this context? Why is it so hard to understand that the machinery of our institutions can injure men as permanently as it does women? We know, for instance, that both male and female children are permanently injured by familial abuse and violence and "normal" cruelties of family life. Why, then, do we find it hard to see that grown men, as well as women, can be crippled by childhood, or that they often end up on the edges of society, unable to play expected roles in a world that has betrayed them? . . .

The fact is that most such men seem to have tried to make a go of things, and many are willing to try again. But if others have given up . . . , is that really astonishing? The curious world we've compounded in America of equal parts of freedom and isolation and individualism and demands for obedience and submission is a strange and wearing mix, and no one can be startled at the number of victims or recalcitrants it produces or at those who can't succeed at it.

Finally, I must add one more thing. Whatever particular griefs men may have experienced on their way to homelessness, there is one final and crippling sorrow all of them share: a sense of betrayal at society's refusal to recognize their needs. Most of us—men and women—grow up expecting that when things go terribly wrong someone, from somewhere, will step forward to help us. That this does not happen, and that all watch from the shore as each of us, in isolation, struggles to swim and then begins to sink, is perhaps the most terrible discovery that anyone in any society can make. When troubled men make that discovery, as all homeless men do sooner or later, then hope vanishes completely; despair rings them round; they have become what they need not have become: the homeless men we see everywhere around us.

What can be done about this? What will set it right? One can talk, of course, about confronting the root causes of marginalization: the failure of families, schools and communities; the stupidities of war, racism and discrimination; social and economic injustice; the disappearance of generosity and reciprocity among us. But what good will that do? America is what it is; culture has a tenacity of its own; and though it is easy to call for major kinds of renewal, nothing of the sort is likely to occur.

That leaves us with ameliorative and practical measures, and it will do no harm to mention them, though they too are not likely to be tried: a further reformation of the welfare system; the federalization of assistance to single adults; increases in the amount and duration of unemployment insurance; further raises in the minimum wage; expanded benefits for vets; detox centers and vocational education for those who want them; the construction of the kinds of low-cost hotels and boarding houses where men in trouble once stayed.

And remember that back in the Depression when the welfare system was established, it was paralleled by programs providing work for men: the Civilian Conservation Corps and the Works Progress Administration. The idea seems to have been welfare for women, work for men. We still have the welfare for women, but where is the work for those men, or women, who want it? Why no one is currently lobbying for contemporary forms of those old programs remains a mystery. Given the deterioration of the American infrastructure—roads, bridges, public buildings—such programs would make sense from any point of view.

But beyond all this, and behind and beneath it, there remains the problem with which we began: the prejudices at work in society that prevent even the attempt to provide solutions. Suggestions such as those I have made will remain merely utopian notions without an examination and renovation of our attitudes toward men. During the past several decades we have slowly, laboriously, begun to confront our prejudices and oppressive practices in relation to women. Unless we now undertake the same kind of project in relation to men in general and homeless men in particular, nothing whatever is going to change. That's as sure as death and taxes and the endless, hidden sorrows of men.

PETER SINGER

Famine, Affluence,
and Morality

PETER SINGER teaches philosophy and directs the Center for Human Bioethics at Monash University in Australia. His best-known work is *Animal Liberation* (1975). He has written widely on civil disobedience and medical ethics.

As I write this, in November 1971, people are dying in East Bengal from lack of food, shelter, and medical care. The suffering and death that are occurring there now are not inevitable, not unavoidable in any fatalistic sense of the term. Constant poverty, a cyclone, and a civil war have turned at least nine million people into destitute refugees; nevertheless, it is not beyond the capacity of the richer nations to give enough assistance to reduce any further suffering to very small proportions. The decisions and actions of human beings can prevent this kind of suffering. Unfortunately, human beings have not made the necessary decisions. At the individual level, people have, with very few exceptions, not responded to the situation in any significant way. Generally speaking, people have not given large sums to relief funds; they have not written to their parliamentary representatives demanding increased government assistance; they have not demonstrated in the streets, held symbolic fasts, or done anything else directed toward providing the refugees with the means to satisfy their essential needs. At the government level, no government has given the sort of massive aid that would enable the refugees to survive for more than a few days. . . .

What are the moral implications of a situation like this? In what follows, I shall argue that the way people in relatively affluent countries react to a situation like that in Bengal cannot be justified; indeed, the whole way we look at moral issues—our moral conceptual scheme—needs to be altered, and with it, the way of life that has come to be taken for granted in our society. . . .

I begin with the assumption that suffering and death from lack of food, shelter, and medical care are bad. I think most people will agree about this, although one may reach the same view by different routes. I shall not argue for this view. People can hold all sorts of eccentric positions, and perhaps from some of them it would not follow that death by starvation is in itself bad. It is difficult, perhaps impossible, to refute such positions, and so for brevity I will henceforth take this assumption as accepted. Those who disagree need read no further.

My next point is this: if it is in our power to prevent something bad from happening, without thereby sacrificing anything of comparable moral importance, we ought, morally, to do it. By "without sacrificing anything of comparable moral importance" I mean without causing anything else comparably bad to happen, or doing something that is wrong in itself, or failing to promote some moral good, comparable in significance to the bad thing that we can prevent. This principle seems almost as uncontroversial as the last one. It requires us only to prevent what is bad, and not to promote what is good, and it requires this of us only when we can do it without sacrificing anything that is, from the moral point of view, comparably important. I could even, as far as the application of my argument to the Bengal emergency is concerned, qualify the point so as to make it: if it is in our power to prevent something very bad from happening, without thereby sacrificing anything morally significant, we ought, morally, to do it. An application of this principle would be as follows: if I am walking past a shallow pond and see a child drowning in it, I ought to wade in and pull the child out. This will mean getting my clothes muddy, but this is insignificant, while the death of the child would presumably be a very bad thing.

The uncontroversial appearance of the principle just stated is deceptive. If it were acted upon, even in its qualified form, our lives, our society, and our world would be fundamentally changed. For the principle takes, firstly, no account of proximity or distance. It makes no moral difference whether the person I can help is a neighbor's child ten yards from me or a Bengali whose name I shall never know, ten thousand miles away. Secondly, the principle makes no distinction between cases in which I am the only person who could possibly do anything and cases in which I am just one among millions in the same position.

I do not think I need to say much in defense of the refusal to take proximity and distance into account. The fact that a person is physically near to us, so that we have personal contact with him, may make it more likely that we *shall* assist him, but this does not show that we *ought* to help him rather than another who happens to be further away. If we accept any principle of impartiality, universalizability, equality, or whatever, we cannot discriminate against someone merely because he is far away from us (or we are far away from him). . . .

There may be a greater need to defend the second implication of my principle— that the fact that there are millions of other people in the same position, in respect to the Bengali refugees, as I am, does not make the situation significantly different from a situation in which I am the only person who can prevent something very bad from occurring. Again, of course, I admit that there is a psychological difference between the cases; one feels less guilty about doing nothing if one can point to others, similarly placed, who have also done nothing. Yet this can make no real difference to our moral obligations. Should I consider that I am less obliged to pull the drowning child out of the pond if on looking around I see other people, no further away than I am, who have also noticed the child but are doing nothing? One has only to ask this question to see the absurdity of the view that numbers lessen obligation. . . .

The view that numbers do make a difference can be made plausible if stated in this way: if everyone in circumstances like mine gave £5 to the Bengal Relief Fund, there would be enough to provide food, shelter, and medical care for the refugees; there is no reason why I should give more than anyone else in the same circumstances I am; therefore I have no obligation to give more than £5. Each premise in this argument is true, and the argument looks sound. It may convince us, unless we notice that it is based on a hypothetical premise, although the conclusion is not stated hypothetically. The argument would be sound if the conclusion were: if everyone in circumstances like mine were to give £5, I would have no obligation to give more than £5. If the conclusion were so stated, however, it would be obvious that the argument has no bearing on a situation in which it is not the case that everyone else gives £5. This, of course, is the actual situation. . . .

The outcome of this argument is that our traditional moral categories are upset. The traditional distinction between duty and charity cannot be drawn, or at least, not in the place we normally draw it. Giving money to the Bengal Relief Fund is regarded as an act of charity in our society. The bodies which collect money are known as "charities." These organizations see themselves in this way—if you send them a check, you will be thanked for your "generosity." Because giving money is regarded as an act of charity, it is not thought that there is anything wrong with not giving. The charitable man may be praised, but the man who is not charitable is not condemned. People do not feel in any way ashamed or guilty about spending money on new clothes or a new car instead of giving it to famine relief. (Indeed, the alternative does not occur to them.) This way of looking at the matter cannot be justified. When we buy new clothes not to keep ourselves warm but to look "well-dressed" we are not providing for any important need. We would not be sacrificing anything significant if we were to continue to wear our old clothes, and give the money to famine relief. By doing so, we would be preventing another person from starving. It follows from what I have said earlier that we ought to give money away, rather than spend it on clothes which we do not need to keep us warm. To do so is not charitable, or generous. Nor is it the kind of act which philosophers and theologians have called "supererogatory"—an act which it would be good to do, but not wrong not to do. On the contrary, we ought to give the money away, and it is wrong not to do so. . . .

The conclusion remains: we ought to be preventing as much suffering as we can without sacrificing something else of comparable moral importance. This conclusion is one which we may be reluctant to face. I cannot see, though, why it should be regarded as a criticism of the position for which I have argued, rather than a criticism of our ordinary standards of behavior. Since most people are self-interested to some degree, very few of us are likely to do everything that we ought to do. It would, however, hardly be honest to take this as evidence that it is not the case that we ought to do it.

It may still be thought that my conclusions are so wildly out of line with what everyone else thinks and has always thought that there must be something wrong with the argument somewhere. In order to show that my conclusions, while certainly contrary to contemporary Western moral standards, would not have seemed so extraordinary at other times and in other places, I would like to quote a passage from a writer not normally thought of as a way-out radical, Thomas Aquinas.

> Now, according to the natural order instituted by divine providence, material goods are provided for the satisfaction of human needs. Therefore the division and appropriation of property, which proceeds from human law, must not hinder the satisfaction of man's necessity from such goods. Equally, whatever a man has in superabundance is owed, of natural right, to the poor for their sustenance. So Ambrosius says, and it is also to be found in the *Decretum Gratiani:* "The bread which you withhold belongs to the hungry; the clothing you shut away, to the naked; and the money you bury in the earth is the redemption and freedom of the penniless."

I now want to consider a number of points, more practical than philosophical, which are relevant to the application of the moral conclusion we have reached. These points challenge not the idea that we ought to be doing all we can to prevent starvation, but the idea that giving away a great deal of money is the best means to this end.

It is sometimes said that overseas aid should be a government responsibility, and that therefore one ought not to give to privately run charities. Giving privately, it is said, allows the government and the noncontributing members of society to escape their responsibilities.

This argument seems to assume that the more people there are who give to privately organized famine relief funds, the less likely it is that the government will take over full responsibility for such aid. This assumption is unsupported, and does not strike me as at all plausible. The opposite view—that if no one gives voluntarily, a government will assume that its citizens are uninterested in famine relief and would not wish to be forced into giving aid—seems more plausible. . . .

Another, more serious reason for not giving to famine relief funds is that until there is effective population control, relieving famine merely postpones starvation. If we save the Bengal refugees now, others, perhaps the children of these refugees, will face starvation in a few years' time. In support of this, one may cite the now well-known facts about the population explosion and the relatively limited scope for expanded production.

This point, like the previous one, is an argument against relieving suffering that is happening now, because of a belief about what might happen in the future; it is unlike the previous point in that very good evidence can be adduced in support of this belief about the future. I will not go into the evidence here. I accept that the earth cannot support indefinitely a population rising at the present rate. This certainly poses a problem for anyone who thinks it important to prevent famine. Again, however, one could accept the argument without drawing the conclusion that it absolves one from any obligation to do anything to prevent famine. The conclusion that should be drawn is that the best means of preventing famine, in the long run, is population control. It would then follow from the position reached earlier that one ought to be doing all one can to promote population control (unless one held that all forms of population control were wrong in themselves, or would have significantly bad consequences). . . .

A third point raised by the conclusion reached earlier relates to the question of just how much we all ought to be giving away. One possibility, which has already been mentioned, is that we ought to give until we reach the level of marginal utility—that is, the level at which, by giving more, I would cause as much suffering to myself or my dependents as I would relieve by my gift. This would mean, of course, that one would reduce oneself to very near the material circumstances of a Bengali refugee. It will be recalled that earlier I put forward both a strong and a moderate version of the principle of preventing bad occurrences. The strong version, which required us to prevent bad things from happening unless in doing so we would be sacrificing something of comparable moral significance, does seem to require reducing ourselves to the level of marginal utility. I should also say that the strong version seems to me to be the correct one. I proposed the more moderate version—that we should prevent bad occurrences unless, to do so, we had to sacrifice something morally significant—only in order to show that even on this surely undeniable principle a great change in our way of life is required. On the more moderate principle, it may not follow that we ought to reduce ourselves to the level of marginal utility, for one might hold that to reduce oneself and one's family to this level is to cause something significantly bad to happen. Whether this is so I shall not discuss, since, as I have said, I can see no good reason for holding the moderate version of the principle rather than the strong version. Even if we accepted the principle only in its moderate form, however, it should be clear that we would have to give away enough to ensure that the consumer society, dependent as it is on people spending on trivia rather than giving to famine relief, would slow down and perhaps disappear entirely.

GARRETT HARDIN

Lifeboat Ethics

GARRETT HARDIN is Emeritus Professor of Human Ecology at the University of California at Santa Barbara. He has researched and written extensively on human ecology and evolution.

Environmentalists use the metaphor of the earth as a "spaceship" in trying to persuade countries, industries and people to stop wasting and polluting our natural resources. Since we all share life on this planet, they argue, no single person or institution has the right to destroy, waste, or use more than a fair share of its resources.

But does everyone on earth have an equal right to an equal share of its resources? The spaceship metaphor can be dangerous when used by misguided idealists to justify suicidal policies for sharing our resources through uncontrolled immigration and foreign aid. In their enthusiastic but unrealistic generosity, they confuse the ethics of a spaceship with those of a lifeboat.

A true spaceship would have to be under the control of a captain, since no ship could possibly survive if its course were determined by committee. Spaceship Earth certainly has no captain; the United Nations is merely a toothless tiger, with little power to enforce any policy upon its bickering members.

If we divide the world crudely into rich nations and poor nations, two thirds of them are desperately poor, and only one third comparatively rich, with the United States wealthiest of all. Metaphorically each rich nation can be seen as a lifeboat full of comparatively rich people. In the ocean outside each lifeboat swim the poor of the world, who would like to get in, or at least to share some of the wealth. What should the lifeboat passengers do?

First, we must recognize the limited capacity of any lifeboat. For example, a nation's land has a limited capacity to support a population and as the current energy crisis has shown us, in some ways we have already exceeded the carrying capacity of our land.

ADRIFT IN A MORAL SEA

So here we sit, say 50 people in our lifeboat. To be generous, let us assume it has room for 10 more, making a total capacity of 60. Suppose the 50 of us in the lifeboat see 100 others swimming in the water outside, begging for admission to our boat or for handouts. We have several options: we may be tempted to try to live by the Christian ideal of being "our brother's keeper," or by the Marxist idea of "to each according to his needs." Since the needs of all in the water are the same, and since they can all be seen as "our brothers," we could take them all into our boat, making a total of 150 in a boat designed for 60. The boat swamps, everyone drowns. Complete justice, complete catastrophe.

Since the boat has an unused excess capacity of 10 more passengers, we could admit just 10 more to it. But which 10 do we let in? How do we choose? Do we pick the best

10, the neediest 10, "first come, first served"? And what do we say to the 90 we exclude? If we do let an extra 10 into our lifeboat, we will have lost our "safety factor," an engineering principle of critical importance. For example, if we don't leave room for excess capacity as a safety factor in our country's agriculture, a new plant disease or a bad change in the weather could have disastrous consequences.

Suppose we decide to preserve our small safety factor and admit no more to the lifeboat. Our survival is then possible, although we shall have to be constantly on guard against boarding parties.

While this last solution clearly offers the only means of our survival, it is morally abhorrent to many people. Some say they feel guilty about their good luck. My reply is simple: "Get out and yield your place to others." This may solve the problem of the guilt-ridden person's conscience, but it does not change the ethics of the lifeboat. The needy person to whom the guilt-ridden person yields his place will not himself feel guilty about his good luck. If he did, he would not climb aboard. The net result of conscience-stricken people giving up their unjustly held seats is the elimination of that sort of conscience from the lifeboat.

This is the basic metaphor within which we must work out our solutions. Let us now enrich the image, step by step, with substantive additions from the real world, a world that must solve real and pressing problems of overpopulation and hunger.

The harsh ethics of the lifeboat become even harsher when we consider the reproductive differences between the rich nations and the poor nations. The people inside the lifeboats are doubling in numbers every 87 years; those swimming around outside are doubling, on the average, every 35 years, more than twice as fast as the rich. And since the world's resources are dwindling, the difference in prosperity between the rich and the poor can only increase.

As of 1973, the U.S. had a population of 210 million people, who were increasing by 0.8 percent per year. Outside our lifeboat, let us imagine another 210 million people (say the combined populations of Colombia, Ecuador, Venezuela, Morocco, Pakistan, Thailand and the Philippines) who are increasing at a rate of 3.3 percent per year. Put differently, the doubling time for this aggregate population is 21 years, compared to 87 years for the U.S. . . .

In sharing with "each according to his needs," we must recognize that needs are determined by population size, which is determined by the rate of reproduction, which at present is regarded as a sovereign right of every nation, poor or not. This being so, the philanthropic load created by the sharing ethic of the spaceship can only increase.

THE TRAGEDY OF THE COMMONS

The fundamental error of spaceship ethics, and the sharing it requires, is that it leads to what I call "the tragedy of the commons." Under a system of private property, the men who own property recognize their responsibility to care for it, for if they don't they will eventually suffer. A farmer, for instance, will allow no more cattle in a pasture than its carrying capacity justifies. If he overloads it, erosion sets in, weeds take over, and he loses the use of the pasture.

If a pasture becomes a commons open to all, the right of each to use it may not be matched by a corresponding responsibility to protect it. Asking everyone to use it with discretion will hardly do, for the considerate herdsman who refrains from overloading the commons suffers more than a selfish one who says his needs are greater. If everyone would restrain himself, all would be well; but it takes only one less than everyone to ruin a system of voluntary restraint. In a crowded world of less than perfect human beings, mutual ruin is inevitable if there are no controls. This is the tragedy of the commons.

One of the major tasks of education today should be the creation of such an acute awareness of the dangers of the commons that people will recognize its many varieties. For example, the air and water have become polluted because they are treated as commons. Further growth in the population or per-capita conversion of natural resources into pollutants will only make the problem worse. The same holds true for the fish of the oceans. Fishing fleets have nearly disappeared in many parts of the world, technological improvements in the art of fishing are hastening the day of complete ruin. Only the replacement of the system of the commons with a responsible system of control will save the land, air, water and oceanic fisheries. . . .

LEARNING THE HARD WAY

What happens if some organizations or countries budget for accidents and others do not? If each country is solely responsible for its own well-being, poorly managed ones will suffer. But they can learn from experience. They may mend their ways, and learn to budget for infrequent but certain emergencies. For example, the weather varies from year to year, and periodic crop failures are certain. A wise and competent government saves out of the production of the good years in anticipation of bad years to come. Joseph taught this policy to Pharaoh in Egypt more than 2,000 years ago. Yet the great majority of the governments in the world today do not follow such a policy. They lack either the wisdom or the competence, or both. Should those nations that do manage to put something aside be forced to come to the rescue each time an emergency occurs among the poor nations?

"But it isn't their fault!" Some kindhearted liberals argue. "How can we blame the poor people who are caught in an emergency? Why must they suffer for the sins of their governments?" The concept of blame is simply not relevant here. The real question is, what are the operational consequences of establishing a world food bank? If it is open to every country every time a need develops, slovenly rulers will not be motivated to take Joseph's advice. Someone will always come to their aid. Some countries will deposit food in the world food bank, and others will withdraw it. There will be almost no overlap. As a result of such solutions to food shortage emergencies, the poor countries will not learn to mend their ways, and will suffer progressively greater emergencies as their populations grow.

POPULATION CONTROL THE CRUDE WAY

On the average, poor countries undergo a 2.5 percent increase in population each year; rich countries, about 0.8 percent. Only rich countries have anything in the way of food reserves set aside, and even they do not have as much as they should. Poor countries have none. If poor countries received no food from the outside, the rate of their population growth would be periodically checked by crop failures and famines. But if they can always draw on a world food bank in time of need, their population can continue to grow unchecked, and so will their "need" for aid. In the short run, a world food bank may diminish that need, but in the long run it actually increases the need without limit.

Without some system of worldwide food sharing, the proportion of people in the rich and poor nations might eventually stabilize. The overpopulated poor countries would decrease in numbers, while the rich countries that had room for more people would increase. But with a well-meaning system of sharing, such as a world food bank, the growth differential between the rich and the poor countries will not only persist, it will increase. Because of the higher rate of population growth in the poor countries of the world, 8 percent of today's children are born poor, and only 12 percent rich. Year by year the ratio becomes worse, as the fast-reproducing poor outnumber the slow-reproducing rich.

A world food bank is thus a commons in disguise. People will have more motivation to draw from it than to add to any common store. The less provident and less able will multiply at the expense of the abler and more provident, bringing eventual ruin upon all who share in the commons. Besides, any system of "sharing" that amounts to foreign aid from the rich nations to the poor nations will carry the taint of charity, which will contribute little to the world peace so devoutly desired by those who support the idea of a world food bank. . . .

OVERLOADING THE ENVIRONMENT

Every human born constitutes a draft on all aspects of the environment: food, air, water, forests, beaches, wildlife, scenery and solitude. Food can, perhaps, be significantly increased to meet a growing demand. But what about clean beaches, unspoiled forests, and solitude? If we satisfy a growing population's need for food, we necessarily decrease its per capita supply of the other resources needed by men.

India, for example, now has a population of 600 million, which increases by 15 million each year. This population already puts a huge load on a relatively impoverished environment. The country's forests are now only a small fraction of what they were three centuries ago, and floods and erosion continually destroy the insufficient farmland that remains. Every one of the 15 million new lives added to India's population puts an additional burden on the environment, and increases the economic and social costs of crowding. However humanitarian our intent, every Indian life saved through medical or nutritional assistance from abroad diminishes the quality of life for those who remain, and for subsequent generations. If rich countries make it possible, through foreign aid, for 600 million Indians to swell to 1.2 billion in a mere 28 years, as their current growth rate threatens, will future generations of Indians thank us for hastening the destruction of their environment? Will our good intentions be sufficient excuse for the consequences of our actions? . . .

IMMIGRATION VS. FOOD SUPPLY

World food banks *move food to the people*, hastening the exhaustion of the environment of the poor countries. Unrestricted immigration, on the other hand, *moves people to the food,* thus speeding up the destruction of the environment of the rich countries. We can easily understand why poor people should want to make this latter transfer, but why should rich hosts encourage it? . . .

I can hear U.S. liberals asking: "How can you justify slamming the door once you're inside? You say that immigrants should be kept out. But aren't we all immigrants, or the descendants of immigrants? If we insist on staying, must we not admit all others?" Our craving for intellectual order leads us to seek and prefer symmetrical rules and morals: a single rule for me and everybody else; the same rule yesterday, today and tomorrow. Justice, we feel, should not change with time and place.

We Americans of non-Indian ancestry can look upon ourselves as the descendants of thieves who are guilty morally, if not legally, of stealing this land from its Indian owners. Should we then give back the land to the now living American descendants of those Indians? However morally or logically sound this proposal may be, I, for one, am unwilling to live by it and I know no one else who is. Besides, the logical consequence would be absurd. Suppose that, intoxicated with a sense of pure justice, we should decide to turn our land over to the Indians. Since all our other wealth has also been derived from the land, wouldn't we be morally obliged to give that back to the Indians too?

PURE JUSTICE VS. REALITY

Clearly, the concept of pure justice produces an infinite regression to absurdity. Centuries ago, wise men invented statutes of limitations to justify the rejection of such pure justice, in the interest of preventing continual disorder. The law zealously defends property rights, but only relatively recent property rights. Drawing a line after an arbitrary time has elapsed may be unjust, but the alternatives are worse.

We are all the descendants of thieves, and the world's resources are inequitably distributed. But we must begin the journey to tomorrow from the point where we are today. We cannot remake the past. We cannot safely divide the wealth equitably among all peoples so long as people reproduce at different rates. To do so would guarantee that our grandchildren, and everyone else's grandchildren, would have only a ruined world to inhabit.

To be generous with one's own possessions is quite different from being generous with those of posterity. We should call this point to the attention of those who from a commendable love of justice and equality, would institute a system of the commons, either in the form of a world food bank, or of unrestricted immigration. We must convince them if we wish to save at least some parts of the world from environmental ruin.

Without a true world government to control reproduction and the use of available resources, the sharing ethic of the spaceship is impossible. For the foreseeable future, our survival demands that we govern our actions by the ethics of a lifeboat, harsh though they may be. Posterity will be satisfied with nothing less.

ANDREW CARNEGIE

Wealth

ANDREW CARNEGIE (1835–1919) was a Scottish-born U.S. businessman and philanthropist. His Pittsburgh-based company, the Carnegie Steel Company, introduced the Bessemer process of making steel to the United States and was merged with the United States Steel Company upon Carnegie's retirement. He is well known for donating hundreds of libraries to towns and schools throughout the United States and England, and he is the author of a number of books, including *Triumphant Democracy* (1886) and *The Empire of Business* (1902).

The problem of our age is the proper administration of wealth, so that the ties of brotherhood may still bind together the rich and poor in harmonious relationship. The conditions of human life have not only been changed, but revolutionized, within the past few hundred years. In former days there was little difference between the dwelling, dress, food, and environment of the chief and those of his retainers. The Indians are today where civilized man then was. When visiting the Sioux, I was led to the wigwam of the chief. It was just like the others in external appearance, and even within the difference was trifling between it and those of the poorest of his braves. The contrast between the palace of the millionaire and the cottage of the laborer with us today measures the change which has come into civilization.

This change, however, is not to be deplored, but welcomed as highly beneficial. It is well, nay essential, for the progress of the race, that the houses of some should be homes for all that is highest and best in literature and art, and for all the refinements of civilization, rather than that none should be so. Much better this great irregularity than universal squalor. Without wealth there can be no Maecenas. When these apprentices rose to be masters, there was little or no change in their mode of life, and they, in turn, educated in the same routine succeeding apprentices. There was, substantially, social equality, and even political equality, for those engaged in industrial pursuits had then little or no political voice in the State.

But the inevitable result of such a mode of manufacture was crude articles at high prices. Today the world obtains commodities of excellent quality at prices which even the generation preceding this would have deemed incredible. In the commercial world similar causes have produced similar results, and the race is benefited thereby. The poor enjoy what the rich could not before afford. What were the luxuries have become the necessities of life. The laborer has now more comforts than the farmer had a few generations ago. The farmer has more luxuries than the landlord had, and is more richly clad and better housed. The landlord has books and pictures rarer, and appointments more artistic, than the King could then obtain.

The price we pay for this salutary change is, no doubt, great. We assemble thousands of operatives in the factory, in the mine, and in the counting-house, of whom the employer can know little or nothing, and to whom the employer is little better than a myth.

All intercourse between them is at an end. Rigid Castes are formed, and, as usual, mutual ignorance breeds mutual distrust. Each Caste is without sympathy for the other, and ready to credit anything disparaging in regard to it. Under the law of competition, the employer of thousands is forced into the strictest economies, among which the rates paid to labor figure prominently, and often there is friction between the employer and the employed, between capital and labor, between rich and poor. Human society loses homogeneity.

The price which society pays for the law of competition, like the price it pays for cheap comforts and luxuries, is also great; but the advantages of this law are also greater still, for it is to this law that we owe our wonderful material development, which brings improved conditions in its train. But, whether the law be benign or not, we must say of it, as we say of the change in the conditions of men to which we have referred: It is here; we cannot evade it; no substitutes for it have been found; and while the law may be sometimes hard for the individual, it is best for the race, because it insures the survival of the fittest in every department. We accept and welcome, therefore, as conditions to which we must accommodate ourselves, great inequality of environment, the concentration of business, industrial and commercial, in the hands of a few, and the law of competition between these, as being not only beneficial, but essential for the future progress of the race. Having accepted these, it follows that there must be great scope for the exercise of special ability in the merchant and in the manufacturer who has to conduct affairs upon a great scale. That this talent for organization and management is rare among men is proved by the fact that it invariably secures for its possessor enormous rewards, no matter where or under what law or conditions. The experienced in affairs always rate the MAN whose services can be obtained as a partner as not only the first consideration, but such as to render the question of his capital scarcely worth considering, for such men soon create capital; while, without the special talent required, capital soon takes wings. Such men become interested in firms or corporations using millions; and estimating only simple interest to be made upon the capital invested, it is inevitable that their income must exceed their expenditures, and that they must accumulate wealth. Nor is there any middle ground which such men can occupy, because the great manufacturing or commercial concern which does not earn at least interest upon its capital soon becomes bankrupt. It must either go forward or fall behind: to stand still is impossible. It is a condition essential for its successful operation that it should be thus far profitable, and even that, in addition to interest on capital, it should make profit. It is a law, as certain as any of the others named, that men possessed of this peculiar talent for affairs, under the free play of economic forces, must, of necessity, soon be in receipt of more revenue than can be judiciously expended upon themselves, and this law is as beneficial for the race as the others.

Objections to the foundations upon which society is based are not in order, because the condition of the race is better with these than it has been with any others which have been tried. Of the effect of any new substitutes proposed we cannot be sure. The Socialist or Anarchist who seeks to overturn present conditions is to be regarded as attacking the foundation upon which civilization itself rests, for civilization took its start from the day that the capable, industrious workman said to his incompetent and lazy fellow, "If thou dost not sow, thou shalt not reap," and thus ended primitive Communism by separating the drones from the bees. One who studies this subject will soon be brought face to face with the conclusion that upon the sacredness of property civilization itself depends—the right of the laborer to his hundred dollars in the savings bank, and equally the legal right of the millionaire to his millions. To those who propose to substitute Communism for this intense Individualism the answer, therefore, is: The race has tried that. All progress from that barbarous day to the present time has resulted from its displacement. Not evil, but good, has come to the race from the accumulation of wealth by those who have the ability and energy that produce it. But even if we admit for a moment that it might be better for the race to discard its present foundation, Individualism—that it is a nobler ideal that man should labor, not for himself alone, but in and for a brotherhood of his fellows, and share with them all in common, realizing Swedenborg's idea of Heaven, where, as he says, the angels derive their happiness, not from laboring for self, but for each other—even admit all this, and a sufficient answer is, This is not evolution, but revolution. It necessitates the changing of human nature itself—a work of aeons, even if it were good to change it, which we cannot know. It is not practicable in our day or in our age. Even if desirable theoretically, it belongs to another and long-succeeding sociological stratum. Our duty is with what is practicable now; with the next step possible in our day and generation. It is criminal to waste our energies in endeavoring to uproot, when all we can profitably or possibly accomplish is to bend the universal tree of humanity a little in the direction most favorable to the production of good fruit under existing circumstances. We might as well urge the destruction of the highest existing type of man because he failed to reach our ideal as to favor the destruction of Individualism, Private Property, the Law of Accumulation of Wealth, and the Law of Competition; for these are the highest results of human experience, the soil in which society so far has produced the best fruit. Unequally or unjustly, perhaps, as these laws sometimes operate, and imperfect as they appear to the Idealist, they are nevertheless, like the highest type of man, the best and most valuable of all that humanity has yet accomplished.

We start, then, with a condition of affairs under which the best interests of the race are promoted, but which inevitably gives wealth to the few. Thus far, accepting conditions as they exist, the situation can be surveyed and pronounced good. The question then arises—and, if the foregoing be correct, it is the only question with which we have to deal—What is the proper mode of administering wealth after the laws upon which civilization is founded have thrown it into the hands of the few? And it is of this great question that I believe I offer the true solution. It will be understood that *fortunes* are here spoken of, not moderate sums saved by many years of effort, the returns from which are required for the comfortable maintenance and education of families. This is not *wealth,* but only *competence,* which it should be the aim of all to acquire.

. . . Indeed, it is difficult to set bounds to the share of a rich man's estate which should go at his death to the public through the agency of the state, and by all means such taxes should be graduated, beginning at nothing upon moderate sums to dependents, and increasing rapidly as the amounts swell, until of the millionaire's hoard, as of Shylock's at least

> "—The other half
> Comes to the privy coffer of the state."

This policy would work powerfully to induce the rich man to attend to the administration of wealth during his life, which is the end that society should always have in view, as being that by far most fruitful for the people. Nor need it be feared that this policy would sap the root of enterprise and render men less anxious to accumulate, for to the class whose ambition it is to leave great fortunes and be talked about after their death, it will attract more attention, and, indeed, be a somewhat noble ambition to have enormous sums paid over to the state from their fortunes.

There remains, then, only one mode of using great fortunes; but in this we have the true antidote for the temporary unequal distribution of wealth, the reconciliation of the rich and the poor—a reign of harmony—another ideal, differing, indeed, from that of the Communist in requiring only the further evolution of existing conditions, not the total overthrow of our civilization. It is founded upon the present most intense individualism, and the race is prepared to put it in practice by degrees whenever it pleases. Under its sway we shall have an ideal state, in which the surplus wealth of the few will become, in the best sense, the property of the many, because administered for the common good, and this wealth, passing through the hands of the few, can be made a much more potent force for the elevation of our race than if it had been distributed in small sums to the people themselves. Even the poorest can be made to see this, and to agree that great sums gathered by some of their fellow-citizens and spent for public purposes, from which the masses reap the principal benefit, are more valuable to them than if scattered among them through the course of many years in trifling amounts.

The best uses to which surplus wealth can be put have already been indicated. Those who would administer wisely must, indeed, be wise, for one of the serious obstacles to the improvement of our race is indiscriminate charity. It were better for mankind that the millions of the rich were thrown into the sea than so spent as to encourage the slothful, the drunken, the unworthy. Of every thousand dollars spend in so-called charity today, it is probable that $950 is unwisely spent; so spent, indeed, as to produce the very evils which it proposes to mitigate or cure. A well-known writer of philosophic books admitted the other day that he had given a quarter of a dollar to a man who approached him as he was coming to visit the house of his friend. He knew nothing of the habits of this beggar; knew not the use that would be made of this money, although he had every reason to suspect that it would be spent improperly. This man professed to be a disciple of Herbert Spencer; yet the quarter-dollar given that night will probably work more injury than all the money which its thoughtless donor will ever be able to give in true charity will do good. He only gratified his own feelings, saved himself from annoyance—and this was probably one of the most selfish and very worst actions of his life, for in all respects he is most worthy.

In bestowing charity, the main consideration should be to help those who will help themselves; to provide part of the means by which those who desire to improve may do so; to give those who desire to rise the aids by which they may rise; to assist, but rarely or never to do all. Neither the individual nor the race is improved by alms-giving. Those worthy of assistance, except in rare cases, seldom require assistance. The really valuable men of the race never do, except in cases of accident or sudden change. Every one has, of course, cases of individuals brought to his own knowledge where temporary assistance can do genuine good, and these he will not overlook. But the amount which can be wisely given by the individual for individuals is necessarily limited by his lack of knowledge of the circumstance connected with each. He is the only true reformer who is as careful and as anxious not to aid the unworthy as he is to aid the worthy, and perhaps, even more so, for in alms-giving more injury is probably done by rewarding vice then by relieving virtue.

Thus is the problem of Rich and Poor to be solved. The laws of accumulation will be left free; the laws of distribution free. Individualism will continue, but the millionaire will be but a trustee for the poor; intrusted for a season with a great part of the increased wealth of the community, but administrating it for the community far better than it could or would have done for itself. The best minds will thus have reached a stage in the development of the race in which it is clearly seen that there is no mode of disposing of surplus wealth creditable to thoughtful and earnest men into whose hands it flows save by using it year by year for the general good. This day already dawns. But a little while, and although, without incurring the pity of their fellows, men may die sharers in great business enterprises from which their capital cannot be or has not been withdrawn, and is left chiefly at death for public uses, yet the man who dies leaving behind him millions of available wealth, which was his to administer during life, will pass away "unwept, unhonored, and unsung," no matter to what uses he leaves the dross which he cannot take with him. Of such as these the public verdict will then be: "The man who dies thus rich dies disgraced."

Such, in my opinion, is the true Gospel concerning Wealth, obedience to which is destined some day to solve the problems of the Rich and the Poor, and to bring "Peace on earth, among men Good-Will."

AMARTYA SEN

Property and Hunger

AMARTYA SEN teaches economics at Harvard University. His recent publications include *Commodities and Capabilities* (1985), *The Standard of Living* (1987), and *On Ethics and Economics* (1987). Sen has also conducted research on the role of rationality in social behavior.

In an interesting letter to Anna George, the daughter of Henry George Bernard Shaw wrote: "Your father found me a literary dilettante and militant rationalist in religion, and a barren rascal at that. By turning my mind to economics he made a man of me." I am not able to determine what making a man of Bernard Shaw would exactly consist of, but it is clear that the kind of moral and social problems with which Shaw was deeply concerned could not be sensibly pursued without examining their economic aspects. For example, the claims of property rights, which some would defend and some (including Shaw) would dispute, are not just matters of basic moral belief that could not possibly be influenced one way or the other by any empirical arguments. They call for sensitive moral analysis responsive to empirical realities, including economic ones.

Moral claims based on intrinsically valuable rights are often used in political and social arguments. Rights related to ownership have been invoked for ages. But there are also other types of rights which have been seen as "inherent and inalienable," and the American Declaration of Independence refers to "certain unalienable rights," among which are "life, liberty and the pursuit of happiness." The Indian constitution talks even of "the right to an adequate means of livelihood." The "right not to be hungry" has often been invoked in recent discussions on the obligation to help the famished.

RIGHTS: INSTRUMENTS, CONSTRAINTS, OR GOALS?

Rights can be taken to be morally important in three different ways. First, they can be considered to be valuable *instruments* to achieve other goals. This is the "instrumental view," and is well illustrated by the utilitarian approach to rights. Rights are, in that view, of no intrinsic importance. Violation of rights is not in itself a bad thing, nor fulfillment intrinsically good. But the acceptance of rights promotes, in this view, things that are ultimately important, to wit, utility. Jeremy Bentham rejected "natural rights" as "simple nonsense," and "natural and imprescriptible rights" as "rhetorical nonsense, nonsense upon stilts." But he attached great importance to rights as instruments valuable to the promotion of a good society, and devoted much energy to the attempt to reform appropriately the actual system of rights.

The second view may be called the "constraint view," and it takes the form of seeing rights as *constraints* on what others can or cannot do. In this view rights *are* intrinsically important. However, they don't figure in moral accounting as goals to be generally promoted, but only as constraints that others must obey. As Robert Nozick has put it in a powerful exposition of this "constraint view": "Individuals have rights, and there are things no person or group may do to them (without violating their rights)." Rights "set the constraints within which a social choice is to be made, by excluding certain alternatives, fixing others, and so on."

The third approach is to see fulfillments of rights as goals to be pursued. This "goal view" differs from the instrumental view in regarding rights to be intrinsically important, and it differs from the constraint view in seeing the fulfillment of rights as goals to be generally promoted, rather than taking them as demanding only (and exactly) that we refrain from violating the rights of others. In the "constraint view" there is no duty to help anyone with his or her rights (merely not to hinder), and also in the "instrumental view" there is no duty, in fact, to help unless the right fulfillment will also promote some other goal such as utility. The "goal view" integrates the valuation of rights—their fulfillment and violation—in overall moral accounting, and yields a wider sphere of influence of rights in morality.

I have argued elsewhere that the goal view has advantages that the other two approaches do not share, in particular, the ability to accommodate integrated moral accounting including inter alia the intrinsic importance of a class of fundamental rights. I shall not repeat that argument here. But there is an interesting question of dual roles of rights in the sense that some rights may be *both* intrinsically important and instrumentally valuable. For example, the right to be free from hunger could—not implausibly—be regarded as being valuable in itself as well as serving as a good instrument to promote other goals such as security, longevity or utility. If so, both the goal view and the instrumental view would have to be simultaneously deployed to get a comprehensive assessment of such a right. This problem of comprehensiveness is a particularly important issue in the context of Henry George's discussion of rights, since he gave many rights significant dual roles.

The instrumental aspects is an inescapable feature of every right, since irrespective of whether a certain right is intrinsically valuable or not, its acceptance will certainly have other consequences as well, and these, too, have to be assessed along with the intrinsic value of rights (if any). A right that is regarded as quite valuable in itself may nevertheless be judged to be morally rejectable if it leads to disastrous consequences. This is a case of the rights playing a *negative* instrumental role. It is, of course, also possible that the instrumental argument will *bolster* the intrinsic claims of a right to be taken seriously. I shall presently argue that such is the case in George's analysis with the right of labor to its produce.

There are two general conclusions to draw, at this stage, from this very preliminary discussion. First, we must distinguish between (1) the intrinsic value of a right, and (2) the overall value of a right taking note *inter alia* of its intrinsic importance (if any). The acceptance of the intrinsic importance of any right is no guarantee that its overall moral valuation must be favorable. Second, no moral assessment of a right can be independent of its likely consequences. The need for empirical assessment of the effects of accepting any right cannot be escaped. Empirical arguments are quite central to moral philosophy.

PROPERTY AND DEPRIVATION

The right to hold, use and bequeath property that one has legitimately acquired is often taken to be inherently valuable. In fact, however, many of its defenses seem to be actually of the instrumental type, e.g., arguing that property rights make people more free to choose one kind of a life rather than another. Even the traditional attempt at founding "natural property rights" on the principles of "natural liberty" (with or without John Locke's proviso) has some instrumental features. But even if we do accept that property rights may have some intrinsic value, this does not in any way amount to an overall justification of property rights, since property rights may have consequences which themselves will require assessment. Indeed, the causation of hunger as well as its prevention may materially depend on how property rights are structured. If a set of property rights leads, say, to starvation, as it well might, then the moral approval of these rights would certainly be comprised severely. In general, the need for consequential analysis of property rights is inescapable whether or not such rights are seen as having any intrinsic value.

Consider Henry George's formula of giving "the product to the producer." This is, of course, an ambiguous rule, since the division of the credits for production to different causal influences (e.g., according to "marginal productivities" in neoclassical theory, or according to human efforts in classical labor theory) is inevitably somewhat arbitrary, and full of problems involving internal tensions. But no matter how the ambiguities are resolved, it is clear that this rule would give no part of the socially produced output to one who is unemployed since he or she is producing nothing. Also, a person whose productive contribution happens to be tiny, according to *whichever* procedure of such accounting we use, can expect to get very little based on this so-called "natural law." Thus, hunger and starvation are compatible with this system of rights. George thought that this would not occur, since the economic reforms he proposed (including the abolition of land rights) would eliminate unemployment, and provision for the disabled would be made through the sympathetic support of others. These are empirical matters. If these empirical generalizations do not hold, then the outlined system of rights would yield a serious conflict. The property rights to one's product (however defined) might be of some intrinsic moral importance, but we clearly must also take note of the moral disvalue of human misery (such as suffering due to hunger and nutrition-related diseases.) The latter could ever plausibly be seen as having more moral force than the former. A positive intrinsic value of the right to one's product can go with an overall negative value, taking everything into account.

I have tried to argue elsewhere—not in the context of disputing these moral theories but in trying to understand the causation of famines in the modern world—that famines are, in fact, best explained in terms of failures of entitlement systems. The entitlements here refer, of course, to legal rights and to practical possibilities, rather than to moral status, but the laws and actual operation of private ownership economies have many features in common with the moral system of entitlements analyzed by Nozick and others.

The entitlement approach to famines need not, of course, be confined to private ownership economies, and entitlement failures of other systems can also be fruitfully studied to examine famines and hunger. In the specific context of private ownership economies, the entitlements are substantially analyzable in terms, respectively, of what may be called "endowments" and "exchange entitlements." A person's endowment refers to what he or she initially owns (including the person's own labor power), and the exchange entitlement mapping tells us what the person can obtain through exchanging what he or she owns, either by production (exchange with nature), or by trade (exchange with others), or a mixture of the two. A person has to starve if neither the endowments, nor what can be obtained through exchange, yields an adequate amount of food.

If starvation and hunger are seen in terms of failures and entitlements, then it becomes immediately clear that the total availability of food in a country is only one of several variables that are relevant. Many famines occur without any decline in the availability of food. For example, in the Great Bengal famine of 1943, the total food availability in Bengal was not particularly bad (considerably higher than two years earlier when there was no famine), and yet three million people died, in a famine mainly affecting the rural areas, through rather violent shifts in the relative purchasing powers of different groups, hitting the rural laborers the hardest. The Ethiopian famine of 1973 took place in a year of average per capita food availability, but the cultivators and other occupation groups in the province of Wollo had lost their means of subsistence (through loss of crops and a decline of economic activity, related to a local drought) and had no means of commanding food from elsewhere in the country. Indeed, some food moved *out* of Wollo to more prosperous people in other parts of Ethiopia, repeating a pattern of contrary movement of food that was widely observed during the Irish famines of the 1840s (with food moving out of famine-stricken Ireland to prosperous England which had greater power in the battle for entitlements). The Bangladesh famine of 1974 took place in a year of *peak* food availability, but several occupation groups had lost their entitlement to food through loss of employment and other economic changes (including inflationary pressures causing prices to outrun wages). Other examples of famines without significant (or any) decline in food availability can be found, and there is nothing particularly surprising about this fact once it is recognized that the availability of food is only one influence among many on the entitlement of each occupation group. Even when a famine *is* associated with a decline of food availability, the entitlement changes have to be studied to understand the particular nature of the famine, e.g., why one occupation group is hit but not another. The causation of starvation can be sensibly sought in failures of entitlements of the respective groups.

The causal analysis of famines in terms of entitlements also points to possible public policies of prevention. The main economic strategy would have to take the form of increasing the entitlements of the deprived groups, and in general, of guaranteeing minimum entitlements for everyone, paying particular attention to the vulnerable groups. This can, in the long run, be done in many different ways, involving both economic growth (including growth of food output) and distributional adjustments. Some of these policies may, however, require that the property rights and the corresponding entitlements of the more prosperous groups be violated. The problem, in fact, is particularly acute in the short run, since it may not be possible to engineer rapid economic growth instantly. Then the burden of raising entitlements of the groups in distress would largely have to fall on reducing the entitlements of others more favorably placed. Transfers of income or commodities through various public policies may well be effective in quashing a famine (as the experience of famine relief in different countries has shown), but it may require substantial government intervention in the entitlements of the more prosperous groups.

There is, however, no great moral dilemma in this if property rights are treated as purely *instrumental*. If the goals of relief of hunger and poverty are sufficiently powerful, then it would be just right to violate whatever property rights come in the way, since—in this view—property rights have no intrinsic status. On the other hand, if property rights are taken to be morally inviolable irrespective of their consequences, then it will follow that these policies cannot be morally acceptable even though they might save thousands, or even millions, from dying. The inflexible moral "constraint" of respecting people's legitimately acquired entitlements would rule out such policies.

In fact this type of problem presents a *reductio ad absurdum* of the moral validity of constraint-based entitlement systems. However, while the conclusions to be derived from that approach might well be "absurd," the situation postulated is not an imaginary one at all. It is based on studies of actual famines and the role of entitlement failures in the causation of mass starvation. If there is an embarrassment here, it belongs solidly to the consequence-independent way of seeing rights.

I should add that this dilemma does not arise from regarding property rights to be of intrinsic value, which can be criticized on other grounds, but not this one. Even if property rights *are* of intrinsic value, their violation may be justified on grounds of the favorable consequences of that violation. A right, as was mentioned earlier, may be intrinsically valuable and still be justly violated taking everything into account. The "*absurdum*" does not belong to attaching intrinsic value to property rights, but to regarding these rights as simply acceptable, regardless of their consequences. A moral system that values both property rights and other goals—such as avoiding famines and starvation, or fulfilling people's right not to be hungry—can, on the one hand, give property rights intrinsic importance, and on the other, recommend the violation of property rights when that leads to better overall consequences (*including* the disvalue of rights violation).

The issue here is not the valuing of property rights, but their alleged inviolability. There is no dilemma here either for the purely instrumental view of property rights or for treating the fulfillment of property rights as one goal among many, but specifically for consequence-independent assertions of property rights and for the corresponding constraint-based approaches to moral entitlement of ownership.

That property and hunger are closely related cannot possibly come as a great surprise. Hunger is primarily associated with not owning enough food and thus property rights over food are immediately and directly involved. Fights over that property right can be a major part of the reality of a poor country, and any system of moral assessment has to take note of that phenomenon. The tendency to see hunger in purely technocratic terms of food output and availability may help to hide the crucial role of entitlements in the genesis of hunger, but a fuller economic analysis cannot overlook that crucial role. Since property rights over food are derived from property rights over other goods and resources (through production and trade), the entire system of rights of acquisition and transfer is implicated in the emergence and survival of hunger and starvation.

THE RIGHT NOT TO BE HUNGRY

Property rights have been championed for a long time. In contrast, the assertion of "the right not to be hungry" is a comparatively recent phenomenon. While this right is much invoked in political debates, there is a good deal of skepticism about treating this as truly a right in any substantial way. It is often asserted that this concept of "right not to be hungry" stands essentially for nothing at all ("simple nonsense," as Bentham called "natural rights" in general). That piece of sophisticated cynicism reveals not so much a penetrating insight into the practical affairs of the world, but a refusal to investigate what people mean when they assert the existence of rights that, for the bulk of humanity, are not in fact guaranteed by the existing institutional arrangements.

The right not to be hungry is not asserted as a recognition of an institutional right that already exists, as the right to property typically is. The assertion is primarily a moral claim as to what should be valued, and what institutional structure we should aim for, and try to guarantee if feasible. It can also be seen in terms of Ronald Dworkin's category of "background rights"—rights that provide a justification for political decisions by society in abstract. This interpretation serves as the basis for a reason to change the existing institutional structure and state policy.

It is broadly in this form that the right to "an adequate means of livelihood" is referred to in the Constitution of India: "The state shall, in particular, direct its policy towards securing . . . that the citizens, men and women equally, have the right to an adequate means of livelihood." This does not, of course, offer to each citizen a guaranteed right to an adequate livelihood, but the state is asked to take steps such that this right could become realizable for all.

In fact, this right has often been invoked in political debates in India. The electoral politics of India does indeed give particular scope for such use of what are seen as background rights. It is, of course, not altogether clear whether the reference to this right in the Indian constitution has in fact materially influenced the political debates. The constitutional statement is often cited, but very likely this issue would have figured in any case in these debates, given the nature of the moral and political concern. But whatever the constitutional contribution, it is interesting to ask whether the implicit acceptance of the value of the right to freedom from hunger makes any difference to actual policy.

It can be argued that the general acceptance of the right of freedom from acute hunger as a major goal has played quite a substantial role in preventing famines in India. The last real famine in India was in 1943, and while food availability per head in India has risen only rather slowly (even now the food availability per head is no higher than in many sub-Saharan countries stricken by recurrent famines), the country has not experienced any famine since independence in 1947. The main cause of that success is a policy of public intervention. Whenever a famine has threatened (e.g., in Bihar in 1967–68, in Maharashtra in 1971–73, in West Bengal in 1978–79), a public policy of intervention and relief has offered minimum entitlements to the potential famine victims, and thus have the threatening famines been averted. It can be argued that the quickness of the response of the respective governments (both state and central) reflects a political necessity, given the Indian electoral system and the importance attached by the public to the prevention of starvation. Political pressures from opposition groups and the news media have kept the respective governments on their toes, and the right to be free from acute hunger and starvation has been achieved largely because it has been seen as a valuable right. Thus the recognition of the intrinsic moral importance of this right, which has been widely invoked in public discussions, has served as a powerful political instrument as well.

On the other hand, this process has been far from effective in tackling pervasive and persistent undernourishment in India. There has been no famine in post-independence India, but perhaps a third of India's rural population is perennially undernourished. So long as hunger remains non-acute and starvation deaths are avoided (even though morbidity and mortality rates are enhanced by undernourishment), the need for a policy response is neither much discussed by the news media, nor forcefully demanded even by opposition parties. The elimination of famines coexists with the survival of widespread "regular hunger." The right to "adequate means" of *nourishment* does not at all seem to arouse political concern in a way that the right to "adequate means" to *avoid starvation* does.

The contrast can be due to one of several different reasons. It could, of course, simply be that the ability to avoid undernourishment is not socially accepted as very important. This could be so, though what is socially accepted and what is not is also partly a matter of how clearly the questions are posed. It is, in fact, quite possible that the freedom in question would be regarded as a morally important right if the question were posed in a transparent way, but this does not happen because of the nature of Indian electoral politics and that of news coverage. The issue is certainly not "dramatic" in the way in which starvation deaths and threatening famines are. Continued low-key misery may be too familiar a phenomenon to make it worthwhile for political leaders to get some mileage out of it in practical politics. The news media may also find little profit in emphasizing a non-spectacular phenomenon—the quiet survival of disciplined, non-acute hunger.

If this is indeed the case, then the implications for action of the goal of eliminating hunger, or guaranteeing to all the means for achieving this, may be quite complex. The political case for making the quiet hunger less quiet and more troublesome for governments in power is certainly relevant. Aggressive political journalism might prove to have an instrumental value if it were able to go beyond reporting the horrors of visible starvation and to portray the pervasive, non-acute hunger in a more dramatic and telling way. This is obviously not the place to discuss the instrumentalities of practical politics, but the endorsement of the moral right to be free from hunger—both acute and non-acute—would in fact raise pointed questions about the means which might be used to pursue such a goal.

MORAL ASSESSMENT AND SOCIAL RELATIONS

. . . If there is one thing that emerges sharply from the discussion I have tried to present in this paper, it is the importance of factual analysis for moral assessment, including moral scrutiny of the acceptability and pursuit of specific rights. This is so even when the right in question is acknowledged to have intrinsic moral value, since valuing a right is not the same thing as accepting it. To affirm acceptability independently of consequences can be peculiarly untenable, as was discussed in analyzing entitlements and hunger. In assessing the claims of property rights, of the right not to be hungry, the examination cannot be confined to issues of basic valuation only, and much of the challenge of assessment lies in the empirical analysis of causes and effects. In the world in which we live—full of hunger as well as wealth—these empirical investigations can be both complex and quite extraordinarily important. The big moral questions are frequently also deeply economic, social, or political.

Corporate Collectivism
A System of Social Injustice

MICHAEL HARRINGTON, member of the Democratic Socialist Organizing Committee, is also the author of *The Other America* (1981), *Socialism* (1973), *The Twilight of Capitalism* (1976), and other books. He has taught at Queens College, City University of New York, and was chairman of the Socialist Party of the United States from 1968 to 1972.

I do not believe the United States is a free enterprise society. I think the people who want us to use this term wish to rationalize and defend rather than describe the society. There may have been a free enterprise society for five minutes in Great Britain in the nineteenth century, although personally I doubt it. It certainly has never existed in the United States. Among other things, we fought a war, the Civil War, in which one of the issues was free trade versus protectionism. Protectionism won. The infrastructure of our society, the railroad, was built by federal donations. The United States today does not have a free enterprise society in any kind of Adam Smithian sense of the term. Rather, we have gigantic oligopolies administering prices, shaping tastes, working together with an all-pervasive government which follows corporate priorities. Therefore, I suggest that rather than using the term "free enterprise" to describe our system we get closer to reality and call it "corporate collectivism."

I maintain that corporate collectivism, in its historical thrust and tendency, is not compatible with social justice. Moreover, I am absolutely certain that capitalism—corporate collectivism in its latest phase—is coming to an end. As a socialist, I am not necessarily filled with joy at this prospect because there is more than one end possible to this society. The question before us is not *whether* there is going to be a collectivist society in the future, because that is already decided. The real question is, what kind of collectivist society will there be? When we play around with terms like "free enterprise," we ask the wrong questions and cannot possibly come up with the right answers. . . .

CAPITALISM: AN HISTORICAL PERSPECTIVE

What was the principle of precapitalist society? What was the big gulf between capitalist society and previous societies? In all that went before capitalism, the political, the economic, and the social were one. The individual's economic position in society was not independent of his political and social position. If you were a duke, a slave owner, or a member of a mandarin bureaucracy, there was a seamless whole which defined you politically, economically, and socially. In the Middle Ages, a young serf did not decide to try to become a duke. There was only one institution in the Middle Ages which made that possible—the Catholic Church. But, by and large, it was a society where one's economic, political, and social position was fixed at birth and was part of this whole.

As a result, in these precapitalist societies (what Marx called Oriental despotism, and slave society, as well as feudal society), the ruling class had a very specific way of extracting an economic surplus from the direct producers. Feudal society achieved the surplus through force sanctioned by religion. That is to say, the serf labored free for the lord or gave him rent in kind, or later gave him money, because the lord was his military protector, sanctioned by God, in an order which was accepted from the very start.

Capitalism did a number of absolutely magnificent things in terms of those precapitalist societies. First it separated, or as a system had a tendency to separate, the political, economic, and social orders. Properly speaking, social classes are an invention of capitalism. Before capitalism, there were "estates," caste systems, hereditary systems. Only with the advent of capitalism and its separation of the political, economic, and social systems was there a society that offered individual choice, the possibility of mobility, and an opportunity to rise above the status of one's birth.

Second, capitalism normally did not extract a surplus by naked force. That was a great advance. Capitalism is the system which uses economic means to get the surplus out of the direct producer. That is to say, it is based on a contract. It is absolutely true that the contract is utterly unfair, but it is nevertheless a contract, and that means a rise, so to speak, in civil liberties—a rise in the ethical and personal level of the society. The contract is unfair because, in the capitalist mythology, a free worker with nothing to sell but his labor freely contracts with someone who has enormous wealth and who is able to gain a surplus through that contract. It is an unfair contract, but it is a system that works on the basis of contract and law rather than force. . . .

Third, capitalism discovered the social power of people working together. That, I submit, was its economic invention. . . . What capitalism discovered was not technology; it discovered that allowing people to work together enormously increased their productivity. That was social invention. The discovery of the social nature of work, of people working together rather than in isolation, was the decisive moment in the rise of capitalism and, again, an enormous contribution to humankind.

This brings me to the final point of this brief history: the capitalist system bases itself on a contradiction. It is a system which is increasingly and progressively social capitalism. Capitalism is a socializing system. It first socializes work, with entrepreneurs getting artisans together under a single roof, achieving certain economies of scale. Larger entrepreneurs socialize smaller entrepreneurs. There is a tendency toward concentration, toward monopoly, toward oligopoly, cartels, trusts—larger and larger units. . . .

Capitalism is from the very first moment a world system. It reaches all over the world, destroys ancient cultures, and upsets the international balance. It tries to bring the entire world, every last person, into the same integrated unit. Capitalism is profoundly social and profoundly revolutionary. But at the same time that capitalism becomes more social, at the same time that the technological decisions today of a U.S. Steel or an IBM have more social consequences than most of the decisions of state legislatures, the system remains private in its decision making and its allocation of resources and benefits. And there, I suggest, is the genius of capitalism and the contradiction that will destroy it. Here I am using a paradox defined by Joseph Schumpeter, one of the great conservatives of the modern age, but I think it very much in the spirit of my good friend, Karl Marx, viz., that capitalism is destroyed by its success, not its failure. Capitalism so successfully

socializes that the socialized world which it creates becomes incompatible with the institutional decision-making process in private hands.

Finally, I am perfectly aware that capitalism today is no longer run by individual
entrepreneurs making personal decisions. I am perfectly aware that there are huge corporate bureaucracies, technostructures if you want. Of course, corporate bureaucracies
tend to view profit maximizing on a much longer time span than a nineteenth century
robber baron. But what I am saying is, for example, that the American automobile industry still considers the problem of pollution or the problem of automobile safety
from the point of view of making as much money in a sophisticated way as it possibly
can. This is in contradiction with the extremely social system which capitalism creates.

So my first point is this. Capitalism is a magnificent, revolutionary, and liberating
system which, by its own success, becomes conservative and reactionary. It will bring
about its own demise.

CONTEMPORARY CAPITALISM

I call our present system corporate collectivism. Its origins are to be found in three historical periods and the events associated with them. The first period was from about
1880 to 1900, when European and American capitalism went through a crisis which it
solved by monopolies, trusts, and by the intervention of the state, the beginning of the
state's entrance into the economy. The first move toward corporate collectivism is the
end of the entrepreneurial capitalism at the end of the last century.

The second period was World War I, a tremendous watershed. Here I use the rather
classical, conservative, contemporary economist Hicks as my source. Hicks points out
that during World War I, the government had to mobilize the war effort. This brought
about the discovery of military socialism, the capacity of the state to administer the
economy. There had been government intervention into the economy before World
War I, particularly social welfare intervention under Bismarck in Germany and Lloyd
George in Britain. But in World War I, government actually operated industries. For
example, the railroads were run by the United States government. That was, Hicks says,
the beginning of an administrative revolution in which the state learned its capacity
for economic intervention.

The third period was during the Great Depression of the 1930's, when Keynesianism
triumphed in its most conservative variant. In the 1930's, some nations began to understand that the government had to be responsible for the economic management of the
macro-economy. . . .

This Keynesian revolution in its democratic variant, particularly in its American
variant, was conservative. Many in the United States, including conservatives, think that
Keynes was some kind of radical. I suggest they read his life. Keynes was not only a
theorist, he was a man who made money for himself and various charitable causes for
which he worked as an investment advisor. Keynes was an upper-class aristocratic
snob who regarded the workers as a bunch of boobs and who said that he was a Keynesian precisely because he was not a socialist.

Now there are Keynesians who, in my opinion, are much better than Keynes. But
American conservatives will have to learn one of these days that the ideology of
conservatism in the late twentieth century is Keynesianism or at least conservative

Keynesianism. The point of Keynesianism was that the corporate infrastructure was fundamentally sound and that all the government did, merely by fiscal and monetary policy, was to match the macro-aggregates of supply and demand through public and private investment at a full employment level. But the assumption behind Keynes' policy, and particularly behind the Roosevelt New Deal version of Keynesianism, was that the basic investment decisions are made by corporations and that the government simply creates an environment in which they will be able to carry out that function.

So Keynesianism, I suggest, has this profoundly conservative aspect. It has another aspect—an aspect which makes any government, including a liberal government, a hostage to the corporations. I take a very wise sentence from a contemporary German sociologist, Klaus Hoffa: "The capitalist state is not itself a capitalist." That is to say, the capitalist state is dependent for the success of its policies on the private sector. In this society of supposed equals, some people are more equal than others. When a John Kennedy is elected in 1960 or a Jimmy Carter in 1976, they must assure themselves of the cooperation of the corporate community because that community makes investment decisions, and private investment decisions are the key to full employment.

I therefore suggest that the concept of "trickle down," the concept of the government rewarding the corporate rich more than anyone else, is not a policy of American society. It is *the* policy of American society. The policy is imposed upon this society by the fact that corporations are in charge of the investment process. Therefore, if one considers the Kennedy/Johnson tax cuts, as has Leon Keyserling, who was chairman of the Council of Economic Advisors under Truman, one finds that the rich received much more than anyone else. Indeed, I would suggest to you that the welfare state does much more for the corporate rich than for anybody else.

For now, I just want to focus on the fact that macroeconomic policy has to be pro-corporate. If we elected a government in the United States composed solely of left-wing trade union leaders, militant civil rights advocates, feminists and reformers, but kept corporations in charge of investment, that government would be nicer to corporations than to workers or minorities or women or to the people in general—not because it sold out but because that is the reality of government in our society. What I am saying is: the political freedom of society is profoundly restricted by the economic and social institutions. So it is that today in Great Britain a Socialist Chancellor of the Exchequer, a former member of the Young Communist League, is presiding over increasing unemployment and holding wages down as a socialist policy. Under the circumstances in Britain, corporate people are more important than working people; people in board rooms are more important than unemployed people. That is built in, I suggest, to this kind of society.

This leads me to a proposition about the kinds of decisions that are made in our society. I am not suggesting that there is a capitalist conspiracy, that there are a bunch of bloated plutocrats in top hats who sit around the table in the morning and say, "Let us now go and see how we can do harm to the weak and the poor in this society." What I am saying is that there is a structure of power that dictates pro-corporate outcomes to democratically elected representatives. . . .

In conclusion, the issue before American society is not whether there will be national economic planning. We already have it. Our problem is that the plan on which we operate today proceeds according to the priorities of a hidden agenda. That hidden agenda, which has a remarkable consistency, is that government shall on all major decisions maximize corporate priorities. I suggest therefore that the issue is whether the plan will become democratic with a small "d," transparent and open, or whether it will remain bureaucratic and secret.

And, in terms of that point, one last unkind word for the American corporation. I believe the American corporation is now becoming decadent. The typical corporate executive, after reading the *Wall Street Journal* editorial in the morning about the glories of free enterprise and the free market system, immediately tries to figure how to get another subsidy from the government. There is a sense—and please understand me clearly, because there are enormous differences between the United States and the Soviet Union—but there is a sense in which executives in the United States are increasingly playing the role that commissars play in the Soviet Union. They act as a bureaucratic elite with a government at their disposal, taking money from the people to fulfill their priorities and their interests and to make their decisions.

My second point, then, is that capitalism, which was such a magnificent and revolutionary system, has by its very socialization now created a corporate collectivist society in which government and the corporations cooperate with the public's money on the basis of corporate priorities. . . .

THE ALTERNATIVES TO CAPITALISM

What are the alternatives? What would be a perspective for freedom and social justice in the modern world? Now let me state at the outset that I am a socialist, a democratic socialist. That is, I do not regard any of the totalitarian societies which claim to be socialist as being socialist. I think they are bureaucratic collectivisms, not democratic and free collectivisms. But much of what I am going to say does not require that you be a socialist to agree with me. . . .

The principle of the alternative to corporate collectivism, it seems to me, is the democratization of economic and social decision making. This is the fundamental principle that one then wants to follow in absolutely every aspect of the society. Under capitalism, by an (I hope) imperishable conquest of the human spirit, the idea of political freedom came into being, and we are eternally in the debt of the capitalist society for that. But now the concept of freedom and democracy must be applied to areas in which capitalism never applied it. Unless we democratize our increasingly collectivist state, which acts on the basis of a hidden agenda, we will lose freedom. Therefore, I believe that the democratization of economic and social power is the fundamental principle.

Now let me suggest some very specific ways that this can be done. First, there is a very moderate bill to which the Democratic Party platform was formally committed in 1976 and which a good many Democrats are busily running away from as fast as they possibly can. The bill is the Hawkins–Humphrey Full Employment Bill. It is a bill for the most conservative modicum of liberal capitalist planning. It says that the President of the United States every year will make an analysis of all the investment decisions, public and private, that can be anticipated for that year, add up those investment decisions, and discover what level of unemployment will result, given the population, technology, and so on. If adult unemployment exceeds 3 percent, which in plainer English is about 4 percent total unemployment, then the President is required by law to present to the Congress in an annual message those programs which will make up the shortfall and reduce unemployment to 4 percent or 3 percent adult unemployment. It is a very modest bill. It is viewed in some quarters as being practically the equivalent of Bolshevism. But it would begin to attack the most outrageous and abiding evil in this society today, its high level of unemployment, which is not randomly distributed but particularly discriminates against minorities, youth, and women. . . .

The problem is that many people are now saying we cannot do that, and some of them are liberals. Charles Schultze of the Brookings Institution says, in effect, that American society requires 5 percent unemployment in order to function. He maintains that as soon as we get to 5.5 percent unemployment, the inflationary tendencies become so strong that we must give up our campaigns against unemployment in order to fight inflation. This implies that the people composing that reserve army of the unemployed, as Marx would describe it—this reserve army which is disproportionately black, Hispanic, female, and young—will pay for the struggle against inflation.

In conclusion, I suggest three propositions. First, capitalism was a magnificent advance for mankind, but a contradictory advance because it was a system of private socialization. The socialization brought enormous successes, but the private socialization has brought us intolerable contradictions. Second, the contemporary manifestation of the contradictions of private socialization are seen in an American system that is not a free enterprise system but a corporate collectivist system in which government honestly, sincerely, and non-conspiratorially follows corporate priorities because they are natural in this society. Third, the alternative, the way to pursue freedom in the late twentieth century, is to democratize economic and social as well as political institutions.

If we ask: "Shall we have free enterprise or shall we have collectivism?" we have asked a meaningless question, because there is no free enterprise today. There can be no free enterprise given the scale of our technology, given the interdependence of our world. Richard Nixon planned as much as Lyndon Johnson. . . . It is not that people sell out. This is the basic thrust of our society.

Therefore, I think the question, as is often the case, is at least as important as the answer. I would reformulate the question and say the true question before us today in terms of freedom and social justice is: "Will the collectivist economic and social and political structure, which is emerging right now in front of our very eyes, be bureaucratically run by a united front of corporations and government on the basis of a hidden agenda moving toward a post-capitalist bureaucratic collectivist society run by the grandchildren of the executives?" Or is it possible for the collectivism which is emerging here and now to be democratized, to be subjected to the will of the people instead of its dominating the people? It is that second possibility that I am for, that I pose in terms of ethics and freedom and social justice. I am not sure it can prevail. I am not sure it will prevail. The one thing that I am sure of is that it is the only way for freedom to survive in the modern world.

CHAPTER 13

Who Should Decide When I Die?

Medical ethics is almost as old a field as medicine itself. One of the earliest documents concerning medicine is the Hippocratic oath, a set of ethical standards for the practice of medicine laid down by the Greek physician Hippocrates about 400 B.C. Important as such ethical guidelines were then, they are even more important now. Medicine is much more effective now than it was even a century ago, when there was little that could be done for most illness and injury. Accordingly, we have become far more dependent on the medical establishment to maintain the quality and extend the duration of our lives.

At the same time, medical technology has advanced to a point that the very concepts that have historically framed our moral sensibilities seem in need of drastic redefinition, or abandonment. Even the concept of death has been stretched almost beyond recognition by the wide availability of mechanical means for prolonging cellular activity in the human body. Perhaps a hypothetical example will bring into focus the sorts of problems that our culture must face in reaching anything like a clear view of the proper ends of medicine.

Jack O'Conner, age 51, has worked for 32 years as a machinist for a local manufacturing company. Outside of his work, he exercises occasionally, but not with much enthusiasm. He has been married, if not happily, at least to the same person, for 29 years, and has three children: Kathleen, 17, Sean, 19, and Maureen, 22. He and his family are covered by the standard health insurance offered by his company and they have generally breezed through their regular medical checkups without issue. Nevertheless, because his own father died young, Jack worries about his health, sometimes excessively. He has remarked to his regular physician that if he is dying, he doesn't want to know about it. These remarks have always been an occasion for lighthearted banter between Jack and Dr. Fine. But now Jack has cancer.

Dr. Fine decides to take Jack's expressed wishes seriously; she doesn't know Jack's wife or children and does not feel she can breach confidentiality by contacting them directly. She knows that Jack will die within six months, and she has seen many cases in which a patient who was informed of his imminent death went into a depression that ruined, literally, the rest of his life. She decides not to tell Jack that he has cancer.

Consequently, three months later when Jack is admitted to the hospital, he is not well prepared to make important decisions regarding the course of his treatment. He quickly degenerates to a state of severe, unremitting pain, which is treated with heavy doses of narcotic pain relievers. The medication brings some relief from pain, but the combined effect of the medication and the pain makes it impossible for Jack to discuss coherently his disease or his treatment.

Dr. Fine would like to enroll Jack in an experimental program at one of the other local hospitals. Unfortunately, Jack's medical insurance does not pay for "exotic" treatment. Last year Jack's neighbor, also a machinist, but at a different local plant, became seriously ill and was referred to a specialist in San Francisco. But his insurance covered such referrals, whereas Jack's does not. Consequently, Dr. Fine can do littler more than alleviate Jack's increasing pain and the other symptoms of his physical decline.

Within a month, Jack spends his days and nights racked with excruciating pain the is increasingly unresponsive to larger and larger doses of medication. In his few marginally coherent moments, he pleads to be relieved of his pain and to die in peace. The doctors agree that if Jack's heart stops, they will not resuscitate him, and that if he stops breathing, they will not place him on a mechanical respirator. Nevertheless, his

608 Chapter 13 | Who Should Decide When I Die?

body stubbornly lives on. Jack's wife and children plead with the doctors to give him a lethal injection. But the law, or the doctor's conception of it, and their ethical code, will not permit them either actively to cause his death (even though that is the only thing that would relieve his suffering) or intentionally to fail to treat him as fully as possible so long as he continues breathing and his heart beats. They remark on the possibility of a miracle.

Five weeks later, Jack's body dies. He has spent nine weeks in the hospital, eight of them in intensive care. The hospital bill is nearly $300,000, of which Jack's insurance pays 80%. His family is responsible for the remaining $60,000 which, conveniently, is precisely the amount of the life insurance policy that Jack carefully maintained during the 25 years since he first began paying for it. All of us who participate in health insurance paid the remaining $240,000 of Jack's hospital bill.

The case of Jack O'Conner illustrates three of the issues that are discussed in the readings in this chapter. First, was it permissible for Dr. Fine to withhold from Jack, on his request, the information that he had cancer? If she were right about the quality of his life after her diagnosis, does that justify her decision not to tell him the truth about his illness? This practice has been referred to as a form of **paternalism** in medicine, in which doctors—rightly or wrongly—impinge on the autonomy of patients by withholding information from them. In his selection, Allen Buchanan argues that withholding the truth from patients is a common practice in medicine, but that the justifications usually given for this practice are insufficient. He concludes that doctors ought to tell their patients the truth about their illnesses. In a rebuttal of Buchanan's position, Donald Vandeveer argues that at least one justification for withholding the truth from patients survives Buchanan's argument: patients have the right to contract with their physicians to have potentially distressing information withheld from them. Such contracts, Buchanan argues, reinforce rather than undermine the patient's autonomy. If he is right, we are left with at least one area in which physicians are permitted, even obligated, not to tell their patients the truth about their illnesses.

A second issue that Jack's case raises is the cost of medical care. Jack's treatment and care were enormously expensive to him, to his family, and to the rest of us who share the financial burden of his health care through insurance and government health programs. Moreover, if he could have afforded it, Jack could have tried a new sort of treatment that offered more hope of a cure. His neighbor, a person of similar talents and needs, was fortunate enough to have more comprehensive health insurance that paid for such treatment. Should the availability of health care be a matter of how much money a person has or whom a person works for? Or is health care a basic need that should be guaranteed equally to all? Dan E. Beuchamp claims that our present health-care system is based on a social ethic of "market-justice" that protects the majority and the most powerful from the burdens of equitable health care. He argues that we need to develop a public-health ethic that would emphasize prevention and collective responsibility rather than autonomy and individual liberty. Loren E. Lomasky claims to the contrary that we simply could not pay for equity at the level of care that the more privileged of our society currently enjoy. We should, he argues in his selection, let individuals—rather than government—make their own choices about health care, based on their ability to pay. In order to protect the poor, Lomasky suggests a system of health-care vouchers to be used in a medical marketplace. He therefore squarely opposes the sort of national health-care system proposed by Beauchamp.

A third issue that Jack's case raises concerns the nature of his death. Jack lived much longer than he wanted to, lost to relentless pain at great financial cost. As an alternative, he could, at a point at which his death was inevitable, simply have requested a lethal injection. Our current laws and codes of medical ethics do not permit this on the grounds that a doctor may not intentionally bring about the death of a patient. To do so would legally and, it is claimed, morally constitute murder. In many circumstances, Jack's for example, a doctor is permitted not to treat a patient for whom treatment would only prolong life. A huge amount of legal and moral weight is placed on this critical distinction between actively causing a person's death and passively, through inaction, allowing a person to die. James Rachels proposes in a crisp selection that it is a distinction without a difference. He agrees that "active euthanasia" and "passive euthanasia" are legally different. But by spelling out for us some of the consequences of trying to hold on to such a legal distinction, he argues that there is no moral basis for it. In her response to Rachels' argument, Bonnie Steinbock claims to the contrary that the distinction between active and passive euthanasia can be supported in cases in which the patient refuses treatment and in cases in which, like Jack's, the purpose of failing to treat a patient is not the termination of life, but rather the reduction of pain.

The Chapter ends with two articles that deal not so much with particular questions but rather with the structure of concepts that leads us to think about these questions as we do. Virginia L. Warren argues that the very framing of issues often reveals "sexist ethics." For example, she sees the focus on paternalism in medicine as a preoccupation with issues of authority and power—characteristically masculine approaches. She then explores what an alternative medical ethic might look like if it were created in response to central themes in feminist philosophy. The novel result suggests quite different approaches to moral problems in the conduct of medicine.

Finally, Daniel Callahan's article questions our prevailing concept of the aim of medical practice. He argues, in response to costs of medical care that we cannot possibly pay, that we must adopt a view of medical care that is not focused exclusively on the goal of curing illness. His startling proposal is that we employ age as a specific criterion in the allocation of medical treatment. His proposal has been nearly unspeakable in current political circles, but his thoughtful and sensitive defense of it challenges our thinking both about equity in the allocation of resources and about the ends of medicine.

ALLEN BUCHANAN

Medical Paternalism

ALLEN BUCHANAN is a philosopher who is interested in medical ethics. He was a member of the President's Commission for the Study of Ethical Problems in Medicine, Bio-Medicine, and Behavior. He has taught at the University of Minnesota and at the University of Arizona.

I

There is evidence to show that among physicians in this country the medical paternalist model is a dominant way of conceiving the physician-patient relationship. I contend that the practice of withholding the truth from the patient or his family, a particular form of medical paternalism, is not adequately supported by the arguments advanced to justify it. Beyond the issue of telling patients the truth is the distinction between "ordinary" and "extraordinary" therapeutic measures, a distinction which, I argue, both expresses and helps to perpetuate the dominance of the medical paternalist model.

There are two main types of arguments against paternalism. First are the arguments that rely upon a theory of moral rights rooted in a conception of personal autonomy. These arguments are more theoretically interesting and perhaps in the end they are the strongest arguments against paternalism. Second are the arguments that meet the paternalist on his own ground and then attempt to cut it from beneath him by showing that his arguments are defective. I shall concentrate on the second type of antipaternalist argument because I wish my arguments to have some practical effect, and I believe that this goal can best be achieved if they are directed against paternalist justifications which are actually employed by the practitioners of medical paternalism. . . .

II

Paternalism is usually characterized as interference with a person's liberty of action, where the alleged justification of the interference is that it is for the good of the person whose liberty of action is thus restricted. To focus exclusively on interference with liberty of *action* however, is to construe paternalism too narrowly. If a government lies to the public or withholds information from it, and if the alleged justification of its policy is that it benefits the public itself, the policy may properly be called paternalistic.

On the one hand, there may be a direct connection between such a policy and actual interference with the citizen's freedom to act. In order to withhold information from the public, agents of the government may physically interfere with the freedom of the press to gather, print, or distribute the news. Or government officials may misinform the public in order to restrict its freedom to perform specific acts. The police, for example, may erect signs bearing the words "Detour: Maintenance Work Ahead" to route unsuspecting motorists around the wreckage of a truck carrying nerve gas. On the other hand, the connection between withholding of information and actual interference with freedom of action may be indirect at best. To interfere with the public's freedom of information the government need not actually interfere with anyone's freedom to act—it may simply not divulge certain information. Withholding information may preclude an *informed* decision, and it may interfere with attempts to reach an informed decision, without thereby interfering with a person's freedom to decide and to act on his decision. Even if I am deprived of information which I must have if I am to make an informed decision, I may still be free to decide and to act.

Granted the complexity of the relations between information and action, it seems plausible to expand the usual characterization of paternalism as follows: paternalism is interference with a person's freedom of action or freedom of information, or the deliberate dissemination of misinformation, where the alleged justification of interfering or misinforming is that it is for the good of the person who is interfered with or misinformed. The notion of freedom of information is, of course, unsatisfyingly vague, but the political examples sketched above along with the medical examples to follow will make it clearer. We can now turn to a brief consideration of evidence for the claim that medical paternalism is a widespread phenomenon in our society.

III

The evidence for medical paternalism is both direct and indirect. The direct evidence consists of the findings of surveys which systematically report physicians' practices concerning truth-telling and decision-making and of articles and discussions in which physicians and others acknowledge or defend paternalistic medical practices. The indirect evidence is more subtle. One source of indirect evidence for the pervasiveness of medical paternalist attitudes is the language we use to describe physician-patient interactions. Let us now consider some of the direct evidence.

Though there are many ways of classifying cases of medical paternalism, two distinctions are especially important. We can distinguish between the cases in which the patient is legally competent and those in which the patient is legally incompetent; and between those cases in which the intended beneficiary of paternalism is the patient himself and those in which the intended beneficiary is the patient's guardian or one or more members of the patient's family. The first distinction classifies cases according to the *legal status of the patient*, the second according to the *object of paternalism.*

A striking revelation of medical paternalism in dealings with legally competent adults is found in Donald Oken's essay, "What to Tell Cancer Patients: A Study of Medical Attitudes." The chief conclusion of this study of internists, surgeons, and generalists is that ". . . there is a strong and general tendency to withhold" from the patient the information that he has cancer. Almost 90 percent of the total group surveyed reported that their usual policy is not to tell the patient that he has cancer. Oken also notes that "no one reported a policy of informing every patient." Further, Oken reports that some physicians falsified diagnoses.

> Some physicians avoid even the slightest suggestion of neoplasia and quite specifically substitute another diagnosis. Almost everyone reported resorting to such falsification on at least a few occasions, most notably when the patient was in a far-advanced stage of illness at the time he was seen.

The physicians' justifications for withholding or falsifying diagnostic information were uniformly paternalistic. They assumed that if they told the patient he had cancer they would be depriving him of all hope and that the loss of hope would result in suicidal depression or at least in a serious worsening of the patient's condition. . . .

There is also considerable evidence of medical paternalism in the treatment of legally incompetent individuals through the withholding of information from the patients or their guardians or both.

The law maintains that it is the parents who are primarily responsible for decisions concerning the welfare of their minor children. Nonetheless, physicians sometimes assume primary or even total responsibility for the most awesome and morally perplexing decisions affecting the welfare of the child.

The inescapable need to make such decisions arises daily in neonate intensive care units. . . . A. Shaw notes that some physicians undertake the responsibility for making decisions about life and death for defective newborns in order to relieve parents of the trauma and guilt of making a decision. He cites the following comment as an example of this position.

> At the end it is usually the doctor who has to decide the issue. It is . . . cruel to ask the parents whether they want their child to live or die. . . .

The growing literature on life or death decisions for defective neonates reveals more complex paternalistic practices. Some physicians routinely exclude parents from significant participation in decision-making either by not informing the parents that certain choices can or must be made, or by describing the child's condition and the therapeutic options in such a skeletal way as to preclude genuinely informed consent.

A case cited by Shaw is a clear example of a physician withholding from parents the information that there was a choice to be made.

> Baby A was referred to me at 22 hours of age with a diagnosis of esophageal atresia and tracheo-esophageal fistula. The infant, the firstborn of a professional couple in their early thirties had obvious signs of mongolism, about which they were fully informed by the referring physician. After explaining the nature of the surgery to the distraught father, I offered him the operative consent. He pen hesitated briefly above the form and then as he signed, he muttered, "I have no choice, do I?" He didn't seem to expect an answer and I gave him none. The esophageal anomaly was corrected in routine fashion, and the infant was discharged to a state institution for the retarded without ever being seen again by either parent. . . .

Not every case in which a physician circumvents or overrides parental decision-making is a case of paternalism toward the parents. In ignoring the parents' primary legal responsibility for the child, the physician may not be attempting to shield the parents from the burdens of responsibility—he may simply be attempting to protect what he perceives to be the interests of the child.

These examples are presented, not as conclusive evidence for the claim that paternalist practices of the sorts discussed above are widespread, but as illustrations of the practical relevance of the justifications for medical paternalism, which I shall now articulate and criticize.

IV

In spite of the apparent pervasiveness of paternalistic practices in medicine, no systematic justification of them is available for scrutiny. Nonetheless, there appear to be at least three main arguments which advocates of paternalism could and sometimes do advance in justification of withholding information or misinforming the patient or his family. Since withholding information seems to be more commonly practiced and advocated than outright falsification, I shall consider the three arguments only as justifications of the former rather than the latter. Each of these arguments is sufficiently general to apply to each of the types of cases distinguished above. For convenience we can label these three arguments (A) the Prevention of Harm Argument, (B) the Contractual Version of the Prevention of Harm Argument, and (c) the Argument from the Inability to Understand.

The Prevention of Harm Argument is disarmingly simple. It may be outlined as follows.

1. The physician's duty—to which he is bound by the Oath of Hippocrates—is to prevent or at least to minimize harm to his patient.
2. Giving the patient information X will do great harm to him.
3. (Therefore) It is permissible for the physician to withhold information X from the patient.

Several things should be noted about this argument. First of all, the conclusion is much weaker than one would expect, granted the first premise. The first premise states that it is the physician's *duty* to prevent or minimize harm to the patient, not just that it is *permissible* for him to do so. However, since the weaker conclusion—that withholding information is permissible—seems more intuitively plausible that the stronger one, I shall concentrate on it.

Second, the argument as it stands is invalid. For the claims that (1) the physician's duty (or right) is to prevent or minimize harm and that (2) giving information X will do the patient great harm, it does not follow that (3) it is permissible for the physician to withhold information X from the patient. At least one other premise is needed: (2') giving information X will do greater harm to the patient on balance than withholding the information will.

The addition of (2') is no quibble. Once (2') is made explicit we begin to see the tremendous weight which this paternalist argument places on the physician's power of judgment. He must not only determine that giving the information will do harm or even that it will do great harm. He must also make a complex comparative judgment. He must judge that withholding the information will result in less harm on balance than divulging it. Yet neither the physicians interviewed by Oken nor those discussed by Shaw even mention this comparative judgment in their justifications of withholding information. They simply state that telling the truth will result in great harm to the patient or his family. No mention was made of the need to compare this expected harm with harm which might result from withholding the information, and no recognition of the difficulties involved in such a comparison was reported. . . .

In order to justify withholding the diagnosis of terminal cancer from the patient the physician must not only determine that informing the patient would do great harm but that the harm would be greater on balance than whatever harm may result from withholding information. Since the notion of "great harm" here is vague unless a context for comparison is supplied, we can concentrate on the physician's evidence for the judgment that the harm of informing is greater on balance than the harm of withholding. Oken's study showed that the evidential basis for such comparative judgments was remarkably slender.

> It was the exception when a physician could report known examples of the unfavorable consequences of an approach which differed from his own. It was more common to get reports of instances in which different approaches had turned out satisfactorily. Most of the instances in which unhappy results were reported to follow a differing policy turned out to be vague accounts from which no reliable inference could be drawn.

Oken then goes on to focus on the nature of the anticipated harm.

> It has been repeatedly asserted that disclosure is followed by fear and despondency which may progress into overt depressive illness or culminate in suicide. This was the opinion of the physicians in the present study. Quite representative was the surgeon who stated, "I would be afraid to tell and have the patient in a room with a window." When it comes to actually documenting the prevalence of such untoward reactions, it becomes difficult to find reliable evidence. Instances of depression and profound upsets came quickly to mind when the subject was raised, but no one could report more than a case or two, or a handful at most. . . . The same doctors could remember many instances in which the patient was told and seemed to do well. . . .

Consider the case of a person with terminal cancer. To eliminate the complication of interpersonal net harm comparisons, let us suppose that this person has no relatives and is himself legally competent. Suppose that the physician withholds information of the diagnosis because he believes that knowledge of the truth would be more harmful than withholding the truth. . . . Even if we view this judgment of comparative harm as a purely clinical judgment—more specifically a clinical psychiatric judgment —it is difficult to see how the physician could be in a position to make it. But it is crucial to note that the notions of harm and benefit appropriate to these deliberations are not exclusively clinical notions, whether psychiatric or otherwise. In taking it upon himself to determine what will be most beneficial or least harmful to this patient the physician is not simply making ill-founded medical judgments which someday might be confirmed by psychiatric research. He is making *moral* evaluations of the most basic and problematic kind.

The physician must determine whether it will be better for the patient to live his remaining days in the knowledge that his days are few or to live in ignorance of his fate. But again, this is a gross simplification: it assumes that the physician's attempt to deceive the patient will be successful. E. Kübler-Ross claims that in many, if not most, cases the terminally ill patient will guess or learn his fate whether the physician withholds the diagnosis from him or not. Possible harm resulting from the patient's loss of confidence in the physician or from a state of uncertainty over his prospects must be taken into account.

Let us set aside this important complication and try to appreciate what sorts of factors would have to be taken into account in a well-founded judgment that the remainder of a person's life would be better for that person if he did not know that he had a terminal illness than if he did.

Such a judgment would have to be founded on a profound knowledge of the most intimate details of the patient's life history, his characteristic ways of coping with personal crises, his personal and vocational commitments and aspirations, his feelings of obligation toward others, and his attitude toward the completeness or incompleteness of his experience. In a society in which the personal physician was an intimate friend who shared the experience of families under his care, it would be somewhat more plausible to claim that the physician might possess such knowledge. Under the present conditions of highly impersonal specialist medical practice it is quite a different matter.

Yet even if the physician could claim such intimate personal knowledge, this would not suffice. For he must not only predict, but also *evaluate*. On the basis of an intimate knowledge of the patient as a person, he must determine which outcome would be *best* for that person. It is crucial to emphasize that the question which the physician must pose and answer is whether ignorance or knowledge will make possible a life that is better *for the patient himself.* The physician must be careful not to confuse this question with the question of whether ignorance or knowledge would make for a better life for the physician if the physician were terminally ill. Nor must he confuse it with the question of whether the patient's life would be a *better life*—a life more valuable to others or to society—if it ended in ignorance rather than in truth. The question, rather, is whether it would be better *for the patient himself* to know or not to know his fate.

To judge that a certain ending of a life would be best for the person whose life it is, is to view that life as a unified process of development and to conclude that that ending is a fitting completion for that process. To view a human life as a unified process of development, however, is to view it selectively. Certain events or patterns of conduct are singled out as especially significant or valuable. To ascertain the best completion of a person's life for that person, then, is to make the most fundamental judgments about the value of that person's activities, aspirations, and experiences.

It might be replied that we do make such value judgments when we decide to end the physiologic life of a permanently comatose individual. In such cases we do make value judgments, but they are not judgments of this sort. On the contrary, we believe that since this individual's experience has ended, his life-process is already completed.

When the decision to withhold information of impending death is understood for what it is, it is difficult to see how anyone could presume to make it. My conjecture is that physicians are tempted to make these decisions in part because of a failure to reflect upon the disparity between two quite different kinds of judgments about what will harm or benefit the patient. Judgments of the first sort fall within the physician's competence as a highly trained medical expert. There is nothing in the physician's training which qualifies him to make judgments of the second sort—to evaluate another human being's life as a whole. Further, once the complexity of these judgments is appreciated and once their evaluative character is understood, it is implausible to hold that the physician is in a better position to make them than the patient or his family. The failure to ask what sorts of harm/benefit judgments may properly be made by the physician in his capacity as a physician is a fundamental feature of medical paternalism.

There is a more sophisticated version of the attempt to justify withholding of information in order to minimize harm to the patient or his family. This is the Contract

Version of the Prevention of Harm Argument. The idea is that the physician-patient relationship is contractual and that the terms of this contract are such that the patient authorizes the physician to minimize harm to the patient (or his family) by whatever means he, the physician, deems necessary. Thus if the physician believes that the best way to minimize harm to the patient is to withhold information from him, he may do so without thereby wronging the patient. To wrong the patient the physician would either have to do something he was not authorized to do or fail to do something it was his duty to do and which was in his power to do. But in withholding information from the patient he is doing just what he is authorized to do. So he does the patient no wrong.

First of all, it should be noted that this version is vulnerable to the same objections just raised against the non-contractual Argument from the Prevention of Harm. The most serious of these is that in the cases of paternalism under discussion it is very doubtful that the physician will or even could possess the psychiatric and moral knowledge required for a well-founded judgment about what will be least harmful to the patient. In addition, the Contract Version is vulnerable to other objections. Consider the claim that the patient-physician relationship is a contract in which the patient authorizes the physician to prevent or minimize harm by whatever means the physician deems necessary, including the withholding of information. This claim could be interpreted in either of two ways: as a descriptive generalization about the way physicians and patients actually understand their relationship or as a normative claim about the way the physician-patient relationship should be viewed or may be viewed.

As a descriptive generalization it is certainly implausible—there are many people who do not believe they have authorized their physician to withhold the truth from them, and the legal doctrine of informed consent supports their view. Let us suppose for a moment that some people do view their relationship to their physician as including such an authorization and that there is nothing morally wrong with such a contract so long as both parties entered into it voluntarily and in full knowledge of the terms of the agreement.

Surely the fact that some people are willing to authorize physicians to withhold information from them would not justify the physician in acting toward other patients as if they had done so. The physician can only justify withholding information from a particular patient if this sort of contract was entered into freely and in full knowledge *by this* patient.

What, then, is the physician to do? Surely he cannot simply assume that all of his patients have authorized him to withhold the truth if he deems it necessary. Yet if in each case he inquires as to whether the patient wishes to make such an authorization, he will defeat the purpose of the authorization by undermining the patient's trust.

There is, however, a more serious difficulty. Even the more extreme advocates of medical paternalism must agree that there are some limits on the contractual relationship between physician and patient. Hence the obligations of each party are conditional upon the other party's observing the limits of the contract. The law, the medical profession, and the general public generally recognize that there are such limits. For example, the patient may refuse to undergo a certain treatment, he may seek a second opinion, or he may terminate the relationship altogether. Moreover, it is acknowledged that to decide to do any of these things the patient may—indeed perhaps must—rely on his own judgment. If he is conscientious he will make such decisions on consideration of whether the physician is doing a reasonable job of rendering the services for which he was hired.

There are general constraints on how those services may be rendered. If the treatment is unreasonably slow, if the physician's technique is patently sloppy, or if he employs legally questionable methods, the patient may rightly conclude that the physician has not lived up to the implicit terms of the agreement and terminate the relationship. There are also more special constraints on the contract stemming from the special nature of the problem which led the patient to seek the physician's services in the first place. If you go to a physician for treatment of a skin condition, but he ignores that problem and sets about trying to convince you to have cosmetic nose surgery, you may rightly terminate the relationship. These general and special constraints are limits on the agreement from the patient's point of view.

Now once it is admitted that there are any such terms—that the contract does have some limits and that the patient has the right to terminate the relationship if these limits are not observed by the physician—it must also be admitted that the patient must be in a position to discover *whether* those limits are being observed. But if the patient were to authorize the physician to withhold information, he might deprive himself of information which is relevant to determining whether the physician has observed the limits of the agreement.

I am not concerned to argue that authorizing a physician to withhold information is logically incompatible with the contract being conditional. My point, rather, is that to make such an authorization would show either that (a) one did not view the contract as being conditional or that (b) one did not take seriously the possibility that the conditions of the contract might be violated or that (c) one simply did not care whether the conditions were violated. Since it is unreasonable to expect a patient to make an unconditional contract or to ignore the possibility that conditions of the contract will be violated, and since one typically does care whether these conditions are observed, it is unreasonable to authorize the physician to withhold information when he sees fit. The Contract Version of the Argument from the Prevention of Harm, then, does not appear to be much of an improvement over its simpler predecessor.

There is one paternalist argument in favor of withholding of information which remains to be considered. This may be called the Argument from the Inability to Understand. The main premise is that the physician is justified in withholding information when the patient or his family is unable to understand the information. This argument is often used to justify paternalistic policies toward parents of defective infants in neonate intensive care units. The idea is that either their lack of intelligence or their excited emotional condition prevents parents from giving informed consent because they are incapable of being adequately informed. In such cases, it is said, "the doctrine of informed consent does not apply."

This argument is also vulnerable to several objections. First, it too relies upon dubious and extremely broad psychological generalizations—in this case psychological generalizations about the cognitive powers of parents of defective neonates.

Second, and more importantly, it ignores the crucial question of the character of the institutional context in which parents find themselves. To the extent that paternalist attitudes shape medical institutions, this bleak estimate of the parental capacity for comprehension and rational decision tends to be a self-fulfilling prophecy. In an institution in which parents routinely sign operation permits without even having seen their newborn infants and without having the nature of the therapeutic options clearly explained to them, parents may indeed be incapable of understanding the little that they are told.

Third, it is a mistake to maintain that the legal duty to seek informed consent applies only where the physician can succeed in adequately informing parents. The doctor does not and cannot have a duty to make sure that all the information he conveys is understood by those to whom he conveys it. His duty is to make a reasonable effort to be understood.

Fourth, it is important to ask exactly why it is so important not to tell parents information which they allegedly will not understand. If the reason is that a parental decision based on inadequate understanding will be a decision that is harmful to the *infant*, then the Argument from the Inability to Understand is not an argument for paternalism toward *parents*. So if this argument is to provide a justification for withholding information from parents for *their* benefit then the claim must be that their failure to understand will somehow be harmful to *them*. But why should this be so? If the idea is that the parents will not only fail to understand but become distressed because they realize that they do not understand, then the Argument from the Inability to Understand turns out not to be a new argument at all. Instead, it is just a restatement of the Argument from the Prevention of Harm examined above—and is vulnerable to the same objections. I conclude that none of the three justifications examined provide adequate support for the paternalist practices under consideration. If adequate justification is to be found, the advocate of medical paternalism must marshal more powerful arguments.

V

So far I have examined several specific medical paternalistic practices and criticized some general arguments offered in their behalf. Medical paternalism, however, goes much deeper than the specific practices themselves. For this reason I have spoken of "the medical paternalist model," emphasizing that what is at issue is a paradigm, a way of conceiving the physician-patient relationship. Indirect evidence for the pervasiveness of this model is to be found in the very words we used to describe physicians, patients, and their interactions. Simply by way of illustration, I will now examine one widely used distinction which expresses and helps perpetuate the paternalist model: the distinction between "ordinary" and "extraordinary" therapeutic measures.

Many physicians, theologians, ethicists, and judges have relied on this distinction since Pius XII employed it in an address on "The Prolongation of Life" in 1958. In reply to questions concerning conditions under which physicians may discontinue or refrain from initiating the use of artificial respiration devices, Pius first noted that physicians are duty-bound "to take the necessary treatment for the preservation of life and health." He then distinguished between "ordinary" and "extraordinary" means.

> But normally one is held to use only ordinary means—according to circumstances of persons, places, times, and culture—means that do not involve any grave burden for oneself or another.

Though he is not entirely explicit about this, Pius assumes that it is the right of the physician to determine what will count as "ordinary" or "extraordinary" means in any particular case.

In the context of the issue of when a highly trained specialist is to employ sophisticated life-support equipment, it is natural to assume that the distinction between "ordinary" and "extraordinary" means is a distinction between higher and lower degrees of technological sophistication. The Pope's unargued assumption that the medical specialist is to determine what counts as "ordinary" or "extraordinary" reinforces a technological interpretation of the distinction. After all, if the distinction is a technological one, then it is natural to assume that it is the physician who should determine its application since it is he who possesses the requisite technical expertise. In my discussions with physicians, nurses, and hospital administrators I have observed that they tend to treat the distinction as a technological one and then to argue that since it is a technological distinction the physician is the one who should determine in any particular case whether a procedure would involve "ordinary" or "extraordinary" means.

Notice, however, that even though Pius introduced the distinction in the context of the proper use of sophisticated technical devices and even though he assumed that it was to be applied by those who possess the technical skills to use such equipment, it is quite clear that the distinction he explicitly introduced is not itself a technological distinction. Recall that he defines "ordinary" means as those which "do not involve any grave burden for oneself or another." "Extraordinary" means, then, would be those which do involve a grave burden for oneself or for another.

If what counts as "extraordinary" measures depended only upon what would constitute a "grave burden" to the patient himself, it might be easier to preserve the illusion that the decision is an exercise of medical expertise. But once the evaluation of burdens is extended to the patient's family it becomes obvious that the judgment that a certain therapy would be "extraordinary" is not a technological or even a clinical, but rather a *moral* decision. And it is a moral decision regardless of whether the evaluation is made from the perspective of the patient's own values and preferences or from that of the physician.

Even if one is to evaluate only the burdens for the patient himself, however, it is implausible to maintain that the application of the distinction is an exercise of technological or clinical judgment. For as soon as we ask what would result in "grave burdens" for the patient, we are immediately confronted with the task of making moral distinctions and moral evaluations concerning the quality of the patient's life and his interests as a person.

When pressed for an explanation of how physicians actually apply the distinction between "ordinary" and "extraordinary" therapeutic measures, the director of a neonate intensive care unit explained to me that what counts as "ordinary" or "extraordinary" differs in "different contexts." Surgical correction of a congenital gastrointestinal blockage in the case of an otherwise normal infant would be considered an "ordinary" measure. But the same operation on an infant with Down's syndrome would be considered extraordinary.

I am not concerned here to criticize the moral decision to refrain from aggressive surgical treatment of infants with Down's syndrome. My purpose in citing this example is simply to point out that this decision *is* a moral decision and that the use of the distinction between "ordinary" and "extraordinary" measures does nothing to help one make the decision. The use of the distinction does accomplish something though: it obscures the fact that the decision *is* a moral decision. Even worse, it is likely to lead one to mistake a very controversial moral decision for a "value-free" technological or clinical decision. More importantly, to even suggest that a complex moral judgment is a clinical or technological judgment is to prejudice the issue of *who* has the right to decide whether life-sustaining measures are to be initiated or continued. Once controversial moral decisions are misperceived as clinical or technological decisions it becomes much easier for the medical paternalist to use the three arguments examined above to justify the withholding of information. For once it is conceded that his medical expertise gives the physician the right to make certain decisions, he can then argue that he may withhold information where this is necessary for the effective exercise of this right. By disguising complex moral judgments as medical judgments, then, the "ordinary/extraordinary" distinction reinforces medical paternalism.

VI

In this paper I have attempted to articulate and challenge some basic features of the medical paternalist model of the physician-patient relationship. I have also given an indication of the powerful influence this model exerts on medical practice and on ways of talking and thinking about medical treatment.

There are now signs that medical paternalism is beginning to be challenged from within the medical profession itself. This I believe, is all to the good. So far, however, challenges have been fragmentary and unsystematic. If they are to be theoretically and practically fruitful they must be grounded in a systematic understanding of what medical paternalism is and in a critical examination of justifications for medical paternalist practices. The present paper is an attempt to begin the task of such a systematic critique.

DONALD VANDEVEER

The Contractual Argument for Withholding Medical Information

DONALD VANDEVEER teaches philosophy at North Carolina State University. He has undertaken research in political philosophy, ethics, and medical ethics and has published widely in these areas.

Paternalistic grounds for justifying presumptively wrongful treatment of competent adults are widely looked upon as suspect. Allen Buchanan, in an instructive and generally careful essay, has shown that the presence of paternalistic attitudes and paternalistic treatment is not uncommon in physicians' dealings with their patients. In particular he contends that "the practice of withholding the truth from the patient or his family, a particular form of medical paternalism, is not adequately supported by the arguments advanced to justify it." Buchanan distinguishes two types of arguments which may be advanced against paternalism. The first sort would appeal to a theory of moral rights and would seek (I presume, although Buchanan does not say so explicitly) to show that instances of medical paternalism unjustifiably infringe one or more rights of the patient. Assuming the absence of an adequate defense of a full-blown theory of moral rights Buchanan prefers to advance an alternative critique. He seeks to show that "paternalist justifications which are actually employed by the practitioners of medical paternalism" are inadequate. Contrary to Buchanan's claims I shall show that (1) his attack on one attempt to justify the physician's withholding of information in a restricted range of cases is wrongheaded and that there is in fact a strong presumption that it is permissible and (2) the physician's withholding information in these cases is not appropriately described as "medical paternalism."

I

Buchanan observes that paternalism is usually characterized as "interference with a person's liberty of action, where the alleged justification of the interference is that it is for the good of the person whose liberty is thus restricted." Regarding the focus on liberty of *action* as too narrow, he prefers to include the withholding of information under similar conditions as also an instance of paternalistic interference. The characterization of paternalism is thus revised to include "interference with a person's freedom of action or freedom of information, or the deliberate dissemination of misinformation." I shall not object here to this extension of the more usual characterization.

After instructively documenting a tendency among physicians to attempt to justify withholding, or even falsifying, diagnostic information from their patients, Buchanan attempts to show the inadequacy of three arguments advanced to defend such practices. My focus will be solely on what he labels "the Contractual Version of Prevention of Harm Argument." It is worth quoting here his formulation of what I shall henceforth refer to as the Contractual Argument:

> The idea is that the physician-patient relationship is contractual and that the terms of this contract are such that the patient authorizes the physician to minimize harm to the patient (or his family) by whatever means he, the physician, deems necessary. Thus if the physician believes that the best way to minimize harm to the patient is to withhold information from him, he may do so without thereby wronging the patient. To wrong the patient the physician would either have to do something he was not authorized to do or fail to do something it was his duty to do and which was in his power to do. But in withholding information from the patient he is doing just what he is authorized to do. So he does the patient no wrong.

Buchanan raises a series of objections against this argument. The first is one that may be brought against the claim that the physician may and ought to treat the patient in whatever way will be "least harmful" even in cases where there is no contractual agreement as described above. So a physician may legitimately withhold diagnostic information if he deems it the least harmful course of action. Buchanan objects that "it is very doubtful that the physician will or even could possess the psychiatric and moral knowledge required for a well-founded judgment about what will be least harmful for the patient." Elsewhere he emphasizes that a physician's judgments about certain matters are problematic—for example, when the judgment is made that a patient is likely to become fearful and develop a despondency which may progress into depressive illness (or culminate in suicide) if certain information is revealed to him (say he has terminal cancer). Such judgments, in Buchanan's view, involve *psychiatric generalizations* made typically on the basis of scanty evidence. He claims, further, that *even if* a physician is in a position to reliably predict, he may simply be assuming that suicide "is not a rational choice" for the patient. Buchanan is correct, I believe, in judging that the physician who decides to withhold information on such grounds must make difficult empirical judgments and also difficult evaluative judgments about which alternative will be "least harmful" on balance for the patient. Several points, however, seriously weaken Buchanan's first objection to the Contractual Argument. Buchanan's reservations, if correct, serve only as a counsel of caution to the conscientious physician who wants to do what is least harmful to the patient. They do not show that it is impossible for a physician to arrive at a reasonable judgment that withholding information will be least harmful to the patient. Second, a physician may be in no more difficult position to make this judgment than the patient himself. Physicians are more likely, on average, than patients to have had training in psychiatric or psychological theory relevant to predicting the consequences of revealing disturbing information to patients. Further, they are more likely to have observed the effects of doing so in a wide variety of cases than laypersons. More significant, perhaps, is the point that as the Contract Argument is described, the patient has authorized the physician to minimize harm to the patient by *whatever means the physician deems necessary.* The contract is not and could not plausibly be one where the physician is authorized to act only on *correct* judgments. It must be an authorization for the physician to act only on the basis of what *he believes to be* a well-founded judgment. If the physician does so, he does not violate the terms of the contract *even if,* as it turns out, his judgment is not well-founded. That such judgments are difficult to make or that a physician may have failed to make one would not, thereby, show that he has done a wrong to his patient. An unwise judgment is not necessarily an unconscientious, negligent, or reckless one.

A second objection proposed by Buchanan is that not all patients understand their relationship with their physician to be one where they have authorized him (or her) to withhold information when deemed necessary to minimize harm. So the physician, it is implied, cannot assume the existence of such a contract with a particular patient unless it is clear that *this* patient has contracted freely and with full knowledge that he has done so. These points are surely correct. It should be clear, however, that neither supposition undermines the Contractual Argument for it purports to justify withholding information *only* when there *is* a contractual authorization to do so. Again, we can only advise caution for physicians who may be tempted to assume authorization when there is inadequate reason to make such an assumption. Buchanan's claims may also be taken to urge patients to make explicit agreements with physicians so that there are no false or unfounded assumptions about the reciprocal rights and duties of the contracting parties. Since such matters are often not well defined, the point is well taken. Once more, it does not strike a blow against the Contractual Argument.

Buchanan presses his point further by claiming that if the physician inquires in each case whether the patient wishes to authorize the withholding of certain information "he will defeat the purpose of the authorization by undermining the patient's trust." If correct this claim shows, not that the Contractual Argument is unsound, but that such contracting is not likely to occur or that there is a reason to avoid forming such contracts. Hence, claims that such a contract was agreed upon ought to be viewed skeptically. The claim that such inquiries do or would undermine the patient's trust is itself, I think, a dubious empirical generalization although I cannot disprove it. A patient asked by his physician if he wishes to have possibly disturbing diagnostic information withheld from him when the physician may judge its revelation harmful to him would be inclined to judge that his physician is conscientious and principled, that he is a person unwilling to treat a patient in a presumptively wrong manner in the absence of his express consent to such a policy. Such an inquiry would tend to confirm a patient's hope that his physician respects the patient's right to decide how he shall be treated and will not treat him in a suspect way just because the physician judges it to be "for the patient's own good." That is, the inquiry would support the claim that the physician was *not* a member of the fraternity of paternalists.

Buchanan claims, however, that there is yet "a more serious difficulty." He states that even extreme advocates of medical paternalism must agree that there must be some limits on the contractual relationship between patient and physician. In particular, the patient needs to be able to determine whether the physician is observing the limitations imposed by the contractual relationship. If the patient authorizes the physician to withhold information he may deprive himself of the information necessary to determine *whether or not* those limits are being observed. In Buchanan's view such an authorization would show that "(a) one did not view the contract as being conditional or that (b) one did not take seriously the possibility that the conditions of the contract might be violated or that (c) one simply did not care whether the conditions were violated." Thus, it is concluded that it is unreasonable to authorize the physician to withhold information when he sees fit. There are difficulties with this line of thought.

Surely, it cannot be maintained that the patient should do nothing which would make it impossible or difficult to determine whether contractual limits are being observed. If so, the patient would never submit to anesthesia which would, after all, impair his ability to oversee a surgeon's procedure. More importantly it is possible that a patient might authorize the withholding of information and yet the conditions mentioned in (a), (b), and (c) are not true of the patient. For example, I might want certain information revealed to me and other information not revealed. Recognizing the benefits frequently associated with the "placebo effect" I may reasonably prefer not to be told when a placebo has been prescribed as part of my treatment. Also, I may recognize my penchant for undue anxiety and worry over the fact that certain of my symptoms are suggestive but not conclusive evidence of the presence of some dreaded disease. Hence, I may choose to remain ignorant of such matters until the physician is certain of its presence. Further, if my affairs are in order, I may even prefer to live out my last days falsely hopeful of recovery even when the physician is certain that I have terminal cancer. These preferences for ignorance with regard to a certain range of information may be made clear to the physician in a contract. With regard to certain matters I may authorize the physician to use his best judgment about whether it will be least harmful to disclose or to withhold information. Ignorance is not always bliss, but an individual may prefer ignorance under certain conditions. The nature of the contract made would obviously depend on one's preferences and one's degree of trust and confidence in the judgment of one's physician.

Thus, whether or not the physician wrongfully withholds information will depend on the nature of the contract. It may authorize and require disclosure of certain information *and also* authorize and require the withholding of other information. An interesting result shows up here. If I contract *not* to be informed of terminal cancer should I have it and the physician later decides that my *not* being informed of this fact is more harmful to me on balance than my being informed and he thus informs me his *disclosure* would be *paternalistic interference* with my chosen course, with my freedom to choose what information I shall receive. Hence, it is misleading to focus solely on the cases of withholding information or giving misinformation proceeding from paternalistic motives as actions requiring justification. Disclosing information may also be a paternalistic act and, possibly, an unjustifiable form of paternalism.

Buchanan maintains that "it is unreasonable to authorize the physician to withhold information when he sees fit." If he means "whenever, without qualification," I certainly agree. I have tried to show how it may be reasonable to authorize withholding information on certain matters. Hence, withholding information need not be paternalistic interference, and, indeed, disclosure may be. That depends on the nature of the contract, whether its authorizations are reasonable or not.

II

In view of the preceding remarks my second basic point can be defended more briefly. It is that in a certain range of cases where the physician withholds information from the patient, we do not have a case of medical paternalism. Hence, a justification for doing so is not a justification of medical paternalism.

As noted earlier, since Buchanan regards the (partial) characterization of paternalism as interference with "freedom of action" as too narrow, he expands the characterization to include "freedom of information, or the deliberate dissemination of misinformation." For reasons mentioned "freedom of information" may be understood to mean "freedom to be provided with information" or "freedom to not be subjected to information." Whether the disclosure of information or its being withheld is an *interference* depends on whether what the physician does violates the terms of the contract which, if well-made, will express the patient's preference for ignorance or disclosure, or some combination thereof. Hence, what the patient prefers and consents to is a crucial determinant in deciding whether a physician *interferes* with the patient, and, therefore, whether the physician *paternalistically interferes* with the patient. If a patient contracts to authorize his physician to withhold information under certain conditions, then the physician's doing so *under those conditions* is not a case of interference and, hence, not paternalistic interference. It is rather a case of compliance with the terms of the contract and not appropriately adduced as an instance of "medical paternalism" The withholding of information in such a case may even be an act the physician reluctantly agrees to but, in order to respect his *patient's* judgment about what is "for his (the patient's) own good," he complies with such a wish. So the withholding of information need not be paternalistic at all and, if it is justified, may be justified because it is the honoring of a contractual agreement, a respecting of the patient's autonomy rather than an overriding or disregarding of it.

If my arguments succeed, they are of course compatible with the overly neglected fact that medical paternalism is not uncommon and that purported justifications of it bear critical attention. If such paternalism is suspect, as I believe, it is important to identify ways of minimizing or avoiding it. In fact the making of explicit contracts with adequate checks on compliance by both parties seems just such a way of doing so. Whether any particular physician-patient relationship involves a contract of this more or less ideal sort is an empirical question about which I have avoided generalizing. A purported justification of a particular withholding of information may fail in its appeal to contractual authorization to do so simply because there has been no such contractual authorization. The remedy for practices lacking such authorization may be an increased turn toward the making of such contracts. The Contractual Argument, then, proffers not a justification of paternalistic interference, but rather a non-paternalistic justification of treating patients in ways that, abstractly considered, would be judged presumptively wrong. As such it is not vulnerable to the sorts of objections which may be brought against purported justifications of genuinely paternalistic treatment of patients.

DAN E. BEAUCHAMP

Public Health as Social Justice

DAN E. BEAUCHAMP writes on medical policy.

Anthony Downs has observed that our most intractable public problems have two significant characteristics. First, they occur to a relative minority of our population (even though that minority may number millions of people). Second, they result in significant part from arrangements that are providing substantial benefits or advantages to a majority or to a powerful minority of citizens. Thus solving or minimizing these problems requires painful losses, the restructuring of society and the acceptance of new burdens by the most powerful and the most numerous on behalf of the least powerful or the least numerous. As Downs notes, this bleak reality has resulted in recent years in cycles of public attention to such problems as poverty, racial discrimination, poor housing, unemployment or the abandonment of the aged; however, this attention and interest rapidly wanes when it becomes clear that solving these problems requires painful costs that the dominant interests in society are unwilling to pay. Our public ethics do not seem to fit our public problems.

It is not sufficiently appreciated that these same bleak realities plague attempts to protect the public's health. Automobile-related injury and death; tobacco, alcohol and other drug damage; the perils of the workplace; environmental pollution; the inequitable and ineffective distribution of medical care services; the hazards of biomedicine—all of these threats inflict death and disability on a minority of our society at any given time. Further, minimizing or even significantly reducing the death and disability from these perils entails that the majority or powerful minorities accept new burdens or relinquish existing privileges that they presently enjoy. Typically, these new burdens or restrictions involve more stringent controls over these and other hazards of the world.

This somber reality suggests that our fundamental attention in public health policy and prevention should not be directed toward a search for new technology, but rather toward breaking existing ethical and political barriers to minimize death and disability. This is not to say that technology will never again help avoid painful social and political adjustments. Nonetheless, only the technological Pollyannas will ignore the mounting evidence that the critical barriers to protecting the public against death and disability are not the barriers to technological progress —indeed the evidence is that it is often technology itself that is our own worst enemy. The critical barrier to dramatic reductions in death and disability is a social ethic that unfairly protects the most numerous or the most powerful from the burdens of prevention.

This is the issue of justice. In the broadest sense, justice means that each person in society ought to receive his due and that the burdens and benefits of society should be fairly and equitably distributed. But what criteria should be followed in allocating burdens and benefits: Merit, equality or need? What end or goal in life should receive our highest priority: Life, liberty or the pursuit of happiness? The answer to these questions can be found in our prevailing theories or models of justice. These models of justice, roughly speaking, form the foundation of our politics and public policy in general, and our health policy (including our prevention policy) specifically. Here I am speaking of politics not as partisan politics but rather the more ancient and venerable meaning of the political as the search for the common good and the just society.

These models of justice furnish a symbolic framework or blueprint with which to think about and react to the problems of the public, providing the basic rules to classify and categorize problems of society as to whether they necessitate public and collective protection, or whether individual responsibility should prevail. These models function as a sort of map or guide to the common world of members of society, making visible some conditions in society as public issues and concerns, and hiding, obscuring or concealing other conditions that might otherwise emerge as public issues or problems were a different map or model of justice in hand.

In the case of health, these models of justice form the basis for thinking about and reacting to the problems of disability and premature death in society. Thus, if public health policy requires that the majority or a powerful minority accept their fair share of the burdens of protecting a relative minority threatened with death or disability, we need to ask if our prevailing model of justice contemplates and legitimates such sacrifices.

MARKET-JUSTICE

The dominant model of justice in the American experience has been market-justice. Under the norms of market-justice people are entitled only to those valued ends such as status, income, happiness, etc., that they have acquired by fair rules of entitlement, e.g., by their own individual efforts, actions or abilities. Market-justice emphasizes individual responsibility, minimal collective action and freedom from collective obligations except to respect other person's fundamental rights.

While we have as a society compromised pure market-justice in many ways to protect the public's health, we are far from recognizing the principle that death and disability are collective problems and that all persons are entitled to health protection. Society does not recognize a general obligation to protect the individual against disease and injury. While society does prohibit individuals from causing direct harm to others, and has in many instances regulated clear public health hazards, the norm of market-justice is still dominant and the primary duty to avert disease and injury still rests with the individual. The individual is ultimately alone in his or her struggle against death.

Barriers to Protection

This individual isolation creates a powerful barrier to the goal of protecting all human life by magnifying the power of death, granting to death an almost supernatural reality. Death has throughout history presented a basic problem to humankind, but even in an advanced society with enormous biomedical technology, the individualism of market-justice tends to retain and exaggerate pessimistic and fatalistic attitudes toward death and injury. This fatalism leads to a sense of powerlessness, to the acceptance of risk as an essential element of life, to resignation in the face of calamity, and to a weakening of collective impulses to confront the problems of premature death and disability.

Perhaps the most direct way in which market-justice undermines our resolve to preserve and protect human life lies in the primary freedom this ethic extends to all individuals and groups to act with minimal obligations to protect the common good. Despite the fact that this rule of self-interest predictably fails to protect adequately the safety of our workplaces, our modes of transportation, the physical environment, the commodities we consume, or the equitable and effective distribution of medical care, these failures have resulted so far in only half-hearted attempts at regulation and control. This response is explained in large part by the powerful sway market-justice holds over our imagination, granting fundamental freedom to all individuals to be left alone—even if the "individuals" in question are giant producer groups with enormous capacities to create great public harm through sheer inadvertence. Efforts for truly effective controls over these perils must constantly struggle against a prevailing ethical paradigm that defines as threats to fundamental freedoms attempts to assure that all groups—even powerful producer groups —accept their fair share of the burdens of prevention.

Market-justice is also the source of another major barrier to public health measures to minimize death and disability—the category of voluntary behavior. Market-justice forces a basic distinction between the harm caused by a factory polluting the atmosphere and the harm caused by the cigarette or alcohol industries, because in the latter case those that are harmed are perceived as engaged in "voluntary" behavior. It is the radical individualism inherent in the market model that encourages attention to the individual's behavior and inattention to the social preconditions of that behavior. In the case of smoking, these preconditions include a powerful cigarette industry and accompanying social and cultural forces encouraging the practice of smoking. These social forces include norms sanctioning smoking as well as all forms of media, advertising, literature, movies, folklore, etc. Since the smoker is free in some ultimate sense to not smoke, the norms of market-justice force the conclusion that the individual voluntarily "chooses" to smoke; and we are prevented from taking strong collective action against the powerful structures encouraging this so-called voluntary behavior. . . .

The prestige of medical care encouraged by market-justice prevents large-scale research to determine whether, in fact, our medical care technology actually brings about the result desired—a significant reduction in the damage and losses suffered from disease and injury. The model conceals questions about our pervasive use of drugs, our intense specialization, and our seemingly boundless commitment to biomedical technology. Instead, the market model of justice encourages us to see problems as due primarily to the failure of individual doctors and the quality of their care, rather than to recognize the possibility of failure from the structure of medical care itself. Consequently, we seek to remedy problems by trying to change individual doctors through appeals to their ethical sensibilities, or by reshaping their education, or by creating new financial incentives. . . .

Public Health Measures

I have saved for last an important class of health policies—public health measures to protect the environment, the workplace, or the commodities we purchase and consume.

Are these not signs that the American society is willing to accept collective action in the face of clear public health hazards?

I do not wish to minimize the importance of these advances to protect the public in many domains. But these separate reforms, taken alone, should be cautiously received. This is because each reform effort is perceived as an isolated exception to the norm of market-justice; the norm itself still stands. Consequently, the predictable career of such measures is to see enthusiasm for enforcement peak and wane. These public health measures are clear signs of hope. But as long as these actions are seen as merely minor exceptions to the rule of individual responsibility, the goals of public health will remain beyond our reach. What is required is for the public to see that protecting the public's health takes us beyond the norms of market-justice categorically, and necessitates a completely new health ethic.

I return to my original point: Market-Justice is the primary roadblock to dramatic reductions in preventable injury and death. More than this, market-justice is a pervasive ideology protecting the most powerful or the most numerous from the burdens of collective action. If this be true, the central goal of public health should be ethical in nature: The challenging of market-justice as fatally deficient in protecting the health of the public. Further, public health should advocate a "counter-ethic" for protecting the public's health, one articulated in a different tradition of justice and one designed to give the highest priority to minimizing death and disability and to the protection of all human life against the hazards of this world. . . .

Ideally . . . the public health ethic is not simply an alternative to the market ethic for health—it is a fundamental critique of that ethic as it unjustly protects powerful interests from the burdens of prevention and as that ethic serves to legitimate a mindless and extravagant faith in the efficacy of medical care. In other words, the public health ethic is a *counter-ethic* to market-justice and the ethics of individualism as these are applied to the health problems of the public.

This view of public health is admittedly not widely accepted. Indeed, in recent times the mission of public health has been viewed by many as limited to that minority of health problems that cannot be solved by the market provision of medical care services and that necessitate organized community action. It is interesting to speculate why many in the public health profession have come to accept this narrow view of public health—a view that is obviously influenced and shaped by the market model as it attempts to limit the burdens placed on powerful groups.

Nonetheless, the broader view of public health set out here is logically and ethically justified if one accepts the vision of public health as being the protection of all human life. The central task of public health, then, is to complete its unfinished revolution: The elaboration of a health ethic adequate to protect and preserve all human life. This new ethic has several key implications which are referred to here as "principles": 1) Controlling the hazards of this world, 2) to prevent death and disability, 3) through organized collective action, 4) shared equally by all except where unequal burdens result in increased protection of everyone's health and especially potential victims of death and disability.

These ethical principles are not new to public health. To the contrary, making the ethical foundations of public health visible only serves to highlight the social justice influences as work behind pre-existing principles.

Controlling the Hazards

A key principle of the public health ethic is the focus on the identification and control of the hazards of this world rather than a focus on the behavioral defects of those individuals damaged by these hazards. . . .

Public health should—at least ideally—be suspicious of behavioral paradigms for viewing public health problems since they tend to "blame the victim" and unfairly protect majorities and powerful interests from the burdens of prevention. It is clear that behavioral models of public health problems are rooted in the tradition of market-justice, where the emphasis is upon individual ability and capacity, and individual success and failure. . . .

Prevention

Like the other principles of public health, prevention is a logical consequence of the ethical goal of minimizing the numbers of persons suffering death and disability. The only known way to minimize these adverse events is to prevent the occurrence of damaging exchanges or exposures in the first place, or to seek to minimize damage when exposures cannot be controlled.

Prevention, then, is that set of priority rules for restructuring existing market rules in order to maximally protect the public. These rules seek to create policies and obligations to replace the norm of market-justice, where the latter permits specific conditions, commodities, services, products, activities or practices to pose a direct threat or hazard to the health and safety of members of the public, or where the market norm fails to allocate effectively and equitably those services (such as medical care) that are necessary to attend to disease at hand.

Thus, the familiar public health options:

1. Creating rules to minimize exposure of the public to hazards (kinetic, chemical, ionizing, biological, etc.) so as to reduce the rates of hazardous exchanges.
2. Creating rules to strengthen the public against damage in the event damaging exchanges occur anyway, where such techniques (fluoridation, seat-belts, immunization) are feasible.
3. Creating rules to organize treatment resources in the community so as to minimize damage that does occur since we can rarely prevent all damage.

Collective Action

Another principle of the public health ethic is that the control of hazards cannot be achieved through voluntary mechanisms but must be undertaken by governmental or non-governmental agencies through planned, organized and collective action that is obligatory or non-voluntary in nature. This is for two reasons.

The first is because market or voluntary action is typically inadequate for providing what are called public goods. Public goods are those public policies (national defense, police and fire protection, or the protection of all persons against preventable death and disability) that are universal in their impacts and effects, affecting everyone equally. These kinds of goods cannot easily be withheld from those individuals in the community who choose not to support these services (this is typically called the "free rider" problem). Also, individual holdouts might plausibly reason that their small contribution might not prevent the public good from being offered.

The second reason why self-regarding individuals might refuse to voluntarily pay the costs of such public goods as public health policies is because these policies frequently require burdens that self-interest or self-protection might see as too stringent. For example, the minimization of rates of alcoholism in a community clearly seems to require norms or controls over the substance of alcohol that limit the use of this substance to levels that are far below what would be safe for individual drinkers.

With these temptations for individual noncompliance, justice demands assurance that all persons share equally the costs of collective action through obligatory and sanctioned social and public policy.

Fair-Sharing of the Burdens

A final principle of the public health ethic is that all persons are equally responsible for sharing the burdens—as well as the benefits—of protection against death and disability, except where unequal burdens result in greater protection for every person and especially potential victims of death and disability. In practice this means that policies to control the hazards of a given substance, service or commodity fall unequally (but still fairly) on those involved in the production, provision or consumption of the service, commodity or substance. The clear implication of this principle is that the automotive industry, the tobacco industry, the coal industry and the medical care industry—to mention only a few key groups—have an unequal responsibility to bear the costs of reducing death and disability since their actions have far greater impact than those of individual citizens.

DOING JUSTICE: BUILDING A NEW PUBLIC HEALTH

I have attempted to show the broad implications of a public health commitment to protect and preserve human life, setting out tentatively the logical consequences of that commitment in the form of some general principles. We need however, to go beyond these broad principles and ask more specifically: What implications does this model have for doing public health and the public health profession?

The central implication of the view set out here is that doing public health should not be narrowly conceived as an instrumental or technical activity. Public health should be a way of doing justice, a way of asserting the value and priority of all human life. The primary aim of all public health activity should be the elaboration and adoption of a new ethical model or paradigm for protecting the public's health. This new ethical paradigm will necessitate a heightened consciousness of the manifold forces threatening human life, and will require thinking about and reacting to the problems of disability and premature death as primarily collective problems of the entire society.

These new definitions would reveal the collective and structural aspects of what are termed voluntary risks, challenging attempts to narrowly and persuasively limit public attention to the behavior of the smoker or the drinker, and exposing pervasive myths that "blame the victim." These collective definitions and descriptions would focus attention on the industry behind these activities, asking whether powerful producer groups and supporting cultural and social norms are not primary factors encouraging individuals to accept unreasonable risks to life and limb, and whether these groups or norms constitute aggressive collective structures threatening human life.

A case in point: Under the present definition of the situation, alcoholism is mostly defined in individual terms, mainly in terms of the attributes of those persons who are "unable" to control their drinking. But I have shown elsewhere that this argument is both conceptually and empirically erroneous. Alcohol problems are collective problems that require more adequate controls over this important hazard.

This is not to say that there are no important issues of liberty and freedom in these areas. It is rather to say that viewing the use of, for example, alcohol or cigarettes by millions of American adults as "voluntary" behavior, and somehow fundamentally different from other public health hazards, impoverishes the public health approach, tending . . . to divorce the behavior of the individual from its social base.

In building these collective redefinitions of health problems, however, public health must take care to do more than merely shed light on specific public health problems. The central problems remain the injustice of a market ethic that unfairly protects majorities and powerful interests from their fair share of the burdens of prevention, and of convincing the public that the task of protecting the public's health lies categorically beyond the norms of market-justice. This means that the function of each different redefinition of a specific problem must be to raise the common and recurrent issue of justice by exposing the aggressive and powerful structures implicated in all instances of preventable death and disability, and further to point to the necessity for collective measures to confront and resist these structures.

I also believe that the realism inherent in the public health ethic dictates that the foundation of all public health policy should be primarily (but not exclusively) national in locus. I simply disagree with the current tendency, rooted in misguided pluralism and market metaphors, to build from the bottom up. This current drift will, in my opinion, simply provide the medical care industry and its acolytes (to cite only one powerful group) with the tools necessary to further elaborate and extend its hegemony. Confronting organizations, interests, ideologies and alliances that are national and even international in scope with such limited resources seems hopelessly sentimental. We must always remember that the forces opposed to full protection of the public's health are fundamental and powerful, deeply rooted in our national character. We are unlikely to successfully oppose these forces with appeals or strategies more appropriate for an earlier and more provincial time.

Finally, the public health movement must cease being defensive about the wisdom or the necessity of collective action. One of the most interesting aspects of market-justice—and particularly its ideological thrusts —is that it makes collective or governmental activity seem unwise if not dangerous. Such rhetoric predictably ignores the influence of private power over the health and safety of every individual. Public health need not be oblivious to the very real concerns about a proliferating bureaucracy in the emergent welfare state. In point of fact, however, the preventive thrust of public health transcends the notion of the welfare or service state and its most recent variant, the human services society. Much as the ideals of service and welfare are improvements over the simply working of market-justice, the service society frequently functions to spread the costs of public problems among the entire public while permitting the interests, industries, or professions who might remedy or prevent many of these problems to operate with expanding power and autonomy.

CONCLUSION

The central thesis of this article is that public health is ultimately and essentially an ethical enterprise committed to the notion that all persons are entitled to protection against the hazards of this world and to the minimization of death and disability in society. I have tried to make the implications of this ethical vision manifest, especially as the public health ethic challenges and confronts the norms of market-justice.

I do not see these goals of public health as hopelessly unrealistic nor destructive of fundamental liberties. Public health may be an "alien ethic in a strange land." Yet, if anything, the public health ethic is more faithful to the traditions of Judeao-Christian ethics than is market-justice.

The image of public health that I have drawn here does raise legitimate questions about what it is to be a professional, and legitimate questions about reasonable limits to restrictions on human liberty. These questions must be addressed more thoroughly than I have done here. Nonetheless, we must never pass over the chaos of preventable disease and disability in our society by simply celebrating the benefits of our prosperity and abundance, or our technological advances. What are these benefits worth if they have been purchased at the price of human lives?

LOREN E. LOMASKY

Medical Progress and National Health Care

LOREN E. LOMASKY is a professor of philosophy at the Bowling Green State University. His interests are in the fields of ethics and social philosophy and he has done research in natural-rights theory and in the ethical basis of health-care allocation.

An individual's access to medical care should not be determined exclusively by his ability to pay the going price. From this starting point, alternatives beckon. One is the traditional system of health-care delivery within which eleemosynary [nonprofit] and religious institutions are prominent in providing medical services to those unable to pay. Before the emergence of modern medicine the poor could not expect treatment equivalent to that received by the rich, but this was a general disability of poverty, not specifically a problem of medical access. Indeed, in an era when health care had little positive correlation with health outcomes and hospitals were chiefly places where one went to die, inequities in the provision of medical services were among the least of the burdens borne by the poor.

MEDICAL PROGRESS AND THE "RIGHT" TO HEALTH CARE

The ability of medicine to produce favorable results has increased exponentially in this century. At the same time, for understandable reasons, dissatisfaction with the traditional model has also increased. It is criticized as being too haphazard and arbitrary. More fundamentally, it is argued that medical care is a good to which individuals have a right, and that it ought to be distributed impartially in line with the criterion: to each according to his need. Medical care is not simply one consumer good among others; because it bears so directly on life itself as well as the ability to lead a good life, medical care cannot be left to the vagaries of the market.

But this argument is met with a counterargument that also emphasizes the role of rights. Medical services are, after all, not endowments provided cost-free by a bountiful nature. Rather, they are made available in finite quantities by individuals who must expend effort to produce them. The state can enforce equity in the delivery of these services only by coercing service providers, taxpayers and would-be recipients. State-controlled health care is thus founded on widespread rights violations.

When right contends with right, the heroic seek victory, the wary hunt for accommodation. It is wariness that will be pursued here.

A RIGHT TO WHAT?

It should be obvious that no claim of the form, "persons have a right to X" can be addressed without determining what kind of entity X is. Unless one is clear about what type of good health care is, resulting appraisals of its value and proper apportionment are hobbled. It will be suggested below that arguments for the provision of national health care pay insufficient attention to the changed and changing nature of health care. . . .

The first large-scale campaign for universal health insurance in the United States dates back to World War I. At that time Americans were far less wealthy than they are now. Paradoxically, however, they were better equipped to provide genuinely full and equal access to health services. Medicine's power to intervene effectively in crises was then extremely limited. Patients recovered in short order or died, in either case removing themselves from the need for ongoing attention. Chronic diseases, especially those associated with aging, were predominantly dealt with outside of medical contexts. In consequence, little extra benefit could be accorded the richest patients beyond what was available to those of more modest means.

In the last quarter of the twentieth century, however, there exist numerous high technology procedures that can be provided to only a fraction of those who could benefit from them. Computerized axial tomography, organ transplants, and coronary arteriograms are but three conspicuous therapeutic measures whose use is limited by financial or biological factors. It is incumbent upon those who demand that medical care of the highest quality be universally provided as a matter of right to explain how this can be done. And if it cannot, which would they dispense with: equity or the lives that could be saved by selective use of expensive technology? (I shall return later to this dilemma.)

The preceding remarks suggest that there is a wide gulf between medical care being an important human *interest* or *need* and its being a *right*. Interests admit of a wide range of degree and can be freely traded off, one for another. Needs are interests that possess a high degree of urgency, but carry no explicit entitlement to the goods or services of other people. Rights, though, are demands that others *must* comply with; where compliance is impossible or unwarranted, no right exists.

THE WELFARE CASE FOR A NATIONAL HEALTH PROGRAM

Even if health care in all its dimensions cannot, strictly speaking, be made out to be a human right, proponents of a national health program can argue that it is a good that ought to be provided to all irrespective of the ability to pay. Economic impoverishment would no longer follow in the wake of major illness. Government would be able to address directly the problem of ever rising costs instead of trying to influence at arm's length the fragmented health care industry. Finally, a more rational allocation of scarce medical resources to those who are most in need of them would be achieved. The de facto rationing of services by the market would be replaced by explicit consideration of how most equitably to optimize benefits for a given level of expenditure.

Major medical treatments *are* enormously expensive; for many persons the expense occasioned by an illness is its most persistent burden. We are all roughly equal in our vulnerability to debilitating disease or accident. Therefore, everyone would receive benefit from a national health plan that removed the threat of impoverishment as a consequence of medical disability. But this end can be achieved equally well by less sweeping measures. The risk of large economic loss can easily be guarded against by insurance. Its characteristic function is to protect against infrequent, unpredictable events which, when aggregated over a large population, are statistically regular.

Medical insurance is readily available in a variety of forms from private insurance companies. Like fire, automobile, and life insurance, it offers a means for persons to pool economic risks that are too great to hazard on an individual basis. Health maintenance organizations (HMOs) represent another and growing means by which prepayment allows individuals to spread risks. (In addition, HMOs offer service providers added inducement to economize on hospital stays and questionable surgical intervention, thus moderating overall medical expenditures.) The special problems of the poor can be met by cash grants or by health-care vouchers exchangeable for prepaid services. Given the availability of these sharply focused means for dealing with unpredictable expense, the threat of major economic loss cannot provide a sound justification for a national health program.

Ever-rising total health care expenditure creates a different dilemma, one that is also far more unyielding. As long as the demand for medical services (especially those embracing high technology) keeps growing, continuous cost increases largely represent an efficient response to consumers' preferences. Of course, these preferences can be questioned. Critics of prevailing practices have frequently argued that a more rational allocation of resources would redirect funds away from costly acute intervention procedures to preventive medicine and health education. However, even if this shift in emphasis could be carried out, benefits might prove to be less than anticipated. Annual physical checkups have long been advocated as worthwhile prophylaxis. Although they clearly impose substantial burdens on health care delivery systems, there is little evidence demonstrating significant health gains. . . .

Education to alter unhealthy lifestyles would undoubtedly have a momentous positive impact—if we know how to provide it. Wide dissemination of the relevant information may accomplish little: there is probably not a smoker in the country unaware of cigarettes' deleterious effects or a motorcyclist uninformed about the dangers of riding helmetless. In a free society there are limits to how much good one can do for another who is not very interested.

Governmental control typically features politically motivated decisions and cozy relationships between an industry and its regulators that work against economic efficiency. In addition, there are good reasons to believe that a national health program would be even *more susceptible* to escalating costs than most federal ventures. First, to be workable it would need the support of health professionals. It is therefore unlikely that they will be pressured to accept lower fees in order to realize monetary savings. Witness the boon to physicians' incomes provided by Medicare. Second, few citizens clamor for the purchase of another battleship, and even highly subsidized train fares move few people out of automobiles and airplanes. But health care is a commodity that most people desire. To lower or eliminate out-of-pocket expenses for it will predictably increase demand and thus further burden the public purse. Costs may be shared more evenly, but they will not be small.

The only way a nationalized program can realistically hope to keep costs in line is to enforce strict schedules of permissible treatments for all illnesses. These would be established on the basis of empirical studies detailing cost-effectiveness—assuming that political pressures to act otherwise are avoided. Therapeutic measures failing to come up to the stipulated benefit-per-dollar level would simply be disallowed. In effect, the goal of moderating overall costs would be subsumed under that of equitable rationing. So, if the case for a national health program can be made at all, it is on the grounds of enforcing the equal provision of health services based solely on need.

EQUALITY AND HEALTH CARE

The case for equality in the delivery of health-care services may be presented as simply one specification of the general brief for economic equality. But then it is subject to all the standard criticisms that beset rigid egalitarianism. If equality of condition is to be enforced, the liberty to pursue projects that generate differential rewards must be restricted. Substitutes must be found for the motivating force provided by the desire to better one's estate and the fear of seeing it diminished. The intuition that some merit more than others in return for greater effort or services rendered must be set aside. In short, the single-minded pursuit of equality is exceedingly costly in terms of other values surrendered, other goods forgone.

An alternative defense focuses on the special nature of health. The value of experiencing grand opera, vintage Chablis, a Yankee-Red Sox doubleheader or a trek up a mountain will vary greatly from individual to individual. Differences in talents and preferences will render ludicrous any program intent on providing these goods in equal measure to the entire populace. It is clearly preferable to allow individuals to pursue them as they will. But health is different. Whatever else one wants, good health is not only wanted but needed. Failure in securing it jeopardizes all other attainments. Moreover, its absence is rarely an indication of culpability; it is bad luck. Coordinated activity of men in civil society cannot abolish luck but it can ameliorate the stark randomness of its effects. The case for treating health care as a public good, subsidized by the common treasure, is that to do so is the most effective way we have of counteracting the vagaries of nature and providing each person with the preconditions for living a satisfying life. . . .

Being the sole possessors of a right to exercise coercion, governments are obliged to undertake the functions of protection, apprehension, and punishment that citizens are prohibited from carrying out on an individual basis. There exists no similar necessity that states monopolize the provision of health services. Health may indeed be a primary human good, but whether it is distributed centrally or by independent contractors is irrelevant to the continued existence of a political order. That is not to deny that states have obligations to their citizenry respecting health care delivery. A state acts unjustly if it forbids crucial health services to some or all persons or if it promotes economic inequalities that deprive disadvantaged social classes of adequate medical care. It should be noted though that unjust health policies may appear either in states with comprehensive national health care or those without it. In either, services may be discriminatorily distributed, subverted for political ends, irrationally regulated, or irresponsive to consumer demand. The desirability of national health care cannot be deduced from a pure philosophical theory of justice; rather, its desirability hinges on whether, in the actual world, it promises to promote a fair and efficient allocation of resources. . . .

COLLECTIVE VS. PRIVATE CHOICE: SOME EXAMPLES

A foretaste of the difficulties that would regularly confront a nationalized health program is provided by the debate over Medicaid funded abortion. Each year the nation is treated to a ritualized congressional confrontation that changes no minds, produces no consensus, yet paralyzes essential legislative operations throughout its duration. Few can believe that this public fanning of already polarized attitudes is worthwhile; yet there seems to be no way to avoid it so long as the provision of specific medical services to the poor remains an item for legislative decision. The right of women to procure abortions may have been conclusively established by judicial action, but a democracy must also recognize the right of individual citizens to participate in processes determining how their tax monies will be spent. Either the public treasure will release funds to pay for abortion or it will not; room for compromise is narrowly constricted.

Entirely removing abortion related issues from the public agenda may be neither feasible nor desirable. But this especially futile contest is the direct product of choosing to meet the health needs of the poor through a centrally funded and regulated program. If Medicaid and related welfare measures were replaced by a negative income tax or some other device guaranteeing all persons a minimally adequate income, recipients would be free to purchase those goods and services of greatest personal urgency. Poor persons, if they so chose, could avail themselves of abortions on the same basis as other members of the population. A less sweeping alteration of current welfare programs would be to provide health care vouchers. In either case, we would be spared a situation in which others decide for the poor what specific services they can or cannot have. Perhaps these proposed alternatives are defective on other grounds, but they do point up the advantages of leaving medical questions that touch on basic values up to individual discretion.

By means of amniocentesis, dozens of hereditary fetal traits can presently be detected. They range from its sex to the presence of debilitating diseases such as Tay-Sachs or mongolism. Occasionally the procedure is useful for diagnosing a condition that can be treated in utero, but it is also employed to procure information on which the decision whether or not to abort will be based. Will a national health program routinely provide amniocentesis when abortion is intended if results are negative? Or will it attempt somehow to keep to a middle course, allowing procedures leading to the abortion of severely incapacitated fetuses but not, say, those of the parentally disfavored sex? Alternatively, a cost-conscious program could require as a condition of coverage that women at risk undergo amniocentesis and abortion when a live birth will entail huge medical costs. These hypothetical policies are not of equal likelihood, but any one of them would engender pitched battles whose outcome would certainly leave large sections of the population dissatisfied. Pollyannas may expect the passage of time to ease these problems. Just the reverse will be the case: as techniques of genetic screening and engineering become more sophisticated, moral quandaries will ineluctably multiply. Sometimes polarization is the inescapable consequence of forging a national policy, but in this case divisiveness can be minimized by leaving decisions in the hands of private citizens.

The other end of human existence has also been profoundly affected by advances in medical capabilities. The hospital has replaced the home as the usual place to die, and it is increasingly the case that the exact time of death is a matter for choice. Biological function can be preserved in so attenuated a state that physicians have been forced to move toward a redefinition of "death" in order to avoid the ghoulish indefinite preservation of living corpses. But most ethical dilemmas surrounding death and dying are untouched by semantic legerdemain. Unless one supposes that each advance in the power to sustain life creates a corresponding imperative for its universal employment—and also creates the funds to pay for them—there is no simple answer to the question of when to extend life and when to terminate it. Here I shall sidestep substantive matters to raise instead a procedural issue: to what extent is it desirable that government intrude upon deliberations at the edge of life?

It is unrealistic to deny that the state does have some legitimate interests. Inevitably it must confront practices that raise the specter of homicide. The law must also establish standards concerning informed consent and the contractual obligations obtaining between patient and physician. But beyond staking out legal terrain within which concerned parties can take their bearings, government may move in either of two opposed directions: it can issue detailed regulations pertaining to the application of lifesaving technology or, within broad guidelines, it can return decision-making prerogatives to individual patients, their families and physicians. For two major reasons, the latter course is to be preferred whenever possible.

First, individual discretion promotes autonomy. Persons differ in their judgments concerning the conditions under which life is no longer worth living. They will also vary in their willingness to forgo other possible satisfactions for the sake of securing incremental health gains. A liberal society is one that values the ability of individuals to direct their own lives. One significant way in which this value can be pursued is to allow people to determine for themselves what course their medical treatments will take. A recent expression of this policy is the granting of legal status to "living wills," documents that spell out conditions under which the signator desires that heroic medical procedures be terminated. The gradual development of hospice programs also provides enhanced opportunities for terminally ill patients to take charge of their own destinies. Instead of being shunted aside as medicine's embarrassing failure, the hospice patient is encouraged to accept the fact of his upcoming death and to influence the conditions under which he will depart from life. As technology continually enlarges the scope for intervention into the process of dying, further methods will be required to ensure that the party most directly affected is able to play a significant role.

Second, an active governmental role in mandating standards for care poses the same danger of political disruption that has already been experienced in the case of publicly funded abortion. All citizens have a fundamental stake in how they and their loved ones will die. Decisions in this sphere do not come easily under the best of circumstances. But burdens will be exacerbated if matters of personal decision are transformed into public policy questions. Regulation is, in essence, inflexible. If national standards are to be formulated that adjudicate among basic and deeply felt values, diverse groups will want to see their own attitudes enshrined in law. A zero-sum game will develop in which one side's gain is another's loss, and so each will attempt to use the political machinery for its own ends.

If the state assumes full responsibility for the provision of health services, it will be unable to avoid dictating standards for the utilization of life sustaining services. Extraordinary means for staving off death are inordinately costly both in monetary terms and in demands placed upon highly trained personnel. If the ability of patients to pay is entirely removed as a factor influencing their use, there will be an increased call for their employment. To remain solvent, a national health program will have to contain some formula for determining when the cost of procuring and employing expensive technology are justified by realizable benefits. If such a formula is not to be subverted from within, little room for exceptions can be permitted. Whatever structure emerges is sure to leave many health professionals and consumers dissatisfied. They will be informed that their own personal discretion must give way to considerations of the public good—as defined by a distant bureaucracy. . . .

Deciding when treatment shall cease involves ethical questions of considerable magnitude. A yet more vexing range of dilemmas surround triage: the selection of some for treatment when not all can be saved. If resources are indispensable to a group of persons at peril but too limited to accommodate all, to save one life is to sacrifice another. Our moral principles are severely strained by circumstances that require the balancing of one innocent life against another. Such choices, however, promise to intrude upon us increasingly.

Two classic examples of triage are the dangerously overloaded lifeboat and the harried medic patching up the wounded on a battlefield. Whatever is done, some salvageable lives will be forfeited. The dreadfulness of these choices, though, is somewhat softened by the urgency of a crisis: action must be immediate and there is little luxury for reflective deliberation. If called upon to justify his actions, an agent could plead that he was reacting instinctively to the needs of the moment.

Contemporary medical technology is responsible for triage situations of a rather different character. A mechanism is devised that is effective against some previously untreatable condition. Unfortunately, only a small percentage of those afflicted can receive treatment. Who shall be allowed to live? Here decision-makers are dealing with a series of events predictable well in advance. Not enmeshed in a precipitously developing crisis, they are privileged to assume the role of detached administrator. There is, however, a price to be paid for this relative ease: whatever standards are developed and employed are subject to close scrutiny. Those disfavored in the selection process are perfectly entitled to ask why. Persuasive answers will not be easily forthcoming. . . .

Should triage decisions be left to numerous private groups acting independently, or should responsibility be assumed by a national health care delivery board? The latter would, I believe, be a profoundly unsatisfactory state of affairs. The least of its drawbacks is that treatment decisions would be thrust into the arena of public choice where diverse groups would lobby intensively for special consideration. It requires little imagination to foresee the young, those with dependents, military veterans, persons holding responsible positions, and others all claiming to merit a preferred status. A policy of random selection might appease these contending forces, but it also might appear to each of them as unjustly slighting legitimate merit. The trouble arises precisely because no process of choice presents itself as clearly superior; whichever method is imposed will be open to objections rendering it unstable.

Consider a further complication: wealthy individuals may not be content to leave their survival to the vagaries of a national health care system. Suppose they choose to go outside of the system to procure lifesaving technology; how will authorities respond? If the rich are allowed carte blanche, the egalitarianism of national health care is compromised in a context where the stakes are no less than life and death. If outside access is forbidden by law, the situation is even more anomalous. Persons who are entitled to spend their money for utterly frivolous purposes will be precluded from using it to remain alive. No compensating gain for the poor would be realized—unless a surrender to envy is counted as a gain. . . .

Triage is never unproblematic, but on what basis could a creature of the state adopt *any* principle of selection? Whoever is excluded can justifiably complain that he is thereby being disadvantaged by the very institution whose special duty is to extend equal protection to all persons. The essential point is not that government will do a poorer job of allocating lifesaving technology than would non-governmental units—although, given the nature of the political pressures to which it is subject, it very well might—but that *this is a singularly inappropriate area for any governmental choice*, no matter how conscientiously it is made. Neutrality among all citizens is a political ideal that is easily subverted and, once breached, difficult to restore. I suggest that this ideal is well worth preserving, and that to establish a precedent of forcing the state to determine that some named individuals shall live and others die is to do that ideal possibly irreparable damage. When such decisions have to be made, it is far better that they be carried out by non-public boards not constrained by obligations of equal protection to an entire citizenry. Flexibility is enhanced, and the implications of unsavory choices are localized.

One objection to this argument is that government can and should avoid the necessity of triage by providing resources sufficient to accommodate all patients. Indeed, precisely this intent motivated the passage of the 1972 legislation providing dialysis treatment to all end-stage renal disease sufferers in need of it. Could not a well-funded national health-care program act similarly in all other cases?

The answer is no. There are some shortages that not even unlimited finances can eliminate. The number of persons who can be benefited by organ transplants already exceeds the available supply. As further advances in immunosuppression and surgical technique are realized, the disparity will grow. Transplantable hearts cannot be produced by governmental edict. Further, there is always a gap between the time the procedure is experimentally introduced and its widespread implementation.

In the real world, finances are not unlimited. Money used to counter one life-threatening syndrome is unavailable for others. For example, the huge infusion of Medicare funds for kidney disease sufferers could have been devoted to the comparably expensive treatment of hemophiliacs. That it was not may be due only to the greater muscle of the kidney disease lobby. Even if sufficient funds to eliminate all triage situations could be raised, it does not follow that to do so is advisable. A commitment to treat every salvageable patient will shortchange other legitimate health goals as well as competing goods in other spheres. An ironic result of nationalized health care might be that to avoid the undoubted evil of governmental triage, grotesque misallocations of resources will ensue. Is it really desirable that education, housing and general economic advancement be penalized so that a 110-year old patient can receive his third kidney transplant and second artificial heart?

NATIONAL HEALTH CARE AND NON-STANDARD OPTIONS

The terms with which a debate is pursued can become frozen while the underlying real dimensions continue to change. This has been the fate of the case for national health care. Its desirability cannot be assessed in a vacuum, as the nature of the commodity health care evolves so too do reasons for and against its provision by the state. The most revolutionary development in medical practice since national health care was initially broached is the increasing prominence of *non-standard options*. By "non-standard option" I mean a medical service possessing the following three features: (1) Each occasion on which it is delivered entails great expense; (2) It has little effect on mortality or morbidity configurations for the population as a whole; (3) Individuals who receive the service are substantially benefited or perceive themselves to be substantially benefited.

Proliferation of non-standard options bedevils egalitarianism in health care delivery. A system that undertook to fulfill all requests on the basis of demonstrated need at no charge to recipients would soon be bankrupt. If non-standard options were excluded from the system but could be secured privately, major inequalities in health-care delivery would thereby be reintroduced. Finally, if non-standard options that cannot be offered to all are forbidden to all, government is placed in the uncomfortable position of abridging the liberty of citizens to preserve health and life.

Health-care delivery has often been cited as an area in which the case for equality is especially convincing, even self-evident. In an important paper, Bernard Williams has maintained that, "leaving aside preventive medicine, the proper ground of distribution of medical care is ill health: this is a necessary truth." I have argued that it is not a necessary truth but rather a seductive falsehood based on an obsolete model of medical care. It does indeed seem intolerable that anyone should die or continue to suffer from disease when, for a relatively small expenditure, his plight can be alleviated. Even on coldly economic grounds, it is irrational not to invest a sum that will be returned many times over in a life of increased productivity. But non-standard options do not fit this model. Their opportunity costs are extremely high, they rarely provide restoration to full health, and the need for them continually outstrips the available supply.

SUGGESTIONS FOR A MEDICAL MARKETPLACE

I have been arguing that national health care is an idea whose time has come—and gone. That should not be interpreted as a brief for the status quo. Ongoing expansion of the medical role argues against imposing uniformity in the delivery of health services. It is not enough, however, to reject national health care; positive steps should be taken to enable consumers to choose for themselves the goods and services they most want. This requires a genuine marketplace: a sector in which alternative products are offered and where those who receive a good are the ones who pay for it. I conclude with five brief suggestions concerning how diversity and consumer sovereignty can be enhanced.

First, there are better and worse means by which society can respond to the health needs of the poor. Routing all medical care through a monolithic national health service has already been amply criticized. Somewhat preferable would be the provision of a suitably defined "minimum decent standard" of health care. One drawback of this proposal is that not all will agree on what counts as minimally decent. The acrimonious debate over Medicaid funded abortion is a case in point. Also, the poor will still be precluded from acting on their own preferences. Therefore, I suggest instead a cash grant or voucher program enabling the poor to purchase their own medical services on a prepaid basis. How generous this program should be is a crucial question that cannot be explored in this paper.

Second, influential health-care spokespersons should avoid making extravagant claims heralding the accomplishments of highpowered medicine. Such statements lead to unrealistic expectations on the part of consumers and consequent pressure upon the health care system to deliver more than it is capable of providing. Newly developed technology provides genuine health gains, but its effect on mortality and morbidity are inconsequential compared to the dramatic gains realized between the 1930s and 1950s. Predictions are hazardous, but we very probably have reached a point of drastically diminishing returns on the health care dollar. Pessimism concerning future health gains need not follow: health care is not the same as health. There are a great number of steps individuals can take to live longer and healthier lives: avoid smoking, eat breakfasts, get and stay married (especially significant for males), sleep at least seven hours each night, consume alcohol in moderation. These "life-style" patterns are free of cost, undeliverable by professionals, but wonderfully responsive to individual choice. Because what individuals can do for themselves far exceeds what can be done for them, we ought to begin to emphasize the former.

Third, there is need to expand the variety of health-insurance policies and other prepaid packages. Not everyone needs or desires the same level of coverage. I see no reason to suppose that consumers are generally unable to choose rationally how much of their resources to devote to health goods. Nor is there any evidence that welfare gains are realized if central planning boards are vested with the responsibility for such choices. Some persons are very sensitive to increased probabilities of an extended life span; they ought to have the opportunity to purchase expensive policies that include coverage for a wide range of non-standard options. Those who place a premium on present consumption should be free to devote only a minimal amount of income to health care coverage. Both will thus be able to maximize expected utility while assuming responsibility for their own choices. A not incidental benefit is that triage dilemmas will be minimized; or rather, *individuals will be making such decisions for themselves* through genuine market arrangements. The prospective demand for some item of expensive lifesaving technology will tend to create its own supply.

Fourth, consumers of medical services will never reclaim control of their health care programs until what Charles Fried characterizes as "a guild system as tight and self-protective as any we know" is broken. Physicians make virtually all medical decisions and are loath to relinquish any of this power either to public agencies or to consumers. Even the choice of a primary care physician is usually made blind because organized medicine has traditionally execrated advertising or any other means which would afford consumers the basis for making a cost-conscious selection. Physicians' domination of health-care delivery is made possible by a legal structure that grants them unparalleled powers to control entry into the profession, set fees, and regulate their own practice. The results are remarkably high incomes and an almost total immunity from normal market forces. Numerous steps could be undertaken to transform this cartel into competitive purveyors of service to an informed clientele: eliminating all bans on advertising, easing the formation of HMOs and other alternatives to fee-for-service medicine, eliminating or drastically abridging entry restricting requirements, allowing patients and pharmacists more say in the selection of prescription drugs, and enabling other health professionals to provide services that do not require a physician's expertise.

Fifth, what ought to be done to hold down the nation's spiraling medical bill? Nothing. To be more precise, external bureaucratic regulation is the wrong prescription for the ills of our health care delivery system. If, as I have suggested above, consumers are afforded the opportunity to make informed purchases in a genuine medical marketplace, they will be able to determine what percentage of their income is devoted to health care. Is 5% of GNP too little, 15% too much? I suggest that there is no a priori answer to these questions. Health care is one among many services persons can choose for themselves in whatever quantity they desire—if they are given the chance to do so.

JAMES RACHELS

Active and Passive Euthanasia

JAMES RACHELS is a professor of philosophy at the University of Alabama in Birmingham who has written extensively on ethical issues. This selection is taken from his influential book, *The End of Life*.

The distinction between active and passive euthanasia is thought to be crucial for medical ethics. The idea is that it is permissible, at least in some cases, to withhold treatment and allow a patient to die, but it is never permissible to take any direct action designed to kill the patient. This doctrine seems to be accepted by most doctors, and it is endorsed in a statement adopted by the House of Delegates of the American Medical Association on December 4, 1973:

> The intentional termination of the life of one human being by another—mercy killing—is contrary to that for which the medical profession stands and is contrary to the policy of the American Medical Association.
>
> The cessation of the employment of extraordinary means to prolong the life of the body when there is irrefutable evidence that biological death is imminent is the decision of the patient and/or his immediate family. The advice and judgment of the physician should be freely available to the patient and/or his immediate family.

However, a strong case can be made against this doctrine. In what follows I will set out some of the relevant arguments and urge doctors to reconsider their views on this matter.

To begin with a familiar type of situation, a patient who is dying of incurable cancer of the throat is in terrible pain, which can no longer be satisfactorily alleviated. He is certain to die within a few days, even if present treatment is continued, but he does not want to go on living for those days since the pain is unbearable. So he asks the doctor for an end to it, and his family joins in the request.

Suppose the doctor agrees to withhold treatment, as the conventional doctrine says he may. The justification for his doing so is that the patient is in terrible agony, and since he is going to die anyway, it would be wrong to prolong his suffering needlessly. But now notice this. If one simply withholds treatment, it may take the patient longer to die, and so he may suffer more than he would if more direct action were taken and a lethal injection given. This fact provides strong reason for thinking that, once the initial decision not to prolong his agony has been made, active euthanasia is actually preferable to passive euthanasia, rather than the reverse. To say otherwise is to endorse the option that leads to more suffering rather than less, and is contrary to the humanitarian impulse that prompts the decision not to prolong his life in the first place.

Part of my point is that the process of being "allowed to die" can be relatively slow and painful, whereas being given a lethal injection is relatively quick and painless. Let me give a different sort of example. In the United States about one in 600 babies is born with Down's syndrome. Most of these babies are otherwise healthy—that is, with only the usual pediatric care, they will proceed to an otherwise normal infancy. Some, however, are born with congenital defects such as intestinal obstructions that require operations if they are to live. Sometimes, the parents and the doctor will decide not to operate, and let the infant die. Anthony Shaw describes what happens then:

> When surgery is denied [the doctor] must try to keep the infant from suffering while natural forces sap the baby's life away. As a surgeon whose natural inclination is to use the scalpel to fight off death, standing by and watching a salvageable baby die is the most emotionally exhausting experience I know. It is easy at a conference, in a theoretical discussion to decide that such infants should be allowed to die. It is altogether different to stand by in the nursery and watch as dehydration and infection wither a tiny being over hours and days. This is a terrible ordeal for me and the hospital staff—much more so than for the parents who never set foot in the nursery.

I can understand why some people are opposed to all euthanasia, and insist that such infants must be allowed to live. I think I can also understand why other people favor destroying these babies quickly and painlessly. But why should anyone favor letting "dehydration and infection wither a tiny being over hours and days"? The doctrine that says that a baby may be allowed to dehydrate and wither, but may not be given an injection that would end its life without suffering, seems so patently cruel as to require no further refutation. The strong language is not intended to offend, but only to put the point in the clearest possible way.

My second argument is that the conventional doctrine leads to decisions concerning life and death made on irrelevant grounds.

Consider again the case of the infants with Down's syndrome who need operations for congenital defects unrelated to the syndrome to live. Sometimes, there is no operation, and the baby dies, but when there is no such defect, the baby lives on. Now, an operation such as that to remove an intestinal obstruction is not prohibitively difficult. The reason why such operations are not performed in these cases is, clearly, that the child has Down's syndrome and the parents and the doctor judge that because of that fact it is better for the child to die.

But notice that this situation is absurd, no matter what view one takes of the lives and potentials of such babies. If the life of such an infant is worth preserving what does it matter if it needs a simple operation? Or, if one thinks it better that such a baby should not live on, what difference does it make that it happens to have an unobstructed intestinal tract? In either case, the matter of life and death is being decided on irrelevant grounds. It is the Down's syndrome, and not the intestines, that is the issue. The matter should be decided, if at all, on the basis, and not be allowed to depend on that essentially irrelevant question of whether the intestinal tract is blocked.

What makes this situation possible, of course, is the idea that when there is an intestinal blockage, one can "let the baby die," but when there is no such defect there is nothing that can be done, for one must not "kill" it. The fact that this idea leads to such results as deciding life or death on irrelevant grounds is another good reason why the doctrine would be rejected.

One reason why so many people think that there is an important moral difference between active and passive euthanasia is that they think killing someone is morally worse than letting someone die. But is it? Is killing, in itself, worse than letting die? To investigate this issue, two cases may be considered that are exactly alike except that one involves killing whereas the other involves letting someone die. Then, it can be asked whether this difference makes any difference to the moral assessments. It is important that the cases be exactly alike, except for this one difference, since otherwise one cannot be confident that it is this difference and not some other that accounts for any variation in the assessments of the two cases. So, let us consider this pair of cases:

In the first, Smith stands to gain a large inheritance if anything should happen to his six-year-old cousin. One evening while the child is taking his bath, Smith sneaks into the bathroom and drowns the child, and then arranges things so that it will look like an accident.

In the second, Jones also stands to gain if anything should happen to his six-year-old cousin. Like Smith, Jones sneaks in planning to drown the child in his bath. However, just as he enters the bathroom Jones sees the child slip and hit his head, and fall face down in the water, Jones is delighted; he stands by, ready to push the child's head back under if it is necessary, but it is not necessary. With only a little thrashing about, the child drowns all by himself, "accidentally," as Jones watches and does nothing.

Now Smith killed the child, whereas Jones "merely" let the child die. That is the only difference between them. Did either man behave better, from a moral point of view? If the difference between killing and letting die were in itself a morally important matter, one should say that Jones's behavior was less reprehensible than Smith's. But does one really want to say that? I think not. In the first place, both men acted from the same motive, personal gain, and both had exactly the same end in view when they acted. It may be inferred from Smith's conduct that he is a bad man, although that judgment may be withdrawn or modified if certain further facts are learned about him— for example, that he is mentally deranged. But would not the very same thing be inferred about Jones from his conduct? And would not the same further considerations also be relevant to any modification of this judgment? Moreover, suppose Jones pleaded, in his own defense, "After all, I didn't do anything except just stand there and watch the child drown. I didn't kill him; I only let him die." Again, if letting die were in itself less bad than killing, this defense should have at least some weight. But it does not. Such a "defense" can only be regarded as a grotesque perversion of moral reasoning. Morally speaking, it is no defense at all.

Now, it may be pointed out, quite properly, that the cases of euthanasia with which doctors are concerned are not like this at all. They do not involve personal gain or the destruction of normal healthy children. Doctors are concerned only with cases in which the patient's life is of no further use to him, or in which the patient's life has become or will soon become a terrible burden. However, the point is the same in these cases: the bare difference between killing and letting die does not, in itself, make a moral difference. If a doctor lets a patient die, for humane reasons, he is in the same moral position as if he had given the patient a lethal injection for humane reasons. If his decision was wrong—if, for example, the patient's illness was in fact curable—the decision would be equally regrettable no matter which method was used to carry it out. And if the doctor's decision was the right one, the method used is not in itself important.

The AMA policy statement isolates the crucial issue very well; the crucial issue is "the intentional termination of the life of one human being by another." But after identifying this issue, and forbidding "mercy killing," the statement goes on to deny that the cessation of treatment is the intentional termination of a life. This is where the mistake comes in, for what is the cessation of treatment, in these circumstances, if it is not "the intentional termination of the life of one human being by another"? Of course it is exactly that, and if it were not, there would be no point to it.

Many people will find this judgment hard to accept. One reason, I think, is that it is very easy to conflate the question of whether killing is, in itself, worse than letting die, with the very different question of whether most actual cases of killing are more reprehensible than most actual cases of letting die. Most actual cases of killing are clearly terrible (think, for example, of all the murders reported in the newspapers), and one hears of such cases every day. On the other hand, one hardly ever hears of a case of letting die, except for the actions of doctors who are motivated by humanitarian reasons. So one learns to think of killing in a much worse light than of letting die. But this does not mean that there is something about killing that makes it in itself worse than letting die, for it is not the bare difference between killing and letting die that makes the difference in these cases. Rather, the other factors—the murderer's motive of personal gain, for example, contrasted with the doctor's humanitarian motivation—account for different reactions to the different cases.

I have argued that killing is not in itself any worse than letting die; if my contention is right, it follows that active euthanasia is not any worse than passive euthanasia. What arguments can be given on the other side? The most common, I believe, is the following:

> The important difference between active and passive euthanasia is that, in passive euthanasia, the doctor does not do anything to bring about the patient's death. The doctor does nothing, and the patient does of whatever ills already afflict him. In active euthanasia, however, the doctor does something to bring about the patient's death: he kills him. The doctor who gives the patient with cancer a lethal injection has himself caused his patient's death; whereas if he merely ceases treatment, the cancer is the cause of the death.

A number of points need to be made here. The first is that it is not exactly correct to say that in passive euthanasia the doctor does nothing, for he does do one thing that is very important: he lets the patient die. "Letting someone die" is certainly different, in some respects, from other types of action—mainly in that it is a kind of action that one may perform by way of not performing certain other actions. For example, one may let a patient die by way of not giving medication, just as one may insult someone by way of not shaking his hand. But for any purpose of moral assessment, it is a type of action nonetheless. The decision to let a patient die is subject to moral appraisal in the same way that a decision to kill him would be subject to moral appraisal: it may be assessed as wise or unwise, compassionate or sadistic, right or wrong. If a doctor deliberately let a patient die who was suffering from a routinely curable illness, the doctor would certainly be to blame if he had needlessly killed the patient. Charges against him would be appropriate. If so, it would be no defense at all for him to insist that he didn't "do anything." He would have done something very serious indeed, for he let his patient die.

Fixing the cause of death may be very important from a legal point of view, for it may determine whether criminal charges are brought against the doctor. But I do not think that this notion can be used to show a moral difference between active and passive euthanasia. The reason why it is considered bad to be the cause of someone's death is that death is regarded as a great evil —and so it is. However, if it has been decided that euthanasia—even passive euthanasia—is desirable in a given case, it has also been decided that in this instance death is no greater an evil than the patient's continued existence. And if this is true, the usual reason for not wanting to be the cause of someone's death simply does not apply.

Finally, doctors may think that all of this is only of academic interest—the sort of thing that philosophers may worry about but that has no practical bearing on their own work. After all, doctors must be concerned about the legal consequences of what they do, and active euthanasia is clearly forbidden by the law. But even so, doctors should also be concerned with the fact that the law is forcing upon them a moral doctrine that may be indefensible, and has a considerable effect on their practices. Of course, most doctors are not now in the position of being coerced in this matter, for they do not regard themselves as merely going along with what the law requires. Rather, in statements such as the AMA policy statement that I have quoted they are endorsing this doctrine as a central point of medical ethics. In that statement, active euthanasia is condemned no merely as illegal but as "contrary to that for which the medical profession stands," whereas passive euthanasia is approved. However, the preceding considerations suggest that there is really no moral difference between the two, considered in themselves (there may be important moral differences in some cases in their *consequences*, but, as I pointed out, these differences may make active euthanasia, and not passive euthanasia, the morally preferable option). So, whereas doctors may have to discriminate between active and passive euthanasia to satisfy the law, they should not do any more than that. In particular, they should not give the distinction any added authority and weight by writing it into official statements of medical ethics.

BONNIE STEINBOCK

The Intentional Termination of Life

BONNIE STEINBOCK teaches philosophy at the State University of New York at Albany. She is the author of *Killing and Letting Die* (1980).

According to James Rachels and Michael Tooley, a common mistake in medical ethics is the belief that there is a moral difference between active and passive euthanasia. This is a mistake, they argue, because the rationale underlying the distinction between active and passive euthanasia is the idea that there is a significant moral difference between intentionally killing and intentionally letting die. "This idea," Tooley says, "is admittedly very common. But I believe that it can be shown to reflect either confused thinking, or a moral point of view unrelated to the interests of individuals." Whether the belief that there is a significant moral difference (between intentionally killing and intentionally letting die) is mistaken is not my concern here. For it is far from clear that this distinction *is* the basis of the doctrine of the American Medical Association which Rachels attacks. And if the killing/letting die distinction is not the basis of the AMA doctrine, then arguments showing that the distinction has no moral force do not, in themselves, reveal in the doctrine's adherents either "confused thinking" or "a moral point of view unrelated to the interests of individuals". Indeed, as we examine the AMA doctrine, I think it will become clear that it appeals to and makes use of a number of overlapping distinctions, which may have moral significance in particular cases, such as the distinction between intending and foreseeing, or between ordinary and extraordinary care. Let us then turn to the statement, from the House of Delegates of the American Medical Association, which Rachels cites:

> The intentional termination of the life of one human being by another—mercy-killing—is contrary to that for which the medical profession stands and is contrary to the policy of the American Medical Association.
>   The cessation of the employment of extraordinary means to prolong the life of the body when there is irrefutable evidence that biological death is imminent is the decision of the patient and/or his immediate family. The advice and judgment of the physician should be freely available to the patient and/or his immediate family.

Rachels attacks this statement because he believes that it contains a moral distinction between active and passive euthanasia. . . .

I intend to show that the AMA statement does not imply support of the active/passive euthanasia distinction. In forbidding the intentional termination of life, the statement rejects both active and passive euthanasia. It does allow for ". . . the cessation of the employment of extraordinary means . . ." to prolong life. The mistake Rachels and Tooley make is in identifying the cessation of life-prolonging treatment with passive euthanasia or intentionally letting die. If it were right to equate the two, then the AMA statement would be self-contradictory, for it would begin by condemning, and end by allowing the intentional termination of life. But if the cessation of life-prolonging treatment is not always or necessarily passive euthanasia, then there is no confusion and no contradiction.

Why does Rachels think that the cessation of life-prolonging treatment is the intentional termination of life? He says:

> The AMA policy statement isolates the crucial issue very well; the crucial issue is "the intentional termination of the life of one human being by another". But after identifying this issue, and forbidding "mercy-killing", the statement goes on to deny that the cessation of treatment is the intentional termination of a life. This is where the mistake comes in, for what is the cessation of treatment, in these circumstances, if it is not "the intentional termination of the life of one human being of another"? Of course it is exactly that, and if it were not, there would be no point to it.

However, there *can* be a point (to the cessation of life-prolonging treatment) other than an endeavor to bering about the patient's death, and so the blanket identification of cessation of treatment with the intentional termination of a life is inaccurate. There are at least two situations in which the termination of life-prolonging treatment cannot be identified with the intentional termination of the life of one human being by another.

The first situation concerns the patient's right to refuse treatment. Both Tooley and Rachels give the example of a patient dying of an incurable disease, accompanied by unrelievable pain, who wants to end the treatment which cannot cure him but can only prolong his miserable existence. Why, they ask, may a doctor accede to the patient's request to stop treatment, but not provide a patient in a similar situation with a lethal dose? The answer lies in the patient's right to refuse treatment. In general, a competent adult has the right to refuse treatment, even where such treatment is necessary to prolong life. Indeed, the right to refuse treatment has been upheld even when the patient's reason for refusing treatment is generally agreed to be inadequate. This right can be overridden (if, for example, the patient has dependent children) but, in general, no one may legally compel you to undergo treatment to which you have not consented. "Historically, surgical intrusion has always been considered a technical battery upon the person and one to be excused or justified by consent of the patient or justified by necessity created by the circumstances of the moment. . . ."

At this point, it might be objected that if one has the right to refuse life-prolonging treatment, then consistency demands that one have the right to decide to end his life and to obtain help in doing so. The idea is that the right to refuse treatment somehow implies a right to voluntary euthanasia, and we need to see why someone might think this. The right to refuse treatment has been considered by legal writers as an example of the right to privacy or, better, the right to bodily self-determination. You have the right to decide what happens to your own body, and the right to refuse treatment in an instance of that more general right. But if you have the right to determine what happens to your body, then should you not have the right to choose to end your life, and even a right to get help in doing so?

However, it is important to see that the right to refuse treatment is not the same as, nor does it entail, a right to voluntary euthanasia, even if both can be derived from the right to bodily self-determination. The right to refuse treatment is not itself a "right to die"; that one may choose to exercise this right even at the risk of death or even *in order to die*, is irrelevant. The purpose of the right to refuse medical treatment is not to give persons a right to decide whether to live or die, but to protect them from the unwanted interferences of others. Perhaps we ought to interpret the right to bodily self-determination more broadly so as to include a right to die: but this would be a substantial extension of our present understanding of the right to bodily self-determination, and not a consequence of it. Should we recognize a right to voluntary euthanasia, we would have to agree that people have the right not merely to be left alone, but also the right to be killed. I leave to one side that substantive moral issue. My claim is simply that there can be a reason for terminating life-prolonging treatment other than "to bring about the patient's death".

The second case in which termination of treatment cannot be identified with intentional termination of life is where continued treatment has little chance of improving the patient's condition and brings greater discomfort than relief.

The question here is what treatment is appropriate to the particular case. A cancer specialist describes it in this way:

> My general rule is to administer therapy as long as a patient responds well and has the potential for a reasonably good quality of life. But when all feasible therapies have been administered and a patient shows signs of rapid deterioration, the continuation of therapy can cause more discomfort than the cancer. From that time I recommend surgery, radiotherapy, or chemotherapy only as a means of relieving pain. But if a patient's condition should once again stabilize after the withdrawal of active therapy and if it should appear that he could still gain some good time, I would immediately reinstitute active therapy. The decision to cease anticancer treatment is never irrevocable, and often the desire to live will push a patient to try for another remission, or even a few more days of life.

The decision here to cease anticancer treatment cannot be construed as a decision that the patient die, or as the intentional termination of life. It is a decision to provide the most appropriate treatment for that patient at that time. Rachels suggests that the point of the cessation of treatment is the intentional termination of life. But here the point of discontinuing treatment is not to bring about the patient's death but to avoid treatment that will cause more discomfort than the cancer and has little hope of benefiting the patient. Treatment that meets this description is often called "extraordinary". The concept is flexible, and what might be considered "extraordinary" in one situation might be ordinary in another. The use of a respirator to sustain a patient through a severe bout of respiratory disease would be considered ordinary; its use to sustain the life of a severely brain damaged person in an irreversible coma would be considered extraordinary.

Contrasted with extraordinary treatment is ordinary treatment, the care a doctor would normally be expected to provide. Failure to provide ordinary care constitutes neglect, and can even be construed as the intentional infliction of harm, where there is a legal obligation to provide care. The importance of the ordinary/extraordinary care distinction lies partly in its connection to the doctor's intention. The withholding of extraordinary care should be seen as a decision not to inflict painful treatment on a patient without reasonable hope of success. The withholding of ordinary care, by contrast, must be seen as neglect. Thus, one doctor says, "We have to draw a distinction between ordinary and extraordinary means. We never withdraw what's needed to make a baby comfortable, we would never withdraw the care a parent would provide. We never kill a baby. . . . But we may decide certain heroic intervention is not worthwhile."

We should keep in mind the ordinary/extraordinary care distinction when considering an example given by both Tooley and Rachels to show the irrationality of the active/passive distinction with regard to infanticide. The example is this: a child is born with Down's syndrome and also has an intestinal obstruction which requires corrective surgery. If the surgery is not performed, the infant will starve to death, since it cannot take food orally. This may take days or even weeks, as dehydration and infection set in. Commenting on this situation, Rachels says:

> I can understand why some people are opposed to all euthanasia, and insist that such infants must be allowed to live. I think I can also understand why other people favor destroying these babies quickly and painlessly. But why should anyone favor letting "dehydration and infection wither a tiny being over hours and days"? The doctrine that says that a baby may be allowed to dehydrate and wither, but may not be given an injection that would end its life without suffering, seems so patently cruel as to require no further refutation.

Such a doctrine perhaps does not need further refutation; but this is not the AMA doctrine. For the AMA statement criticized by Rachels allows only for the cessation of extraordinary means to prolong life when death is imminent. Neither of these conditions is satisfied in this example. Death is not imminent in this situation, any more than it would be if a normal child had an attack of appendicitis. Neither the corrective surgery to remove the intestinal obstruction, nor the intravenous feeding required to keep the infant alive until such surgery is performed, can be regarded as extraordinary means, for neither is particularly expensive, nor does either place an overwhelming burden on the patient or others. (The continued existence of the child might be thought to place an overwhelming burden on its parents, but that has nothing to do with the characterization of the means to prolong its life as extraordinary. If it had, then *feeding* a severely defective child who required a great deal of care could be regarded as extraordinary.) The chances of success if the operation is undertaken are quite good, though there is always a risk in operating on infants. Though the Down's syndrome will not be alleviated, the child will proceed to an otherwise normal infancy.

It cannot be argued that the treatment is withheld for the infant's sake, unless one is prepared to argue that all mentally retarded babies are better off dead. This is particularly implausible in the case of Down's syndrome babies who generally do not suffer and are capable of giving and receiving love, of learning and playing, to varying degrees.

In a film on this subject entitled, "Who Should Survive?", a doctor defended a decision not to operate, saying that since the parents did not consent to the operation, the doctors' hands were tied. As we have seen, surgical intrusion requires consent, and in the case of infants, consent would normally come from the parents. But, as their legal guardians, parents are required to provide medical care for their children, and failure to do so can constitute criminal neglect or even homicide. In general, courts have been understandably reluctant to recognize a parental right to terminate life-prolonging treatment. Although prosecution is unlikely, physicians who comply with invalid instructions from the parents and permit the infant's death could be liable for aiding and abetting, failure to report child neglect, or even homicide. So it is not true that, in this situation, doctors are legally bound to do as the parents wish.

To sum up, I think that Rachels is right to regard the decision not to operate in the Down's syndrome example as the intentional termination of life. But there is no reason to believe that either the law or the AMA would regard it otherwise. Certainly the decision to withhold treatment is not justified by the AMA statement. That such infants have been allowed to die cannot be denied; but this, I think, is the result of doctors misunderstanding the law and the AMA position.

Withholding treatment in this case is the intentional termination of life because the infant is deliberately allowed to die; that is the point of not operating. But there are other cases in which that is not the point. If the point is to avoid inflicting painful treatment on a patient with little or no reasonable hope of success, this is not the intentional termination of life. The permissibility of such withholding of treatment, then would have no implications for the permissibility of euthanasia, active or passive. . . .

Someone might say: Even if the withholding of treatment is not the intentional termination of life, does that make a difference, morally speaking? If life-prolonging treatment may be withheld, for the sake of the child, may not an easy death be provided, for the sake of the child, as well? The unoperated child with spina bifida may take months or even years to die. Distressed by the spectacle of children "lying around, waiting to die", one doctor has written, "It is time that society and medicine stopped perpetuating the fiction that withholding treatment is ethically different from terminating a life. It is time that society began to discuss mechanisms by which we can alleviate the pain and suffering for those individuals whom we cannot help."

I do not deny that there may be cases in which death is in the best interests of the patient. In such cases, a quick and painless death may be the best thing. However, I do not think that, once active or vigorous treatment is stopped, a quick death is always preferable to a lingering one. We must be cautious about attributing to defective children *our* distress at seeing them linger. Waiting for them to die may be tough on parents, doctors and nurses—it isn't necessarily tough on the child. The decision not to operate need not mean a decision to neglect, and it may be possible to make the remaining months of the child's live comfortable, pleasant and filled with love. If this alternative is possible, surely it is more decent and humane than killing the child. In such a situation, withholding treatment, foreseeing the child's death, is not ethically equivalent to killing the child, and we cannot move from the permissibility of the former to that of the latter. I am worried that there will be a tendency to do precisely that if active euthanasia is regarded as morally equivalent to the withholding of life-prolonging treatment.

VIRGINIA L. WARREN

Feminist Directions in Medical Ethics

VIRGINIA L. WARREN teaches philosophy at Chapman College in California. She writes on ethics and feminist philosophy.

We might as well admit it. Medical ethics has grown a bit stale. Hot new topics continue to arise—such as whether to withhold artificial food and fluids from patients, or to "harvest" organs for transplant from fetuses and anencephalic newborns. But calling on the same list of Basic Moral Principles does not produce the thrill it once did, though the issues are as significant and heart-breaking as ever. My aim here is to see whether feminism can suggest some new directions for medical ethics, and for philosophical ethics generally.

I shall begin with two disclaimers. First, I am *not* claiming that a feminist medical ethics must develop in any particular ways, only that certain paths are suggested by feminism. Second, I am *not* claiming that these possibilities could *only* have come from a feminist perspective. These directions may, for example, reinforce some ideas from Marxism or from the holistic health movement. I have no desire to plant a flag on the moon and claim, "Feminists got here first." I do hope, however, that the speculations emerging from the cross-fertilization of medical ethics and feminism will bear fruit.

"SEXIST ETHICS"

Before pondering what a feminist medical ethics might look like, however, muse about what a *Sexist Ethics* might be like. My aim is neither to condemn philosophic ethics through caricature, nor to search for sexist villains. The sexism—of which I, too, am guilty—is mostly unintended. Rather, I want to spur the imagination. What would academic moral philosophy be like if it were sexist? Let us begin with *substance*—with what questions and solutions are discussed. Later we will consider *process:* how moral debates are conducted. And, should the resulting picture fit real life, let us recognize it.

First, a Sexist Ethics would use a male perspective to frame moral questions and to shape solutions. Magicians know to keep the audience's attention away from the action. But moral philosophers may be magicians who have tricked even themselves by concentrating on the topic at hand, without asking which topic most deserves study or what will result from approaching this topic this way. In a Sexist Ethics, moral questions would often involve competitions for power, status or authority. For example, the autonomy-paternalism debate in medical ethics concerns who has the moral authority to make the final decision: patient or physician. And solutions to moral problems would often downplay or ignore the interests of women (and children). For example, when medical costs are contained by sending hospital patients home "quicker and sicker," family members—usually females—must nurse them at home. This unpaid labor—by mothers, wives, daughters, and daughters-in-law—needs to be given more weight. Even now, women's work is often "invisible."

Second, a Sexist Ethics would never appear sexist. It would be clothed in a cloak of neutrality because favoring some group or position would be unthinkable. The dominant trend in philosophical ethics has been to regard people as best able to decide what is moral when least tied to place and time, when least connected through ties of partiality to family and community. Ideal moral decision-makers are viewed as common denominators—e.g., rational egos (Kant) or calculators of utility—who are more likely to adopt the proper universal perspective when the veneer of particularity is stripped away.

Two distortions may result from this approach to ethics. First, although some moral agents may adopt a common denominator moral perspective without feeling that anything of value is lost, others may feel the loss intensely. The reason for this loss is that persons whose unique experiences have been largely omitted from the dominant culture—e.g., women, Blacks, gay males and lesbians—may find the stripping away of particularity from the moral observer to be anathema to self. By subtracting those features that shed light on their experience and life, such individuals may become, at least in part, invisible to themselves.

A second distortion may arise because adopting a universal perspective toward moral situations tends to (although it does not need to) reveal generic persons and relationships whose psychological subtleties have been washed away. Specifically, the fact that human beings are gendered is likely to be deemed irrelevant to moral deliberation. It is too bad if the stereotypic woman—with all her reproductive organs, emotions, and kinship ties to particular others—does not fit the category of Plain Wrap Human Being. Of course, men are also gendered. Sexist Ethics would not take sufficient account of males *qua* males, any more than it does of females *qua* females. Ironically, distortion may be the likely result of our trying so hard not to distort.

Third, a Sexist Ethics would frame the ethical debate so that women would be kept on the defensive. Women would spend much time for little gain. A Sexist Ethics would seduce women to work within its framework by offering hope for improvement—but only if they did not rock the patriarchal boat too vigorously. "Strive for *equality* with men," it would say, "and all will be well. There is no need for more fundamental change." Such a domesticated ethics would, for example, allow women and men to compete equally for the positions of nurse and physician, without questioning the roles themselves, which were founded on an unequal power relationship between females and males.

Women might be kept on the defensive in another way: topics chosen for moral debate might have the unintended effect of fanning the flames of sexism. In moral philosophy in the past fifteen years, the two most commonly discussed topics concerning women have been abortion and preferential hiring. In both cases, women's interests and rights are pitted against the interests and rights of "innocent" others: fetuses, and young (white) male applicants to law or medical school who are not principally responsible for the worst sexist practices.

The central place of preferential hiring in the "contemporary moral issues" literature is particularly instructive. Women (and minorities) studying preferential hiring are made to feel how many expectations of males (and whites) they are crushing, and how much hostile backlash awaits, if they push too hard to be let into the club. With sexism (and racism) so prevalent, it border on the scandalous that so much philosophical energy is focused on preferential hiring. For, while this issue clearly merits attention, it directly affects a relatively small percentage of job-holders for brief periods, mainly in decisions about hiring and promotion. I say this even though I know that believing that one has been, or might be, passed over for a desired job may profoundly affect one's self-conception and self-worth; hence, the *indirect* effects of a policy of preference may extend far beyond the period of hiring.

My point is threefold. First, enough moral philosophers have focused so narrowly on preferential hiring and on whether white males are wronged by it that the full burden on women (and minorities) of sexist (and racist) practices tends to get insufficient attention. . . . Second, the preferential hiring debate is inflammatory because a zero-sum, us-against-them attitude is presupposed, and often goes unchallenged. Alternative, non-zero-sum approaches to ending discrimination and to securing women's (and minorities') rightful interests usually go unexplored. Third, even if the preferential hiring debate (framed now in terms of justice and utility) were resolved one way or the other, that would not help people of different genders (and races) to *relate* to each other better on the job: to respect each other, and to overcome suspicion and hostility. . . .

In addition to substantive questions about the rightness of actions, *how* philosophical ethics is done—the process—is important. First, the theories and arguments of Sexist Ethics would be used as weapons in a competitive power struggle. Participants in the ethical debate would have an ulterior purpose. Over and above seeking the truth about what is morally right, they would want to win the debate, including to look good at someone else's expense. Second, the "star" system would be part of the Sexist Ethics game. In academia, a huge disparity exists between ability and productivity (as judged on a fair merit system), on the one hand, and reputation, on the other. Would-be "stars" aim at advancing their reputations, and at gaining prestige and the power and perquisites which accompany prestige. Thus, over and above any substantive differences between sexist and feminist ethics, we must attend to how the philosophical "ethics game" is played in discussions, at conferences, and in print.

In my view, contemporary philosophical ethics—including medical ethics—has all of the features described under "Sexist Ethics" to *some* degree, even though the intention to be sexist is usually absent. The degree varies dramatically with the topic, the author or speaker, and the occasion. Imagining how philosophical ethics might become increasingly less sexist is the challenge.

FEMINIST MEDICAL ETHICS: WHAT IS STUDIED

Which questions moral philosophers choose to study—and choose not to study—is itself a moral issue, yet one that is hardly ever raised. In this section I will sketch some changes —suggested by feminism—in the questions addressed in medical ethics.

Feminists could add the perspectives of women of different races, classes, sexual preferences, etc., to questions and solutions already discussed in the literature of medical ethics. For example, more weight would be given in cost-cutting debates to the effects on families—especially on female caretakers—of patients released from hospitals earlier.

In addition, feminists could include women's perspectives—along with the perspectives of males *qua* males, and the interests of children—by *posing new questions.*
Carol Gilligan interviewed women who were considering abortion, and listened to how
they framed moral questions and to which moral values they appealed. We, too, need
to listen. I will discuss four categories of new questions: (1) inequalities, (2) sexist occupational roles, (3) personal issues, and (4) relationship issues that do not involve deciding the winner of power struggles.

(1) *Inequalities.* The treatment of women patients, women physicians, and people in
traditionally female occupations such as nursing or social work should be examined.
After exposing any unequal treatment of women in health care, solutions could be
sought. An example of unequal treatment of female patients is the policy in many *in
vitro* fertilization programs of excluding all women who are not married heterosexuals;
that is, only women who want to raise a child with a husband need apply. When this
policy is criticized, one response is to point out the scarcity of places in IVF programs—
with no attempt to defend this particular allocation of scarce resources. The issue is
deflected, but not taken seriously; and male privilege is protected, but not justified.

(2) *Sexist occupational roles.* Historically, the roles of physician and nurse were designed for males and females, respectively. Tasks were assigned based on what was
appropriate masculine and feminine behavior, with nurses expected to defer to physicians. So far, the basic question in nursing ethics has been what hospital nurses should
do when their moral views clash with those of physicians, who have more institutional and legal power.

Moreover, physicians' training is largely theoretical and technological, and they
have final decision-making authority for patient treatment. The role of nurse has always included nurturing patients' psyches (and although much knowledge and skill is
required to perform nurturing tasks well, that is often overlooked and labeled "intuition"); and nurses' decision-making authority is subordinated to "doctor's orders."
This division of labor in health care—based on which gender the role was designed
for—remains, even though an increasing number of physicians are now female. (Male
nurses remain a rarity.)

A second type of new question would go further, examining sexism in occupational
roles. We need to stop segregating nurturing from theory—whether in health care
(the work of nurses and social workers from that of physicians) or in academia (un-
dergraduate teaching from research). Giving females and males equal opportunity to
enter occupations in which nurturing and theory are pulled apart does not solve the
problem. The answer is not to have fifty percent of nurses be caring, responsive males,
while fifty percent of physicians are oriented toward technology and research and
professionally distant—but are female. Nor is the answer to have RNs imitate the
higher paid, higher status, traditionally male occupations; for then the caring tasks
would be delegated to others (e.g., to licensed vocational nurses). Nurturing needs to
be valued more highly, including monetarily, and integrated with technical and theoretical expertise, particularly in medicine. (Nursing is already attempting such integration.) We need to redefine the roles and relationships of all members of the "health
care team," making roles more androgynous.

(3) *Personal issues. . . .* Philosophical ethics routinely ignores the little—and not so
little—domestic problems of life, which I call *"housekeeping issues."* These "personal"
issues contrast with the *"crisis issues"* (e.g., abortion or withdrawal of life-support) that

are the bread and butter of contemporary moral philosophy. Perhaps an analogue to the feminist slogan, "The personal is political," is needed: "The personal is professional." That is, what is "merely" personal may profoundly affect how one acts on and off the job, and thus should play a significant role in professional ethics.

An example of an important housekeeping issue is how to help people *use* such valuable legislation (in California and some other states) as the Durable Power of Attorney for Health Care. Should one become incompetent, a Durable Power specifies what medical treatment one does and does not want, and invests a designated person (e.g., spouse, friend) with the legal authority to make one's other medical decisions. While bio-ethicists have discussed moral reasons for and against passing such legislation (a crisis issue), they rarely address problems of implementation (housekeeping issues). Nor do physicians raise the possibility of signing such a document with patients very often. When physicians do think of it, they may fear that even raising the issue with terminal patients will cause despair and hasten death. Often it is thought of too late: when patients are already comatose, or weakened by illness and confused by drugs. Nor do we help families learn how to discuss such grave matters openly and "before need" (the phrase used in cemetery commercials). If most laypeople are unaware that such legislation exists, they cannot raise the issue of signing a Durable Power with physicians. And few physicians are raising it with them. (Nurses sometimes do, but risk being criticized for encroaching on the physician's prerogative.)

These two categories of moral issues—crisis and housekeeping issues—contrast in several ways.

First, with crisis issues, moral decisions are more or less final. A moral problem arises; one decides; one moves on and feels a sense of progress. With housekeeping issues, however, *the problematic situation is ongoing, rather than resolved once and for all;* and decisions need to be made continually. Job stress, for example, can be contained but not eliminated.

Second, the significance of crisis issues immediately catches our attention. We take pride in facing a difficult challenge. By contrast, housekeeping issues *seem trivial.* Even if we handle these problems well, we feel we have not accomplished much, and others are unlikely to laud our efforts. For example, we discuss crisis issues related to AIDS, such as whether AIDS antibody testing should be mandatory in some cases. But few are discussing housekeeping issues, e.g., how sexually active persons can raise the question of AIDS exposure and protection with prospective sexual partners, while trying to respect privacy and avoid manipulation. Even if housekeeping issues were trivial when considered one at a time, their collective impact on individuals and institutions would be anything but trivial.

Third, crisis issues usually involve a narrow range of alternative actions. By contrast, housekeeping issues commonly *require us to reassess large parts of our lives:* our character traits, how we think about ourselves, and how we relate to others. Their impact is thus felt long after a particular crisis is past. . . .

For example, informed consent is standardly interpreted as a crisis issue: "Was an autonomous and informed consent obtained from the patient before this treatment, or did the physician withhold relevant information or pressure the patient?" Compare this to informed consent interpreted as a housekeeping issue: "How should we foster the conditions which make informed consent more likely?" The whole physician-patient relationship is thereby called into question: How much time should physicians spend with patients, and on whose terms—when it is convenient for the doctor or when the patient is well-rested and psychologically prepared? How involved should physicians be with patients' value choices and anguish? Should the relationship between physicians and nurses be changed so that they can work together more effectively to encourage patient autonomy?

Fourth, crisis issues are more readily handled using such standard moral principles as justice, autonomy, beneficence and non-maleficence, and utility. *Applying these principles to housekeeping issues helps only up to a point.* These principles do not deal satisfactorily with psychological subtleties, especially with the intricacies of longer-term relationships. For example, autonomy and beneficence will offer only rudimentary guidance to a health professional deciding whether and how to approach a specific patient about signing a Durable Power of Attorney. Utilitarians, it is true, hold that the Utility Principle always applies. Yet, reducing character traits and relationships to how much happiness and unhappiness they can be expected to produce seems to me to drain them of much of their significance.

Overall, what are we to make of these housekeeping issues, which refer to one's everyday life and to on-going relationships, and which are routinely overlooked? On a given topic, should housekeeping issues replace crisis issues? Not necessarily. I view it as an open question whether, for a given area, both crisis and housekeeping issues need to be discussed, or whether one of these sets of issues is sufficient. What matters is that we neither ignore important questions, nor distort the moral debate by asking questions in the wrong way—for we sometimes turn housekeeping issues into crisis issues just so they will be resolved.

(4) *Relationship issues that do not involve deciding who wins various power struggles.* The main relationship questions in medical ethics now involve competitions for power, status or authority. Who should have the moral authority to make the final decision: the patient or the physician (in the autonomy-paternalism debate), the physician or the nurse (in nursing ethics)? Relationships are incorrectly assumed to be fine when there is no overt struggle for power.

Moral philosophers should consider ways of resolving power conflicts other than declaring a winner. For example, a strategy of "preventive ethics" could be adopted. Instead of asking who should be "King of the Hill"—physician or patient—ask how the conflict might be prevented in the future. Changes might be needed in medical education or in the social organization of hospitals.

On a larger scale, I believe that the feminist goal of eliminating conflicts over power can be permanently attained only by solving this problem: How can people be helped to develop a sense of self and of self-worth (identity) that is not based on putting down or controlling someone else (power over others)? This question is important because simply trying to eliminate one form of discrimination—against women, gays and lesbians, the disabled—and then another will never have an end. We will be playing musical chairs: there will always be an odd person out. To eliminate discrimination across the board, a radical strategy is needed: educating people to value themselves in a way that does not depend on branding anyone else inferior.

In addition to preventing or eliminating power struggles, other questions about relationships might be asked by a feminist medical ethics. Relationship ethics should discuss openness, responsiveness and caring. For example, how personally involved with patients should health care professionals be in different situations? In order to encourage more sensitivity to their patients and co-workers, how should health care professionals—including physicians—be trained, and what should their working conditions be?

Some issues in medical ethics have been much debated but, in those discussions, crucial questions about relationships have been downplayed or ignored. For example, in the philosophical literature, abortion is often interpreted as a power struggle. Whose rights are more important: the fetus's right to life, if it has one, or the mother's right to autonomously guide her life? What is usually left out of the abortion debate is a network of issues surrounding the parent- (especially mother-) child relationship.

I have been amazed by the casualness with which many opponents of abortion offer adoption as an alternative. Nor have moral philosophers considered the following question in any depth. If a pregnant woman has decided not to abort, when is it morally permissible for her to give up the newborn for adoption? Whenever she wants to? Is adoption permissible only if the baby would be better off being raised by someone else—and, then, only if the mother is unwed? (Can you imagine telling your parents or in-laws that you and your partner have decided to give up their grandchild for adoption? Or telling an older child that its sibling-to-be will be given up for adoption?) Is it permissible for a woman to conceive *in order* that the child be adopted—if everyone, including the child and the adoptive parents, benefit? If it is, then surrogate motherhood (money issues aside) would have a more solid moral foundation. My point is that, regarding abortion and adoption (as well as child custody disputes during divorce), we need to get to the heart of matters of the heart: relationships between parents and children, between life partners, between siblings, between grandparents and grandchildren. At present, we have not identified what the important relationship issues are, nor do we know how to weigh these values against such standard ones as rights, autonomy, and beneficence/utility.

One way to move health care relationships away from the issue of power struggles is to downplay the traditional view of the physician as authority, and to emphasize their role as *educators.* In most fields, teaching non-experts has traditionally been viewed as a female task. Not surprisingly, patient education is often delegated to the predominantly female occupations of nursing and social work.

Observe what happens when informed consent is viewed in terms of an educational model, with the physician as teacher, instead of a medical model, in which treating disease is paramount. Using the medical model, many physicians relate to patients based on whether the interaction will promote patient health. Thus, information is given to patients only if it will not harm the patient's medical condition. For example, a physician might ponder, "Will these facts depress the patient, thereby lowering her immune response?" Moreover, using the medical model, when a patient fails to understand the risks and benefits of alternative treatments, the first explanation is probably psychiatric: the patient is in denial, unable to accept disturbing facts. Maybe, maybe not. Of course people sometimes refuse to hear frightening facts. But, as a teacher, I know how hard it is to communicate even when the subject is emotionally bland, as in logic. Teachers need to repeat, to connect with *this* student's experience, and to get feedback from students so that inaccuracies can be corrected. Teaching skills are hard-won—requiring practice, experimentation, and sensitivity to audience. The medical model downplays the difficulties of teaching well, tends to attribute failures of communication to patients, and lets physicians who are poor teachers off the hook.

In sum, there are many ways to add the perspectives of women to the questions asked in medical ethics. Existing questions can be rethought. And new questions can be posed: about inequality, occupational roles, "housekeeping issues," and relationship issues other than power struggles.

FEMINIST MEDICAL ETHICS: HOW ETHICS IS DEBATED

Over and above which questions are studied, how discussions in moral philosophy are conducted is crucial. I will briefly discuss three feminist themes which suggest directions for how academic medical ethics might be done: (1) diversity, (2) relationships, and (3) basing theory on ordinary experience.

(1) The first theme is *diversity*. Women (and other groups) have had their perspectives and interests minimized or omitted from textbooks and theories. After devising theories that take account of women's experiences, feminist theorists are often ambivalent about establishing these ideas as the paradigm for all humanity. (For example, Gilligan is still working out to what degree the "justice perspective" and the "care perspective" in ethics are both needed, and to what degree they compete.) And rightfully so: feminists know that "one size fits all" usually does not. We need fully to explore the degree to which philosophical ethics should accommodate multiplicity. . . .

We need to explore not only new questions, but also alternative moral principles or values. Those we have now (except in virtue ethics) are best suited to handling conflicts over power and authority. I believe that autonomy, in particular, needs to be reconceived. In medical ethics, the principle of autonomy is most frequently used to fend off others' attempts to make one's decisions. But it may prove wanting as a positive conception of human agency at its noblest. Alternative conceptions might include self-expression (as opposed to self-mastery) or effortlessness (that is, not needing to "make laws for oneself"). More radically, we should question whether the aim is to find one, rather small, set of moral principles or values for everyone (all races, genders, cultures, etc.) at all times in their lives. Some feminists have questioned universalizability or have otherwise tried to find room in moral theory for caring for particular others. Universalizability may indeed be compatible with caring for particular persons. Still, we may seek a tolerable, even desirable, amount of diversity in ethics—both in the normative principles themselves and in the solutions they yield when applied to specific situations—that will not lead to chaos.

(2) A second feminist theme is *relationships*. Accordingly, a feminist approach might examine *how* people in academia relate to each other when discussing ethics.

First, the social interaction occurring during academic debates (written or oral) about ethics should itself be morally evaluated. Did people treat each other with respect? Was good will fostered among the participants? Motives are important. Sometimes, people simply serve as sounding boards for each other as they try to discover what the right response to a morally complex issue is. However, the absence of ulterior motives in ethics discussions is, I suspect, at least as rare in academia as in the rest of life—that is, rare indeed. When participants in moral dialogues have ulterior purposes co-existing with (and sometimes overshadowing) the desire to seek the truth about right and wrong, they are playing a "game": The Ethics Game.

In academia, the Ethics Game is sometimes played to one-up the opposition. The goals include proving oneself right (about what is morally right) *and* proving the "opposition" wrong. Moral theories and arguments are used as weapons. Philosophical reputations are at stake: who can poke holes in the opponent's position and defend an alternative position against all objections—for all to see? Winning may take precedence over truth. Most women and some men feel demeaned by playing this game; they feel sullied when they win, foolish when they lose.

When we think of ulterior motives—anything besides simply seeking the truth about right and wrong—we usually think of bad motives, especially of manipulating others in ways that harm their interests. However, playing the Ethics Game need not be bad; both the intentions and the results may be good. For example, during classroom ethics discussions, teachers often desire (an ulterior motive) that students will learn to express their ideas more confidently in public and increase their self-esteem. Here the Ethics Game is played to encourage trust and respect among participants, instead of scoring points at others' expense. Feminists could explore the moral merits of different variations of the Ethics Game. . . .

(3) A third feminist theme is that *theory should be constructed from one's life experience,* that life precedes theory. In the 1960s and 70s, small consciousness-raising groups were pivotal in spreading the feminist spirit. Accepted ideas in politics, morality, science, and everyday living had to be reexamined; and the bedrock of this critique and exploration was to be each woman's experience. It was thought that feminist theory should *not* come down from on high by "experts" and famous authors, even if they were feminists.

The belief that feminist theory should be grounded on the experiences of ordinary women is not a naive philosophical claim. Feminists know that our experience is shaped, even constructed, by our system of (patriarchal and other) beliefs. Rather, it is a political commitment which accomplishes two things. First, one learns to trust one's own judgment, listening to oneself and to other ordinary folk, even if all the books say otherwise. (Not until I taught my first Philosophy of Women course did I realize that my conception of God was based on my mother—not on my father, as Freud had said.) Second, the authority of established experts—and one's relationship to them— is challenged. If knowledge is power, "life precedes theory" is social revolution.

This social revolution could be extended to academic ethics. Moral philosophy would not be assumed mainly to trickle down from the experts to students. . . . Despite the fact that we philosophers champion "critical thinking," our students are expected, to a great degree, to accept their teachers' framework, methods, and basic assumptions— which form the criteria for doing good philosophy. (How many times did I force students, when they offered moral reasons, to "identify the relevant moral principle" from a short list, before I realized how many of their reasons simply did not fit, unless mutilated?) I have no desire to expel the philosophical baby with the bathwater, but maybe, all along, we have been discarding only part of the water after each bath. It may be time for moral philosophers to question not only the power relationship between physicians and patients, but that between themselves and those they would instruct; and that between themselves and the philosophers (from Plato to Rawls) they turn to for guidance.

CODA

I have described some directions which a medical ethics inspired by the insights of feminism might take. Two overall points will, I believe, prove useful in rethinking philosophical ethics, particularly medical ethics. First, *moral philosophers should decide which moral issues merit attention.* Neglect is not always benign. And raising certain questions—especially in the absence of a wider context—may deeply influence people's beliefs and attitudes. Second, *we need to consider how philosophical moral debates should be conducted,* including how ulterior motives influence us. What we select—and neglect— to study as well as the "games" we play may be sending a message as loud as the words we do speak on ethics. These two points are instances of the claim that *doing philosophy— including moral philosophy—is a part of life, and so may be evaluated morally.*

DANIEL CALLAHAN

Aging and the Ends
of Medicine

DANIEL CALLAHAN received his Ph.D. from Harvard and is director of the Hastings Center for Bioethics. A philosopher by training, he has written extensively on bio-medical ethics and abortion.

In October of 1986, Dr. Thomas Starzl of the Presbyterian-University Hospital in Pittsburgh successfully transplanted a liver into a 76-year-old woman. The typical cost of such an operation is over $200,000. He thereby accelerated the extension to the elderly of the most expensive and most demanding form of high-technology medicine. Not long after that, Congress brought organ transplantation under Medicare coverage, thus guaranteeing an even greater extension of this form of life-saving care to older age groups.

This is, on the face of it, the kind of medical progress we have long grown to hail, a triumph of medical technology and a new-found benefit to be provided by an established entitlement program. But now an oddity. At the same time those events were taking place, a parallel government campaign for cost containment was under way, with a special targeting of health care to the aged under the Medicare program.

It was not hard to understand why. In 1980, the 11% of the population over age 65 consumed some 29% of the total American health care expenditures of $219.4 billion. By 1986, the percentage of consumption by the elderly had increased to 31% and total expenditures to $450 billion. Medicare costs are projected to rise from $75 billion in 1986 to $114 billion in the year 2000, and in real not inflated dollars.

There is every incentive for politicians, for those who care for the aged, and for those of us on the way to becoming old to avert our eyes from figures of that kind. We have tried as a society to see if we can simply muddle our way through. That, however, is no longer sufficient. The time has come, I am convinced, for a full and open reconsideration of our future direction. We can not for much longer continue on our present course. Even if we could find a way to radically increase the proportion of our health care dollar going to the elderly, it is not clear that that would be a good social investment. . . .

Three major concerns have . . . surfaced over the past few years. They are symptoms that a new era has arrived. The first is that an increasingly large share of health care is going to the elderly in comparison with benefits for children. The federal government, for instance, spends six times as much on health care for those over 65 as for those under 18. . . .

The second concern is that the elderly dying consume a disproportionate share of health care costs. . . .

The third concern is summed up in an observation by Jerome L. Avorn, M.D., of the Harvard Medical School:

With the exception of the birth-control pill, each of the medical-technology interventions developed since the 1950s has its most widespread impact on people who are past their fifties—the further past their fifties, the greater the impact.

Many of these interventions were not intended for the elderly. Kidney dialysis, for example, was originally developed for those between the age of 15 and 45. Now some 30% of its recipients are over 65.

These three concerns have not gone unchallenged. They have, on the contrary, been strongly resisted, as has the more general assertion that some form of rationing of health care for the elderly might become necessary. To the charge that the elderly receive a disproportionate share of resources, the response has been that what helps the elderly helps every other age group. It both relieves the young of the burden of care for elderly parents they would otherwise have to bear and, since they too will eventually become old, promises them similar care when they come to need it. There is no guarantee, moreover, that any cutback in health care for the elderly would result in a transfer of the savings directly to the young. Our system is not that rational or that organized. And why, others ask, should we contemplate restricting care for the elderly when we wastefully spend hundreds of millions of dollars on an inflated defense budget?

The charge that the elderly dying receive a large share of funds hardly proves that it is an unjust or unreasonable amount. They are, after all, the most in need. As some important studies have shown, moreover, it is exceedingly difficult to know that someone is dying; the most expensive patients, it turns out, are those who are expected to live but who actually die. That most new technologies benefit the old more than the young is perfectly sensible: most of the killer diseases of the young have now been conquered.

These are reasonable responses. It would no doubt be possible to ignore the symptoms that the raising of such concerns represents, and to put off for at least a few more years any full confrontation with the overpowering tide of elderly now on the way. There is little incentive for politicians to think about, much less talk about, limits of any kind on health care for the aged; it is a politically hazardous topic. Perhaps also, as Dean Guido Calabresi of the Yale Law School and his colleague Philip Bobbitt observed in their thoughtful 1978 book *Tragic Choices,* when we are forced to make painful allocation choices, "Evasion, disguise, temporizing . . . [and] averting our eyes enables us to save some lives even when we will not save all."

Yet however slight the incentives to take on this highly troubling issue, I believe it is inevitable that we must. Already rationing of health care under Medicare is a fact of life, though rarely labeled as such. The requirement that Medicare recipients pay the first $500 of the costs of hospital care, that there is a cutoff or reimbursement of care beyond 60 days, and a failure to cover long-term care, are nothing other than allocation and cost-saving devices. As sensitive as it is to the votes of the elderly, the Reagan administration only grudgingly agreed to support catastrophic health care costs of the elderly (a benefit that will not, in any event, help many of the aged). It is bound to be far more resistant to long-term care coverage, as will any administration.

But there are other reasons than economics to think about health care for the elderly. The coming economic crisis provides a much-needed opportunity to ask some deeper questions. Just what is it that we want medicine to do for us as we age? Earlier cultures believed that aging should be accepted, and that it should be in part a time of preparation for death. Our culture seems increasingly to reject that view, preferring instead, it often seems, to think of aging as hardly more than another disease, to be fought and rejected. Which view is correct? To ask that question is only to note that disturbing puzzles about the ends of medicine and the ends of aging lie behind the more immediate financing worries. Without some kind of answer to them, there is no hope of finding a reasonable, and possibly even a humane, solution to the growing problem of health care for the elderly.

Let me put my own view directly. The future goal of medicine in the care of the aged should be that of improving the quality of their life, not in seeking ways to extend that life. In its longstanding ambition to forestall death, medicine has in the care of the aged reached its last frontier. That is hardly because death is absent elsewhere—children and young adults obviously still die of maladies that are open to potential cure—but because the largest number of deaths (some 70%) now occur among those over the age of 65, with the highest proportion in those over 85. If death is ever to be humbled, that is where the essentially endless work remains to be done. But however tempting that challenge, medicine should now restrain its ambition at that frontier. To do otherwise will, I believe, be to court harm to the needs of other age groups and to the old themselves.

Yet to ask medicine to restrain itself in the face of aging and death is to ask more than it, or the public that sustains it, is likely to find agreeable. Only a fresh understanding of the ends and meaning of aging, encompassing two conditions, are likely to make that a plausible stance. The first is that we—both young and old—need to understand that it is possible to live out a meaningful old-age that is limited in time, one that does not require a compulsive effort to turn to medicine for more life to make it bearable. The second condition is that, as a culture, we need a more supportive context for aging and death, one that cherishes and respects the elderly while at the same time recognizing that their primary orientation should be to the young and the generations to come, not to their own age group. It will be no less necessary to recognize that in the passing of the generations lies the constant reinvigoration of biological life.

Neither of these conditions will be easy to realize. Our culture has, for one thing, worked hard to redefine old age as a time of liberation, not decline. The terms "modern maturity" or "prime time" have, after all, come to connote a time of travel, new ventures in education and self-discovery, the ever-accessible tennis court or golf course, and delightfully periodic but gratefully brief visits from well-behaved grandchildren.

This is, to be sure, an idealized picture. Its attraction lies not in its literal truth but as a widely accepted utopian reference point. It projects the vision of an old age to which more and more believe they can aspire and which its proponents think an affluent country can afford if it so chooses. That it requires a medicine that is singleminded in its aggressiveness against the infirmities of old age is of a piece with its hopes. But as we have come to discover, the costs of that kind of war are prohibitive. No matter how much is spent the ultimate problem will still remain: people age and die. Worse still, by pretending that old age can be turned into a kind of endless middle age, we rob it of meaning and significance for the elderly themselves. It is a way of saying that old age can be acceptable only to the extent that it can mimic the vitality of the younger years.

There is a plausible alternative: that of a fresh vision of what it means to live a decently long and adequate life, what might be called a natural life span. Earlier generations accepted the idea that there was a natural life span—the biblical norm of three score years and ten captures that notion (even though, in fact, that was a much longer life span than was then typically the case). It is an idea well worth reconsidering, and would provide us with a meaningful and realizable goal. Modern medicine and biology have done much, however, to wean us away from that kind of thinking. They have insinuated the belief that the average life span is not a natural fact at all, but instead one that is strictly dependent upon the state of medical knowledge and skill. And there is much to that belief as a statistical fact: the average life expectancy continues to increase, with no end in sight.

But that is not what I think we ought to mean by a natural life span. We need a notion of a full life that is based on some deeper understanding of human need and sensible possibility, not the latest state of medical technology or medical possibility. We should instead think of a natural life span as the achievement of a life long enough to accomplish for the most part those opportunities that life typically affords people and which we ordinarily take to be the prime benefits of enjoying a life at all—that of loving and living, of raising a family, of finding and carrying out work that is satisfying, of reading and thinking, and of cherishing our friends and families.

If we envisioned a natural life span that way, then we could begin to intensify the devising of ways to get people to that stage of life, and to work to make certain they do so in good health and social dignity. People will differ on what they might count as a natural life span; determining its appropriate range for social policy purposes would need extended thought and debate. My own view is that it can now be achieved by the late 70s or early 80s.

That many of the elderly discover new interests and new facets of themselves late in life—my mother took up painting in her seventies and was selling her paintings up until her death at 86—does not mean that we should necessarily encourage a kind of medicine that would make that the norm. Nor does it mean that we should base social and welfare policy on possibilities of that kind. A more reasonable approach is to ask how medicine can help most people live out a decently long life, and how that life can be enhanced along the way.

A longer life does not guarantee a better life—there is no inherent connection between the two. No matter how long medicine enabled people to live, death at any time—at age 90, or 100, or 110—would frustrate some possibility, some as-yet-unrealized goal. There is sadness in that realization, but not tragedy. An easily preventable death of a young child is an outrage. The death from an incurable disease of someone in the prime of young adulthood is a tragedy. But death at an old age, after a long and full life, is simply sad, a part of life itself.

As it confronts aging, medicine should have as its specific goal that of averting premature death, understood as death prior to a natural life span, and the relief of suffering thereafter. It should pursue those goals in order that the elderly can finish out their years with as little needless pain as possible, and with as much vigor as can be generated in contributing to the welfare of younger age groups and to the community of which they are a part. Above all, the elderly need to have a sense of the meaning and significance of their stage in life, one that is not dependent for its human value on economic productivity or physical vigor.

What would a medicine oriented toward the relief of suffering rather than the deliberate extension of life be like? We do not yet have a clear and ready answer to that question, so long-standing, central, and persistent has been the struggle against death as part of the self-conception of medicine. But the Hospice movement is providing us with much helpful evidence. It knows how to distinguish between the relief of suffering and the extension of life. A greater control by the elderly over their dying—and particularly a more readily respected and enforceable right to deny aggressive life-extending treatment—is a long-sought, minimally necessary goal.

What does this have to do with the rising cost of health care for the elderly? Every-thing. The indefinite extension of life combined with a never-satisfied improvement in the health of the elderly is a recipe for monomania and limitless spending. It fails to put health in its proper place as only one among many human goods. It fails to accept aging and death as part of the human condition. It fails to present to younger genera-tions a model of wise stewardship.

How might we devise a plan to limit health care for the aged under public entitle-ment programs that is fair, humane, and sensitive to their special requirements and dignity? Let me suggest three principles to undergird a quest for limits. First, govern-ment has a duty, based on our collective social obligations to each other, to help people live out a natural life span, but not actively to help medically extend life beyond that point. Second, government is obliged to develop under its research subsidies, and pay for, under its entitlement programs, only that kind and degree of life-extending tech-nology necessary for medicine to achieve and serve the end of a natural life span. The question is not whether a technology is available that can save the life of someone who has lived out a natural life span, but whether there is an obligation for society to pro-vide them with that technology. I think not. Third, beyond the point of natural life span, government should provide only the means necessary for the relief of suffering, not life-extending technology. By proposing that we use age as a specific criterion for the limitation of life-extending health care, I am challenging one of the most revered norms of contemporary geriatrics: that medical need and not age should be the standard of care. Yet the use of age as a principle for the allocation of resources can be perfectly valid, both a necessary and legitimate basis for providing health care to the elderly. There is not likely to be any better or less arbitrary criterion for the limiting of resources in the face of the open-ended possibilities of medical advancement in therapy for the aged.

Medical "need," in particular, can no longer work as an allocation principle. It is too elastic a concept, too much function of the state of medical art. A person of 100 dying from congestive heart failure "needs" a heart transplant no less than someone who is 30. Are we to treat both needs as equal? That is not economically feasible or, I would argue, a sensible way to allocate scarce resources. But it would be required by a strict need-based standard.

Age is also a legitimate basis for allocation because it is a meaningful and universal category. It can be understood at the level of common sense. It is concrete enough to be employed for policy purposes. It can also, most importantly, be of value to the aged themselves if combined with an ideal of old age that focuses on its quality rather than its indefinite extension. . . .

The elderly will not be served by a belief that only a lack of resources, or better financing mechanisms, or political power, stand between them and the limitations of their bodies. The good of younger age groups will not be served by inspiring in them a desire to live to an old age that will simply extend the vitality of youth indefinitely, as if old age is nothing but a sign that medicine has failed in its mission. The future of our society will not be served by allowing expenditures on health care for the elderly end-lessly and uncontrollably to escalate, fueled by a false altruism that thinks anything less is to deny the elderly their dignity. Nor will it be served by that pervasive kind of self-serving that urges the young to support such a crusade because they will eventu-ally benefit from it also.

We require instead an understanding of the process of aging and death that looks to our obligation to the young and to the future, that recognizes the necessity of limits and the acceptance of decline and death, and that values the old for their age and not for their continuing youthful vitality. In the name of accepting the elderly and repudiating discrimination against them, we have mainly succeeded in pretending that, with enough will and money, the unpleasant part of old age can be abolished. In the name of medical progress we have carried out a relentless war against death and decline, failing to ask in any probing way if that will give us a better society for all age groups.

The proper question is not whether we are succeeding in giving a longer life to the aged. It is whether we are making of old age a decent and honorable time of life. Neither a longer lifetime nor more life-extending technology are the way to that goal. The elderly themselves ask for greater financial security, for as much self-determination and independence as possible, for a decent quality of life and not just more life, and for a respected place in society.

The best way to achieve those goals is not simply to say more money and better programs are needed, however much they have their important place. We would do better to begin with a sense of limits, of the meaning of the human life cycle, and of the necessary coming and going of the generations. From that kind of a starting point, we could devise a new understanding of old age.

COPYRIGHTS AND ACKNOWLEDGMENTS

CHAPTER 3

CHAPTER 4

CHAPTER 5

CHARLES FRIED   "The Evil of Lying" Reprinted by permission of the publishers from *Right and Wrong* by Charles Fried, Cambridge, Mass.: Harvard University Press, Copyright © 1978 by the President and Fellows of Harvard College.

THOMAS E. HILL, JR.   "Autonomy and Benevolent Lies" From *Journal of Value Inquiry* vol. 4, no. 4 (Winter 1970) pp. 243–57. Reprinted by permission of Kluwer Academic Publishers.

HENRY SIDGWICK   "The Duty of Veracity" From *Methods of Ethics* by Henry Sidgwick, Macmillan London.

ANNETTE BAIER   "Trust and Anti-Trust" From *Ethics and Personality*, Deigh, ed. Reprinted by permission of The University of Chicago Press.

HARRY FRANKFURT   "Reflections on Bullshit" Reprinted by permission of Harry Frankfurt.

CHAPTER 6

JOHN HOSPERS   "Profits and Liberty" From *Libertarianism* by John Hospers. Reprinted by permission.

KARL MARX   "Alienated Labor" From *The Economic and Philosophic Manuscripts of 1864*, ed. Dirk J. Strunk, tr. Martin Miligan, International Publishers (New York) 1964. Reprinted by permission.

ENRIQUE DUSSELL   "The Economics of Liberation" From *Philosophy of Liberation*, tr. Aquilina Martinez and Christine Morkovsky, Orbis Books (New York) 1985. Reprinted by permission.

MANUEL VELASQUEZ   "International Business, Morality, and the Common Good" Reprinted by permission of Manuel Velasquez.

JOANNE B. CIULLA   "Insider Trading: The Secret Seduction" Originally published in *The Ethics of Organizational Transformation: Mergers, Takeovers, and Corporate Restructuring*, W.M. Hoffman, R. Frederick, and E.S. Petry, eds. (Quorum Books, an imprint of Greenwood Publishing Group, Inc., Westport, CT, 1985), pp. 213–219. Copyright © by the Center for Business Ethics at Bentley College. Reprinted with permission; all rights reserved.

ROBERT C. SOLOMON   "The Aristotelian Approach to Business" From *Ethics and Excellence: Cooperation and Integrity in Business* by Robert Solomon. Copyright © 1992 by Robert Solomon. Used by permission of Oxford University Press, Inc.

JOHN LADD   "Bhopal: An Essay on Moral Responsibility and Civic Virtue" Reprinted by permission of the *Journal of Social Philosophy*.

MARK ALFINO   "Information Rights and the Information Manager" From *Journal of Information Ethics*, vol. 1 © 1992 and vol. 2:1 © 1993 by permission of McFarland & Company, Inc., Publishers, Jefferson NC 28640.

CHAPTER 7

JOHN RAWLS   "Justice as Fairness" *The Philosophical Review* 67 (1958), pp. 164–94. Reprinted by permission.

C H A P T E R   8

C H A P T E R   9

MARILYN FRYE "Sexism" From *The Politics of Reality: Essays in Feminist Theory,* The Crossing Press Feminist Series, 1983. pp. 17–40. Reprinted with permission.

CARYL RIVERS "Put the Blame on Eve, Boys" From *Slick Spins and Fractured Facts* by Caryl Rivers. Copyright © 1996 by Columbia University Press. Reprinted with permission of the publisher.

JACOB JOSHUA ROSS "Gender Differences" Reprinted with the permission of The Free Press, a division of Simon & Schuster from *The Virtues of the Family* by Jacob Joshua Ross. Copyright © 1994 by Jacob Joshua Ross.

LINDA A. BELL "Racism, Sexism, and the Ideal of Equality" From *Rethinking Ethics in the Midst of Violence,* Rowman and Littlefield, 1993, pp. 63–80. Reprinted by permission.

C H A P T E R 1 0

SUN TZU "The Art of Warfare" From *The Art of Warfare* by Roger Ames, edit., trans. Copyright © 1993 by Ballantine Books, Inc. Reprinted by permission of Ballantine Books, a division of Random House, Inc.

SAM KEEN "The Enemy as Abstraction" Excerpt from *Faces of the Enemy: Reflections of the Hostile Imagination* by Sam Keen. Copyright © 1986 by Sam Keen. Reprinted by permission of HarperCollins Publishers.

JOHN MCMURTRY "The Military Paradigm" Reprinted from John McMurtry, "Rethinking the Military Paradigm," *Inquiry,* vol. 34, 1991, pp. 415–432, by permission of Scandinavian University Press, Oslo, Norway.

LOIS PINEAU "Date Rape: A Feminist Analysis" From *Law and Philosophy* no. 8 (1989), pp. 217–43. Reprinted by permission of Kluwer Academic Publishers.

ALBERT CAMUS "Reflections on the Guillotine" From *Resistance, Rebellion, and Death* by A. Camus, trans. J. O. O'Brien. Copyright © 1960 by Alfred A. Knopf, Inc. Reprinted by permission of the publisher.

BAT-AMI BAR ON "Why Terrorism is Morally Problematic" From Claudia Card, ed., *Feminist Ethics,* University Press of Kansas (Lawrence), 1991, pp. 107–125.

C H A P T E R 1 1

ALLEN GINSBERG "Ballade of Poisons" From *Collected Poems 1947–1980* by Allen Ginsberg. Copyright © 1978 by Allen Ginsberg. Reprinted by permission of Harper-Collins Publishers.

TOM REGAN "The Nature and Possibility of an Environmental Ethic" Reprinted by permission of Tom Regan.

PETER SINGER "Not For Humans Only: The Place of Non-humans in Environmental Issues" is taken from *Ethics and Problems of the 21st Century* edited by K. E. Goodpaster and K. M. Sayre. © 1979 by University of Notre Dame Press. Reprinted by permission of the publisher.

ALDO LEOPOLD "The Land Ethic" From *A Sand County Almanac: And Sketches Here and There* by Aldo Leopold. Copyright 1949, 1977 by Oxford University Press, Inc. Reprinted by permission.

MARK SAGOFF "Animal Liberation and Environmental Ethics: Bad Marriage, Quick Divorce" Reprinted with the permission of the Institute for Philosophy and Public Policy, School of Public Affairs, University of Maryland, from Mark Sagoff, "Animal Liberation and Environmental Ethics: Bad Marriage, Quick Divorce" *Report from the Institute for Philosophy and Public Policy* vol. 4, no. 2 (Spring 1984).

ANNETTE BAIER "For the Sake of Future Generations" Reprinted by permission of Waveland Press, Inc. from Tom Regan, *Earthbound: Introductory Essays in Environmental Ethics.* (Prospect Heights, IL: Waveland Press, Inc., 1990). All rights reserved.

MARTI KHEEL "The Liberation of Nature: A Circular Affair" From *Environmental Ethics* vol. 7, no. 2 (Summer 1985) pp. 135–49.

CHAPTER 12

JOHN D. JONES "Multiculturalism and Welfare Reform" From *Philosophy in the Contemporary World*, vol. 1, no. 2 (Summer 1994) pp. 11–18. Reprinted by permission.

NANCY FRASER "Women, Welfare, and the Politics of Need Interpretation" From *Unruly Practices: Power, Discourse, and Gender in Contemporary Social Theory* by Nancy Fraser. (University of Minnesota Press, 1989) pp. 144–153. Reprinted by permission.

PETER MARIN "Homelessness and Welfare: The Prejudice Against Men" From "The Prejudice Against Men" by Peter Marin from the July 8, 1991 issue of *The Nation.* Reprinted with permission from *The Nation* magazine. © The Nation Company, L.P.

PETER SINGER "Famine, Affluence, and Morality" *Philosophy and Public Affairs*, vol. 1, no. 3, 1972. Copyright © 1972 by Princeton University Press. Reprinted by permission of Princeton University Press.

GARRETT HARDIN "Lifeboat Ethics" Reprinted by permission of Garrett Hardin.

AMARTYA SEN "Property and Hunger" From *Economics and Philosophy*, vol. 4 (1988), pp. 57–68. Copyright © Cambridge University Press. Reprinted with the permission of Cambridge University Press.

MICHAEL HARRINGTON "Corporate Collectivism: A System of Social Injustice" From *Ethics, Free Enterprise, and Public Policy: Original Essays in Moral Issues in Business* by Richard T. DeGeorge and Joseph A. Pilchler. Copyright © 1978 by Oxford University Press, Inc. Reprinted by permission.

CHAPTER 13

ALLEN BUCHANAN "Medical Paternalism" From *Philosophy & Public Affairs* vol. 7, no. 4 (Summer 1978) Copyright © 1978 by Princeton University Press. Approximately 12 pages reprinted by permission.

DONALD VANDEVEER "The Contractual Argument for Withholding Medical Information" From *Medical Ethics: A Philosophy and Public Affairs Reader.* Copyright © 1982 by Princeton University Press. Reprinted by permission.

DAN E. BEAUCHAMP "Public Health as Social Justice" Reprinted with permission from *Inquiry* 13: 3–14 (March 1976), © Blue Cross and Blue Shield Association.

LOREN E. LOMASKY "Medical Progress and National Health Care" From *Philosophy & Public Affairs* vol. 710, no. 1 (1980). Copyright © 1980 by Princeton University Press.

JAMES RACHELS "Active and Passive Euthanasia" From *The New England Journal of Medicine* vol. 292, 1975, pp. 78–80. Reprinted by permission.

BONNIE STEINBOCK "The Intentional Termination of Life" Reprinted with permission from *Ethics in Science and Medicine* (now *Social Science and Medicine*) vol. 6 (1979) Copyright © 1979 Pergamon Press PLC. Reprinted by permission.

VIRGINIA L. WARREN "Feminist Directions in Medical Ethics" From *Hypatia* vol. 4, no. 2 (Summer 1989) Reprinted by permission.

DANIEL CALLAHAN "Aging and the Ends of Medicine" From *Annals of the New York Academy of Sciences* vol. 530 (June 15, 1988) Reprinted by permission.